# Gettysburg

A New Look at George Armstrong Custer versus Jeb Stuart in the Battle's Climactic Cavalry Charges

Phillip Thomas Tucker

STACKPOLE
BOOKS
*Guilford, Connecticut*

Published by Stackpole Books
An imprint of The Rowman & Littlefield Publishing Group, Inc.
4501 Forbes Blvd., Ste. 200
Lanham, MD 20706
www.rowman.com

Distributed by NATIONAL BOOK NETWORK
800-462-6420

Copyright © 2019 by Phillip Thomas Tucker

All photos from the author's collection
Maps by Hal Jespersen, www.cwmaps.com

*All rights reserved.* No part of this book may be reproduced in any form or by any electronic or mechanical means, including information storage and retrieval systems, without written permission from the publisher, except by a reviewer who may quote passages in a review.

British Library Cataloguing in Publication Information available

**Library of Congress Cataloging-in-Publication Data available**

ISBN 978-0-8117-3853-8 (hardcover)
ISBN 978-0-8117-6892-4 (e-book)

∞™ The paper used in this publication meets the minimum requirements of American National Standard for Information Sciences—Permanence of Paper for Printed Library Materials, ANSI/NISO Z39.48-1992.

To Edward G. Longacre, PhD, and to the "Dean" of
Civil War Cavalry Historians.
And to "Ohio Fats."

# Contents

| | | |
|---|---|---|
| *Introduction* | | 1 |
| 1 | One of the Youngest Generals in the Annals of American History | 45 |
| 2 | Chasing a Golden Dream in Pushing North | 115 |
| 3 | Young Custer's Greatest Challenge | 159 |
| 4 | Custer Audaciously Leads the Way with the 7th Michigan Cavalry | 299 |
| 5 | The Day's Greatest Crisis: Custer Leads the Charge of the 1st Michigan Cavalry | 337 |
| *Epilogue* | | 387 |
| *Notes* | | 403 |
| *Index* | | 439 |

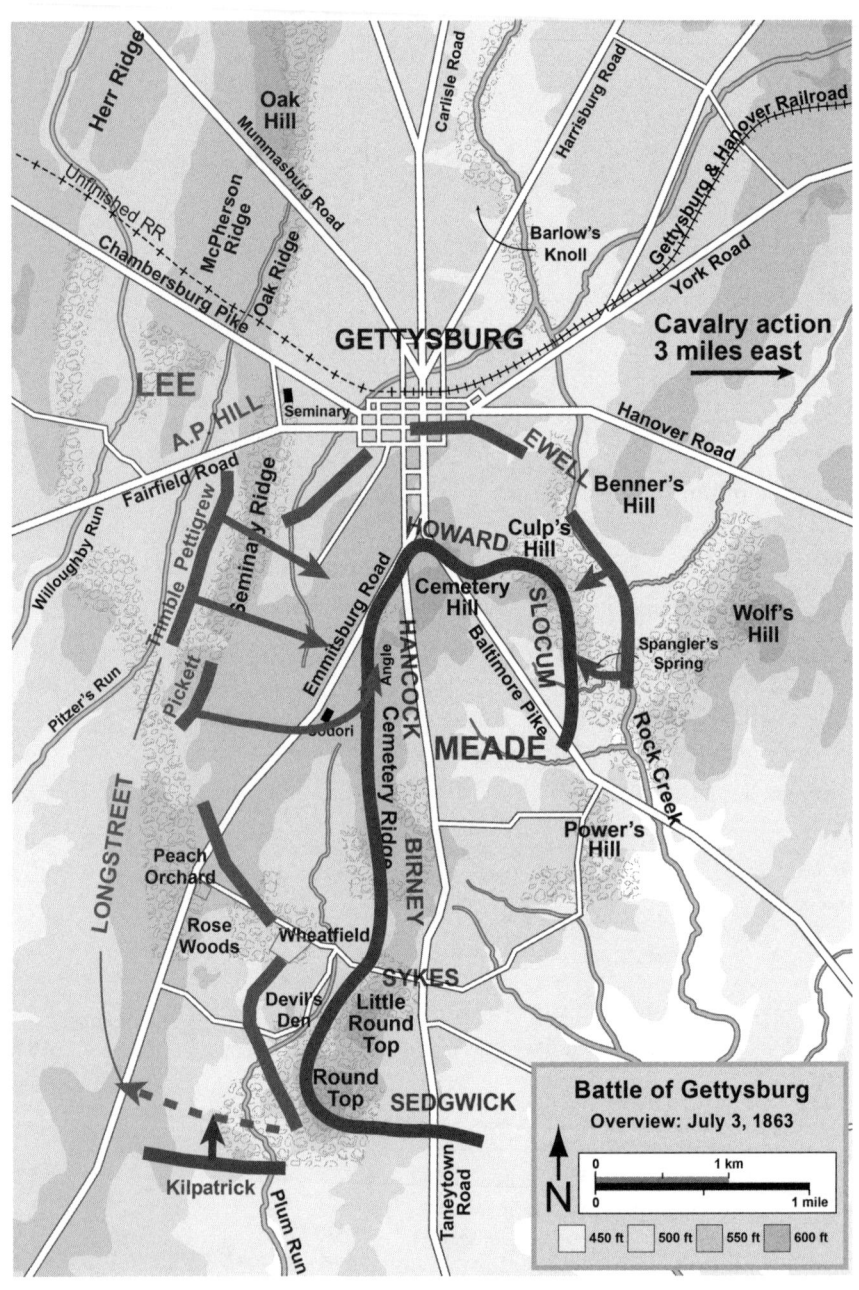

**Gettysburg Battle Map, Day 3**
The general tactical situation of both armies on the final day at Gettysburg, July 3, 1863.

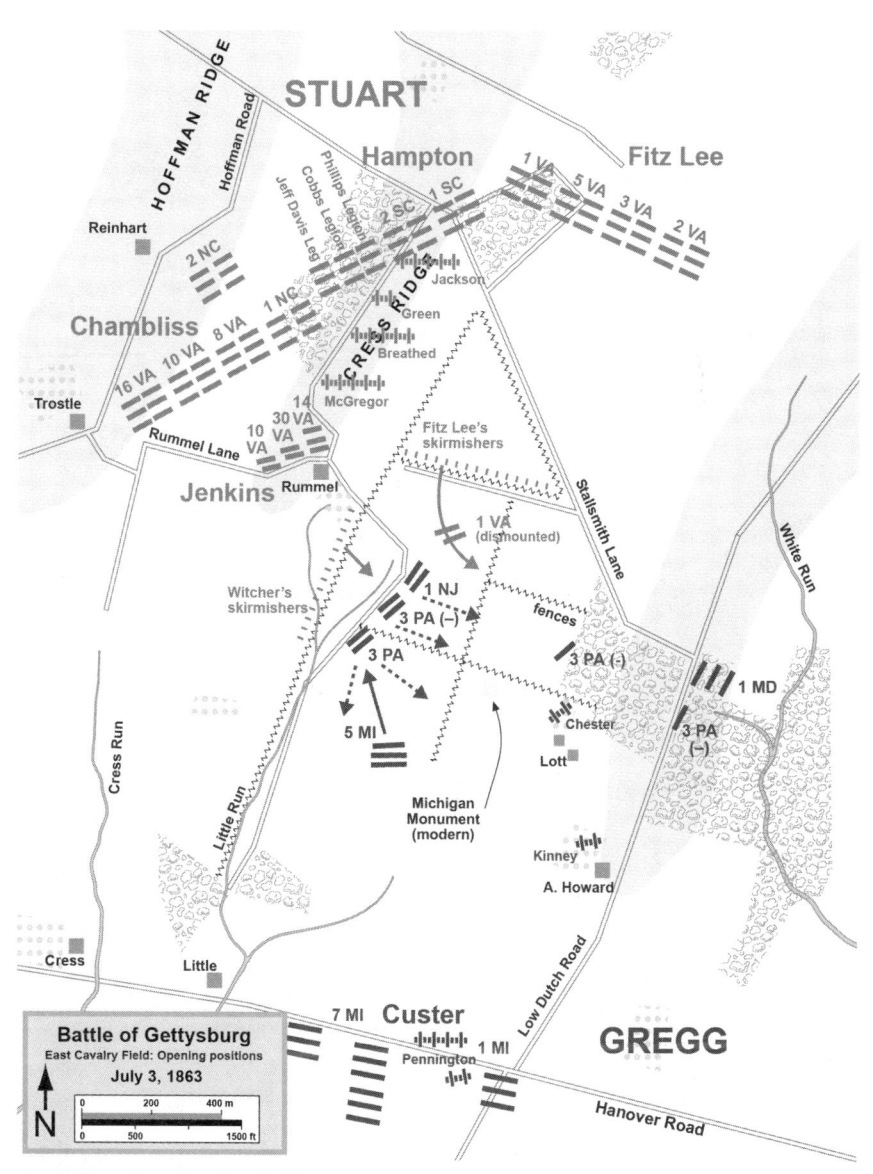

**Gettysburg East Cavalry Field 1**
Early positions of both sides on the East Cavalry Field during the early afternoon of July 3, 1863.

**Gettysburg East Cavalry Field 2**
The general tactical situation when Brigadier General George Armstrong Custer leads the daring saber charge of the 7th Michigan Cavalry straight north to push the encroaching Rebels back to buy precious time for the Union.

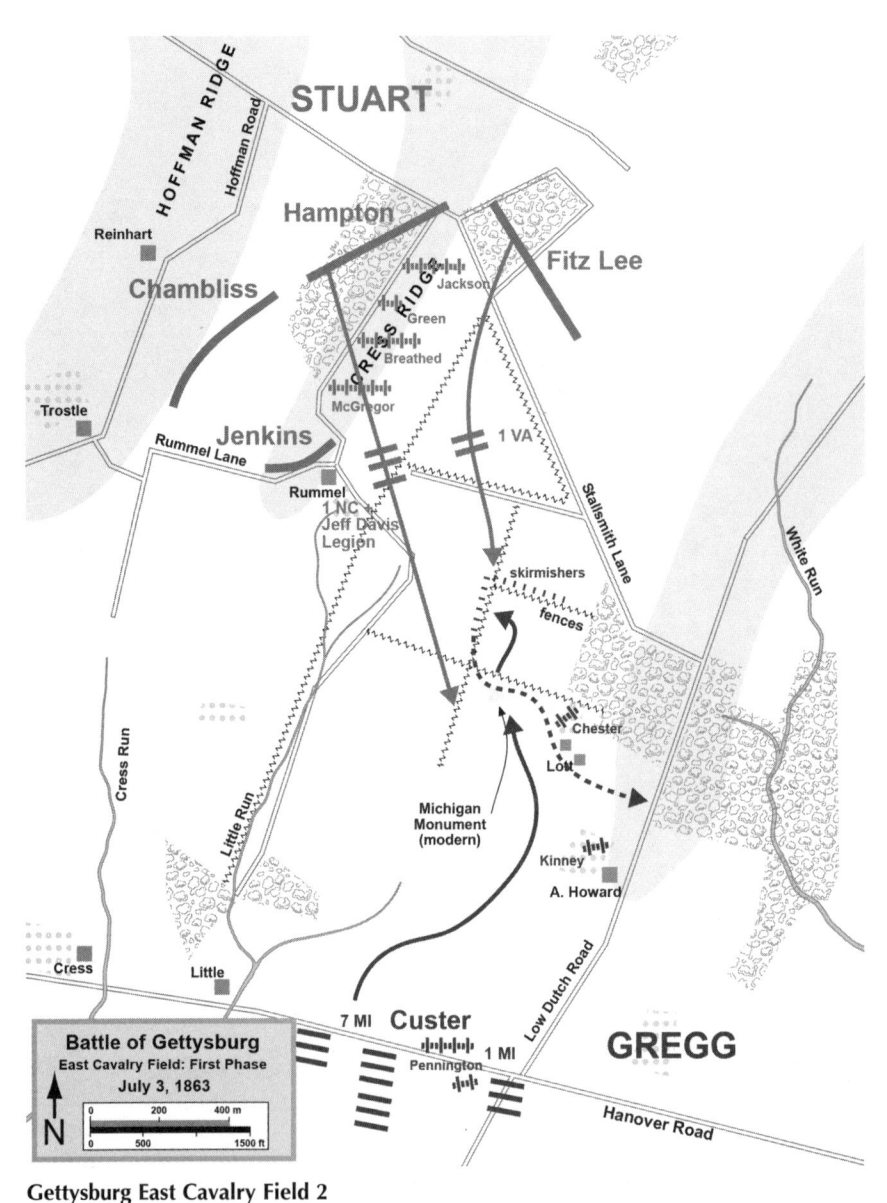

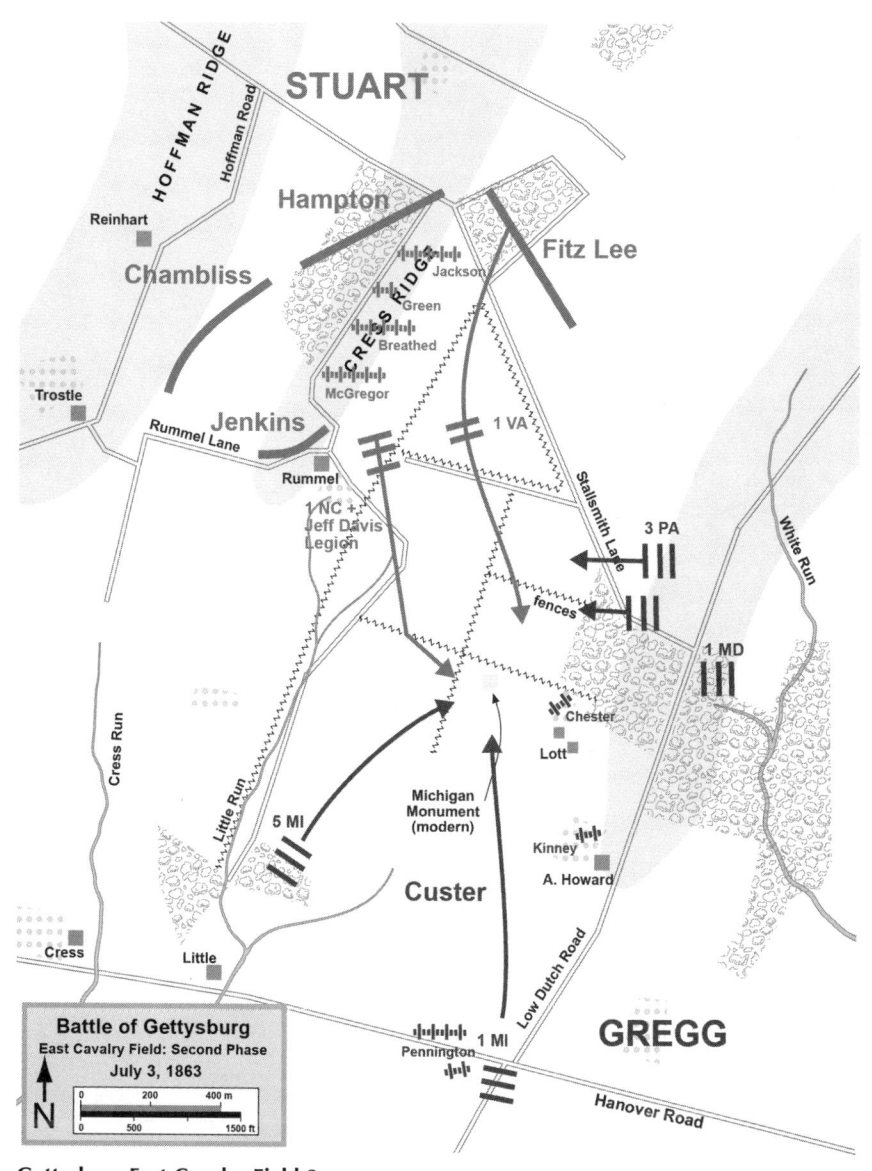

**Gettysburg East Cavalry Field 3**
Brigadier General George Armstrong Custer leads the saber charge of the 1st Michigan Cavalry straight north to hurl aside the strongest Confederate offensive effort of the day on the East Cavalry Field. Custer saved the day by leading this audacious saber attack to protect the strategic crossroads—the Hanover Road and the Low Dutch Road—and the two Union horse batteries that were in peril.

# Introduction

$\mathcal{U}$nfortunately, in one of the great ironies of American history and national memory, most of the millions of people who have visited the Gettysburg battlefield have not been aware that cavalry was even present or played a key role on the final day of America's most epic and famous battle. In a striking paradox, a far smaller number of visitors to this hallowed ground in Adams County, Pennsylvania, have realized that the Union cavalry of Gettysburg not only played key roles on the afternoon of July 3, 1863, but also made the most crucial contribution to the victory, and far more than the much-celebrated role of Federal cavalry on the first day of the Battle of Gettysburg on July 1.

But in fact more than six thousand of the South's finest cavalry, under its most famous cavalry leader, Major General James Ewell Brown (Jeb) Stuart, had been ordered by General Robert E. Lee to play an all-important role in conjunction with the army's overall offensive effort on July 3. As so often in the past and in the finest offensive tradition, Lee was once again thinking in true Napoleonic terms during the final day at Gettysburg—the largest battle ever fought on the North American continent—in what was basically another Waterloo-like showdown in overall strategic terms because this was the Confederacy's last chance to win it all, when a desperate Lee, who knew it was now or never, ordered Stuart to embark upon a vital mission: to strike the Army of the Potomac's rear in conjunction with Pickett's Charge on the critical third day, which represented Lee's final chance for victory.

In going for broke, Lee knew exactly what was needed to reap a decisive victory on this crucial final day, and that was that his cavalry, the South's finest, had to play its key offensive part in close conjunction with his other two arms—infantry and artillery—in a bid to defeat the Army of the Potomac in his final offensive effort, because he correctly sensed that the golden tactical opportunity (a weak opposing army on the ropes after having been repeatedly assaulted and battered on the two previous days) would never come again for the outgunned and manpower-short Confederacy, which was on the road to extinction during a brutal war of attrition during America's bloodiest war, if victory was not secured at Gettysburg.

However, the resulting clash of cavalry on the East Cavalry Field, three miles east of Gettysburg, has been long underappreciated by generations of historians. This striking contradiction has partly developed because no battle in the annals of American history has been more shrouded in layers of romance and myth than the climactic three-day clash that raged in the fields, hills, and forests of Gettysburg. Even some of the most celebrated Union heroes of this battle have been the mere products of decades of excessive glorification and mythmaking. But this misguided focus that created some of the most famous leaders at Gettysburg was not the case with regard to the man who commanded the army and won the battle, Major General George Gordon Meade.

Instead of having been rightfully elevated to near the top of the list of saviors who played a leading role in winning victory at Gettysburg, General Meade's vital contributions have been largely overlooked and overshadowed for a wide variety of reasons, although he perhaps contributed more to winning the final victory than anyone else, a development that exemplifies but one—at the highest level—of the many striking contradictions and ironies about the battle that have continued to this day.

For example, the famous statue of General Gouverneur K. Warren was erected atop Little Round Top more than a century ago at a time when he was widely viewed as having saved the day at Gettysburg on July 2, 1863. But in the shifting currents of fickle popularity and hero worship of Gettysburg's idols based on the most recent historical trends, Warren fell out of favor in regard to the popular belief that he had played the leading role in saving the Union left on the crucial second day in favor of the most recent savior of the day, Colonel Joshua Lawrence Chamberlain. Fueled by popular media, the Maine colonel reached a new height of popularity in the 1990s that had been seldom equaled, evolving into a cultlike status. Chamberlain commanded the 20th Maine Volunteer Regiment when he allegedly saved the day by ordering and leading the charge of the Maine regiment down the slope of Little Round Top on the left flank of Colonel Vincent Strong's defending brigade (Third Brigade of Major General James Barnes's First Division, Fifth Corps, Army of the Potomac) that held the strategic hilltop at the southern end of the battle line.

But in fact and contrary to popular belief, Chamberlain never ordered—a fact verified by a number of his own men, including officers and the second in command of the regiment—one of the most celebrated charges during the bloody three days at Gettysburg as believed. Literally becoming a matinee idol to an adoring public, Chamberlain's rise to prominence in the late twentieth century resulted largely from the popular 1994 movie *Gettysburg* in which the colonel's role was much embellished and exaggerated. However, to many modern Americans, he was portrayed in the film and then seen as nothing less than a saint in shining armor in regard to his celebrated July 2, 1863, role, and even a Christ-like figure who walked on water—or on the rocky slopes of Little Round Top in this case—like the ancient miracle worker.

How could such extensive distortions have occurred in the first place, because the Battle of Gettysburg has been the most written about engagement in American history and the most decisive clash of arms during the four years of war? Why has romantic myth and legend been allowed to take center stage and dominate the historical record, besides the fact that America needed new heroes in a most non-heroic age. First and foremost, the 1994 movie *Gettysburg* was based on a 1977 work of fiction, *The Killer Angels* by Michael Shaara, whose overly dramatic and highly embellished portrayals, especially of Colonel Chamberlain, were accepted as fact, becoming holy gospel to an uncritical public in need of heroes in an age sorely lacking in heroes. Warren and Chamberlain are the most obvious examples in regard to the tenacious defense of the Union left about how the popularity and cultlike worship of Gettysburg heroes has changed with the times and almost on a whim, almost as if orchestrated by a savvy Madison Avenue marketing firm.

Even politics and economics have become key factors in the profitable equation that has led to the creation of popular Gettysburg heroes. And as could be expected, the highly profitable Gettysburg tourist industry has thoroughly cashed in by the crass exploitation and promotion of the newest popular Gettysburg hero, who was transformed into a cash cow for the Gettysburg tourist industry. Colonel Chamberlain and his saintly image—he had everything but the golden halo in his commercialized image—were catapulted into the historical stratosphere, resulting in the most popular cult figure for throngs of Gettysburg worshippers.

Therefore, the tourist industry of Gettysburg—more of a vast commercial enterprise than a historical town in the traditional sense because the small community's economy is based upon the National Battlefield Park—has sold everything imaginable to the masses to make a steady stream of money off the latest Gettysburg hero: Colonel Chamberlain T-shirts, coffee mugs, key chains, refrigerator magnets, photographs, posters, artwork, and a seemingly endless number of souvenirs that are still sold at the tourist shops (tourist traps) that line the visitor-filled streets of Gettysburg. To capitalize on the Chamberlain craze that has continued to this day with only slightly less capitalist vigor and enthusiasm, a host of popular Civil War artists likewise cashed in to reap their own profits. They wasted little time in completing their latest works of art that focused on excessively glorified Colonel Chamberlain portraits and the charge of the 20th Maine down the rocky slope of Little Round Top to save the day as described in *The Killer Angels*. In many ways, Gettysburg has all the superficial and crass qualities of a mini-Tinseltown (the fantasy-fueled Mecca of Hollywood, California), which created a surreal landscape of a make-believe world (not unlike the Disney empire in Orlando, California) by producing popular films, including about comic book heroes, mostly based on works of fiction.

Absolutely nothing has been off limits during the process of the seemingly endless promotion of Gettysburg's newest commercialized god created to be dutifully worshipped by the adoring masses. Therefore, hordes of aggressive marketers of Gettysburg cashed in for decades on the so-called savior of Little Round Top, when the true heroes who won the day at Little Round Top on Meade's left flank have been largely forgotten—Colonel Strong Vincent, the talented commander of his hard-hitting brigade, who gained the high ground of Little Round Top just in the nick of time, and Ireland-born Colonel Patrick Henry "Paddy" O'Rorke, who led the 140th New York Volunteer Infantry in a determined counterattack that truly won the day on the southern end of the army's overextended battle line.

The popular heroes created by Shaara's revered work of fiction, which the 1994 movie faithfully followed in promoting these fictional views, generated profits on a scale that made this a most highly profitable big business. Following this popular trend of cashing in on the latest media-generated heroes, nonacademic Civil War presses and their mostly non-PhD authors then profited from a thriving cottage industry based on the latest hero worship of the most recent cast of Gettysburg celebrities created by this popular book of fiction and the movie.

Like the much-embellished Colonel Chamberlain as a result of the film *Gettysburg*, so this fictional work and the movie based on it created still another hero, Brigadier General John Buford, who was also cynically marketed by the Gettysburg cash-making machine. He commanded the First Cavalry Division, and his dismounted troopers performed magnificently in slowing the Confederate advance with a series of defensive stands on the morning of July 1 to buy time for the arrival of the vanguard of the army's infantry. Like Chamberlain, this Kentucky-born cavalryman was elevated to cult status by the excellent and memorable performance of deep-voiced and handsome Sam Elliott, who emerged as the film's finest actor in *Gettysburg* in playing the character of Buford. Elliott's fine acting ensured that a number of writers and historians shortly exploited the film's popularity by their increased focus on Buford.

Like the Colonel Chamberlain cult, partly because there was never a General Meade cult and probably never will be, so the John Buford cult developed and was similarly exploited in full by opportunistic writers and Gettysburg's marketplace for commercial gain. In this way, so the Buford cult was thoroughly exploited by these amateur historians and their obliging presses—concerned mostly about making as much money as possible—which churned out one John Buford book after another to make a quick, easy buck by creating another cottage industry like the lucrative Chamberlain market. Therefore, the film *Gettysburg* created two cash cows, Chamberlain and Buford, which have continued to garner revenues for the souvenir shops and writers to this day.

All of these modern media developments have revealed the principal weaknesses of the overworked Gettysburg field of study, its authors, and its publishers, who support themselves—financially and in regard to their respective reputations—by exploiting whatever the latest and most fashionable trend of Gettysburg hero worship, even if the idol is not always deserving of cult status, a classic case of history having been dictated and transformed by the sheer power of commercialism and profits like the rows of gaudy tourist shops that line Gettysburg's streets block after block. Exploiting the Gettysburg aura, these businesses even include a popular family restaurant with the appropriate name of "General Pickett's Buffet."

All in all, therefore, not only in regard to the small town of Gettysburg in general, but also largely its historiography—especially its excessive need to focus on the profit-garnering process of hero worship of the latest popular trend and marketable personalities that have become fashionable due to the most recent film or book—has been excessively commercialized to a degree unlike at any other historical site in America. The usual divisions that once existed between genuine history and crass commercialism, especially in regard to the most recently celebrated Gettysburg heroes like Chamberlain and Buford, have been erased until they have become one in the same because of the pursuit of the almighty dollar.

Much like the unfortunate historical fate of obscurity for General Meade and Colonel O'Rorke in truly saving the day, the most forgotten hero of the Battle of Gettysburg just happened to be one of the most well-known figures in American history and the subject of seemingly countless biographies over an extended period. In one of the greatest paradoxes of not only the Civil War but also of American history, a newly minted brigadier general named George Armstrong Custer, only twenty-three, was one of the unsung heroes of the largest and most important battle ever fought on the North American continent. This striking, if not unparalleled, contradiction in the historical record of Gettysburg has existed because the young native Ohioan, who hailed from the hill country of east central Ohio, did much more than simply rise to the fore on the battlefield like so many other brigade commanders (Chamberlain was only a regimental commander) during the three bloody days at Gettysburg. Quite simply and more than any other cavalry Federal officer, Custer truly saved the day for the Union in the dramatic showdown on the East Cavalry Field.

While Chamberlain rewrote his official reports and embellished them to bolster his own historical image in regard to saving the day at Little Round Top, Custer did not exaggerate or rewrite his report, which was filled with praise for others, after the Battle of Gettysburg. However, in one enduring mystery, Custer's official battle report of the third day at the East Cavalry Field became "lost." When the 128 volumes of *The War of the Rebellion: A Compilation of the Official Records of the Union and Confederate Armies* were printed by the U.S. government from 1880 to 1901, Custer's report about what happened on the East Cavalry Field, when he commanded the Michigan Cavalry Brigade with skill and distinction in a key combat situation, was missing. Almost incredibly, Custer's report was never published by the U.S. government for reasons that are unknown to this day. Of course, the absence of Custer's report about the largest cavalry action at Gettysburg on July 3, 1863, has played a role in obscuring the importance of not only the young brigadier general's role, but also the cavalry showdown in the Army of the Potomac's rear to make the East Cavalry Field contest the most forgotten clash of importance at Gettysburg.

Even more, the vital role of young Brigadier General Custer at Gettysburg was minimized by even the government, partly because he had become the convenient scapegoat for the highest levels of government, the top military and civilian leaders, including President Ulysses S. Grant, and misguided policies for the disaster at Little Bighorn on June 25, 1876. After all, seemingly everyone needed a scapegoat, and Custer became the ideal one because he obviously could not defend himself. Therefore, a dark stain had been applied to the Custer name by the summer of 1876—America's Centennial year—and becoming the politically based scapegoat severely tarnished his image and role at Gettysburg. The myth of Custer as the supreme bungler, faulty tactician, and overly ambitious fool had taken a firm hold in leading military and civilian circles by the turn of the century, when new American heroes, from both the North and the South, arose to the fore during the Spanish-American War, and the old Civil War wounds between North and South were healed by the new patriotism born of a new Manifest Destiny, when America continued its westward push into the Pacific.

For such reasons, what has been most overlooked and ignored by large numbers of Gettysburg historians for generations, including today, was the fact that Custer played a leading role in saving the day in a truly critical situation on July 3, 1863. All in all, therefore, the general obscurity of the remarkable performance of young Brigadier General Custer at Gettysburg is not only one of the great paradoxes in American military history, but it also represents an incredible success story in the tradition of Horatio Alger. In fact and in truth, Custer's performance on July 3 far exceeded what was achieved by the much-celebrated professor (Chamberlain) from Bowdoin College, New Brunswick, Maine, which was a magnet for the aristocratic sons of the political social elite, and by the privileged son of a leading politician in Buford's case.

Chamberlain and Buford, Gettysburg's most recent heroes who have evolved into cult figures, were members of America's political and social elite, unlike the more homespun and less educated Custer, who was a lowly westerner without lofty expectations. In contrast, Custer was truly a common man with a most common background from a remote region of rural America. Only the opportunities provided by the war elevated Custer to a lofty level because he took full advantage of what was presented to him. In this sense, Custer's overall personal story fell into the realm of the essence and historic promise of America, which allowed talented men to rise on their own abilities (a true meritocracy), unlike in the class-based countries of Europe, including the western democracies.

Indeed, Custer's rapid rise was as sudden as it was meteoric in the early summer of 1863, and he demonstrated its legitimacy at Gettysburg. This son and grandson of hardworking blacksmiths and the decidedly provincial product of a small Ohio town, New Rumley, had been suddenly appointed to the lofty rank of brigadier general only a few days before he faced his greatest and most important challenge of the Civil War. Here, on the crucial third day at Gettysburg, Custer, whose cadet career at West Point was marred by a long list of seemingly endless infractions, not only met but also reached out to grab his personal destiny during the most decisive clash of arms in the annals of American history.

As if deemed by fate and almost by accident when everything was at stake on the all-important third day when General Lee and his Army of Northern Virginia went for broke in a final bid to win it all, Custer suddenly faced one of the most crucial situations during the final day of the most important battle that ultimately decided America's destiny and defined the nation anew. The new brigadier general's boyish looks, which advertised that he was one of the youngest generals in American military history, seemed to bode ill for his upcoming decision making on the all-important final day at Gettysburg because of his lack of experience while commanding his brigade of Michigan cavalry (the 1st, 5th, 6th, and 7th Michigan Volunteer Cavalry of the Michigan Cavalry Brigade) in a vital situation of extreme importance in the right-rear of the Army of the Potomac.

For ample good reason by the red, warm dawn of July 3, 1863, Custer was already called the "boy general," and his older Michigan troopers of his crack Wolverine Brigade still looked at him with a mixture of amazement and amusement. Indeed, with long yellow hair, freckles, smooth complexion, and fair skin, Custer certainly looked the part of the "boy general" to his mostly older Michigan men from across the state. Both men and women of the day thought Custer possessed a feminine appearance because of his overall attractiveness, which was distinctive among the mostly bearded military men of the officer corps. Custer stood out in part because he never wore a beard, as if still a fumbling cadet at West Point.

Because he had been appointed to brigadier general only a few days before, which had left him with no time to secure the regular uniform of a one-star general according to regulations, Custer compensated by having designed one of the most distinctive and flamboyant uniforms to highlight his handsome features and a slim, athletic physique that made him a splendid horseman. He made himself deliberately conspicuous on the battlefield to his men so that they could more easily see and follow him in the heat of action. Custer understood that he had to perform exceptionally well on the battlefield, because he would inevitably become an easy target of ridicule for his outlandish and unconventional uniform if he met with failure on the field of strife.

But most importantly, Custer possessed exactly what was needed by his Michigan troopers and the Army of the Potomac in the defense of the crucial intersection of the Hanover Road and the Low Dutch Road in Meade's right-rear on the afternoon of July 3. Here, he demonstrated that he was an exceptionally intelligent, aggressive, tactically flexible, fiercely ambitious, and audaciously brave leader. Most of all, he excelled in part because of his determination to prove himself to his men, commanders, friends, future wife (Elizabeth "Libbie" Bacon back in Monroe, Michigan) and her disapproving wealthy father, Judge Daniel Bacon, because of his class disparity concerns in regard to the lowly blacksmith's son, and a legion of skeptics. They all, except for Libbie, doubted the young man's abilities and skills. Even having graduated last—the infamous "goat"—of his class at West Point (class of 1861) called for great personal redemption on Gettysburg's final day. Therefore, a good many things still haunted Custer on July 3, but they were positive catalysts in regard to propelling him to excel in a crisis situation.

Here, in the Army of the Potomac's rear on July 3, he possessed a golden opportunity to exorcise a good many demons by a single means that required skill and aggressiveness: reaping an important victory in Meade's vulnerable rear by halting the South's premier cavalryman, when the Union army was fighting for its life in attempting to withstand the offensive blows of the most aggressive and successful general in America. As ordered by Lee, Stuart needed to capture the key intersection of the Hanover and Low Dutch Roads to continue his mission of gaining the Baltimore Road to the southwest to strike Meade's rear on Cemetery Ridge. Quite simply, he could not leave large numbers of Union cavalry in his rear that would become vulnerable when he led thousands of troopers and horse artillery toward the Army of the Potomac's vulnerable rear, while Pickett's Charge struck from the other direction, thus setting the stage for the climactic cavalry clash at the East Cavalry Field on July 3.

Given this key situation, this flamboyant youth and near West Point failure, without sufficient experience in commanding a full cavalry brigade in a major battle, was about to do the impossible on the soil of Adams County. Fortunately for the Union, Custer was a natural leader of men and a true lover of war, who possessed ample skill and abilities and who actually excelled in crisis situations. Custer demonstrated as much when the life of the battered Army of the Potomac hung in the balance on July 3, when Lee was going for broke as never before.

With his hard-hitting style, Custer also shattered the myth that the importance of cavalry had been significantly reduced in this war because of the less favorable open terrain of America's battlefields—as compared to the more open plains of central Europe, where Napoleon Bonaparte's cavalry had reached the pinnacle of its effectiveness—and because of advances in military technology in a new age of much-improved mass infantry firepower with the rifled musket. Custer demonstrated that the mounted charge (the sheer shock power of the saber attack) combined with the mobility, flexibility, and firepower of dismounted troopers armed with fast-firing repeating rifles could reap an important victory on the battlefield, deftly combining the best Napoleonic cavalry tactics with more modern tactics.

All in all, Custer had been seemingly placed by the gods of war in the most dramatic of stages in the army's rear during the final showdown. After Lee had emerged victorious on the first and second days but without achieving a decisive success, he then planned to deliver his offensive masterstroke to destroy Meade's reeling army, now stationary and barely holding its own, on July 3. At this time, the Army of the Potomac was on the ropes and hanging onto the advantages of the high ground, especially along the sprawling length of Cemetery Ridge. Lee was determined to split the battered army in two at all costs. Located just east of this suddenly strategic crossroads town in southeastern Pennsylvania, the East Cavalry Field provided the first large and dramatic stage upon which Custer was suddenly thrust by the twisting contours of the war's fast-paced developments and seemingly by fate itself. Most importantly, this was no ordinary role that he played during the showdown between the army's opposing cavalry. Custer had been placed in the most crucial of roles several miles behind Meade's thin defensive lines at a time when Lee relied on all available forces, especially his main body of cavalry under Stuart—which had been absent during the first two days—for his greatest offensive effort of the war and his most desperate bid to win it all.

The vital mission of the South's top cavalry commander was to eventually slip around the Union cavalry posted to guard the Army of the Potomac's right flank and to deliver, in the astute words of one of America's top historians, James M. McPherson, "the coup de grace to the Yankees desperately engaged with Pickett and Ewell in their front"—the largest cavalry attack of Lee's finest horsemen into Meade's rear in conjunction with Lee's greatest offensive effort, Pickett's Charge.

Most importantly, Custer thwarted the ambitions of not only Stuart but also General Lee by successfully protecting the strategic crossroads of the Hanover and Low Dutch Roads to make sure that thousands of Rebel cavalrymen never rode toward Meade's rear to deliver a devastating blow during the most important battle ever fought on the North American continent. Custer possessed an unprecedented opportunity, and he took full advantage. He succeeded in proving to his superiors that their promotion of him at age twenty-three was not a mistake, performing beyond all expectations during the most decisive battle of the Civil War.

If one of the youngest generals to wear a brigadier general's star in the annals of American history had failed to live up to expectations on that third day, Custer might well have just faded away into dark obscurity (a fate that he feared). In fact, there probably would have been no famous "Custer's Last Stand"—one of the most written about chapters of the Old War and in American military history—played out in tragic fashion on the afternoon of June 25, 1876, in a remote region of the Montana Territory.

Clearly, for a variety of abundant reasons, young Custer had a great deal to prove to himself and others on the decisive afternoon of July 3, and his exceptional tactical and leadership performance has revealed his high motivations and abilities as one of the army's best young commanders. After all, he had graduated last in his West Point class of 1861, a most promising class of ambitious young men, including many of whom had performed well in the war after gaining higher rank.

And as a strange fate would have it, the Army of the Potomac, the Battle of Gettysburg, and perhaps even the Union itself depended on what this much-maligned "goat" of the class of 1861 could accomplish against the odds in the army's right-rear to thwart the most legendary Confederate cavalry commander, Stuart, of the most winning army in the Civil War. For these reasons, and contrary to the views of today's dissenters who still believe that what happened on the East Cavalry Field was of relatively little importance, Major

General George Gordon Meade emphasized in volume 2 of his *Life and Letters of George Gordon Meade* how the climactic cavalry fight in his army's rear was "an extremely important cavalry engagement." Meade's statement was well founded. After all, the legendary Stuart and his cavalry of "Invincibles" were in fact acting in conjunction with the massed infantry formations of Pickett's Charge in a planned and coordinated offensive effort to cut the Army of the Potomac in half, the antitheses of so many of today's armchair historians and Civil War bloggers, who still believe that they somehow know differently from General Meade and other top leaders, including the men who served with distinction in the cavalry corps.

Ironically, generations of historians, even those who have long focused on Gettysburg history, have largely overlooked the importance of the cavalry clash—far more crucial than the largest cavalry battle of the war, which had been at Brandy Station the previous month—just east of Gettysburg on the all-important afternoon of July 3, when General Lee mounted his greatest offensive effort. This glaring omission in the historical record has primarily developed because of two main developments: (1) the excessive focus of historians on Stuart's lengthy and time-consuming raid, which deprived Lee of his best cavalry and more reliable "eyes and ears" during the first two days of the Battle of Gettysburg, and (2) the focus of generations of historians on the dramatic story of Pickett's Charge, which has cast a giant shadow over all other sectors on the final day of the epic contest, especially in regard to the East Cavalry Field just three miles to the east.

This development has been the greatest irony of the most written about battle in American history, because the cavalry clash at the East Cavalry Field certainly deserves more than a brief mention or an obscure footnote in the historical record, as has so often been the case in the past, because it was in fact the most forgotten turning point of the most important battle ever fought on American soil. And as noted, Custer was not only at the center of the action but played the most important role in thwarting the South's greatest cavalrymen on this afternoon of decision.

After more than a century and a half, incredibly, this is the first book devoted solely to the supreme importance of the timely contributions of young Brigadier General Custer that ensured a decisive Union victory during the most crucial battle of the Civil War. Because of Custer's contributions in leading the Michigan Cavalry Brigade and in skillfully orchestrating the hard-hitting power of the cavalry, especially the saber charge on more than one occasion, together with the horse artillery for maximum impact to significantly influence the course of the Battle of Gettysburg, an all-important contribution was made that has been long minimized or ignored by generations of historians in one of the great paradoxes of Civil War history and memory and has continued to the present day. This glaring omission—the greatest single missing piece of the Gettysburg puzzle in regard to an extremely important event that played a large role in determining the outcome of America's fate and future—has served as the genesis for the writing of this book about the most overlooked chapter of not only the Gettysburg story, but also this Custer story, *Custer at Gettysburg*.

In consequence and for the first time, this book will go into greater detail and analysis than any other previous study in regard to the crucial contributions of the tactically gifted "boy general" on the decisive afternoon of July 3, 1863. The overall goal of this author has been to rightfully place Custer's contributions in a proper historical perspective to end an ongoing debate that no longer rightfully deserves any serious consideration: the supreme importance of what happened on the East Cavalry Field. After all, Custer's amazing success in the Army of the Potomac's rear could not have been more timely, having a dramatic impact on the final outcome of the largest battle in American history, because the threat to Meade's army could hardly have been more formidable: thousands of the South's best cavalry leaders and men, who were bolstered by ample artillery that could have inflicted unprecedented damage on the Union rear.

Erected in 1889, a majestic monument—a decorative granite column—to honor Custer and his Michigan Brigade perhaps said it best in regard to the overall importance of these often-overlooked contributions to a decisive Union victory: "This monument marks the field where the Michigan Cavalry Brigade under the gallant leader General George A. Custer rendered signal and distinguished service in assisting to defeat the further advance of a numerically superior force under the Confederate General J. E. B. Stuart, who in conjunction with Pickett's charge" posed the greatest threat to the Army of the Potomac's life on July 3, 1863. However, no statue of Custer—or Stuart for that matter—can be found today on the battlefield of Gettysburg, unlike many other Union and Confederate generals, still another factor that has doomed Custer and the fight on the East Cavalry Field to an entirely undeserved obscurity.

Despite the importance of Custer's contributions on the East Cavalry Field that protected the army's rear when its weak right-center was hit by thousands of the attackers of Pickett's Charge, relatively few tourists who annually descend upon the hallowed ground of Gettysburg—America's most popular battlefield—are even aware that Custer, despite holding a brigadier general's rank and commanding an elite brigade of Michigan troopers, was even on the field of action. And even fewer tourists realize that he played the leading role in the battle on the East Cavalry Field, when America's fate hung in the balance and its destiny was determined.

What other overlooked factors can possibly explain this glaring contradiction in the historical record that has led to gross distortions even in regard to the most written about battle of the Civil War? In many ways, the East Cavalry Field is truly the overlooked stepchild of the Gettysburg battlefield and its more famous sites, such as Little Round Top and the Devil's Den, that were in the eye of the storm on the bloody afternoon of July 2.

Located three miles northeast of Cemetery Ridge where Pickett's Charge was finally repulsed while thousands of cavalrymen battled tenaciously to protect the Army of the Potomac's vulnerable rear, the relative obscurity of the East Cavalry Field is one of the great paradoxes of Gettysburg historiography, because the more famous events (Pickett's Charge) that played out just to the southwest have completely overshadowed the crucial clash of cavalry that helped to decide America's future more than imaged by most historians of the outdated traditional school. The stirring drama and pathos of Pickett's Charge have cast a giant shadow over the importance of what happened on the East Cavalry Field to distort the focus of generations of historians by providing a thorough and permanent misdirection.

First and foremost, the veterans of both sides and government officials during the postwar period played leading roles in orchestrating and manipulating the historical record for posterity by deliberately taking the steps to create the famous "high-water mark of the Confederacy," where they themselves (civilians!) decided that this was where the turning point of the great battle was located. In the end, therefore, perhaps nothing has more thoroughly obscured the fighting in other key sectors, especially in regard to the East Cavalry Field, than the overemphasis of this designated spot—the famous clump of trees and Angle—at Meade's right-center on Cemetery Ridge.

This early manipulation of the historical record by historians, veterans, and civilians, especially newspaper reporters, can perhaps best be seen in the immortal name chosen for Lee's final assault on the last day, Pickett's Charge. But Major General George Edward Pickett led only three Virginia brigades, which was the minority of attackers in Pickett's Charge. But like Lee, Pickett was a Virginian, and so were his men, ensuring a disproportionate focus on this state and its residents because of the powerful Virginia press and Virginia-first historians, who wrote most of Civil War history, especially the "Lost Cause" promoters, well into the second half of the twentieth century.

Consequently, according to traditional history, the Virginians of Pickett's Charge reached true glory on July 3, almost as if no other troops, including even thousands of attackers from North Carolina who advanced in large numbers north of Pickett, participated in the famous assault—a revealing example of how history has been thoroughly manipulated and used to promote state and personal agendas from an extremely narrow and agenda-driven prism. And, as noted, the Virginia school of Civil War history in the postwar period was all powerful, overshadowing not only the North Carolinians but also troops from other states in Pickett's Charge—a great misfortune. Because of their disproportionate influence both during and after the war, it was the Virginians' version of events at Gettysburg that became the established traditional history that has dominated a distorted field of study to this day.

Of course, it was certainly true that the heroics and courage of the Virginia troops was worthy of celebration, which was successfully employed by the ever-influential Virginia school of "Lost Cause" historiography to bolster the cultural concept of the alleged nobility of the moral superiority of the Virginia soldiers and the Southern people in general, qualities and myths that were memorialized in the postwar period to no end. It was this excessive glorification of the Southern soldier that resulted in the erection of Confederate statues in town squares across the South.

But what has been most forgotten was the fact that this seemingly endless glorification of the Virginians of Pickett's Charge provided what was basically the most highly effective cover-up of the greatest military failure that has been relegated to historical obscurity—the antithesis of the glorification of Pickett's Charge that excessively garnered the spotlight—when the South's greatest national hero (Stuart, who was second only to General Lee) failed both the army and the nation by having his worst day as a cavalry commander. What happened in the right-rear of the Army of the Potomac had to be covered up and silenced by Southern leaders, including Lee, and the excessive postwar glorification of Pickett's Charge succeeded in thoroughly masking Stuart's dismal failure.

After all, the story of the East Cavalry Field was about Union heroics that won the day, not Southern heroics. Therefore, not only on the afternoon of July 3, but also in creating the overlapping layers of romantic myth that reached new heights after the war, Pickett's Charge and the climactic fight on the East Cavalry Field (two climaxes, one infantry and the other cavalry) were not only closely connected, but also deeply interwoven to a degree not appreciated by generations of historians. However, while one of these climactic events has been endlessly celebrated by generations of historians, the other has been largely forgotten.

All in all, and for a host of reasons, this is the most ironic development of the three days' contest at Gettysburg because the fighting on the East Cavalry Field, located around three miles behind Cemetery Ridge just to the southwest, was not only directly related to Pickett's Charge, but also had a truly symbiotic connection and relationship. As directed by General Lee on the night of July 2 at his headquarters located in the Widow Mary Thompson's house on the crest of Seminary Ridge, Major General Stuart, reinforced until he possessed four cavalry brigades and four batteries and a section of Louisiana artillery, was ordered to strike with his veteran cavalry, known as the "Invincibles" because of so many past successes, into the Army of the Potomac's rear. As Lee realized, the often-defeated army, which was now perched on the best available high ground, was now commanded by a novice (Major General George Gordon Meade, whom President Abraham Lincoln had appointed only a few days before) and hence extremely vulnerable, especially to a cavalry strike from the rear after the army had been under assault over the previous two days.

Generations of historians, especially Southerners who fully embraced the "Lost Cause" myths, have made the mistake of either entirely overlooking or minimizing the considerable threat posed by the combat capabilities of Stuart's Cavalry Corps at this time. To be sure, Stuart's men and horses were worn out and in relatively bad shape from an arduous campaign, but so was the Union cavalry, which had shadowed the Rebel horse soldiers who had screened the advance of Lee's infantry.

Most of all, Stuart's cavalrymen possessed the potential to deliver a decisive blow from the rear, and an overpowering one, when the battered infantrymen who defended Cemetery Ridge were exceptionally vulnerable. Thousands of veteran Southern cavalrymen—the finest horsemen of not only the Army of Northern Virginia, but also of the Confederacy—were made more formidable because Stuart possessed the guns of the famous Stuart Horse Artillery Battalion and other artillery units—four batteries in total and a section of Louisiana artillery. These guns were manned by seasoned artillerymen and officers, who relished nothing more than the tantalizing opportunity to open fire on the Union rear (an artilleryman's dream come true) from the east at the decisive moment to assist Pickett's attackers striking from the west. In one of the most bizarre omissions in Gettysburg historiography, historians have long overlooked the seriousness of the threat of not only thousands of Stuart's cavalrymen, but also well-trained artillerymen, whose fire could have torn holes in the Army of the Potomac's rear to create widespread devastation and panic among the defenders when they were most vulnerable.

In the past, nothing had been able to stop the full force of Stuart's cavalry, including his crack artillery arm of highly effective horse artillery, when unleashed in full force on the offensive, until the fateful afternoon of July 3 at the East Cavalry Field. Indeed, at that critical time, something unprecedented occurred when Custer and his Michigan troopers ended not only Lee's and Stuart's, but also the South's, lofty ambitions of winning a decisive victory at Gettysburg on the fatal third day. Therefore, this cavalry showdown was not only a true turning-point moment in the Battle of Gettysburg, but the most decisive clash of arms during the four years of war, and also in American history. And, most importantly, the young brigadier general who accomplished more in regard to stopping and thwarting Stuart's and Lee's ambitious tactical design that targeted Meade's rear was George Armstrong Custer.

However, even more ironically, it was another famous clash of arms that has cast the largest shadow, after Pickett's Charge, to diminish the importance of Custer's role in the Army of the Potomac's rear on the third day: Little Round Top. More recently, popular novels, such as Michael Shaara's *The Killer Angels* (1974), and the movie *Gettysburg* (1993), based on Shaara's book, have inexplicably left Custer's role completely out of the public view and even further removed from the realm of popular memory by creating an entirely new cast of heroes, especially Colonel Joshua Lawrence Chamberlain.

As noted, he commanded the 20th Maine Volunteer Infantry during the famous showdown on Little Round Top on Meade's extreme left on the afternoon of July 2. By way of the modern media, including film and books, Chamberlain was made into nothing short of a superhero for leading the attack that he, in fact, never ordered or led at a time when the attackers (the 15th Alabama Infantry Regiment) were already withdrawing because of high losses, lack of ammunition, and lack of water in their canteens during one of the year's hottest days, while Custer led two dramatic saber charges (first with the 7th Michigan Cavalry and then with the 1st Michigan Cavalry), when outnumbered—unlike Chamberlain in defending the southern side of Little Round Top against the 15th Alabama—to thwart Stuart's far larger and more serious attempt to strike the rear of the vulnerable Army of the Potomac.

Nevertheless, and as noted, Custer and the East Cavalry Field have been mostly forgotten to this day in popular memory and imagination, unfairly relegated to general obscurity in one of the most bizarre cases of inversion of history in America's saga. Reading Shaara's best seller, which won the Pulitzer Prize for Fiction in 1975, and watching the movie *Gettysburg* have succeeded in leaving millions of viewers with the distinct impression that Custer was not even present on the field, and especially that he certainly played no important role on the crucial afternoon of July 3. In the triumph of popular fiction that evolved into popular history in a seamless transition, colorful and romantic fiction—like a cheap romance novel penned by a hack author with a vivid imagination—has effectively replaced solid history in the popular imagination in regard to the most important cavalry clash during the most important battle of the Civil War. In regard to filmmakers, the Vietnam era antiestablishment film *Little Big Man* (1970) has also succeeded in having left an enduring image of Custer as nothing more than a conceited, buffoonish clown—a gross distortion and misrepresentation from a Hollywood scriptwriter—instead of a savior on the third day at Gettysburg.

In still another striking paradox to obscure his vital contributions to a decisive success in the army's rear on a day of decision, Custer's primary opponent cast a giant shadow on what happened on July 3. Unlike young Custer, who commanded the Michigan Cavalry Brigade during his first major battle and when he was still unknown in the North and a recent dismal failure at West Point, General Stuart was already a national hero across the South. He had become an idol and legend of his Southern republic for his many daring cavalry feats since 1861, while compiling an unparalleled record of success. In contrast, Custer, an eager new brigadier general and anxious for recognition, badly wanted to prove his worth to his men and even himself, while Stuart enjoyed the peak of his lofty reputation and amazing career as the South's top cavalryman.

As demonstrated in full on July 3, Custer was a dynamic cavalry leader on the rise, while Stuart's fortunes were in the process of spiraling downward, thanks in large part to what this young brigadier general from Ohio accomplished against the odds when the Southern army's finest cavalrymen were defeated for the first time in a fair and open-field fight in a major battle of extreme importance. At this time, it was almost as if the gods of war had turned their smiles away from the once-favored Stuart, because he had basked in fame for nearly two years, to shine on a new leader who had been suddenly thrust into the spotlight—a dramatic reversal of fortunes best symbolized by the importance of what happened on the East Cavalry Field. Unlike Custer, who miraculously survived one fight after another despite leading daring charges from 1863 to 1865, General Stuart was fated to be mortally wounded by one of Custer's Michigan men in May 1864 at Yellow Tavern, Virginia, where the iconic Southern leader suffered still another stunning defeat like he had at the East Cavalry Field on July 3, 1863.

General Stuart's death at age thirty-two only added to the considerable romance surrounding the Army of Northern Virginia's top cavalryman, and his legend grew to such heights, both during and after the war, to ensure that his list of critical failures in such a key situation as at the East Cavalry Field were forgotten, especially since they were covered up by General Lee for the overall good of the army and nation. After all, General Lee knew that his reeling army and nation needed to come together and that there was no time for either culprits or scapegoats after the Gettysburg defeat and the repulse of his second invasion of the North, especially when combined with the fall of strategic Vicksburg, Mississippi, which cut the Confederacy in half.

Most of all at such a crucial time in the life of the infant nation, the army's foremost leaders, especially the ever-popular "gay cavalier," who symbolized the revered concept of Virginia nobility and aristocratic warriors, simply could not be sacrificed on the altar of official and public criticism when the Confederacy was fighting for its very life during its darkest days before 1865. And General Stuart's lofty reputation and image were part of the Old Dominion's pantheon of sacred heroes, who were revered by the Southern people. Even Stuart's disastrous June 1863 raid, when he had needed instead to provide

Lee with a flow of reliable intelligence during the first two days of fighting at Gettysburg, also cast a giant shadow over Stuart's failures on the final day, directing the focus of generations of historians away from the East Cavalry Field. But in truth, Stuart's greatest failure came on the East Cavalry Field, and it was a decisive one.

Ironically, while Stuart escaped becoming a national scapegoat and then became glorified to new heights because of his wartime death and the rise of the postwar "Lost Cause" romance that celebrated all things Confederate, Custer was destined to not be so fortunate in the historical record during the decades following the Civil War. The extensive writings of extremely partisan and mythmaking "Lost Cause" authors glorified Stuart to no end and continued to catapult him into the lofty realm of the upper strata of Confederate heroes. In overall moral terms that justified this glorification in Southern minds, he was viewed as the embodiment of Southern manhood and served as an iconic idol.

Like Lee's own long list of mistakes at Gettysburg, so Stuart's failures on the afternoon of July 3 were conveniently overlooked and covered up almost before the last shot had been fired. In consequence and as already mentioned, Stuart's reputation as the South's greatest of all cavaliers only increased in the postwar years, when Confederate mythmaking reached new heights of truly outlandish, if not ridiculous, proportions. Out of necessity, Stuart's glorification excluded the true story of what happened in the Army of the Potomac's rear on July 3, which was another factor that ensured that Custer's achievements in saving the day rapidly faded away in the popular memory, a strange case of historical osmosis that has grossly distorted the historical record.

Still other factors guaranteed that Custer's key contributions to the decisive victory were forgotten by generations of Americans, including many people in the North. Ironically, Custer's own penchant for writing and his longtime ambition of becoming a successful author might well have played a part in distracting him from the grim realities that lay in store for him in the Little Bighorn valley on the afternoon of June 25, 1876. With his customary ambition and hard work ethic that continued throughout his life, Custer began to write his war memoirs about his Civil War days for the popular *Galaxy Magazine*, which was published in New York City. The first five installments of his eagerly awaited memoir appeared in issues during March, April, May, and June 1876 to the delight of an eager reading public. Almost incredibly, Custer wrote whenever the best opportunity and extra time were presented on the march to a cruel rendezvous with destiny at the Little Bighorn.

Of course, the profit-focused editors of *Galaxy* were as ambitious as Custer, and they planned for regular installments of his Civil War memoir to be published in their popular magazine. But Custer's tragic death with more than two hundred ill-fated troopers of five 7th Cavalry companies abruptly ended those ambitious plans. In the end, Custer only completed his war memoirs through the beginning of the 1862 Peninsula Campaign. He completed his work with the Battle of Williamsburg, which was fought on the Virginia Peninsula on May 5, 1862, near the beginning of the Peninsula Campaign. Therefore, Custer never wrote about his greatest success during the war years, which was his remarkable performance on the East Cavalry Field at Gettysburg. Not having the full story of Custer's role on the afternoon of July 3, 1863, was still another factor that has obscured the importance of what he achieved against the odds and the South's best cavalryman at Gettysburg.

Most of all, Custer has been unfairly judged and condemned in the historical record for the misjudgments and mistakes—fairly normal under the circumstances because of faulty army intelligence and the entirely unpredictable behavior of Northern Great Plains warriors—that he committed on his last day in the Montana Territory. Indeed, one of America's most famous battles—although actually nothing more than a large skirmish and entirely insignificant—has also played a large part in obscuring Custer's all-important success on the third day at Gettysburg. This most famous clash in the lengthy history of America's Indian Wars—the iconic "Custer's Last Stand," which was Custer's most dismal performance of his career—all but guaranteed the permanent distortion of the historical record in regard to Custer's July 3 role by casting the largest shadow over his stirring performance in the Army of the Potomac's rear.

The Battle of the Little Bighorn raged with an intensity unprecedented in the history of the Indian Wars on the hot afternoon of June 25, 1876, and the tragic results shocked America to the core after Custer was wiped out with five companies of his 7th Cavalry during the greatest victory achieved by Native Americans—thanks to many modern weapons, especially the fast-firing Henry rifle—during the centuries of America's relentless westward expansion. To this day, and especially in regard to his stirring role at Gettysburg, Custer is still best known for having led his hard-riding troopers straight into the depths of the Little Bighorn's timbered valley in an audacious attack on the immense Sioux and Cheyenne village that resulted in one of the greatest military disasters in America's saga. Custer's ignominious demise in short order has remained one of the most hotly debated mysteries in American military history.

The seemingly endless controversies surrounding Custer and the famous fight along the Little Bighorn have remained alive to this day because there were no survivors in his immediate command of five companies. This monumental fiasco—not only resulting from Custer's own decision making but also from the failures of his high-ranking superiors in faraway headquarters and top 7th Cavalry lieutenants, who found a perfect lone scapegoat in Custer to mask their own failures—has led to enduring misconceptions and misinterpretations (part of the enduring Custer myth) that have persisted to this day. First and foremost, because the fight reached legendary mythical status and proportions, the Little Bighorn disaster forever branded Custer with the most simplistic of explanations: the ultimate fool, a terrible tactician, and a bungler of the first magnitude, who lacked common sense as a battlefield commander. What was established was the enduring popular myth of the mindless glory hunter, who got all his men killed for no other reason than his own soaring ambitions.

Of course, such a simplistic analysis of the many complex factors that ensured defeat at the Little Bighorn was simply not the case, and Custer proved that he was the antithesis of this portrayal by his superior battlefield performances from 1863 to 1865. After all, Custer had fully demonstrated that he was an aggressive, flexible, skillful, and fast-thinking battlefield commander of both cavalry and horse artillery during some of the war's most severe battles, especially at Gettysburg.

Contrary to the popular stereotypes that became the traditional views about the Little Bighorn disaster, Custer certainly was not a narrow-minded and tactically inflexible commander who could do nothing but launch mindless frontal charges in blind fashion at every possible opportunity. Nevertheless, the traditional stereotypes, misconceptions, and myths have continued to dominate our view of the simplistic Custer to this day because of the flood of literature—historical and fictional—about "Custer's Last Stand" that has flowed steadily for nearly a century and a half, the antithesis of Custer's crucial role and performance on the third day at Gettysburg.

All in all, this largely one-sided Custer historiography has thoroughly twisted the truth to transform one of America's most capable cavalry commanders of the Civil War, especially at Gettysburg, into nothing more than a blunderer without an ounce of military talent as a battlefield commander and tactician. This popular portrayal was no accident, providing the perfect scapegoat that had been needed by the army, its leaders, and even the president, Ulysses S. Grant, to hide their own long list of mistakes and failures that ensured that Custer rode to his doom in the Montana Territory and never returned from the Little Bighorn valley. Consequently, Custer has become the symbol of folly and unprecedented disaster in popular culture to this day—the popular myth that has obscured his key July 3, 1863, performance in an entirely disproportionate manner.

Evolving from America's iconic hero of the Civil War years to the alleged lone architect of one of the most famous disasters in American military history has occurred because of the mythmaking and longtime disproportionate focus of historians on only a very short fight of little importance—unlike the all-important clash on the East Cavalry Field—in a remote region seen by very few Americans. Probably no figure in America's saga has been more maligned than Custer has for what happened during only a few hours along the Little Bighorn. Like President Grant, historians have pointed their fingers of blame at Custer. Decade after decade, they have faithfully and predictably poured forth a voluminous amount of writings about Custer's failures in what was little more than a hot firefight by Civil War standards, to negate the true extent and importance of his success at Gettysburg. Consequently, what has resulted has been one of the greatest distortions in American history in regard to one of America's most famous military leaders.

Nevertheless, in the ultimate irony, Custer is still best remembered in the twenty-first century for his worst day—June 25, 1876—for his performance in a small-scale battle of absolute insignificance, while ignoring his most important success as a military commander on his finest day, July 3, 1863, during the dramatic cavalry showdown that helped to decide America's fate. This gross, if not perverse, distortion has obscured what Custer accomplished against the odds at Gettysburg to save the day in the army's rear.

Even more paradoxical, Custer had been widely viewed as America's premier Indian fighter when events at the Little Bighorn proved quite the opposite. Ironically, stemming from the legacy of the Civil War years, but more in 1864 and 1865 than in 1863, Custer continued to possess this lofty reputation on the western plains even when he lacked the proper level of experience and record of achievement as an Indian fighter. Ironically, Custer had been widely viewed, even by his own Michigan men, as a commander who lacked the necessary level of experience when he gained the rank of brigadier general at age twenty-three and achieved the most important success of his career.

Still another factor—a most unfortunate one—has also emerged to deny Custer the well-deserved laurels for what he achieved on July 3: today's cyber-propagandists. Therefore, this book is a corrective history, because the internet has provided a forum for cliques of self-serving individuals with aggressive agendas to deny Custer his due for what he achieved at Gettysburg. Unfortunately, this situation is especially the case in the Gettysburg field, which is quite unlike any other—cliquish, incestuous, clannish, and dominated by an old-boy network of self-serving authors and bloggers who have deemed themselves the leading experts in their respective fields despite the lack of proven expertise—partly because of the financial rewards connected to this lucrative field. In corrupt collusion, they have long worked closely hand in hand (like a political propaganda organization) not only to promote but also to constantly reinforce their work, including books that have minimized the significance of Custer's role on July 3 to emphasize the alleged superiority of their own self-serving side of history on the internet (today's ultimate propaganda tool of manipulation, especially in the hands of anonymous critics who desire a nonthinking compliance to their will and self-serving personal views by way of censure through aggressive criticism).

These well-organized Civil War blogs not only endlessly promote the party line in the politicizing and propagandizing of history, but also smear historians who have dared to challenge the organized group think that is linked to the prestige, profits, and reputations of these clannish authors and publishers—an old Soviet Union kind of eliminating competition to protect their own books, even if out of date. These well-organized internet cronies discredit (by creating "reasonable doubt," since some of these people are lawyers and cyber-bullies) any historian who has dared to overturn their outdated, self-serving views by piling on an avalanche of coordinated, well-organized and even scripted comments to corrupt historical truths, new ideas, and contrary views to set back generations of Civil War historiography—sheer propaganda, more political than historical—of the twenty-first century.

Even more, and in the most shameful form of self-interest, they have discredited the very men who fought at the East Cavalry Field with great heroism by dismissing their personal words from their writings that indicate the cavalry battle's supreme importance in Meade's rear by accusing them of false claims—armchair and latter-day manipulators of the truth without PhD or military, especially combat, experience or expertise. To defend their self-serving positions, they simply dismiss out of hand the contradictory accounts of veterans, including generals and army commanders, whom they are not in agreement with in the form of censure: basically a silencing of history. But in fact these veterans' postwar accounts, including not only Union regimental, brigade, and division commanders but also even General George Gordon Meade himself, are more accurate and more faithful representations of the truth than many of the too often self-serving officers' reports in the *Official Records of the War of the Rebellion*. Postwar Union accounts are more reliable and accurate than the romanticized accounts of "Lost Cause" sentimentalists and apologists, who have excessively glorified the Southern experience, including on the battlefield.

Today, and almost tragically, no social media or blog has been more intolerant, agenda driven, and aggressive than those self-serving authors and their publishers (usually old friends with self-serving agendas) and their cronies to safeguard their reputations and profits than those who have been determined to deny George Armstrong Custer's role in stopping Stuart at the East Cavalry Field.

Despite reliable existing evidence that has emphasized quite the opposite in regard to the true story of what happened in the Army of the Potomac's rear, a number of nonprofessional Civil War authors—rather than PhDs—and nonacademic publishers have made a cottage industry based on the proposition that Stuart never possessed the key mission of attacking into the Union army's rear, and hence Custer's role was not important in any way, shape, or form—one of the greatest modern Gettysburg myths that has continued to be perpetuated by these self-serving activists to this day. They have aggressively attempted to rewrite history in a cyber-revisionism that has resulted in creating myths. And these myths have to be protected by their self-serving creators at all costs.

More political than historical and much like the entirely wrongheaded Holocaust deniers with their sinister motivations, this anti-Stuart-in-the-rear school of active bloggers (a small number of non-academics who have been partly revealed by a prosecutorial aggressiveness usually only seen in the courtroom until the age of social media was thoroughly exploited by these modern propagandists) have attempted to rewrite history to support their book sales and have inflated their reputations created by their blogs, where the twisting of the truth has become a well-honed art form by skilled propagandists—an old Soviet Union style of silencing fundamental historical truths to protect their own reputations, egos, and books. But all the self-serving mythmakers on the Civil War blogs cannot erase the words or destroy the reputations of the men who fought at Gettysburg and who knew the truth of the situation. And they cannot eliminate fundamental historical truths, including from the often-ignored winner of the Battle of Gettysburg, General Meade, who certainly knew the truth long before Civil War blogs.

In fact, one of the reasons that Lee might well have decided against Longstreet's alternate strategy on July 3 of marching around the Round Tops in an attempt to gain the enemy's rear was because he had already decided upon a wiser and more sensible tactical plan: striking into Meade's rear with his newly arrived cavalry—the army's finest horsemen, who had rejoined the army on July 2—under the South's finest cavalry commander, Stuart. Even more, today's dissenters have claimed that Stuart's only role was to chase down the remains of a defeated army if Pickett's Charge had succeeded, without understanding that the horses of the Southern cavalry were too exhausted after the recent eight-day raid to have performed such a demanding mission as the pursuit of a defeated army. Therefore, Stuart's mission was a strike because this was the most important day of the war, in which Lee was going for broke.

Again, these extremely aggressive bloggers and social media players who are so fanatically devoted (more for personal reasons than professional or historical ones) to routinely dismissing Stuart's key role of striking into Meade's rear in conjunction with Pickett's Charge out of hand not only lack military experience but also know little if anything of horses or the animals' level of endurance, which is made worse by their obvious lack of understanding of Napoleonic tactics and the fundamental realities of what actually happened on the East Cavalry Field. It is a supreme irony that those individuals who claim to be cavalry experts today on the East Cavalry Field story are urban types and mostly professionals, including self-serving lawyers, who work in cities and have never ridden a horse in their lives or know intimately about the nuances of nature—the essence of the so-called "city slickers." Dynamic leaders like Custer and Stuart would have dismissed the life work of these modern cavalry blogger types out of hand for a host of obvious reasons because of the depth of their lack of personal and intimate knowledge as self-appointed cavalry experts who actually know nothing on any level about true warfare or cavalry other than what they have seen in movies or imagined in their heads.

Even more, these social media manipulators have failed to acknowledge the superior offensive power—even if Southern horses were worn, they were no more exhausted than those of Union troopers, including Custer's men—of Stuart's Cavalry Corps. This routine tendency to overlook the combat prowess of Stuart's Cavalry Corps is especially the case in regard to the expert gunners of Stuart's famed horse artillery, which was perhaps the best artillery arm in the Army of Northern Virginia. Even firing at long range, these cannon worked by veterans could have wreaked havoc by firing into the rear of Meade's army, especially in support of charging Rebel cavalry. Significantly, Stuart's artillery also could have fired upon any Union reinforcements dispatched to support the men defending the copse of trees and Angle sector at the so-called "high-water mark of the Confederacy."

Most importantly, what needs to be remembered about what happened on July 3 in the Army of the Potomac's rear was that it was no ordinary success and that Custer was largely responsible for winning on that day in the army's rear, and this fact was acknowledged by the men who fought at Gettysburg. Indeed, Custer played the largest role in protecting and saving the Union rear on that climactic third day, when everything was at stake. Custer aggressively led his Michigan Cavalry Brigade with a rare blend of skill and audacity to thoroughly outperform the most legendary cavalry commander of the day, General Stuart. Significantly, unlike in Custer's case, Stuart and his horsemen in gray and butternut were considered invincible by the time of the Gettysburg campaign, and they enjoyed legendary reputations that had preceded them to the East Cavalry Field. In no uncertain terms, Custer certainly proved that these were nothing more than long-existing myths during a key turning point on the climactic third day, while verifying that a new day had come for the Union cavalry.

Against the odds, the youngest general officer of the Army of the Potomac, Custer, accomplished the impossible by playing the leading role in stopping Lee's finest and more numerous cavalry from achieving its much-anticipated tactical surprise by striking into the rear of Meade's army to change the course of the Battle of Gettysburg. Consequently, it is now time for a new and closer look at the key role played by one of the most controversial generals in American history, and to explore why his July 3 performance was so important in regard to the overall outcome of the war's most decisive battle—the genesis and fundamental thesis of this groundbreaking book.

Ironically, as incorrectly believed by highly respected theorists of the time and many leading historians to this day, Custer proved that the traditional Napoleonic cavalry charges, especially the saber attack, of massed horsemen were not obsolete or hopelessly out of date on the third day. Stuart relied on his greatest cavalry charge of massed horsemen in a final bid to smash through Custer and his men that would have opened the way to the Union rear to assist Lee's desperate effort to split Meade's army in two. However, on this day of destiny, he was thwarted by two saber charges—first by the 7th Michigan Cavalry and then the 1st Michigan Cavalry—led by Custer himself, and especially the last one that met Stuart's last and mightiest offensive effort.

Clearly, Custer possessed a set of hard-hitting Napoleonic tactics of his own when he met Stuart's best offensive effort head-on with his own offensive effort that proved more than a match for the "Invincibles." However, Custer relied on much more than headlong cavalry charges in his tactical bag of tricks that saved and won the day in the army's rear. Significantly, he proved to be a highly skilled and flexible tactician, who knew how to outmaneuver and outflank the enemy while utilizing the advantages of dismounted cavalry and the firepower of his veteran horse artillery that supported his Michigan Brigade. Throughout July 3, he skillfully utilized the benefits of superior firepower—the accurate fire of rifled horse artillery and the fast-firing Spencer repeating rifles of his tough Wolverines—which ensured that Custer's troopers would not be outflanked or pushed aside on July 3, despite Stuart's best efforts. Therefore, in overall tactical terms and in masterfully orchestrating not only cavalry but also artillery together as one in a unified team in defense of the strategic crossroads of the Hanover and Low Dutch Roads, Custer masterfully combined old tactics of the Napoleonic era with the new tactics of the first modern war to stop the determined efforts of the best cavalry leader and the most experienced Southern cavalry during the dramatic showdown on the East Cavalry Field.

Like on no other battlefield in a high-stakes situation of extreme importance, which was the antithesis of what happened along the Little Bighorn in the ugliest of small-scale fights with no glory, Custer rose splendidly to the challenge in this first large-scale fight when the fate of the Union and the battle hung in the balance. If not for Custer's timely and skillful actions on the East Cavalry Field, the case can be made that there might well be no United States of America today as we know it. Of course, the establishment of two neighboring republics would have changed not only the course of American history, but also world history.

Most importantly, what Custer fully demonstrated on the afternoon of July 3 was the fact that he was well on his way to becoming one of the finest cavalry commanders on either side during the Civil War, the antithesis of today's common perception of him as the symbol of folly and hubris that paved the way for one of America's most iconic military disasters. Ironically, quite unlike today, the people—both military and civilian—of the 1860s knew the real Custer and his all-important tactical and leadership contributions at Gettysburg without the significant distortions of time, politics, and personal agendas.

For the first time, therefore, this book will reveal in great detail how the Battle of Gettysburg would not have been won by the Union without the timely and key contributions of one of America's youngest generals and the alleged architect of defeat at the Little Bighorn, and how his key role at Gettysburg helped to pave the way to Appomattox Court House in the end. For such reasons, this book will not be still another traditional and standard biography of Custer's life (far too many of these books already exist) with the usual rehashing of the same well-known information that has already been presented in a seemingly endless number of books released generation after generation. Most of all, the overall purpose of this current work has been to present as many new insights and views as possible to reveal the supreme importance of Custer's contributions on July 3, when everything was at stake for not only the young man from Ohio, but also for the American nation during the war's most important battle.

In a thoughtful essay written by Emory M. Thomas that appeared in Gabor S. Boritt's *The Gettysburg That Nobody Knows* (1997), this award-winning historian concluded quite correctly how on July 3,

> Stuart had the greater opportunity [and] had Stuart been able to overwhelm his enemies [Custer], the direction of his advance would have carried his troopers into the rear of those Federal foot-soldiers on Cemetery Ridge. And had Pickett's Charge succeeded in breaking the Union battle line, Stuart would have been in the right place at the right time to provide a rout. Stuart might have become the hero of a climactic battle that destroyed Meade's army and quite possibly won the war. Even had Pickett failed as he did, Stuart still had the chance to thunder down on the Federal infantry posted on Cemetery Ridge and rescue the day for the Confederacy [when Generals] Pickett and Stuart would have shaken hands on Cemetery Ridge and prepared to destroy portions of Meade's army at their leisure.

But relying on a powerful mixture of bold offensive tactics, tactical flexibility, dismounted cavalry, the superior firepower of repeating rifles, mobility, and a skillful use of well-served horse artillery, Custer made sure that this distinct possibility never happened, and thankfully so for the Army of the Potomac and the Union. But of course Custer was not solely responsible for this outstanding success because of his highly capable division commander, Brigadier General David McMurtrie Gregg, who made key leadership decisions that ensured Custer's success and the overall saving of the day in the army's rear. In many ways, Gregg was the mastermind of the overall battle, but Custer was the tool that fulfilled Gregg's tactical wishes and desires while also relying on his own abilities to complement his superior's efforts. But to be sure, Custer conducted his own battle in defending the strategic crossroads before the belated arrival of the ailing Gregg, who did not appear on the field until the early afternoon. In addition, Custer was blessed with having commanded excellent fighting men—the crack troopers of the Michigan Cavalry Brigade, which became the best mounted combat unit of the Army of the Potomac, thanks largely to Custer's dynamic leadership.

Nevertheless, no battle in the annals of American history has been more dominated by myths and conceptions as the bloody three days at Gettysburg, and the legacy of Custer's notable achievements at Gettysburg paid a high price of being relegated to the historical shadows because of a host of enduring myths. The vast majority of these romantic myths and fallacies, which have grossly distorted the truth of the historical record of Gettysburg, were born from the words of former officers on both sides who exaggerated their roles, while criticizing and minimizing the roles of their own comrades.

Meanwhile, during the postwar period, the South excessively glorified its leaders, especially Lee but also Stuart, disguising their failures, especially at Gettysburg, under layers of romance and myth. In a not unique American phenomenon, the winning side dominated the future writing and created the enduring myths, distortions, and misconceptions in the process of attacking opponents in print and justifying their own actions. But what was most ironic was the fact that Custer's role was not embellished or glorified, but ignored even by the winners, despite the fact that his performance rightly deserved greater recognition.

While Stuart was widely condemned for his ill-fated June raid that denied Lee his services on July 1 and July 2, he escaped condemnation for what was his greatest failure. Condemning Stuart's failure on the final day at Gettysburg would have exposed the central weaknesses and failures of Lee's tactical plan, and Lee was above reproach and all criticism, because the South had transformed him into a saintly hero and romantic symbol of the people's revolution. Therefore, in the end, a silence fell upon what happened on the East Cavalry Field while Pickett's Charge became immortalized, and fundamental truths faded away in the mists of time. For such reasons, the most forgotten turning point of the war actually occurred three miles behind the Union lines on the final day at the East Cavalry Field.

For a host of reasons, Custer has been relegated into the part of a secondary player at Gettysburg, while a cast of Union heroes, including those leaders who embellished their personal achievements to glorify themselves and their actions, rose to the fore. Consequently, the mere thought—even today—that Custer might have played a key and leading role at Gettysburg became incongruous with the overall negative image and stereotype of the tactical blunderer who led five 7th Cavalry companies to annihilation under the hot Montana sun. Therefore, the myths of Little Bighorn combined with the myths of Gettysburg (twin legacies of two wars) to deny Custer the proper recognition of his achievements in an extremely important tactical situation on the final day at Gettysburg.

But in truth, Custer was a gifted and smart tactician and dynamic leader of men, who followed him without hesitation, as was demonstrated on the East Cavalry Field. Even more, Custer's personality also played a factor in his amazing success in the vulnerable rear of the Army of the Potomac. Unlike Stuart, whose reputation had been long considerably inflated by an adoring Southern press and the admiring Southern people as Lee's top cavalry commander, Custer was still an unknown when he led his men on the East Cavalry Field. But contrary to the Southern stereotypes about one of their greatest leaders, Custer was more stable and had more common sense than Stuart, and he was more down to earth partly because of his humble past as the son of the village blacksmith in a rural community—key qualities that made him extremely reliable, mature, and sensible beyond his years, and an excellent commander of cavalry in a key battlefield situation, including on July 3.

Most of all, Custer was an aggressive man of action in early July 1863, rather than one that had been largely created by the day's popular media and by legions of fawning admirers as Stuart had, who allowed his lengthy list of past successes to go to his head by the time of the showdown on the East Cavalry Field. Much like General Ulysses S. Grant, and contrary to the enduring image that he was little more than an overdressed, elitist flop from West Point, Custer was a commonsense westerner who had known a host of setbacks and low points during his difficult and challenging life, a situation quite unlike Stuart, who began life on top as a privileged member of the Virginia upper class and the top levels of society.

As mentioned, Custer was a small-town product of east central Ohio, and this humble background reflected some of the best qualities of a young America on the rise and this frontier environment, where the cherished values of courage, self-sufficiency, and hard work still thrived, and more than in the east. Like Grant, who was also basically a sensible common man of the western soil from the raw lands of the Mississippi Valley, such humble roots helped to ensure that Custer never became complacent and rested on his laurels like Stuart, who had allowed himself to be seduced by his past successes by the time of the Gettysburg campaign. And unlike the popular Custer bashing that has long proclaimed him as the foolish, even stupid, author of the most famous defeat in the history of the West, Custer was practical, intelligent, and thoughtful to an inordinate degree on July 3, 1863, the key requirements that were necessary for the winning victory by an unknown young brigadier general over Lee's close friend, Stuart, who held the lofty rank of major general—a living legend—in the Army of the Potomac's rear, when Lee was going for broke as never before.

For such reasons, this current book has been written to fill key gaps in not only Custer's historiography, but also Gettysburg historiography by taking the closest look and keenest focus on Custer's role on July 3, 1863. Therefore, this book is not another history of Custer, because many highly capable and competent authors have already thoroughly covered the same well-trod ground, although many of them have been guilty of either overlooking or minimizing the supreme importance of what happened on the East Cavalry Field.

When all of the dense layers of myths, misconceptions, and stereotypes are finally swept away after having existed for so long, a new bright light and fresh view can be shed on the significance of Custer's overall contributions at Gettysburg on both a tactical and strategic level. Indeed, Custer's leading role was one of extreme importance, and more than previously realized by the vast majority of historians, including experts in Civil War and Little Bighorn history. In saving the day in the army's rear on July 3, Custer made the correct tactical decisions and personally led two key cavalry charges, which ensured that the South's best cavalrymen never attacked into the Union rear.

Therefore, to get to hidden truths beyond the myths and misconceptions, the story of Gettysburg has to be told anew and from an entirely fresh perspective to reveal the most overlooked and hidden chapter of the largest battle ever fought on the North American continent. This fundamental truth requires a new look at not only Custer but also the climactic showdown of cavalry in the army's rear on the war's most decisive afternoon—the most important one in the Confederacy's short lifetime, when the destiny of a nation hung in the balance. To truly understand what happened on July 3 and why it happened that way, it is essential to view Custer's role from an entirely new perspective in regard to the crucial showdown on the East Cavalry Field to reveal the true story of the decisive Union victory in the Army of the Potomac's rear.

For more than a century and a half, the romance and glorification that has surrounded the South's greatest cavalry hero, the plumed Virginia cavalier who had known fame without limits, has also obscured what was his greatest failure in his military career on the afternoon of July 3. For more than a century, this excessive deification of Stuart has played a large role in obscuring the fundamental truths about what happened on the East Cavalry Field and the overall importance of Custer's role, because Stuart's failures were an ugly reality that needed to be silenced by top Confederate leadership, including General Lee, for the overall good of the Confederate nation and for the people's morale to continue the struggle to the bitter end.

Consequently, for a host of reasons, especially in regard to enduring historical myths and misconceptions, it is now time to take a closer look at Custer and his actions during his first major battle, without the omnipresent shadow of the most disastrous single day of his career on June 25, 1876. After all, that day occurred more than a dozen years after the final showdown on the third day at Gettysburg. But there existed a strong connection between July 3, 1863, and that final day amid the rolling hills of the Montana Territory, because Custer hoped to recapture the kind of important victory—not to mention his long-lost youth when he had been twenty-three and his wish for once again gaining national recognition with a sparkling victory as during the Civil War—that he had won on another hot afternoon in Adams County, Pennsylvania, around two thousand miles to the east.

In a strange symbiotic relationship, if young Custer had not won glory on the afternoon of July 3, 1863, he probably would not have commanded the 7th Cavalry, and his five companies would not have been wiped out on an obscure, grass-covered hilltop. Indeed, in many ways, Custer was still searching for the glory he had first found on the East Cavalry Field when he rode into the Little Bighorn valley on June 25, 1876, and that earlier glory had long passed him by. But, of course, what Custer at age thirty-six, prematurely balding and having lost the handsomeness of his youth, was searching for was now well beyond his reach and had already passed him by like his long-vanished youth on that remote Ohio frontier, although he almost certainly never realized these basic truths until it was far too late.

Indeed, Custer's relentless search for the same kind of sparkling victory that he had won at Gettysburg led him with too few men into a strange and isolated place that he had never seen before—the remote valley of the Little Bighorn—and into the midst of a powerful opponent, whom he did not understand like the Rebels of old, and straight to a cruel fate that ended his career. Custer's youthful optimism and pursuit of what was unattainable to him—another day of glory like on July 3, 1863—came far too late, because his youth and the distant memories of the East Cavalry Field could no longer be regained by one of the North's greatest heroes, no matter how hard he tried.

Despite the overall importance of what occurred on the East Cavalry Field, this special place where one of the war's greatest cavalry clashes was fought has long remained one of the most obscure and least visited spots on the Gettysburg battlefield generation after generation—the antithesis of Pickett's Charge. Ironically, this development has occurred only because Custer's vital role in thwarting what had been envisioned by Lee and Stuart—formerly a highly effective and winning team of fellow Virginians—as delivering the masterful "coup de grace," in the words of Professor James M. McPherson, to the Army of the Potomac has long been underappreciated.

At long last, therefore, it is time for Custer to receive the long overdue recognition that he rightly deserves in regard to his vital contributions in saving the day in the army's rear at Gettysburg. However, to this day, Custer has continued to be seen and judged by what happened at the most mythical defining moment (June 25, 1876) in American history, while his role on July 3, 1863, was a true defining moment in the nation's history but has been forgotten. In the end, generations of writers and historians have embraced the myths and romance of a meaningless battle along the Little Bighorn, while ignoring Custer's decisive role in the most crucial battle in a true turning-point moment in American history.

Ironically, Stuart's monumental failures during the Gettysburg campaign—better known for his embarrassment at Brandy Station and then his ill-timed June raid rather than what happened on July 3—have obscured the man who played the largest role in winning the day in the Army of the Potomac's rear. But while Stuart and his image were elevated even higher in the pantheon of great Confederate leaders after the war, partly because of his 1864 death, to become a Southern martyr and iconic saintlike figure, the supreme importance of Custer's role on July 3 faded away, while his death in the Montana Territory doomed him to greater controversy than ever before. If he had been killed in the war like Stuart instead of at the Little Bighorn, then the significance of Custer's contributions on the critical third day would not have been so thoroughly forgotten.

In another striking paradox, the focus of historians has been incorrectly pointed in the wrong direction by concentrating on how Stuart failed Lee by his eight-day absence from the army during his overly ambitious raid that deprived Lee of his "eyes and ears," when the army's commander actually possessed sufficient cavalry to lead his advance deeper into Pennsylvania and gather intelligence, a case of Lee having badly misused his existing cavalry that magnified the fact that he had delegated too much authority (a fundamental weakness in leadership that applied to his other top lieutenants and which came back to haunt him at Gettysburg) to Stuart. But Stuart's greatest failure was on July 3, 1863, when he let Lee and the Army of Northern Virginia down by a disastrous performance on all levels in an absolutely crucial situation. Therefore, in the end, Stuart was not as much wrong in conducting his raid as he has been long branded by generations of historians, and these errors were not as great as the ones he made on July 3.

Ironically, Stuart has not been blamed for his greatest failure of all—in fact, of his entire career—in one of the most astounding paradoxes of Civil War historiography. This situation has revealed another myth regarding July 3, 1863: the myth that Stuart was the greatest of all cavalry commanders, which was not the case. He had one of his worst days when facing Custer, who outthought and outfought him, when it counted the most. Of course, Stuart was truly an outstanding cavalry commander in the early part of the war, but this was certainly not the case by the time of the decisive showdown at Gettysburg.

Fortunately for the Union, while Stuart was experiencing a sharp decline in both abilities and reputation at this time, July 3 presented Custer with the first opportunity for him to truly shine. In this sense, the climactic showdown on the East Cavalry Field represented a classic case of an upcoming man of the future meeting a complacent man (a case of hubris from garnering so many successes and accolades) because of too much praise, if not outright glorification, in the past, and with predictable results.

Nevertheless, to this day, Stuart is still viewed as the greatest cavalry commander of the Civil War, while Custer is seen by many as one of the greatest failures because of the disaster along the Little Bighorn, a bizarre inversion of historical realities and events only because Stuart's dismal failure and Custer's sparkling success in the Army of the Potomac's rear have been obscured to this day—additional evidence that Henry Ford was correct when he famously said that "all history is bunk."

In today's antiheroic age when even social media has become more important to me-first people and culture than authentic heroes and traditional American values, which have continued to decline at a rapid rate at this time, George Armstrong Custer now seems terribly outdated and little more than an anachronism from a bygone age, of no importance or relevance in the twenty-first century. During the nineteenth century, Americans had needed heroes in the so-called winning of the West, and Custer served as the ideal martyr to the American people when he was killed at the Little Bighorn.

As much as Custer has been ridiculed and condemned beginning in the second half of the twentieth century for his Manifest Destiny–inspired role, he actually helped to create the modern America that we know today because of what he achieved in ensuring the defeat of Lee's and Stuart's secret plan on July 3. Custer gave the war-weary people of the North new and brighter hopes for the successful waging of America's most costly war to the bitter end, emerging as an authentic war hero during the most traumatic period of America's history.

Quite simply, Custer's role on the afternoon of the last day at Gettysburg was a classic case of the axiom "cometh the hour, cometh the hour": the man and his hour indeed having met in the Army of the Potomac's rear, when everything was at stake for the fate of two nations. In the words of Brigadier General Fitzhugh Lee, who commanded one of Stuart's best cavalry brigades, from a letter, Stuart's crucial mission and primary purpose was "effecting a surprise in the enemy's rear," when the weary defenders of Cemetery Ridge faced thousands of attackers in Lee's great offensive effort, Pickett's Charge. This desperate crisis situation that Custer successfully met in the army's rear provided the opportunity that literally placed Custer squarely on the path of becoming one of the war's most talented cavalry commanders. Fortunately for the Army of the Potomac, Custer was exactly the right man at the right place and at the right time in a tactical and crisis situation that caused him to boldly and correctly twice disobey his orders from a superior, because he believed that he was right—he was—and he knew that the day's greatest crisis was about to play out in Meade's right-rear and not farther south where he had been ordered to rejoin his own division under Brigadier General Judson Kilpatrick.

Even more, Custer seems to have been motivated like ancient Achilles, the greatest of the Greek heroes and warriors, who made his fateful choice between achieving glory or obscurity. But unlike Achilles, who fell to rise no more in the Trojan War, Custer survived the bloodiest war in American history to finally succumb to an opponent who was considered unworthy (ironically, much like Stuart and his men viewed the hated Yankees at the time of the Battle of Gettysburg), which was certainly not the case. Indeed, if not for this son of a lowly blacksmith from a small Ohio town in the middle of nowhere in an amazing battlefield performance that defied all the odds and expectations, "Mr. Lincoln's army" might not have emerged as the winner of the most important battle in American history. Quite simply, no brigadier general officer, especially a newly minted one and only twenty-three, had a more disproportionate impact in the nation's most important battle on a decisive field of strife in America's saga than Custer on that afternoon.

But despite commanding an inferior force against Stuart's "Invincibles," and by relying on aggressiveness and tactical flexibility, he successfully blocked and parried Stuart's best offensive efforts, which were calculated to deliver the final blow that would have led to the Army of the Potomac's destruction. In the end, and despite being one of the youngest generals in the annals of American history, Custer played the largest role in saving the day on the East Cavalry Field.

While Custer is forever known for his famous "Last Stand" at a time when he had ample experience and hard-earned renown across America for his Civil War exploits, his far more important "First Stand" in defending the vital intersection of the Hanover and Low Dutch Roads has been long minimized and forgotten. Consequently, a seemingly endless number of books have focused on the well-known story of the "Last Stand," while overlooking Custer's far more important "Last Stand" of all on the afternoon of July 3 and a true day of decision, a classic case of myth superseding history while obscuring a host of fundamental truths.

The story of Gettysburg has been the most written about subject in the annals of Civil War historiography, and hundreds of books have focused on the struggle for possession of the vital ten roads that intersected at Gettysburg, which made this town suddenly so strategically important. But, ironically, these books have not focused on one of the most important chapters of the Battle of Gettysburg—the relatively forgotten struggle in the Army of the Potomac's rear, which was absolutely crucial in regard to the battle's overall outcome. Seemingly endless numbers of books and even a popular film, the 1994 movie *Gettysburg*, which is still played nonstop in major gift shops and bookstores in Gettysburg to this day, have endlessly praised the defensive stand of Brigadier General John Buford's men of the First Cavalry Division on the first day, while the most important and more crucial cavalry stand at Gettysburg actually came two days later at the East Cavalry Field.

Despite being based on a novel from the 1970s, this movie made a hero of not only Buford for his July 1 performance but, as mentioned, also Chamberlain for his role at Little Round Top on July 2. Therefore, for a new generation of Americans, Buford, not Custer, emerged as the cavalry savior at Gettysburg and Chamberlain the infantry savior at Gettysburg. Therefore, historians of Union cavalry at Gettysburg have focused on the wrong day and the wrong commander at the wrong time in regard to the most decisive contribution to Union success at Gettysburg—a most ironic development that has obscured fundamental historical truths to this day.

What was noticeably absent in this film—based upon a book of fiction—was anything about Custer or the all-important fight on the East Cavalry Field, almost as if it never existed. Instead, the film focused on the traditional story of Pickett's Charge without any hint of Stuart's vital role on July 3, thus presenting only half of the story of Lee's offensive effort on July 3, with the usual romance and glorification. Ironically, this film is still respected and considered definitive, especially in regard to Chamberlain's overly embellished role, which was presented in the most dramatic possible fashion. In this regard, Buford, Chamberlain, Little Round Top, and Pickett's Charge have all cast a giant shadow, obscuring Custer's role, which was left out of the film and a large number of books—basically a historical silencing and perhaps the most bizarre anomaly in Gettysburg and Civil War historiography. Hundreds of books about Custer's Last Stand have never mentioned his most important "First Stand," which was a decisive turning point in America's most decisive battle.

How could the blundering tactical architect of the so-called "massacre" at Little Bighorn have saved the day at Gettysburg with brilliant tactics? This is a historical question and incongruity that helped to ensure the longtime silencing of Custer's magnificent performance on the third day at Gettysburg. Even the East Cavalry Field itself betrayed Custer and his memory by its obscure location three miles from the main battlefield, whereas the clump of trees located at the famous Angle has been long celebrated as the "high-water mark" and turning point of the battle. Instead, there are no large clumps of trees, Angle, or "high-water mark" monument on the East Cavalry Field, which bestows the mistaken impression of an entirely insignificant backwater without anything of importance whatsoever having occurred there—the last existing major myth about the Battle of Gettysburg, which has continued to endure to this day.

As it exists today, this development has been largely the result of the early and disproportionately powerful influence of the press of Richmond, Virginia—the capital of the Confederacy—in promoting Virginia heroics in Pickett's Charge and emphasizing the glory won by three Virginia brigades of Pickett's Division in a tragic defeat, which is the traditional view escalated to new heights by the embellished romance of the "Lost Cause," historians, and writers of fiction during the postwar years and well into the twentieth century. The same case could not be made by the "Lost Cause" mythmakers in regard to the most dismal failure—which was considered less heroic—of one of the South's greatest heroes, Stuart.

Consequently, in the end, the defeat of Stuart's "Invincibles" in the Army of the Potomac's rear was ignored and then forgotten in what was a deliberate silencing at the highest levels of Southern military and civilian leaders out of necessity for sound political, military, and domestic reasons—basically a cover-up of what was in truth the greatest and most significant cavalry failure of the Civil War, because Stuart was largely responsible for this monumental setback of extreme importance. After all, Stuart was a revered Virginian, like Lee, and both revered iconic heroes escaped blame for the disaster on July 3 that ended the invasion of Pennsylvania in the most dismal manner.

Most importantly, in the end, the clash of cavalry on the East Cavalry Field was nothing less than America's most decisive cavalry battle in which a recent staff officer and a mere captain saved the day for the Union by relying on skill, leadership ability, and aggressive Napoleonic era tactics, which, ironically, were reborn in Meade's rear in an open-field setting of a broad plain that was traditionally Napoleonic and unlike the norm in Virginia. But all of this has been forgotten because Custer lives in immortality today because of the worst day of his career at the Little Bighorn, while his finest hour on July 3 has faded away to dark obscurity. While almost every American knows about Custer at the Little Bighorn and about the Battle of Gettysburg, his vital role in saving the day at Gettysburg is not generally known or appreciated today.

Therefore, no battlefield in America should be more closely identified with Custer and appreciated for his outstanding success during the war years than the East Cavalry Field. Even more ironic, if Custer had been killed on July 3, 1863, his role and memory would rank high as a primary savior at Gettysburg and would be celebrated as such—and not Buford and Chamberlain, who enjoyed long lives to embellish their roles at Gettysburg, unlike Custer.

Unlike at the Little Bighorn, Custer applied his experience and West Point lessons, which paid immense dividends, to reap a most impressive success when it was needed most by General Meade and the Army of the Potomac. Paradoxically, by way of largely Napoleonic tactics that thwarted the ambitious Lee-Stuart plan to strike the Army of the Potomac's rear, Custer proved that a bright future for the Union cavalry had come at long last. Fortunately for him, and unlike at the Little Bighorn and contrary to the myth that his 7th Cavalry was an elite regiment in June 1876, Custer commanded a truly elite command at Gettysburg. Custer's four hard-hitting regiments of the Michigan Cavalry Brigade were perhaps the best cavalry command in the Army of the Potomac, thanks partly to the fact that so many troopers were armed with the fast-firing Spencer rifle and carbine, a seven-shot repeating rifle. Quite simply, Custer was destined to never command better troopers than his beloved Wolverines, and they performed magnificently on the third day of the battle.

Here, during his finest hour at the most forgotten turning point of the Battle of Gettysburg on the East Cavalry Field, Custer played the leading role in ending the greatest threat to Meade's rear, ensuring that the attackers of Pickett's Charge were systematically cut to pieces by Cemetery Ridge's defenders. The same cannot be said of either John Buford on July 1 or Joshua Chamberlain on July 2, when they both faced less formidable odds and lesser challenges in less important situations than Custer. Therefore, it is a mistake for historians to have placed Chamberlain and Buford above Custer.

Indeed, in truth in regard to the performance of the cavalry arm alone, the forgotten crucial role played by Custer superseded in importance the celebrated role of John Buford, thanks to the excesses and embellishments of the popular Shaara novel and the movie *Gettysburg*. Had Custer failed on the afternoon of July 3, then John Buford—and also Chamberlain for that matter—would have been basically forgotten and relegated to little more than mere footnotes in today's history books, and they would never have emerged as cult heroes of the battle. This situation has once again demonstrated that no battle in American history has been more romanticized and dominated by layers of myth, which not only have continued to exist to this day, but also have continued to rise from misinformation and ignorance.

Therefore, as much as possible, this book has been written to set the historical record straight and to restore an extremely important chapter of Gettysburg history beyond the realms of cult worship, the most recent fashionable trends in history, and crass commercialism that have long obscured fundamental truths in the annals of Gettysburg history. For these reasons, almost every visitor to the Gettysburg battlefield today knows about the so-called "high-water mark of the Confederacy" at the copse of trees on Cemetery Ridge, but little, if anything, about what happened on the East Cavalry Field, although these two dramatic showdowns were closely related because they were part of the same strategy from the fertile tactical mind of the army's commander.

In consequence, the overall purpose of this book is not to tell the traditional story of Custer's life, because of the seemingly endless number of books that already have been devoted to this subject, but to explore those long-overlooked factors that explain how and why Custer enjoyed the finest day of his Civil War career on July 3 while commanding his brigade in his first major battle. This analysis has required an extremely close and detailed look at not only the men of the Michigan Cavalry Brigade, but also his opponents—Stuart and his "Invincibles"—to understand why Custer was so successful in thwarting the greatest threat posed to the Army of the Potomac's rear during the three days at Gettysburg.

On July 3, Custer was mostly responsible for defending the key intersection of the Hanover and Low Dutch Roads in Meade's right-rear, which had been targeted by Stuart and Lee on the night of July 2, before the final attack into the Union army's rear. Even when officially relieved with the arrival of two reinforcing brigades and knowing that he was disobeying orders from his own division commander, Custer still refused to depart this vital sector, knowing that the key to the upcoming fight in Meade's right-rear was in retaining possession of the crossroads.

Most of all, it was Custer's successful defense of this strategic crossroads that thwarted the lofty tactical ambitions of Lee and Stuart for striking a devastating blow in Meade's rear in conjunction with Pickett's Charge. In the end, Custer's aggressiveness sabotaged the best-laid plans of Lee and Stuart—who were considered to be the two greatest strategic and tactical minds in the South—to literally save the day for the battered Army of the Potomac. Therefore, Custer's performance was more important than any other Union cavalry general at Gettysburg, including the much-celebrated role of John Buford on July 1, 1863, despite the fact that he missed participating in the two most important days of the battle. In the end, Custer achieved his greatest success by refusing to obey orders from his own division commander not once but twice. However, he gained the approval in regard to both decisions from the commander of another division (Second Division) outside his own Third Division, an unparalleled audacity for the newly appointed brigadier general, who risked his career in a classic case of moral courage on two fronts.

Even more and as noted, Custer then ensured that Stuart's ambition of gaining Meade's rear was thwarted by leading two of the most important and dramatic saber charges—one with the 7th Michigan Cavalry and the next one with the 1st Michigan Cavalry—during the four years of war to save the day for the Army of the Potomac during its most crucial hour. In the end, no one was more responsible for this remarkable success than Custer, while thousands of Stuart's veteran troopers and the batteries of his famed horse artillery and other artillery units posed the greatest threat to Meade's rear. Because Stuart possessed seasoned batteries, the cavalry threat that he possessed in regard to Meade's rear complemented the massive array of artillery that supported Pickett's Charge by softening up the defenders and their thin line. In this most optimistic scenario, the hard-pressed lines of the Army of the Potomac on Cemetery Ridge would be sandwiched between guns and cavalry on the east and guns and infantry from the west, if everything had gone according to plan, if not for Custer's contributions to completely frustrate the loftiest of Southern ambitions on July 3.

Therefore, this book will focus on the final dramatic showdown on the East Cavalry Field instead of the well-known details of Custer's life, because this subject has been the most untold chapter of what was truly a high point of his early military career. In addition, this work is not involved in the usual promotion of the traditional hero worship of Custer that has so often marred past works, but will focus on an amazing tactical performance on what was the most important single day of the Civil War. Therefore, *Custer at Gettysburg* will explore the key factors that explain why he proved so successful on the afternoon of July 3, including analyzing the weaknesses of his opponent. In general, Stuart's character was less pristine than that of Custer, who has long been seen as possessing more character flaws—a view that conforms to existing stereotypes of the simplistic, rash commander who needlessly sacrificed the lives of his men—and this analysis partly explains what happened on the East Cavalry Field and why.

Largely because Stuart's bold plan to strike into the Army of the Potomac's rear was a secret expedition that was an independent operation but was planned to be unleashed in conjunction with Pickett's Charge, its presence in the official records is lacking, a situation that has bestowed the mistaken impression that the East Cavalry Field showdown was totally insignificant and nothing more than mindless combat to protect just the flank and not at all about the real mission of striking Meade's rear—one of the greatest misconceptions and fallacies of Civil War historiography.

But what can never be denied was the fact that Stuart was in Meade's rear and in position to deliver an offensive blow of extreme importance at the key moment—the exact tactical situation and location where he needed to be, because Lee himself had ordered Stuart to perform this mission on the crucial third day that would separate winner from loser at Gettysburg. Quite simply, the climactic showdown on the East Cavalry Field was all about causing havoc in Meade's rear to assist Pickett's Charge and not about protecting a flank, which was of no importance if Lee's offensive was not successful on July 3. Therefore, in the true Napoleonic tradition, Stuart was focused on striking the Army of the Potomac's vulnerable rear, because he was ordered to do so by Lee on the night of July 2, 1863, and this offered the best chance of achieving a decisive success.

In addition and partly because of these reasons, a number of problems still exist in the historical record, and the exact details of the climactic fight in Meade's rear have remained tactically confusing to this day—ironically, more in regard to the tactics rather than in regard to Stuart's overall goal of striking Meade's rear. Even one of the leading experts on the story of Union cavalry in the Civil War, Stephen Z. Starr, had no choice but to honestly admit the problems about telling the story of the tactical aspects of the fighting on the East Cavalry Field. He admitted in absolute truth how the "precise sequence of events is unclear" because of the contradictory and conflicting accounts not only from both sides, but also often from the same side.

In addition, even highly respected memoirs, especially the ones penned decades after the battle—even the famous Captain James H. Kidd's memoir, which was published nearly half a century after July 3, 1863—which have long seemed most reliable, should be seriously questioned because they have also presented a good deal of contradictory information. Then, after Custer was killed on that ill-fated June afternoon at the Little Bighorn, the formal oral addresses that were presented at Gettysburg for veterans' groups often came from individuals who seemingly were trying to gain more credit for themselves for what happened on July 3 in the absence of Custer's voice to claim otherwise. Therefore, the author has also attempted to rely only upon the most accurate information, including a previously unpublished account of the battle written on July 4, 1863, from the *Detroit Free Press*, July 15, 1863, that was written by the "special" correspondent under the heading of "From the Michigan Cavalry."

For more than 150 years, many historians have theorized about the exact causes of Confederate defeat. Many ideas have been explored except one: The Confederacy died of the myth of the superiority of its cavalry that was no longer the case by the time of the dramatic showdown on the East Cavalry Field, and the Army of Northern Virginia and the South paid a high price for this myth. Custer delivered the final death stroke to one of the longest-existing myths—cavalry superiority—upon which the Confederacy and her people had long felt supremely confident during the most important battle of the war.

But most of all, this book will finally give Custer, who was a more complex personality—thoughtful and analytical—than has been generally presented in the usual one-dimensional caricature of him, his just due during the most important campaign—the scene of his first charge in a major battle—in his finest hour, which was the antithesis of the disaster along the Little Bighorn (the scene of his last charge), when the Army of the Potomac's life was at stake as never before. Even President Abraham Lincoln marveled at how Custer led charges "with a whoop and a shout," and this was especially the case when he led not only the 7th Michigan Cavalry, but also the 1st Michigan Cavalry in two saber charges in crucial situations on his finest day, when his best qualities as a dynamic leader and gifted tactician rose to the fore.

Indeed, these were no two ordinary charges led by Custer but represented key turning points in the all-important battle in the Army of the Potomac's rear. It was largely these two bold saber charges—first by the 7th Michigan Cavalry and then by the 1st Michigan Cavalry—led by Custer that were most responsible for thwarting Stuart's and Lee's offensive plan of striking into the Army of the Potomac's rear. Most importantly, these two timely and hard-hitting attacks were the forgotten offensive tactics that led to Custer's saving the day behind Meade's lines.

Ironically, Custer proved that offensive Napoleonic cavalry tactics, which revealed the wisdom of the considerable shock power of the frontal attack in an open-field fight, were not at all obsolete in America's first modern war under the proper circumstances, by leading these two saber charges—exactly what was needed in a crisis situation—of a bygone era to win the day, a highly unusual case of Custer thwarting Lee's Napoleonic tactics by his own Napoleonic tactics that were bolder than Stuart's own. In the end, it was Custer and his crack Michigan Brigade, which suffered nearly 90 percent of the Union cavalry losses on the East Cavalry Field to reveal a most disproportionate sacrifice, which resulted in the saving of the day in Meade's rear.

Consequently, this book presents a new view of Custer beyond the simplistic caricature created by generations of novelists, historians, and filmmakers during the final day of the epic showdown at Gettysburg, when a twenty-three-year-old brigadier general saved the day in the army's rear by thwarting the day's greatest threat by his usual aggressiveness and tactical skill. All in all, this is the story of a true American odyssey, when Custer—who was not trapped in his own popular image and string of past successes like Stuart was, who had been seduced by the adulation—had his finest day when leading a brigade in his first major battle against the South's most legendary cavalry commander.

Instead, Custer was a free thinker who was mentally and tactically flexible, who as much outthought as he outfought his opponent during one of the most crucial moments of the war. Perhaps historian Gregory J. W. Urwin said it best in emphasizing in his classic work *Custer Victorious: The Civil War Battles of General George Armstrong Custer*: "The Battle of Gettysburg was over, and thanks to George Armstrong Custer and his Michigan Brigade, as much as to any other commander and command in the Army of the Potomac, it was a Union victory." Indeed, the dramatic story of the showdown on the East Cavalry Field was not as much a case where Stuart had failed Lee and the army but where Custer had saved the day for Meade and the Army of the Potomac. What began on the East Cavalry Field was the beginning of Custer's emergence as the celebrated hero of his generation—a meteoric leap for a very young man.

While Stuart and his cavalrymen experienced their worst day, the Union cavalry enjoyed its finest day, and against the odds, at the East Cavalry Field in Meade's rear, the one-sided development and winning equation for which the young Custer was most responsible because he served as the hard-hitting hammer during the tactical chess game. However, much credit goes to his division commander, Brigadier General David McMurtrie Gregg, for allowing Custer the opportunity to excel. Indeed, the insightful and prophetic Gregg first made the decision that the strategic crossroads of the Hanover and Low Dutch Roads, where he had skirmished the day before, had to be defended at all costs. But it was Custer whom Gregg used as his effective sledgehammer to achieve his tactical objectives, including leading charges against the odds. Indeed, Gregg and Custer were kindred spirits on July 3 and fought together as a highly effective team that operated smoothly, in striking contrast to Stuart and his top lieutenants, who performed more poorly than the boys in blue.

Most importantly, because of what Custer accomplished on the afternoon of the third day, Stuart never embarked upon the relatively short ride southwest in only a brief time across the gently rolling and open ground without any obstacles or Union soldiers on Cemetery Ridge's east side that led to the Army of the Potomac's rear, as would have happened if Custer and his Wolverines had been pushed aside as so confidently expected by the highest levels of Southern leadership during one of the great cavalry clashes of the Civil War.

Indeed, General Meade and the Army of the Potomac were saved by the cavalry, and no Union officer was more responsible for this success than Custer, who masterfully defended the strategic crossroads and led two cavalry charges that played the leading role in ensuring that Stuart and thousands of his cavalrymen never struck the Army of the Potomac's rear, a rare and unprecedented success of so few men having accomplished so much and to a degree that was not seen in any other major battle of such importance during the Civil War.

All in all, this was a remarkable achievement because the most irresistible and defiant physical force of nature that stood between Stuart and thousands of his veteran troops and the rear of the hard-pressed Army of the Potomac was Custer, who outdueled and outmaneuvered the South's best cavalry leaders when America's fate hung in the balance.

Ironically, what has been most forgotten is the fact that Custer played the key cavalry role in the climactic showdown, which also played a leading role in ultimately determining the fate of slavery, because his vital contribution in the righteous crusade to destroy America's most horrific institution has been completely obscured by the popular dark imaginary of Custer as the hater of Native Americans (which was never the case) and an imperialistic crusader in buckskin who met a just fate at the Little Bighorn. Quite simply, Custer struck a decisive blow against slavery on the afternoon of July 3, 1863, but this fact has been mostly obscured by the developments beyond his control during his post–Civil War career.

Even more ironic, a larger number of books have been written about Custer and his post–Civil War career (the much-maligned "glory hunter," which far more correctly fit Stuart than Custer during the Gettysburg campaign) than any other subject in the storied history of the American West. But significantly, this is the first book ever devoted to taking an extremely detailed and close look at Custer and his vital contributions on a single day during the Civil War. Likewise, the popular myth and misconception that Stuart's July 3 mission was nothing more than a task of only defending Lee's left flank—an impossibility under the crucial circumstances of Lee's greatest offensive effort in which he planned to utilize his infantry, artillery, and cavalry to maximize his offensive capabilities because this was his last bid to win it all (the purpose of marching north of the Potomac River on the most ambitious campaign of the war was to win a decisive victory before it was too late because the South could not win a long war of attrition) in what was basically a pincer movement from the west and the east—has played its part in obscuring the overall importance of Custer's role.

All in all, young Custer's success in rising to the supreme challenge at Gettysburg made a mockery of his long list of failures at West Point, where he earned the ignominious title as the "goat" (ironically, like George E. Pickett—class of 1846—who, of course, is best known for Pickett's Charge, which Custer ensured that Stuart and his men never assisted in any way, shape, or form) of his class of 1861. Custer's performance on July 3 was a truly remarkable success in thwarting Stuart's most determined offensive efforts—leading two saber charges of his own with the 7th Michigan Cavalry and then the 1st Michigan Cavalry—to buy the precious time to ensure that Stuart never reached the Army of the Potomac's rear, possibly the last tactic expected by Stuart and his top commanders in such a key situation, when it seemed as if the strategic crossroads in Mead's rear would inevitably fall to the massive last offensive launched by Lee's finest cavaliers.

Most of all, this book is the unforgettable story of a classic case of a phoenix rising from the ashes of a miserable West Point career that would have certainly ended abruptly in considerable embarrassment and disgrace if Confederate cannon had not opened fire at Fort Sumter and given him the opportunity to rise high on his own merits, which were demonstrated in full on the East Cavalry Field. Here, Custer was more responsible for saving the day in the Army of the Potomac's rear than any other Union commander, when everything was at stake for the American nation. Indeed, as mentioned, on July 3, 1863, it was more a case of Custer succeeding in his crucial mission of stopping Stuart's best efforts to strike a decisive blow in Meade's rear than the failure of the best cavalry in the Confederacy—a testament to Custer's invaluable and decisive role in ensuring that the Union won its greatest victory of the war at Gettysburg.

Phillip Thomas Tucker, PhD<br>
Washington, DC<br>
March 1, 2019

c 1 ɔ

# One of the Youngest Generals in the Annals of American History

In the first volume of his classic two-volume work, *The Union Cavalry in the Civil War: From Fort Sumter to Gettysburg, 1861–1863*, historian Stephen Z. Starr perhaps best summarized the fundamental truth about the all-important cavalry clash in the Army of the Potomac's rear on the afternoon of July 3, 1863. In his astute on-target analysis, he concluded correctly in answering one of the most crucial questions about the three days of intense combat that swirled in and around Gettysburg, Pennsylvania, from July 1 to July 3: "What was the result of the fight? Stuart's claim that he was only protecting the left flank of the Confederate army is not worth a moment's credence. The course of the battle from its beginning makes it evident that [Stuart's] objective was to brush [Brigadier General David McMurtrie] Gregg [and Brigadier General George Armstrong Custer] out of the way and attack the rear of Meade's infantry on Cemetery Ridge, at the same time that it was attacked frontally by Pickett. In this he clearly failed."[1]

Corporal James Henry Avery's words about the importance of the tenacious cavalry struggle that was played out on the East Cavalry Field, Gettysburg, echoed those of historian Starr. A member of the 5th Michigan Cavalry of the famed Wolverine Brigade, which was led capably and with consummate skill by young Brigadier General George Armstrong Custer on the third day at Gettysburg, he wrote in his journal, with the commonsense insight and knowledge that existed in the ranks of the enlisted men, of General Robert E. Lee, "who was trying to push around the [rear right] flank of our army" to strike the rear.[2]

Even more, Avery correctly emphasized in his journal how if the bold plan of General Lee and Major General James Ewell Brown (Jeb) Stuart "had succeeded [on the last day at Gettysburg, then they] would probably have beaten us" and "won the Battle of Gettysburg."[3] Major General Stuart's faithful adjutant who served on his staff in a capable manner, Major Henry Brainerd McClellan, emphasized how Stuart's tactical objective was to unleash "an attack upon the enemy's rear."[4]

In the end, of course, there was never any Confederate cavalry and horse artillery attack on Meade's rear during the dramatic showdown, and Pickett's Charge went ahead on its own across the open fields of early summer without any assistance from the east: a tactical situation that ensured a miserable failure and a bloody repulse. Historian Edward G. Longacre, the dean of Civil War cavalry studies during the Gettysburg campaign, concluded that the Union's combined defensive and offensive efforts on the East Cavalry Field on July 3 were decisive: "Stuart's attempt to reach the rear of Meade's army in time to influence the outcome of Robert E. Lee's grand offensive had failed."[5]

But who was mostly responsible for Stuart's dismal failure and this all-important success in the Army of the Potomac's rear on the crucial third day at the Battle of Gettysburg that was a key turning point of the most important battle on the North American continent? In one of the seemingly most improbable and impossible developments, the primary architect of the most important cavalry victory at Gettysburg was a young man of only twenty-three years of age, and he had been a brigade commander only a few days when he and his Wolverine (Michigan) Brigade rose magnificently to the stern challenge on July 3, 1863. To the surprise of many Americans today, George Armstrong Custer was the name of this idealistic, romantic-minded youth from a remote area in the isolated depths of middle America, which was still considered the West in 1860.

Few Americans of the Civil War period rose up from greater obscurity than Custer, who was a small-town product from the heavily timbered hill country of east central Ohio. He was too young to have served in any of America's previous fighting that resulted in victory deep in the heart of the Republic of Mexico during the Mexican-American War of 1846–1848. Even more, he was the son of a lowly village blacksmith in New Rumley, Ohio. Custer's humble social and economic background could not have been more mundane or obscure. As an energetic teenager who did not reveal much promise, he had proven himself not suitable for teaching school, farming the land, or being an apprentice to a cabinetmaker, largely because of his fun-loving and nonserious nature. And he wanted no part of the blacksmith's trade, which guaranteed long and dreary hours in the blacksmith's shop. Under the circumstances, what was this fun-loving, immature, undisciplined, girl-happy, and idealistic young man to do in life when his prospects for any kind of true personal success, especially professional, were extremely low?

As fate would have it, Custer's long list of liabilities and disadvantages began to be transformed into positive assets when he realized that he needed a much better education to succeed in life than found on the isolated Ohio frontier. This mature realization revealed that rising ambition, a growing drive to succeed, and depth of character burned behind the happy-go-lucky facade of the fun-loving young man without a care in the world. But his large family lacked the funds and connections—social, political, or economic—necessary for the advancement of Custer's education to any higher level beyond the area's common schools.

## THE SOLUTION

In consequence, only one possible solution remained for the starry-eyed youth under the circumstances. He, of course, could only advance in life if he could obtain a free quality education, and only one place in America provided an education of extremely high quality on a scale unknown in the backwoods of Ohio: the United States Military Academy at West Point, New York. However, obtaining entry into that prestigious institution seemed all but impossible for a young man with so few prospects. But the seemingly endless obstacles and disadvantages for any chance of getting ahead in life only fueled Custer's determination to succeed and overcome what were nothing less than impossible odds—the key quality that was the trademark of Custer's personality, which was destined to serve him extremely well on future battlefields, including in the epic clash of arms at Gettysburg.

First and foremost, Custer faced a seemingly insurmountable political hurdle in regard to gaining the finest free education that was available in America at the time. Members of the Custer family at New Rumley, Ohio, were well known to be die-hard Democrats, led by their outspoken patriarch and Custer's father, Emmanuel. As the ever-talkative and popular blacksmith of New Rumley who had cornered business for miles around, he tirelessly fitted and nailed iron shoes on horses' hooves for a living with the same enthusiasm that he talked about national politics. Politics was Emmanuel's burning passion. A vexing political situation also posed an obstacle to Custer's ambitions because his local congressman, John A. Bingham, was an extreme Republican of aristocratic tastes and inclinations. Even more, he detested Democrats, especially common, working-class men like Emmanuel and his brood of equally politicized children. In fact, he was well known for possessing his own passion, which was "an avowed hatred of Democrats, such as the Custers'."[6]

Therefore, the political dilemma of young Custer seemed insurmountable because of the formidable twin obstacles of politics and economics.

However, this most disadvantageous of situations only made the young man more determined to succeed in the end, revealing the true depth of his character. Indeed, he "appeared to have no chance against such overwhelming odds, but—a true Custer—he threw caution to the winds and wrote Congressman Bingham, requesting an interview when he next returned to Cadiz [Ohio] from Washington."[7]

Due to a most favorable impression—confident, spunky, and intelligent—that he made with Congressman Bingham because he had been able to express himself much better in writing than in oral communication, as revealed with additional correspondence with the congressman, Custer's life changed forever when he overcame the odds by officially gaining entry into America's prestigious military institution of higher learning atop the bluffs overlooking the Hudson River. In his own words: "In June 1857, I entered the Military Academy at West Point as a cadet, having received my appointment thereto through the kindness of Hon. John A. Bingham, then representing in Congress the district in Ohio in which I was born, and in which I had spent almost my entire boyhood. The first official notification received by me of my appointment to the Military Academy bore the signature of Jefferson Davis, the Secretary of War [and the future president of the Confederacy] in the cabinet of President James Buchanan."[8]

Destined to graduate last in his class of 1861 of thirty-four members, Custer summarized his West Point experience—a rocky road—with a mixture of honesty and humor, which dominated life in his large family, because of the large number of demerits he had accumulated by only halfheartedly applying himself to the serious business of meeting the academy's high standards of excellence: "My career as a cadet had but little to commend it to the study of those who came after me, unless as an example to be carefully avoided. The requirements of the academic regulations, a copy of which was placed in my hand the morning of my arrival at West Point, were not observed by me in such a manner at all times as to commend me to the approval and good opinions of my instructors and superior officers. My offences against law and order were not great in enormity, but what they lacked in magnitude they made up in number."[9]

But in these words largely written to amuse readers, Custer left out what was actually most important for achieving success in the future. Despite his dismal performance as a cadet and a long list of demerits earned at West Point that left behind one of the worst records in the academy's history, Custer understood a most important quality for the creation of a successful battlefield commander. Winning at war was about much more than shiny buttons, neat uniforms, and excessive attention to precise details and parade-ground appearances, especially when it came to one's appearance at inspection. He instinctively knew that what a man achieved on the battlefield was what really mattered, and, in his mind, playing soldier boy for stuffy old officers of a bygone era at West Point was simply not that significant. He was not impressed by the academy's lofty standards and mocked them with his boyish contempt and inattention to details.

Quite simply, Custer learned only what he wanted to learn at West Point, or what he felt was most useful in the future as a battlefield commander. Most importantly, what has been most overlooked in his graduating last in his class was the fact that he fully incorporated and absorbed in totality the academy's esprit de corps and a warrior's ethos (the real purpose of West Point), and these key qualities had nothing to do with an excessive number of demerits. Inside and out, and although his own superiors and instructors were not fully aware of this fact, Custer was already a model soldier at heart and in spirit, which was what really mattered most of all on the battlefield. Not revealed by his long list of demerits, he possessed the soul of a true soldier.[10]

Nevertheless, Custer's career nearly ended in disgrace because of a gross violation of duty when he failed to perform his assigned responsibilities as the officer of the guard: not halting a fistfight that had broken out between two cadets and not arresting them as required by regulations. In Custer's own words, "the instincts of the boy prevailed over the obligations of the officer of the guard [and] I pushed my way through the surrounding line of cadets [and then] called out loudly, 'Stand back, boys; let's have a fair fight.'"[11]

The sudden appearance of two regular officers caught Custer, who loved nothing more than watching a good fight, in the process of grossly neglecting his duties as the officer of the guard. The following morning, Custer was formally arrested and assigned to his tent. Then a court-martial was prepared to determine Custer's fate, which almost certainly would be a dark one: expulsion from West Point. But the young man's good fortune—that was destined to become legendary in the years ahead until June 25, 1876—rose to the fore in timely fashion, when most needed by him. In Custer's own words: "Within a few hours of my arrest the long-expected order came, relieving my class from further duty at West Point, and directing the members of it to proceed to Washington and report to the Adjutant General of the Army for further orders. My name, however, did not appear on the list [because] I was to be detained to await the application of the commandant for a court-martial to sit on my case [and shortly thereafter] I was arraigned with all the solemnity and gravity which might be looked for in a trial for high treason. . . . The trial was brief." This was because he pleaded guilty.[12]

But, as mentioned, the often-reoccurring phenomenon known as "Custer's Luck" came into play once again to his advantage in a seemingly impossible situation, because my classmates who had preceded me to Washington interested themselves earnestly in my behalf [and] some of them had influential friends there, and it was but a few days after my trial that the superintendent of the Academy received a telegraphic order from Washington, directing him to release me at once, and order me to report to the Adjutant-General of the Army for duty. This order practically rendered the actions and proceedings of the court-martial in my case nugatory. The record, I presume, was forwarded to the War Department, where it probably lies safely stowed away in some pigeonhole. What the proceeding of the court or their decision was, I have never learned.[13]

As destiny would have it, Custer's timing could not have been better in regard to his ambition, which was to serve his country on the battlefield. He had narrowly avoided an abrupt end to his military career and to his growing visions of achieving glory on the battlefield in the sacred war to save the Union, which he loved with a passion like his father. Therefore, thankful to his lucky stars that had not deserted him in his darkest hour when expulsion from the United States Military Academy seemed inevitable, he "left West Point on the 18th of July for Washington, delaying a few hours that afternoon on my arrival in New York to enable me to purchase . . . my lieutenant's outfit of sabre, revolver, sash, spurs, etc. Taking the evening train for Washington [DC], I found the cars crowded with troops, officers and men, hastening to the capital."[14]

Against the odds, Custer was at last going to war with his career and reputation intact. As a kind fate would have it, a far greater measure of good fortune lay in store for Custer in the days ahead. But this development was no accident as long assumed, especially by his detractors. Custer was smart, ingenious, and resourceful to the point that he made his own luck, a rare quality that served him extremely well throughout the war years. And he took advantage of every possible opportunity, combining a laser-like focus with an iron determination that also helped to pave the way to his successes from 1861 to 1865. Custer's rise and success have often been incorrectly identified as nothing more than "Custer's Luck," without any connection to the key personal qualities that were actually responsible for manufacturing his good fortune.

For the first time, Custer took what he had learned at West Point seriously, once he was away from the academy's hallowed halls, and incorporated those lessons into his personal conduct and behavior to a degree that would have astounded those mocking and haughty cadets, whose behavior was more disciplined to garner far fewer demerits, who he had known at the academy on the Hudson River: a most timely transformation of a young man who now took himself and the military most seriously during wartime, unlike at West Point, because the life of the nation was at stake.

By his own actions, he was about to enter upon the fast track for future advancement by way of demonstrated abilities and a series of extremely fortunate developments, taking advantage of every opportunity that was presented to him. Ironically, even the humiliating West Point court-martial that had nearly ended his career proved to be a lucky stroke in the end, because it allowed him to appear in Washington, DC, on his own without class members. Due to this unique situation, Custer was in a position to stand out from other West Point graduates and become conspicuous to a degree that elicited a "special attention" not enjoyed by his fellow class members.[15]

But still another factor benefited young Custer, who fully appreciated the fact that his dismal "career as a [West Point] cadet had but little" to provide as a lesson, "unless as an example to be carefully avoided," as had penned the native Ohioan with open honesty tinged with humor.[16] Since he was a contrarian and unorthodox by nature, which partly explained his embarrassing West Point experiences and lack of earning distinction, Custer was actually able to turn the negatives of having been the "goat" (ranked last in his class of 1861) into positives, employing the overall academy experience to fuel his motivation and desire to succeed. What could not be denied was the fact that the typical "goat" of West Point was a resourceful and ingenious survivor, who had basically beaten the hierarchical system based on an almost unreal level of excellence, which was a requirement ignored, if not mocked, by Custer in overall conceptual terms by his unorthodox behavior.

Therefore, the real achievement of the "goat" was in becoming a master in the clever art of dodging, outsmarting, and outmaneuvering a system that was established to thoroughly crush the last vestiges of individuality, personal identity, and unorthodox inclinations in the name of mindless conformity and automatic acceptance of the endless rules of a hierarchical system. Therefore, to Custer, the ultimate survivor who had barely managed to get through the rigors of West Point by living on the dangerous edge of expulsion, the "goat" status was a badge of honor that represented a significant accomplishment in the end. In this sense, the act of "graduating last at West Point [was] not a badge of shame but a mark of achievement" that engendered a certain sense of perverse pride and achievement. This contrarian mind-set and understanding served Custer well in the days ahead, including in the dramatic showdown at Gettysburg.[17]

With a confidence that was in contrast to his poor West Point record, the newest second lieutenant, who had become a member of the 2nd United States Cavalry, reported to the adjutant general in Washington, DC, for assignment. Here he was surprised when an officer in charge at the office suddenly asked, "Perhaps you would like to be presented to General Scott, Mr. Custer?" General Winfield Scott, the highest-ranking military man in the United States, was America's greatest living military hero since George Washington and a living legend for stirring battlefield performances that dated back to the War of 1812. An old infantryman of the regular army, he was the revered leader of America's armies, despite his many outdated and traditional views, including that the cavalry arm of the U.S. Army was not important for winning this war between brothers. In Custer's words, "in the youthful minds of the West Point cadets [including himself] Scott was looked up to as a leader whose military abilities were scarcely second to those of a Napoleon," who was still highly revered across the breadth of America.[18]

Of course, Custer fairly leaped at the opportunity and "joyfully assented," wrote the young second lieutenant of another fortunate, but unexpected development.[19] And a good many more fortunate developments were shortly forthcoming for the young man. During the formal conference with General Scott, Custer was surprised when the highly respected general suddenly said, "I desire to send dispatches to General [Irvin] McDowell [an Ohio-born West Pointer who was assigned to defend Washington, DC, and commanded the North's primary eastern army that was about to be defeated in the Battle of First Manassas in the war's first major battle], and you can be the bearer of them."[20]

Custer delivered his official dispatches to McDowell's headquarters without incident after riding through the hostile Virginia countryside from the nation's capital. He arrived in time to witness the first major disaster suffered by the overconfident Union forces along a muddy Virginia creek called Bull Run on July 21, 1861. In his own words about the fiasco at First Manassas, Custer was shocked by what happened so quickly to the boys in blue at the hands of an amateur army of Southerners: "The cry of 'We're flanked! We're flanked!' passed from rank to rank, the Union lines, but a moment before so successful and triumphant, threw down their arms, were seized by a panic, and began a most disordered flight. All of this occurred almost in an instant of time. No pen or description can give anything like a correct idea of the rout and demoralization that followed."[21]

Destined to serve him well, Custer learned an invaluable lesson from the fiasco at First Manassas. As he penned of the lesson that he never forgot at a time when Colonel James Ewell Brown Stuart (a West Pointer who was known far and wide simply as "Jeb") commanded the 1st Virginia Cavalry, or the so-called Black Horse Cavalry, with skill that resulted in his promotion to brigadier general while on the road to gaining iconic hero status across the South: "The value of discipline was clearly shown in this crisis by observing the manner of the few regular troops, as contrasted with the raw and undisciplined three months' men. The regular soldier never for a moment ceased to look to their officers for orders and instructions, and in retiring from the field, even amid the greatest disorder and confusion of the organizations near them, they preserved their formation, and march only as they were directed to do."[22]

In much the same way, the North also learned its lessons from the disastrous loss during the war's most major clash of arms at First Bull Run, taking the war more seriously and realizing that it would not be over in a matter of months as everyone had originally expected. In the words of Willard Worcester Glazier, 2nd New York Cavalry, Army of the Potomac, Stuart's "Black Horse Cavalry of Virginia, at Bull Run, unmatched by any similar force on our side, had demonstrated the efficiency and importance of this branch of the service, and our authorities began to change their views . . . to encounter the chivalrous Black Horse Cavalry" in the future.[23] After the fiasco at First Manassas, the war became far bloodier, revealing the folly of civil war to both the North and the South.

## DECISIVE SPRING AND SUMMER 1863

Ironically, no great battle would have ever been fought for three bloody days among the fertile fields, ridges, and hilltops of Adams County, southeastern Pennsylvania, at Gettysburg, if not for the ever-growing threat posed to a strategic town on the east bank of the Mississippi River, the defensive bastion of Vicksburg, Mississippi. At long last, and unlike in the eastern theater where his Army of the Potomac continued to fail to deliver a knockout to General Robert E. Lee's Army of Northern Virginia, President Abraham Lincoln had found his best general in the West, Ulysses S. Grant.

A veteran of the Mexican-American War in which he had made a name for himself by demonstrating heroism and resourcefulness, Grant was a practical and commonsense westerner and, most of all, a tough and hard-nosed fighter, invaluable qualities that were shared by Custer in part because of comparable western and West Point experiences. Grant was exactly the man for the job of capturing the all-important bastion of Vicksburg, because he was an ingenious and tactically flexible commander. If Grant's army and the Union navy on the western waters captured Vicksburg and then gained control of the "Father of Waters" during the 1863 campaign, then the Confederacy would be cut in two. As a younger man who had journeyed down the brown waters of the wide Mississippi to New Orleans on a makeshift flatboat from the fertile fields of Illinois, Lincoln realized early on the importance of the broad expanse of the Mississippi and how this brutal war could be won if the river was completely controlled by the Union navy to cut the Confederacy in half.[24]

Therefore, the Confederacy and the Richmond government faced an escalating threat of the first magnitude after General Grant's forces crossed the

Mississippi like a flood from the lowlands of eastern Louisiana in a bold operation to catch the Confederates by surprise. After gaining the high ground on the river's east side, Grant then won the hard-fought battle of Port Gibson, Mississippi, on May 1, 1863. In a brilliant campaign that reminded him of General Winfield Scott's march west across the country to Mexico City when he was a young lieutenant fresh out of the hallowed halls of West Point, nothing could stop a relentless General Grant when he was on the move and sensed a good tactical opportunity. He fully exploited a fumbling Confederate political and military leadership at the highest levels from Mississippi to Virginia.

Keeping his opponents confused and guessing about his next tactical move, Grant had maneuvered rapidly and with great skill into the rear of Vicksburg's defending army. After winning victories at Champion's Hill on May 16, 1863, and along the Big Black River, situated just east of Vicksburg, the following day, Grant pushed the reeling Confederate army westward to trap it inside Vicksburg with its back to the Mississippi, a fatal entrapment that ensured the eventual demise of an entire army that was destined to surrender on the Fourth of July 1863, which was the day after the East Cavalry Field showdown at Gettysburg.

President Jefferson Davis, who felt the mounting political pressure and public criticism of Grant's winning ways on the soil of his own home state and eventually on his own beloved plantation of Brierfield, held high-level military conferences in Richmond, Virginia. He hoped to develop a solution before it was too late. But this was already too little, too late, because Davis had neglected the western theater, in part because Grant's fast-paced tactics had so thoroughly caught Confederate leadership, especially in Mississippi, by surprise. Most importantly, the Confederacy could now be severed in half by Grant's forces to ensure the permanent isolation of the vast trans-Mississippi theater, which hastened the day when the Confederate experiment in nationhood ended in miserable failure.

Vicksburg's fate was already sealed thanks to Grant's tactical brilliance and Confederate incompetence at the highest levels. General Robert E. Lee, the most winning general in the South, had a solution, and President Davis could always count on his top commander for answers, as in the past. With his typical audacity, and returning to an old plan that he had envisioned even before winning the sparkling victory in the woodlands of Chancellorsville in May 1863, Lee proposed to push north with his Army of Northern Virginia into western Maryland and then into Pennsylvania during his second invasion of the North in the hope of relieving pressure on Vicksburg and winning a decisive victory on northern soil to reverse the war's course that was going against the Confederacy. The recent success at Chancellorsville had opened the door to a much more aggressive strategy, including one that was calculated to take the pressure off Richmond, both the capital and its beleaguered leaders, especially President Davis, who was becoming the most convenient scapegoat for every new Confederate defeat.

Despite having nearly met with disaster near the town of Sharpsburg in western Maryland in the showdown with the Army of the Potomac at the Battle of Antietam on September 17, 1862, General Lee still dreamed of winning a decisive victory on northern soil. Lee had seemingly forgotten that he had been fortunate to escape back to the safety of Virginia when his battered army limped to the south side of the Potomac River. Ignoring his close call with disaster in the pristine farmlands of Washington County, Maryland, Lee was not hesitant to once again throw the dice in the risky bid of hopefully winning a decisive victory on northern soil to reverse the war's course that was going against the South, before it was too late for the Confederacy.

Despite initially desiring to send reinforcements to Vicksburg's defending army rather than launching another risky northern invasion beyond the Potomac River, President Davis embraced Lee's sheer audacity and aggressiveness, because these factors were the keys to so many past successes reaped by the South's best general. He envisioned the reaping of victories on northern soil to sap the will of the war-weary northern populace to prosecute the war, to fuel greater criticism against Lincoln, to embolden the so-called Peace Party of the dissatisfied North, and to prove to Europeans, especially to the leaders of England and France, that the Confederacy might still win this lengthy struggle for survival.

For all of these reasons, Lee possessed relatively little choice but to launch his second invasion of the North, because the manpower-short South was trapped in a lengthy war of attrition that it could not win unless a decisive knockout blow was delivered to the Army of the Potomac on northern soil. But this offensive movement was a risky gamble of the first magnitude, because the increasingly desperate Confederacy possessed far less resources and could not afford to suffer a sharp setback that would damage morale and credibility across the Atlantic. Quite simply, therefore, General Lee, the Army of Northern Virginia, and the Confederacy were going for broke as never before in the summer of 1863.[25]

And although it seemed improbable at the time, George Armstrong Custer, who was about to become a young cavalry brigade commander of Wolverine troopers, was fated to play a key role in the most decisive clash of arms on the last of the bloodiest three days of the war at Gettysburg. As he had written in a prophetic letter to his half-sister Lydia-Ann Kirkpatrick-Reed of Monroe, Michigan, from the United States Military Academy, describing an entirely realistic understanding of the depth of the sectional crisis: "It is useless to hope the coming struggle will be bloodless or of short duration. Much blood will be spilled and thousands of lives, at the least, lost. If it is to be my lot to fall in the service of my country and my country's rights I will have no regrets."[26]

## TIMELY CAVALRY REFORMS

A central mystery had long haunted the bluecoat troopers of the often-defeated cavalry of the Army of the Potomac. Perhaps Lieutenant Willard W. Glazier, 2nd New York Cavalry, Army of the Potomac, said it best. He emphasized how "it has been a source of wonderment to us, that while the efficiency of the infantry is known to depend largely upon its organization into brigades, divisions, and corps . . . the same [case was] not [known to] be true of the cavalry."[27]

Quite simply, the North had mismanaged its cavalry arm from the beginning, reducing its overall effectiveness in the midst of wartime. The years 1861 and 1862 had clearly demonstrated that the Army of the Potomac's cavalry had failed miserably to perform up to its potential, like the army itself, which was unable to win decisive victory, while the cavalry arm of the Army of Northern Virginia—which was considered to be the best cavalry in the world—seemingly always prevailed. These developments were inevitable because the American nation had badly neglected its cavalry since its last major conflict, the Mexican-American War (1846–1848), where the potential of cavalry was not exploited or utilized, a trend that continued during the early years of the Civil War. In this sense, the United States had learned the wrong lessons from that victorious war, which had been won deep in the heart of Mexico, ensuring that its cavalry was wholly unprepared for the extensive challenges of the Civil War.

However, the South—more of a horse-based society and culture than the North—had fully maximized the potential of its cavalry forces from the beginning, unlike the North. One secret of the success of Lee's cavalry arm had been its steady growth and heightened efficiency, because it had been properly organized by 1862 under the able leadership of Major General James Ewell Brown (Jeb) Stuart. Stuart's Cavalry Division, Army of Northern Virginia, had mushroomed into six brigades by the time of the Gettysburg campaign in preparation for the stern challenges that lay ahead.

In this sense, much of Stuart's soaring fame had been won because of the superior organizational structure of the army's cavalry compared to that of the Army of the Potomac, which seemed cursed with losing. Stuart and Lee benefited from the fact that the six cavalry brigades functioned like one in the capacity of an independent cavalry corps, especially after gaining proper corps strength of half a dozen brigades. This organizational structure maximized the full potential of the cavalry arm, and it paid almost immediate dividends.

Fortunately for the inefficient Union army's cavalry—which had never been used properly, to the delight of Stuart, whose long list of successes had come much easier in consequence—Major General Joseph K. Hooker worked on making lasting improvements to the cavalry after he took command of the Army of the Potomac from the fumbling Major General Ambrose E. Burnside during the last week of January 1863. A likeable West Pointer who was entirely unsuited to command the army and win decisive victories on the battlefield, as recently demonstrated in the slaughter and disastrous defeat at Fredericksburg in December 1862, Burnside never made the grade. He failed to meet lofty expectations that were too often confused with his likeable ways—one of the worst of all ways to judge the quality and character of a general, when depth of character and tactical skill were required instead of a breezy charm and appealing smile.

The floundering, inept Army of the Potomac had witnessed a case of musical chairs when it came to commanders who had failed miserably when facing the hard-hitting Army of Northern Virginia under Lee. On November 7, 1862, Burnside had replaced the "Young Napoleon" who had failed to win victories that were once so optimistically expected by President Lincoln.

Major General George Brinton McClellan, Burnside's friend, had been sacked by Lincoln, and for ample good reason. Both once highly touted generals, first "Little Mac," who proved his excessive caution and penchant for failing to exploit golden opportunities to reap significant victories from the onset of the Peninsula Campaign to the Antietam campaign, and the personable Rhode Islander, who bestowed the name of "sideburns" to the American lexicon, had failed to deliver a knockout blow during the bloody year of 1862.

As was fully evident to the frustrated President Lincoln and the War Department, McClellan had demonstrated that he was no Napoleon during the Peninsula Campaign and at Antietam to make a mockery of his "Young Napoleon" nickname. Following suit after Burnside's failures, especially in having launched suicidal assaults in repeated fashion at Fredericksburg, Hooker had been recently vanquished in the dark forests around Chancellorsville, Virginia, in early May 1863—the magnificent, but costly, victory achieved by Lee that bestowed the opportunity for his army to march north from the Fredericksburg area and invade the North for a second time. None of these Union commanders before Hooker had bothered to improve the organizational structure of the Army of the Potomac's cavalry by creating a cavalry corps, which was urgently needed.

Despite his bombastic boasts and outward overconfidence that resulted in an entirely unwarranted swagger that amused more sensible officers, the overconfident General Hooker failed to measure up to the considerable challenge of defeating the masterful Lee. He proved to be more of a talker—like the equally overconfident McClellan—and braggart than a hard-nosed fighter in the no-nonsense manner of Grant. Lee exploited the considerable weaknesses of the self-proclaimed "Fighting Joe" Hooker, who proved to be a featherweight against his heavyweight opponent during the showdown at Chancellorsville, when he had initially possessed the advantage by gaining Lee's rear. But Lee's quick reaction and aggressiveness had quickly frozen Hooker into a defensive stance to pave the way for his eventual defeat, after "Fighting Joe" lost his nerve west of Fredericksburg.

Because of Hooker's failures, especially at Chancellorsville, the general has been unfairly painted as a complete disaster and the worst possible commander of the Army of the Potomac by generations of historians. Unfortunately, in this regard, they have thrown out the baby with the bathwater, because Hooker possessed talents not displayed on the battlefield. Before he exposed the full array of his considerable weaknesses as a battlefield commander at Chancellorsville, Hooker made an extremely important contribution in dramatically improving the army's capabilities, especially in regard to the cavalry arm during the first week of February 1863. He aggressively took the organizational steps that were absolutely necessary for the overall improvement of the quality of the army's cavalry.

More than anyone else, "Fighting Joe," who perhaps should have been known as "Administrative Joe," was responsible for having significantly upgraded the army's cavalry months before Lee's troops pushed north in the hope of winning a decisive victory rather than the usual pyrrhic successes like at Chancellorsville, which had been too costly to the South's limited supply of manpower. Before he had lost the Battle of Chancellorsville and proved himself unworthy of his badly misplaced "Fighting Joe" nickname, Hooker's smart organizational decisions proved of immense importance for the future of the army's cavalry, although these have been often overlooked by historians who have long focused only on the general's follies.

Indeed, to his great credit, Hooker had recognized early the urgent need to improve the combat capabilities of his cavalry arm, which had not been properly utilized since the war's beginning, unlike in the South, to Stuart's supreme advantage. For instance, at the Battle of Antietam on September 17, 1862, near the little town of Sharpsburg, western Maryland, the sizeable force of the Union cavalry had been wasted in being assigned in a stationary position to protect lengthy rows of Union batteries—not under any threat at the time—aligned on the east side of Antietam Creek.

Instead of playing an aggressive role in this battle and perhaps turning the tide in the Union's favor, more than four thousand Union cavalrymen had remained aligned in neat rows like they were on a parade ground, in case the massed artillery was attacked by Lee, whose force was too weak for offensive operations. Then, nearly two months later at the Battle of Fredericksburg, Virginia, Union cavalry had played still another comparable spectator role of no importance. At that time, the army's cavalry remained on the other side (east) of the Rappahannock River near the booming artillery arrayed on the heights, when a stubborn Burnside repeatedly hurled his troops over the broad killing fields to suffer his greatest defeat on bloody December 13, 1862. In both major battles, the losses to the immobile cavalry arm were minuscule, while the hard-fighting infantry, including commands like the Irish Brigade, Second Corps, had been slaughtered in unprecedented numbers.

Clearly, a new spirit of aggressiveness and an organizational enhancement of the cavalry's combat capabilities had been required, not only in 1862, but also from the war's beginning. The South had been a much more militarized society than the North during the antebellum period, and militia functions, especially cavalry, were prominent in antebellum society. Because of a mostly rural geography, a poor road system, and a lack of public transportation, unlike in the North, the reliance on horses for individual transportation had been greater in Southern society over the course of generations. In addition, many Southern men performed their civic duty by serving on mounted slave patrols to safeguard the countryside from the threat of slave revolts, while serving as members of paramilitary organizations.

Therefore, throughout 1861 and 1862, the North had thoroughly underutilized its cavalry arm and in the wrong manner—mostly for scouting and reconnaissance—because of the mistaken concept that cavalry was not as important as infantry, thanks to the advances of modern weaponry. Meanwhile, the South had fully maximized the potential of its cavalry arm to achieve impressive results by more fully appreciating the importance of cavalry on multiple levels, after having organized the cavalry arm in a manner that allowed it to be employed more aggressively to achieve significant results. General Hooker, therefore, had determined early on to accomplish the same for the Union cavalry arm.

As mentioned, by early 1863, Hooker knew that he needed to maximize the potential of the army's cavalry, after having learned some hard lessons from its more skilled cavalry opponent. For too long, Stuart and his cavalry had their way with the Union cavalry, prevailing with an ease that bred a great deal of overconfidence. In fact, the audacious Stuart had twice ridden circles—the last one just after the Battle of Antietam, which had taken the bold Rebel horsemen into Pennsylvania—around the Army of the Potomac with daring impunity. In doing so, he mocked the Union cavalry's inability and futility, which was only too obvious to one and all. Each time, Stuart had easily slipped away from the grasp of his bluecoat pursuers with little loss of life or risk to his fast-moving and wide-ranging command. The cavalry arm of the North's primary army was repeatedly embarrassed by failing to inflict a mortal blow on Stuart and his raiders, who were like gray ghosts. For such reasons, not long after taking command of the Army of the Potomac, Hooker issued his General Orders No. 6, on February 5, 1863. He initiated the organizational and administrative reforms that resulted in nothing short of a "miracle," greatly enhancing the combat capabilities of the often-defeated Army of the Potomac, especially in regard to the cavalry, capabilities that were destined to rise to the fore at Gettysburg on July 3.

General Hooker had quickly made up for the failures of previous commanders, who had allowed the cavalry arm to languish to new lows. Unlike Lee's cavalry, which was concentrated, and although best known for his organizational skills, General McClellan had early made the mistake of having his cavalry divided, assigned to infantry commands, and burdened with administrative assignments, which greatly diminished its overall potential as a legitimate combat command.

General Hooker's initiatives were not revolutionary. He basically followed the cavalry model of General Lee's Army of Northern Virginia because of its outstanding successes. But these improvements were timely and all important, especially with the most decisive campaign of the war on the horizon. In a stroke of organizational brilliance, Hooker grouped together all of the divergent elements of the army's troopers—three previously unconnected and unrelated cavalry brigades—into a single cavalry corps that was equivalent to the army's infantry corps. In this way, more than nine thousand Federal troopers of the army's cavalry became an independent command to enhance its potential and combat capabilities just in time for the stern challenges of the Gettysburg campaign.

Such a centralized cavalry organization was absolutely necessary because the Union cavalry had been so often embarrassed and humiliated by Stuart and his hard-riding cavaliers. For the first time, Hooker had created a serious fighting force rather than an idle nonplayer in crucial battles. As noted, this timely creation of a truly independent cavalry corps instilled new life, spirit, and energy into the army's much-maligned cavalry. Unlike at Antietam and Fredericksburg, consequently, the Union cavalry was destined to play an all-important role at Gettysburg, especially on the third day of the epic confrontation that decided the fate of America.

Like their flamboyant commander, General Stuart, who possessed a flair for the dramatic like Custer, Southern cavalrymen of the Army of Northern Virginia had become supremely confident and cocky from their long list of successes at the expense of the much-maligned Union cavalry arm from 1861 to 1862. But now a new day was beginning to dawn as the result of Hooker's February 5, 1863, orders for reform. Demonstrating insight and forward thinking when it was most needed on the eve of the Gettysburg campaign, Hooker also strengthened the overall quality of his cavalry arm with the addition of better horses and weapons that outmatched his opponent. Often overlooked by careless commanders, medical care was also improved to keep men and horses in the best shape possible for meeting the stiff rigors of hard campaigning, because healthy horses and troopers were necessary to reap victory on the battlefield.

Most of all, Hooker smartly concentrated his horsemen into what was most desperately needed at this time, an independent cavalry corps that greatly enhanced the cavalry's overall potential and combat capabilities to a degree not previously seen. At long last, the formerly restricted Union cavalry was liberated from the control of infantry leaders, who commanded brigades, divisions, and corps and possessed little knowledge of cavalry. After all, many of these infantry commanders were well known for their prejudice and contempt for mounted service in a traditional interservice rivalry that had long existed.

After the creation of the cavalry corps that began to breathe new life and an all-important esprit de corps into the Union cavalry, all that was needed to complete the crucial reform of the cavalry arm was the appointment of a new generation of up-and-coming young men of promise blessed with tactical skills and aggressive instincts—new generals who were more energetic than the older generation and possessed new attitudes about how to wage the art of war with vigor and intensity. These younger and more aggressive leaders—just what the cavalry corps needed at this time—were now required to command the brigades of the new cavalry corps for the all-important summer campaign of 1863.

All in all, what Hooker created before the showdown at Gettysburg was a hard-hitting strike force under the capable Alfred Pleasonton, who commanded the cavalry corps with the rank of major general by the time of the Gettysburg campaign, to finally match the combat capabilities of Stuart and his troopers, who had long exploited the vulnerabilities and weaknesses of the Union cavalry. To his credit, Hooker had taken the much-needed steps toward finally stopping this disastrous trend and downward spiral of the cavalry arm.[28]

But Hooker was not entitled to all the credit for these achievements. He had benefited from organizational ideas submitted by General Pleasonton. As the ambitious Pleasonton penned on December 1, 1862, with considerable insight, "To obviate some of the defects existing at present in our cavalry organization [he emphasized that] the cavalry is a distinct arm of the service . . . that can only be properly discharged under an organization conformable to those duties. It is, therefore, recommended that such legislation be obtained as will give the cavalry a corps organization [and] our cavalry can be made superior to any now in the field by organization, which permits great freedom and responsibility to its commanders, subject to the commanding general."[29]

Fortunately for the Union, General Hooker had not only listened but also acted accordingly to enhance his cavalry's combat capabilities. From this point forward, the Union cavalry was well on its way to becoming truly superior for the first time in the war. Indeed, Willard W. Glazier, 2nd New York Cavalry, emphasized the importance of Hooker's timely changes, because

> Hooker [brought] about the desired result; and, at last, the Cavalry Corps of the Army of the Potomac is organized, and General George D. Stoneman for its commanding general. By this change [cavalry] regiments which have been scattered here and there on detached service are brought together, and made to feel the enthusiasm which numbers generally inspire, especially when those numbers are united into a system [and] under this new regime some very beneficial changes have been wrought. Schools and camps of instruction have been established, with a more rigid discipline than before, and boards of examination [were established so that] old and incompetent officers have been dismissed, or have slunk away before this incisive catechism, giving way generally to intelligent, young, and efficient men, who, placed at the heads of regiments and brigades, gave promise of success in the struggles that await us.[30]

And in time, Custer was destined to become the foremost of this new breed of dynamic young leaders of outstanding promise and ability, commanding a crack brigade of Michigan troopers by the time of the Battle of Gettysburg.

The morale and enthusiasm of the average troopers for the newly formed cavalry corps was additionally increased on April 6, 1863, when President Lincoln reviewed the twenty-one cavalry regiments of Stoneman's command. The Kentucky-born president was duly impressed by the imposing sight of the "well filled and drilled" regiments that were more ready for the challenges of the upcoming campaign than at any time in the past.[31] Clearly, and unappreciated by Stuart and his men, who had been spoiled by their repeated successes, which they believed would continue forever, everything possible was being accomplished to make the Union cavalry as formidable as possible to meet future challenges—a case of perfect timing with the most important campaign of the war on the horizon.

Even the Prussian officer, Heros von Borcke, who served on General Stuart's staff and carried a lengthy (forty-two-inch) sword manufactured in Solingen, Germany, lavished considerable praise on the much-maligned General Hooker for his timely contributions: "Great credit, however, was due to him for having availed himself of the interval of inaction to improve his cavalry, which was now completely recruited, men and horses, and augmented by fresh brigades."[32] Indeed, unknown to Stuart, who still basked in a long list of past successes, a new day had come at long last for the often-defeated Union cavalry.

Willard W. Glazier, 2nd New York Cavalry, summarized the situation and emphasized the importance of a central organization for the Federal cavalry that was destined to pay high dividends at Gettysburg: "The Rebel cavalry under Stuart has long been organized into an efficient body, which, at times, has sneered at our attempts to match them; and yet they have been made to feel, on some occasions, that we are a growing power [while] the general successes of the Rebel army have made them all very insolent, in the hope that final victory is already in their grasp."[33] This pervasive attitude was a fatal hubris that was destined to rise to the fore at Gettysburg on July 3, 1863, to reduce its overall effectiveness north of the Potomac and far from the friendly confines of Virginia during the most important day of the war.

Indeed, unrealized by Stuart and his men at the time, the days of glory for the Southern cavalry arm were being relegated to a place in the distant past and memory by the time of the all-important campaign of 1863. Therefore, the ever-insightful Lee sensed that a significant change was in the air and that a key equation had already begun to turn against Stuart and his cocky cavaliers, although they still had not realized it—realities that would emerge during the course of the Gettysburg campaign. This was a day of reckoning that Lee had long feared, because it meant the war was still steadily evolving into an entirely new phase and certainly not in the South's favor. For the first time and for good reason, therefore, General Lee was worried about the increased aggressiveness, new confidence, and enhanced combat capabilities of the Union cavalry after General Hooker's timely reforms had been initiated and as early as May 9, 1863.[34]

## THE MOST SURPRISING OF PROMOTIONS

One of the most important decisions in the history of the Army of the Potomac was hardly noticed at the time and is almost completely forgotten today. Major General George Gordon Meade, who has seldom received the credit that he deserved for what he accomplished during the Gettysburg campaign, wisely sought to improve the overall quality of his cavalry arm before embarking on the march north in pursuit of the Army of Northern Virginia. By this time, Lee's army had gotten the jump on the Northern army.

Shortly after Meade was appointed as the army's new commander under Lincoln's decision received on June 27 at Frederick, Maryland, after the army had advanced north to his location in western Maryland, Meade held a high-level conference with Major General Pleasonton, who now commanded the cavalry corps, after Stoneman had been sacked for failing to meet expectations. Getting a good feel for the shape of the army that he now commanded, Meade talked at length to Pleasonton to gain needed information about the cavalry arm. They agreed that changes to the army's cavalry were necessary for the coming campaign.

Most importantly, the open-minded Meade agreed to Pleasonton's suggestion that a new generation of young and aggressive leaders was now necessary to lead the seasoned brigades of the cavalry corps, after removing older officers who were less capable and aggressive. Captain Custer, one of the three recommended "Young Turks" who were serving as lowly staff officers for generals, was recommended without any reservation by Pleasonton. In this regard, Custer was fortunate. General Pleasonton was more than a friend, and he considered the young man born in Ohio to be his surrogate son. Therefore, Pleasonton recommended Custer to General Meade during their conference. However, Pleasonton's admiration of the young man was well founded, because it was based on previous demonstrations of Custer's skills, courage, and abilities on the battlefield and in trying situations.

In short order, Meade accepted all of Pleasonton's astute recommendations to advance his three most promising cavalry captains to the rank of brigadier general—an unprecedented request not found in the annals of American military history—during the most important campaign of the war. He emphasized to Meade that Custer, 5th United States Cavalry; Elon J. Farnsworth, 8th Illinois Cavalry; and Wesley Merritt, 2nd United States Cavalry were the chosen ones who were needed to take charge of brigades to defeat the South's best cavalry leaders, who had become legendary at this time.

To his credit, Meade wasted no time, which was of the essence, when his army was about to meet the Army of Northern Virginia. Within only hours after gaining command of the Army of the Potomac, Meade wired the War Department in Washington, DC, about the recommended promotions. Fortunately for the Army of the Potomac, no objections were raised by General Henry W. "Old Brains" Halleck in Washington because so much was at stake for the Union.

Without waiting for an official response, Meade and Pleasonton, who both realized what had to be done for the good of the army and the nation, smartly moved ahead with their on-target plans in regard to the reorganization of the cavalry corps and the placement of new cavalrymen, including Custer, in command of their respective brigades. Meanwhile, another young man and West Pointer of Scotch-Irish descent, Judson Kilpatrick, took command of the reconstituted Third Division of Pleasonton's Cavalry Corps. Such timely decisions by Pleasonton and Meade were one of the fundamental keys to future success, including in regard to the performance of the army's cavalry at Gettysburg on July 3.[35]

Clearly, urging the promotion of three young captains to the rank of brigadier general—an almost unbelievable jump in rank that was not previously known in the army—was a bold decision by General Pleasonton. Quite simply, he risked his reputation by placing his faith in three young captains. This was especially the case in regard to Custer, who left behind a dismal record of subpar performances at West Point, and who had never previously commanded a full brigade of cavalry. However, this initiative was in keeping with the earlier initiatives that had been undertaken by General Hooker for regimental examining boards of officers to dismiss older and incompetent cavalry officers and replace them with young men of a new generation, who were aggressive, competent, and, most importantly, fighters.

Fortunately for Custer, one of the army's best cavalry brigades, the Michigan Cavalry Brigade, which had been created in February 1863, possessed one of these older commanders, Brigadier General Joseph T. Copeland. He had been the first commander of the 5th Michigan Cavalry. At age fifty, he was twice the age of most of the young troopers in the ranks. A former judge and lawyer of a bookish nature, Copeland was hardly a fighter type, which was what was needed to achieve battlefield success. From Pontiac, Michigan, he was more of a politician, administrator (he had organized the 5th Michigan Cavalry), and paper pusher than a dynamic leader.

In a long overdue action, therefore, Copeland was relieved of command of the Michigan Cavalry Brigade not long before the opening guns of Gettysburg roared in Adams County, Pennsylvania. When Pleasonton asked Custer which brigade he wanted to command to begin his career as the army's youngest brigadier general, he named the Michigan Brigade without any hesitation. And he got his wish to ensure an ideal match between an aggressive commander and excellent fighting men.[36] With all the good news, Custer wrote about one of the most joyous days of his life: "To say I was elated would faintly express my feelings."[37]

Shortly to earn renown across the North as the "boy general with the golden locks," Custer was officially appointed to the rank of brigadier general at age twenty-three on June 28, 1863, in "Special Orders No. 175." This order had been dispatched from General Meade's headquarters at Frederick, Maryland. Custer was officially given command of the Second Brigade (Michigan Cavalry Brigade of four regiments—the 1st, 5th, 6th, and 7th Michigan Cavalry—while Farnsworth commanded the First Brigade), Third Division, which was led by Brigadier General Judson Kilpatrick. At almost the last minute, Pleasonton's Cavalry Corps became more ready and better prepared for the stern challenges of the Gettysburg campaign. Clearly this was one of the most spectacular rises in rank in the history of the Army of the Potomac, and Custer basked in his good fortune that astounded one and all, including the native Ohioan himself.

In a single day, young Custer jumped in rank from a mere captain to a brigadier general in a truly astounding promotion that was not even imaginable or conceivable by military men in prewar days.[38] This impressive rise in rank was not only unprecedented but also almost unbelievable, especially to other general officers who were older and had served for long periods before promotion. Even the editors of the *Monroe Commercial* in Monroe, Michigan, expressed disbelief over the rapid rise of one of their own, an adopted son from Ohio: "Upon the first appearance of the report that Captain Custer had been made a brigadier general of Cavalry, we were in some doubt as to its genuineness."[39]

As could be expected and as noted, Custer was just as shocked by the rapid promotion: "I had not the most remote idea that the president would appoint me, because I considered my youth, my low rank and what is of great importance at times & recollection that I have not a single 'friend at Court.'"[40] In fact, Custer had been so stunned by the news of his lofty promotion that he at first thought that it was a joke.[41] Indeed, a disillusioned Custer had been only recently concerned that "his career was standing and he was forever doomed to serve some general as a glorified messenger boy," while his West Point classmates, who now served on both sides, had moved up in rank and position.[42]

What other factors can explain Custer's promotion to such a lofty rank? First, fate itself seems to have come to Custer's rescue from his lowly position as a mere captain with a terrible West Point record—which was a source of considerable embarrassment—because of the outright failures of others. A former trooper of the 6th New York Cavalry explained General Pleasonton's determination to promote "the three or four 'boys' for high command [which] was based on the fact that he found himself unable to get any sharp and effective work out of the elderly and over cautious colonels and generals in command of his divisions and brigades [because they] were so cautious and safe that there was no getting a hard fight out of them."[43]

In Custer's own words in explaining his remarkable rise in such a short time, especially since he had been first commissioned as a lowly second lieutenant upon leaving West Point for the seat of war far away and then had served in low but highly visible positions for high-ranking commanders: "Until the commencement of the skirmishes preliminary to and immediately preceding the battle of Gettysburg, my service was principally that of a staff officer, during which period I served on the staffs of General [Philip] Kearney, [William F.] (Baldy) Smith, [Edwin V.] Sumner, [George B.] McClellan, and Pleasonton, in the order named. While on staff duty I usually accompanied the reconnaissances and expeditions conducted by the cavalry, and to this in a great measure was due my subsequent promotion to the grade of general officer, and my assignment to a cavalry command."[44]

But in fact Custer was guilty of excessive modesty, which was a sterling quality contrary to the stereotypical image of the egotistical Custer, who has almost always been viewed as possessing excessive vanity and pride. For instance, he never mentioned anything about the stirring role he played in the largest cavalry of the war at Brandy Station on June 9, 1863, when he was in the foremost of the combat, including leading charges. In the end, Custer's legendary "luck" had not been responsible for his dramatic rise, as has long been generally assumed.

For a lengthy period of time, General Pleasonton had been greatly impressed by Custer's high level of energy, tactical ability, and skill on the battlefield, including in crisis situations. Therefore, he had early realized that Custer was just the kind of dynamic young leader needed to lead a full brigade as a brigadier general. During the great cavalry clash at Brandy Station, Custer had played a role in which the Union cavalry had achieved what had never been previously accomplished: getting the best of Stuart and his so-called "Invincibles."[45] Ironically, and as a strange fate would have it, Custer's earliest interest in the military had been sparked in his hometown of New Rumley, Ohio, when he had watched the drilling and marching of the local militia unit called the "New Rumley Invincibles."[46] However, the sobriquet for Stuart's men still applied, which was never the case for those local Ohio boys, who had long played at being soldiers to the delight of the locals, including the Custer family.

But now Custer commanded a full brigade. As he wrote in a late letter to his half-sister on July 26, 1863, revealing his excessive modesty, which indicated a quiet strength of character in this ambitious man of twenty-three: "You have heard of my good fortune [which is] promotion to a Brigadier-General. I have certainly great cause to rejoice. I am the youngest General in the U.S. Army by over two years, in itself something to be proud of [and] my appointment dates from the 20th of June," 1863.[47] In another letter, Custer explained to Libbie Bacon of Monroe, Michigan, how "I owe it all to Gen'l [Alfred] Pleasonton [who] has been more like a father to me than a Gen'l."[48]

These words were no exaggeration, and they revealed Custer's ability to forge deep and lasting relationships with higher-ranking officers based on mutual respect and admiration. First and foremost, he had been forced to overcome army politics that had stopped the careers of a good many officers. Custer's career had been at a dead end because his previous mentor, General McClellan, had been removed after his failure to destroy Lee's army during the Maryland campaign. When McClellan was sacked by the frustrated President

Lincoln, who had tried everything to transform "Little Mac" into a winner and finally gave up betting on a loser, Custer's career was seemingly over since he had served on the general's staff and had been reduced in rank from captain back to lieutenant in consequence.

Even more, he greatly admired the removed general, who had fallen out of favor. And Custer was a Democrat like McClellan, who planned a national political career to challenge Lincoln for office in 1864—a double disadvantage that seemed impossible to overcome for someone of his young age. And because the governor of Ohio was a Republican and governed a Republican administration, Custer realized that he could not gain command of an Ohio regiment. Therefore, Custer's home state was eliminated from a career choice because of politics. But his adopted state of Michigan, where he had spent time at Monroe while living with his older half-sister, also presented an obstacle because the state was even more Republican than Ohio, which was closer to the South, in overall sentiment. However, everything changed for Custer when he was first noticed by Alfred Pleasonton, a fellow West Pointer (class of 1844), who admired Custer's daring and bravery that he had witnessed in the heat of combat.[49]

Once again, Custer was being modest when it came to emphasizing that Pleasonton was solely responsible for his rise, because it had actually been much more than a very good personal relationship that was the root of Custer's rapid promotion. For good reason, Pleasonton had been Custer's greatest supporter and advocate, but only after the sterling qualities of the young man had already been repeatedly demonstrated on the battlefield, including in the great clash of cavalry at Brandy Station in June 1863. Quite correctly, he was early convinced that Custer possessed all the necessary qualities to lead a cavalry brigade with distinction, because of what he had proven as a leader of men on the battlefield, where he displayed a feisty fighting spirit— "he loved battle"—that was irrepressible.

Quite simply, Custer was every inch a fighter, like another native Ohioan, Grant. Even more, Pleasonton was desperate to infuse new life into his cavalry arm and to enhance the overall combat capabilities of the much-derided cavalry corps. And the energetic, intelligent, and aggressive Custer was exactly the kind of new man that was needed if a new day were to finally come for the often-defeated Union cavalry.[50]

Clearly, what he had demonstrated before his promotion to brigadier general had been the antithesis of his earlier shameful experience at the United States Military Academy. Custer realized that his West Point career had only provided to future cadets "an example to be carefully avoided."[51] Ironically, the cadets of his class of 1861, including Patrick Henry "Paddy" O'Rorke, who was fated to die heroically while playing a leading role in saving the day on Little Round Top, Gettysburg, on July 2, 1863, had marched off to war with the motto that had not applied to Custer: "Promotions or a coffin!"[52] More importantly, Custer had also graduated with a classmate and a friend who was destined to provide him with invaluable artillery assistance on July 3, Captain Alexander Cummings McWhorter Pennington, who graduated eighteenth in the class of 1860.[53]

In regard to the upcoming clash at Gettysburg, General Pleasonton's decision and the organizational changes within the cavalry corps could not have been more timely or important for Custer in personal and professional terms. His star was on the rise, and it was destined to go even higher in the years ahead. Custer's timing could not have been better because of the extensive transformation that had taken place to improve the army's cavalry arm. After all, the past failures, embarrassments, and defeats of the Union cavalry of the Army of the Potomac had created the environment that emphasized the need for drastic changes, because the cavalry arm had never fulfilled its potential. In this regard, Custer's timing and luck certainly applied because he was a fortunate beneficiary of these changes.

Even more, in facing the challenges of the greatest threat posed by the most winning general in America, Pleasonton and Meade were of a like mind in ensuring that the best cavalry commanders advanced in rank before meeting Lee's famous cavalry under Stuart, because this might be the last campaign if the Army of Northern Virginia proved victorious, as optimistically envisioned in Richmond and army headquarters. Therefore, the old leaders who had failed to excel had been replaced by a younger generation of men—best personified by Custer—who were now aggressive and hard-nosed fighters like Stuart and his seasoned commanders.

Ironically, the critical situation that the army faced with Lee's invasion of Pennsylvania was not unlike what had developed during the rise of Napoleon and his young commanders, especially his famous marshals, including men who had been commoners, who became the best military leaders in Europe after the French Revolution had eliminated upper-class officers of the aristocracy. Like Custer, Napoleon's timing had proved most fortunate, because the egalitarian sentiments and then republican excesses of the French Revolution had eliminated the largely inefficient officer corps of the privileged aristocratic elite.

What was replaced in both cases—in the age of Napoleon and at the midway point of America's bloodiest war—was a mostly inferior officer corps of older and less capable men with younger, more dynamic and gifted leaders, especially in regard to the cavalry arm in Napoleon's army and the Army of the Potomac. A new day had come, and fortunately for the Union, it came immediately before the showdown at Gettysburg.[54]

Indeed, throughout the family's history, which extended back to the Rhineland of Germany, no Custer had risen so high, so far, and so fast as this twenty-three-year-old when he attained the lofty promotion of brigadier general, which caught everyone by surprise. The Custer family was typically rural and a poor one of Harrison County, Ohio—although not fully realized by its members at the time—and known for its self-sufficient and subsistence existence in a small-town environment. This economic factor had ensured that the Custer family had been long part of the flood of the American people pushing toward the setting sun during the course of westward movement. The first Custer, George Armstrong Custer's great-grandfather, like his grandfather, hailed from the fertile lands of western Maryland and served as a noncommissioned officer in the Maryland militia. He was an average settler of humble origins and certainly not an "officer and a gentleman" of a higher class that filled the officer ranks of the European armies.

The father, Paul Custer, of Custer's father—Emmanuel Henry Custer—had migrated west to Berks County, Pennsylvania, which was located just northwest of Philadelphia. However, the family returned to western Maryland, where Emmanuel had been born at Cresaptown on December 10, 1806. Vigorous and full of life, which had caused him to forsake his low expectations of life in his father's community, Emmanuel had pushed west in search of a brighter future like his ancestors. He had crossed the imposing Alleghany Mountains, consisting of parallel ridges that were heavily timbered and pointed northward. Setting down roots, Emmanuel eventually settled on the high ground of the small town of New Rumley, Ohio.

Here, amid the rural countryside of east central Ohio, which was more hilly terrain than farther west where the lands of the Ohio Valley eventually became more level the farther one journeyed toward the Mississippi River, including prairie lands, Emmanuel's enterprising uncle Jacob had laid out the town of New Rumley in 1813. This settling of New Rumley occurred during the War of 1812, which was a dangerous period in the Ohio Valley because of Native American alliances with the British. Many settlers of German heritage had settled in this part of Ohio, like the Custer family. Here, in Harrison County, Teutonic farmers had transformed this region of the Ohio frontier into a land of plenty and high productivity. The enterprising Custer family—hardworking and industrious—traced its ancestry to a small northwest German town, where the lack of opportunities had led to the ultimate solution of the Custer family immigrating to America to begin again.

Being the son of the lowly village blacksmith and farmer (he had saved enough money as a blacksmith to fulfill his life's dream—like most Americans—of purchasing his own farm, although of small size) at New Rumley was not exactly a promising start for George Armstrong Custer. Here, on the Ohio frontier, he was born in a large, two-story clapboard house on December 5, 1839, to Emmanuel and his attractive second wife, Maria Ward Kilpatrick. She was a widow—formerly married to Israel R. Kilpatrick—with two children. Of course, Maria needed a provider like Emmanuel needed a wife for himself and his three children from his first wife, Matilda Viers, who died in the mid-1830s. Because two children had died in infancy, George became the oldest son of Emmanuel and Maria.

The product of two distinctive people—Pennsylvania Dutch (German) and Scotch-Irish—who had settled on the Ohio frontier, Custer had inherited the good looks of his pretty mother and the blondness of his father's Teutonic side of the family. Maria was of a pious nature, and this was not lost on her son. She was an attractive, thin, and curly haired widow of Scotch-Irish descent with a loving nature. Both Emmanuel and Maria were widowers with children, and the two families of five children were united as one after Emmanuel again took the plunge after his first wife had died in 1835. The household of blacksmith Emmanuel, who was popular in the local community and was the only "smithy" for miles around, which ensured a steady income, was merry and full of life.

The children of both families considered themselves equal members of the same family, with the usual divisions and jealousies, but they all got along very well. Blond like his father, who was a devout Methodist and who liked to wear his hair long like his pioneer ancestors, George Armstrong Custer was called "Autie" by the close-knit family because of the boy's own early mispronunciation of Armstrong. He had been named in honor of a preacher in the hope of his pious parents that a future avocation in the service of God was in his future. From both sides of the family, Custer inherited the gaiety of the local Scotch-Irish and the businesslike Teutonic meticulousness and "a certain tenacity of purpose" from his father, which served him extremely well, including at Gettysburg.

Emmanuel, a strict follower of the Holy Bible like his devout wife, wanted "my boys to be, foremost, soldiers of the Lord" in the never-ending war against the Devil's wiles. George, as the big brother, became close to Thomas "Tom" Ward Custer. George's little brother, who eventually became the black sheep of the family, was destined to emerge as a Civil War hero and winner of two Medals of Honor. He became the highest-decorated Union officer of the Civil War—the Audie Murphy of World War II fame of his day. A healthy rivalry existed between the two brothers, despite the fact that they were very much alike. They shared a common bond, mutual admiration, and love, which all but ensured that they were both killed while battling the Cheyenne and Sioux warriors together on the famous "Last Stand" ridge that overlooked the Little Bighorn River on June 25, 1876. They were the closest brothers of the Custer family, and the fact that they died together was a most symbolic ending for both of them. Ironically, George and Tom had survived some of the hardest-fought battles of the Civil War, only to die with their command, which included other Civil War veterans, on June 25, 1876.

But unlike his younger brother Tom, George was much different from his father. He wanted nothing to do with a lifetime of preaching and farming the black soil of east central Ohio. An early love for all things military first began when his father took him to watch the drills of the citizen-soldiers of the ragtag New Rumley militiamen, who were more at home on parade grounds and at picnics and social events than on the battlefield. This experience helped to set the stage for Custer's diligent efforts to gain entry into the United States Military Academy.

From the beginning, Custer was lucky in life, because he was the couple's first child to survive, after the first two had died in infancy. Inside the sprawling two-story house in New Rumley, Custer enjoyed an extended family with the three children from his father's first marriage (half brothers and sisters) and nearly as many children from the widow's family to create a household of endless activity, pranks, and laughter. He became the pet of his doting parents, the fun-loving Emmanuel who was basically a grown-up boy, and his older siblings on both sides of this extended family.[55]

Blessed with piercing blue eyes and curly blond hair, Custer was lively and handsome when he grew into early manhood, appealing to the girls of all classes. Despite his "sharp, fox-like nose," one of Custer's students where he taught at the Beech Point school near the small town of Athens, Ohio, Sara McFarland, emphasized, "What a pretty girl he would have made."[56] John A. Bingham, who had nominated Custer for entry into West Point, went a step further by writing how the young man was as "beautiful as Absalom with his yellow curls."[57]

## THE PRETTIEST GIRL IN MONROE

Custer's humble roots and lower-class status of a western blacksmith and farmer's son had done nothing to engender a sense of inferiority in him, at least on the surface. But of course the young man's aggressiveness and ambition were direct compensations for his less than distinguished past. However, Custer's high level of self-assurance stemmed partly from the fact that he was so solidly grounded in a vibrant family life, where deep love and understanding had long existed in abundance. He hailed from a home of loving parents and siblings, and this nurturing environment was little different from the close-knit environment of farm families all across eastern Ohio. Perhaps Custer's mother, Maria Ward Custer, said it best in a heartfelt letter: "I was not fortunate enough to have wealth to make home beautiful, always my desire. So I tried to fill the empty spaces with little acts of kindness."[58]

A development that was only a matter of time for an ambitious young man of lowly background from a remote part of rural America, Custer's family's low standing in society early caused him difficulties in his love life. He aspired higher, and this included his social and romantic life. Custer eventually desired not only a wife of a higher social standing than his own, but he also had to have the prettiest girl in the entire town of Monroe. This was Custer's second home, where he lived in the house of his older half-sister.

Monroe was nestled in Michigan's southeastern corner and located on the western shore of Lake Erie. Monroe County's largest town, which was situated on the banks of the river Raisin that emptied only a short distance away into the giant lake after a 140-mile journey through southeast Michigan, possessed a reputation for its attractive belles. And the vivacious Elizabeth Bacon was at the top of the social, economic, and political heap of the most appealing women in the county.

Elizabeth was the most cultured and the brightest belle of all Monroe County—a great prize to any young man, as evident from a long list of her admirers and suitors. Because of her pleasing personality, winning ways, sense of humor, and "lovely temperament," Elizabeth was irresistible to most young men of Monroe. The only daughter of four children who had been born to the autocratic judge, Libbie was the only fortunate survivor at a time when childbirth was extremely dangerous to both mother and child. Unfortunately for Custer, Daniel Stanton Bacon was one of the sternest judges in Michigan, and he was an aristocratic snob. Elizabeth was at the center of Monroe's active social world. She moved smoothly in the community's upper strata without engendering the usual jealousy and envy among her peers.

Since their formal introduction at the Boyd Seminary in Monroe on a late November 1862 evening, and barely two months after the bloodiest day—September 17, 1862—of the war, the dashing Captain Custer had set his sights on Elizabeth Bacon. However, in his ardent pursuit of Libbie with his customary enthusiasm, Custer had aimed too high, or so it seemed, because he "was from the wrong side of the tracks." A highly respected community leader who enjoyed the upper-class elite of Monroe, and of a well-known and lofty political, social, and financial status, Judge Daniel Stanton Bacon bristled at the attention this young man lavished upon Libbie because Custer lacked the social and personal background suitable for his daughter, who had been initially resistant to the young captain's considerable charms for some of the same reasons. She was torn between her father's will and that of Custer for an extended period, including at the time of the showdown at Gettysburg.

Of course Bacon, a probate court judge, who had been a member of the Michigan Territory Legislature before statehood came in 1837, was only trying to protect his only daughter because of Custer's reputation as a drinker, hell-raiser, and womanizer. Not known for his sense of humor or for a lack of awareness of strict lines of class distinction, he possessed not only the arrogance of a prosperous man from a small town, but he also looked back with pride upon his family's early New England roots. Quite simply, he was an elitist. While Bacon was one of the most respected men in Monroe and a member of the upper-class elite, Custer's father was nothing more than a lowly "village smithy," with almost too many children to feed and clothe.

In fact, the Custer family and the Bacon family could not have been more different: A fun-loving sense of humor, merriment, and pranks distinguished the Custer clan, while Judge Bacon's excessive authority cast an austere and solemn tone over his family. Libbie's father had spoiled his only child, but this usually corruptive influence had not affected her in a negative way. But as could be expected, he posed the major obstacle in the path of romantic bliss between Custer and the woman of his dreams. Blessed with a sweet disposition and temperament, a good head on her shoulders, popular among both men and women, and a lover of the arts, Libbie was quite a remarkable young woman of her time, as Custer fully appreciated. Custer had never met anyone quite like Libbie Bacon, whom he had targeted with a laser-like focus as he did in advancing his military career.

In part because of his daughter's sterling qualities, Bacon's opposition to Custer was so strong that it not only backfired by driving Libbie closer to Custer, which is so often the case in love affairs, but it also revealed an excessive emotionalism when it came to his own daughter. Behind the stoic professional and upper-class veneer was a man of intense passions, unlike his more analytical and sensible daughter, who was wise and mature beyond her years. In emotional terms, the death of Daniel's wife had unhinged him. When his wife died of disease during the summer of 1854, Bacon left his home, moved into a Monroe hotel, and sent his daughter, age twelve, off to the best local boarding school. For reasons more psychological than personal, Bacon's unrelenting antagonism and hostility toward Custer was excessive by any measure. The mere concept that this upstart member of the lower class—and a roving soldier at that—might be his son-in-law possessed a degree of shock potential that proved nearly as great as his wife's death.

As fate would have it, Bacon and Custer were actually much alike in some fundamental ways because they were self-made men, which also might well have partly explained the depths of the judge's opposition. After all, Bacon had also been a young man on the rise at one time. But while Custer was a westerner from Ohio, Bacon was an easterner, which was another factor in his opposition to Custer to some degree. As a young man and the son of a physician, he had departed his father's house in Onondaga County, New York, where Syracuse served as the county seat, and moved west—from Maryland to Ohio—like members of the Custer family. Beginning as a teacher and then a farmer of the fertile lands of Michigan's Raisin River country near Lake Erie, he had prospered a great deal in the West, unlike the Custer family. Clearly, the autocratic judge meant to protect the comfortable and prestigious world, including his close-knit family, which he had created by hard work and dedication. The judge never trusted Libbie's many suitors, even refusing her requests to go sleigh riding in mixed company and to dances, especially in his own house where it was forbidden.

Of all of Libbie's suitors—she had many young handsome men, including a young minister and a lecherous teacher, if the latter had been successful in his pursuit of Libbie (the future Mrs. Custer). By the time of the war's outbreak, the judge most of all feared that his only daughter would fall prey to the romantic image of a handsome, dashing man in a fancy uniform. He correctly recognized this kind of attraction as his levelheaded daughter's only Achilles' heel when it came to young men. Judge Bacon, therefore, correctly saw Custer, among all his pretty daughter's suitors, as the greatest threat and hoped that he might just go away. But the ever-relentless Custer was not the kind of man to go away discouraged and defeated in any single-minded pursuit on or off the battlefield.[59]

However, in regard to his personal life, Custer actually needed formidable obstacles and barriers—even Libbie, who was not initially impressed with him since he was just another in a long line of suitors and because she dutifully hoped to fulfill her father's ambitions for her, which excluded soldier boys who might be killed at any time—because they only fueled his greater efforts to overcome the most daunting roadblocks that had been placed in his path. Clearly, despite facing resistance from the judge and a considerable social disparity, Custer was not to be denied. In typical audacious fashion and not wasting time, he proposed marriage to Libbie on their second meeting. All in all, Custer was driven by the combined fuel of ambitions and obstacles that worked closely together within him in symbiotic fashion to create a steely determination both on the battlefield and in regard to his love life.

Custer confidently believed that he could not only overcome Libbie's other suitors despite her beauty and upper-class status, but also the opposition of the judge, who was one of the most powerful and influential men in Monroe, as well as any of Libbie's remaining reservations while her keen intellect wrestled with the pull of her soft heart. Realizing her vulnerability, Libbie's own doubts were well placed because she had never previously known a soldier, a vocation that was considered low on America's social ladder and almost contemptible because of the taking of the so-called "king's shilling." At this time, the popular concept was that such men as Custer were only serving in the military because they had been unable to excel in the civilian world.

Most importantly, in regard to Custer's first major battle (Gettysburg) as the Michigan Cavalry Brigade's commander, he was highly motivated to win victory to impress not only the love of his life, but also her father, who was still convinced that the young soldier was not good enough for his daughter's hand. Custer fully realized that he needed to reap splendid successes on the battlefield to remove the last obstacles and doubts of not only the judge but also his daughter. In this sense, Custer was fighting two wars at the same time, one against the Confederates and the other behind the scenes against the obsessively class-conscious judge, who was concerned that his family's high social standing might be blemished.

What cannot be denied was the fact that Custer's overly aggressive pursuit of Libbie and his quest for her love served as a powerful motivation for him to perform skillfully and heroically to win her hand and live happily ever after, according to the romantic fairy tale. After all, this idealistic scenario was all part of the thinking of young males of the Civil War generation. In the end, therefore, perhaps the outcome of the fight on the East Cavalry Field in the Army of the Potomac's rear was partly determined in some degree by the influence of the pretty young daughter of an arrogant Michigan judge, because of Custer's desire to win the hearts of both Daniel and Libbie.[60]

As Custer knew, Libbie felt deeply—"I like him very well"—as she wrote in a letter to her shocked father, in part because his excessive attentions and endless flattery had thoroughly "spoiled" her for other men. As she had written prophetically in an 1862 letter to her father, now even more adamant that his daughter should no longer see the dashing Captain Custer, who had already captured her heart, although she was still trying hard to resist his considerable well-honed charms—he was an experienced ladies' man—which had already overwhelmed her: "Do not blame Captain Custer. He has many fine traits and [the town of] Monroe will yet be proud of him."[61]

But Libbie was still conflicted and undecided about the relentless pursuit of Custer by the time of the Gettysburg campaign. In her confidential journal, Libbie, still tormented and torn between her warm heart and her sensible head, admitted, "I am trying hard to tear Autie's image from my heart."[62]

Custer was fully aware of the situation resulting from Libbie's indecisiveness, partly because of her father's excessive resistance, and how the judge was the most serious threat to his romantic ambitions, when his intentions were entirely honorable, in contrast to what the cynical judge and other Bacon family members believed was the case. Therefore, in the end, Custer fully realized that he would have to win the hand of his lady by what he could accomplish on the battlefield, including the most important battle of America's most murderous war. To secure what he desired in his heart, he knew that he had to make a national name for himself so that Judge Bacon and the town of Monroe would hear about his achievements and be proud. Libbie knew as much, and she was convinced that he would succeed in the future. She believed in this excessively bold young man named Custer, and she would not be disappointed.[63]

In this sense, the Battle of Gettysburg was destined to be a great testing of Custer's fate in regard to his love life, which could only be saved by winning victory on the field of strife. Indeed, it was not long after the dramatic showdown on the East Cavalry Field on July 3, 1863, that Judge Bacon's seemingly insurmountable opposition to the young upstart from a lowly background finally crumbled, and he accepted Custer as truly worthy of his only daughter's hand in marriage.[64] Quite simply, Custer was a winner, and he fully demonstrated as much to one and all in the end, beginning at Gettysburg.

## THE ELITE MICHIGAN CAVALRY BRIGADE

But to be fair, Custer could not win glory on the battlefield and make a great name for himself without an elite command of fighting men who possessed a well-deserved reputation for excelling in combat. In this regard, he was most fortunate in commanding some of the best fighting cavalrymen of the North: a full brigade of Michigan men whose combat prowess and elite qualities were unmatched in the cavalry arm. Michigan, which only became a state in late January 1837, produced 90,000 volunteers for the Union in total, and 14,700 of these men of the infantry, cavalry, and artillery died during the war years, despite a population of under one million in 1860. These included many recent immigrants (an estimated four thousand Ireland-born Michiganders served the Union, including a fair number in the four regiments of Custer's Michigan Cavalry Brigade), not only from the east, especially New York, but also from Germany and England.

From the beginning, these Michigan men were highly motivated to join the fight to save the Union and to demonstrate the value of their state that was still relatively new to the cherished Union. Because it was still largely undeveloped and rural—much like the South—and still very much a frontier state in 1861, skill in horsemanship and transportation by horseback were still all important and a regular feature of everyday life in Michigan, unlike in the more urbanized northeast. Therefore, Michigan early on led the North in supplying cavalrymen to the war effort. In fact, Michigan was destined to provide more mounted men than any other state in proportion to the size of its population.

And no troopers in the Army of the Potomac were better fighting men than Custer's 1st, 5th, 6th, and 7th Michigan Cavalry Regiments, of a brigade that was created shortly before the dramatic showdown at Gettysburg.

Most importantly, and not surprisingly, therefore, perhaps no fighting men from Michigan played a more crucial role in the war than the Michigan Cavalry Brigade, especially on the last day at Gettysburg, July 3, 1863, when everything was at stake during the dramatic showdown on the East Cavalry Field in the Army of the Potomac's rear. Under Custer's leadership, the Michigan Cavalry Brigade evolved into a truly crack command of elite fighting men, who served in perhaps the finest Union volunteer cavalry regiments during the four years of war—a fact that was demonstrated by thwarting Generals Lee's and Stuart's ambitions in the rear of the Army of the Potomac on the crucial afternoon of the third day at Gettysburg.

Michigan's contributions came early in the war to reveal the extent of its patriotism and desire to save the Union. President Abraham Lincoln received the majority of the state's votes for president, which partly indicated the state's strong antislavery roots and enthusiasm to preserve the Union at all costs. A much-relieved Lincoln praised the Michiganders because they were some of the first Union troops to arrive in Washington, DC, to protect the capital in mid-May 1861.[65]

Like many other men from Michigan, the state's senator Zachariah Chandler wrote philosophically in a letter of how the blood of both traitors and patriots needed to be shed in order to liberally water "the Tree of Liberty," and this required a good deal of "bloodletting" that was necessary for the good of the nation and to preserve the republican experiment in liberty.[66]

The hard-fighting 24th Michigan Volunteer Infantry, consisting mostly of hardy farm boys (which included 135 sets of brothers) from Wayne County, Michigan, evolved into one of the most famous infantry regiments of the Civil War. These Wolverines served in perhaps the best fighting command of the elite Iron Brigade, or the "Black Hat" Brigade. They won a widespread reputation for combat prowess in some of the hardest-fought battles in the eastern theater while wearing the 1858 Model Hardee dress hat for which these crack fighting men were well known to both sides. The worthy counterparts of the elite infantrymen of 24th Michigan, known as the "black hatters," were the elite Michigan cavalrymen of the four regiments of Custer's Brigade.[67]

Symbolically, Custer wisely gave his Michigan men a distinct appearance in a unique way that mirrored the distinctive look of the soldiers of the Iron Brigade. Because he realized that the high black hats of the 24th Michigan soldiers was a morale builder that bolstered the command's esprit de corps, Custer knew that the Michigan cavalrymen of his Wolverine Brigade likewise needed something unique in their appearance to forge greater solidarity and fighting spirit; historically, a distinctive uniform or a part of military apparel had long denoted elite soldiers, who basked in their enhanced and elevated status as superior fighting men. Therefore, Custer eventually had red ties, which were worn around the neck, made for his men to match his own bright red tie that made his own uniform distinctive. These red ties bestowed a distinctive appearance that enhanced the morale and fighting spirit of his Wolverine command.[68]

But more importantly, and thanks to Custer's leadership, the regiments (the 1st, 5th, 6th, and 7th Cavalry Regiments of the Michigan Cavalry Brigade, which was formed not long after General Joseph "Fighting Joe" Hooker was relieved of command of the army by President Lincoln) became the most elite fighting cavalry force of the Army of the Potomac—a direct and worthy counterpart of the Iron Brigade. In regard to the word "Iron," this distinctive name, which emphasized the combat prowess of some of the army's hardest-fighting infantrymen, might well have applied to the Michigan troopers of Custer's Brigade by the time of the Gettysburg campaign.

As members of an elite cavalry brigade destined to achieve glory, beginning on the afternoon of July 3, 1863, when everything was at stake in the Army of the Potomac's rear, on battlefields across the South, these brave troopers were Custer's finest fighting men—especially when compared to the famed 7th Cavalry of Little Bighorn fame—that he ever commanded in his lengthy career that extended a decade after the Civil War. Quite simply, the Wolverines were members of the "best [Union cavalry] brigade" of the eastern theater.[69] Indeed, this elite command of Michigan troopers garnered the reputation as "the hardest-fighting cavalry brigade of the war," thanks in no small part to Custer's leadership and hard-hitting style.[70]

But in the days before the bloody showdown at Gettysburg, the Michigan Brigade of four cavalry regiments—recruited at different times and with different periods of military service before brigaded together—had yet to prove itself as a fighting unit. The showdown in Adams County, Pennsylvania, on July 3, 1863, was destined to be its first fight together as a four-regiment brigade. And symbolically, in the same way, Custer had to prove himself to his men because of his age and inexperience. But most of all, the young man's rapid advance in rank was sure to cause a great deal of skepticism, jealousy, and envy, if not outright hatred among the older members of the general officer corps and among regimental commanders and other brigade leaders. Regardless of what Custer achieved in the name of saving the Union, therefore, he was still in many ways a marked man because his opponents were watching his every move. In this regard and ironically, there was a somewhat deeper level of a more personal animosity forthcoming for Custer from his fellow generals than from the enemy, because the Southerners' hostility and desire to eliminate him was not as intimate and personal.

A careful student of the nuances of human nature, Custer had no illusions that he was due for a hostile reception upon taking command of his brigade, perhaps including deliberate sabotage to some degree, and he would be closely watched for committing any flaws or errors on the battlefield, which would be magnified by those who were less capable and, hence, jealous. But he remained confident in his own abilities to win over his men, including the Michigan officers who had been passed over in his taking command of the Wolverine Brigade. Custer was therefore determined to do all that he could to win over hearts and minds and change the views of the inevitable legion of skeptics and critics, especially older and more experienced officers, because of what he knew he could accomplish on the battlefield, where it mattered the most: "I should soon have them clapping me on the back and giving me advice."[71]

While Custer was certainly a war lover to an excessive degree compared to most others, he was not a hater of the enemy, a key distinction for understanding the thinking and attitude of one of the most remarkable cavalry commanders of the Civil War. Custer described the depth of his sincere feelings about the enemy when he assisted an injured Captain John W. "Gimlet" Lea of a North Carolina regiment. One of Custer's West Point friends, Lea had been wounded at the Battle of Williamsburg at the beginning of the 1862 Peninsula Campaign.

Custer provided timely assistance to the captive officer, despite the gentlemanly protests of the proud Captain Lea: "When we first saw each other he shed tears and threw his arms about my neck, and we talked of old times [and] I carried his meals to him, gave him stockings of which he stood in need, and some money. This he did not want to take, but I forced it on him. He burst into tears and said it was more than he could stand. . . . The bystanders looked with surprise when we were talking, and afterwards asked if the prisoner were my brother."[72]

Custer's friendliness toward the enemy was not changed as the war lengthened and became more terrible. He somehow remained unchanged by the war's horrors, maintaining his boyish ideals and enthusiasm for life. As he penned in a letter to relatives not long after the Battle of Antietam, Washington County, Maryland, on September 17, 1862: "Enclosed I send you a small strip of silk which I tore from a rebel flag at the battle of Antietam, pronounced 'An-tee-tam,' an Indian name. . . . I accompanied a rebel Colonel, a Lieutenant and several prisoners, under a flag of truce inside the rebel lines. I found several who were acquainted with my classmate and friends . . . and we had an hour's social chat, discussing the war in a friendly way. And we exchanged cards."[73]

## COMMON, BUT EXCEPTIONAL, MICHIGAN TROOPERS

As mentioned, Custer was blessed when it came to commanding a truly elite fighting force, which rose magnificently to the fore on the third day at Gettysburg. But what factors were responsible for making these Michigan men elite fighters and the army's best troopers? How could they possibly have become crack fighting men and performed so much by the time of their first major battle at Gettysburg on July 3, 1863? These are important questions seldom explored by historians when telling the often-overlooked story of the East Cavalry Field fight. Again, Custer deserves the lion's share of recognition for what he accomplished at Gettysburg, but he could not have succeeded without the highly motivated and crack fighting men of the 1st, 5th, 6th, and 7th Michigan Cavalry. All in all, the development of an elite soldiery lay largely in the Wolverines' unique backgrounds, which set them apart from eastern soldiers. Quite simply, it was the forge of the western and frontier experiences that played a part in transforming these Michigan men into a superior soldiery, who rose splendidly to the challenge—like their young commander—at Gettysburg.

Indeed, the overall high quality and resourceful nature of the Michigan troopers that made them such excellent fighting men was partly born of the western and frontier experiences, which provided a toughening process as well as nurturing a strong sense of patriotism and devotion to a land, where a self-made man could rise high in life by hard work and ambition. The mysterious new lands that lay beyond the western horizon had beckoned another generation of optimistic Americans to continue the nation's historic push west into the pristine countryside and wilderness of the Michigan Territory, which had been created by Congress in 1805, during the 1820s, 1830s, and 1840s.

Most of all, Custer's Michigan troopers were tough, resilient, and hardened men from a state that was still frontier-like at the time of the Civil War. They were true pioneers in a rugged land, covered in virgin white pine forests, once highly prized by the early French because of the lucrative fur trade (beaver was the fashionable fur that was worn across Europe, especially in regard to hats) that had led to the early establishment of Detroit, located on the eastern lower peninsula. Detroit had long served as the crucial gateway to all of Michigan. In the pioneer tradition, the men of Michigan were resourceful, hardworking, and known for their ingenuity in having tamed a wilderness nestled in the midst of the sprawling Great Lakes—Lake Michigan on the west, Lake Huron on the northeast, and Lake Erie on the southeast.

Long coveted by the English, French, Canadians, Americans, and, of course, the original inhabitants, Native Americans like the Potawatomi, Chippewa, and Ottawa, these rich lands along the expansive lakes of fresh water were exceptionally fertile—a glacial loess soil—which had drawn early settlers like a magnet. Consequently, a new generation of Americans had migrated west by wagon, horse, and along the Erie Canal, which was opened in 1825, to this agricultural "El Dorado." These settlers journeyed to the Michigan Territory not only from the east, but from the south in Illinois, Indiana, and Ohio, from west to east. Because so many rivers, clear and fast moving, flowed into the Great Lakes, the pristine lands, including stretches of prairie, around these watercourses were luxurious and fertile and early settlers benefited from the lucrative Great Lakes trade centered at Detroit.

For such reasons, these early settlers, who found a fertile land of endless bounty, understood why Michigan, because of its strategic location in the heart of Great Lakes country, had long been a bone of contention in the imperial struggle between France and England in their long wars for empire and control of the North American continent. But in the end, it was the success of the settlers, small farmers, and lumbermen who harvested the tall, straight pines that seemed to touch blue skies, and the hardworking boatmen who plied the clear rivers and the broad Great Lakes, that had transformed Michigan into a state.

These were the common people who conquered a land of plenty to fulfill their own personal versions of the American Dream, when idealistic visions of a bright future had no end for these hardworking eternal optimists. Most importantly, these resourceful men brought a can-do spirit and never-say-die qualities that created a rugged individualism born of their western and frontier experiences—a forge of adversity and seemingly endless challenges that resulted in a toughening process and created strength of character—that significantly bolstered the ranks of the Michigan Cavalry Brigade and was a perfect match for their aggressive fellow westerner from a rural and frontier-like environment, Custer, who was considered one of them because of his close connections to Monroe, Michigan.[74]

This rugged land of westerners was a land of die-hard patriots who were determined to do whatever was necessary to save the Union during the exciting spring of 1861 when the call to arms was issued after the firing of Confederate cannon on Fort Sumter in Charleston, South Carolina. As emphasized by the words of the editor of the *Grand Rapids Enquirer* of Grand Rapids, Michigan: "It is our duty and that of every patriot citizen to adhere to his loyalty and uphold his country's flag" to save the sacred Union.[75]

No city in Michigan was more central to the inspirational story of Custer's Michigan Cavalry Brigade than Grand Rapids, which was located around thirty miles east of Lake Michigan and northwest of Detroit, Michigan. This community took its name from the Grand River, which gave life to the thriving town. Despite being the second-largest city in Michigan by the time of the Civil War, Grand Rapids still possessed a number of distinctive frontier-like qualities after having been settled in the 1830s. At this time, the Grand River Valley was considered the "garden of Michigan," becoming a magnet for a generation of optimistic settlers. By 1860, around eight thousand residents called Grand Rapids—known as the "Valley City," and the largest city in northwest Michigan—their home.[76]

But more importantly, Grand Rapids might well have been known as "Michigan's Horse Soldier City" that had no peer in the sprawling state. In the war's beginning, cavalry service was extremely popular, and the ranks of Michigan's first cavalry regiment were quickly and easily filled for the creation of the 1st Michigan Cavalry. This fine regiment became part of Custer's crack Wolverine Brigade, and the command arose magnificently to the challenge of July 3, 1863. The 1st Michigan Cavalry was filled with zealous men from Grand Rapids, which was situated opposite Milwaukee, Wisconsin, and located on the other side of Lake Michigan, and from other communities, mostly small towns, across the state, including Detroit. The 1st Michigan Cavalry was dispatched to Washington, DC, in late September 1861 and represented Michigan with a great deal of pride and abundant enthusiasm. As mentioned, these were no ordinary men but represented the hardiness of not only the West, but also the frontier environment. For such reasons, one recruiter with insight had specifically targeted frontier backwoodsmen, who were "not only first class riders, but also crack shots."[77]

A worthy companion regiment of the 1st Michigan Cavalry for service in Custer's Wolverine Brigade, the 6th Michigan Cavalry was created for the express purpose of enhancing the often-defeated cavalry arm of the Army of the Potomac. Tall, handsome, and distinguished by a command presence that inspired respect, Colonel Russell A. Alger, an expert horseman and dynamic commander, led the more than one thousand troopers of the 6th Michigan Cavalry. This fine regiment was organized at Grand Rapids. Alger benefited from a fine officer corps of young men of promise.

Leading the boys of Company B, Captain Peter A. Weber possessed prior military experience, but as an enlisted man in an infantry regiment and then the 2nd Michigan Cavalry. He was one of the finest officers in Colonel Alger's command. Nearly as capable as Weber on the battlefield, Captain Henry E. Thompson led Company A with consummate skill, and his men would follow him to hell and back if necessary. The regiment was officially mustered into service in mid-October 1862, just in time for the great challenge of the Gettysburg campaign.[78]

The resourcefulness and ingenuity that the men of Custer's Brigade had gained from the demanding experiences of life on the western frontier had been early exhibited. Lieutenant Samuel Harris, 5th Michigan Cavalry, who had journeyed west from Vermont in January 1837—when Michigan became a state, losing its territorial status—was one such individual, demonstrating flexibility and ingenuity both on and off the battlefield. When he arrived at his unit's campgrounds just outside of Detroit, Michigan, with nearly 120 new recruits for the 5th Michigan Cavalry, Harris found only a barren cornfield for training, "with nothing to shelter us." Fortunately a supply of timber arrived on the second day, and Harris, the only officer present, then organized the construction of a large barracks to house his men, completing a sturdy structure in record time and in typical frontier fashion.[79]

Sergeant George Thomas Patten was a common soldier, but exceptional in a number of ways, of the Michigan Cavalry Brigade. He has provided a good representative example of the high quality and caliber of Custer's men in the ranks. After all, Custer could not have performed his amazing feats at Gettysburg, especially two headlong saber charges against the odds, without such highly motivated and self-sacrificing troopers, who served faithfully in the ranks. As he fully appreciated, Custer was most fortunate because he commanded such high-quality men on the afternoon of July 3, 1863.

Like the vast majority of the men who served in the Michigan Cavalry Brigade, George Thomas Patten, 6th Michigan Cavalry, was an ordinary American of middle-class status and a humble farmer who tilled the soil of the place that he loved—the occupation of the majority of the Civil War generation. Quite simply, he was an ordinary man who suddenly found himself in extraordinary times, and he arose splendidly to the challenge like his comrades. As a sad fate would have it, he was destined to be killed near the end of the Gettysburg campaign in mid-July 1863 at Falling Waters, Maryland, during a reckless charge in leading a mere handful of brave Wolverines upon Lee's strong rearguard with no chance of succeeding.

Embarking on the noble and idealistic crusade to save the Union, Patten volunteered to serve his country with great enthusiasm, enlisting on September 6, 1862, not long before the bloody Battle of Antietam. But Patten would not live another year, dying far from home at age twenty-eight while carrying the Holy Bible that his wife had given him on the regiment's departure from Grand Rapids, where the regiment had been organized. Sergeant Patten's death in western Maryland was not the only tragedy to strike this devout farming family like a thunderbolt. His pretty wife and childhood sweetheart, whom he had married on May 5, 1859, and described as "so good and patriotic wife," Lydia A. Denton-Patten, died of tuberculosis on April 1, 1863. This tragedy fueled Patten's sense of fatalism, if not a desire to rejoin her in the other world, far from the horrors of war.

The two parents left behind a son, whom his father had lovingly called "Little Georgie," age three. The history of the Patten family had centered on the high hopes of finding greater opportunities by migrating west like so many other Americans of the Civil War generation. They had moved from New York (a quarter of Michigan's population was from New York in 1860) and headed for the bountiful lands of Kent County, Michigan, in the summer of 1839. There, not far from Lake Michigan, which lay to the west in the appropriately named Alpine Township, they had found a pristine land covered by a carpet of white pine forests filled with game and the golden promise of a brighter future. In the bountiful land that had to be cleared of virgin timber, the Patten family had made their dream come true by making a decent living from the apple, pear, and peach orchards that were situated on the choice ground on Peach Ridge and the surrounding area that provided great abundance.[80]

A true patriot who loved the Wolverine State, Patten was hardworking and intelligent. Therefore, he won appointment to the key position of quartermaster sergeant of the 6th Michigan Cavalry and served capably in that role. He earned the rank of first sergeant of Company B on April 1, 1863, just before the beginning of the Gettysburg campaign. But he would not bask in the good fortune and advancement for long. He received a letter (ironically postmarked the same day as his promotion, and a sad missive that revealed his life's greatest tragedy, while he was serving far from home) from his mother, who wrote her most heartfelt words: "My Dearest Son; it is with the most profound and deepest regret that I must be the one to tell you of the dreadful fate of our dearest love and beautiful wife. On this day, April 1, 1863, Lydia went on to the Lord in her sleep after a short but dreadful illness. . . . Dad and I, and little Georgie were at her side when she passed away, and her last words were to tell you she loves you so very much, and if she does not make it through, as sure as there are angles in heaven, she will be at your side for all eternity."[81]

Corporal James Henry Avery, Company I, 5th Michigan Cavalry, was another typical faithful follower of Custer, who greatly benefited from such dedicated men in the ranks of his Wolverine Brigade. Born in Troy, New York, located on the east bank of the Hudson River just north of Albany, Avery was a highly motivated and die-hard cavalryman, the key qualities that were secrets to the amazing success of the Michigan Cavalry Brigade, especially on the third day at Gettysburg. Like so many other Michiganders, Avery was a farmer who had moved west to Michigan to begin anew in the tradition of America's historic expansion toward the setting sun. He had migrated to the fertile lands of Kent County, Michigan, in 1859 as a newly married man who was eager for a fresh start in a bountiful land. At age twenty-four in mid-August 1862, he enlisted in the ranks of the 5th Michigan Cavalry and then gained a well-deserved promotion to corporal in the first month of 1863.[82]

By any measure, the 5th Michigan Cavalry was one of the best regiments of the hard-fighting Wolverine Brigade, despite having been only recently organized in the summer of 1862. Of the more than 250 cavalry regiments that served the Union, this excellent cavalry regiment was destined to rank number three in the total number of troopers who were killed on the field of strife—a distinguished sacrifice and the most notable distinction that spoke directly to the command's fighting spirit and combat prowess.

If the 5th Michigan Cavalry was perhaps the finest regiment of Custer's Michigan Brigade, as was partly demonstrated during the combat on the East Cavalry Field on July 3, 1863, then the 7th Michigan Cavalry was not far behind. The 7th Michigan Cavalry was organized at Grand Rapids not long before the beginning of the 1863 Gettysburg campaign. But despite the command's experience by the time of the showdown at Gettysburg, its overall quality was not at all lacking in any regard. Again, the superior quality of the men in the ranks certainly applied to the 7th Michigan Cavalry, and this fact was fully demonstrated in the regiment's first major battle, at Gettysburg.

By this time, the bloody battles of Antietam, Fredericksburg, and Chancellorsville had ensured that there were few fair-weather troopers who had enlisted in the ranks after these nightmarish slugfests. Without receiving bounties for enlistment and knowing that enlisting for service in the faraway eastern theater ensured that many of these men would never return to Michigan, they fully realized this fact, unlike the soldiers who had enlisted in 1861, when naive volunteers had believed that the war would be won in only a few months and in a practically bloodless manner. Most of all, these late-enlisting Wolverines were determined to see a long and grim job completely through, and they were highly motivated by a single cause: to save the Union at any cost.

One Michigan officer of this regiment was so determined to create an elite soldiery at Grand Rapids that he carried a pocket full of rocks to hurl at full force at any young recruit of the 7th Michigan Cavalry troopers who made a clumsy mistake on the drill field. Evidently, this officer's unorthodox method of instilling discipline was effective, because regimental members were extremely well drilled by the time the 7th Michigan Cavalry journeyed to Washington, DC, to join the Army of the Potomac.[83]

However, the men of the 1st Michigan Cavalry had already established an elite reputation before the formation of the Michigan Brigade because it had been the first Wolverine command to serve in the eastern theater. Here, the Wolverines had early made their presence felt and won a name for themselves. In this regard, a case can be made that the sister regiments of the 1st Michigan Cavalry learned a good deal from this older command, including what was necessary for meeting the challenge of the final day at Gettysburg.[84]

As could be expected, older officers, who were naturally envious of the new commander, who almost looked like he had yet to shave, were shocked at Custer's young age of twenty-three, when he earned his promotion to brigadier general. But what has been most often overlooked by historians was the fact that he was looked upon like an older father figure by the teenagers who served in the 7th Michigan's ranks. But these teenagers made good fighting men, and some of them demonstrated outstanding leadership ability during the showdown at Gettysburg. By the spring of 1863, "two beardless youths" had become sergeants in the 7th Michigan Cavalry.[85]

In a May 15, 1863, letter to his mother, one of these young sergeants explained his harrowing experiences after one fight with Virginia guerrillas not long before the command's first major battle at Gettysburg: "I was shot in the leg slightly in a fight we had yesterday morning. . . . It is a simple flesh wound, and I will be laid up for only a short time. I rode four miles on horseback after I was shot."[86]

Clearly, this teenage sergeant was a tough soldier, and he reflected the character and quality of the hard-fighting Michigan Brigade, a premier combat unit, in general. But he revealed his youth when he added at the end of his letter what was foremost on his mind at this time after having long eaten bacon and tasteless hardtack while recovering in the hospital: "P.S.—If you could manage to send me a box of grandmother's custard pies, they would be highly appreciated."[87]

But rather than this young trooper who possessed a sweet tooth, the true quality—hard and tough—of these Michigan men can be seen in the words of young Private William Glover Gage, Company C, 7th Michigan Cavalry. After having enlisted at age eighteen, he was known as "Glover" to his comrades. From a rather sheltered background, he was shocked by his rough-edged comrades, who were some tough characters. In a letter he penned to his father, he described how he had taken his advice in regard to "avoiding bad company," emphasizing with some surprise how "there are so many mean men in the Co. [C] [that] there is hardly a decent private in it."[88] Quite simply, these Wolverines, rawboned and rough edged in reflecting the rigors and challenges of the western experience, possessed a Michigan toughness not known in the east.

But of course an excellent officer core was also key to the overall success of the Michigan Cavalry Brigade, which explained why it evolved into an elite unit and excelled on the East Cavalry Field on July 3, 1863. Dark haired and presenting a striking appearance, Captain Peter A. Weber, 6th Michigan Cavalry, was one of the most capable leaders of not only the regiment, but also of Custer's Wolverine Brigade. For good reason, James Harvey Kidd, 6th Michigan, described him as "the heroic Weber" and "the gallant Major

Weber."[89] Kidd's own background partly reflected the stern demands of the western frontier experience, having been connected to the "lumbering and mercantile business in the pine woods of northern Michigan" before the war.[90]

A model soldier in every respect, Captain Weber's sterling qualities that had earned him a promotion to major were exhibited in full when he played a key role on July 3, 1863. He helped save the day by informing Custer about the hidden presence of thousands of Stuart's men (four cavalry brigades and four batteries and a section of Louisiana guns) in the forests atop Cress's Ridge in Meade's right-rear and near the strategic crossroads of the Hanover and Low Dutch Roads. As the popular company (B) commander of the 6th Michigan Cavalry, Weber was a dynamic man of action and a hard-nosed fighter in the Custer mold, and the two men were kindred spirits. They worked together as a highly effective team on the East Cavalry Field on Gettysburg's bloody third day, when everything hung in the balance.

But ironically, the captain's darkly handsome and overall placid appearance gave little hint of the abundance of abilities and skills that existed deep inside the young man from Grand Rapids. He looked even younger than his years. Even more, Weber's prewar background indicated very little, if anything, of what lay inside him: a highly capable and dynamic leader who was absolutely fearless on the field of strife. A scholar and lover of learning, he was the librarian at the Grand Rapids Library Association in Grand Rapids, Michigan. Trim and athletic, Weber's sense of duty and morality had been well established before the war. He was the main provider for his widowed mother and two sisters, which engendered a maturity well beyond his years and a great sense of responsibility that helped to forge a natural leader.[91]

Captain Weber possessed one basic flaw, and it was one that was destined to cost him his life—he was too brave and daring for his own good. In one of the most audacious charges of the war, Weber led fifty-six troopers of Companies B and F, 6th Michigan Cavalry, into the midst of two entire Confederate brigades—Lee's rearguard—that caught by surprise at Falling Waters (also known as the Battle of Williamsport), Maryland, on July 14, 1863. However, this was a suicidal charge, with Weber leading the way. Weber evidently believed that the Army of Northern Virginia was on the ropes and vulnerable while crossing the Potomac River on a pontoon bridge during its escape to Virginia, after it had been mauled during three days of brutal combat at Gettysburg.

Captain Weber, of course, was mistaken in his optimism, but he sensed a tactical opportunity by striking the rear guard of a battered army. For his heroics in leading the charge and attacking impossible odds with only a relative handful of Michigan men, Weber was shot in the head and killed while leading his band of Wolverine troopers. Like no other junior officer, Weber personified the Michigan fighting spirit against any odds.[92]

## SUPERIOR WEAPONRY THAT CONTRIBUTED TO ELITENESS

The troopers of the 5th Michigan Cavalry and 6th Michigan Cavalry—while the men of the 1st Michigan Cavalry and 7th Michigan Cavalry were trained in the fine art of conducting the saber charge, which was put to good use by Custer on the afternoon of July 3, 1863—evolved into elite fighting commands in part because its members were armed with the seven-shot Spencer repeating rifle. These fast-firing weapons greatly enhanced the regiment's combat capabilities because of the massive amount of firepower that was unleashed by these deadly weapons. Quite simply, the Spencer was the best breech-loading firearm in America by 1863, and the Wolverines embraced the fast-firing weapon like a lover, while Lee's cavalry paid a heavy price for this love affair.

Connecticut-born Christopher Spencer, whose mechanical and innovative genius, combined with a tireless Puritan work ethic, paid immense dividends for Custer on July 3, 1863, was the inventor who had created the spring-loaded, seven-shot tubular magazine that he placed in the wooden butt of this deadly weapon. Like the fast-firing Winchester rifle, the Spencer's level action ejected the spent metal cartridge with a smooth and rapid ease to chamber a fresh round for firing to ensure a rapid rate of fire.

Making its first appearance on the battlefield in 1862, the Spencer repeating rifle, the first mass-produced magazine-loading firearm, was a new weapon that was nothing less than exceptional and a killing machine in the hands of experienced Michigan cavalrymen. However, the use of the Spencers was limited by Union cavalry in 1863, except for a select few troopers. But fortunately for the Union, an estimated 3,500 Spencers were in the hands of the Union cavalry during the three days of the bitter combat at Gettysburg. Most importantly, Custer possessed hundreds of troopers, especially the Wolverines of the 5th Michigan Cavalry, who were armed with this superior weapon. As demonstrated to the shock of Confederate soldiers who felt its merciless wrath, this was the most lethal hand weapon that could be found on any Civil War battlefield. As fate would have it, and unfortunately for Stuart and his outgunned men, Custer's troopers made the superior firepower of the Spencer felt in full on the East Cavalry Field on July 3.

Most importantly, in the hands of one of Custer's veterans, the Spencer fired as many as twenty rounds a minute, transforming the Michigan men into a lethal machine, and exactly when it mattered most at Gettysburg. One of the enduring myths of the Battle of Gettysburg was that the fast-firing Spencers made the most decisive impact by Brigadier General John Buford's cavalrymen of the First Cavalry Division, Major General Alfred A. Pleasonton's Cavalry Corps, Army of the Potomac, on the morning of July 1, a much celebrated action that has completely—and unfairly so—overshadowed the more important role of the Spencer in a more vital situation in the hands of Custer's Michigan men on July 3. This distortion of the historical record was one of the great ironies of the Battle of Gettysburg.[93]

Corporal James Henry Avery, 5th Michigan Cavalry, penned in his journal of the exciting moment when these new weapons were handed out to the enthusiastic volunteers: "The issuing of arms was the first thing, each man getting a Spencer rifle of seven shots, a revolver of five shots, and a sabre. This made each man almost an arsenal. Our rifles were found too long and heavy for cavalry and were changed for the Spencer carbine, a very nice, light arm. These guns are what caused the Michigan Brigade [in the beginning] to be called by the rebs [Brigadier General Judson] 'Kilpatrick's Seven Shooting Devils,'" [because] after they had a taste of our fire, they asked what kinds of guns we had, to load on Sunday and shoot all the week."[94] For instance, one dazed Confederate asked a Union officer with utter amazement, "What kind of *Hell-fire* guns have your men got?"[95]

But at Gettysburg, these Michigan troopers were "Custer's Seven Shooting Devils," whose superior firepower was one of the forgotten keys to a remarkable success achieved by Custer on the East Cavalry Field. Corporal Avery summarized how the key influence of Custer was still another factor that led to the making of an elite command: "The Michigan Cavalry Brigade, known to the world as one of the best and most effective bodies of troops . . . selected as it was from the best material, and commanded by the best officers [especially Custer] to be found; armed with the most approved arms."[96]

Quite simply, large numbers of Custer's Michigan men were armed with the "most formidable cavalry weapons of this day of destiny, the seven-shot Spencer rife and Spencer carbine, and this superior firepower maximized their numbers and combat capabilities to a considerable extent."[97] The Wolverines of Custer's Michigan Cavalry Brigade were even more formidable because they possessed "some of the best [horses that] could be found in Michigan."[98]

The feisty spirit of Michigan's fighting men can be seen in the actions and words of a young soldier who had been saddled by his proud parents with the name of First Sergeant William Shakespeare of Kalamazoo, Michigan. The degree of harassment that he endured in school for having been named after the most famous writer of English literature can only be surmised.

Like so many other youths, he had enlisted at age seventeen during the spring of 1861. He suffered multiple wounds, including two shattered thighs, of the most serious nature in a hard-fought battle in 1863, after which the experienced physician at a Union field hospital solemnly pronounced that young Shakespeare, who was slightly built and now covered with ugly wounds from the fire of large-caliber Confederate muskets, could not possibly survive and was destined to die. This grim conclusion was derived from a hasty conference by a number of seasoned and capable medical men at the field hospital. Because Private William Shakespeare's death seemed only a matter of time, one Union physician from Detroit penned (Shakespeare was unable to write because of his serious condition) a sad letter to the young man's mother in Kalamazoo, describing the seemingly inevitable tragic fate of death for her teenage son. Before sealing the envelope of the letter, the Union surgeon read the letter to First Sergeant Shakespeare, who already looked like a corpse while lying in a seemingly comatose state.

But suddenly coming to life upon hearing the spoken words of the last letter to his mother read to him out loud, Shakespeare was alarmed, if not upset. He therefore asked the expert medical man if he could add some last words to the letter to his mother. The young man was granted permission by the surprised Union surgeon, who could hardly believe the sudden resurrection of the young Wolverine. Hardly able to write, First Sergeant Shakespeare scribbled his words slowly and with great difficulty: "Do not be alarmed, dear mother, the doctor is mistaken, I am going to get well and come back to you." In the end, Shakespeare fulfilled his solemn promise to his mother, because he had defied authority and the odds—the essence of the feisty Michigan trooper, who was dominated by a never-say-die spirit.[99]

Significantly, a comparable defiance in the face of the odds and irrepressible fighting spirit was exhibited in full by Custer and his men on the afternoon of July 3, 1863. For such reasons, the Michigan troopers were destined to gain a well-deserved reputation among Stuart's Rebel troopers as "the flying devils of Michigan."[100]

But of course these were not "devils" but devout men of quality, courage, and character. Not long after his promotion to brigadier general, Custer knew that he needed to appoint a group of capable staff officers to assist him and his efforts in the upcoming showdowns with the boys in gray and butternut. At the age of twenty-three, Custer was not afraid to appoint even younger men to his staff if they possessed sterling qualifications and ample potential. He appointed the following staff members, who were destined to play key roles during the hard-fought contest on the East Cavalry Field: Captain G. A Drew, 6th Michigan Cavalry, to assistant inspector general; Lieutenant R. Baylis, 5th Michigan Cavalry, to acting assistant adjutant general; and Lieutenant William H. Wheeler, 5th Michigan Cavalry, and Lieutenant William Colerick, 1st Michigan Cavalry, as aides-de-camp.[101] Two Norvell brothers also served on Custer's staff, Edwin Forrest Norvell, aide-de-camp, and Dallas Norvell. They were two of six Norvell brothers who fought to save the Union.[102]

Another young staff officer shortly joined Custer's staff. Lieutenant Edward G. Granger, a Detroit man, had enlisted in the 5th Michigan Cavalry at the young age of nineteen in August 1862. Well educated at quality schools, including the Agricultural College of the State of Michigan, and thanks in part to political connections, he began his service on behalf of his country as a rookie second lieutenant. In late August 1863, Granger was destined to be appointed to Custer's staff. He demonstrated outstanding ability and promise as one of Custer's faithful aides until fatally cut down on an assignment in mid-August 1864.[103]

As Granger penned of his good fortune in an August 22, 1863, letter to his cousin Emma Walker, "The day before yesterday I received an order detailing me as an Aid de Camp on the staff of General Custer commanding the Michigan Brigade, consisting of the First, Fifth, Sixth and Seventh Regiments of Michigan Cavalry."[104]

A more average Wolverine who fought on the East Cavalry Field can be found in Private Henry McKinstry. He hailed from Capac, Michigan, and served in the ranks of the 5th Michigan Cavalry. McKinstry traced his lineage back to Scotland before the family migrated south to north Ireland around 1669. His modern descendant, Neil McKinstry, emphasized how during the decisive showdown on July 3, 1863, "Custer and his men were instrumental in preventing [General] Stuart from getting around the Union Right Flank [when he was] trying to get to the Union rear in support of General Pickett's charge."[105]

## RARE LEADERSHIP QUALITIES

Custer became idolized because of his leadership abilities and his audacious courage demonstrated on the battlefield, and this was especially the case in regard to the showdown on July 3. In the same letter, young Lieutenant Edward G. Granger described Custer in glowing terms that emphasized the young commander's quality and character, including how he treated fellow officers as brothers, which was another secret of his success: "The General is a gentleman as well as a brave soldier and good officer."[106]

In another letter written the following month, Lieutenant Granger provided a more thorough description of Custer and against emphasized his often overlooked redeeming qualities: "First and foremost, of course, as to my present brilliant position [of aide-de-camp] on the Staff of Brig. Gen. Custer—It is a very pleasant position, indeed, as the General is one of the most perfect *Gentlemen* I have met in the Army. . . . Gen. Custer is one of the 'fighting Generals' of whom we read so much and see so little: but there is no doubt about his fighting qualities, for his command has not been in a single engagement in which he has not been under fire."[107]

In this same letter, Lieutenant Granger provided a vivid description of the dynamic, Ohio-born general whom he so greatly admired, like the other men of the Michigan Cavalry Brigade: "The General is a young man of three and twenty, nearly six feet tall and well made, complexion red, eyes blue, hair yellow and hanging in curls on his shoulders, mustache & imperial of the same elegant color, dresses in velveteen with an indefinite number of yards of gold-lace on the sleeve of his jacket as an indication of rank, but when dressed for review makes by far the most splendid appearance of any officer I have seen—morals West Point—manners perfect—temperament lively & full of fun."[108]

Trooper Samuel Harris, 5th Michigan Cavalry, also presented a portrait of Custer that emphasized his audacity and boldness both on and off the battlefield. He described Custer as "a slim young man with almost flaxen hair, looking more like a big boy [who had] the cheek of a government mule."[109] A proud New York cavalryman, Henry C. Meyer, described Custer as an officer of Pleasonton's staff at the beginning of the Gettysburg campaign, before the native Ohioan's promotion to brigadier general: "When Custer appeared he at once attracted the attention of the entire command. . . . He was dressed like an ordinary enlisted man, his trousers tucked in a pair of short-legged government boots, his horse equipments being those of an ordinary wagonmaster. He rode with a little rawhide whip stuck in his bootleg, and had long yellow curls down to this shoulders, his face ruddy and good-natured."[110]

Most appropriately, Custer possessed the superior western qualities and characteristics of not only the enlisted men, but also the Michigan Cavalry Brigade's officers. Quite simply, he was a Wolverine himself for all practical purposes. Hailing from a frontier-like environment in the West, these highly motivated Wolverine officers were resourceful and rugged individualists. An important ingredient that made them such high-quality officers both on and off the battlefield, these determined men carried the essence of the frontier and western experience with them to the battlefields of the eastern theater. Indeed, in the revealing words of one man who was not guilty of exaggeration in regard to analyzing the impressive qualities of the Michigan Cavalry Brigade's officers, who were as tough and reliable as the men in the ranks: "Our officers are not the men to be tampered with, as more than one hoary-headed traitor can testify. . . . They perform their duties fearlessly."[111]

In the very beginning of taking over command of the Michigan Cavalry Brigade, Custer's calculated effort to make himself conspicuous to his men was not without risk. In the insightful words of a former member of the 6th New York Cavalry: "The boy general looked so pretty and effeminate, so unlike the stern realities of war, that he was certain to be quizzed and ridiculed unmercifully, unless he could compel the whole army to respect him. There was envy enough [among other officers, especially older ones with more experience] about his sudden elevation, as it was. . . . The very assumption of his peculiar and fantastic uniform, was a challenge to all the world to notice him. He must do something brilliant, to justify the freak. Imitating as he did the splendor of appearance of Murat, he must equal him in deeds, if he did not wish to be set down for a carpet knight."[112]

Indeed, Marshal Joachim Murat, one of Napoleon's most flamboyant commanders, had commanded the finest cavalry of Europe, and Napoleon relied upon his hard-hitting ways to reap his dramatic victories across Europe.[113] In much the same way, senior commanders, from General Pleasonton to General Gregg, relied on Custer at Gettysburg on the final day as Napoleon had relied upon the handsome Murat, who loved nothing more than to lead a cavalry charge.[114] This historical legacy was still another strong motivation that caused Custer to rise splendidly to the challenge on the afternoon of July 3, because he basked in Napoleonic analogies and the new burden of responsibility delegated to him.

## SURPRISE AT BRANDY STATION

As fate would have it, young Custer was destined to face no ordinary opponent at Gettysburg on July 3, 1863. Far and wide and almost since the war's beginning, General Stuart was considered to be "the best cavalry commander in the world."[115]

This was especially the case in regard to Stuart's lofty reputation in 1862, but the crucial year of 1863 was destined to forever change the equation. The war had changed and become more deadly and businesslike by the spring of 1863, while Stuart remained the same romantic-minded cavalier and outrageous dandy he had been since the war's beginning. And he dressed the part of the gay cavalier, wearing the gaudiest of possible uniforms and behaving in an extremely flamboyant fashion that shocked many observers. While the war was about the serious business of killing as many opponents as possible in a nightmarish war of attrition during the first of all modern wars that no longer had any room for romance or illusions, Stuart still played the part of the romantic and gallant cavalier to excess. Stuart even wore gauntlets of white buckskin, gold spurs that sparkled in the sunlight, plenty of gold braid, a gray cloak trimmed in scarlet and with a fur collar, and a large, high, curling ostrich feather and gold star clasp that kept one side of his hat up. While not as flamboyant as Murat, the marshal of a humble social background, like Custer, would have admired Stuart's dress and showboating.

Even more unnecessary and taking the extremes of gaudiness to new heights while more serious-minded Southern officers looked on in amazement, Stuart also sometimes wore red and blue flowers—given to him by the seemingly endless number of admiring ladies—and brightly colored ribbons that he wore proudly in the lapel of his uniform coat. Even while the ridicule increased about his endless love of frivolities as the war lengthened and became the bloodiest in American history, Stuart seemed never to notice or care about the frowns from the nonromantics, as if increasingly lost in a seductive world of adulation and romance that seemed to have no end. Not exactly to his credit, and unfortunately for General Lee and the Army of Northern Virginia, Stuart soaked up too much of the fame and basked in the acclaim to an excessive degree, and far more than what was usual for a successful commander. Quite simply, he had been seduced by not only his successes, but also by the adulation that had made him the most famous cavalryman of the South. As the days passed, Stuart demonstrated more glaring examples of inner weaknesses and flaws of character that were destined to rise to the fore on July 3, 1863.

To the fullest, and like no other commander in the Army of Northern Virginia, Stuart played the part of the noble knight-turned-cavalier to the hilt, while soaking up the heady acclaim and the ringing cheers of a thankful Southern people, especially the seemingly countless numbers of pretty girls. Stuart returned the warm feelings to these young women by an outrageous level of flirting—according to the value systems of a conservative society—seldom seen in Lee's army, despite a loving and admiring wife, Flora, who was considered "homely," and small daughter, Little Flora, back home in Virginia. The open flirting and budding romances made the Virginia dances and nights memorable to Stuart, who loved the lavish praise and attention. Quite simply, he had become an idol and star of the Confederacy. Such a never-ending flow of adulation proved extremely seductive because of inherent vulnerabilities that were revealed in Stuart's character.[116]

Even a married and devout member of John Bell Hood's famed Texas Brigade, Army of Northern Virginia, was shocked by Stuart's behavior in public with the attractive ladies, when the flirting and dancing that went late into the night intoxicated the so-called gay cavalier more than the strongest Kentucky whiskey. This South Carolina–born soldier, an adopted Texan named John Camden West, saw Stuart in all his glory on a train ride from Richmond in late May 1863. He wrote to his wife with some understatement how "General J. E. B. Stuart was aboard and appeared to be very fond of ladies and flowers." Quite simply, by the crucial year of 1863, Stuart had been thoroughly seduced by not only his string of successes, but also the throngs of attractive ladies, especially the youngest—much younger than his good, but more homely, wife back at home—and prettiest ones of the South.[117]

Stuart attended so many balls and social functions, especially at the highest levels of society in the capital of Richmond, that he gained a reputation as "the gayest of the gay"—not exactly the best qualities needed by the ever-sober Lee, who ignored and tolerated the considerable excesses of his top cavalryman because he still operated at a high level.[118] Although there has been found "no concrete evidence that he ever plucked any forbidden fruit from the tempting orchard of women through which he strolled" like a God, the possibility does exist that he took advantage of the situation because the opportunities that were presented to him were endless.[119]

Especially in the early part of the war, all of this excessive pomp and unbridled flamboyance were relatively harmless and even positive—actually good for overall morale purposes among the troopers and Southern people in general—in purely military terms. But this situation was only the case as long as Stuart performed well on the battlefield, as in the past. There was always the possibility that Stuart's excessive focus on the romantic side of war might evolve over time into something more troublesome to supersede the much more serious side of war on an unconscious level and erode that new seriousness in the art of war fighting that was now necessary to prevail in what had become a vicious war to the death.

By early 1863, the war had changed dramatically—unlike Stuart, who continued to act as if he believed that it was still 1861—because there was no longer any chance or hope for compromise or negotiation in the most murderous conflict in American history. Unfortunately for the South, and as his growing number of critics noticed to their dismay, if not alarm, Stuart had not only not changed, but had seemingly become even more flamboyant as the war gradually began to turn against the Confederacy. In fact, this development might have become an ugly reality because he realized that the South had little chance of winning: a fatalistic realization that in part reflected the inherent and inevitable sense of "gloom" of a conquered people from a tragic past that had been endured by Stuart's Scottish lowland and Scotch-Irish ancestors from the green rolling hills of north Ireland.[120]

The most recent and truly alarming evidence that Stuart's lofty reputation was no longer justified and that he had been seduced by his past successes to the point of engendering a dangerous level of hubris was demonstrated in full in the broad fields at Brandy Station, Virginia, in June 1863. Here, just northwest of Fredericksburg and just east of the Blue Ridge Mountains, which were the easternmost chain of the Appalachians, Stuart had recently learned a bitter lesson about how thoroughly the war had changed forever. Stuart and his cavalry had been dispatched west in the second week of May by Lee, not only to keep watch on the Union cavalry, but also to lead what became the first phase of the army's advance north into Pennsylvania before the infantry moved out in the hope of catching General Hooker by surprise. Meanwhile, Lee's army remained at Fredericksburg.

Seasoned units of Southern cavalry had been concentrating around Culpeper courthouse, which was around forty miles (a leisurely two-day ride) slightly northwest of Fredericksburg, for the offensive operations north of the Potomac River that might decide the war. In addition, the rolling fields of lush clover of Culpeper County around the town of Culpeper—Brandy Station, a railroad depot from which it had earned its name, was located just to the northeast—allowed Stuart's horses, which were in overall poor shape, to gain extra strength and vitality for the great challenges that lay ahead during a new campaign that was guaranteed to be hard and long.

Timely intelligence—including a captured letter to a civilian in which Stuart bragged that a large concentration of Southern cavalry would arrive to end any future Union cavalry raids that might devastate the area—about the sudden grouping of thousands of Rebel cavalrymen was a tipoff that Lee was about to make a bold move from Fredericksburg. General Hooker was more than wary. Thanks to the recent intelligence reports, which alarmed him, Hooker already realized as much in regard to Confederate intentions. While Lee hoped to surprise Hooker by pushing north to exploit his success at Chancellorsville by launching a new campaign north of the Potomac, Hooker smartly spied the opportunity to surprise a complacent Lee and one of his top lieutenants, Stuart. Ironically, Stuart was even more overconfident than Lee, despite his isolation around Culpeper.

Like no other previous Army of the Potomac commander in regard to boldly utilizing the army's cavalry in an aggressive manner, Hooker issued instructions to his top cavalryman, Pleasanton, to descend upon the advanced force of extremely complacent Rebel cavalry and "destroy" them. This ambitious tactical objective was made easier by the fact that Stuart had been seduced by the awe-inspiring majesty of the recent cavalry reviews that were impressive martial displays right out of the history books about Napoleon's glory days. But that more romantic time of Napoleon was no more, and Stuart was gradually becoming an anachronism in this first of all modern wars, when the old glory of 1861 and 1862 was not only out of date, but it was also too late to reclaim even by Lee's most dashing cavalier.

Instead of exercising proper vigilance and focusing on preparing for the most challenging and important campaign of the war, Stuart committed the cardinal sin of letting his guard down when he conducted grand reviews of his cavalry to reveal the depth of his hubris, which had reached a new high. Here, nestled between the Rappahannock River and the town of Culpeper, he held the first grand review of his large concentration of cavalry on May 22, which only fueled his desire to conduct additional reviews, which were also transformed into gaudy shows.

The next review was conducted on June 5, and General Lee was invited to attend along with the general public. But Lee was unable to be present for the gala affair because he was focused on serious work, unlike his top cavalryman, who basked in the limelight. Therefore, without Lee's mature presence, and ignoring the demanding realities of the serious business of preparing for the second northern invasion, Stuart foolishly reduced his combat capabilities by conducting each new review without concern for the future. These festive reviews consisted of excessive exhibitions of mock charges and firing of cannon, the unleashing of "Rebel yells," and riding horses at a gallop until the animals were worn out by wasteful efforts for no gain except to excite the onlookers, especially the ladies.

While three military brass bands played martial airs and proud Southern officers were dressed in their finest uniforms as if for an inspection, these well-attended reviews evolved into grand social events that were attended by a throng of admirers from Richmond. Stuart's reviews, especially the firing of the twenty-four guns of his horse artillery in a waste of precious ammunition that would be badly needed at Gettysburg, especially on the final day, swept over the sprawling fields of grass and clover that stretched below Fleetwood Hill, where spectators crowded on the grassy slopes.

Stuart had become the grand master conductor of the most fashionable and gaudy show of the season, and the excesses of frivolity only continued with the grand ball that was held afterward and went deep into the night. Stuart seemed lost in the heady fog of the pageantry of war and the seemingly endless praise, the pretty ladies who loved to kiss him and he them, and the rich food and strong drink. What was clear to many shocked observers, including grizzled veterans in the enlisted ranks, was that this was no way to win a war. Such outlandish displays of martial prowess were fine in 1861, but they were now badly out of date because the war had changed. Most of all, this was now a bitter war of attrition in which the top priority was to kill as many of the enemy as possible. Stuart was proving that the war's changes and new realities had already passed him by, because he continued to relive the heady days of 1861 as if the romance of war had never ended.

Too many sparkling successes had come much too easily for such an extended period that Stuart saw the war as little more than a game, a sporting event in which he was always the winner at center stage. As a natural showboat with a badly inflated ego, he was at his finest when the majesty and pageantry of war were resurrected for his many excited admirers at Brandy Station. But despite the appearances of strength on display during the reviews, which awed spectators, military and civilian, to bestow a greatly inflated confidence for easy victories in the future over the Union cavalry as so often in the past, the South's most famed cavalryman, commanding his five cavalry brigades that had been reinforced with additional cavalrymen for the challenges of the upcoming northern campaign, was not ready for the war's new and even harsher realities.

Clearly, Stuart's greatest weakness was his excessive fondness for showmanship and pomp that had been personified in his unrestrained and inflated flamboyance, which he loved to no end. On the eve of the army's greatest challenge, at a time when the South's cavalry combat capabilities were still in the overall process of an unseen but steady erosion during a lengthy war of attrition, Stuart was not at all concerned about the extra wear and tear on the horses, both his cavalry and horse artillery, or on his troopers during these grand reviews, which lasted for extended periods and included mock charges at full gallop.

All in all, fatal flaws were revealed during the hours of merrymaking as the post-review social events had become more important than the deadly art of war in a conflict that had become more vicious and horrible than at any time up to that point. Stuart was extremely vulnerable to all the flattery and accolades in overall psychological terms, which was revealed by his penchant for basking in the unnecessary excessiveness of the grand reviews—three in total from late May to early June—before admiring crowds filled with the prettiest ladies of Richmond and the surrounding area. The general public was especially awed by the grand review that had been staged on the broad fields of the Auburn Plantation of John Minor Botts on June 5. After the last review on June 8, which was witnessed by General Lee, who had wisely emphasized that the cavalrymen were not to waste their energy in galloping—Stuart loved to unleash mock cavalry charges—to save the energy and strength of the horses, the worn troopers and horses finally gained much-needed rest from the dusty ordeals in the day's intense heat.

However, as fate would have it, this rest period after the largest grand cavalry reviews of the war was too brief for Stuart's men. Orders were finally passed from cavalry encampment to encampment of more than twelve thousand troopers to push north on the following morning, June 9, and cross Beverly Ford over the Rappahannock to launch the Pennsylvania invasion proper.

As during the 1862 Maryland campaign, Stuart's mission was once again to screen the army's advance north beyond the Potomac River toward where lofty Confederate ambitions and dreams were focused, as in the past. Never had the army's cavalry strength been greater, fueling not only overconfidence but also hubris in the glory-seeking mind of the South's idol, General Stuart.

Meanwhile, the increasingly aggressive General Pleasonton, who was determined to ascertain Lee's exact intentions—either another cavalry raid or the vanguard of the army's next invasion of the North—and to prove his worth to General Hooker, had already made his own preparations for his boldest operation. He was about to launch a surprise attack on Stuart's silent encampments of weary troopers at Brandy Station, which was located just south of the Rappahannock River in Culpeper County, by sending his cavalry across two fords of the river on this very morning. Sleepy Brandy Station had been named for serving as a stop on the Orange and Alexandria Railroad and for the area's tasty apple brandy—seemingly the most unlikely of places for the largest cavalry battle of the Civil War.[121]

On the morning of June 9, and sensing a golden opportunity to strike a confident commander and his highly touted cavalry, which had slipped into a considerable degree of hubris by this time, Pleasonton unleashed his cavalry corps across the Rappahannock simultaneously at two inadequately defended points along Stuart's weak defensive line: Beverly Ford, which was located north of Brandy Station, and Kelly's Ford, just to the south. Headquartered on the high ground of Fleetwood Hill, which overlooked the wide plain covered in broad fields and grassy meadows, General Stuart was caught completely by surprise by the blue onslaught of howling cavalrymen.

Worst of all, hubris had reached such airy new heights at Stuart's headquarters that any thought of Union cavalry as capable of posing a serious threat to the South's finest cavalry was routinely dismissed with a laugh by the boys in gray and butternut. What cannot be denied was the fact that General Stuart had been most fortunate on June 9, because he had been so thoroughly caught by surprise and barely recovered from the shock in time to mount a belated defensive effort. After having been completely outsmarted, he nearly suffered not only the greatest defeat ever inflicted upon Lee's cavalry but also an absolute disaster.

Carelessly left on the main road near the river and Beverly Ford without infantry protection while the artillery horses, which had been worn out by the recent reviews, grazed in nearby fields and pastures on the warm night of June 8, Stuart's Horse Artillery, aligned in neat rows, lay exposed for the taking—a degree of folly that had been allowed for reasons that are unknown to this day. In consequence, sixteen guns of the Stuart Horse Artillery, under the command of Major Robert Franklin Beckham, were nearly captured at the attack's beginning because they were located so near the main river crossing point of any threat that might emerge.

So complete was the surprise achieved by the onslaught of thousands of bluecoat troopers that some of Stuart's horse artillerymen, who had been worn out during the reviews from riding at the head of the column and then hastily deploying their guns to fire rounds to amuse the spectators, were nearly captured in their beds with their blankets spread on the ground. In a letter to his wife, Captain Leonard Williams, 2nd South Carolina Cavalry, of Brigadier General Wade Hampton's Brigade, described how Stuart's Horse

Artillery—badly needed for July 3—had to be saved from the grasp of the Federal troopers. He emphasized how Hampton's regiments "rescued the day [and not General Stuart because Hampton] and his brigade distinguished themselves and made the most brilliant of charges and saved our artillery and Stuart's headquarters" on Fleetwood Hill, which was destined to be the key high ground and most strategic position during the Battle of Brandy Station.[122]

In a classic understatement, one of Stuart's horse artillerymen, George Michael Neese, summarized how Stuart's famed "horse artillery has been permitted to roost a little too near the lion's lair."[123] Of course this carelessness was an inexcusable mistake made by Stuart, which was only one of many errors made that were most alarming, boding ill for the Gettysburg campaign.

In the end, the hard-fighting Hampton and his fine non-Virginia brigade (mostly Carolina boys) had saved the day and the much-touted Virginians, while bailing out his idealized Virginia commander by some magnificent charges long remembered by fortunate survivors. In a candid letter to his wife, Captain Charles Minor Blackford, 2nd Virginia Cavalry, Brigadier General Fitzhugh Lee's Virginia Brigade, revealed the full truth of what had happened at Brandy Station during fourteen hours of the most intense cavalry combat of the Civil War: "The cavalry fight at Brandy Station can hardly be called a *victory*. Stuart was certainly surprised and but for supreme gallantry of his subordinate officers [especially Hampton and the troopers of his command] it would have been a day of disaster and disgrace. . . . Stuart is blamed very much," because he had been more obsessed with the pageantry of reviews than the more serious and less glamorous side of war.[124]

The upset editor, Virginia-born Edward Alfred Pollard, a proud University of Virginia and William and Mary College man, of the *Richmond Examiner*, published one of the most scathing critiques of Stuart as the head of the "much puffed [up] cavalry" of the Army of Northern Virginia: "The more the circumstances of the late affair at Brandy Station are considered, the less pleasant do they appear [and Stuart's cavalry] has been twice, if not three times, surprised since the battles of last December [1862] and such repeated accidents can be regard as nothing but the necessary consequences of negligence and bad management. If the war was a tournament invented and supported for the pleasure and profit of a few vain and weak-headed officers, these disasters might be dismissed with compassion. But the country pays dearly [and] it is high time that this branch of the service be reformed."[125] This harsh analysis was not only no exaggeration, but it was also only the beginning of Stuart's follies that marred Lee's second invasion of the North. The new nation was about to pay a far higher price for Stuart's failures in the upcoming Gettysburg campaign.

Perhaps a Jewish Confederate named Raphael J. Moses, a native of Charleston, South Carolina, said it best in regard to Stuart. Proud of three sons who faithfully served the Confederacy, Moses was one of the best officers of the commissary department, serving as the chief commissary officer of General James Longstreet's First Corps. With keen insight, he penned an on-target evaluation of Stuart: "a splendid Cavalry Officer, but, oh, how frivolous. . . . His favorite passion when not dancing with the girls was to have his banjo player thrum and sing. . . . He is vain and frivolous," to seemingly no end.[126]

In a March 1863 letter, a somewhat shocked Charles William Trueheart, who hailed from the port of Galveston, Texas, wrote about the January 1863 wedding of "Cousin Lizzie" that he attended in Hanover County, Virginia, where he saw Stuart in action that had nothing to do with fighting the Yankees: "Maj Gen'l Stewart [Stuart], Brig. Gen'l Fitzhugh Lee, and several other military gentlemen were among the guests present. The former [Stuart], though a married man, is very fond of the young ladies generally, and takes the liberty of kissing all the pretty ones I notice. He and his staff rode forty miles through the mud to attend this wedding."[127] Clearly, Stuart would certainly go the extra mile to attend merrymaking when pretty young ladies were present and affection was freely dispersed.

Even one of Stuart's greatest admirers, his early adjutant William Willis Blackford, admitted in defense of his beloved superior, while revealing Stuart's most glaring personal shortcomings, which he never disguised: "General Stuart had a warm heart, and though a member of the church . . . he was fond of gay company and of ladies' society and of music and dancing."[128] In fact, Stuart's activities with the ladies and the colorful reviews to impress them had played a part in eroding the already fragile capabilities of his cavalry and horse artillery for entirely unnecessary reasons on the eve of the war's most important campaign. After the post-review balls that went late into the night, like the drinking and flirting with the pretty girls, "while they [including Stuart] danced, many of his enlisted men tending their horses grumbled about Stuart's wearing out men and horseflesh for meaningless pomp."[129]

Of course, in his scathing editorial, which emphasized that reform of the cavalry arm was necessary because of the close brush with disaster at Brandy Station, the same Richmond editor, Pollard, hinted in no uncertain terms and with keen insight that Stuart needed to be replaced before it was too late. But it was already too late, because the first phase of the Gettysburg campaign was underway. General Lee, his army, and the South would have to make the best of their deeply flawed chief cavalryman, who loved attention. In many ways, the string of past successes had thoroughly spoiled Stuart, who had once been a strict West Pointer and a model of caution. But those days were no more and in the past, when victory had been easier.

All in all, Stuart had become a victim of the adulation and glorification that had created a mythical image of him across the South, and he now tried to live up to that lofty romantic image of the South's foremost cavalier, which was a virtual impossibility. He was no longer the same man whom Captain Charles Minor Blackford described in a September 1861 letter, saying Stuart "is very young, only twenty-eight but he seems a most capable soldier, never resting, always vigilant, always active."[130]

Quite simply, Stuart had been spoiled by his impressive successes, and he was no longer that same kind of commander needed for the great challenges that lay ahead north of the Potomac River. What happened at Brandy Station left a degree of not only shock, but also trauma that deflated some of the overconfidence of Stuart's so-called "Invincibles"—a sobriquet that no longer applied as it had in the past. The old confidence and swagger had been eroded not only by a war of attrition but also by Stuart's gradual regression as the finest cavalry leader of the South. After all, for the first time in the war, lamented George Michael Neese, who could hardly believe the new reality, like so many of Stuart's men who were stunned by the ugly truth of Brandy Station, "the Yanks rushed us out of camp this morning before breakfast."[131]

But the irate editor of the *Charleston Mercury* of Charleston, South Carolina, perhaps said it best in a scathing analysis that shocked the Southern people and alerted them to a host of new and ugly realities that boded ill for the ambitious invasion north of the Pennsylvania: Stuart and his men "were disgracefully surprised. General Lee, it is said, has censured Stuart severely. He deserved it [partly because] Stuart's head has been turned by the ladies and the newspaper claquers of his [famous] raids. . . . He has been having big cavalry reviews for the benefit of the ladies and the enemy [General Pleasonton]. At the last review he appeared in grand style, with boquets [sic] pinned plentifully upon his person—much to the disgust of General Lee, as people of [the] Culpepper area."[132]

And this unprecedented disaster and close brush during a serious defeat at Brandy Station just before the war's most important campaign represented an ominous indication that the commander of Lee's cavalry now seemed more interested in conducting reviews "inspiring enough to make even an old woman feel fightish," in the humor-laced words of Neese.[133] But after the complete surprise of Stuart and what came close to becoming an unprecedented disaster that might well have sabotaged Lee's entire invasion plan, what could no longer be denied was the fact that "never again would the Confederate cavalry dominate its Northern counterpart [because] the tide had finally turned for the Federal troopers and against Stuart and his men."[134]

In regard to the mounted arm of both armies, the currents of the tide of war were moving swiftly and rapidly changing, and cavalry commanders who failed to adjust to these changes were increasingly vulnerable. While the Southern cavalrymen continued to bask in their much-inflated sense of superiority that was more a thing of the past than Stuart and his troopers could imagine, the Union cavalry had succeeded in changing by quickly adapting to new challenges in businesslike fashion after learning from the long list of its past mistakes and failures, which was always the best school of the warrior, but only if the lessons were heeded in a timely manner to adapt to new realities.

In contrast and like Stuart, the Southern cavalry had not changed because it had been too successful in the past, and no one, including Lee, saw any need for change because of those past successes. After all, Stuart and Lee believed that they possessed the best cavalry not only in America but also in the world. This was the kind of hubris that caused Stuart to so fondly relish mock cavalry charges and the firing of his horse artillery during reviews, when he needed to have his artillerymen and cavalrymen engaged in target practice and other serious exercises to enhance their combat capabilities instead of diminishing them for no positive result during a lengthy war of attrition.

Time was already running out for Stuart and the Confederacy, although neither fully realized that fact. Stuart had still not learned his lesson from the close call at Brandy Station, because the hardest lesson of all was still to come on the afternoon of July 3, 1863, in the Army of the Potomac's rear, when everything was at stake.

## A CASE OF REMARKABLY GOOD TIMING

Besides the arrival of a new day, Custer was fortunate in another regard by the time he took command of the Michigan Cavalry Brigade near the beginning of the Gettysburg campaign, when Meade's headquarters was located at Frederick, Maryland. This lengthy war of attrition had gradually taken a serious toll on the combat capabilities of the Southern cavalry arm, which was made considerably worse by Stuart's hubris. Therefore, the lengthy list of past cavalry successes had come at a high cost in manpower, especially in the officer corps, during America's bloodiest war.

Most recently, the devastating losses in manpower and horses at Brandy Station on bloody June 9 could not be replaced in time for the Pennsylvania invasion, and this situation was especially the case among veteran members of Stuart's officer corps that had been mauled there. Therefore, some of Stuart's finest officers never saw Pennsylvania in the decisive year of 1863 because of the terrible rate of attrition, while Custer's Michigan Cavalry Brigade had been spared from the bloodletting of the war's largest cavalry battle and the heavy losses suffered there by Stuart.

By the time of the Gettysburg campaign, and despite appearances as presented in Stuart's recent reviews on the grassy plain, the ranks of the most successful cavalry arm in America and the pride of the South were in relatively bad shape, because this most grueling of all of America's wars was in its third year. A large part of the problem for Stuart was the Confederate policy of cavalrymen supplying their own horses from home, while the U.S. government relied on a more centralized and systematic means of procurement that effectively provided its cavalrymen with horses—an increasingly important difference during a lengthy war of attrition.

In contrast, Southern troopers without horses (their own personal property and not government owned like in the Union cavalry) were given extended leaves to go home—to all points of the Confederacy, including west of the Mississippi—to secure mounts. Of course this situation meant that many veteran troopers were always absent from the ranks, because no self-respecting cavalryman wanted to be assigned to the hated infantry (too much marching on foot) if he failed to secure a replacement mount. But these organizational differences in the respective cavalry arms reflected the fact that the South was an agrarian nation, and the national government and state governments—after all, they had originally seceded in the name of states' rights—lacked the means to play a more centralized and, hence, effective role in supplying cavalrymen like the northern war machine, which was unsurpassed.

The popular Prussian officer, called "Von" by the boys, attached to Stuart's headquarters staff and a former member of the 2nd Brandenburg Dragoons, Major Johann Heinrich Heros von Borcke, who was destined to fall wounded in the hot clash at Middleburg, Virginia, just before the Battle of Gettysburg, described how the "condition of our horses continued to grow worse and worse, especially in [Brigadier General Wade] Hampton's brigade, on which was imposed the fatiguing duty of picketing nearly forty miles of the Rappahannock [and in February 1863] it was a mournful sight to see more than half the horses of this field command totally unfit for duty, dead and dying animals lying about the camps in all directions. One regiment lost thirty-one horses in less than a week."[135]

The warm weather of 1863 had brought the arrival of a fresh growth of clover and grass that allowed for some improvement in the horses' overall health and welfare, but this was not enough because Stuart had been too active in overusing his hard-riding force during the winter.[136] Of course, the shortage of horses had not only reduced the combat capabilities of the Confederate cavalry proper, but also the horse artillery that closely supported Stuart's three brigades, under Brigadier Generals Wade Hampton and William Henry Fitzhugh "Rooney" Lee, on the battlefield. A member of Stuart's Horse Artillery battalion concluded how "horses in the Confederacy had become scarce" by the summer of 1862, and "we were compelled to take the field [in August] with only half the number of horses required to place our cannoneers on horseback."[137]

Of course, the major battles of the eastern threat had deeply culled the horses of both Stuart's cavalry and horse artillery during this war of attrition that seemed to have no end. In an understatement, one of Stuart's gunners concluded, "The wear and tear of the Chancellorsville campaign [in the spring of 1863] had been seriously destructive of horseflesh and material."[138]

Stuart and Lee believed that confiscated northern horses would fill the void, serving as a motivation for the launching of raids into the North, including the 1862 Maryland invasion and then into Pennsylvania the following year. While northern horses were eagerly secured by Stuart's cavalry units and horse artillery, they proved inadequate in the long term because they were too big and strong—traditional plow horses long used to hoeing rows in the Pennsylvania soil—compared to smaller and lighter Southern horses. One of Stuart's artillerymen, therefore, explained, "Numbers of horses had been taken from Pennsylvania farmers [during raiding in the 1862 Maryland Campaign, but] we discovered that we had been badly cheated by swapping horses, for these [northern horses] were too heavy and cumbersome for rapid movement, and many of them fell by the wayside."[139]

As noted, the ever-increasing shortage of horses in the Southern army was due to more than the Confederate government policy of troopers supplying their own horses, which proved entirely inadequate, especially after the first two years of this war of attrition. Quite simply, the first two years of the conflict's seemingly endless demands had already consumed the best horseflesh of the Confederacy, especially in the trans-Mississippi theater, during this lengthy war of attrition. Indeed, the South could not compete with the opposing cavalrymen, who rode fresh horses supplied by their government and who had new weapons produced by an industrial giant. Surviving mounts of Rebel troopers from 1861 and 1862 had aged considerably by the third year of the war, losing strength, vitality, and agility. Even more, Confederate cavalryman without horses—killed in battle or dead of sickness—had to return home on lengthy absences that sapped the manpower strength of Lee's cavalry, damaged morale, and reduced overall effectiveness, because many men stayed home longer than was required or authorized.

Because of the omnipresent horse shortage faced by Stuart, the average trooper expressed his concerns that the recent grand reviews at Culpeper were nothing more than useless displays and meaningless exertions that only wore out the horses and the men, when the time had come to preserve every ounce of their strength for their greatest of challenges that lay ahead, the Pennsylvania campaign.[140] Ironically, while Stuart's reviews had been overall detrimental in regard to war-waging capabilities, the reviews of the new Union cavalry corps, including by President Lincoln, had the opposite effect of improving morale and confidence among the boys in blue, when it was most needed in preparation for the most important campaign of the war.[141]

The Confederate secretary of war officially authorized the purchase of one thousand horses in Texas to supply Stuart's cavalrymen and horse artillerymen, but the much-needed mounts from Texas never reached the Army of Northern Virginia in time for the Gettysburg campaign. Union successes, especially at Vicksburg, Mississippi, and later Port Hudson, Louisiana, which won the Mississippi River for the Union, ensured that receiving any horses from the trans-Mississippi for Lee's army was a complete impossibility.[142]

This requirement of only one thousand horses was not only far too little, far too late, but also, most revealing the securing of large numbers of horses was simply not possible any longer in war-torn Virginia. In contrast to the inefficiency of the Confederate troopers in supplying their own horses as required by official government policy, the North's war machine of a vast industrial, assembly-line-like system provided everything needed by the Union cavalryman, who basked in abundances and surpluses until waste became a problem. During the war, an estimated one and a quarter million horses and mules were supplied by the U.S. government to fuel the relentless march of its war machine, including the showdown at Gettysburg. Most importantly, Federal cavalrymen did not have to be released from duty to return home to secure new mounts like the South's misguided, if not disastrous, policy, if their horses died of disease or were killed in battle.[143]

But, most of all and despite being outnumbered, young Brigadier General Custer was destined to possess a distinct psychological advantage over his opponent in regard to the upcoming showdown at Gettysburg, and for a variety of reasons. Because of the humiliation that he had suffered at Brandy Station after having been caught by surprise and nearly defeated in disastrous fashion, the cocky General Stuart—not even what happened at Brandy Station had discouraged him—was certain to be overly aggressive whenever the decisive moment came for him to win the kind of glory that would make the critical politicians and people of the South, especially the vindictive journalists who had condemned his performance and even suggested reform of the cavalry arm, forget all about that place called Brandy Station. Despite his inflated ego and overconfidence in the capabilities of his cavalry corps, the humiliation of Brandy Station still nagged at Stuart's heart and soul in the summer of 1863, and he was overeager to redeem himself on northern soil.[144]

## COMMON VIRGINIA TROOPER

The mostly Virginia troopers of Stuart's command represented a wide variety of men from different places and cultures beyond the common and popular stereotypes of cracker culture. Born in Germany, Lieutenant Hermann Schuricht, 14th Virginia Cavalry of Brigadier General Albert G. Jenkins's Brigade of five Old Dominion units, faithfully kept a war diary, which was filled with his personal thoughts and views written in a neat German script.[145] Germans, of course, served in the Union cavalry, including one horse soldier who showed no mercy in battle. Less ruthless Union comrades intervened when this "infuriated German . . . was trying to sabre a [wounded] Confederate boy" instead of taking him captive.[146]

Unlike the men of Custer's newly formed Michigan Cavalry Brigade, Stuart's troopers were more war weary in general than the members of the Union cavalry because they had fought in some of the major battles of the war from the beginning, and their distant homelands in both the eastern and western theaters had been invaded in many cases. The increasing slaughter of this war had affected the morale and spirits of these hard-fighting Rebels, especially after having buried so many friends and comrades in soil on both sides of the Potomac River.

Captain Richard Henry Watkins served with pride in leading the troopers of Company K (the Prince Edward Dragoons), 3rd Virginia Cavalry. While he fought under Stuart, his wife Mary Watkins remained at home near Meherrin, Prince Edward County, Virginia, and raised their three daughters on her own. While making a living as an attorney, Richard had married his wife in a modest Presbyterian church in August 1858. Like the equally religious Sergeant George Thomas Patten, 6th Michigan Cavalry, he also served in a quartermaster capacity in his hard-riding Company K, and then as assistant quartermaster of regimental headquarters.[147]

In a letter to his "Precious Mary," Captain Watkins was horrified by the war's ever-increasing viciousness, which resulted in the war's bloodiest day at Antietam: "We left a portion of our wounded in the hands of the enemy. Our dead, so far as I know, were buried. . . . The feeling of hatred on both sides is becoming intensified and the battles more fierce and desperate."[148]

As in the great killing fields of Antietam on September 17, 1862, so the Battle of Chancellorsville had stunned Captain Watkins, who wrote on May 4, 1863: "Another great battle has been fought, another horrible scene of carnage and bloodshed. . . . Genl [Jonathan Thomas] Stonewall Jackson lost an arm and Genl. [J. E. B.] Stuart took command of his [Second] corps [and] the slaughter on both sides has been terrific."[149] As noted, Chancellorsville had been nothing more than a pyrrhic victory for the South, but a most costly one in officers and enlisted men, who simply could not be replaced. Lee had narrowly missed destroying the Army of the Potomac at Chancellorsville. He therefore was infuriated by the bungling among his generals that had allowed Hooker's troops to slip away from his grasp and to the north side of the Rappahannock River. An angry Lee had chastised one officer by declaring what he also could have said repeatedly in regard to the Battle of Gettysburg: "You have again let these people get about away [and] I can only tell you what to do, and if you do not do it [then] it will not be done."[150]

One infantryman from Michigan described in a letter the body-strewn field of Williamsburg, Virginia, on the Virginia Peninsula during the Army of the Potomac's ambitious bid to capture the Confederacy's capital, after the Confederate army had withdrawn northwest from Yorktown, Virginia, and the battle raged on May 5, 1862: "In one instance a Michigander and an Alabamian [who had] thrust a bayonet through each other lay dead [with each] still grasping his bayonet."[151]

But like Custer, this Michigan man had died in what he believed was the holy cause of saving the Union. Custer, likewise, was highly motivated to save the fractured republic and shared this view with his equally determined Wolverines. As he penned in a letter to Judge Bacon, expressing his foremost sentiments, "The Union—it was the Union we were fighting for!"[152] From the beginning and like Custer, Libbie's father, a cynical realist, had early understood the high cost that would be required to put down the rebellion, while most others on both sides were wrapped in patriotic idealism. And in a letter that he penned to his sisters in New York from his home in Monroe, Michigan, the judge emphasized, "It is a formidable rebellion, and it will take time, lives, and treasure to put it down."[153]

## CUSTER LEARNS OF THE HORRORS OF WAR

George Armstrong Custer, while serving as a member of the 2nd United States Cavalry, had witnessed his first pitched battle after his baptismal fire at First Manassas on July 21, 1861, before learning more of the war's horrors at the Battle of Williamsburg at the beginning of the Peninsula Campaign. The spirited performance of Union troops in winning victory at Williamsburg on the Virginia Peninsula had mocked the prevailing Southern myth, as Custer, who had been promoted to captain from a lowly lieutenant's rank, emphasized that the "Yankees cannot stand [the] cold steel" of Confederate bayonets.[154]

In this battle on the narrow, heavily wooded peninsula that led to Richmond, Custer never forgot how the Rebels had attacked with spirit when he and his comrades had "the opportunity, for the first time, of hearing the

Southern yell, which ever afterward was made an important auxiliary in every charge or assault made by the Confederates."[155] Of course, Custer heard the famous Rebel yell a good many times on the afternoon of July 3, 1863, and it had become a familiar sound by that time to the young man, who was not at all unnerved by the piercing sound that split the air when Southern veterans were unleashed with fixed bayonets and flashing sabers.

Like other boys in blue and as noted, Custer had learned of the horrors of war as early as the disaster at First Manassas. But significantly, he failed to become jaded or depressed or to lose his high spirits or sense of humor as time passed and the body counts increased month after month. Instead, and despite its surreal horrors, the war seemed to rejuvenate him and lift his morale because he was the consummate man on a holy mission. Clearly, Custer was in his element in a wartime environment in which he excelled, and this quality never left him. While saddened and realistic about the war, he was not sickened by the awful destructiveness of it, like so many other men, who became disillusioned by the spectacle of ever-widening carnage. Despite all that he had seen and experienced in this so-called brothers' conflict, Custer never lost his sense of romance and drama, especially for the headlong cavalry charge—one of the forgotten keys to his success.

Instead, Custer had evolved into what can only be described as a war lover, but one not completely immune to the war's horrors because he maintained a warrior ethos and saw Southerners as brothers in arms. In this regard, Custer was able to compartmentalize his feelings and sensibilities, which allowed him to continue to fight with zeal and enthusiasm. But he most of all respected the men who died for their country, home, and family, which allowed a sentimentalism to rise to the fore. In an April 20, 1862, letter to his half-sister, Custer wrote, "The day before yesterday we buried our dead slain in the skirmish, in the clothes they wore when killed, each wrapped in his blanket. No coffin. It seemed hard, but it could not be helped. Some were quite young and boyish. . . . One, shot through the heart, had been married the day before he left Vermont. Just as his comrades were about to consign his body to the earth, I thought of his wife, and, not wishing to put my hands in his pockets, cut them open with a knife, and found knife, porte-monnaie and ring. I then cut off a lock of his hair and gave them to a friend of his from the same [Vermont] town who promised to send them to his wife. As he lay there I thought of that poem: 'Let me kiss him for his mother . . .' and wished his mother were there to smooth his hair."[156]

By the time of the Antietam campaign, and despite the war's bloodiest single day at the Battle of Sharpsburg (Antietam), Custer was still consumed with the romantic images of the glory of war, while he had served faithfully as a staff officer of his beloved General McClellan. In another letter, signed

"Brother Armstrong," to the family of his half-sister in Monroe, he described excitedly, "We have fought three battles, one the greatest [Antietam on September 17, 1862] ever fought on the continent."[157]

In another letter to the Monroe family members before the end of September 1862, Custer had rejoiced in a trophy that mitigated the awful extent of the slaughter in the fields, meadows, and woodlots of Washington County, western Maryland: "Enclosed I send you a small strip of silk which I tore from a rebel flag at the battle of Antietam, pronounced 'An-tee-tam,' an Indian name."[158]

But Custer's deepest and most unshakeable sentiments about war, especially in regard to cavalry charges, were revealed in a letter the same year that the Battle of Gettysburg was fought: "Oh, could you [Annette Humphrey] but have seen some of the charges that were made! While thinking of them I cannot but exclaim 'Glorious War!'"[159]

Custer was not basking in ideal romance or nostalgia like a mindless schoolboy, despite looking and often acting very much like one. He was a realist and a pragmatist when it came to war, but never a cynic. On July 3, 1863, in leading the 7th Michigan Cavalry and then the 1st Michigan Cavalry in headlong charges that helped to save the day in the vulnerable rear of the Army of the Potomac, he was about to demonstrate that nothing was more hard-hitting and more powerful than a headlong cavalry charge, because this most aggressive of cavalry tactics delivered an unparalleled amount of "the deadly shock" power. Custer knew that this awesome shock power was the true key to victory, and this enduring faith never left him during the course of the war.[160] For this reason, Custer was totally committed and destined to transform the Michigan Cavalry Brigade into "the most feared and effective Northern cavalry command" of the Civil War, especially in regard to its offensive capabilities.[161]

## DOMINANT NAPOLEONIC INFLUENCES

For the Civil War generation, no single military or historical influence was more important in having molded the thinking of the average Union officer than those stemming from Napoleon. This was especially the case in regard to the cavalry arm, which had reached its peak under the most brilliant military man of the nineteenth century, Napoleon Bonaparte. Napoleon's dominance of Europe and the art of waging masterful warfare resulted in an era that became known as the age of Napoleon. Therefore, based on Napoleonic lessons that had proven true more than two generations ago, America's drill manuals and books of doctrine emphasized that the cavalry charge was absolutely necessary for achieving success on the battlefield.

Napoleon's sparkling successes across Europe had resulted in part because he possessed not only the best cavalry in Europe, but also because he utilized the shock power of the cavalry charge to the fullest. Custer's knowledge and lessons of war stemmed from his own readings of Napoleonic history and his West Point education, which incorporated the military campaigns of the greatest military genius of the nineteenth century. In regard to cavalry tactics, Custer was nearly as aggressive and tactically insightful as Napoleon's top cavalryman, Marshal Joachim Murat, whose humble background—the son of an innkeeper—was as lowly as that of Custer, who was a blacksmith's son—factors that fueled the lofty ambitions of both cavalrymen, who became the most popular cavaliers among the people of their respective generations.

Like Custer, Murat was handsome and dashing and rode like the wind at the head of the cavalry charge. Murat became the most famous cavalryman of Europe, as Custer was destined to become the most famous cavalryman of the North by the last campaigns of the Civil War. Most importantly, Murat and Custer believed in their own personal destinies and mystical alignment of the stars, which they believed had marked them for greatness, and the hard-hitting cavalry charge was the avenue that led to the fame and glory of both men.

Knowing the wisdom of a superior organizational structure to most fully utilize the effectiveness of his cavalry arm, Napoleon had organized his cavalry into corps in order to enhance and maximize their offensive capabilities. Napoleon's massed cavalry had been repeatedly unleashed to deliver devastating blows against lengthy lines of enemy infantry, which had also been heavily pounded by the fire of massed artillery, including highly mobile flying artillery, for an effective one-two punch—hard-hitting shock tactics that produced victorious results time and time again across Europe and against the leading monarchies.

Ironically, these lethal Napoleonic cavalry tactics that had long proved successful had fallen out of favor by the time of the Civil War, on the mistaken assumption that the importance and effectiveness of cavalry had been drastically reduced by the advance of modern weaponry—superior firepower—and the lack of suitable terrain in the South, especially Virginia, for cavalry. Young cavalry leaders, especially Custer, proved that these generally accepted belief systems were myths, especially on the third day at Gettysburg. Like Murat, Custer relied on the shock power of the cavalry charge, which was one secret of his success on July 3, 1863.

The War Department in Washington, DC, had dispatched promising cavalry officers to France to incorporate the emperor's cavalry lessons into the axioms codified in *A System of Military Tactics* (published in three volumes titled *Cavalry Tactics* by the U.S. secretary of war Joel R. Poinsett in February 1841), which were thoroughly embraced by the American military system during the decades before the war. These cavalry axioms were taught to the cadets, including Custer, who learned about the supreme importance of the shock value of the cavalry charge at the United States Military Academy. For the most part, these four influential volumes, published from 1841 to 1862, were merely an English translation of the French cavalry tactical system—a French dragoon manual—which was considered the best in Europe. These became known as "Poinsett tactics" to the cavalrymen of the prewar army. This highly respected study served as a central foundation for the writing of other manuals that became standards of doctrine during the Civil War years.

Therefore, the tactical concept of massed cavalry employed to smash through lines of infantry defenders evolved into the basic role of cavalry for generations, especially during the Civil War, on both sides of the Atlantic. These time-honored and widely accepted Napoleonic concepts had resulted in dramatic victories across the central plains of Europe and had transformed Napoleon into an enduring legend that was alive and well in Custer's mind and was omnipresent during the dramatic showdown on the afternoon of July 3, 1863.[162]

This was not a surprising development because Custer was thoroughly influenced by Napoleonic history from an early date, and this historical legacy played a factor in his early interest in military life and in attending West Point. When he had gone to school in Monroe, Michigan, and lived for more than half a decade with his half-sister, Lydia-Ann, who had married David Reed, Custer often read historical fiction and popular military romance instead of his assigned dry textbooks. Hidden under his geography book, Custer especially enjoyed reading the exciting words from Charles Lever's popular novel *O'Malley, the Irish Dragoon*, which he had sneaked into the classroom. During his readings, which fueled his imagination to soaring heights, Custer learned about the adventuresome life of Irishman Charles O'Malley of the 14th Light Dragoons, during the age of Napoleon. This hard-riding dragoon unit fought against Napoleon's French invaders in Spain and Portugal during the Peninsular War.[163]

But of course Custer's most extensive knowledge of Napoleonic tactics had been gained at West Point, where those tactical and strategic lessons of a bygone era were still revered. However, in a supreme irony, as emphasized by historian Kevin M. Sullivan in his excellent book *Custer's Road to Disaster*, Custer performed poorly in the study of cavalry tactics at West Point because his "inner drive to excel in areas of military learning was not present. All of this held little significance for him when compared to the actual hands-on preparation for the battlefield," including the third day at Gettysburg.[164]

Ironically, in a strange way, Custer's lack of serious study of cavalry tactics at West Point paid dividends, because the first of all modern wars represented a host of new challenges and new situations for which there was no standard formula that might serve as a solution. Therefore, Custer even benefited from his thorough lack of knowledge of the past to a degree, which allowed him to be more original and flexible in tactical terms on the battlefield, including at Gettysburg, when fast-paced situations developed that called for the kind of novel solutions that were not found in the outdated textbooks used at West Point. But, at the same time, Custer never forgot what he had learned from his readings, both at West Point and on his own, about the famous French cavalry (light and heavy, and including the units of the famed Imperial Guard) in the Napoleonic era, and these were put to extremely good use by him on July 3, 1863.[165]

Appropriately, Congressman John A. Bingham, who had nominated Custer for entry into the hallowed halls of West Point, wrote in regard to the young man, "I heard of him after the First Battle of Bull Run [First Manassas]. In the report of that miserable fiasco he was mentioned for bravery. A leader was needed to re-form the troops, and take them over a bridge. Like Napoleon at Lodi [where the young native Corsican fought against the Austrians on May 10, 1796, in today's northern Italy and where he captured the bridge over the Adda, which was a tributary of the Po] young Custer sprang to the front—and was a hero."[166]

To be fair, Stuart was just as courageous as Custer, but his bravery had nearly cost him his life in this same fight at First Manassas. During the heat and confusion of battle, Stuart had ridden at the head of his 1st Virginia Cavalry into the midst of a group of fine-uniformed Zouaves and yelled, "Don't run, boys. We're here!" However, Stuart had made the mistake of thinking that these were Alabama Zouaves, when in fact they were New York Zouaves. This error in judgment nearly cost Stuart his life in the first major battle of the war.[167]

## ⌐ 2 ⌐

# Chasing a Golden Dream in Pushing North

*W*hile the fast-fleeing life of a besieged Vicksburg hung in the balance, and in the hope of saving the flickering existence of the strategic bastion on the Mississippi, General Robert E. Lee continued to lead his Army of Northern Virginia northward in the bold movement that resulted in sweeping west of the main Union force at Fredericksburg. Meanwhile, at the executive mansion on East Clay Street in Richmond, an anxious President Jefferson Davis worried about Vicksburg's fate and that of the entire trans-Mississippi if the defensive bastion on the "Father of Waters" fell and then the last Southern defensive position of Port Hudson, Louisiana, was likewise captured—the scenario guaranteed to give the North complete control of the Mississippi River. Davis wondered if he had made a mistake by agreeing to another risky invasion of the North, when he had been initially against such a desperate offensive thrust because he had preferred to send reinforcements to the ill-fated Vicksburg army.

With high hopes for reversing the tide, General Richard S. Ewell's Second Corps—Stonewall Jackson's old command before his death at Chancellorsville—led the long columns of infantry along the dusty roads that led north to the promised land. As during the Maryland campaign, Stuart's troopers led the way to screen the army's movements from prying Yankee eyes because Lee planned to use the mountains and the Shenandoah Valley to cover his push north into the depths of western Maryland. As in previous ambitious movements north, Stuart's veteran cavalry was ordered to protect the army's right flank on the east, keep Union cavalry at a distance, and guard the key mountain passes through which Federal troops could pour to attack the army during the march north and down the Shenandoah Valley to fulfill the great dream of reaching Pennsylvania.

This most ambitious of invasions had pumped new life and optimism into Lee's army, serving as an intoxicant that propelled the hard-marching Southern troops onward with muskets on their shoulders. Heady visions burned brightly in the ranks of the Army of Northern Virginia, including the hope and distinct possibility of capturing Harrisburg, the capital of Pennsylvania on the Susquehanna River; the city of Philadelphia; and then perhaps even Washington, DC, in the end, if everything went well. This was the high tide of Confederate fortunes in the eastern theater, and it was destined to never come again to the infant republic that was fighting for its life in a lengthy war of attrition.[1]

As usual and despite the recent humiliating setback suffered at Brandy Station, General Stuart was overconfident for success north of the Potomac, almost as if he was embarking upon another glorious excursion rather than the war's hardest-fought and most challenging campaign that was destined to prove unprecedented in these regards. With colorful banners flying in the warm air of early June, Stuart pushed north not only with excessive enthusiasm, but also with a shopping list from his homespun wife Flora for the purchase of domestic things—including needles, black silk for a dress, and shoe buttons—to secure from northern merchant shops, perhaps from the fancy stores of Philadelphia or Washington, DC, if captured.[2]

Ironically, hopes for Vicksburg holding out against the odds were still high among the common soldiers in the army's ranks, without realizing that the fortress overlooking the Mississippi had been surrounded by the ever-capable Grant and was already doomed. Captain Leonard Williams, who rode his horse Ruby in the dusty column of the 2nd South Carolina Cavalry, Wade Hampton's Brigade, and whose younger brother was destined to lose his foot at Gettysburg, wrote to his wife, Anna Olivia Laval Williams, in a June 8, 1863, letter, of his optimism for Vicksburg's future: "We have many rumors from Vicksburg of a most cheering character, but . . . there is no doubt that Grant's army has been severely cut up [not the case] by [General] Kirby Smith [(not the case) and] I think our prospect is brightening if Grant's army can be destroyed" deep in Mississippi.[3]

But what was happening in faraway Mississippi was not the concern of Stuart and his troopers, because they faced their own unique challenges and growing problems. By this time, the cavalry arm of the Army of Northern Virginia had been steadily eroded in a lengthy process that began long before the showdown at Vicksburg. A captain of the 2nd Virginia Cavalry, Fitzhugh Lee's Brigade, perhaps said it best in a letter: "My company is becoming smaller and smaller through sickness, wounds and lack of horses, chiefly the latter. . . . I believe this is the only army in history where the men have to furnish their own horses and it is the main weakness of our cavalry. To me to lose a horse is to lose a man, as they cannot afford [due to inflation of Confederate currency] a remount and new recruits with horses of their own are almost nil."[4]

Even more, the war's length and its accompanying demands and horrors, which had intensified along with its unprecedented challenges, had taken a severe toll on the hardened veterans of Stuart's cavalry. Ironically, some of this wear and tear had been unnecessary, when the cavalry had been overused in chasing Stuart's so-called glory. Even more, increasing numbers of lower-class men of Stuart's command began to understand how this was a rich man's war and a poor man's fight, while the lists of killed and wounded of the common soldiers steadily grew to levels unimaginable in the war's beginning. The war's surreal horrors for the average Rebel cavalrymen of Stuart's command can be understood by the words of one Yankee trooper about an early 1863 fight just before the awful bloodletting of the Gettysburg campaign: "Some Rebel heads were fearfully gashed and mangled [by saber blows], one of them exhibiting his low jaw-bone not only dislocated, but almost entirely severed with one determined blow from the strong hand of a cavalryman."[5]

Of course, the largest cavalry clash of the war at Brandy Station had produced greater horrors on a larger scale. During the close-quarter combat that raged with an unprecedented intensity at Brandy Station, acting major Rufus Barringer, 1st North Carolina Cavalry, Hampton's Brigade, was shot off his warhorse when the lead "ball struck him in the back of his upper jaw and passed out at the front part of his mouth knocking out most of his upper teeth."[6]

No-quarter warfare had become another indication that the war had reached new levels of viciousness by the time of the showdown at Brandy Station. One New York trooper, Henry C. Meyer, was shocked at Brandy Station when he "saw a Confederate officer sabre a man . . . and although the man begged for quarter, I saw this officer strike him twice after he offered to surrender."[7]

In a case of bad timing, the savage fighting at Brandy Station had unmercifully culled Stuart's ranks of some of the best men and officers. Stuart lost more than five hundred troopers in having barely held his own against the onslaught of a determined opponent. The veteran officer corps of the South's premier cavalry arm had been cut to pieces during the largest cavalry combat of the war, which provided no glory or positive results. Leading Southern cavalry officers had led their men with great courage and desperation to reverse the disastrous course at Brandy Station on June 9, 1863, which was only achieved at a frightfully high price. Some of Stuart's finest officers were fatally cut down during the intense hand-to-hand combat, including General Wade Hampton's younger brother, South Carolina–born Lieutenant Colonel

"Frank" Hampton of the 2nd South Carolina Cavalry, and young, promising Colonel Solomon Williams, who led the 2nd North Carolina Cavalry with distinction. Williams had fallen at the head of the charge of an entire brigade when a Yankee bullet passed through his head. And a number of other top Rebel cavalry commanders were cut down in battling what seemed like too many Yankee troopers to count.

These lost, tired veterans, especially officers, would be badly needed in the showdown at the Army of the Potomac's rear at Gettysburg on July 3. In a glum June 10, 1863, letter, one Confederate chaplain, James B. Taylor Jr., of one of Stuart's Virginia regiments—the 10th Virginia Cavalry of W. H. F. "Rooney" Lee's Brigade—lamented what was "the longest and most hotly contested cavalry battle of the war [on June 9, but] we have to lament the loss of many gallant officers and privates, some killed and others permanently disabled. . . . We have to regret the temporary loss of our general (W. H. F. Lee), who was wounded in the thigh, and the death of Colonel [Solomon] Williams (of our brigade)" during the intense combat of charge and counter-charge across the open fields of Brandy Station.[8]

Without exaggeration, Lieutenant Willard W. Glazier, a former schoolteacher, of the 2nd New York Cavalry, summarized how the splendid performance of the Union cavalry at Brandy Station had resulted in a "glorious fight, in which the men of the North had proved themselves to be more than a match for the boasted Southern chivalry" that had become an outdated concept in the first of all modern wars, and one that was destined to become even more challenged in the days ahead.[9] Henry C. Meyer, another New York trooper, explained how the climactic battle "was also a great benefit to our troops engaged, in giving them experience in fighting in large bodies mounted, with sabres, and added much to their confidence, as we demonstrated in later engagements," especially Gettysburg.[10] As noted, Stuart was humiliated as never before, having been caught completely by surprise at Brandy Station and losing not only the battle but also his adjutant and personal papers that were captured by the Yankees.[11]

But ironically, while Confederate cavalry combat capabilities, especially in regard to the tactical offensive, continued to steadily decline with each passing day, the overconfidence and hubris of Stuart and his men, who had been spoiled by too many past successes, continued to reach new heights, an extremely dangerous situation in regard to the mind-set of Stuart and his troopers on the eve of the war's most important campaign, because of the extent of the unprecedented challenges that would be presented and because their illusions were out of date.[12]

For such reasons, one member of the Stuart Horse Artillery, Henry Matthews, summarized how not only in regard to the horse artillery, but also the

Southern cavalry in general, "The men and horses were in a deplorable condition, totally unfit for the great invasion of [the state of] Pennsylvania," when everything was at stake north of the Potomac River.[13]

Ironically, General Lee had long known as much, possessing a realistic understanding of the cavalry arm's limitations that had continued to grow over time. As noted, therefore, one of the principal reasons for launching the invasion of Pennsylvania was for the express purpose of confiscating a sufficient number of horses to replace the depleted mounts and to improve the ever-diminishing combat capabilities of Stuart's cavalry.[14]

As fate would have it, there were no solutions to this central dilemma of an ugly reality that steadily eroded the combat capabilities and effectiveness of the South's most fabled cavalry. Too little, too late, General Stuart had written to the Confederate Congress to advocate the creation of the much-needed position of "veterinary surgeon" to serve with each cavalry brigade on April 16, 1863, because "the amount of saving on horseflesh to the Confederacy by a competent Veterinary Surgeon to each Brigade would be incredible."[15] General Stuart was correct, but it was too late because of the launching of the Pennsylvania invasion when time was not on the side of the Army of Northern Virginia and its cavalry arm.

In the same month, one South Carolina Confederate penned in a prophetic April 10, 1863, letter about his optimism for the upcoming northern campaign in which he anticipated that Stuart would play a leading role in the winning of additional glory north of the Potomac River: "I may be mistaken, however, for 'Bob Lee, Jeb Stuart and [?]' may become restless on account of the inactivity of [General] Hooker and strike a streak for parts unknown."[16]

Custer demonstrated his own restlessness, if not recklessness, during the push toward Gettysburg. While still serving on Pleasonton's staff as a captain not long before his promotion to brigadier general, Custer continued to take personal risks, including unnecessary ones, as if bored with time-consuming standard procedures. He had not yet learned to minimize risks, but this was all part of proving himself and attempting to make a name for himself, especially to his superiors.

Therefore, one New York cavalryman described with amazement how Captain Custer embarrassed himself before a large number of troopers, when taking an unnecessary risk:

> While on this march [north near the beginning of the Gettysburg campaign] we came to a stream [and while] the horses [were allowed] to drink, Custer, for some reason, concluded to go in on the other side of the stream, riding in alone to allow his horse to drink. He did not know how deep the water was, and after his horse was satisfied, instead of returning by the way he went in, concluded to cross the stream and come out on our side. The

water was deeper than he anticipated and his horse nearly lost his footing. However, when he got to our side, he urged his horse to climb out at a point where the bank was steep. In this effort he fell over backward, Custer going out of sight in the water. In an instant, however, he was up on his feet and the horse struggled out amid the shouts of the spectators, when, mounting his horse, the march was resumed. The dust at this time was so thick that one could not see more than a set of fours ahead, and in a few minutes, when it settled on his wet clothes and long wet hair, Custer was an object that one can better imagine than I can describe.[17]

Almost certainly, Custer experienced a sense of humiliation that he hoped to wipe away in the next major battle—Gettysburg.

## STUART LAUNCHES HIS ILL-FATED AND OVERLY AMBITIOUS RAID

On June 23, in his overconfidence, if not the hubris that had long infected Stuart to ensure faulty decision making by the time of the Gettysburg campaign, General Lee committed his greatest folly of the Pennsylvania campaign, even before the Army of Northern Virginia had crossed the Potomac River. At this time, Stuart was more than happy to ride away from the growing critics in the army, and farther away still from the rising tide of ridicule of the Richmond newspapers, with the opportunity to win laurels to compensate for his supreme humiliation at Brandy Station. In fact, Stuart never needed to conduct a successful raid more than at this time, and he took advantage of what was presented to him during this push north.

But the concept of allowing Stuart to ride away from the army like he was going to a picnic or wedding was a mistake, which was more pronounced because Lee had marched north in what was his most desperate, ill-fated bid to win it all. Appreciating how well his top cavalryman had performed in the past, including the first northern invasion that had ended in the killing fields of Antietam on September 17, 1862, an overconfident Lee made the mistake of delegating too much authority and initiative (his greatest weakness as a military commander in regard to dealing with his top lieutenants, especially favored ones like Stuart) in the Southern gentleman tradition to Stuart by allowing him to embark with three of his seven cavalry brigades on a wide-ranging assignment.

Stuart was to ride away from the Army of Northern Virginia, cross the Potomac, and push into western Maryland in still another ambitious "ride" around the enemy in the hope, in the commander's words, of "doing them all the damage you can," as in the past. Yet another lengthy ride around the

Union Army was Stuart's old formula for inviting acclaim and glory that would garner for him the leading headlines of newspapers across the South. But time was now more precious than in the past, because this was the South's last chance to win it all. All in all, this was a bad time for risk taking and gambling when it was unnecessary. But Lee was a gambler by nature and instinct, and that only increased during this winner-take-all campaign.

For the third time, which was an indication in itself that he was pushing his luck to the limit, Stuart planned to ride between the northward-advancing Army of the Potomac, pushing through western Maryland and Washington, DC, in pursuit of Lee's army, in the hunt for opportunities to cause damage in General Hooker's rear. At this time, Lee and Stuart believed that nothing was impossible, without considering how thoroughly the Southern cavalry had been overused and worn down over the past campaigns, including during the previous winter. Indeed, Stuart's cavalry had been gradually, if not insidiously, eroded and faced significantly reduced overall combat capabilities—the deep-seated internal weaknesses that had been overlooked in the atmosphere of heady, if not unrealistic, optimism at headquarters because of not only the army's past victories but also the cavalry's continued string of successes that were fully expected to continue by one and all.

However, to be fair to Lee and Stuart, this ambitious plan looked most promising on paper and in the cozy comfort of headquarters. And of course these were jubilant days when future victories on northern soil seemed to lie just over the horizon because of the past cavalry successes that were still talked about with unbridled enthusiasm throughout the army. After all, Stuart was leaving Lee with the majority of the cavalry (four brigades) to guard the mountain passes of Maryland and Pennsylvania, while Lee took only three brigades—his best brigades of Brigadier Generals Wade Hampton, Fitz Lee, and W. H. F. "Rooney" Lee (one of Robert E. Lee's talented sons), which was now commanded by Colonel John Randolph Chambliss Jr. And it was agreed that Stuart would be allowed to conduct his raid as long as he returned in time to provide service in guarding Lee's right flank when the army advanced into Pennsylvania, and then to eventually link with the army's lead Second Corps under newly married "Dick" Ewell, which led the way north for the Army of Northern Virginia.

But both of these fellow Virginians and West Pointers, an unbeatable team in the past, including as recently as the victory at Chancellorsville, were unrealistic, if not naive, in their boundless expectations based largely on a lengthy string of past successes. For one thing, Stuart was no longer that same successful cavalry leader who had long reaped praise across the South, because the horrors of this cruel war, especially the deaths of close friends, had changed him, like so many others caught up in events beyond their control. Too many close friends and comrades had been lost at Brandy Station, and Stuart had only himself to blame, which induced a sense of guilt.

Even more, the rising tide of sharp and stringing criticism—Stuart was extremely sensitive to these mounting accusations from not only the popular press, especially in the nation's capital on the James River, but also from the Southern people and from the army's ranks—about what happened at Brandy Station had hurt his pride and tarnished his prestige. And Stuart was determined to regain what he had lost so suddenly at Brandy Station. A glorious raid and another wide ride around the Army of the Potomac would certainly restore Stuart's reputation and prestige that had been so badly stained by the recent near disaster at Brandy Station.

Leaving a sufficient amount of cavalry (the majority of the army's horse soldiers) to screen Lee's continued advance north and acting upon his commander in chief's discretion and with his usual unbridled confidence and enthusiasm, Stuart embarked upon another ambitious raid with his three brigades on June 25. He planned to ride either entirely around or though Hooker's army that was advancing north through Maryland, depending on the amount of resistance encountered along the way and available opportunities that could be exploited.

In addition, Stuart was to gather vital intelligence about the exact movements of the Army of the Potomac and to do damage to Hooker's lines of communications to cause confusion to delay the pursuit of Lee's army. Then, after performing his mission of causing damage and exploiting existing opportunities because Lee's orders were deliberately vague to bestow greater flexibility, Stuart was then to return north to protect the army's right during the push toward Harrisburg. As mentioned, he was then eventually to link with General Ewell's Second Corps that was leading the advance of Lee's army on Pennsylvania soil. All in all, this was a tall order that involved covering many miles, which required a considerable length of time: factors of space and time that Lee and Stuart had underestimated and minimized to an excessive degree. Quite simply, Stuart could not afford to make any mistakes because the margin of error was extremely thin when venturing north of the Potomac River.

Even more, General Lee, who was an optimist by nature, had overlooked existing problem signs in his top cavalryman that had been revealed in full at Brandy Station, and these were most disturbing if placed under a microscope and carefully analyzed to reveal a host of ugly truths. Nevertheless, partly because of his close friendship with Stuart and his dependence on him, Lee simply overlooked these alarming red flags about his top cavalry commander and the increasing combat prowess of the Union cavalry. Out of necessity and from his pressing, if not urgent, requirement to win victory north of the

Potomac, Lee overlooked what had happened at Brandy Station on that fateful June 9 as if it had never happened.

As Lee was about to learn the hard way, and much like the overall inferior performance of his top lieutenants in the upcoming showdown at Gettysburg, bestowing broad discretionary power to an excessively vain, extremely ambitious, and wildly overconfident commander like Stuart, who needed to be held on a tight leash, especially at this time in his hunt for redemption for his dismal performance at Brandy Station, and turning him loose to ride east and away from the army, especially into enemy territory, was not only a most risky proposition, but also folly. Lee overlooked the obvious increase in his top cavalier's inherent weaknesses, which had been steadily rising to the fore, as a commander and person, who was guilty of an excessive love of the limelight and accolades from the press. In his vain search for glory and redemption in this campaign far from Richmond, Stuart was destined to ride farther away from the army and south all the way to the outskirts of Washington, DC.[18]

As noted, the central concept—at least in theory—for unleashing a raid at this time seemed most promising in discussions at Lee's headquarters, when the sense of optimism could not have been higher. Everything and anything seemed possible in the heady days during the confident march toward Pennsylvania with impunity and with no opposition in sight. But things began to go awry from the beginning of Stuart's new mission, offering a host of ill omens that were conveniently ignored by an overly confident leadership. Two days were wasted when Stuart was forced to conceal his forces to avoid detection from advancing Union troops, when time was of the essence and absolutely crucial. Most of all, Stuart needed to conduct his raid and return to the army as soon as possible, but he acted as if time was almost not important.

In the words of one of Stuart's staff officers, Theodore S. Garnett Jr., who had been born in Richmond, Virginia, which revealed the heady optimism at the time:

> Raiding was Stuart's hobby, and one which he rode with never failing persistence. What a glorious opportunity was now offered for the indulgence of his love! The country had been dazzled by his adventurous rides around McClellan's army . . . but [now] here was an undertaking which, if attended with anything like the success of the former, would eclipse in brilliance and real importance any exploit of the war. The capture of supplies for the enemy, the interruption of their communication with the government at Washington, the probability of effecting an entrance into that city itself, and finally the moral effect of such boldness upon the mind of the people both North and South were, no doubt, some of the chief inducements with General Stuart. General Lee entrusted the matter entirely to General Stuart's discretion. He left Stuart at liberty to do as he pleased.[19]

In the end, General Lee had made a grave mistake, allowing his usually good judgment to forsake him at a time when he could not afford to make errors because everything was at stake during his second invasion of the North.

In a letter to his wife, Captain Richard H. Watkins, 3rd Virginia Cavalry, Fitzhugh Lee's Brigade, described the entire course of Stuart's bold raid over an extensive area that was destined to become the most controversial excursion of his career and for ample good reason:

> Genl Stuart commenced his 2nd raid into Pennsylvania [when] we left Loudoun County [Virginia and] went back almost to Warrenton [Virginia, and then] came into Fairfax [and] approached within 6 miles of Alexandria [Virginia and then] U turned almost to Drainesville [Virginia], crossed the Potomac at midnight [and] then went in the direction of Washington City to Rockville [Maryland and here] too a train of almost 180 wagons & almost 1200 mules with a good number of prisoners [and] then went in the direction of Baltimore [Maryland] till we approached within 15 or 20 miles of that city [and then] turned off to the Pennsylvania line west of Hanover, Penn: where we had a sharp cavalry fight and took several prisoners, went from there to Westminster [Maryland] and then [all the way north] to Carlisle [Pennsylvania and north of Gettysburg where they] found a large force of infantry [militia] at Carlisle, called upon the surrender of the town which was refused & the town shelled by Genl. Stuart & the public buildings burned. We then came across in the direction [south] of Gettysburg and joined [Lee's main] forces, the raid occupying 10 days during which time we marched the whole of each day & the while of six nights & the half of one or two others [and] our only time for sleep being whilst our horses were grazing or feeding in the day.[20]

But the damage had been done, because Stuart had started too late with his three cavalry brigades and lost two days in the beginning to avoid detection, as mentioned. He made the mistake of keeping the slow-moving (pulled by balky mules) captured wagon train with him, riding too many miles over a vast stretch of countryside, and having no idea of the location of either army, even while he rode in between them—essentially a wild goose chase of epic proportions. Worst of all, retaining the captured wagon train was absolute folly, because Stuart's column could only move at the speed of the slow-moving wagons drawn by troublesome mules known for their stubbornness and balkiness.

A concerned member of Major General George E. Pickett's Division, Lieutenant John E. Dooley, who was the son of poor Irish immigrants who had successfully transformed their lives in Richmond and succeeded admirably to make the immigrant's dream come true in the city along the James River, lamented, "There are also from seven to ten thousand cavalry who should be with us but who, under the command of their dashing general, are far away towards Washington City, leaving our infantry and artillery unguarded in flank and rear, and stripping our cautious Lee of sufficient force to explore the exact position of his enemy."[21]

General Stuart had been caught in a time-consuming fiasco of his own making, and the Army of Northern Virginia paid dearly for his long absence. During the lengthy raid that lasted nearly a week and a half, Stuart had worn out his men and horses to drastically reduce their overall combat capabilities in his far-flung raid that achieved only minimal results, and nothing of importance.

As noted, Stuart had driven his men and horses too long and hard in the futile effort to locate Lee's army and in the bid to link with Ewell's Second Corps that had been advancing on Harrisburg, which had sent him farther north and above Lee's army, an exhausting effort and frantic search in which Stuart floundered in the dark and unfamiliar territory. After hearing local rumors that Ewell's infantry had reached Carlisle, Pennsylvania, located just southwest of the state capital of Harrisburg and around thirty miles north of Gettysburg, Stuart wasted even more precious time leading his troopers northwest and away from Lee's army and Gettysburg, where he was urgently needed because the commanding general could not gain adequate intelligence about the enemy's exact location and intentions.

For all of these reasons, by the time of the all-important cavalry showdown that was destined to occur in the Union army's rear on July 3, Captain Watkins lamented in a letter, "My company [K, 3rd Virginia Cavalry, Fitzhugh Lee's Brigade] has dwindled to about 10 or 15, the horses of the rest having completely broken down."[22] But perhaps one of Stuart's Virginia artillerymen, George Michael Neese, said it best in a classic understatement in regard to the high price paid by the troopers and their horses during the wide-ranging raid that had taken the gray-and-butternut troopers nearly all the way to Washington, DC: "Raiding with Stuart is poor fun and a hard business."[23]

And of course Stuart's troopers were in as bad a shape as the horses, if not worse. Sergeant James M. Pugh, 1st North Carolina Cavalry, Hampton's Brigade, wrote in a letter, "I am completely broken down for I have been going day and night . . . in Maryland and Pennsylvania" during this ill-fated campaign.[24] Another cavalryman with Stuart complained, "No man can stand more, and I never wish to be called on to stand this much again [and I] rode three [horses] down" during the nine days of what was Stuart's folly.[25]

Clearly, Stuart and his three brigades of troopers were in overall poor condition after not only the raid but also the exhaustive search to locate Lee's army that had consumed nearly a week and a half in total. As noted, the overall capabilities of Stuart's cavalry had been gradually reduced over the last year, including the past winter when, in the words of Lieutenant Willard W.

Glazier, who had been born in St. Lawrence County, New York, in 1841 and served in the 2nd New York Cavalry, Army of the Potomac, the "Rebel cavalry has been very active all winter, as may be seen by the many raids," including all the way to Chambersburg, Pennsylvania, and then his celebrated "Christmas Raid" on Dumfries, Virginia, which was located just north of Fredericksburg, launched by Stuart. But, as noted, this gradual decline of combat capabilities was imperceivable to Stuart, who believed that he could accomplish anything, which had become a dangerous delusion by the time of the Gettysburg campaign.[26]

But perhaps the greatest irony was that Stuart was the target of a greater amount of criticism than he had ever received for his wide-ranging raid that gained no significant results, although he had been unleashed by Lee, who possessed a sufficient amount of cavalry to have gathered an adequate amount of intelligence. The cavalry that had remained behind should have been placed in the front of the army instead of rearward, but such was not the case for reasons still not entirely understood to this day. In the end, Stuart deserved considerable blame for the length of his absence, but not expressly for the launching of his raid, which had been ordered by Lee in order to exploit opportunities in the Army of the Potomac's rear. In the end, Stuart rightfully deserved the greatest amount of criticism of all for what he failed to accomplish on the afternoon of July 3.[27]

An insightful Major John Cheves Haskell, a South Carolinian who was not enamored by either Virginians or West Pointers, especially when combined in one as in Stuart's case, made the correct measure of Stuart at an early date that boded ill for the great cavalry showdown on the afternoon of July 3: "He was a remarkable mixture of a green, boyish, undeveloped man. . . . To hear him talk no one would think that he could ever be anything more than a dashing leader of a very small command, with no dignity and much boastful vanity."[28] Quite simply, Stuart was lacking in character, after having been corrupted in a number of ways by this brutal war to the death.

As demonstrated throughout the Gettysburg campaign, Haskell's insightful and mature analysis was right on target. After Stuart's near brush with disaster at Brandy Station, no one said it better than the incensed editor of the *Charleston Mercury*, Charleston, South Carolina, with his right-on-target analysis: "Stuart's head has been turned by the [many] newspaper" articles, especially in the Richmond publications.[29] But his most damaging words presented a most significant insight, which was not even fully appreciated or understood by Generals Lee and Stuart, as demonstrated in this all-important campaign, when the Army of Northern Virginia could no longer afford to make grievous mistakes, especially time-consuming ones: "Cavalry were intended to decide and complete victories—not to ride around."[30] These words revealed that both Lee and Stuart were equally at fault in regard to poor decision making for the launching of this ill-fated raid.

In a supreme irony, the means by which Stuart had acquired recognition and fame throughout the army and the South had led to greatly reduced combat capabilities of his cavalry immediately before the most decisive cavalry action of not only the Battle of Gettysburg, but also the entire war. Quite simply, by this time, fate itself and the gods of war had effectively removed their favor and turned against Stuart, who had been seduced by too many past successes and the seemingly endless adulation of an entire people, with a swiftness that left him without any answers or clues about what had happened. Instead of Stuart, an equally bold but younger cavalier, whose career as a brigade commander was just beginning, was now favored by the fickle hands of fate: George Armstrong Custer. In a summer 1863 letter, Custer revealed his personal life philosophy and general "disposition," as he called it, which served him so well, including at Gettysburg, because he most of all wanted to be "the same soldier I now try to be. . . . Do not fear for me. I may lose everything, yet there is a strange, indescribable something in me that would enable me to shape my course through life, cheerful, if not contented."[31] By these words, Custer demonstrated a strength of character that was now lacking in Stuart, who had become trapped by his own inflated image.

## A BETTER CAVALRY LEADER THAN STUART, BRIGADIER GENERAL WADE HAMPTON

By this time and as noted, Stuart was in many ways the victim of his own success, and now he was trapped by the heady fame and adulation—very much a victim of his past glory—that seemed to have no end until he met with his greatest embarrassment at Brandy Station. Having graduated thirteenth in his West Point class of 1854 (seven years before Custer), Stuart had not been impressed by the new cocky products that were being turned out by West Point on an annual basis—an elitist attitude that almost certainly now applied to Custer in Stuart's mind. As he penned in a Christmas Day 1851 letter that was not a vote of confidence for young Custer, who was as green as a gourd in regard to commanding a full brigade: "For one to succeed here [at West Point] all that is required is an ordinary mind and application."[32]

Also by these words, Stuart unwittingly verified how his own top lieutenant, Wade Hampton of South Carolina and a non–West Pointer, was better qualified than he was by the time of the Gettysburg campaign. However, ironically and fortunately for the Union, Lee's most capable cavalryman, who allowed his actions rather than his words to speak for themselves, at this time was not in charge of his cavalry arm, a situation that immensely benefited Custer during the final showdown on the afternoon of July 3.

A dynamic and gifted man of vast wealth (thanks partly to a number of intelligent and industrious ancestors who had early migrated to the South Carolina frontier, where some family members had been killed by the Cherokee while attempting to tame the wilderness), and blessed with a classical education from the finest schools, Wade Hampton was a mature man of the South Carolina planter class without a West Point education. Despite his forty-five years, or perhaps because of them, he served extremely well in the capacity of Stuart's senior brigadier general. While Stuart basked in the national spotlight and soaked up lavish praise, the businesslike Hampton focused on the serious business of winning victories on the battlefield. In the heat of battle and like Custer, Hampton led from the front, joining his men to fight like a common soldier, while giving no hint of his aristocratic background. He was not the kind of leader who remained safely in the rear at headquarters. The family's fantastic wealth had been founded on the growth of short-staple cotton, an early reliance that reaped a vast fortune because of the efficiency of the newly invented cotton gin and large numbers of slaves.

Hampton, born in the bustling port of Charleston in 1818, possessed a level of stability and maturity in greater abundance than found in Stuart, because Stuart's past successes—quite unlike Custer, who had yet to prove himself as a brigade commander—had gone to his head. Because of their wide differences in backgrounds, including in regard to the United States Military Academy, and personalities, Stuart and Hampton were not close because they were so different. However, they worked extremely well together as a formidable team of professional soldiers. Unlike Stuart, Hampton detested the limelight and publicity, including even the attentions of admiring women, because he knew that they had nothing to do with winning decisive victory—the very antithesis of Stuart. In this regard, Hampton possessed a single-minded pursuit, unlike Stuart, who had been seduced by the adulation, and nothing could get in the way of achieving victory.

However, by the time of the Gettysburg campaign, the personal (or off-battlefield) relationship between Hampton and Stuart had broken down to a new low because of the Virginia and West Point cronyism that too often came at the proud South Carolinian's expense. For good reason, he resented the open favoritism shown to Stuart and other Virginia commanders by Lee, the consummate Virginian. And he increasingly clashed and argued, including about the overuse of his non-Virginia cavalry brigade of South Carolina, Mississippi, Georgia, and North Carolina cavalrymen, while the Virginia cavalry brigades did nothing or much less arduous duty with Stuart, who always favored Virginians. These wide differences of opinions and personality clashes steadily increased over time between the two cavaliers until Hampton was heartily sick of Stuart and the disproportionate influence of the powerful Virginia and West Point clique that dominated the army.[33]

While Hampton was not a self-made man in the traditional sense, he was an original and was self-taught as a military officer, despite a political career in which he won distinction in the House of Representatives in the state capital at Columbia, South Carolina. Hampton basked in the heroics and sacrifices of his South Carolina ancestors. He owned and cherished the sword of his cavalryman grandfather who had commanded the hard-riding cavalry of General Thomas Sumter, who was known as the "Fighting Gamecock," when he had terrorized British and Tory forces across South Carolina. Of course, it was Sumter's name that graced the fort in Charleston Harbor when Confederate cannon opened fire to begin the most nightmarish war in American history in April 1861.

Most importantly, Brigadier General Hampton had emerged as a gifted and brilliant cavalry commander. And of course Stuart benefited immensely from his high quality as a brigade commander—the finest general officer of the seasoned leaders of his three brigades. A natural tactician and outdoorsman, including when he had thoroughly enjoyed hunting black bears on his sprawling Mississippi lands (twelve thousand acres in 1860, and he owned more than one thousand slaves in the Magnolia State alone, when he had been initially anti-secessionist—a lukewarm Unionist—and openly against the reopening of the horrific slave trade), but he also enjoyed the pursuit of game in South Carolina's pine forests.

He therefore intimately understood terrain with keen and well-honed insights. Hampton benefited from a wide array of tactical and battlefield instincts that Stuart had only learned in the classrooms of West Point. He had first served at the Battle of First Manassas, where he was wounded while commanding the famous Hampton Legion of South Carolina troops. Therefore, by the time of the Gettysburg campaign and for a host of reasons, Hampton "loomed as Stuart's heir apparent." By this time, he was a talented man on the rise like Custer, who was nearly half the age of the dynamic Hampton, of outstanding ability and rare talents as a battlefield commander.[34]

Despite being a wealthy member of the aristocratic upper class of South Carolina, Hampton was a remarkable man of the people, and he possessed a genuine common touch that was real, not like a typically self-serving politician with soaring ambitions. In many ways, consequently, he was the antithesis of the stereotypical Southern elitist aristocrat in the traditional sense. Despite his wealth, Hampton still maintained some of the common-man touch of his enterprising frontier ancestors, who were self-made men who had helped to tame the South Carolina wilderness—one source of his popularity with the troopers of his brigade. Hampton, a die-hard South Carolinian who loved his homeland, was a rarity in having risen high in the Virginia-dominated army, excelling among the upper circles of the West Pointers and earning their respect in the process.

Hampton's younger brother, Lieutenant Colonel "Frank" Hampton, had early served in his command, along with his son, dark-haired—like his father—Lieutenant William Preston Hampton. Dimming Wade's natural optimism more than having received his second wound during the Peninsula Campaign, Frank Hampton, at age thirty when second in command of the 2nd South Carolina Cavalry that served as an elite regiment in Hampton's brigade, had been killed at Brandy Station. And Hampton's son, who was called Preston, was fated to die at age twenty in October 1864. Ironically, this was the same dismal year that General Stuart was mortally wounded at Yellow Tavern and shortly thereafter died, shocking the Southern nation. As could be expected, Preston's tragic loss was destined to be the most severe blow ever received by his doting father. Preston served with distinction beside his dynamic father as a reliable aide-de-camp. The young man was known for his abilities, his tireless assistance to his father, and his feisty fighting spirit that only the Yankees could extinguish with a bullet.[35]

Even a member of Stuart's own staff recognized the full range of Brigadier General Wade Hampton's unsurpassed abilities, which exceeded those of the highly touted Stuart, especially now with his abilities on a gradual decline. Therefore, Major Henry Brainerd McClellan wrote in regard to Stuart's disastrous raid in June 1863, which deprived Lee of his finest three brigades of cavalry and top horse commander for an extended period, "It was the absence of Stuart himself that he felt so keenly; for on him he had learned to rely to such an extent that it seemed as if his cavalry were concentrated in his person, and from him alone could information be expected. Hampton or Fitz Lee, better than anyone else, would have supplied Stuart's place to the commanding general."[36]

But ironically, it was none other than Libbie Bacon-Custer, based on insightful knowledge and after her marriage to Custer, who said it best in a May 22, 1864, letter to her parents of Stuart's eventual tragic fate and of a truth that was fully demonstrated at Gettysburg: "J. E. B. Stuart is really dead! But our men are sorry, for they consider Wade Hampton who will succeed him a superior officer."[37] Indeed, almost certainly, the wiser and more stable Hampton would not have committed the same sins as Stuart during the Gettysburg campaign, which might have changed the course of the war. Quite likely, if Hampton had commanded the cavalry instead of Stuart, then one Virginia officer would never have penned in a June 30, 1863, letter, with a mixture of surprise and incredulousness during the absence of Lee's top cavalier and the army's best cavalry brigades: "Stuart's whereabouts is unknown."[38]

## FITZHUGH LEE

Commanding Stuart's all-Virginia Brigade, Brigadier General Fitzhugh "Fitz" Lee was second only to Hampton in regard to leadership and tactical abilities while leading his all–Old Dominion Brigade (the 1st, 2nd, 3rd, 4th, and 5th Virginia Cavalry). If anything happened to Stuart and Hampton, Fitz would almost certainly take over Lee's Cavalry Corps in what would be a seamless transition. Lee's pedigree was impressive. He was part of the cherished first families of Virginia at a time when social background and pedigree still meant a great deal in the Army of Northern Virginia. Fitz was the grandson of Robert E. Lee's father, Henry "Light Horse Harry" Lee, who had emerged as one of George Washington's finest cavalry leaders when a young republic had fought for its existence against a mighty empire.

As the nephew of the army's commander, Fitz had lived up to the loftiest expectations of his family and ancestry, which would have made "Light Horse Harry" proud. His rise in this people's army had been impressive by any measure. Fitz earned a brigadier general's rank in the summer of 1862. He was even more lighthearted, personable, and merry than Stuart. He became known as the "Laughing Cavalier" in consequence. But he was every inch a fighter and a model soldier, whose standards were high. Like Lee and Stuart, he had graduated from West Point in 1854, where he did not excel in the almost nonchalant manner of Custer and also racked up a lofty total of demerits. Also like Custer, the equally high-spirited and fun-loving Fitz had preferred reading popular fiction rather than devoting himself to the diligent study required by the academy's high standards.

A native of Fairfax County, Virginia, and born just west of Alexandria, Virginia, which was a leading port on the Potomac River, he had served in the prewar U.S. cavalry against Native Americans on the western frontier, unlike Custer, who had been too young for prewar service. During and after the Gettysburg campaign, the handsome, dashing Fitz led his 1st, 2nd, 3rd, 4th, and 5th Virginia Cavalry with distinction in one campaign after another. The lively and gregarious Fitz was popular and greatly admired by Stuart and the entire command. Like Custer, he loved to play practical jokes and possessed a good sense of humor that often rose to the fore to break the monotony of camp life. He had been groomed for high command by Stuart himself, and Lee was more than able to lead the entire command with consummate skill.[39]

## THE STAGE IS SET

Even before the nasty Yankee surprise at Brandy Station where he had to fight for his command's existence and his own reputation while under attack, Stuart was guilty of an increasing degree of having "acted precipitately in some situations, risking undue harm to his command [and] his penchant for grandstanding, behavior that more conservative solders like Hampton found boorish and immature."[40]

In striking contrast, the mature and dynamic Hampton—more of a comparable counterpart to Custer than Stuart in regard to capabilities—was a diehard revolutionary, whose commitment to the struggle was total. Despite the setbacks and high losses of a merciless war of attrition, he had never lost his unbounded optimism for the South's final victory. Early in the war, Hampton had written with unbounded confidence in a letter to his sister, "I look to the breaking up of the Yankee government and it will be a blessing to mankind, when this occurs."[41] And now in 1863, Hampton still felt the same, because he believed that this was a holy war and a great moral crusade to save the South. Such sentiments motivated Hampton to rise to the challenge on the East Cavalry Field on the critical third day at Gettysburg.

Little did Brigadier General Hampton realize when he wrote his letter in January 1862 that he would have the opportunity to deliver that decisive blow in just more than a year and a half in an obscure place in Adams County, Pennsylvania. At that time, Hampton was destined to play a leading role in the great cavalry clash in the Army of the Potomac's rear, when he led the final offensive effort to eliminate Custer and his feisty Wolverines and other defenders from the strategic crossroads of the Hanover and Low Dutch Roads.[42]

And of course Custer likewise had no idea at the time of his own key role on July 3, 1863, when he wrote to his sister in a typically boyish letter from West Point, revealing his strict and moral side and his paternal sense in regard to his younger siblings back home: "I am surprised at Pop [the devout Emmanuel] not signing my permit to use tobacco. I said distinctly I did not want tobacco for myself, but for my room-mate who smokes, and would get me things I want. . . . Because [younger brothers] Tom and Bos [Boston Custer] . . . are at home where they can control them, are allowed to smoke and chew, but because I am way off here by myself, where I need a permit to use tobacco, they refuse to give me one. . . . Nothing can induce me to use tobacco, either in smoking or chewing. I consider it a filthy, if not an unhealthy practice. I can say what few of my age can—I never chewed tobacco in my life. Tell Bos he must quit using tobacco."[43]

## BLOODY FIRST DAY AT GETTYSBURG, JULY 1

While General Stuart had committed the folly of a wide-ranging raid that wasted too much time for meager results while depriving Lee of his finest cavalry, the Virginia troopers of Brigadier General Albert G. Jenkins's Brigade of Virginians had performed well in having led the advance of General Richard S. Ewell's Second Corps north and all the way to the outskirts of Pennsylvania's capital of Harrisburg. Lieutenant Hermann Schuricht penned with pride in his diary in a graceful German script on June 29 how the hard-riding Virginians "viewed the city of Harrisburg and its defenses. This was the farthest advance made by any Confederate troops during the campaign" north of the Potomac River.[44]

In early summer, the landscape of Adams County, Pennsylvania, where Gettysburg had long served as the county seat, was not only pristine but also quite beautiful in what was essentially an agricultural paradise for the hard-working German and Scotch-Irish farmers who lived there. Like his comrades, a young Catholic Rebel soldier, who was a member of the 1st Virginia Infantry, Brigadier General Lewis Armistead's Brigade, of Major General George E. Pickett's Division—all Virginians—and from Richmond, was astounded by the natural beauty of the Keystone State. He wrote of how "the wheat fields are every where nearly ripe for harvesting, and all around plenty appears to bless the fertile land [and admired] these rich fields of wheat [grown by] these Thrifty German farmers," who had transformed this region into a place of plenty.[45] Gunner Neese, of Stuart's Horse Artillery, marveled at how "the barns look like churches" because of their size and sturdy construction, with large stone foundations.[46]

Serving in the ranks of the 2nd New York Cavalry, Lieutenant Willard W. Glazier described how "Gettysburg, the capital of Adams County, [was] a rural village of about three thousand inhabitants, beautifully situated among the hills, which, though quite lofty, are generally well cultivated."[47]

One of the enduring myths and legends about the Battle of Gettysburg was that this epic clash of arms first erupted because the Confederates were allegedly in search of shoes and headed for Gettysburg to obtain much-needed footwear. But such was not the case. The Battle of Gettysburg never began because Lee's foremost troops of Lieutenant General Ambrose Powell Hill's Third Corps moved east on a mission to secure shoes, as long thought. These vanguard troops of Lee's army—now strung out along dusty roads to the west—met the bluecoat troopers of Brigadier General John Buford's cavalry west and northwest of Gettysburg on the morning of July 1 to open the battle, but this was not an advance launched to obtain shoes. Consequently, as long believed, the Battle of Gettysburg never began because of "a shopping trip gone bad."[48]

Fortunately for General Meade and the Union, Custer and his cavalrymen were near Gettysburg and available on July 1, after the sharp cavalry clash at Hanover, Pennsylvania, on June 30. In the words of Corporal James Henry Avery, who emphasized in his journal how at Hanover, "here too, our boy General Custer took command of the Michigan Brigade; it was a good beginning . . . on June 30, 1863 [and] we moved toward Gettysburg [then on] July 1st, we began to hear the boom of guns at Gettysburg and were hurried forward to take positions on the right of the infantry, a point we reached none too soon."[49]

North of Gettysburg, meanwhile, in his futile search for the Army of Northern Virginia and especially Ewell's Second Corps, Stuart was still befuddled about the exact location of either army. Ironically, the man whose career had been created by having long provided General Lee with updated intelligence of a timely nature not only left his commander without his most reliable "eyes and ears," but also continued to operate blindly and flounder in his embarrassing inability to find Lee and his army.

Completely unaware that the largest battle ever to be fought on the North American continent had already began around twenty-five miles to the south, Stuart skirmished with raw Pennsylvania militiamen, who had been dispatched from Harrisburg. Incensed over developments beyond his control, Stuart had targeted the U.S. cavalry barrack at Carlisle on July 1, when the bloody first day at Gettysburg erupted in full fury.

Stuart had known the Carlisle barracks from his prewar cavalry days in 1859, and his father-in-law, the father of his adoring wife Flora, had once commanded this United States military post located north of Gettysburg. Stuart wasted more time in reducing the post in a mini-siege with a hail of artillery fire because his men desperately needed provisions and rations, hurling 134 shells at the obstinate garrison that refused to surrender.

In consequence, an angry Stuart became frustrated to the point that he ordered the torching of the Carlisle barracks. In a seemingly ill-fated campaign in which everything had gone wrong for him, Stuart suffered still another humiliation for the South's most legendary cavalryman, who must have looked back fondly on his glory days of 1861 and 1862, when the Yankees seldom refused to surrender.

Of course, Stuart was also upset because General Ewell and his Second Corps, leading the army's advance, were not found at Carlisle. But by this time, the guns of Gettysburg were roaring to the south. In the words of Sergeant Robert Scott Hudgins, of Company B, 3rd Virginia Cavalry, Fitzhugh Lee's Brigade, and who hailed from the Tidewater lands of the Hampton, Virginia, area: "We had heard firing off toward Gettysburg and wondered what was going on. Soon an orderly to Col. [Thomas T.] Munford [arrived and] delivered an order for us to proceed by forced march to Lee's assistance [and] we withdrew from Carlisle and began our march [to the south after breaking off the fight]. We proceeded at a trot, pushing our fatigued animals as much as we dared, for they had been constantly on the march during the last ten days."[50]

At long last, Stuart had been enlightened about the army's whereabouts. This sergeant, Robert Scott Hudgins, of the 3rd Virginia Cavalry, described the rapid southward push toward Gettysburg "in the hot July sunshine [of July 2], interrupted only for our horses to drink from the many streams crossing the road along the way. We could hear the distant rumble of the cannon around Gettysburg, which reminded us of the grim business we would face upon our arrival there."[51]

But upon finally reaching Gettysburg in the early afternoon of July 2, Stuart's men were covered in dust and sweat, and their horses were panting and in poor condition because they had been grossly overused by their glory-seeking commander during his wild chase to reap laurels at any cost. Stuart placed his foremost men—those who had best been able to keep up with the rapid push south—on the army's left. A veteran artilleryman of Stuart's Horse Artillery, Henry Matthews, admitted in exhausted resignation the extensive wear and tear on the command: "No one except those who were on this expedition can imagine the condition of the men and horses."[52] Lieutenant George W. Beale, 9th Virginia Cavalry, "Rooney" Lee's Brigade, described how, "from our great exertion, constant mental excitement, want of sleep and food, the men were overcome and so tired and stupid as almost to be ignorant of what was taking place around them."[53] Stuart ordered his men to dismount and rest for the night on the Confederate left near Gettysburg, while the worn horses were allowed to graze in the open fields, and captured cattle, which had been rounded up from farmers' fields, were slaughtered for rations.[54]

Meanwhile, despite being about to command a full brigade (the 1st, 5th, 6th, and 7th Michigan Cavalry) in his first major battle on July 3, 1863, Custer remained supremely confident for success. Despite the repeated losses suffered by the Army of the Potomac in bloody 1862, Custer was never "to lose or lessen my faith, my firm belief and conviction, that the cause of the Union was destined in the end to triumph over all obstacles and opposition."[55] Custer believed every word of what he had written, and it was this supreme faith that motivated him to great exertions at Gettysburg.

Interestingly, this firm conviction and sense of optimism of newly appointed Brigadier General Custer was the antithesis of the belief system of General Stuart, who correctly understood the ugly truth of a lengthy war of attrition and that the South was on the losing end of a grim equation that was bound to condemn the Confederacy to the ash bin of history. In this sense, Stuart was a fatalist who masked his gloom with a cheery exterior. In a confidential letter to his brother, Stuart wrote, "I realize that if we oppose force to force we cannot win, for their resources are greater than ours."[56] Suffering her own mental anguish, Libbie also possessed a negative but realistic streak that contrasted with Custer's boyish optimism, admitting in 1863 that the "worst thing about loving a soldier is that he is as likely to die as to live."[57]

But most of all and like Custer, Stuart still had faith in what the tactical offensive could achieve, especially in regard to the cavalry charge. In fact, nothing was more important in regard to the two objectives now possessed by Stuart: to redeem his reputation and to play a key role in reaping a decisive success, especially after his humiliation at Brandy Station, his missed connection with General Ewell, and the disastrous raid that had left Lee blind about the enemy's position and disposition. But Stuart felt optimistic if he could get an opportunity to engage the Union cavalry in a large showdown like that at Brandy Station. Stuart's own words from July 1863 about what he knew was necessary for success revealed his faith in the tactical offensive: "An attack of cavalry should be sudden, bold and vigorous. The cavalry which arrives noiselessly but steadily near the enemy, and then, with one loud yell leaps upon him without a note of warning, and giving no time to form or consider anything but the immediate means of flight, pushing him vigorously every step with all the confidence of victory achieved, is the true cavalry."[58]

General Stuart had suffered like his men in the ranks. Exhausted and frustrated like his troopers, Stuart had carried the hope of redeeming himself during the lengthy ride south toward Lee's army from Carlisle since around midnight. Stuart was so worn out that he had dismounted beside the dusty road with the dawn of July 2 and leaned against a tree to obtain some much-needed rest while wrapped in his cape to ward off the early morning chill. All the while, Stuart's troopers had remained far behind on the dusty road.[59]

Meanwhile and quite unlike Stuart's men, Custer and his troopers gained ample rest, rations, and time to ready themselves on the night of July 2 for the great challenge of July 3. As Corporal James Henry Avery, 5th Michigan, penned in his journal, "The night passed peacefully, though quickly, to the sleeping men, many of whom were to awake for the last time on earth in the early dawn" of the third day at Gettysburg.[60]

Custer and his men rested assured and confident on the night of July 2 because the quartermaster wagon train containing ammunition reserves for the Michigan Cavalry Brigade had reached Hanover on July 2. This train was now in an advanced position to supply Custer's troopers with supplies of ammunition for whatever fighting was required on July 3. Therefore, Brigadier General Judson Kilpatrick, who commanded the Third Cavalry Division, which included Custer's Second Brigade, was ready for action and on high alert, with the realization that this contest in Adams County was now going to be a three-day battle and bloody slugfest, after he had received orders from Pleasonton "to move as quickly as possible toward Gettysburg."[61]

While Stuart was tired and frustrated during the long ride south to Gettysburg from Carlisle, the young man who was destined to meet Lee's most idolized cavalry chieftain on the East Cavalry Field was cocky and confident for success. Custer's training at West Point had already paid dividends, and he was destined to benefit accordingly on the field of Gettysburg. He had much to prove. From the beginning, therefore, Custer faithfully adhered to what he had learned at West Point because he was now on his own for the first time in commanding a full brigade of Wolverines at a time when mistakes could not be made because too much was at stake.

Therefore, he closely embraced an enduring faith that he had gained at West Point, whose lessons had seeped into his heart and mind to possess his very soul, unlike when he had served as a cadet at the United States Military Academy, when he had compiled a truly disgraceful record: "From the very nature of the military rule which governs and directs the movements and operations of an army in time of war, it is essentially requisite to success that the will of the general in command shall be supreme, whether or not he possesses the confidence of his subordinates. To enforce obedience to his authority, no penalty should be deemed too severe." Clearly, Custer was now a changed man from his embarrassing days at West Point where he lacked any hint of seriousness in his endeavors, which ensured that he became the much-mocked "goat" of his class of 1861, because he had been forged by the stern realities and challenges of war by this time.[62]

But even more, Custer maintained his faith in a higher power just before entering the Battle of Gettysburg, and this faith served him well on a moral and spiritual level. Despite his rakish appearance and war-loving demeanor, which resulted in an inspiring command presence, he was a true holy warrior, imbued with a strong religious faith, which was contrary to his popular image today.

As he later explained to Libbie in a letter that revealed his spiritual side, which he closely embraced in this lengthy war of attrition that culled so many young men from the ranks:

> I have always felt an utter contempt for those who, under the cloak of piety, conceal base designs. The infidel has a stronger claim on my respect than he who professes insincerely. It may seem strange to you, dear girl, that I, a non-professing (tho not an unbeliever) Christian, should so ardently desire you to remain so. I have never prayed as others do. Yet, on the eve of every battle, in which I have been engaged, I have never omitted to pray inwardly, devoutly. Never have I failed to commend myself to God's keeping, asking him to forgive my past sins, and to watch over me

while in danger [and then] to receive me if I fell while caring for those near and dear to me. After having done so all anxiety for myself, here and hereafter, is dispelled. I feel that my destiny is in the hands of the Almighty. This belief, more than any other fact or reason, makes me brave and fearless as I am.[63]

Quite simply, Custer was like a Crusader of old because he believed that he was engaged in a holy cause, and he fought like a true holy warrior.[64]

## TENSE LATE NIGHT CONFERENCE BETWEEN OLD FRIENDS

General Lee had proved on July 1 and July 2 why he had become the most successful commander in the history of American arms. He had masterfully exploited tactical opportunities to the fullest in the pursuit of decisive victory, and he came close to achieving success on both days by relying on the tactical offensive. He possessed an army with legendary offensive capabilities, and these had been demonstrated in full on the first two days of bloodshed. Nevertheless, he had narrowly missed achieving his primary goal and obsessive desire to deliver a mortal blow to the Army of the Potomac, especially on the crucial second day when he came close to breaking Meade's battle line along the sprawling length of Cemetery Ridge and turning his left flank.

For these reasons, Lee was even more determined to deliver a masterstroke on July 3, which was now the day of decision and the last opportunity for him to finally unleash what he envisioned as his knockout blow from which Meade's army would never recover. The long march north by his army was a quest to get the army into a key position to deliver this killer blow. Quite simply, there was no tomorrow for Lee and the Army of Northern Virginia, and the clock was ticking on the young life of the beleaguered Confederacy. Lee knew it was literally a case or now or never for July 3.

There was plenty of time for Lee to yet win this unresolved battle on the final day, if everything went according to his complex plan to win it all by unleashing his greatest offensive effort. Coming so close to decisive victory after having ordered a series of assaults on the afternoon of July 2 had only made Lee more eager and aggressive to reap decisive success on July 3. Although extremely frustrated in having come so close to achieving final victory on the second day, Lee was in high spirits despite the ever-increasing amount of frustration stemming from the missed opportunities of the past two days, because he knew that he still controlled the field and that the Army of the Potomac was on the ropes. He knew that General Meade, a cautious, careful, and extremely capable commander, was now left with no choice but to remain on the defensive by holding the high ground and hoping for the best. Lee possessed the initiative and momentum of continuing his hard-hitting brand of offensive warfare, because he could now more freely maneuver at will, especially now that he possessed his finest cavalry brigades—the three absent commands—and his top cavalry commander.

General Meade wisely prepared for what he knew was as inevitable on July 3 as the sun rising in the east: Lee's all-out offensive effort in his final and most determined attempt to deliver a knockout blow to the battered Army of the Potomac, which was just barely hanging on to its high-ground perches—Cemetery Hill, Culp's Hill, and Cemetery Ridge—to survive the bloody showdown with the South's most winning commander. For all of these reasons, General Stuart was destined to be a key player in Lee's all-out offensive plans on July 3, because the army's commander was determined to go for broke to win it all on the final day. In this regard, there was no resource left for General Lee, the Army of Northern Virginia, and the South but to go for broke as never before and when everything was at stake. For the Confederacy, July 3 was the right moment at the right place to launch the offensive effort that was calculated to win the South's greatest victory of the war.

Most of all, Stuart needed to be a key player in Lee's greatest offensive effort. Galloping west in the humid blackness of the night of July 2 and through the open countryside of Adams County and down the dusty Chambersburg Pike that followed the top of Seminary Ridge, Stuart rode at a brisk pace toward General Lee's headquarters located just northwest of Gettysburg. For miles behind the general who had performed well below Lee's expectations on almost every level from the beginning of this campaign, a good many of Stuart's exhausted cavalrymen and horse artillerymen were still strewn out on the road leading from Carlisle to Gettysburg during the race to rejoin the army before it was too late.

Since learning of the heavy fighting at Gettysburg while at Carlisle to the north as noted, Stuart had ridden south to reach his commander in chief as soon as possible. During the first two days of combat, a frustrated Lee had been incredulous because he had heard nothing from Stuart for nearly a week and a half, and he had been forced to fight "blind" in attempting to deliver a killing blow to the Army of the Potomac. And now Stuart was finally riding west to return to the headquarters of the army that he should never have left in the first place, but without any useful information or intelligence for Lee.

After having gained the army's left and leaving his foremost men—the column was strewn out for miles—near the intersection of the Hunterstown and York Turnpike, Stuart was accompanied by at least one trusty staff officer, his adjutant, during the late nighttime ride west along the York Turnpike. Understandably under the circumstances, he was eager to finally meet his anxious commanding officer, who might well have been pacing back and forth at headquarters by this time. No doubt and for good reason, Stuart was gripped with nervous tension about meeting his revered commander, whose sense of indignation, if not anger, had grown day after day from his long absence. Most of all, Lee had continued to lament Stuart's absence during the first two days of the most important battle ever fought on the North American continent, wondering what had happened to the army's top cavalryman when he was needed most.

By this time, Lee was seething with frustration and almost certainly some degree of anger—an emotion that he had long sought hard to control and almost certainly kept in check on this occasion, despite popular myths to the contrary. Nevertheless, the tension was high at the headquarters, which was located on the crest of Seminary Ridge just northwest of Gettysburg. The dust-covered Stuart, who had been absent from the army for too long, to the point that even the average Confederate infantryman was asking his whereabouts, was therefore taken by surprise by the cold reaction he received from his old friend and revered mentor when he finally entered Lee's headquarters, where courtly manners and gentlemanly diplomacy had long become legendary even to lowly couriers.

After all, Lee and Stuart possessed the closest relationship among all the army's top lieutenants, extending back to the 1850s, when the mere thought of a possible civil war had been dismissed as an absolutely ridiculous concept. At that time, Lee had been the lieutenant colonel of the crack United States dragoon regiment in which his fellow Virginian, Lieutenant Stuart, served as a lieutenant during duty in the West. In many ways, this friendship between Lee and Stuart had endured year after year with deep affection, and not unlike father and son. But late on the night of July 2, this long-existing bond between the two Virginians was severed to a degree not imagined possible by Stuart, who had long basked in Lee's good graces and affectionate glow like a true golden boy. But Stuart's long absence from the army had changed everything, because he had let down not only Lee but also the army at the most crucial time.

Consequently, Stuart's reception at Lee's headquarters on the Chambersburg Pike that led west to the Cumberland Valley was not only chilly but also embarrassingly tense, to a degree unprecedented for the sensitive cavalier, who received the most severe rebuke of his career in the manner of a mentor toward a naughty student. Stuart made the embarrassing scene even worse by offering a most ill-timed and long-winded explanation of his inexplicable absence of nearly a week and a half, but it was too late for excuses by this time.

As Lee fully realized, the damage to the army and his decision-making process in tactical terms had already been done, and the last two days of combat could not be changed. He had been forced to fight the most important battle of the war without his three finest cavalry brigades, under Brigadier Generals Hampton, "Rooney" Lee, and Fitzhugh Lee, although the four cavalry brigades that had been left with the army could have been employed in a more aggressive manner instead of remaining too long in the army's rear. Other veteran batteries of Stuart's Horse Artillery had also lingered too long in the army's rear far west of Gettysburg, and they were destined not to be available for Stuart's use on July 3, when needed the most on this day of decision.

On the crest of Seminary Ridge barely an hour before midnight, Lee and Stuart held their late-night conference in the stone house that had so suddenly become important in this war. Situated on Seminary Ridge and overlooking the surrounding picturesque countryside of rolling fields of wheat standing high and nearly ready for harvest by industrious farmers and their helpers, including free blacks, this little home was owned by Widow Mary Thompson, age sixty-nine.

Far removed from the front lines to the east, the Thompson house was safely out of harm's way, although situated on the main road leading into Gettysburg from the northwest. General Lee had chosen an ideal location for his headquarters, which he had occupied since the first day's battle on July 1, when the engagement had erupted unexpectedly and not only without his knowledge, but also without his choosing. Stuart had noticed that a neat row of white tents of Lee's faithful staff officers, a dignified group of men who were supremely devoted to the army's commander, were clustered around the Thompson house in a parklike setting. Ironically, this modest house had been owned since January 1846 by Pennsylvania congressman Thaddeus Stevens, who was denounced by a gunner of Stuart's Horse Artillery as "that vile old sinner and Southern hater."[65]

Here, at the quiet of the Thompson house, Lee laid out a bold plan that demonstrated the wisdom of his earlier words in regard to the Southern people: "Believe me, sir, the business of this generation *is* the war."[66]

Lee spoke the words of a distinguished Mexican-American War veteran and a career military officer. However, the serious business of war was not the business of all members of the South. A number of ethnic groups were represented in Stuart's ranks, especially the Irish, Scotch-Irish, and Germans. However, one ethnic group, because of its overall small numbers, was especially underrepresented in the ranks of Stuart's cavalry. In the words of historian Robert N. Rosen: "There were a few Jewish officers in the Confederate cavalry. Exceptional riding skill, which few Jewish Southerners possessed, was a prerequisite for a cavalry officer. An urban and mercantile people, Jewish Southerners were rarely qualified to command these units."[67]

## STUART HEAVILY REINFORCED FOR
## A SECRET OFFENSIVE MISSION

Although often overlooked by historians in regard to its overall significance for the events to come in the Army of the Potomac's rear on July 3, this late-night conference between Lee and Stuart was of extreme importance because of the creation of Gettysburg's most secret and overlooked complex plan. Late on the warm night of July 2, Lee immediately got down to business because he had already decided to recommit his forces to the tactical offensive by the time of Stuart's arrival, when he emphasized with a rare sternness that told Stuart that he meant business of extreme importance: "Let me ask your help now. We will not discuss this [absence] matter further. Help me fight these people."[68]

These are the most direct surviving words to Stuart from General Lee, who wrote out no orders for Stuart on the night of July 2 or the morning of July 3, or they simply have not survived, especially if they were deliberately destroyed by Stuart because this was a secret mission. What these oral directives from Lee emphasized was that the army's cavalry must launch the tactical offensive to strike a decisive blow into the Army of the Potomac's rear. But in fact Stuart was about to be assigned to not only play a key role on July 3, but, most importantly, "Stuart would have a chance to clinch the victory," when everything was at stake.[69] Stuart's own adjutant, Major Henry Brainerd McClellan, revealed as much in regard to the importance of the battle plan targeting the enemy's most vulnerable point, emphasizing how Stuart's mission was to unleash "an attack upon the enemy's rear."[70]

Most of all, at this time, Lee was convinced that the Army of the Potomac was vulnerable to an even greater offensive blow on the third day, after the pounding it had taken and the high losses it had suffered during the last two days. Quite simply, Lee was going for broke as never before in a most impressive career that was distinguished by one victory after another because of a masterful reliance on the tactical offensive. Therefore, while Ewell's Second Corps attacked Meade's right at the break of dawn on the third day, Lee planned to deliver the main blow by striking the Federal center in the belief that Meade had sufficiently reinforced the high ground on his line's southern and northern ends that had been hard hit, especially Little Round Top on the south.

Clearly, Lee was desperate, because he knew that he might never again possess an opportunity to inflict a decisive blow on the North's principal army in the east. And, most of all, this all-important requirement now called for hitting the Union center with almost everything he had available in a determined bid to split Meade's army in two. In unleashing his most powerful blow and striking from the west with a formidable array of massed infantry, he was now relying heavily on his last infantry reserve, the three Virginia brigades of General George Edward Pickett's Division, to spearhead the attack.

This seasoned division had missed the surreal carnage of the first two days of bitter combat, and these Virginians could thank their lucky stars. Almost by accident, therefore, Pickett's Division had become the army's strategic reserve, and Lee was determined to use it in the manner of Napoleon's use of the elite troops of the Imperial Guard. Napoleon had long pampered his veterans of the Imperial Guard, including the famed "Old Guard" (the most seasoned fighting men and hence older in age) and the "Young Guard" (the finest recruits of each annual crop of young men from the French population), which was basically a separate army that the emperor relied on to reap decisive victory in key battlefield situations.

And now Stuart, who was available and ready for action on July 3, possessed a sufficient amount of veteran cavalry, led by top lieutenants of outstanding ability, especially Hampton, that had not been engaged on July 1 and July 2; in essence, the strategic cavalry reserve, including veteran horse artillery batteries, that Lee could now utilize in full in the manner of a strategic reserve of infantry like Pickett's Division, which had become a strategic reserve quite by accident. At this time to Lee, the overall offensive effort that targeted Meade's center (eventually the right-center at the time the massive infantry assault was unleashed) made good sense—instead of the long-emphasized folly of frontal assault across open ground, since rifled muskets had made such attacks largely obsolete—but only if Stuart's cavalry, and its accompanying guns of the famed Stuart Horse Artillery (basically flying artillery) and other artillery units, were also unleashed from the east at the same time in a coordinated effort to avoid another disaster of unsupported frontal assaults like Waterloo on June 18, 1815, in Belgium, because uncoordinated attacks across open ground were absolute folly. Like Pickett's Division, so Stuart's cavalry brigades were to be utilized like a strategic reserve in the manner of Napoleon's Imperial Guard—crack troops who were thrown into the fray at a critical moment to reap a decisive success—but in attacking from the opposite direction.

Therefore, Stuart's more than six thousand troopers were ordered by Lee to attack Meade's rear while Ewell struck the defenders of Culp's Hill on the north and Pickett's Charge targeted the Army of the Potomac's midsection along Cemetery Ridge. In traditional terms and throughout the course of western military history, especially during the Napoleonic era, the largest reserve of cavalry was often saved for the express purpose of delivering a decisive blow because of its unparalleled shock value. And, most importantly, Lee now possessed exactly what he needed (a strategic reserve of cavalry) to make his offensive blow most effective in the Army of the Potomac's rear, Lee's final opportunity to deliver a decisive attack, but an even more powerful one than on the previous day and from the opposite direction: the unleashing of Stuart's cavalry from the east, which was guaranteed to catch the Federals from the rear and completely by surprise.

At this time, because they had been part of the ill-fated raid for nearly the last week and a half, Stuart now possessed only two batteries of his horse artillery—Captains William Morrell McGregor (only a section of guns) and Marylander James Williams Breathed, who was also of Scottish descent. McGregor, like General Ewell, had lost a leg in Lee's last northern invasion (the 1862 Maryland campaign), but he was still serving his country and leading by example. Therefore, to fulfill his key mission in the Army of the Potomac's rear, Stuart needed to have more artillery, especially fresh gunners and horses, to deliver a heavier blow on Meade's rear. After all, McGregor's and Breathed's units, representing Virginia and Maryland, respectively, men and horses, were in overall bad shape by this time.

After the death of the legendary Alabamian Major John Pelham, who was the true founder and revered leader of the Stuart Horse Artillery and had recently been killed during the fighting at Kelly's Ford on March 17, 1863, Major Robert Franklin Beckham became his replacement. He faithfully continued the tradition of what was one of the most celebrated units in the Army of Northern Virginia, and Stuart's guns packed a powerful punch, especially if the guns of his horse artillery were trained on the rear of Meade's defenders on the high ground on July 3. The veteran gunners of Stuart's famed "Hoss" (the horse artillery) were determined to maintain their lofty reputations under the leadership of the chief of the Stuart Horse Artillery, Beckham.

To provide Stuart with even more muscle for his upcoming role to wreak havoc in the Union army's rear, therefore, General Lee prudently assigned General Albert G. Jenkins's cavalry brigade—a fresh command of Virginians that had not seen combat either on the first or second day—to Stuart, as well as Captain Thomas E. Jackson's Charlottesville (Virginia) Battery (two 3-inch guns and two howitzers), which had accompanied Jenkins's Brigade to Gettysburg. As importantly, this was a large Old Dominion brigade of around 1,300 cavalrymen who were experienced and highly disciplined—an invaluable reinforcement for Stuart to accomplish great things in the Union army's rear on July 3, as Lee envisioned with clarity at the Widow Thompson house. Therefore, in total, Stuart would now possess more than six thousand men of four cavalry brigades and four batteries and a section of artillery—the most men of the cavalry and artillery that he had commanded during the last ten days. The tantalizing prospect of this combined force of cavalry and artillery striking into the rear of Meade's army would lead to the kind of victory that would ensure that Lee became the George Washington of a new nation, if everything went according to his most ambitious plan of war.

Because of the late hour of the Lee-Stuart conference at the Widow Thompson house, the seasoned troopers of General Jenkins's Brigade, "an especially tightly run outfit," joined Stuart on the morning of July 3 to ensure that his command possessed additional manpower, including a powerful artillery punch. Jenkins's Brigade of Virginians was in good shape, having been assigned to Ewell during his push northeast toward Harrisburg, and had primarily engaged in foraging for provisions for themselves and the Second Corps. A capable cavalryman of Scotch-Irish heritage born in Wayne County, Virginia (now West Virginia), Colonel Milton Jameson Ferguson was officially in command of the brigade, after General Jenkins had been wounded on July 2.

In overall terms, Ferguson was a fine replacement, because Jenkins was a lawyer and politician whom Stuart looked upon with disdain because of the undisciplined behavior of his freewheeling troopers from the mountains of western Virginia and their commander's limitations. But much of Stuart's disdain stemmed from a West Point and Virginia Tidewater contempt that applied to all mountain people, who were considered poor "white trash" by the Southern elites. Most importantly, Jenkins's Virginians were tough fighting men, and that was all that mattered for July 3.

Jenkins's Virginians were a nice complement to Stuart's mostly Virginian cavalry brigade (William Henry Fitzhugh "Rooney" Lee—a Harvard man who was the second son of the army's commander and first cousin to Fitzhugh Lee—whose brigade had been part of the recent ill-fated raid) under Colonel John Randolph Chambliss Jr. Chambliss was a Virginia native and a capable West Pointer (class of 1853) who was destined to shortly gain promotion to brigadier general. He had risen splendidly to the challenge at Brandy Station, leading the brigade of "Rooney" Lee after the revered general had been wounded by a bullet in the leg. Chambliss performed equally well during the Gettysburg campaign, ensuring that he shortly gained the hard-earned and well-deserved rank of brigadier general. But unkind fate awaited the hard-fighting Chambliss. He was destined to be killed while battling for his country in the months ahead.

## AMPLE ARTILLERY

In regard to artillery for his key mission on July 3, Stuart also gained permission from Lee to secure additional guns for Ewell's Second Corps, which was one-third (artillery) of the offensive effort—artillery, infantry, and cavalry—and included Pickett's Charge and Stuart's strike from the rear. Clearly, making extremely sound tactical sense, this was to be a united offensive effort of all three arms on the early morning of the third day, as originally planned by Lee. The new guns would augment the strength of Stuart's Horse Artillery to pack a greater offensive punch for the attack into Meade's rear at the moment of decision.

Never forgetting the remarkable success of the U.S. Army's "flying artillery"—commanded by mostly young West Pointers—of the Mexican-American War, therefore, Stuart added a section of guns (two 3-inch rifles and two 10-pounder Parrott rifles) from Captain Charles A. Green's Louisiana Guard Battery to increase his artillery arm for this all-important mission. Stuart gained these Pelican State guns from Major General Jubal Anderson Early's Division of Ewell's Second Corps. The Louisiana gunners, who wore Pelican State buttons, were veterans. Most importantly, they had not been worn out in Stuart's time-consuming raid over much of the surrounding countryside.

With offensive operations in mind, Lee had wisely bolstered Stuart with not only additional cavalry, but also extra artillery at the last minute for unleashing the offensive in Meade's rear. Therefore, on July 3, Stuart possessed two of his horse artillery batteries—Captain McGregor's 2nd Stuart Virginia Horse Artillery and Captain Breathed's 1st Stuart Virginia Horse Artillery—and also Captain Jackson's Charlottesville "Kanawha" Virginia Horse Artillery and Captain William H. Griffin's 2nd Baltimore Maryland Horse Artillery and, as noted, the section of Louisiana artillery. The Charlottesville Battery was from the same Divisional Artillery Battalion, under Lieutenant Colonel Hilary Pollard Jones, as the section of Louisiana guns of Ewell's corps. Therefore, Stuart now commanded four batteries and the section of Louisiana artillery to inflict maximum damage in the Union army's rear.

Clearly General Lee, a distinguished veteran of the Mexican-American War, envisioned a hard-hitting offensive strike, including with guns in the manner of "flying artillery," in Meade's rear. Because everything was at stake, he embraced this bold concept in full—in keeping with his offensive-minded decisions on the crucial third day—in conjunction with his main offensive effort from the west, Pickett's Charge. In the words of Professor James M. McPherson, one of America's leading Civil War historians, Lee gave Stuart the crucial mission of striking the Union rear to deliver the "coup de grace" to destroy the Army of the Potomac in one knockout punch.

For this express purpose of attacking Meade's vulnerable rear on July 3, Stuart was destined to possess the army's largest reserve (basically a strategic reserve) of cavalry and artillery (both the units of his command and from other units—artillery and cavalry—that equated to more than six thousand men), not only in overall numbers, but also in regard to the number of fresh soldiers, both cavalrymen and artillerymen, because they had not been decimated in the combat of July 1 and 2, which had been the sad fate of the majority of Lee's units, including commands other than the three brigades of Pickett's Division that were ordered to be part of Pickett's Charge, who were in overall bad shape.

As Lee fully realized at this time, the most important offensive strike of the army's cavalry reserve that could possibly be performed by Stuart, whose command had been strengthened with additional guns and cavalry units for his secret mission, was to attack in conjunction with Ewell's corps on the north and Pickett's Charge to the south in the bid to pierce Meade's center and unhinge the two wings of the Army of the Potomac and divide it in two—the key to decisive success.

This bold concept was truly Napoleonic, and Lee's plan on July 3 was classically Napoleonic, revealing his admiration of the audacious native Corsican and the time-honored lessons of double-shock tactics that had long proved so effective on the battlefield: the cavalry delivering the major blow by the headlong charge with cavalrymen relying on the saber—but now the revolvers and carbines of Stuart's troopers that made the cavalrymen doubly lethal—and the employment of "flying artillery," which the emperor had long utilized with great skill by advancing the guns close to the enemy's ranks to blast away at close range and slaughter opposing infantrymen.

Lee had learned the nuances of the French language and greatly admired Napoleon and even French cultural ways—considered the epitome of sophistication and refinement by the Western world—at West Point, including the reading of military texts in French. After all, Napoleon was the master of employing the shock tactics of cavalry and artillery to reap dramatic victories across the breadth of Europe, and these enduring tactical lessons were never lost to Lee, especially at Gettysburg.

As noted, General Lee had fought the two previous days without Stuart's cavalry, and now they were available for the first time on the final day, and Lee was determined to exploit them in full. To have not fully utilized thousands of seasoned cavalrymen of Stuart's four available brigades and the available guns, mostly of the Stuart Horse Artillery Battalion and other artillery units, to the maximum in a last-ditch offensive bid to break through the rear of the Union lines would have been little short of criminal neglect under the circumstances, when everything was at stake, including the Confederacy's future.

Indeed, for the first time on the field of Gettysburg on July 3, Lee held two all-important high cards of troops—one was his last fresh strategic reserve of infantry (Pickett's Division) not engaged in combat on the first two days, and the other was his cavalry, also not previously employed—that were ready for the July 3 challenge.

But most importantly, the one feature of the ambitious tactical potential to deliver the most shock power and the most effective offensive blow on July 3 when Lee was forced to go for broke was the cavalry arm, especially if unleashed to attack the Union rear in conjunction with Pickett's Charge: two forces striking from opposite directions in what was basically a pincer moment from west and east. While traditional infantry tactics of the Napoleonic era had been largely negated by the advances of modern weaponry, especially the rifled musket, such was not the case in regard to cavalry, which retained its traditional hard-hitting "shock" power, including the saber charge, as in the Napoleonic era. In fact, Stuart's cavalry possessed far more punch in regard to modern firepower in the form of the six-shot revolver, which unleashed a high rate of fire, and these modern weapons were especially effective at close range.

As in the glory days of Napoleon when the "sun of Austerlitz" had shone so brightly when Napoleon orchestrated his tactical masterpiece at Austerlitz in early December 1805, the key to reaping decisive victory was still "the deadly shock" of the headlong cavalry charge, which was bolstered by an adequate amount of supporting fire of the "flying artillery," to hit Union infantry facing the wrong way (west), which were even more vulnerable to a surprise cavalry strike from the rear. The rare tactical formula, classically Napoleonic in every way, shape, and form, presented an unprecedented tactical opportunity to win it all on a day that Lee had decided to go for broke as never before. He fully understood how this was the long-sought tactical equation to reap decisive success on July 3: a surprise cavalry attack from the rear in conjunction with Pickett's Charge.

Therefore, because Stuart possessed his best cavalry of four brigades and more than four batteries, which represented considerable firepower for the climactic showdown on July 3, this was a golden opportunity to yet win the day based on all that Lee had learned in the past, including the best lessons of Napoleonic warfare. Lee had not forgotten that Napoleon's amazing successes in no small part lay in the fact that he had masterfully utilized the superior mobility and firepower of the "flying artillery" while relying on swift movements with artillery and cavalry. Napoleon had benefited from commanding the finest cavalry in all of Europe, led by his most fiery marshal, Murat, when employed aggressively, which was usually the case. And no one had been bolder and more aggressive than Murat, who possessed many of Custer's aggressive instincts, which rose to the fore on the field of strife. He had led the French cavalry to victory with reckless bravery that won admiration from friend and foe, including even from the Cossacks during the ill-fated 1812 invasion of Russia.

Impatient for success since July 1 and now especially eager to strike a blow of a decisive nature because he felt that victory was well within his grasp, the ever-optimistic Lee was much like Napoleon in regard to his aggressiveness and well-honed tactical skills. The overall tactical situation that existed on the third day led in only one direction and to only one possible solution for reaping decisive victory: the unleashing of his most powerful tactical offensive with his last available reserves—infantry and cavalry in conjunction—because the successes of the first two days needed to be exploited to the fullest, since he knew that there was no tomorrow for the Army of Northern Virginia and the Confederacy. For these reasons, the thought of allowing his entire cavalry arm to languish in the relatively nonproductive role of merely guarding Ewell's flank—when in fact Ewell's corps had been originally ordered to attack Culp's Hill on the morning of the third day in conjunction with Pickett's Charge and Stuart—on the most important day of the war was an utter impossibility under such circumstances, because Lee realized that the winner would take all on July 3.

In Lee's agile mind, consequently, the final day was a gift from above because he possessed a strategic reserve (Pickett in regard to infantry and Stuart in regard to cavalry) that had not been engaged on the first two days, and because it represented a golden opportunity to win it all by unleashing one final offensive to reap all the dividends, which could not have been higher. After all, this strategic objective had been the South's entire motivation behind launching the Pennsylvania Campaign, which was the army's most desperate offensive effort of the war because everything was now at stake. In this sense, and unlike the two previous days, Lee was confident of reaping a decisive success. In fact, he was too confident, like his top cavalryman, Stuart.

After Pickett's Division, which was his only fresh infantry division, thus ensuring its role as a strategic reserve to spearhead the offensive effort from the west, Lee now possessed his last and largest non-infantry reserve of a one-two punch—four veteran cavalry brigades and the veteran gunners of mostly Major Robert Franklin Beckham's Stuart Horse Artillery Battalion (officially the Divisional Artillery Battalion) of Stuart's Division that had long demonstrated the superiority of their mobility (basically "flying artillery") in having accompanied Stuart on his raids and other veteran artillery units—that promised to deliver the greatest shock value and hardest hitting capabilities on the battlefield as in centuries past. Therefore, Lee possessed what he now needed most of all to deliver a decisive blow from not one but two directions: reserves that included all three arms—infantry, cavalry, and artillery—for unleashing the army's greatest offensive effort in the final decisive showdown upon which so much now depended.

But significantly, as General Lee understood, these last remaining combat capabilities and resources of reserves—infantry, cavalry, and artillery—had to be utilized in full to reap a decisive success. Most of all, Stuart's cavalry certainly could not be wasted in a great, but indecisive, cavalry clash—like the war's largest cavalry clash at Brandy Station, which had only proved that the Union cavalry had considerably improved since the heady days of 1861, as Lee and leaders in Richmond had long feared. Therefore, it was literally now or never for the combined effort of cavalry, infantry, and artillery to work closely together to inflict a mortal blow to the Army of the Potomac, because this was a golden opportunity that would never come again, as Lee correctly sensed.

After two days of bloody combat, everything was now on the line because the decisive showdown at Gettysburg "had not yet reached a conclusion, and Lee now had both Stuart's command and Pickett's fresh division available. Securing a major victory on North soil would bring new political, diplomatic, and even military variables into play—and the possibility of securing one still existed. That, of course, was the driving reason he had taken his army north that summer" of decision.[71]

In consequence, historian Gregory J. W. Urwin, in his fine book *Custer Victorious: The Civil War Battles of General George Armstrong Custer*, summarized Stuart's key mission and the Lee-Stuart plan: "His object was to go around the rear of the Army of the Potomac and get among its lines of communication and supply. This was not to be another glory-hunting raid. Having tested Meade's right and left, General Robert E. Lee believed he could punch a hole through his center and was readying eleven infantry brigades for the grand assault Major General George A. Pickett would lead on Cemetery Ridge. With Pickett clawing through the front and Stuart whirling in from behind, the Army of the Potomac would be cut in half, thrown into a panic, and the South would gain the decisive victory she needed to win the war."[72]

And in the words of the leading authority of the Gettysburg campaign, Edwin B. Coddington, in his classic work, *The Gettysburg Campaign: A Study in Command*, emphasized how "General Stuart, who had finally ridden into Gettysburg [and] had consulted with General Lee about operations for July 3 [and] though a late arrival for the battle, Stuart's unerring eye and quick appreciation of the controlling topographical features in a strange land quickly showed him where he could best use the cavalry for an offensive movement. He and Lee worked out a scheme to put Stuart's entire cavalry force in a position from which he could separate the Union cavalry from the main body of the army and at the proper moment swoop down onto its rear."[73] In his analysis, Coddington had merely followed the words of Stuart's trusty adjutant, Major Henry Brainerd McClellan, who emphasized as much in regard to the Lee-Stuart plan to strike into the Army of the Potomac's rear.[74]

Indeed, during the late July 2 conference at the Thompson house on Seminary Ridge and thanks to a good topographical map, Lee and Stuart had spied the advantages of Cress's Ridge, around three miles southeast of Gettysburg and behind Meade's right, anchored on Cemetery Hill to the west and Culp's Hill to the east. Therefore, they devised their ambitious offensive plan of hitting Meade's vulnerable rear based on the advantages offered by this high-ground perch.[75]

In a reflective moment, General Lee had recently emphasized to Major General Isaac R. Trimble, who was now about to lead troops in Pickett's Charge, of his main ambition not long before the first shots of the Battle of Gettysburg were fired in anger, and now, after the first two days of combat, he was even more desirous of this result "to end the war if Providence favours us."[76]

As in the past, General Lee was indeed relying on "Providence," but not to the point that he was not doing everything possible to maximize his offensive capabilities, especially in regard to Stuart's cavalry, to ensure that he won a decisive victory. Ironically, some historians have assumed that Lee was fundamentally passive in allowing God to perform miracles, except for the unleashing of Pickett's Charge, because of this belief and faith in Providence. But nothing could have been farther from the truth. Consequently, he was now relying on all available reserves of all branches to win the decisive victory that he envisioned, ensuring that Stuart's cavalry was to be a key player in the final showdown, when Lee was going for broke.

Clearly, Lee was determined to strike the offensive blow "to end the war" on July 3, which meant that he had absolutely no choice but to fully utilize Stuart's cavalry in the most aggressive way as a strategic reserve to deliver the "coup de grace," which called for a tactical offensive role of the cavalry in conjunction with Pickett's Charge to break the Union defensive line from two directions—because it was the best existing tactical choice for winning decisive victory—in conjunction with the attack of Ewell's Second Corps on the north at Culp's Hill, a one-two punch from two directions (east and west) that was calculated to win it all because there was no tomorrow for the beleaguered Confederacy and its ill-fated eastern army that would never again possess the opportunity to deliver a knockout blow to the Army of the Potomac.

For such reasons and as noted, Lee had ordered that Brigadier General Albert G. Jenkins's Virginia cavalry brigade, which had been attached to General Ewell's Second Corps during the push north all the way to the Pennsylvania capital of Harrisburg, join Stuart for his key mission of attacking Meade's rear. By any measure, this was a crucial addition, because Jenkins's Virginia cavalrymen (three regiments and two battalions) had not been bloodied in the holocaust at Gettysburg, when almost all of Lee's units had been hard hit by the second day's end. Therefore, this was still another force of fresh fighting men that fit the requirements of a strategic reserve—like Pickett's Division but by accident rather than original design—that was ready for Lee's final gamble on the third day.

As could be expected on a day of decision in which the winner would take all and the stage was set for the full utilization of his cavalry arm, General Lee's background as an old cavalryman had clearly risen to the fore. Lee's decision to utilize Stuart in an offensive role would have made his father, a hero of the Revolutionary War, proud. After all, General Henry "Light Horse Harry" Lee had been one of the best Southern cavalry leaders of the American Revolution and had battled for liberty with a passion, a most distinguished ancestry that might have partly explained the closeness of the bond between Stuart and Lee. Like Napoleon, whose campaigns across Europe, even in Russia, he had studied at West Point, Lee knew that the key to victory lay in effectively utilizing all three arms of his army—infantry, cavalry, and artillery—to the fullest in regard to the tactical offensive—the real, and mostly forgotten, key to Napoleon's successes across Europe—and now he possessed his last reserves (Pickett's Division and Stuart's Cavalry Division), which were relatively fresh, for striking from two directions.

General Lee correctly saw that his lack of reaping a decisive success on the first and second days, on which he had come close to victory, was because he had been unable to properly coordinate his attacks and employ all three arms in the proper Napoleonic manner of a truly unified and closely coordinated offensive effort. But Lee and Stuart realized that the traditional cavalry charge had little, if any, chance for success against infantrymen, armed with modern weaponry, when they held good defensive positions on high ground from the front.

But catching the enemy's infantry by surprise by striking the enemy's rear was a different matter altogether, and this tactic dramatically altered the equation to negate not only the advantages of Meade's defensive positions on the high ground, but also the advanced weaponry in the hands of thousands of bluecoat defenders. Quite simply, a surprise cavalry attack into the enemy's rear, when Meade's defenders were facing west and confronting Pickett's Charge, was nothing less that the key tactical formula for decisive success, transforming a certain defeat—if cavalry attacked in front in such an unfavorable situation against a high-ground defensive position aligned with long lines of defenders—to almost certain victory of a decisive nature.[77]

America's respected dean of Civil War cavalry studies, especially in regard to the Gettysburg campaign, Edward G. Longacre, PhD, emphasized the powerful shock of a cavalry charge: "When horses gallop en masse, they generate a momentum that is often uncontrollable. The power they wield is capable, if the conditions are right, of surmounting every obstacle."[78] And this situation was doubly the case in regard to the hard-hitting and shock power of a sweeping cavalry attack if unleashed into the Union rear of the enemy infantry, especially bluecoats aligned in defensive positions and looking the other direction. Quite simply, no tactic could inflict a more decisive knockout blow and greater shock than an attack of cavalry into the rear of an unsuspecting enemy in defensive positions to negate the high-ground advantage and modern weaponry, especially if coordinated closely with an infantry onslaught in front—the exact situation of Meade's defenders who held the high ground along Cemetery Ridge, and the fundamental basis of Lee's battle plan for July 3.[79] The same gifted Civil War cavalry historian, a longtime Department of Defense historian in Virginia, emphasized how Lee's orders to Stuart at the Thompson house headquarters were "to deal Meade an unexpected blow" from the rear.[80]

Therefore, for General Stuart to "clinch the victory" by striking Meade's rear, Lee "had concentrated virtually all his cavalry under Stuart, giving him [Brigadier General Albert G.] Jenkins' newly-arrived [Virginia] brigade to increase Stuart's forces to 6,000 men."[81] A revered member of Stuart's staff, Major Henry Brainerd McClellan felt added confidence for success on July 3 because General "Jenkins' brigade . . . was added to Stuart's command" for the all-important mission of striking the rear of Meade's army.[82]

Again to reveal that he and Lee were kindred spirits in regard to their offensive-minded thoughts about the supreme importance of unleashing an overpowering tactical offensive effort, Stuart had long emphasized the wisdom of such a successful tactical masterstroke—especially an attack into an enemy's rear—of the cavalry charge that was "sudden, bold, and vigorous. The cavalry . . . arrives noiselessly but steadily near the enemy, and then, with one loud yell leaps upon him without a note of warning."[83]

In Lee's tactically flexible mind, the plan (Gettysburg's most secret plan and mission of supreme importance) that he and Stuart had created at the Widow Thompson's house was calculated to be the winning tactical formula for decisive success on the third day, if Stuart could gain the Union rear in time—in conjunction with Pickett's Charge—to deliver the "coup de grace" in the words of Professor James M. McPherson, a PhD and Pulitzer Prize winner. But as Lee realized and no doubt emphasized during the late-night conference, now there could be no more mistakes, delays, or miscalculations made by Stuart in his all-important offensive effort, because this was the last opportunity to win a decisive success by delivering the maximum offensive effort.[84]

As fate would have it, and although no one realized it at the time, Custer and Stuart were on a collision course and headed for a rendezvous with destiny in the rear of the Army of the Potomac. As Custer had written in an earlier letter of the situation that now applied to dawn July 3 for him and his brigade of Wolverines: "Much blood will be spilled [and] if it is to be my lot to fall in the service of my country and my country's rights I will have no regrets."[85]

## NO WRITTEN ORDERS FOR A SECRET MISSION

Unfortunately, in regard to Stuart's orders, the exact words spoken at this high-level conference between Lee and his top cavalryman at the small stone house located immediately on the north side of the Chambersburg Turnpike, which was the main western approach that led into Gettysburg, are not precisely known, because they have not been preserved. Perhaps historian Jeffry D. Wert said it best: "Evidently, Lee gave him [Stuart] verbal orders, as no written ones or dispatches seem to exist."[86]

But we do know that this was the first, best, and almost certainly last opportunity for Lee to have presented Stuart with his full set of instructions for July 3, and they were based on a desperate aggressiveness, if not sheer audacity, for winning it all on the final day, because this was the Army of Northern Virginia's last chance.

What we do know is that in this key situation, the four finest brigades of the South's cavalry, and two batteries of the famed Stuart Horse Artillery Battalion and the guns of other units (four batteries and the section of Louisiana guns in total) were ordered by Lee to play a vital role in the army's rear. This formidable fighting force under Stuart consisted of significant combat capabilities of both cavalry and artillery that had been enhanced for a final day's showdown in which everything had to be hurled forth during what was General Lee's greatest offensive gamble of his career. All details of this bold plan and secret mission of Stuart striking into the Army of the Potomac's rear were agreed upon by Lee and Stuart at the Thompson house on the night of July 2.

The exact details of this audacious offensive plan for Stuart to attack into the rear of the Army of the Potomac were discussed at the Widow Thompson house and presented in oral, not written, form. Most of all, and unlike on the first two days, Lee desired a "proper concert of action" from all three branches of his army—artillery, infantry, and cavalry—on the decisive third day. As noted, Lee planned for Ewell's Second Corps to attack Meade's right anchored on Culp's Hill at daylight on July 3, while the infantry, mostly of Longstreet's First Corps, delivered the main blow against Meade's center (eventually the right-center was targeted after adjustments) on the belief that this sector had been previously weakened to bolster the hard-hit flanks, the result of Rebel assaults on July 2.

Again, this was an orally communicated plan—a secret that was possessed by only a handful of officers (initially only Stuart) for obvious security reasons—that was never put into writing in official form for what Stuart was to accomplish on July 3. The fact that the exact details of this ambitious plan of attacking into the Army of the Potomac's rear from the east was never written down or has not survived created a situation that has led generations of historians, especially today's self-serving bloggers with personal agendas to protect their reputations and egos, to mistakenly conclude that there was no plan for Stuart to attack with four brigades and four batteries and a section of Louisiana guns in the Union army's rear, when in fact that was precisely the mission of the South's most famous cavalier and the army's finest cavalry, an entirely hollow, if not ridiculous, general assumption in regard to a day of decision when Lee had no choice but to go for broke as never before because he realized (like Stuart) that this was the Confederacy's last chance to achieve a decisive success before this lengthy war of the attrition doomed the South to destruction, which was only a matter of time.[87]

Indeed, what was not in doubt was the simple fact and undeniable reality that the bold plan of striking into Meade's rear was urgently required because the "exigencies of the moment [had] compel[led] [Lee] to call upon Stuart and his cavalry [four brigades] to perform important missions" on July 3, and these were decidedly offensive.[88] As mentioned, Stuart's adjutant revealed as much in his memoirs, when he wrote how Stuart's plan was to charge "upon the enemy's rear."[89]

As noted, "Lee's deep and abiding interest in the battles of the Great Captains [especially Napoleon] was never more apparent than it was on July 2, 1863. The attack against Cemetery Ridge was . . . similar to Napoleon's [tactical] formula for victory during the second day of fighting at Wagram [in 1809, but Lee] wanted to do more than simply copy Napoleon's epic 1809 battle plan [because] Lee planned to utilize and maximize all three of his combat arms (artillery, infantry, and cavalry) in order to gain a decisive success. This is why Lee sent Stuart and his cavalry on a sweeping end run around Ewell's left flank with orders to threaten the Federal rear."[90] But in fact this evaluation by a modern historian was actually a considerable underestimation of Stuart's crucial role—to deliver the "coup de grace"—that was even more hard hitting in regard to Lee's main offensive effort before Cemetery Ridge.

Historian Stephen W. Sears emphasized in his popular book *Gettysburg* how "Stuart's objective—'pursuant to instructions from the commanding general' [in General Stuart's own words about his set of instructions that were received from Lee late on July 2 at the Widow Thompson house]—was apparently to push aside any cavalry screen he found and reach the Baltimore Pike and the Federals' vulnerable rear."[91]

Agreeing with Sears and other leading historians, Bradley M. Gottfried, a gifted scholar, emphasized how Stuart's mission "was [to get] in position and ready to attack the Federal rear. According to the plan, the Confederates would send out a strong and aggressive skirmish line . . . to preoccupy the Federal horsemen [and Custer], then they would swing around their flank" and gain Meade's rear.[92]

Another historian, David F. Riggs, emphasized in more detail that was right on target: "Stuart attempted to strike the rear of the Army of the Potomac at the same time Pickett made his well-known charge upon its center on Cemetery Ridge. Had Stuart broken through this outnumbered but determined band of Union cavalrymen, Pickett's Charge might have been a decisive victory instead of the defeat" on July 3.[93] Likewise, historian Thom Hatch wrote how "Stuart's part in this offensive would be to wade into the Union rear in coordination with Pickett's charge that afternoon. . . . This one-two punch would, in Lee's opinion, ultimately result" in victory.[94]

Most importantly, these talented historians, including respected academics and top scholars with PhDs, are all in agreement with Stuart's adjutant, Henry Brainerd McClellan, who was in the know. He wrote how Stuart's objective was to unleash "an attack upon the enemy's rear."[95] Historian Edward G. Longacre wrote how Stuart was determined "to meet his commander's expectations, ensuring a coordinated effort on many fronts against Meade's battered ranks [and] to circumvent the Union right by a march out the York Pike, then across the fields into Meade's rear [and] if his path were not blocked, Stuart anticipated delivering a blow both psychologically and physically destructive, one that would compel Meade to quit the high ground and perhaps retreat to less defensible positions farther south."[96]

Professor James M. McPherson, a scholar and PhD revered for his historical expertise and insights on both sides of the Atlantic, emphasized as much in his usually accurate analysis that has made him the top Civil War historian of his generation: "While Pickett attacked the Union center and Ewell rolled up the right, Lee intended the 6,000 troopers of Major-General 'Jeb' Stuart's cavalry to circle around north of the Union right flank and come in on the rear of the Union position to give the coup de grace to the Yankees desperately engaged by Pickett and Ewell in their front."[97]

As noted, revered historian Edwin B. Coddington wrote how at the Thompson house, Stuart "and Lee worked out a scheme to put Stuart's entire cavalry force in a position [to eventually] swoop down onto" the rear of the Army of the Potomac.[98]

Another historian described how "General Stuart's original plan called for an avoidance of an engagement with Federal cavalry. The high ground of Cress Ridge was to act as a screen for his cavalry. Skirmishers on the edge of the woods [atop Cress's Ridge] would engage Federal skirmishers if the latter were in the vicinity. Meanwhile, Stuart's cavalry would reach the Baltimore Road unobserved and be in position to create panic with the Federal's rear on Cemetery Ridge."[99]

Despite limited knowledge about the larger strategic situation that was available to the men in the ranks, even a lieutenant of the 5th Michigan,

Samuel Harris, knew as much in regard to Stuart's tactical intentions and goals. He emphasized how Stuart was targeting the rear of the Army of the Potomac, and he was determined "to break through our lines and get to our trains."[100] Of course, Harris had no idea of the full extent of Lee's plans for Stuart, who acted on the express "instructions from the commanding general" that were given to him orally by General Lee at the Widow Thompson house conference, to strike the army's rear by hitting the infantry defending Cemetery Ridge.[101]

One of Stuart's most capable staff officers, William Willis Blackford, emphasized how the most important role of cavalry, especially at Gettysburg, came "in the supreme moment, in the crisis of battle, when victory is hovering over the field, uncertain upon which standard to alight—when the reserves are brought into action and the death struggle has come, *then* the cavalry comes down like an avalanche [and] with splendid effect."[102]

Indeed, for all practical purposes, Stuart's cavalry and horse artillery were actually Lee's final strategic reserves of non-infantry to be committed to the tactical offense in conjunction with Pickett's Charge to achieve a decisive blow to win it all: a strike from the rear that would deliver the "coup de grace" that Lee was convinced would bring the ultimate and unprecedented victory.[103]

Because this was a secret mission of four cavalry brigades, not all of Stuart's staff officers had been apprised of the complexities of this tactical plan, evidently for fear that one of them might be captured and then might allow the crucial intelligence about the secret plan to leak out. In his postwar memoirs, and without full knowledge of the plan's exact details, Major Henry Brainerd McClellan concluded, "Stuart's object was to gain position where he would protect the left of Ewell's corps, and would also be able to observe the enemy's rear and attack it in case the Confederate assault [Pickett's Charge] on the Federal lines were successful. He proposed, if opportunity offered, to make a diversion which might aid the Confederate infantry to carry the heights held by the Federal army," which was holding defensive positions along Cemetery Ridge.[104]

Given the ample evidence, Stuart had been presented his set of assigned orders at the Thompson house conference by General Lee to strike the Union army's rear rather than having orders relayed by courier or staff officer in the early hours of July 3. And this requirement meant avoiding a major clash of cavalry in Meade's rear that would be time consuming and result in high losses, because Stuart's mission was to strike the rear to the southwest along Cemetery Ridge and not engage in another Brandy Station–like slugfest that no longer brought easy or decisive results because of the great improvement of the Union cavalry's overall quality. Because he had decided to go for broke, Lee needed every good fighting man, including the troopers and artillerymen of Stuart's veteran command, for this last supreme effort to win it all on northern soil.[105]

In fact, Lee now needed Stuart, his four brigades of elite cavalry, and the available batteries of the Stuart Horse Artillery Battalion and other artillery units (four batteries and the Louisiana section of guns in total) more than ever before to deliver a decisive stroke in the Union rear, because of what had happened at Chancellorsville to diminish the overall chances for success at Gettysburg.

The accidental loss of Stonewall Jackson, who had long served magnificently as Lee's top lieutenant and a master of the tactical offensive, in the darkening woodlands of Chancellorsville forced more responsibility on Stuart to play a more active and leading role on the final day. The thought—as endlessly emphasized by the aggressive Stuart-in-the-rear deniers, who have long hoped to silence fundamental historical truths—that Lee would not have planned to use all of his available fresh troops, especially cavalry, now that he possessed thousands of his best cavalrymen and the most capable cavalry commander, in a maximum offensive effort on the final day, is an entirely outdated concept that borders on the ludicrous.

Because this offensive effort was Lee's last opportunity to win it all, as he instinctively sensed, he was not about to allow any available troops, including one of his top lieutenants, to play an idle role far beyond the main offensive effort on the war's most crucial day and the last opportunity he would ever be presented north of the Potomac, an unthinkable situation and tactical reality because Lee had decided to launch the invasion of Pennsylvania for the express purpose of delivering a knockout blow before time and all of the past opportunities had run out for the South. Quite simply, it was now or never for Lee, the Army of Northern Virginia, and the Confederacy, and Lee fully realized as much.

For this fundamental reason, Lee utilized every combat-ready brigade—infantry and cavalry—that was available because everything was at stake on the final day. After the battle, Lee's relationship with Pickett reached a new low because of the destruction of his Virginia Division during Pickett's Charge on the afternoon of July 3 that received no support from Stuart as planned by Lee. Therefore, Lee had attempted to explain and "assure" Pickett that his men were not sacrificed—as Pickett believed—because "he had ordered every brigade in the army" to charge Cemetery Ridge on the afternoon of July 3.[106] And this included Stuart's four brigades of his finest cavalry and accompanying horse artillery. Clearly Stuart had been assigned a very special mission for the third day.[107]

c 3 ɔ

# Young Custer's Greatest Challenge

As fate would have it, while the Army of the Potomac was moving north in pursuit of Lee's army, Custer, only twenty-three, was about to be thrust into the most important battle of the war in command of a brigade whose members he hardly knew. After his appointment to brigadier general on the same day, Custer rode north from Frederick through the night to take command of the Michigan Cavalry Brigade in the daylight hours of June 29, which was only four days before his greatest challenge on July 3.[1]

He could not have been more proud of himself and his men, who were highly motivated and eager for a fight with Johnny Reb, while longing for "the whole rebel army" to be near.[2] As Custer revealed in a letter to a family member, who was astounded—like almost everyone else—by the young man's rapid rise to a brigadier general's rank, "I have certainly great cause to rejoice [because] I am the youngest General in the U.S. Army by over two years. . . . My brigade is composed entirely of Michigan troops except my Artillery which belongs to the regular Army."[3]

Ironically, a good many of his Michigan men were not initially impressed with Custer, who was now the army's youngest general, because of his youth and inexperience in commanding a brigade. Corporal James Henry Avery, 5th Michigan Cavalry, described how "our boy General Custer first took command of the Michigan Brigade" and hardly appeared worthy of command.[4] In the words of one Michigan trooper: "It was here that the brigade first saw Custer. . . . I heard a voice new to me, directly in rear of the portion of the line where I was, giving directions for the movement in clear, resonant tones, and in a calm confident manner, at once resolute and reassuring. Looking back to see whence it came, my eyes were instantly riveted upon a figure only a few feet distant, whose appearance amazed if it did not for the moment amuse me. It was he [Custer] who was giving the orders. At first, I thought he might be a staff officer, conveying the commands of his chief."[5] Meanwhile, other Michigan men laughed to themselves and joked when beyond Custer's hearing, while asking, "Who is the child?" and "Where is his nurse?"[6] All in all, it was not a very encouraging beginning for the upstart brigadier general, but Custer knew that he must prove himself more than ever before.

Meanwhile, the slaughter of July 2 had left both armies exhausted from the bitter combat that had raged fiercely over the possession of fields, dark woodlots, and rocky hills, especially Little Round Top on the southern end of the battle line. But only the infantry and artillery on both sides had taken a beating on this bloody Thursday, when Lee had hoped to destroy Meade's army by turning his left on the south. All the while, the opposing cavalry of both sides had been spared the terrible bloodletting that had unmercifully culled the ranks on the second day. Brigadier General John Buford's First Division of Pleasonton's Cavalry Corps had been ordered to the rear to refit and to lick its wounds, after having fought tenaciously to buy precious time on July 1, allowing the first of Meade's infantry to reach the field. After a job well done on the first day, Buford's men departed the field for additional participation in the battle just before noon on the morning of July 2. And of course Stuart's cavalry had arrived late on July 2 and had yet to strike a blow.[7]

Around noon on July 2, Brigadier General David McMurtrie Gregg's Second Cavalry Division, a third of Pleasonton's Cavalry Corps of three divisions, had taken a guardian position to protect Meade's right-rear east of Gettysburg. But as he fully realized, Gregg's immediate forces were too small for this assignment because of recent skirmishing in this area on the afternoon of July 2, indicating that this was a strategic place worth fighting for, and because one of his three brigades was still off in the rural countryside of western Maryland to protect a supply depot located a good distance from Gettysburg.

Therefore, just before midnight, General Pleasonton had wisely ordered Brigadier General Judson Kilpatrick's Third Cavalry Division of two brigades, including Custer and his Michigan Brigade, to ride south from its position at Huntersrown to link with and reinforce Gregg, who was Kilpatrick's superior by right of seniority, to protect the Army of the Potomac's rear, which "was considered vulnerable to assault by either J.E.B. Stuart or his infantry comrades" of Ewell's Second Corps.[8]

Demonstrating his usual wisdom, General Meade, who possessed a low opinion of cavalrymen in general and Pleasonton specifically, wanted to keep his "glorified staff officer," in his ever-critical opinion, close to the army's rear for protection just in case Lee planned to perform the tactical tricks for which he was famous, most recently at Chancellorsville.[9]

Fortunately, a "special" correspondent for the *Detroit Free Press* accompanied Custer and his Michigan Cavalry Brigade men (hence this article's subject heading, "From the Michigan Cavalry") at this phase of the Gettysburg campaign, and his revealing account of the campaign and battle was published in the July 15, 1863, edition of this newspaper and not in any book until the publication of this current book in 2019. How long this journalist, identified only as "A" at the end of his column, was with the Wolverines is not known. His account is important because it is basically a letter that was penned on the day after the battle, July 4, when everything was still fresh and clear in his mind, unlike some of the postwar memoirs that were written long after the war and often strayed from the facts. Riding with the men of the Michigan Brigade, the journalist wrote how "we marched all night" and through the darkness on the early morning of Friday, July 3.[10]

Indeed, throughout the warm Pennsylvania night that was the last for a good many Michigan men, Custer's Wolverine Brigade led the way for Kilpatrick's Third Cavalry Division on the ride south from Hunterstown. With Custer at the head of the column, the troopers rode across the York Road and then the Hanover Road, while steadily moving south down the length of the rear of the Army of the Potomac, whose troops were now transfixed in high-ground defensive positions anchored on Cemetery Hill, Culp's Hill, and Cemetery Ridge. Meade was holding to precious high ground with a tenacious grip, knowing that Lee was going to throw everything he had available at the battered Army of the Potomac on July 3.

Not long before the red sunrise of July 3, Custer and his weary troops, along with the rest of Kilpatrick's Division, finally halted their trek south at a dusty crossroads, where a hostelry stood and was known as Two Taverns on the Baltimore Pike. Here, southeast of Gettysburg, halfway between Gettysburg and Littlestown, seven miles south of Hunterstown, and almost directly east of the Round Tops at the southern end of Meade's lengthy and overly extended battle line based on Cemetery Ridge, the sore Michigan men finally got off their horses, which were in need of rest and fodder.

At this obscure place named for two ramshackle buildings seemingly situated in the middle of nowhere, General Kilpatrick's weary troopers were united with Gregg's cavalrymen, who were encamped in the open fields nearby on both sides of the turnpike. The special correspondent of the *Detroit Free Press* wrote how Custer's troopers had pushed south "all night and effected a junction with our troops at daylight on Friday morning" to gain this remote position behind Meade's line. Because the call to duty could happen at any moment depending on where the next threat emerged, orders were issued for the bluecoat cavalrymen to keep their horses saddled.

After gaining only about two hours of rest, in the early morning light, young buglers in blue at last aroused the dust-stained troopers of Kilpatrick's Division to their feet, when the day's heat and humidity were already on the rise. On the warm morning of July 3, Pleasonton ordered Kilpatrick's men of Brigadier General Elon John Farnsworth's First Brigade of four regiments, Third Cavalry Division, to ride west to protect the army's left-rear and support Meade's defensive lines behind the twin elevations, Big Round Top and Little Round Top. As mentioned, these high-ground positions anchored the left of Meade's sprawling battle line. Little Round Top was located just north of the higher elevation—its twin—covered in timber, and commanded the valley of Plum Run to the west. As usual and in keeping with his personality, Kilpatrick was in a great hurry to prove himself on the last day at Gettysburg, and Farnsworth's weary men led the way to the new assignment at the southern end of Meade's sprawling battle line.

Custer had been alerted because he had been ordered shortly to follow the First Brigade, Kilpatrick's Third Division and his troopers. However, the Michigan men continued to sleep and rest in thankful repose after having been on the move and fighting since June 29. But as fate would have it, Custer and his boys of the Second Brigade, Third Cavalry Division, were not going west with Kilpatrick to the southern end of Meade's overextended battle line as expected with its sister brigade on this day of destiny.

Proving that he was a smart, innovative thinker, Gregg balked at the new instructions to follow Kilpatrick. Gregg knew that the Two Taverns position on the Baltimore Road and the southern end of the battle line were the wrong places for his troopers. He believed correctly that the Hanover Road sector, where he had skirmished with the Rebels on the previous day, to the north, was the most important position because it guarded a more strategic location in Meade's right-rear, which were his original orders before having been directed to move west with Kilpatrick to the southern end of the battle line.

With prophetic insight gained in part from skirmishing during the previous afternoon, Gregg was still worried about the sector west of the Low Dutch Road and the threat closer to Gettysburg that was almost sure to come from that direction. Gregg possessed an intimate sense that the key to the upcoming fight in the army's rear was about to be waged over the possession of the critical intersection of the Hanover and Low Dutch Roads.

He also knew that his men were exhausted and still needed to rest from a long campaign that had been most demanding on troopers and horses. Most of all, Gregg wisely realized that he needed to maintain his advanced position to the north instead of heading south. In consequence, he also knew that he required a good many more men to adequately guard Meade's right-rear at this key point of the vital intersection because of the enemy's activity in this area during the past twenty-four hours.

In consequence, Gregg was determined to delay in carrying out his order, to buy time so that he remained sufficiently close to the strategic crossroads to orchestrate its protection. He then wisely sent a courier to Major General Pleasonton's headquarters on Cemetery Hill to emphasize his different tactical thinking based on existing realities in his front to the commander of the newly formed cavalry corps. Most of all, General Gregg knew that he could not afford to miscalculate or make a tactical mistake based on any erroneous opinion or the folly of overconfidence, especially when so much was at stake.

Commanding the Second Division, General Gregg then received a response from Pleasonton by messenger that emphasized how he had to adhere to orders, but he could order one of Kilpatrick's brigades to eventually move north with them and then replace him on the right-rear, which was his ultimate destination. As fate would have it, Custer and his troopers were the only men available at Two Taverns at this time, because Kilpatrick and Farnsworth's brigade, even some of Custer's foremost troopers, had already moved west to protect the army's left flank and were absent from Two Taverns since just after daylight on July 3.

But fortunately for the Union in regard to the upcoming defense of the strategic intersection of the Hanover and Low Dutch Roads in Meade's right-rear, Custer and his foremost men had not yet moved out of Two Taverns, located on the Baltimore Turnpike, in following Kilpatrick on the ride to the southern end of Meade's army, when one of Gregg's aides suddenly arrived. He had been dispatched by the general to search for any available reinforcements for the upcoming defense of the strategic crossroads in Meade's right-rear. The messenger reached Two Taverns in the early morning light of the third day with Pleasonton's orders for Kilpatrick to reinforce Gregg with a brigade.

Despite his recent head injuries suffered at Hunterstown when he had led the charge of a small number of troopers of the 6th Michigan Cavalry and was unhorsed in a close brush with death, Custer made a bold decision on his own: He would remain in place to serve under Gregg and the Second Cavalry Division and not his own Third Cavalry Division commander, Kilpatrick, who was a good distance away by this time. Custer decided not to obey the orders of his own division commander to rejoin his own command, because he was convinced that he was needed in a more crucial sector. As fate would have it, Custer's main force had been in column and about to move out to join Kilpatrick, and only his foremost troopers had ridden away when Gregg's messenger had arrived at Two Taverns.

In overall strategic terms, Custer entirely agreed with Gregg's tactical thinking and smart initiative to protect the army's right-rear in the Hanover Road sector—specifically the strategic intersection of the Hanover and Low Dutch Roads, where Gregg had skirmished with the Rebels on the previous afternoon—about three miles east of Gettysburg, which was absolutely vital to hold on to with a tight grip. Revealing exactly why the insightful Pleasonton had originally promoted such a young and inexperienced man to the rank of brigadier general, Custer was full of fight and desired to meet the enemy— Stuart's much-touted cavaliers—as soon as possible at the most strategic point in the army's right-rear.

Far from the stereotypical image of the emotion-driven and thoughtless fighter with the instinct of a fighting gamecock, Custer's clearheaded and wise decision to remain with Gregg and follow the fortunes of the Second Cavalry Division—instead of his own Third Cavalry Division—revealed the extent of his analytical abilities and tactical insights instead of a case of mindlessly following orders. He would not rejoin his division under Kilpatrick while the climactic showdown was brewing in another sector. Consequently, Custer "was eager for action, and he sensed that more of it was waiting north than in any other direction," where a crucial defense of Meade's vulnerable right-rear was required.[11]

In this regard, and as would be demonstrated throughout this day of destiny, Custer's overall strategic thinking process and tactical instincts were right on target, revealing that he possessed an amount of good sense and insight that exceed the average young man of twenty-three.[12] Clearly, Custer was precocious and farsighted when it came to his battlefield instincts; quite simply, he was now thinking much more like a brigade commander instead of a staff officer. Serious trouble was on the horizon to the north—not the south—as Custer realized, because, in the words of the *Detroit Free Press* reporter who published his words under the heading "From the Michigan Cavalry," this increasingly hot Friday "was ushered in by heavy cannonading on both sides."[13] Everyone on both sides seemed to instinctively realize that today would be the day that would separate victor from loser in the largest battle ever fought on the North American continent, because Lee was bound to unleash his maximum offensive effort on this final day.

But significantly, this Michigan journalist who was riding with Custer's column explained why Custer's decision, to move northeast from Two Taverns on the Baltimore Turnpike and closer to Gettysburg because of the extent of the formidable tactical challenge that lay ahead at a critical location—the intersection of the Hanover and Low Dutch Roads—that had to be protected at all costs, was so crucial: "Our brigade with one [horse artillery] battery of eight guns was expected to meet and check the enemy's attempt to flank us which we had reason to believe he intended to do."[14]

Perhaps historian James S. Robbins said it best in regard to the overall strategic situation at this time because Stuart and his cavalry were shortly "moving south steadily, nearing Gregg's position [and] Stuart's plan was to swing around the Union right and descend in their rear between the Hanover Road and the Baltimore Pike, to disrupt and divert attention, support Pickett's attack and reduce Meade's freedom of action. Even should Longstreet's assault [Pickett's Charge] fail, penetrating the Union line would have serious consequences."[15]

Most importantly, Custer had made his personal decision to defy Kilpatrick's orders, and he would not rejoin his superior and his own division on the final day at Gettysburg. Instead, he planned to ride northeast from the little, dusty crossroads known as Two Taverns, and he would stick to this bold leadership decision to the last based on the premise that the strategic crossroads was about to become a major bone of contention. Sensing that he was about to engage in the fight of his life in protecting the vulnerable right-rear of Meade's army, Custer hurriedly recalled his foremost Michigan troopers, who had already ridden west with Kilpatrick and Farnsworth to protect Meade's left flank in supportive fashion behind the Round Tops.

On a more immediate level, Custer basked in the glow that he finally possessed his entire brigade of four regiments, and that his Wolverines, who always fought better when together as one to reveal a high level of state pride, were united for the great challenge that lay ahead. Buglers in blue had no need to sound the call of "Boots and Saddles," because Custer's men were already in column and ready to move out. Eager for action and highly motivated, the Wolverines of the 1st, 5th, 6th, and 7th Michigan Cavalry were ready to follow their young brigade commander to hell and back if necessary.

Sensing that he was about to play a key role in the largest battle ever fought on the North American continent despite being promoted to brigadier general and appointed to command a brigade only a few days earlier on a date (June 29) that he never forgot, Custer wasted no time because he knew that time was of the essence. On Custer's orders, the Michigan troopers moved out and headed northeast up the dusty Baltimore Road (the key road Stuart needed to gain to strike Meade's rear after he captured the intersection of the Hanover and Low Dutch Roads) and closer to Gettysburg for their greatest challenge to date—the army's vulnerable right-rear that needed to be guarded from wily veteran Confederate cavalrymen, the best of the Army of Northern Virginia, who were long known to have cunning tricks up their sleeves.

Without sufficient rest and riding worn horses from a long and arduous campaign, Custer led the way northeast instead of west and instead of following Kilpatrick (his own division commander) to the army's left flank as expected by his superior who led the Third Cavalry Division. He rode before his vanguard regiment, the mostly Grand Rapids boys of the reliable 6th Michigan under the command of darkly handsome Colonel Russell A. Alger. Custer headed northeast to reach the strategic intersection of the Hanover and Low Dutch (or Salem Church) Roads, which he and Gregg knew had to be guarded at all costs. After all, this key crossroads was situated closer to Gettysburg, strategically located in Meade's right-rear, and was more strategic than any crossroads to the south, because Stuart needed to possess it to gain the Baltimore Pike and then strike into Meade's rear.[16]

After they had enjoyed their morning coffee and hardtack and a short rest, the men of the Michigan Brigade, in the words of one 5th Michigan Cavalry trooper, were in relatively good shape, while pushing north with Custer leading the way. After the recent march through the Pennsylvania night, they had caught precious hours of much-needed rest while "on the ground to sleep with guns in hand, and without shelter [but] many of whom were to awake [on the morning of July 3] for the last time on earth," and were destined to find a final resting place in Adams County, Pennsylvania.[17]

Meanwhile, while Brigadier General Elon John Farnsworth's men, First Brigade, Kilpatrick's Third Cavalry Division,

> began to deploy in positions selected for them [on the army's left-rear] by Pleasonton's aides, Kilpatrick searched frantically for Custer and could not find him. What had happened to Custer and his entire brigade? Kilpatrick was exasperated.
>
> With the exception of an advance guard that had closed up in Farnsworth's rear, the bulk of the Second Brigade had effectively disappeared as far as Kilpatrick was concerned. It is not known how long it took Kilpatrick to learn about what exactly had lured away almost 2,500 horsemen and a battery of light [horse] artillery

of his entire Second Brigade, Third Division. Instead, Custer's bold decision not to follow Brigadier General Farnsworth, who commanded Kilpatrick's First Brigade as one of the promising "Young Turks," "would prove decisive to Meade's ability to remain at Gettysburg long enough to fight Lee to a conclusion, assured that his army's right flank and rear were protected from attack and overthrow."[18]

Custer was long gone from Two Taverns and on his own contrarian mission that he correctly believed was more important in overall strategic terms than whatever might transpire on the southern end of Meade's battle line. Quite simply, Custer had successfully confronted his first true leadership dilemma in regard to obeying the proper orders or doing what he believed was right. Custer was convinced that he was doing right, adhering to his motto: "Be sure you're right, to go ahead" with what you know to be correct.[19] And

Custer was right on target in his overall analysis of the strategic and tactical situation, because one of the greatest threats to the Army of the Potomac's rear was about to emerge in Meade's right-rear.

## DESTINY CALLS AT A STRATEGIC CROSSROADS IN MEADE'S REAR

In regard to his rapid rise in the ranks to brigade commander, Custer had early on philosophically reasoned about the inevitable added pressure and the greatest leadership challenge of his life by emphasizing with sincere modesty, "I don't know whether or not I am worthy of such promotion; but if they give it to me, I promise that you shall hear of me."[20] Therefore, as noted, Custer had much to prove to himself on the third day at Gettysburg, because doubts among his own men, especially among older officers, lingered, until he demonstrated his tactical gifts as a battlefield commander. But Custer was not lacking in confidence in the face of this stern challenge, because he was determined to not only do his best, but also to make a name for himself.[21]

The afternoon of July 3 was fated to be the day of destiny for Custer and his Wolverine Brigade—a truly elite command—of tough Michigan cavalrymen and a battery of horse artillery, who would exceed his lofty expectations about what these men were capable of achieving on the battlefield. Fortunately for Custer, he possessed a truly elite group of fighting men, including a good many former lumbermen, frontier types, and rugged farm boys who had helped to tame a frontier land of the West.

For the great challenge that lay ahead, these Michigan men possessed high motivations, and Custer appreciated the truly lethal qualities of the Wolverine Brigade that was in the process of becoming a true killing machine. As fate would have it, and in a rather unusual development, Custer actually commanded a brigade that was more formidable because of the distinctive capabilities of two separate units with well-honed specialized qualities—the command's best combat capabilities that he was destined to exploit in full on July 3. The 1st and 7th Michigan Cavalry were two commands—one experienced and the other green, respectively—that had been trained and schooled in the art of launching cavalry saber attacks in the style of the finely uniformed cavalrymen of the Napoleonic era, while the 5th and 6th Michigan Cavalry were armed with fast-firing repeating rifles, which made them ideal dismounted fighting men, who could buy precious time when on the tactical defensive.

All in all, these two strengths—perfectly divided and represented by two regiments each—bestowed Custer with a distinct advantage in the form of an inordinate degree of tactical flexibility in the crucial defense of the strategic crossroads, because he could utilize to the maximum advantage each hard-hitting specialty—either the saber charge or a fast-firing dismounted cavalry—depending on the exact tactical situation, the most pressing tactical requirement, and whatever threat he faced. In consequence, Custer's tactics on July 3 would expertly blend the strengths of both of these combat specialties depending on the tactical situation and the circumstances that confronted him, while also acting like an astute artillery commander by directing orders to his brigade's horse artillery under Captain Alexander Cummings McWhorter Pennington. Appropriately, Pennington was an old West Point classmate and good friend of the new brigade commander.

Even the popular nickname of Custer's hard-fighting brigade was most appropriate because of the ferocity of the powerful and deadly predator, the wolverine, which roamed the depths of the hardwood northern forests with a confident swagger and lethality that was all its own. A member of the weasel family that is fierce and agile when under threat, the feisty wolverine was known to fight off all challengers, even attacking the most dominant and powerful predators, from black bears to grizzly bears, with its ferocious qualities. In much the same way, the high-spirited troopers of the Michigan Brigade were equally ferocious and resourceful when it came to battling Stuart and his men, allowing their never-say-die qualities to rise to the fore.

Significantly for the July 3 showdown, Custer was the ideal leader of these excellent fighting men from Michigan, because he was a perfect match in regard to fighting spirit, high motivation, and determination to succeed at any cost. A 6th Michigan Cavalry captain of the Michigan Brigade described his new brigade commander, who had suddenly arrived on June 29 to take charge of the Second Brigade, Third Cavalry Division, like an experienced brigade commander: "An officer superbly mounted . . . tall, lithe, active, muscular, straight as an Indian and as quick in his movements, he had the fair complexion of a school girl."[22]

But Custer's handsomeness and placid fair features disguised the heart of a die-hard commander and true holy warrior when it came to meeting the enemy on the battlefield. And the Michigan Cavalry Brigade skeptics, mostly jealous officers who were older, learned of the extent of the difference between his almost girlish looks and his fierce fighting qualities at Gettysburg. Ironically, this general impression of Custer by this amused 6th Michigan Cavalry captain was much the same as when he had been an east central Ohio schoolteacher without prospects or a bright future, and one of his students, an admiring Sara McFarland, was envious of Custer's good looks. She never forgot "what a pretty girl he would have made."[23]

But as noted, Custer's boyish good looks were most deceiving. Custer was not only a tenacious fighter, but also a killer with keen and well-honed killing instincts. He had already personally taken the lives of Confederate soldiers in this war, and he viewed these killings of his fellow man as little more than sporting events in which one's manhood was proven according to an ancient warrior ethos. But his greatest opportunity at engaging in close-range combat was yet to come. Custer was destined to be bestowed with an open battleground on July 3 that was ideal for leading cavalry charges like the kind he had read about during the Napoleonic Wars, and he would make the most of his opportunity.[24]

Ironically, Major General Winfield Scott, the old hero of the War of the 1812 and the Mexican-American War and who had commanded all Union armies in the conflict's beginning, had early emphasized what proved entirely untrue at the third day at Gettysburg: "Owing to the broken and wooded Character of the terrain in the field of operations and improvement of rifled weapons, the role of cavalry will be secondary and unimportant."[25] Mirroring the views of European military experts and top American theorists of war, Scott—who had conquered Mexico City in September 1847 in a war in which cavalry was underutilized while following the same route west of the Spanish conquistadors under Hernando Cortez when they had vanquished the Aztec Empire—could not have been more wrong in regard to the upcoming cavalry showdown on July 3.

The dramatic cavalry clash in the Army of the Potomac's rear on the East Cavalry Field in which Custer was destined to play the leading role was to be decided in the open fields and a broad plain like on the European battlefields of old, when Napoleon's cavalrymen, the finest horsemen in all Europe, under Marshal Murat, had become legendary for their outstanding performances and long string of successes.

Generations of European observers, revealing their own cultural bias if not arrogance, generally looked down on Americans as cavalrymen in this war, believing that these New World fighting men were culturally, if not biologically, averse to relying on the cold steel of sabers like the more finely uniformed cavalrymen of the Napoleonic era, especially Murat's famous horse soldiers. Of course, the inference was that the American fighting man lacked courage compared to the European fighting man. After all, the average American troopers certainly looked and acted entirely unlike the much-touted European cavalryman who had ridden to glory into the pages of European history. Europeans considered the American cavalryman of the Civil War to be decidedly inferior in overall quality in tactical terms because they were basically nothing more than mounted infantrymen, who preferred to fight dismounted and to rely on firearms instead of the sweeping cavalry and saber charges to deliver the decisive blow to win the day—an entirely incorrect analysis based on European prejudices that ran deep in part because of the romantic legacies and glories of the Napoleonic past.

For the first time in the largest battle ever fought on the North American continent, the cavalry of both armies were on the field and ready for the final showdown on the all-important last day to decide which side would emerge as the ultimate victor. At this crucial time, the mauled Army of the Potomac was hanging on to the high ground—Cemetery Ridge, Culp's Hill, and Cemetery Hill—for dear life after having suffered heavy losses on the first two days. Most of all, General Meade knew that Lee would not only continue but also maximize his offensive efforts for the third straight day, and they would be even more powerful than on July 2.

But now this Friday of July 3 was different than the previous day, because the cavalry of both armies were about to play a leading role for the first time, and not as dismounted cavalry like Buford's bluecoat troopers on July 1. Instead, in the Army of the Potomac's rear and contrary to the beliefs of European soldiers and observers who were considered the top experts, the cavalrymen on both sides were about to rely largely on sabers to decide the day, when so much was at stake, almost as if it was 1805 or 1812 during the heyday of the Grande Armee instead of more than a half century later in 1863.[26]

Indeed, because of Gregg's and Custer's determination to protect the strategic crossroads in Meade's right-rear, the stage was being set for the final cavalry showdown on a sweltering Friday that was destined to make the largest cavalry clash of the war seem entirely insignificant, because so much less had been at stake during the showdown at Brandy Station. In General Meade's words that hinted of a sense of relief because he could now worry less about the safety of his army's rear on the final climactic day: "By the night of July 2 the whole of the available Federal and Confederate cavalry had either closed in or was closing in on Gettysburg, the major portion of each being actually on the field" for the first time.[27]

Only recently in his journal that revealed the extent of the regiment's confidence in their own abilities and combat capabilities, a corporal of Custer's Michigan Cavalry Brigade, James Henry Avery, 5th Michigan Cavalry, recorded the high level of fighting spirit among these crack Michigan troopers: "We wished the whole rebel army was near, so that our Fifth Michigan Cavalry could whip them, and end the war right there."[28] Corporal Avery had no idea that he and other Wolverines were about to get the opportunity to deny Lee and Stuart the possibility of winning it all on the third day at Gettysburg.

Indeed, Custer and his Michigan men were destined to be presented with an opportunity to fulfill some of that lofty ambition, as emphasized by

Corporal Avery on July 3. And, after the recent organizational reforms that had made the Union cavalry more formidable, as had been demonstrated at Brandy Station, Custer was shortly to be handed an opportunity to truly shine in unprecedented fashion in defense of a vital crossroads, because these timely and much-needed changes granted "great freedom and responsibility" to aggressive commanders in the field, where his tactical abilities and talents could rise to the fore. And Custer was the epitome of an aggressive commander, whose hard-hitting style was equaled by few others.[29]

Likewise, Stuart also possessed a great opportunity to thwart the tactical mission and goals—the defense of the strategic crossroads to protect Meade's rear—of the Union cavalry on the third day, because he would be presented with the chance to redeem himself with the kind of sparkling success that would make everyone forget about Brandy Station and the recent raid that had been barren of results. Stuart's chance was finally about to come at long last, and he was determined to make the most of the opportunity that would be presented to him—ironically, much like Custer, who thought the same way in regard to taking full advantage of what was presented to him on the battlefield. In his official report after the battles of the 1862 Peninsula Campaign that had threatened Richmond, Stuart revealed his sense of frustration in having been presented with no opportunity for unleashing an "overwhelming charge" that might have won the day.[30] And now on July 3, he was about to gain that long-awaited opportunity to win it all by employing the aggressive tactics he loved most.

Indeed, General Stuart embraced his greatest opportunity to reap battlefield glory by unleashing an overwhelming charge into Meade's vulnerable rear with four brigades of cavalry, supported by four batteries and a section of Louisiana artillery from Ewell's Second Corps, on the war's most important day. But ironically, as fate would have it, July 3 was destined to be the most inept and poorly managed battle by Stuart at the worst possible time for the fate of the army and the Confederacy.[31]

But Stuart remained confident in part because he was unaware of the extent of his own deficiencies and liabilities. In a Napoleon-like axiom, Stuart also firmly believed that "he who brings on the field the last cavalry reserve wins the day." And now as Lee had ordered on the night of July 2, Stuart was about to find himself in the exact situation and position—northeast of Gettysburg and within easy striking distance of the Union rear—when it mattered most, since this was the Army of Northern Virginia's last best chance to win it all, a classic case of now or never for the South's primary eastern army.[32] In the words of one historian with a PhD, General Stuart was focused on making the attempt "to slide around Brig. Gen. David Gregg's division, plus Brig. Gen. George A. Custer's brigade," to strike Meade's rear.[33]

Best of all, Stuart planned to charge into Meade's rear to catch the bluecoats by surprise with thousands of veteran cavalrymen, who were bolstered by two batteries of the Stuart Horse Artillery Battalion and other guns of veteran artillerymen. The evolution of modern weaponry, especially the rifled musket that had made the outdated smoothbore musket obsolete, had greatly enhanced firepower until the reality existed that almost any cavalry assault against veteran infantry, especially if in defensive positions on high ground, was doomed even before it was launched.

But such was not the case in regard to Stuart's plans on the third day at Gettysburg. Cavalry charges against seasoned infantrymen in good defensive positions were suicidal, and such headlong attackers were early broken up by concentrated musket and cannon fire, especially by defenders poised on dominant terrain. If he could vanquish the Union cavalry if any were found defending the strategic crossroads in Meade's right-rear, which was sure to be protecting Meade's right, and according to the bold plan developed by him and Lee at the Widow Thompson house on Seminary Ridge, then Stuart would face no Union commands, especially entrenched Federal troops facing westward, to receive his charge to the east. Indeed, Stuart could strike Meade's defenders from the rear by riding across the open and gently rolling terrain that lay in Cemetery Ridge's rear, including where Pickett's Charge had targeted the defensive line—the long-sought and much-needed recipe for the sweetest and most decisive of Southern victories.[34]

## A FORGOTTEN BUT DEEP BOND

It made perfect sense that Stuart and Lee, both proud Virginians and West Pointers, had developed a bold tactical plan at the Thompson house that was based largely on the common belief of both biased men that Virginia troops, both infantry and cavalry, were superior fighting men: infantry (Pickett's three Old Dominion brigades) to strike from the front and mostly Virginia cavalry to strike from behind to deliver a one-two punch.

Another forgotten factor also called for a unified offensive effort by Virginia infantry and cavalry, which would be largely an Old Dominion understanding to win decisive victory for their Virginia-born commanders, both Lee and Stuart, on July 3: deep-seated bonds that had long existed between the Virginians of Pickett's Division and the mostly Virginians of not only Stuart's cavalry but also the Virginia batteries of his horse artillery battalion. In regard to these Old Dominion units, relatives and close friends maintained a close-knit network based on pride in state and loyalty to Virginia, despite serving in different branches—Pickett's infantry regiments and Stuart's cavalry and artillery.

As a true-blue Virginian who always looked at things from a Virginia perspective that often resulted in a routine dismissal of the importance of non-Virginia commands and leaders and other regions of the Confederacy, especially the western theater, Lee's ambitious offensive plan called for the dramatic meeting of Virginians: Stuart from the rear and Pickett from the front on Cemetery Ridge after piercing Meade's center. This crucial point—the key to decisive victory—was emphasized by historian and distinguished professor Emory M. Thomas. He stressed exactly what Lee and Stuart envisioned with clarity in what would be a glorious Virginia-first victory that would have changed the course of the Civil War if Generals "Pickett and Stuart would have shaken hands on Cemetery Ridge and prepared to destroy portions of Meade's army at their leisure."[35]

Friends and relatives in both the enlisted ranks and the officer corps existed in large numbers in Pickett's Division and Stuart's Cavalry Corps. The bond was extremely close between the men of both commands (one infantry and one cavalry). Therefore, a good many men often transferred between the two Old Dominion commands because of the kinship and familial feeling among these combat units. In general, this tight bond that bound the Pickett and Stuart commands seemed to be stronger among the officer corps than the enlisted ranks. A former member of the 6th Virginia Cavalry, Captain James Skinner Oden had served on the staff of General Richard B. Garnett's Virginia Brigade of Pickett's Division before his transfer as captain and assistant quartermaster in the Stuart Horse Artillery in mid-June 1863.[36]

Another favorite officer, Lieutenant Alexander Robinson Boteler Jr., served on the staff of General James L. Kemper, who commanded another one of the Old Dominion brigades of Pickett's Division at Gettysburg. He began a career with the Stuart Horse Artillery after the bloodletting at Gettysburg.[37] And artilleryman William Remsen Lyman had formerly served on General Garnett's staff before becoming an adjutant to Major James Williams Breathed, who commanded the 1st Stuart Horse Artillery of Virginia guns on July 3, 1863.[38]

Other close links that existed between Stuart's cavalry and Pickett's Division abounded in the past to strengthen this familial bond of extreme closeness, forging a natural link between the two commands that would pay dividends on the battlefield on July 3 if they acted in conjunction as planned by the Virginia leadership. William Willis Blackford, the first adjutant of Stuart's 1st Virginia Regiment, was proud of the fact that his brother, Launcelot M. Blackford, served in the ranks of the 24th Virginia Infantry, Pickett's Division.[39]

## HORSE ARTILLERY BATTALION WITH A LEGENDARY REPUTATION

What has been most overlooked by historians about Stuart's potential impact of delivering a powerful blow into the Union rear on July 3, as Lee and Stuart envisioned with tactical clarity at the Thompson house, were the combat capabilities and firepower of his formidable artillery arm that was a natural extension of his cavalry arm, a symbiotic relationship that paid high dividends on the field of battle, which was partly a lesson that Stuart had learned during the Mexican-American War. Especially in 1846 during the early battles along the Rio Grande River, American "flying artillery" had helped to win the day by playing key roles. Napoleon had been the master in the art of effectively employing "flying artillery," and this was not forgotten by Stuart's gunners, who took great pride in their work.

Stuart's horse artillerymen, under the command of capable Major Robert Franklin Beckham, who was a West Pointer, possessed a distinctive esprit de corps of their own, not unlike the Virginians of Pickett's Division, because they gained a reputation for aggressiveness and audacity in the tradition of "flying artillery," hard-hitting qualities that were especially needed for an audacious attack into Meade's rear, because this highly mobile artillery arm was best utilized and most effective in the tactical offensive. It has been estimated that the Stuart Horse Artillery, which possessed more than 2,200 members from beginning to end, fired more shot, shell, and canister than any other artillery command during the four years of war. While this fact cannot be proven with a proper degree of accuracy and might be an exaggeration to some degree, what certainly was not an exaggeration was the fact that Stuart's gunners were some of the best and most experienced artillerymen in the Army of Northern Virginia, exactly the kind of capable gunners who could rise to the challenge and wreak havoc on Meade's vulnerable rear, if they ever obtained the golden opportunity.[40]

Modern naysayers, mostly for self-serving reasons and despite what leading historians have written in the past, are still convinced that Stuart had no plan at all to attack the Union rear by emphasizing that the Confederate cavalry arm was too jaded and weak to have made a significant impact. But of course nothing could have been further from the truth. What they have long overlooked is the fact that the Union cavalry arm was exhausted from overuse by the third day.

To support their narrowly focused views based on selective evidence in attempting to make a weak case, they have always overlooked the most powerful firepower asset possessed by Stuart: four seasoned batteries and the section of Louisiana guns. Unfortunately for General Stuart, the other batteries of his guns of the Stuart Horse Artillery were still scattered by the time of the showdown in Adams County, trailing in the army's rear west of Gettysburg. Therefore, none of Stuart's batteries—those with Stuart and those left with Lee—had reached the field of Gettysburg on July 1. But, as noted, for the goal of striking Meade's rear, Stuart possessed two of these batteries on July 2, and Lee had given him two other batteries and the section of Louisiana guns to strengthen his artillery arm for his most daring offensive operation.

The first of Stuart's batteries, under Captain James Franklin Hart, who had advanced in the rear of Major General James Longstreet's First Corps, which brought up the army's rear, arrived on the battlefield on July 2. But this South Carolina unit—known as the Washington Battery—had played only a support role on the second day, while the struggle for the Peach Orchard, where Longstreet's attack succeeded against defenders of the Third Corps, and Little Round Top held by Fifth Corps men, where "Old Bull" Longstreet's attack failed, roared on that bloody afternoon. Likewise, Captain Thomas E. Jackson's Charlottesville "Kanawha" Battery, also with Jenkins's Brigade, played no role on July 2, but Stuart possessed these four guns for the final day and the challenge that lay ahead. Therefore, as fate would have it, the final day at Gettysburg was the only day on which the Stuart Battalion Artillery was destined to play a key role, and it was the most crucial one—in the Army of the Potomac's rear.

Stuart now possessed batteries that had been on his wide-ranging raid and had been recently assigned to him. On the day of decision, Stuart counted on the four 3-inch ordnance rifles of Captain James Williams Breathed's Virginia Battery, 1st Stuart Horse Artillery; Captain William M. McGregor's Virginia Battery, 2nd Stuart Horse Artillery, which included one Blakely gun, two 12-pounder howitzers, and two 3-inch ordnance rifles of Captain Thomas Edwin Jackson's Virginia Battery, Charlottesville Horse Artillery, which had accompanied General Albert G. Jenkins's cavalry brigade to Gettysburg; and an attached section of guns of the Louisiana Battery under Captain Charles A. Green. He also commanded two 10-pounder Parrott rifles of what was commonly called Green's Battery, Louisiana Guard Artillery. As mentioned, Stuart had secured the guns of this Louisiana Guard Battery from Ewell's Second Corps to bolster his long-arm strength.

Most importantly, these were no ordinary artillery batteries but some of the finest horse artillery in the Army of Northern Virginia. Known as "the Hoss," these fast-moving and lethal guns of the Stuart Horse Artillery Battalion had become legendary by the time of the dramatic showdown at Gettysburg. As mentioned, these guns and seasoned artillerymen of the Stuart Horse Artillery Battalion were under the capable overall command of Virginia-born Captain Robert Franklin Beckham, who called Culpeper County home. Unlike Custer, he had compiled a distinguished record at West Point, especially in mastering the toughest courses of engineering.

Therefore, upon graduating from the United States Military Academy "with distinction" in 1859, Beckham ranked high at sixth in his class. Ironically, the young lieutenant was first assigned to the Corps of Topographical Engineers and reported for duty at Detroit (the hometown of quite a few members of Custer's Wolverine Brigade and top officers) to his new superior, a no-nonsense Captain George Gordon Meade. Even more ironic, Beckham had specifically requested of a Confederate congressman not to be assigned to the artillery![41]

But as a strange fate would have it, Beckham had earned the prestigious appointment to command the famed Stuart Horse Artillery Battalion on April 8, 1863, which was less than three months before the climactic showdown at Gettysburg. At that time, the battalion was created to unify the horse artillery under a single organization. But unfortunately for Confederate fortunes on July 3, Beckham was more of a capable organizer and manager than an astute battlefield commander who possessed the necessary degree of daring—like Custer—when it counted the most at Gettysburg. Unfortunately for him, he was additionally hampered by a heavy shadow in having taken the place of the beloved and highly revered former commander of Stuart's Horse Artillery who had been killed just before the Gettysburg campaign's beginning, the incomparable Major John Pelham. Quite simply, Pelham's exploits could never be matched by Beckham, or anyone else for that matter, and he realized as much, which did nothing to enhance his confidence and fuel his motivations.[42]

Unfortunately for Confederate fortunes in regard to striking the Union army's rear on July 3, some of Beckham's top lieutenants of the Stuart Horse Artillery Battalion were as flawed as battlefield commanders as Beckham. Major James Williams Breathed, born at Fruit Hill, Virginia (in today's West Virginia), commanded the 1st Stuart Horse Artillery at Gettysburg by a quirk of fate. When Stuart had first journeyed east by rail to Richmond to offer his services to the Confederate government, he accidently met Breathed, who was a civilian physician in St. Joseph, Missouri, on the train. The young man was eager to serve the South, and he greatly impressed Stuart by his charm and winning ways. He then enlisted as a private in the 1st Virginia Cavalry, which was commanded by Stuart. Breathed had quickly struck up a friendship with Stuart, who proved to be his mentor, while riding the tracks, and this friendship had fueled his rapid rise.

Always ambitious in regard to achieving higher rank, Stuart had early conceived the wise concept to make his cavalry more formidable by creating a horse artillery command. Revealing a more dramatic rise than Custer even, when he gained his rank to brigadier general on June 29, this lowly private (Custer jumped from captain to brigadier general) named Breathed seemed to Stuart to be the ideal man to command the battery, despite the young man's lack of artillery experience. This glaring example has revealed one of Stuart's central weaknesses as a commander, which was a distinct penchant for promoting unqualified friends and close associates to high rank because he liked them personally, which superseded professional qualifications.

Therefore, Stuart had requested that Breathed be promoted to lieutenant so that he could officially command the battery. But before he gained approval from Richmond, Stuart assigned "Lieutenant" Breathed to the command of the 1st Stuart Horse Artillery, which was Stuart's first battery that supported his cavalry arm. Breathed officially gained a captain's rank in September 1862. Clearly, the young physician had been promoted far beyond his abilities and talents because of Stuart's affection for and friendship with him. As noted, Stuart continued to promote friends without the necessary qualifications and experience, including in the quartermaster department of the Stuart Horse Artillery, and this unfortunate trend, which can be described as personal excess, continued year after year.

To his credit, and in part because of his own shortcomings that were destined to be displayed in full on the crucial third day at Gettysburg in Meade's right-rear, Captain Breathed admitted as much. Because of his failures in rising to the challenge on July 3, 1863, and on other fields, he submitted his resignation on September 25, 1863, less than three months after the Battle of Gettysburg, with an honest admission: "I know I can do better service in another 'arm of the service.'" Like his much-touted superior who was still the toast of the South, Breathed had needed to "do better" at Gettysburg.[43]

Captain Breathed was not the only culprit who failed to rise to the challenge of the critical third day. Other top officers of the Stuart Horse Artillery Battalion were unable to perform up to expectations on July 3. Captain William Morrell McGregor, an Alabamian in an artillery corps dominated by Virginians like the Army of Northern Virginia itself, commanded the 2nd Stuart Horse Artillery of Virginia guns. Only in his early twenties, McGregor led his battery that consisted of seasoned men from the Old Dominion. However, like Beckham, he lacked training at a military school, especially West Point, and he had suffered a severe wound on November 10, 1862. McGregor had been a lawyer before the war.

Despite his promotion to captain in February 1863, McGregor was never quite the same after having been wounded, physically and perhaps mentally in terms of trauma that affected him more in part because the war had become more terrible and bloody. He had also seen a good many friends and associates killed in gory fashion during the first half of the war, sights and experiences that were enough to discourage many good fighting men who found themselves trapped in the midst of the bloodiest war in American history. Like Stuart, Captain McGregor had become a victim of the war in this regard, but he continued to gamely fight on with his heart and Scotch-Irish courage.[44]

Captain Thomas Edwin Jackson, born in Fredericksburg, Virginia, commanded the four Virginia guns of the Charlottesville Battery, which was known as Jackson's Battery and the "Kanawha" Battery. At age twenty-eight, which was older than Captain McGregor, Jackson was still young, and he also failed to measure up to high standards for a variety of reasons. Therefore, in the end, the Jackson Battery was "ill prepared" in regard to training and quality of weaponry for the great challenge on the afternoon of July 3.[45]

Nevertheless, the most important mission of Stuart's Horse Artillery was to provide a key "offensive punch" that could provide a knockout blow, especially if blasting away into Meade's rear to wreak havoc.[46] And now Lee had handed Stuart and his men their greatest opportunity to deliver that knockout blow to the Army of the Potomac in his all-out offensive bid to destroy Meade's army, and Stuart's Artillery would naturally play a large role if they came into range of Meade's rear to hit the unprepared Federals from behind.[47]

## LINGERING MISTAKES AND THE GHOSTS OF BRANDY STATION

Ironically, to a degree unseen in the past and on the eve of his most important assignment of the war, General Stuart was no longer the swaggering cavalier who believed that he and his men could do the impossible against any odds, because of the recent vast improvement of Pleasonton's cavalry. On July 3 for General Lee and his army, therefore, a central question now haunted them: Could the legendary Stuart still rise to the challenge and perform up to his full capabilities as in the past, especially after the near disaster at Brandy Station, where he had been caught by surprise and embarrassed to an unprecedented degree? Was the sharp criticism from the Richmond press true about Stuart's shortcomings and that the cavalry arm needed to be reformed, perhaps including even the need for a new commander?[48]

But it was not just the Richmond newspapers that condemned Stuart, who seemed burdened by a dark fate since the campaign's beginning. For instance, the alarmed editor of the *Charleston Mercury*, Charleston, South Carolina, wrote in no uncertain terms, "If any one asks you about the cavalry fight in Culpepper [Brandy Station], tell 'em we were whipped."[49]

Even an amused Lee mentioned Stuart's principal weakness, which was basically a character flaw of a serious nature that might well cost the army dearly in the future. But of course Lee never imagined that Stuart's character flaws might once again play a part in Confederate defeat, especially of a decisive nature. In a letter to his wife about the series of unnecessary reviews that had set the stage for Stuart to suffer his greatest surprise at Brandy Station on that fateful June 9, a somewhat amused General Lee had written how "Stuart was in all his glory."[50]

But could Stuart now once again become the skillful tactician and legendary fighter of old in what was his most important assignment in delivering a decisive blow in the rear of the Army of the Potomac? Was it possible that Stuart might be able to return to his old highly capable self by eliminating his obsessive focus on the meaningless sideshows, gaudy reviews, pretty ladies, and far-flung raids and redirecting it to the serious business at hand, especially the life or death of the nation? Could he finally silence his critics who had grown in number and boldness in their condemnations since he had been caught by surprise at Brandy Station?

No doubt, the stinging words that he had read in the Richmond newspaper that pronounced him to be nothing more than a "vain and weak-headed" commander of the much-overrated cavalry arm because of his excessive flamboyance and love of pomp continued to linger in his mind. Almost certainly Stuart's confidence had been shaken, and new doubts had caused fissures to crack the once impenetrable high levels of overconfidence, because he knew that some ugly truths and flaws had been badly exposed at Brandy Station. Therefore, as if fearing more criticism, Stuart had wisely refused to allow a Richmond reporter to accompany him on the Gettysburg campaign—a wise decision, especially in regard to his crucial mission on July 3.[51]

After his lengthy raid, which had taken him nearly to the outskirts of Washington, DC, and then north all the way to Carlisle, slightly northeast of Gettysburg, in the vain search for Lee's army before the orders were received to ride south to Gettysburg, the combat capabilities of Stuart's cavalry had been reduced by wear and tear. Because the supplies of horses from states in the trans-Mississippi had ended in the summer of 1862, thanks to Union successes, an estimated half of Stuart's horses consisted of "miscellaneous animals gathered from the Pennsylvania farms," a negative portent of events to come.[52]

Indeed, as earlier emphasized by one of Stuart's artillerymen, the Pennsylvania horses, although larger and stronger in general than Southern horses, especially the "delicately shaped" mounts from South Carolina that were smaller than Virginia Piedmont and Shenandoah Valley horses, were quickly jaded and died. In the end, these oversized animals proved "too heavy and cumbersome for rapid movement" and the demands of raiding and the battlefield.[53]

Because of the lengthy raid and eight-day absence from the army, both men and horses of Stuart's command needed a lengthy respite, but there was no time for rest, because the dawn of July 3 was on the horizon. As fate would have it, a series of events had caught up with Stuart and his troopers. Likewise, the Union cavalry was also worn down from arduous service in this lengthy campaign. Nevertheless, it was a classic case of now or never for the Confederacy, and Stuart and his cavalrymen were finally to have their dramatic stage upon which to win glory, because Lee had bestowed upon them a mission of such vital importance. In an understatement, these "misplaced exertions no doubt stressed Stuart['s] men and animals, who needed days of rest before they would be able to recover their peak efficiency."[54]

Likewise, William Willis Blackford, one of Stuart's best staff officers, lamented how after the intense combat at Brandy Station, "from that time the difficulty of getting remounts acted disastrously upon the strength of our cavalry arm, not only in diminishing the numbers but in impairing the spirit of the men. Many of the men knew that when their horses were disabled they could not get others, and this injured their dash."[55]

Significantly this was not the case with Custer's men or any of the more fortunate troopers of the Army of the Potomac, because remounts were easily secured from the government to increase the confidence and "spirit" of the cavalrymen in the ranks. Ironically, even the success in forcing a tactical draw at Brandy Station—actually a notable moral and psychological victory in itself for the Union cavalry—during Stuart's close brush with absolute disaster left a detrimental tactical legacy that was destined to rise to the fore on the afternoon of July 3 in the rear of General Meade's battle line. Lieutenant Cadwallader J. Iredell, 1st North Carolina Cavalry, boasted in a letter that revealed a dangerous delusion that still existed even after the close call at Brandy Station, "We gave the Yankees a [severe] thrashing [and] whenever we got them in the [open] fields out of the woods, we whipped them cleverly with the Sabre!"[56] But in truth Stuart's alleged victory was not only an illusion but also a most costly setback.

Ironically, the Napoleonic concept of a mass of cavalrymen relying on sabers to charge through an opponent had been recently proved not to be completely outdated during the largest cavalry clash of the battle at Brandy Station. As fate would have it, the upcoming fight in Meade's rear on the third day would primarily be yet another clash of cavalry using sabers in a war where there were "only a few engagements in which the saber figured prominently," but in a fight that was far more important in overall strategic terms than what happened at Brandy Station. But the forthcoming all-important cavalry battle in the Army of the Potomac's rear was destined to be the last major battle in which the saber "figured prominently."[57] Significantly, Custer was the principal author and orchestrator of leading two saber charges that stunned Stuart and his men, who never completely recovered from the shock.[58]

Ironically, Custer was fortunate in this regard. The crack 1st Michigan Cavalry, which had been organized before the formation of the Michigan Cavalry Brigade, "was especially formidable in the saber charge."[59] The romantic appeal of the saber charge of the Napoleonic era acted like an intoxicant on both Union and Confederate horsemen, inspiring them to perform with even more fanaticism and heroics on the battlefield. Dashing Captain Peter A. Weber, who commanded Company B, 6th Michigan Cavalry, and who was fated to play a key role on July 3, 1863, but destined to die barely ten days after the East Cavalry Field fight, emphasized not long before his death, "I want a chance to make one saber charge."[60]

Unfortunately for Stuart on July 3, while the overall combat capabilities of the Confederate cavalry arm continued to decline steadily, the overconfidence, born of too many past successes across Virginia, remained alive and well, as if the glorious times had not changed. But it was no longer those same heady days of 1861 and 1862, when high hopes and optimism abounded. At that time of easy victories, the superiority of Stuart's cavalry was the stuff of legend and the talk of the entire South.

But because of his absence from the Army of Northern Virginia on July 1 and July 2, Stuart had now opened himself up to even more criticism than ever before, including in regard to having been surprised at Brandy Station, because Lee had been forced to fight for two days without the benefits of his best cavalryman and his finest cavalry brigades. Major John Cheves Haskell, a South Carolina College (today's University of South Carolina) man, later wrote with bitterness of the common sentiment that was growing throughout the army and at headquarters: "Again, at Gettysburg, there is no doubt but that we suffered for lack of information. Our cavalry did not give us the timely information, or the time to get ready, which was their chief duty. If Stuart, instead of being miles away, had been in position guarding our advance, giving our infantry warning, engaging the enemy and masking our troops until they all got together, there is every reason to think that we might have crushed the enemy [marching north from western Maryland] in detail."[61]

But this opportunity had slipped away because Stuart and the army's finest cavalrymen were not available to the frustrated commander in chief during the first two days of the dramatic showdown at Gettysburg. Historian Noah Andre Trudeau summarized how "Stuart had badly misread the degree of personal connection his superior [Lee] required [to safeguard against this development. Longstreet] had specifically requested that Stuart select an officer whom Lee knew and trusted, Brigadier General Wade Hampton, to coordinate the [four brigades of] cavalry remaining with the army [but] Stuart's failure to comply embittered Longstreet [and he later] would roundly condemn the cavalryman's vainglorious ride" that reaped no results.[62]

## STUART'S DANGEROUS OBSESSION WITH RESTORING HIS DAMAGED REPUTATION

As during his recent raid to deprive Lee and the army of his presence and finest cavalry brigades for the first two days of Gettysburg, so Stuart continued to focus primarily on his own wants and needs even in regard to his new assignment on July 3. This was additional proof that what had happened at Brandy Station was no accident or fluke but occurred because of his obsessions.

His increasing number of critics in the Richmond newspapers had been correct, because Stuart's lofty fame and reputation had exceeded his true abilities, exposing a host of weaknesses and vulnerabilities that were destined to once again rise to the fore on Gettysburg's final day. For good reason, he still felt the sting of what had happened at Brandy Station far more than the previous day's rebuke by General Lee and the wild ride that had taken him away from the army for nearly a week and a half. Stuart's priorities were still distorted because his ego had been so badly inflated for so long, and these were destined to continue to come at the army's expense on July 3, when a sterling performance from him was required for success.[63]

Indeed, by this time, Stuart was most of all determined "to salvage all of his lost glory . . . to rekindle the fires of adoration that had been ignited a year before when he made the first ride around McClellan [and] perhaps he dwelled on the words of the newspapers [critical over his having been caught by surprise at Brandy Station and his near brush with disaster] from mid-June," when criticism of him had reached a new high.[64] Receiving the kind of ridicule that tore at the heart and soul of this sensitive man, Stuart was now mocked for his nickname, the "Knight of the Golden Spurs."[65]

In Captain Charles Minor Blackford's words, which were right on target, Stuart was still obsessed by his heightened "anxiety to 'do some great thing'" in order to clear his name and restore his damaged reputation.[66]

Stuart was now even more motivated, not only because of having been caught by surprise at Brandy Station, but also because of the degree of personal embarrassment, if not humiliation, he had experienced at Lee's headquarters on the night of July 2. Therefore, instead of marching west toward "the sound of the guns"—the most fundamental of all military tenets and the most time-honored axiom of a good soldier—when Pickett's Charge was unleashed, he would remain focused on achieving glory by defeating Union cavalry in a dramatic open-field fight three miles away and far from where he needed to be. Once again, Stuart would continue to be too far away from Lee and his army on the final day of decision when he could have made a great difference in the battle's outcome.[67]

Ironically, this monumental failure that was destined to come on the third day had already been predicted by Stuart's harshest critics, who were steadily growing in number, including some Richmond journalists like Edward Alfred Pollard. Offering sage portents and new realities that could no longer be denied, these prophetic words revealed that the true Stuart by the time of the war's most important campaign had been long ignored, especially by Lee, who continued to hope for the best in regard to the failing abilities of the flamboyant cavalier in the plumed hat. Indeed, "there was [a rising tide of] civilian opinion . . . to the effect that he was a fine soldier but too reckless, gay, and irresponsible, to be trusted with important operations."[68]

And no cavalry operation was more important for Stuart, Lee, the Army of Northern Virginia, and the Confederacy than the crucial mission in Meade's rear on July 3. And in this regard, Pollard's astute observations were destined to prove right on target in regard to the upcoming cavalry showdown on the third day.

With ample numbers of troopers and artillery, Stuart now possessed the key mission of striking the Union rear, by which he might redeem his reputation by winning not only a great success for himself but also for his army and his nation. He continued to lust for just such a dramatic victory to restore his reputation and prestige, which had been tarnished at Brandy Station and by his failure to link with Lee on the first two days at Gettysburg. Therefore, Stuart could not have been more highly motivated to fulfill his key mission and perform up to expectations on the final day, because he was determined to reclaim what he had lost in less than a month during a grueling campaign in which his own leadership failures had reached an all-time high. And Stuart had only himself to blame for his own failures at both Brandy Station and in regard to his recent raid devoid of important results. Even the Richmond newspapers had openly challenged him to perform some future stirring exploit to demonstrate that he rightly deserved his former lofty reputation, which had been so badly damaged by this time.

As directed by Lee during the nighttime conference at headquarters and as noted, Stuart had been ordered to move his troopers into a "position to advance against the enemy's rear, where it was hoped his appearance would divert Federal attention and reinforcements away from the decisive point the Confederates were attacking along Cemetery Ridge."[69] And, as determined on the night of July 2 at the Widow Thompson house headquarters, this high-ground position was on Cress's Ridge, which was located near the strategic intersection of the Hanover and Low Dutch Roads in Meade's right-rear.[70]

Serving in the ranks of the 2nd New York Cavalry, Willard W. Glazier emphasized how Stuart "hoped to break in upon the flank and rear" of the

Army of the Potomac.[71] Modern historian David P. Bridges described how "Stuart's assignment was to ride into the rear of the Army of the Potomac and create confusion when the primary infantry attack [Pickett's Charge] broke through the center."[72] As mentioned, Edwin B. Coddington, one of the most respected Gettysburg historians, penned how General Stuart's key mission was to "at the proper moment swoop down onto [Meade's] rear."[73]

But Stuart's mission involved a great deal more than indicated by these historians. As noted, Professor James M. McPherson, one of America's leading Civil War historians, was right on target when he wrote that Stuart's vital mission was to deliver the "coup de grace" into the Army of the Potomac's rear at a time when it would never be more vulnerable than when Cemetery Ridge's defenders were facing Pickett's Charge.[74] And another respected scholar and expert on the Gettysburg campaign emphasized how Stuart "had consulted with General Lee about operations for July 3 [on the previous night at the Thompson house and] he and Lee worked out a scheme to put Stuart's entire cavalry force in a position from which he could separate the Union cavalry from the main body of the army and at the proper moment swoop down onto its rear."[75]

But as mentioned, a key question still remained and had yet to be answered: Would Stuart be able to return to his old highly capable self of 1861 and 1862, as Lee believed, when he had become famous across the South, or was his near brush with absolute disaster at Brandy Station and the disastrous raid a negative trend that pointed to additional dismal events and subpar performances yet to come? Was what had happened in the open fields of Brandy Station to shock Stuart and his men an anomaly or the new normal? Clearly, Lee believed it was the former, or he would not have ordered Stuart on such a crucial mission on July 3.

But there were increasing numbers of doubters in the ranks because June 9 had been such a close call for Stuart, who barely had time to pull his boots on in the face of a Union cavalry attack at Brandy Station. Ironically, after all he had previously accomplished, Stuart now found himself having to prove himself all over again—no small challenge because the war had changed, having become more brutal and serious. Even one of Stuart's own staff officers was forced to admit the undeniable truth of Brandy Station, which was most disturbing on a number of levels: "Stuart managed badly that day."[76]

And one of his finest brigade commanders, Wade Hampton, whom Lee and the army actually needed to be in charge of the army's cavalry instead of Stuart, as General Longstreet, Lee's top lieutenant and commander of the First Corps, fully realized, openly expressed his strongly held opinions. Therefore, Longstreet's "report [about Brandy Station] bristled with resentment for General Stuart."[77]

By this time and despite Stuart's best efforts to attempt to stop the increasing flow of rumors about the true extent of his poor performance at Brandy Station, the people of the South had experienced a degree of disillusionment and an unprecedented crisis in confidence, having second thoughts about one of the nation's greatest heroes. Even the editor of the *Richmond Enquirer*, Richmond, Virginia, said, "Gen. Stuart has suffered no little in public estimation" because of what happened at Brandy Station.[78]

And this ugly truth and undeniable reality cut like a sharp knife, because, in the words of one Confederate cavalryman who was right on target in his critical analysis of Stuart, who read these words in ever-increasing fury: "I can't imagine anyone more likely to suffer in his own feelings than Gen. Jeb from the withdrawal of that popular applause which he is so fond of sunning himself in."[79]

Indeed, General Stuart possessed a considerable flaw of character that was becoming increasingly exposed to full view to both friend and foe. Lee's famed cavalry leader was still the man of 1861 and 1862, which was no more, just like the once pervasive view that the South could easily win the war.[80]

## CUSTER THE YOUNG DEMOCRAT

Of course this decline in the lofty reputation of the most highly valued cavalry leader of the South was the antithesis of what Custer was experiencing. He was too young and new in his rank to have generated any favorable or unfavorable impression with the northern public at this stage in the Gettysburg campaign, because he had only recently taken command of the Wolverine Brigade. However, the northern public might have been surprised to learn that the newly appointed brigadier general hailed from a staunchly Democratic family and that Custer's political views had long been Democratic. While teaching the pupils of a common school at Beech Point at Athens, eastern Ohio, during the late fall of 1856, Custer was known to have loudly mocked and ridiculed students because of their strong Republican views, including those who were antislavery. He was even known to loudly denounce what Southerners called the radicalism of the "Black Republicans."[81]

Therefore, it was a supreme irony that the young man who was destined to play a key role on the afternoon of July 3 in saving the day in the Army of the Potomac's rear during the most important battle of a war dedicated to slavery's destruction had been in disagreement with extreme Republican views. Even more ironic, Custer's official letter of appointment to the United States Military Academy had been signed by Secretary of War Jefferson Davis, who had now placed all his hopes on his eastern army's chances of winning a decisive victory in Pennsylvania.[82]

Equally ironic, Custer needed to win a dramatic victory of importance on the afternoon of July 3 because his political views were largely those of the Democratic Party. If he was defeated at Gettysburg on the final day of decision, then a Democrat Party past would surely come back to haunt him to derail his military career. As noted, he hailed from a strongly Democratic family, and he had embraced the Democratic faith like his family members, especially his politically outspoken father, Emmanuel, who preferred discussing politics to eating.

Even more, the young and impressible Custer had served on the staff of General George B. McClellan, who openly opposed President Lincoln long before the president removed him from command of the Army of the Potomac—a long overdue decision after the missed opportunities of the Maryland campaign, where McClellan had failed to destroy the reeling Army of Northern Virginia when it was on the ropes after the war's bloodiest day. McClellan was a handsome, charismatic figure, and Custer fell under his spell.

General McClellan's long list of failures cost Custer his coveted position on the staff of "Little Mac" and strengthened his anti-Republican faith, which had existed since his earliest days. Taking McClellan's side could be expected of Custer, who idolized the man who hated Lincoln with an unbridled passion. After all, McClellan was a mentor and friend. Therefore, an upset Custer had unfairly blamed Lincoln and his administration for removing his beloved general who could not win decisive victory. In truth, McClellan, an arrogant elitist, deserved to be sacked for a good many valid reasons that were almost too many to count. In time, McClellan was destined to become the Democratic candidate for the president's reelection bid in November 1864, revealing the depth of his anti-Republicanism and his hatred of Lincoln.

As the war lengthened and became bloodier, to levels unimaginable in 1861, the anti-Republican sentiment in parts of the North grew in strength. The so-called Peace Party, Peace Democrats, or "Copperhead Party" desired a negotiated settlement to end the war that would have resulted in two neighboring republics to fulfill the loftiest of the Confederacy's ambitions. The outspoken head of the Copperhead Party, or the antiwar Democrats, was Clement L. Vallandigham. He hailed from Custer's own home state of Ohio, which was a fact that also tarnished Custer's reputation and image among the high-ranking Republicans in blue uniforms.

Therefore, the depth of Custer's loyalty to the Republicans and the Lincoln administration was still in doubt to some degree by the time of the Gettysburg campaign because the army was so highly politicized by this time, and these hostile forces would rise to the forefront if he failed to win victories. Indeed, whimpers among some high-ranking officers were already circulating in army circles that Custer was a "McClellan Man" and a "Copperhead."[83]

Ironically, one of the enduring myths about Custer's promotion to brigadier general at age twenty-three was that this rapid rise was due to politics in regard to having cleverly orchestrated his promotion, which was certainly not the case. In fact, the opposite was true, because Custer had risen high on his own merits, despite of the omnipresent factor of politics in regard to his strong sympathies with the Democratic Party and McClellan.[84]

At this time, Custer might not have been aware of the fact that one of the fundamental reasons why President Jefferson Davis and Lee had decided on a second invasion of the North was for the express purpose of bestowing new strength on the Peace Democrats by making the war be felt with more severity by the Union, especially the large northeastern cities like Philadelphia, north of the Potomac River. But of course this ambitious invasion was a most risky undertaking, because any defeat suffered by the Army of Northern Virginia might have the opposite effect of eroding the power of the Copperhead Party and strengthening Lincoln's position to prosecute this brutal war to the bitter end. As penned with considerable insight in his diary, George Templeton Strong was correct when he wrote that "unless rebeldom [Army of Northern Virginia] gain some great decisive success, this move of Lee's [north] is likely to do good by bothering and silencing our nasty peace-democracy."[85]

But Lee, Stuart, and their veteran men in gray and butternut never imagined that they might meet with a decisive reversal north of the Potomac River, because they had won too often in the past and still believed in the outdated concept of Southern superiority on all levels. In fact, a badly misplaced sense of optimism in the army's ranks had never been higher, and it had only grown with every mile marched over Pennsylvania soil that was undefended, when the South's colorful banners had flapped in the wind and seemed to herald great things to come. But was the surprise and shock suffered by Stuart at Brandy Station only an aberration or was it a new reality for the cavalryman whom Lee trusted so completely? Of course no one at the time knew the answer to that question before the dramatic showdown on July 3, especially General Lee.

All the while, Stuart and his cavalrymen and horse artillerymen remained confident for success, as if the nasty surprise at Brandy Station at the hands of the much-disparaged Union cavalry, which had been defeated so often in the past, was nothing more than a fluke that would never happen again. But in truth, and what was entirely unimaginable by Stuart, age thirty, and by his seasoned troopers, the performance and combat prowess demonstrated by the enemy troopers, highly motivated and brave young men from across the North, was anything but a fluke: It was a new reality that boded extremely well for the increasingly confident boys in blue, including the high-spirited Wolverines under the leadership of newly minted Brigadier General Custer, age twenty-three.[86]

## LATE MORNING RIDE FROM GETTYSBURG

To ensure achieving a tactical surprise as Generals Stuart and Lee had envisioned back at headquarters in the little stone house on the high ground of Seminary Ridge on the warm night of July 2, the Confederate cavalry, of course, needed to get the early jump on their opponent and ensure that they would not be seen riding into the Army of the Potomac's rear with the intent of causing great mischief. But unfortunately for Stuart, fate worked against his most ambitious plan (actually the Lee-Stuart plan as originally conceived) from the beginning. Stuart's troopers and horses were so exhausted from the lengthy raid almost all the way to Washington, DC, that they could do little more than sleep and rest to regain their strength on the night of July 2, which was the first night's rest they had gotten in eight days.

For a host of reasons, Stuart missed the opportunity to move into the Union army's rear under the veil of darkness just before the red sunrise brightened a war-torn land on Friday, July 3. The sun dawned bright in a clear sky, promising more scorching weather. But Lee's finest cavalry were destined to move out much too late. Stuart had needed darkness to ensure that the line of direction (initially northeast down the York Turnpike) of his lengthy column of thousands of veteran troopers and horse artillery was not ascertained by Meade. But such was not to be.

Consequently, the precious hours of darkness on the night of July 2 passed by like a soft summer dream with no movement of Southern cavalry, almost as if it did not matter if Stuart finally got his men into position by night or by daylight. But of course his move into Meade's right-rear should have been conducted under the cover of darkness to avoid detection and guarantee a stealthy movement. But such was not the case.

For whatever reason, but evidently because of the state of sheer exhaustion of the officers and men, including at Stuart's headquarters, no one in Stuart's command seemed too concerned about moving with much-needed stealth into Meade's right-rear in the daylight hours—a great mistake that was fated to come back and haunt the cavalrymen from the South. But since the offensive efforts of both Ewell and Pickett's Charge had not been launched with the dawn as planned, Lee might well have sent word to Stuart that he needed to delay his movements because the main offensive effort would not come until much later.

However, requiring a lengthy ride from near Gettysburg on the Confederate left, any such movement into Meade's right-rear was risky because the rising sun of July 3 and clouds of dust, thanks to the lack of rain and a lengthy dry spell, rising above the trees from thousands of horsemen riding northeast across the open ground along the York Turnpike, surrounded by broad farmers' fields of summer, would betray Stuart's column and the direction of its movement to sharp-eyed Federals on the high ground. This exposure would be especially the case in regard to the Yankees atop Cemetery Hill at the north end of Cemetery Ridge. Certainly that was the very last scenario desired by the cavalry commander, who had been assigned orders for his final movements into the Army of the Potomac's rear.[87]

Another culprit in the crucial failure to move to Meade's right-rear under the shielding veil of darkness was logistical. Major Henry Brainerd McClellan described with regret how on "the morning of the 3d several hours were consumed in replenishing the ammunition of the cavalry of Jenkins' [Virginia] brigade [of three regiments and two battalions], command by Colonel M[ilton] J. Ferguson, of the 16th Virginia Cavalry, was added to Stuart's command, but by some bad management was supplied with only ten rounds of cartridges to the man."[88]

Clearly, as if cursed by fate, Stuart was continuing to run into new problems that cost precious time, as throughout this ill-fated campaign thus far from the safe confines of Virginia, where seemingly everything had always worked to perfection for Lee and his cavalry arm. Even more ominous, Stuart for some time had ceased to perform at his best as in the past, as revealed in the near disaster at Brandy Station and the recent ill-fated raid, and Lee seems to have been long oblivious to these disturbing facts for whatever reason. In fact, because of the close father-son relationship between the two Virginians, the army's commander was guilty of continuing to indulge Stuart, while conveniently overlooking his shortcomings and his increasing number of examples of poor judgment that had manifested themselves in shocking fashion in 1863. Lee even continued to look upon Stuart's excessive flamboyance, which bordered on the ridiculous, with the amusement of a doting father allowing the excesses of a spoiled son.

Most recently and as noted, General Lee had given Stuart permission to go ahead with his gaudy reviews just before becoming a victim of the surprise attack at Brandy Station, although he considered it wiser to rest men and horses for the great challenges north of the Potomac that lay ahead. Of course Lee was correct. Unfortunately for the cavalry arm, Stuart had thought otherwise and seems to have cared little about the overall condition of his cavalry and artillery on the eve of the war's most important campaign.

Clearly, Lee, in father-like fashion, was allowing his emotions—which ran deep under the placidity of the Southern gentleman facade—to interfere with his judgment, a dangerous degree of excess for a commander in chief in regard to a top lieutenant, whom he was depending a great deal upon during a risky invasion on northern soil. What was no longer in doubt was the fact that Stuart had become a victim of a steadily creeping hubris that had reached a new high by the time of the Gettysburg campaign.

But even before Stuart was caught by surprise at Brandy Station and before his recent lengthy absence from the army in having ridden too far south and away from the army, Lee missed the ever-growing number of warning signs on the eve of the army's most important campaign of the war. Troubling signs about Stuart's hubris had been on the rise for some time. Lee had been forced to diplomatically soothe Stuart's hurt feelings when he complained that he deserved greater recognition for successfully leading Jackson's Second Corps at Chancellorsville with skill by the war cry "Charge, and remember Jackson!" after Stonewall had been accidently shot by Tar Heel State men in the half-light of thick woodlands. Stuart's ambitions and fame were getting the best of him, especially in 1863. Lee had been forced to keep Stuart in check because of his faulty judgment, which was increasingly on display after winning the great but pyrrhic victory at Chancellorsville.

And before the fateful showdown at Brandy Station, an overeager Stuart had wanted to send his units across the Rappahannock to strike General Gregg's Cavalry—now stronger because it was much better organized for combat operations because of Hooker's timely reforms—as if it were still the days of reaping heady Southern victories of 1861 and 1862. Stuart's proposed attack on the now much more formidable Union cavalry, which had recently moved up the Rappahannock River with newfound confidence, was only guaranteed to stir up a hornet's nest and result in high losses among men and horses on the eve of the army's second crucial invasion of the North—not a wise ambition for Stuart, who still wanted to reap glory to make the headlines of the Richmond newspapers.

In Lee's wise words, written in his usual diplomatic and even gentle style, in response to Stuart's burning desire to win additional accolades like a true glory hunter obsessed with single-minded goals that were too personal for the army's overall good: "I think it would be wise to be quiet and watchful for a little time [and I] think you had better not undertake an expedition at present. Devote your attention to the organization and recuperation of your command."[89] Lee knew what was most important at this time, especially on the eve of the Pennsylvania invasion, unlike Stuart, who should have known better.

All in all, therefore, the alarming list of clear indications in Stuart from May to early July revealed that Lee's top cavalier was no longer the same commander he had once been in his glory days. And ever since the cavalry fight at Brandy Station, the overall quality of the horses of Stuart's men had continued to plummet because of the wear and tear caused by the lengthy campaign over hundreds of miles in Maryland and Pennsylvania, because their commander's soaring ambitions had gotten the best of him.

Such undeniable truths in regard to both top leadership and the overall condition of Stuart's Cavalry Corps did not bode well for Confederate cavalry fortunes on July 3, when everything needed to go right to secure decisive victory. To win victory, Lee most of all needed a top lieutenant of sound judgment like Stonewall Jackson, who could perform up to expectations, unlike Stuart, upon whom the gods of war no longer smiled, a realization that he almost seemed to understand at times, which, however, only caused him to take even greater risks. Everything had changed by July 3, and whatever luck and good fortune Stuart had enjoyed in the past had already deserted him by the time of the most important campaign of the war.

Ironically, President Davis, like Stuart, called Stonewall Jackson's accidental mortal wounding by skittish North Carolina troops in Chancellorsville's darkening woodlands a "national calamity." In Lee's words of deep lament, "such an executive officer the sun never shone on." The sun of July 3 was destined not to shine with an equal luster on Lee's top cavalryman, although he did not yet know that the twisting fortunes of war and the fickle favor of fate had already turned so decidedly against him, and far more than he could possibly imagine at this time.[90]

But what was more disturbing in regard to the upcoming showdown of cavalry in the Army of the Potomac's rear was not Stuart's gradual loss of sound judgment. A new day had come, and the splendid performance of the hard-hitting Union cavalry at Brandy Station had been no anomaly or aberration that could be easily dismissed by Southern leadership. Only recently in the Pennsylvania campaign, one stunned Confederate admitted an ugly reality that was once again about to rise to the fore on the afternoon of July 3: "I had never known the enemy's cavalry to fight so stubbornly or act so recklessly."[91]

In general, Federal cavalry in the eastern theater had not been known to fight with such tenacious qualities in 1861 and 1862. Unfortunately for Stuart and his men, the increasingly capable troopers of Pleasonton's Cavalry Corps, Army of the Potomac, were about to surpass all previous expectations held by the legendary Rebel cavalrymen, especially their commander, who was living the glories of the past.

Stuart and his cavaliers incorrectly believed that July 3 was destined to be another day of glory, when even greater luster would be added to a most distinguished record that extended back to the war's beginning. If everything went according to the ambitious Lee-Stuart plan that had been established in an air of rising confidence during the conference at the Widow Thompson house, then the rising sun of July 3 would be nothing less than the sun of Austerlitz that had blessed Napoleon with his most tactically brilliant victory. At that time in December 1805, Napoleon had outsmarted the top generals and leaders of the mighty Third Coalition to inflict one of the most terrible defeats ever suffered by his opponents, who tangled with the brilliant native Corsican and learned hard lessons in consequence.

Symbolically, and as if offering a portent of another Napoleonic victory, the sun would rise in the same direction that Stuart and his men had initially been ordered to ride—northeast down the York Turnpike—on their most important mission of the war.[92] But entirely unknown to him at the time, Stuart was also destined to eventually ride, after turning south from an initial northeastward course, toward a determined young man: a new brigadier general and a fellow West Pointer, who lived by the personal motto that was destined to serve him extremely well in protecting the vulnerable rear of the Army of the Potomac: "First be sure you're right, then go ahead!"[93]

## EASILY SECURING THE STRATEGIC HIGH GROUND NEAR THE CROSSROADS IN MEADE'S REAR

Eager to redeem himself, General Stuart was ready for his greatest challenge in the mid-morning light, after the lengthy delay that had caused additional frustration for him. However, the failure of Lee's offensive to begin at dawn as planned had allowed him extra time. At last, he was fully prepared for his secret mission in Meade's rear, because he had thoroughly "consulted his topographical maps in order to select the perfect location for an offensive strike" into the rear of the Army of the Potomac.[94]

Finally, after the precious early morning hours of daylight had been wasted away on July 3, Stuart and his men were ready to move out when the bright sun of early summer had risen about midway in the morning sky. Most of the morning had been squandered, and the day's heat was high like the creeping humidity of the third summer of the war, when Stuart finally gave orders to depart the night's encampment in the open fields. Major McClellan, who served on Stuart's staff, described how, "at about noon [actually around mid-morning] Stuart, with Jenkins' and Chambliss' brigades, moved out on the York turnpike, [with the immediate objective] to take position on the left of the Confederate line of battle [while] Hampton and Fitz Lee were directed to follow."[95]

But Stuart now rode forth, northeast and down the York Turnpike, on this crucial mission without two batteries of the famed Stuart Horse Artillery, which were much needed on this day of destiny in the rear of Meade's army. As Major McClellan wrote, two of the best batteries of the Stuart Horse Artillery "had not been able to obtain ammunition, and were left behind, with orders to follow as soon as their [ammunition and caisson] chests were filled."[96]

Stuart, however, was not deterred by the absent artillery or the late start on the most crucial morning in the history of the Army of Northern Virginia, because he was a highly motivated man on a most important mission. Historian Edward G. Longacre perhaps said it best about the high motivations of Lee's top cavalier at this time, because Stuart was "determined to make amends for the anxiety and frustration his ride [raid] around the enemy had caused General Lee. This day he vowed to meet his commander's expectations, ensuring a coordinated effort on many fronts against Meade's battered ranks."[97]

A man on a mission, Stuart rode northeastward toward the mid-morning sun with his lead cavalry brigades in a column, followed by artillery, that extended several miles along the dusty York Turnpike—he was familiar with this road from having already ridden down it, but in the other direction, to meet with General Lee at the Widow Thompson house on the night of July 2, and because of the topographical maps. He was now in command of almost all of Lee's available cavalry for the fulfillment of this crucial mission of striking Meade's rear to inflict as much damage as possible. As usual and despite the belated start on his most important mission of the war, Stuart was confident and optimistic, which was his nature.

Right behind Stuart rode the troopers of Jenkins's Brigade. This command consisted of five Virginia commands (three cavalry regiments—the 14th, 16th, and 17th Virginia Cavalry—and two cavalry battalions—the 34th and 36th Virginia Cavalry—and the Charlottesville, Virginia, "Kanawha" Horse Artillery) and was now officially led by Colonel Milton J. Ferguson, but actually commanded by Lieutenant Vincent Addison Witcher, who served in place of Brigadier General Albert G. Jenkins. Next in column behind Witcher's men came General "Rooney" Lee's Brigade under Colonel John Randolph Chambliss Jr., which consisted of three Virginia regiments and one North Carolina regiment.

Wade Hampton's mostly South Carolina Brigade and Fitz Lee's Brigade (1st, 2nd, 3rd, 4th, and 5th Virginia Cavalry and the 1st Maryland Cavalry Battalion) were also headed for the immediate objective of Cress's Ridge in a separate column behind the hard-riding Virginians. Ironically, the finest brigades, under Brigadier Generals Hampton and Fitzhugh Lee, were not under Stuart's immediate command at this point until they later linked on Cress's Ridge as planned.

Therefore, two separate columns of Lee's best cavalrymen and horse artillery steadily made their way along the York Turnpike to eventually gain a position on the commanding high ground of Cress's Ridge below, or south of, the turnpike and to within just over a mile from the Hanover Road, which roughly paralleled the York Turnpike, to the south. As noted, this heavily wooded ridge was the predesigned meeting point for Stuart's commands to concentrate, which indicated that this had been agreed upon by Lee and Stuart at the Thompson house conference because of its strategic location and thanks to a good topographical map that had revealed to them that Cress's Ridge was the highest ground in the area.[98]

Most importantly and as noted, Stuart already had his immediate tactical objective in mind because he possessed good topographical maps and because this ambitious plan of striking Meade's rear had already been worked out between him and General Lee in detail at the Thompson house on the night of July 2. Stuart also knew that nothing could now stop him from reaching his objective on this morning: the strategic high ground of Cress's Ridge, which was located around three miles southeast of Gettysburg, which overlooked the strategic crossroads of the Hanover and Low Dutch Roads to the south.

Here, located between the York Turnpike to the north and the Hanover Road, which was well within sight from the dominant high ground, just to the south, the dominant heights of Cress's Ridge, situated between the small watercourses of Cress's Ridge to the west and Little's Run, whose clear waters flowed cold from a spring house on the John Rummel (a Pennsylvania German—commonly referred to as Dutch by Americans—like most of the hardworking farmers in this area) farm, to the east, was now the most strategic position in the right-rear of the Army of the Potomac. The open southern slope of Cress's Ridge, situated just below the tree line of the thick woodlands atop the ridge, would provide concealment for thousands of cavalrymen and a commanding high-ground platform for the alignment of artillery that would dominate the open ground below that led south to the strategic crossroads once the fighting began.

The heavily wooded, lengthy, and narrow ridge extended in a southwesterly direction from below the York Turnpike, past the Rummel farm, which was located southwest of the Daniel Stallsmith place and not far below (south) the ridge's wood line, and then continued straight south through the open fields and pastures toward the Hanover Road and the vital crossroads, where this road and the Low Dutch Road intersected.

This strategic high ground of Cress's Ridge overlooked and controlled the lower ground to the south where the crossroads lay vulnerable, as Lee and Stuart had ascertained from a topographical map back at headquarters. With this vital objective in mind, Stuart had already informed General Hampton and Fitzhugh Lee to join him and his foremost brigades on Cress's Ridge, which would provide excellent cover for thousands of troopers. As mentioned, Stuart led the cavalry brigades of Jenkins (Witcher) and Chambliss forward, while his two best brigades under Hampton and Fitzhugh Lee rode belatedly toward the ridge in a separate column. After gaining the good cover provided by the tall trees of Cress's Ridge, Stuart then planned to await the arrival of his other units that would likewise deploy under the cover of the woodlands of Cress's Ridge.

By this time, General Meade had divided his cavalry, and much of it was positioned to the south: Brigadier General Kilpatrick's Third Cavalry Division of two brigades—now located below the Round Tops to protect the army's left-rear and his left flank, which had been battered by Longstreet's attackers, especially in an assault at Little Round Top on the bloody afternoon of July 2. Even more, General Kilpatrick planned to unleash an offensive strike on Lee's right flank, but he would do so without Custer and his wayward Second Cavalry Brigade, Third Cavalry Division, of highly motivated Wolverines, because they had remained at Two Taverns and then moved north toward the strategic crossroads.

Meanwhile, Pleasonton's Second Cavalry Division of three brigades under General Gregg was assigned to guard Meade's right-rear and flank, which was a traditional and customary tactical measure to protect an army's flank with cavalry during a major confrontation. At this time, and as almost certainly expressed by the army's commander at the July 2 conference with Stuart at the Widow Thompson house, Lee almost certainly felt, and correctly so, that Meade's right-rear was more vulnerable than his left-rear—because of Longstreet's July 2 assaults on Houck's Ridge, Devil's Den, and then Little Round Top, where he had attempted to turn the Army of the Potomac's left—and would have drawn reinforcements to bolster this hard-hit position on the army's southern end by now. In regard to the potential threat posed by protective Union cavalry, Lee believed that Meade's right-rear would not be as strong as the left-rear on July 3, which was indeed the case.

In consequence, Kilpatrick faced no threat from Confederate cavalry on the far left on July 3 because Stuart had concentrated his main cavalry force, made stronger with recently added cavalrymen and artillery on Lee's orders, on the north to strike into Meade's rear. Therefore, the way was clear for Kilpatrick—but without Custer and his Michigan Brigade that remained with Gregg—to strike the weary defenders of Major General John Bell Hood's Texas Brigade, Longstreet's First Corps, on the far south of the sprawling battle line. Meanwhile, General Gregg, a native Pennsylvanian, and his Second Cavalry Division had been assigned by Meade to protect the vulnerable right-rear, exactly where the day's greatest cavalry threat was destined to appear. As noted, Gregg had early expressed concern for the vulnerability of this key position at the strategic crossroads of the Hanover and Low Dutch Roads, a source of worry that was well placed, and General Pleasonton eventually wisely concurred as much in the end to ensure the upcoming protective role of Custer and his Wolverines.

As mentioned, this key tactical objective—Cress's Ridge and the strategic crossroads—of General Stuart that needed to be occupied had been ascertained during the recent Lee-Stuart conference at the Thompson house. In the words of historian Edwin B. Coddington in regard to the late-night conference when Stuart and Lee had poured over topographical maps: "Stuart's unerring eye and quick appreciation of the controlling topographical features in a strange land quickly showed him where he could best use his cavalry for an offensive movement."[99] In Stuart's own words, he planned "to effect a surprise upon the enemy's rear."[100] And the key to this bold plan was Lee and Stuart's selection of "the perfect location for an offensive strike" into Meade's rear, and Cress's Ridge fulfilled this requirement because of its proximity to the strategic crossroads.[101]

Therefore, toward the mid-morning sun that hung in a clear sky that promised greater heat on another scorching day that felt as hot as in the lowlands of coastal South Carolina, Stuart and his troops continued to ride northeastward up the York Turnpike with a confidence born of past successes that had been reaped across Virginia, heading for his immediate objective of Cress's Ridge. Stuart, explained Coddington, and "the three brigades of his command and Jenkins' troopers [confidently] rode [along] the York road for about two and a half miles [northeast] beyond Gettysburg before turning off on a crossroads [about two and a half miles east of Gettysburg along a country road, or lane,] to the right, which led him [southeast] to Cress Ridge a mile away. The position controlled a wide area of cultivated fields stretching east toward Hanover and south to the frowning hills of the Union lines," including Cemetery Ridge to the southwest.[102]

In more detail, historian Edward G. Longacre described how after pushing northeastward along the York Turnpike, and thanks to recent intelligence from mounted scouts, Stuart's column led by Lieutenant Colonel Witcher, who now commanded Jenkins's Brigade of Virginia boys (the 14th, 16th, and 17th Virginia Cavalry and the 34th and 36th Virginia Cavalry Battalions), turned southeastward "beside the home of Levi Rinehart [and] descended a country road that led" toward Cress's Ridge.[103]

In his memoirs, Major Henry B. McClellan, a member of Stuart's staff, emphasized as much in describing the course of Stuart's route: "After marching about two and a half miles on the York turnpike, Stuart turned to his right [south] by a country road [Stallsmith Lane] which led past the [Daniel] Stallsmith farm [about a half mile below the York Turnpike] to," in Stuart words, "a commanding ridge which completely controlled a wide plain of cultivated fields stretching towards Hanover on the left, and reaching to the base of the mountain spurs among which the enemy held position."[104]

Cress's Ridge was a long and low elevation, but it was the highest in the area, which explains why Stuart needed to occupy this key high ground because of its nearness to the crossroads that needed to be captured before gaining the Baltimore Road to the southwest and easing behind Meade's Cemetery Ridge position. McClellan continued to describe the terrain in his memoir:

This ridge is known as the Cress Ridge. Its northern end was covered with woods, which enveloped the road by which he approached it, and concealed his presence from the enemy. Near where the woods terminated on the southwest, and on the slope of the hill, stood a stone dairy, covering a spring. On the [open] plain below, and not more than three hundred yards from the foot of the hill, stood a large frame barn, known as the Rummel Barn. A glance satisfied Stuart that he had gained the position he wanted. The roads leading from the rear of the Federal line of battle were under his eye and could be reached by the prolongation of the road by which he had approached. Moreover, the open fields, although intersected by many fences, admitted of movement in any direction.[105]

Continuing his on-target analysis of Lee and Stuart's earlier decision at the Widow Thompson house in regard to securing strategic Cress's Ridge, which ran north–south like so many other ridges, including Cemetery Ridge just to the southwest, in the area, Coddington described the crucial importance of securing this strategic high ground for the future operations that were all important: "With Stuart occupying [Cress's Ridge,] Ewell's left and rear would be secure against attack, but more importantly, Stuart would obtain a view of the routes leading to the enemy's rear."[106]

However, General Stuart's plan "called for an avoidance of an engagement [against General Gregg's troopers, including Custer and his Wolverines, who shortly occupied the crossroads of the Hanover and Low Dutch Roads] with Federal cavalry. . . . The high ground of Cress Ridge was to act as a screen for his cavalry. Skirmishers on the edge of the woods [of Cress's Ridge] would engage Federal skirmishers if the latter were in the vicinity [to hold the crossroads]. Meanwhile, Stuart's cavalry would reach the Baltimore Pike [which roughly paralleled Cemetery Ridge just to the west and ran southeast from Gettysburg and southwest of Cress's Ridge] unobserved and be in position" to strike into Meade's rear.[107]

According to plan, the units of Stuart's command reached Cress's Ridge in piecemeal fashion. While the brigades of Hampton and Fitzhugh Lee still lingered behind and only belatedly reached the strategic high ground of Cress's Ridge, Stuart, with Chambliss's and Jenkins's (Witcher's) Brigades, arrived first. Stuart was riding at the head of Jenkins's Virginia Brigade. As noted, this seasoned Virginia brigade was now temporarily under the command of the capable Lieutenant Colonel Vincent Addison Witcher. Most importantly, they reached their high-ground objective without incident or having encountered any Yankees. To the knowledge of Stuart and his men, no Federals had seen their movement to Cress's Ridge. Clearly, this was a cautious and careful tactic by Stuart in regard to positioning his cavalry in the forests of Cress's Ridge in what was a stealthy and secret movement, because he was not sure of the location and deployment of Union cavalry by Pleasonton.

Brigadier General Hampton, Stuart's top lieutenant, and Fitzhugh Lee would not reach the strategic high ground of Cress's Ridge for another hour or so. Meanwhile, Stuart, his trusty staff, and his foremost Virginia cavalrymen reached the southernmost spur at the edge of the thick woods that crowned the high ground that was located just over a mile north of the strategic crossroads and overlooked the lower ground of the intersection of the Hanover and Low Dutch Roads.

Here, among the tall hardwood trees that provided ideal cover because they were arrayed in dense summer foliage, Stuart ordered his dust-covered men to dismount and then walk their horses through the woods just beyond the edge of the timber so as not to betray their positions to any Federal troops, including pickets, which might be occupying the strategic crossroads. As noted, Stuart knew little, if anything, of Federal cavalry dispositions, and he was determined to maintain secrecy in regard to his future tactical intentions.

Leading the way, Witcher's Virginia men moved west to take position among the timber near the high ground known as Hoffman's Ridge, taking position on Stuart's right and serving as a solid anchor to the new battle line. Colonel Chambliss's Brigade ("Rooney" Lee's Brigade) of three Virginia regiments and a North Carolina regiment followed Jenkins's (Witcher's) Virginians to position their right on Witcher's left. Here, Stuart's line on the right took shape amid the trees and beyond detection. Stuart then directed his troopers to rest in the refreshing cool of the shade among the timber, which was much needed on this scorching day amid the damp summer heat.[108]

Burdened by incomplete knowledge in regard to the location and dispositions of Union cavalry like General Stuart, but knowing enough about Stuart's overall plan to offer perceptive insights, William Willis Blackford, a former Fredericksburg, Virginia, businessman and a respected member of Stuart's staff, described the mission and movements of Stuart's troopers on the morning of July 3: "Stuart moved his command forward on the York road [Turnpike] a couple of miles and placed it in a position to cover the left [Ewell's Second Corps that occupied the north end of Lee's sprawling battle line] of our main line around Gettysburg as well as to threaten the enemy's rear."[109]

Here, northeast of Gettysburg and within striking distance of the all-important Baltimore Road to the southwest, by which he could gain Meade's vulnerable rear on Cemetery Ridge, Stuart felt added confidence in having secured a good strategic "position to the left of General Ewell's left, and in advance of it, where a commanding ridge [Cress's Ridge] completely controlled a wide plain of cultivated fields stretching [east] towards Hanover."[110]

In Stuart's own words from his official report: "On the morning of July 3, pursuant to instructions from the commanding general [from the late July 2 conference at the Widow Thompson house], I moved forward to a position to the left of General Ewell's left, and in advance of it, where a commanding ridge completely controlled a wide plain of cultivated fields stretching toward Hanover, on the left, and reaching to the base of the mountain spurs, among which the enemy held position. . . . I hoped to effect a surprise upon the enemy's rear."[111]

The capable Blackford, who had been born in Fredericksburg, Virginia, on the Rappahannock River in March 1831, was haunted by the eerie quiet of the dark woodlands of Cress's Ridge and the surrounding area that overlooked the open fields, including high-standing crops of wheat, and meadows to the south and leading to the strategic crossroads. First and foremost, he knew that Lee almost always attacked at dawn or in the morning, but the day still remained quiet. Why had Lee not launched his greatest offensive effort in a final effort to secure a decisive victory? This question haunted Blackford, like other veterans in the ranks, because they had anticipated a dawn assault, which was Lee's offensive style. As he penned, "All was quiet for a long time; hour after hour passed and scarcely a gun was heard" on this warm morning in Adams County.[112] A respected member of Stuart's staff, Major McClellan, who served as the major general's capable adjutant, wrote that "when Stuart first reached this place the scene was as peaceful as if no war existed. The extension of the ridge on his right hid from view the lines of the contending armies, and not a living creature was visible on the plain below."[113]

While his men rested quietly under the cool shade of the woodlands located at the southern base of Cress's Ridge after he had carefully placed Jenkins's (Witcher's) and Chambliss's troopers under good cover among the trees, whose green leaves were undisturbed by any refreshing breeze on this intensely hot afternoon, Stuart departed the highest point of the ridge on the south to gain a view of the ground before the strategic crossroads of the Hanover and Low Dutch Roads.

From high ground at the edge of the woods on the spur of the southern slope, Stuart surveyed the open lands of John Rummel and Jacob Lott with his trusty binoculars that he had utilized on previous fields. Cress's Ridge proper was owned by John Rummel and his wife Sarah, while the Lott house stood just west of the Low Dutch Road and just north of the strategic crossroads. First and foremost, Stuart looked for boys in blue that might be guarding the vital road intersection in an attempt to ascertain the location and strength of enemy cavalry that he knew had to be in the area.

From his high-ground perch, Stuart gained a panoramic view of open ground covered in fertile fields and meadows that gently descended south across a pastoral landscape covered with stone fences and post-and-rail fences that were destined to provide good cover for blue and gray troopers amid the open terrain once the battle erupted. Having fought mostly on fields of strife in Virginia, General Stuart—like other commanders, including Custer—had not yet discovered how these fences, especially the ones made of stone, were sturdier and stronger than the split-rail fences in the Old Dominion. Therefore, any Rebel cavalry charge unleashed by Stuart down the open slope—which looked ideal for a sweeping attack to push aside any bluecoats that might advance north from the crossroads—would be disrupted by these manmade obstacles that were more formidable than they appeared at first glance.

From the high-ground vantage point, not a Yankee infantryman or cavalryman was in sight, which delighted Stuart, who realized that he had not lost the race to secure a commanding high-ground position that dominated the crossroads and that his secret mission in Meade's rear had not been betrayed or ascertained by the Yankees, or so it seemed. In keeping with other designations in an area covered mostly by the open farmlands of Adams County, locals knew Cress's Ridge simply by the name of Rummel's Woods, which covered the commanding elevation, including the lowermost southern spur now filled with veteran Rebel cavalrymen (Stuart's right and right-center after the upcoming arrival of Hampton's and Fitzhugh Lee's Brigades, which eventually formed the left-center and left, respectively) who meant to cause great mischief in Meade's rear on July 3. All the while, General Stuart closely surveyed the strategic crossroads to the south, where the Hanover and Low Dutch Roads met—his ultimate objective by which to eventually gain the Army of the Potomac's rear.[114]

In his own words from his report, Stuart emphasized how he now possessed and "commanded a view of the routes leading to the enemy's rear."[115] Indeed, and most importantly in regard to his secret mission, Stuart held the strategic high ground, which he considered "an ideal position" because "it afforded direct access to the Union line to the south" along Cemetery Ridge.[116]

One Union officer described the supreme advantages now enjoyed by Lee's finest cavalry, writing how Stuart "now occupied what is known as Cress's Ridge, about three-fourths of a mile north of Lott's house. On the south-eastern slope of the ridge there were cultivated fields, while its summit was covered with heavy timber. North of this ridge there were open fields, almost surrounded by woods, through which ran a country cross-road leading from the York pike to the Low Dutch road. The place was most admirably adapted to the massing and screening of troops. Behind the woods Stuart, who had come from that direction of Gettysburg along the York pike, concentrated his forces on what was known as the Stallsmith farm."[117]

Ironically, Stuart's troopers, who had so easily gained this key highground position of Cress's Ridge that was located north-northeast of the all-important Baltimore Road and in Meade's vulnerable right-rear, which was the ultimate target for delivering the planned "coup de grace," were mostly armed with six-shot revolvers. The majority of these weapons had been manufactured in the North, and they represented considerable firepower in the hands of these veterans. Relatively few revolvers were produced in the South because it lacked not only resources and experienced machinists, but also mass-production capabilities such as assembly lines, unlike the more industrialized North. Therefore, the .45-caliber army Colt revolver, which packed a punch by having the capacity to unleash half a dozen shots in short order, was the handgun of choice of Stuart's men. During the planned upcoming attack into the defenders' rear, Stuart's battle-hardened men could fire rapidly to deliver six shots, unlike Meade's infantrymen, who were handicapped by carrying only single-shot muskets, which took too much time to reload, as in the days of Napoleon.[118]

Stuart's veterans could therefore inflict considerable damage from small arms alone—not to mention from the fire of the horse artillery—on the bluecoat infantrymen, who were facing west, in the wrong direction in regard to Stuart's surprise attack in the rear of Meade's army when the time came to strike a blow. Unfortunately, the letters and diaries of Stuart's men in the ranks have revealed little of grand strategy or tactics, which was usually the case, because they were not privy to the decision making of the top Confederate leadership during the July 2 conference between Stuart and Lee at the Thompson house, which resulted in Stuart acting "pursuant to instructions" from Lee on the final day at Gettysburg, when everything hung in the balance. And, as could be expected, Stuart had not widely spread the word of his plan for the sake of secrecy, because this was a plan of stealth derived from the fertile minds of two eternal optimists and tactically astute generals, Lee and Stuart.

Normal in such situations, this absence of specific information about the exact details of the tactics for July 3 does not mean that no tactics, especially of an offensive nature, existed for striking Meade's rear. As noted, the men of the enlisted ranks knew little, if anything, about the larger plans of Stuart and Lee because this was, most of all, a secret plan, another key factor that has doomed the importance of the dramatic cavalry showdown on the East Cavalry Field in the historical record.

Knowing nothing about the plan to strike Meade's rear, Sergeant Robert S. Hudgins, 3rd Virginia Cavalry, Fitzhugh Lee's Brigade—which finally began to arrive belatedly at Cress's Ridge after the mostly Old Dominion troopers of Jenkins's (Witcher's) and Chambliss's Brigades had taken their assigned positions in the dense woodlands on the high ground—merely penned, "Our march was uninterrupted as we reached a large field along the York Pike," which was actually the farm lane (Stallsmith Lane) that ran southeast from the pike.[119] Stuart's staff officers shortly directed the late-arriving Hampton's and Fitzhugh Lee's men from the open ground into the sheltering woods of Cress's Ridge, where they were safe from prying Yankee eyes, and formed them amid the trees on the left-center (Hampton) and the left (Fitzhugh Lee).[120]

But Stuart's staff officers possessed a good deal more information about the aggressive battle plan of striking into Meade's rear, unlike Hampton, who evidently knew very little, if anything at all, at this time about the intricate details of the Lee-Stuart plan for striking Meade's rear, because great care had to be taken to safeguard this most secret of plans. Trusty staff officer William Willis Blackford, a tall, slim ex-merchant and a former captain of Company D, 1st Virginia Cavalry (Stuart's old regiment), emphasized how one of Stuart's primary missions was "to threaten the enemy's rear" on the afternoon of July 3.[121]

Indeed, and as mentioned, Stuart's primary "assignment was to ride into the rear of the Army of the Potomac." Stuart was now in a position that "provided a direct route into the center of Meade's rear area, and if Stuart and his troopers could get there, they could wreak havoc on a grand scale."[122] In addition, this fact was verified by Brigadier General Fitzhugh Lee in a most revealing postwar letter, when he wrote how Stuart's principal mission was for "the purpose of effecting a surprise on the enemy's rear."[123] For such reasons and as noted, historian Coddington also emphasized that Stuart's occupation of the lower spur of Cress's Ridge was the key high-ground position that was necessary for any chance of delivering a masterstroke for eventually "swoop[ing] down onto the rear" of the Army of the Potomac.[124]

Now that Stuart had gained an advanced high-ground position before and to the left of Ewell's Second Corps at an elevated point to "obtain a view of the routes leading to the enemy's rear," he felt a measure of added reassurance because he had concealed his troopers and artillery in the thick woodlands that covered Cress's Ridge—including the southernmost spur, which was closest to the strategic crossroads—like a thick green blanket. To deliver his offensive blow to smash into the Army of the Potomac's rear, Stuart had gained Jenkins's seasoned Virginia cavalry brigade, now under Lieutenant Colonel Witcher because the general had been wounded by a shell on July 2 during a personal reconnaissance. As mentioned, the addition of Jenkins's (Witcher's) Old Dominion troopers of three cavalry regiments and two battalions, positioned on the right of Chambliss's regiments, now gave him four brigades—one more than he had taken on his far-flung recent raid—of experienced cavalrymen who were eager to settle old scores after the drubbing that they had taken at Brandy Station.[125]

Just the kind of men needed for the stiff challenges of July 3, the seasoned Old Dominion troopers of General Jenkins's (Witcher's) Brigade were tough and ruthless if necessary, and if ordered to be so by the capable Lieutenant Colonel Witcher. These were hardy mountain boys from western Virginia, which is today's West Virginia. In Franklin County, Pennsylvania, amid the Cumberland Valley directly west of Gettysburg, these cavalrymen had led the army's advance across the Keystone State and scoured towns and homes to return blacks to slavery. Of course, in one of the greatest tragedies of the Gettysburg campaign, it did not matter to these hardened men that they also captured free blacks—not runaway slaves from the South—who had been living on Pennsylvania soil for generations.[126]

Then, during this grueling campaign, the spirits of Jenkins's Virginia men, now under Witcher, had reached a high point upon viewing the capital of Harrisburg, which seemed ripe for the taking, until the command was recalled on July 1 to return to the main army at Gettysburg after the roar of combat was heard on the distant horizon around forty miles to the southwest.[127]

## LEE'S GREATEST OFFENSIVE DELAYED UNTIL EARLY AFTERNOON

Most of all, since he saw no sizeable numbers of Federals around the strategic crossroads to the south, Stuart now needed to know what was happening with the main army to the southwest before Cemetery Ridge, because he had been told in full by Lee about the planned early morning offense, when he was going for broke as never before. And now in occupying the high ground in Meade's right-rear, he could peer southwest to ascertain developments from his perch. Stuart had reason for concern because Lee's offensive plan for July 3 was not developing and moving forward as it was supposed to. For ample good reason, therefore, Stuart was worried about when the main attack would be launched.[128]

As mentioned, Ewell (Second Corps) and Longstreet (First Corps) had not attacked at daylight or throughout the course of the quiet (it was too quiet) morning hours of July 3, as they were supposed to have done according to Lee's plan to strike at dawn. If not informed of the reasons for the delay before embarking upon this mission, therefore, Stuart likely wondered why Lee had not already launched his final all-out assault to destroy the Army of the Potomac. Lee had planned to attack early on July 3, which was usually the case for the ever-aggressive commander, who had once been the superintendent at West Point. After all, Stuart had been informed about the day's plans by him on the night of July 2. But now the front to the west and southwest was eerily silent, as if no great assault had ever been planned by Lee. Clearly something had gone terribly wrong.

For a variety of reasons, Lee's planned, coordinated offense for the early morning had never materialized on the most important day of the war. First, the three seasoned Virginia infantry brigades of Pickett's Division, Longstreet's First Corps, were too late in moving forward that morning to minimize the effectiveness of a strategic reserve in regard to a dawn attack. Longstreet, whom Lee had assigned to orchestrate Pickett's Charge, was not acting with promptness and the necessary diligence because his heart and head were simply not in the tactical offensive. And General Ewell and the veteran troops of his Second Corps had already acted too early (he was to have attacked at daylight in conjunction with Pickett's Charge, according to Lee's plan) by unleashing assaults against Meade's right at Culp's Hill in the early morning blackness even before the dawn of July 3. Therefore, Ewell was not attacking with the dawn as expected with Pickett's Charge, which continued to be delayed for hours.

Even worse in regard to sabotaging Lee's original battle plan were developments in Longstreet's sector proper on the southern end of the lengthy battle line. As Lee discovered when he visited Longstreet's First Corps headquarters just before 5:00 a.m. on the morning of the third day, no orders had been issued by Longstreet to attack as earlier agreed upon by the commander in chief and his top lieutenant, whose reluctance in regard to adhering to Lee's orders for unleashing the tactical offensive had existed during the first two days, and, in fact, the entire campaign. In this regard, nothing had changed on the crucial third day in regard to Longstreet's intransigence, when close coordination on all levels was necessary for Confederate success.

Quite simply, Longstreet continued to be excessively defensive minded, and Lee's aggressiveness was the antithesis of what was demonstrated by the "Old Bull," whose stubbornness had once again risen to the fore. Clearly, Lee's plan, which required a "proper concert of action," including by Stuart from the east, had completely fallen apart to leave Stuart confused and guessing. Once again, General Longstreet, the obstinate Georgian, who was not fond of Virginians and their excessive cronyism, which seemed to have no end, still desired to flank the Union left to the south: a flanking movement that called for bypassing the twin elevation on the south known as the Round Tops.[129]

Incredibly and to Lee's frustration, Longstreet's desire—as on July 2—to embark upon his alternative tactics threw off Lee's plan for a "proper concert of action" from his three main offensive operations that were planned to deliver an overpowering blow: (1) Pickett's Charge to strike Meade's weak right-center, which was now targeted after having been moved farther north from the center proper because of Longstreet's arguments not to include his units in the great attack; (2) Ewell's Second Corps to attack Meade's right flank; and (3) Stuart's cavalry to strike Meade's rear. Therefore, after again deciding against Longstreet's plan, which lacked the required aggressiveness needed to win a decisive success on the third day, Lee and this top lieutenant conferred to make the final arrangements for the assault (now targeting Meade's right-center) and the massive artillery bombardment to precede it. But much precious time had been wasted, and Stuart's own plan of operations was delayed in consequence. In an entirely misplaced delegation of authority, like when he had allowed Stuart to conduct his raid without keeping a tight rein on him, Lee had assigned Longstreet the task of orchestrating Pickett's Charge, which he never wanted to unleash in the first place.

Orders finally reached the artillery and Colonel Edward Porter Alexander, the highly capable young man (a West Pointer—class of 1857—Georgian) in charge of the First Corps' artillery, to begin to make preparations around 9:00 a.m. for unleashing a massive bombardment before Pickett's Charge was ordered to begin. Born in Washington, Georgia, in 1835, "Porter," as he was known to his friends, realized, as Lee had himself, that the best early morning opportunity had already passed. Indeed, there would be no early morning attack as envisioned and planned by Lee, and this eerie morning silence boded ill for Confederate fortunes and confounded Stuart.[130]

As indicated by the lack of firing, this waste of precious time throughout the morning of July 3 perplexed Stuart—and his staff officers—after he had been told by Lee about the planned early morning assault by Longstreet and Ewell during the conference on the night of July 2. Therefore, a concerned Stuart had no choice but to rely on staff officers in the hope of gaining as much information as possible about this vexing situation with the main army to the west and southwest during the course of that warm morning. In the words of William Willis Blackford: "Wishing to know what was going on in the main body of the army, Stuart sent me with a roving commission to find out."[131] Again, Stuart possessed the advantage of having easily secured the high ground, especially in regard to "obtain[ing] a view of the routes leading to the enemy's rear," in historian Coddington's analysis.[132]

Therefore, Blackford rode west toward Gettysburg through the open fields and toward the main army and a front that remained much too quiet. All the while, he was haunted by the eerie quiet, like General Stuart, knowing that something had gone awry and badly with Lee's offensive plan. Blackford wrote how during his mission to ascertain developments in regard to the Army of Northern Virginia's offensive plans, he rode west and toward the army's left wing to determine why Ewell's and Longstreet's planned daylight assaults had not been unleashed as everyone had expected: "All was quiet as if there was not a soldier within a hundred miles, and the country looked so calm and beautiful, dotted over with thrifty farms, that it was hard to realize that nearly a quarter of a million men were met together to settle" the decisive showdown at Gettysburg.[133]

## STUART SIGNALS GENERAL LEE ABOUT GAINING THE UNION ARMY'S REAR

By this time, Stuart had completed the job of forming his troopers on the high ground of Cress's Ridge that dominated the key crossroads of the Hanover and Low Dutch Roads, after "carefully concealing" the troopers of Chambliss's and Jenkins's (Witcher's) brigades of almost all Virginia regiments. Stuart now had to protect his front and make it more secure just in case any Federals in the area decided to attack after he had situated thousands of his men in hidden positions in the timber. Then the most experienced skirmishers of Colonel Jenkins's (Witcher's) Virginians were ordered forward and aligned in the open fields immediately below the wood line along the crest as skirmishers to protect the front, which was standard procedure in an unfamiliar area and not knowing the whereabouts of Pleasonton's Cavalry.

Meanwhile, Stuart's brigades were aligned under the good cover of the woodlands on the southern spur of Cress's Ridge, remaining out of sight from any nearby Federals who might be occupying the strategic crossroads. As noted, the three Virginia regiments and one North Carolina regiment of Chambliss's Brigade ("Rooney" Lee's command) were now aligned on higher ground on the southern spur of Cress's Ridge on the left of Jenkins's (Witcher's) main contingent to the left-rear, or north, of the brigade's skirmishers.

As mentioned, the final alignment of Stuart's men along the length of Cress's Ridge took some time, and longer than expected. After arriving late just after the noon hour, Hampton's Brigade, which consisted of the 1st North Carolina Cavalry, the 1st and 2nd South Carolina Cavalry, two Georgia Cavalry Legions, and one Mississippi Cavalry Legion, extended the line farther north and northeast of Chambliss's Brigade in the woods of the commanding southern spur. Occupying the left-center, Hampton's Brigade, the elite command of Stuart's cavalry, was a most solid anchor of the battle line. Arriving last because the wagons and ambulances with his column had slowed movements was the all-Virginia brigade, except for the 1st Maryland Cavalry Battalion, of darkly handsome Fitzhugh Lee, which arrived late with Hampton's Brigade. Fitzhugh Lee's troopers were then posted in the forest on even higher ground above, or slightly northeast of, Hampton's men to anchor the left of Stuart's line: the most dominant, or highest, position atop the southern end of Cress's Ridge.

In the end, the late arrival of Fitzhugh Lee's Brigade and its placement in line farthest north (on Stuart's left) and farthest from the location of the upcoming fight, or farther—north of—from the strategic crossroads, was actually a blessing in disguise: Stuart now had what was essentially a strategic reserve for the upcoming clash of arms, because his best troopers (Hampton on the left-center and Fitzhugh Lee on the left) held high ground northeast of Jenkins's (Witcher's) Virginia Brigade. Here, just over a mile north of the crossroads of the Hanover and Low Dutch Roads, Stuart waited with his men, hidden in the tall trees and comforting shade that eased the intense heat of another hot day in early July, on the dominant heights that overlooked the low ground of the strategic intersection, where any enemy movements could be easily and early perceived because of the intervening open terrain covered in fields, pastures, and meadows.[134]

After the belated arrival of Hampton's and Fitzhugh Lee's Brigades, Stuart now possessed all of his forces that he needed to perform his vital mission of striking a decisive blow. He had encountered no resistance whatsoever. It seemed as if no sizeable commands of Federals were located anywhere nearby. This situation allowed him the tactical opportunity to make final preparations for leading "an attack upon the enemy's rear," in the words of Stuart's most trusty staff officer, Major Henry Brainerd McClellan.[135]

But first and foremost at this time, Stuart needed to know if any Union cavalry were before him, because he also had been entrusted with protecting Ewell's right flank in conjunction with eventually striking Meade's rear. He still did not know the location of the powerful cavalry arm under Pleasonton. Therefore, the line of Virginia skirmishers positioned just below the trees might draw fire if any Federals, especially their artillery if hidden in the woods around the crossroads, were nearby. Indeed, if any Union artillery was defending the crossroads, it would open first on Colonel Ferguson's (Witcher's) skirmishers. Major McClellan reasoned what Stuart was almost certainly thinking at this time: After he "had gained a favorable position [and] finding that none of the enemy were within sight, he may have desired to satisfy himself whether the Federal cavalry was in his immediate vicinity before leaving [to strike Meade's rear] the strong position he then held" on the southern spur of Cress's Ridge.[136]

If necessary and despite his vital mission to attack Meade's rear, Stuart possessed a degree of tactical flexibility because he was basically leading an independent command. Therefore, he was prepared to fight if necessary by way of his own decision making, depending on the situation that was presented to him, unlike having been caught by surprise and then forced to fight for the life of his cavalry arm as at Brandy Station. But most of all, Stuart realized that he needed to fight only a defensive battle if the Yankees appeared and became aggressive, because his primary mission was to strike the Army of the Potomac's rear.

Keeping his tactical options open, Stuart now set the stage for the upcoming clash of cavalry by initiating it himself, before he felt free to ride west and then southwest to strike Meade's rear along Cemetery Ridge, because he could not allow any large force of Union cavalry to remain in his rear. Indeed, he realized that he could not allow Federal cavalry to attack his rear if he decided to ride west or southwest in targeting Meade's rear. Therefore, Stuart first had to deal with the situation before him since Pleasonton's troopers were almost certainly guarding the flank, because he needed to possess the strategic crossroads before moving out to gain the Baltimore Road and Meade's vulnerable rear, and this tactical situation required defeating any Union force of cavalry that might be occupying the intersection.

Ironically, it was almost as if he had reread the scathing editorial (it certainly still burned into his mind) from the pages of the *Charleston Mercury*, Charleston, South Carolina, about the disastrous fight at Brandy Station, which included the kind of criticism that applied even more now to the recent raid that had taken Stuart too far away from the "blind" army, when Lee had needed his "eyes and ears," while his best cavalry commander and brigades had ridden as far south as nearly to Washington, DC, and also as far north as Chambersburg, Pennsylvania, in attempting to locate the army: "Cavalry were intended to decide and complete victories—not to ride around."[137]

And now Stuart possessed the opportunity to accomplish his greatest feat to date in reaping a decisive success. But first he needed to know of the enemy's numbers, location, and disposition as much as possible, because he might have to fight to gain possession of the crossroads before gaining Meade's rear. Pleasonton's entire Cavalry Corps of three divisions—nearly twelve thousand men—was somewhere in Meade's rear, and it had to be relatively close.

In addition, Stuart also might have feared his own vulnerability because he was no longer mobile—with his four brigades and batteries hidden in the forests of Cress's Ridge—and that was an uncomfortable situation for a commander, who had long relied upon mobility and swift movement to win victory. Quite simply, this was not Stuart's kind of fighting, and he was impatient by nature and inclination.

In this sense, Stuart was adhering to a plan, which seems to suggest that it was more of Lee's than Stuart's design, because it required qualities that fit the more mature Lee, known for his strategic insights and tactical wisdom, far more than the impetuous Stuart. But because no specific tactical details were forthcoming from the Lee-Stuart meeting of July 2, it is not known if the following act that was about to be played out was conceived by Lee, Stuart, or both. But the distinct possibility exists that this forthcoming act was the idea of both Lee and Stuart, and it had been mutually agreed upon by them during their conference at the Widow Thompson house.

Therefore, before the opening of the massive artillery bombardment in preparation for the launching of Pickett's Charge, because the sound of the booming guns could be easily heard, and for a long distance to the west where General Lee was now located, Stuart suddenly ordered a field piece to be pushed from the dense woodlands of Cress's Ridge. This gun was pushed by hand out into the open on the high ground overlooking the strategic crossroads of the Hanover and Low Dutch Roads to the south.

All the while, Stuart made sure that his thousands of cavalrymen remained hidden in the thick woodlands of Cress's Ridge that provided an ideal shelter and screen from Union eyes. Historian Stephen W. Sears described how around 11:30 a.m., and before Lee's massive bombardment in preparation for the unleashing of Pickett's Charge against the vulnerable right-center of Meade's lengthy defensive line that was overextended along Cemetery Ridge, Stuart "fired off his four-round artillery salvo to inform General Lee that he was behind the Yankee army."[138]

From the western side of Cress's Ridge just before the woods that covered the ridgetop like a green shroud, this gun was fired west toward Gettysburg for the express purpose of alerting General Lee, who was now located around three miles distant from Cress's Ridge, because this was a long-awaited signal that both men had agreed upon during their late July 2 conference.[139] In his memoir, Major Henry Brainerd McClellan, who served capably as one of Stuart's trusty staff officers, wrote, "Stuart pushed one of [Captain William H.] Griffin's guns [of the Maryland Battery] to the edge of the woods and fired a number of random shots in different directions, himself giving orders to the gun."[140]

From the limited knowledge that he possessed about Stuart's plan, which was still a closely guarded secret at this time, he later wrote in regard to the firing of the cannon of the 2nd Baltimore, Maryland, Horse Artillery Battery of four 10-pounders as personally directed by Stuart: "I suppose that they may have been a prearranged signal by which he was able to notify General Lee that he had gained a favorable position; or, finding that none of the enemy were within sight, he may have desired to satisfy himself whether the Federal cavalry was in his immediate vicinity before leaving the strong position he then held; and receiving no immediate reply to this fire, he sent for Hampton and Fitz Lee, to arrange for them for an advance and an attack upon the enemy's rear."[141]

But in fact the purpose of the firing of the cannon, a 10-pounder Parrott, was threefold: (1) to make General Lee, now near the front lines before the unleashing of Pickett's Charge instead of back at the Widow Thompson house northwest of Gettysburg, aware of his planned positioning on the high ground of Cress's Ridge behind the Union lines; (2) to bait Federal cavalry to show their strength and dispositions; and (3) to convince any nearby Union cavalry to advance toward him with a degree of overconfidence—the thin line of skirmishers positioned on the high ground just before the tree line of the high ground providing the bait—so that he could ambush them with the larger numbers of his main force of around six thousand men who were hidden in the thick forests that covered Cress's Ridge.

Since his headquarters meeting with General Lee at the Widow Thompson house on the previous night, Stuart had envisioned a grand charge sweeping downhill from the high ground of Cress's Ridge to destroy any Union cavalry forces that were sure to gain possession of the strategic crossroads, which was on lower ground and hence extremely vulnerable. Then he would be free to attack into Meade's rear without having to take the risk of being struck in the rear by any Union cavalry once he had defeated any force sent by Pleasonton.

But first, with time of the essence, Stuart had to alert the Federal cavalry that seemingly only a small number of Rebels (a thin line of dismounted skirmishers on the high ground just in front of the tree line on the crest of Cress's Ridge) were in Meade's rear with only the mission of guarding Ewell's flank, which was not the case, and they were sure to come to secure the crossroads. Basically, he was setting up his tactical trap because both the vital intersection and his skirmishers of Jenkins's (Witcher's) command now served as bait that could not be resisted by Federal cavalry arriving in large numbers.[142]

All the while, thousands of Stuart's men were confident and eager to charge out of the woods to wipe out any unwary Union forces that might well advance too close to the timbered high ground of Cress's Ridge with the mission of pushing aside only a relatively few skirmishers in gray and butternut. Most importantly, at this time, to fulfill Lee's and his top cavalryman's ambitions, Stuart's troopers were highly motivated to strike a blow, because they realized what was at stake on July 3. In the words of Sergeant Robert S. Hudgins, Company B, 3rd Virginia Cavalry, Fitzhugh Lee's Brigade: "We had rejoined Lee, and were looking for a victory to perch on our banners. This was the day that Gen. Pickett" unleashed his offensive effort, when General Lee and the Army of Northern Virginia were going for broke as never before.[143]

Indeed, in a repeat of the cavalry charges and countercharges that had been seen at Brandy Station, the dramatic cavalry showdown was about to erupt around three miles northeast of Gettysburg, and it was now only a matter of time. In consequence, Stuart was naturally overanxious and in a rush to engage and defeat the enemy cavalry, which would then unleash him for his larger mission of striking Meade's rear. Gifted historian Bradley M. Gottfried emphasized how Stuart "fired four shots [from the lone cannon] to inform Lee that he was in position and ready to attack the Federal rear."[144]

Significantly, one of Stuart's best staff officers, the Philadelphia-born Major Henry "Harry" Brainerd McClellan, emphasized as much in regard to Stuart's reasoning and actions. Ironically, Henry's own brother was Captain Carswell McClellan. The captain served as assistant adjutant general on Meade's staff in the epitome of the meaning of the brothers' war, and he had been born in Philadelphia, which was Lee's primary urban target if the Army of the Potomac was defeated on July 3. The capable Major McClellan, of Stuart's staff, had performed heroically at Brandy Station, playing a role in saving the day in a success to ensure that Stuart's cavalry would be allowed the opportunity of July 3.[145] Even more, McClellan was the cousin of General George B. McClellan, who had failed to capture Richmond during the 1862 Peninsula Campaign. Although a former schoolteacher and only twenty-three years of age (the same age as Custer, who had served on General McClellan's staff in 1862), McClellan served Stuart well as his new adjutant during the Gettysburg campaign, helping to make the staff operate more smoothly to meet an unprecedented number of challenges.[146] Significantly, the talented major knew that Stuart's plan was to strike a blow into the rear of the Army of the Potomac and wrote as much in his memoirs, *I Rode with Jeb Stuart*.[147]

McClellan's revealing memoir, providing a wealth of information, has often been ignored by historians for reasons that are entirely unknown to this author. Nevertheless, the myth has been created by some modern historians that Stuart fired the Maryland Battery's 10-pounder not as a signal to General Lee, but merely to draw out the bluecoats. However, this assumption—not even an educated guess based on substantial or accurate evidence—is entirely off base. Perhaps historian Thom Hatch said it best: Adjutant "McClellan [who was not entirely in the know at the time] speculated that the firing of the four rounds may have been a prearranged signal to let General Lee know that Stuart had successfully reached his position at the Union rear. McClellan's assumption rings true. Stuart, the master of stealth, would not have fired the cannons and compromised his position simply to determine the location of his enemy. Jeb knew, after all, that he was at the rear of the Union line. His actions therefore can be interpreted to mean that the cavalry indeed was an integral part of a plan to strike the rear in coordination with Pickett's frontal assault. Lee was now free to carry on with his bold strategy."[148]

In addition, self-serving revisionist historians without PhDs have had a disproportionate influence in promoting their own self-serving agendas with well-organized propaganda on Civil War blogs—where they can mask deep-seated personal motivations by using multiple fake accounts—and have emphasized that Lee was too far away at his headquarters at the Widow Thompson house to have heard Stuart's cannon shots fired from the Maryland artillery piece from the high ground. Again, this was simply not the case and is only the most recent example of revisionist spin or outright propaganda. The sound of a cannon firing from Cress's Ridge carried a long distance to the west, and certainly well within Lee's hearing, before the opening of the artillery bombardment in preparation for unleashing Pickett's Charge.

In fact, Lee was away from his more distant (farther west) headquarters, northwest of Gettysburg and farther away from Cress's Ridge than the front lines, for most of July 3, and farther east and closer to Stuart, because this was the most important day of the war and he was therefore near the front. In the words of West Point graduate, respected historian, and combat veteran Tom Carhart, Stuart "fired cannon shots signaling their arrival to Lee."[149] Another historian correctly concluded that Stuart "fired the shots to inform Lee that the cavalry was in position and ready to attack."[150]

For strange reasons that are inexplicable, modern historians—the armchair types without military experience or academic backgrounds who are the most aggressive cyber-warriors to promote their self-serving agendas by aggressive cyber-propaganda—have found Stuart's decision to fire four shots from the cannon of Captain Griffin's Battery to have been entirely inexplicable. What they have refused to admit was the simple fact that Stuart would have been guilty of the greatest of military sins if he had not signaled Lee to inform him of the presence of his largest force of cavalry on the war's most important day, because he was to act in conjunction with Pickett's Charge. And he knew that he could not leave a powerful force in his rear, and one with great mobility and formidable combat capabilities, to strike him in the rear, if he proceeded toward Meade's rear without inflicting any damage whatsoever on the Union cavalry on that portion of the field. Therefore, Stuart had to initially fight whatever Federal force came his way or defended the strategic crossroads.

## STUART'S TACTICAL TRAP

All in all, General Stuart had developed a clever plan, while keeping his four batteries and one section of artillery and four cavalry brigades hidden under the cover provided by the dense woodlands of Cress's Ridge. He knew that the forthcoming defenders—Custer and his Michigan Brigade, which were shortly to gain permanent possession of the strategic crossroads—would soon be expecting the most likely Confederate threat from the two roads that met on the low ground: either from the north down the Low Dutch Road or from the west down the Hanover Road.

Therefore, if the enemy arrived in force and posed a threat by denying him possession of the strategic crossroads, Stuart then planned to attack between the two anticipated avenues of advance and straight down the open slope toward the crossroads, and from where least expected, hoping to catch the Federals by surprise on the assumption that they had extended their defensive lines too far, their right flank having advanced too far north up the Low Dutch Road and the left flank too far west down the Hanover Road.[151]

As expected, the response to the firing of cannon was not long in coming, while Stuart continued to keep his thousands of cavalrymen hidden among the dense timber of Cress's Ridge.

As noted in regard to tactical options, Stuart planned to hold any Federals who decided to defend the crossroads in place by escalating the skirmish when the Yankees arrived, then depart the cover to the ridge to swing around their left, western, flank and make straight for the Baltimore Road.

To his great credit and in agreement with General Gregg, Custer was determined to secure permanent possession of the strategic crossroads at all costs, because it posed a threat to Meade's rear if gained by Stuart. With his well-honed instincts for battle, he already knew that if Stuart gained this key crossroads, he would possess an avenue to strike into the Union army's rear, because the "Low Dutch Road provided a direct route into the center of" the vulnerable Army of the Potomac to deliver the boldest of strokes from the east.[152]

To make sure that the Federals got within easy striking distance by dangling a tempting target before their eyes, Stuart had sent the dismounted skirmishers of Chambliss's North Carolina and Virginia Brigade and Jenkins's (Witcher's) Virginia Brigade down the slope in a wide skirmish line to protect his front and gain possession of John Rummel's buildings. He wanted especially to secure the huge Dutch-style barn that dominated the northern horizon from the view of the lower ground of the crossroads. These buildings were located just south on high ground on a slight ridge primarily before Chambliss's Virginia and North Carolina Brigade, which held Stuart's right on the southern spur of Cress's Ridge. These buildings needed to be secured because they were situated almost immediately before Stuart's center. If the Federals first gained possession of these buildings, they could use them as a launching pad to strike north a short distance up the slope in an offensive bid to split Stuart's line in two by attacking the center between Hampton's Brigade and Chambliss's Brigade. Even more importantly, the cagy Stuart was deliberately dangling the thin line of these dismounted Virginia men—an ideal target for charging mounted bluecoat troopers—in the open fields before the woods of Cress's Ridge as part of his ambush to lure the smaller number of Federals up the slope to within easy striking distance, where they would be vulnerable on the lower ground.[153]

One of the last Rebels to reach the wooded shelter of Cress's Ridge, veteran Sergeant Robert S. Hudgins, of Fitzhugh Lee's Brigade, which held Stuart's left on the north to Hampton's left on the ridge's higher ground—compared to the position of Jenkins's (Witcher's) Brigade of Virginians—and still hidden among the tall timber, described how not long after his arrival, he and his comrades were about to hear the "scattered skirmishing firing [that] indicated the presence of Yankees [Custer] along the far side of the field" around the crossroads.[154] Hudgins sensed trouble brewing, revealing his veteran instincts. Stuart needed to defeat and then push the Federals aside as quickly as possible to gain the strategic intersection of the Hanover and Low Dutch Roads, which "provided a direct route into the center of Meade's rear area."

Therefore Stuart prepared to order four guns—two ordinance rifles and two 12-pounder howitzers—of Captain Thomas Edwin Jackson's Virginia Battery, which was known as the Charlottesville Horse Artillery or simply Jackson's Battery, into the open to support his skirmishers if a large number of Union cavalry suddenly appeared at the crossroads, as fully expected by this time. Hidden among the trees on the high ground that overlooked the Rummel farm, Jackson's cannon were about to be pushed south from the sheltering timber onto a dominant high-ground perch and into the bright July sunlight for all to see. Here, on an ideal perch for artillery, located just below the thick woods that covered the high ground like a green blanket, these guns that represented the Old Dominion were shortly to realign on the open ground, situated below the forested crest of Cress's Ridge, which overlooked the wide plain and shallow valley, where the strategic intersection was occupied by dismounted Yankee pickets.[155]

From his commanding perch of Cress's Ridge, which ran north–south and provided the Rebels with an ideal location that overlooked the lower-ground intersection of the Hanover and Low Dutch Roads, Stuart now occupied a good concealed position from which to descend from the high ground and eventually ride southwest to gain the Baltimore Road and not only threaten but also "strike Meade's rear to wreck considerable havoc on truly a grand scale." But first he had to push aside any nearby Federal cavalrymen who were protecting Meade's right flank and holding the strategic intersection of the Hanover and Low Dutch Roads, before the final ride southwest to assist the attackers of Lee's main effort (Pickett's Charge) that had been orchestrated to win it all.

Therefore Stuart had created what was essentially an ambush by hiding most of his troopers, especially the elite fighting men of Hampton's and Lee's Brigades, and his ample number of cannon in the thick woods of Cress's Ridge that overlooked the fields to the south, where the key crossroads was in full view across the open fields that descended across open terrain, including a wide plain. With the dismounted men of Jenkins's (Witcher's) and Chambliss's brigades aligned in the open fields in a lengthy skirmish line near the wood line in full sight on the high ground, Stuart had positioned the bait so that the Federal cavalry would engage the Rebels on first sight—seemingly almost a guarantee from a new and overly aggressive brigade commander like Custer.

When the Federals of Gregg's Second Cavalry Division eventually engaged the dismounted skirmishers in sizeable numbers in the open fields, Stuart possessed an option to secure a decisive victory at the crossroads if necessary and depending on the tactical situation and existing opportunities: the unleashing of his mounted troopers of Hampton's and Lee's Brigades (a strategic reserve) from the advantage of the high ground of Cress's Ridge to smash the dismounted Federals—they were certain to be dismounted to engage the dismounted skirmishers of Chambliss and Jenkins (Witcher)—with a mighty blow that would not only destroy the opposition but also secure the strategic crossroads, before riding west to attack into Meade's rear.

Therefore, Stuart's finest troopers, especially the men of Hampton's Brigade—situated between Fitzhugh Lee on its left and Chambliss on its right—were mounted and basically serving in the role of a strategic reserve. Consequently, these regiments remained hidden from view amid the tall timber, and Stuart planned that they should remain concealed and in a good, elevated position because they were his best cavalrymen, who would most likely be ordered to lead the way to the Federal rear—Stuart's primary mission—due to their experience and combat prowess.

Because of the firing of the lone Maryland gun in four directions on Stuart's orders, the largest body of nearby Union cavalrymen of Pleasonton's Corps almost certainly would be quickly drawn to the sudden firing of Confederate artillery—a serious threat indicating that a larger body of the enemy was present nearby to protect the guns—in Meade's rear like a magnet. If there was no reply or appearance of sizeable numbers of Union cavalry, then Stuart planned to ride southwest to strike Meade's rear at the most appropriate time and place in compliance with Lee's orders.

But if Federals appeared in force as expected, then Stuart's plan was to present a weak dismounted force to bait the Federals into attacking uphill with too much confidence and carelessness; then he would unleash his main force of Hampton's and Lee's hard-hitting brigades that would attack from the high ground and the cover of the woods of Cress's Ridge to strike the unsuspecting Yankees with a severe blow that would negate their combat capabilities and manpower, before his all-important ride to the southwest to gain the Baltimore Road and the Union rear after gaining control of the vital intersection of the Hanover and Low Dutch Roads at the field's southern end. Then, once Stuart vanquished any newly arrived Yankees around the intersection, he would have an easy and open avenue to gain the Union rear three miles to the southwest by the time thousands of Rebels of Pickett's Charge struck from the opposite direction.

Some of the exact details of this tactical plan were almost certainly developed by Stuart, because Lee always allowed his top commanders to utilize their own initiative and flexibility, often to an excessive degree, which proved detrimental—like Stuart's recent raid for no gain—and this was especially the case during the three days at Gettysburg. The more cautious Lee almost certainly emphasized that Stuart should only lightly and briefly engage (anything but a large-scale battle) Union cavalry in front and then "slide around" or "swing around their flank," in the words of historian Bradley M. Gottfried, because the Union rear was the real target of opportunity. Therefore, Lee knew that men and horses could not be lost in a large-scale and time-consuming cavalry fight three miles from the Union rear to the east, when time was of the essence. Manpower and energy had to be preserved for the main effort of striking Meade's rear. But a less mature and sensible Stuart was more likely to be sucked into a gradually escalating conflict for the crossroads because he was a fighter by nature, and his pride was at stake, especially after the humiliation at Brandy Station. Therefore, he wanted to redeem himself, and this meant winning glory in manfully vanquishing Yankee cavalry. In this sense, Stuart possessed a mind-set that might cause him to lose sight of his principal mission because of his emotions and bruised ego.

Again like Lee, Stuart did not initially want a major clash with any Union cavalry—especially sizeable numbers of bluecoats—over the possession of the strategic crossroads to sap his strength and combat capabilities, because his primary mission was to proceed onward to strike the Union rear. But Stuart was vulnerable to any escalating contest that might develop for possession of the crossroads, and he knew that he might win victory if he unleashed his strategic reserve—Hampton's and Fitzhugh's Brigade—to deliver a devastating blow. For Stuart, it would be most tempting to engage in a full-scale contest, but initially he wanted no Brandy Station–like slugfest.

Stuart, therefore, wanted to first eliminate any initial Union cavalry opposition and then gain the crossroads by way of a tactical trap that allowed him to preserve as much of his force as possible for the primary mission of attacking Meade's rear. In this tactical scenario, he most likely envisioned only using Fitzhugh Lee's Brigade, his second-best combat unit, to wipe out the Yankees at the crossroads, and saving Hampton's Brigade, his premier combat unit, to spearhead the attack into Meade's rear. Again, Stuart's exact tactical thinking, especially when influenced by his emotions and ego, at this time is not known.

However, in overall terms, this situation was precarious because the forthcoming fight for possession of the little crossroads in Meade's right-rear had the potential to quickly spiral out of control—like at Brandy Station and as an absent Lee had discovered on the first day at Gettysburg when his foremost troops became too aggressive before the army was prepared for a major battle—because Stuart's men, including top officers, were proud fighting men who were eager to gain revenge for their supreme humiliation at Brandy Station, where the bluecoat troopers had taught them a nasty lesson. But this was Stuart's fight from beginning to end, because Lee knew relatively little about the area known today as the East Cavalry Field or Cress's Ridge, because it was unfamiliar territory.

However, as mentioned, Lee possessed a topographical map by which he and Stuart had made their offensive plans at the Widow Thompson house on the night of July 2. Therefore, because he possessed flexibility since Lee expected him to adapt to the tactical situation that would inevitably develop before moving southwest to strike Meade's rear, this was Stuart's battle to orchestrate in tactical terms as he thought was most appropriate under the circumstances in a fluid battlefield situation once the Federal cavalry arrived in force, because Lee was far away and no longer in contact. All in all, this plan was a good one because the situation was fluid and Stuart possessed the strategic high ground—always the way to win a battle—and he knew that the confident Union cavalry would be overly aggressive after a magnificent performance in thoroughly bloodying his cavalry arm at Brandy Station and might well commit tactical mistakes, especially if too aggressive, that could be exploited.[156]

Indeed, as planned from the beginning and eager to make the most of the opportunity, Stuart was in an excellent position atop Cress's Ridge, which he had gained without a single shot fired, to fulfill his overall "assignment [which] was to ride into the rear of the Army of the Potomac" and then "wreak havoc on a grand scale."[157] Indeed, Major Henry Brainerd McClellan emphasized that Stuart's top priority was not to engage in a full-scale battle like at Brandy Station, but "to attack upon the enemy's rear."[158]

General Stuart's chances of achieving a decisive success were increased by the fact that he was about to face cavalry that were in overall bad shape, one of the overlooked factors that came into play during the showdown on the East Cavalry Field. In the past, critics have incorrectly charged that Stuart's effectiveness was too greatly diminished for the key mission of striking Meade's rear, which was certainly not the case, without ever considering how the Union cavalry was in equally bad shape from a grueling campaign in hot, dry weather.

Arriving later on the scene as the belated defenders of the strategic crossroads in Meade's right-rear, a trooper of the 3rd Pennsylvania Cavalry, Colonel John Baillie McIntosh's First Brigade, Brigadier General David McMurtrie Gregg's Second Cavalry Division, Pleasonton's Cavalry Corps, described how by July 3, "we were a sorry-looking body of men, having been in the saddle day and night almost continuously for over three weeks [and] we were much reduced by short rations and exhaustion, and mounted on horses whose bones were plainly visible."[159]

All the while, Stuart envisioned winning a great victory—not only defeating the Union cavalry that protected Meade's right-rear if they appeared in sizeable numbers because he would outnumber them and enjoy the high-ground advantage, but also striking into the Army of the Potomac's rear to deliver the masterstroke "to clinch the victory" on July 3—that would make everyone, from General Lee to the people of the South, forget all about his greatest day of humiliation and embarrassment at Brandy Station.[160]

In consequence, Stuart planned to slip around the Union cavalry and then "reach the Baltimore Road unobserved and be in position to create panic within the Federal's rear on Cemetery Ridge" when Pickett's Charge struck in the greatest offensive effort ever unleashed by Lee and his top lieutenant, Major General James Longstreet, who was in charge of orchestrating the great assault that was calculated to win it all.[161]

But in regard to fulfilling his lofty ambitions of inflicting a decisive blow, Stuart had no idea about the high quality of the feisty Michigan men and their tactically gifted brigade commander, who seemed far too young. Unknown to him and unimaginable at this time, Stuart was about to more than meet his match in this native Ohioan in the struggle for possession of the strategic crossroads. Like Custer, the Wolverine troopers, both officers and enlisted men, were cocky and confident for success. These Michigan men would fight tenaciously like a hungry or cornered wolverine to retain possession of the crossroads if they secured it.

When serving with the large Washington, DC, garrison in the winter of 1862–1863, a group of serious-faced 6th Michigan Cavalry officers, who were now members of Custer's Brigade, had even boasted to Abraham Lincoln in person of the "intention on their part to capture the rebel cavalry leader J.E.B. Stuart," which caused the president to grin in some amusement.[162] But this was exactly the kind of feisty fighting spirit that was needed to beat Stuart and frustrate his lofty ambitions.

As fate would have it, Stuart also did not realize that his primary opponent and the man—the "goat" of his class of 1861, with an almost girlish handsomeness—who was destined to achieve more in thwarting his lofty strategic designs on July 3 was nothing more than a fresh-faced twenty-three-year-old youth, who had come close to being killed in the clash of cavalry at Hunterstown on July 2, when an inordinate degree of luck had saved his life.[163]

But something significant had been demonstrated by Custer, who had led a cavalry attack with too few Michigan men in the sharp clash at Hunterstown, that was destined to rise to the fore on the afternoon of July 3 to mock his West Point failures, youth, and inexperience. He was about to demonstrate in remarkable fashion how one's class ranking and notoriously bad behavior in racking up one of the highest totals of demerits (726 in four years, which included having hair too long and throwing bread in the dining hall) in the history of the United States Military Academy had nothing to do with actual achievements on the battlefield where it mattered most.

Custer had excelled at West Point only by his flexibility and ingeniousness, which had allowed him to survive, if not thrive, and graduate from the academy in the end as the notorious "goat" of the class of 1861. And now he was about to thrive in protecting the vulnerable rear of the Army of the Potomac on the final day at Gettysburg, when everything mattered and counted, unlike in the hallowed halls of West Point. Even more, Custer represented a new generation of fighting men in blue who were much younger and more aggressive than men of the older generation, including Lee and his corps commanders, like the one-legged General Ewell and the fumbling General Stuart to a lesser degree.[164]

## CUSTER SKILLFULLY DEPLOYS AND DEFENDS THE STRATEGIC CROSSROADS

While the defenders along Cemetery Ridge waited patiently but nervously for the unleashing of Lee's greatest offensive of the war, Custer's Brigade of four Wolverine regiments, consisting of around 2,500 men, rode forward on their special mission to guard the crossroads in the rising heat of mid-morning light. Of course, General Kilpatrick was infuriated by Custer's decision not to rejoin his division and instead to stay with another division.

Arriving at the strategic crossroads, Custer was shown his new position by General Gregg's courier, who had guided the new brigade commander and his men to this new location. Gregg's aide knew of this strategic spot from the previous day's skirmishing and from where Gregg had withdrawn after suffering light casualties. With perfect knowledge of the area, he led the foremost Wolverines to the dusty intersection of the Hanover and Low Dutch Roads, which seemed to be located in the middle of nowhere. Here, north of the all-important Baltimore Pike that Stuart wanted to eventually secure before proceeding onward for his main assignment of striking Meade's rear, Custer found a handful of lonely Union pickets who had been left behind at the crossroads by General Gregg from the previous day's skirmishing, when the Second Division had held the strategic intersection.

Most of all, Custer was thankful that no Rebels—only a company or two could have accomplished the job—had advanced down either the Hanover Road or the Low Dutch Road to capture the strategic intersection that lay there for the taking, or were advancing in large numbers off the high ground of Cress's Ridge because he occupied low ground at the crossroads that was most vulnerable. Not liking the looks of the place, especially with his entire brigade not up yet, Custer saw how thoroughly the strategic intersection was dominated by higher ground, especially Cress's Ridge to the north.[165]

Meanwhile, Stuart waited on Cress's Ridge to make his next move and then spring his tactical trap—basically a clever ambush if Custer made the mistake of becoming overly aggressive—from his elevated position that overlooked the key crossroads of the Hanover Road and Low Dutch Road (also known locally as the Salem Road and running north–south to intersect the Hanover Road to the south), which he now needed to capture from the foremost of Custer's troopers after they had arrived "at a trot" in the bright summer light of mid-morning. But Stuart was not primarily focused on a time-consuming struggle for the crossroads per Lee's orders, because he was thinking about turning southwest at the best opportunity to ride to gain the Baltimore Pike and then the Union rear to fulfill his key mission of delivering a devastating blow from the east.

Most importantly and in striking contrast to Stuart's men, the troopers of Custer's Brigade were relatively fresh, even after the fight at Hunterstown on the previous day, but they were still in a worn condition after a vigorous and wide-ranging campaign. At that time, only a relatively few troopers of the 6th Michigan Cavalry had been roughed up when Custer led a foolish headlong charge with a small force against too many opponents without properly gaining intelligence about the enemy's strength and advantageous position. Hoping to obtain a measure of revenge for their bruising at Hunterstown, the troopers of the 6th Michigan Cavalry had appropriately led the advance of Custer's Brigade to the strategic crossroads on this increasingly ever-warming day in the late morning hours.

But how had Custer and his men arrived at the strategic crossroads in the nick of time? Fully understanding the importance of this key position, Brigadier General David McMurtrie Gregg, who had been ordered by Pleasonton to protect the army's right-rear, had retained possession of the strategic intersection of the Hanover and Low Dutch Roads with a small force. Earlier in the morning, when about five miles east of Gettysburg, Gregg had been ordered by Pleasonton to shift closer to the army's right flank at Culp's Hill. But the savvy Gregg, whose well-honed instincts were as right on target today as Custer's own, had wisely balked at the order, knowing that the key to the upcoming fight in Meade's right-rear was destined to be played at the crucial intersection of the Hanover and Low Dutch Roads. A native Pennsylvanian, Gregg was determined to defend the land that he loved, and his motivations could not have been higher at this time when everything was at stake.

With only Colonel John Baillie McIntosh available to him because his other brigade, under Colonel J. Irvin Gregg, was farther down the Baltimore Road, General Gregg had early realized that he had to keep Custer's Brigade with him for any chance of retaining permanent possession of the strategic crossroads. From the beginning, the sage Gregg knew that Custer would be needed by him today because Meade's rear was so vulnerable, and a dramatic showdown of cavalry was destined to come behind the front lines. In this regard, Gregg's instincts were right on target, fortunately for General Meade and the Army of the Potomac.

Because of the growing concern that Stuart was lurking in the area, after receiving a message around noon from Major General Oliver Otis Howard, who commanded the Eleventh Corps and held Cemetery Hill, located at the northern end of Cemetery Ridge, from where Stuart's gray-and-butternut column had been spied riding northeast down the York Turnpike, and that thousands of Rebel cavalrymen were now on the move toward the Union right, General Gregg's adjutant personally directed, on the general's orders, Custer to deploy his Michigan troopers around the crossroads and along the Low Dutch Road. This road ran northeast from the crossroads a short distance to the rear.

Without wasting time or waiting for specific orders, General Gregg had smartly taken the initiative, assuming full responsibility for having boldly ordered Custer's Wolverine Brigade to the crossroads on the John Rummel farm. But, as noted, Custer was anything but a reluctant commander, because he remained eager to defend the crossroads to the last man if necessary because of the overall importance of this key position in the army's vulnerable rear. Above all else, Custer knew that an important fight lay ahead for him and his Michigan boys.

To his great credit and with prophetic insight, Gregg had early realized that he needed a good many more men to guard the army's right-rear to hold the strategic crossroads because of the brewing threat that he believed might descend upon Meade's rear at any moment. Therefore, at great risk to his own career if anything went wrong, Gregg assumed full responsibility for having directed Custer and his brigade to the crossroads, because he had not informed Pleasonton or Kilpatrick, to whose division Custer's Michigan Brigade belonged, of his bold decision. Most of all, he fully realized that no time could be wasted in a fast-moving tactical situation if Stuart was prowling somewhere in the area of Meade's rear with the promise of causing great mischief.

But, especially in the beginning, this was primarily going to be Custer's fight in defending the crossroads—a showdown between Stuart and Custer, or the case of a legendary warrior chieftain and a young, rookie brigade commander. Therefore, on paper, it looked like a great mismatch, but this was not the case.

After all, Gregg was absent from the crossroads and would hold his other units in support after the arrival of all the Wolverines at the key intersection, while the young brigadier general in the outlandish uniform held the key intersection of the Hanover and Low Dutch Roads with his foremost troopers. Here, around three miles east of Gettysburg on the lush acres of John Rummel's farm, which included not only the crossroads but also Cress's Ridge just over a mile to the north to dominate the horizon, Custer knew that he had to hurriedly hurl out his own long lines of Michigan skirmishers, both mounted and dismounted, in every direction, including the rear (clearly Custer was not taking any chances), and deploy his dismounted men to defend the crossroads before the enemy struck to gain this strategic position.

Because he had no idea that Stuart and thousands of his cavalrymen and artillerymen were now hidden in the thick woodlands of Cress's Ridge to the north, Custer wisely remained prudent and careful, because—like Stuart—he was not familiar with this area. He also knew that he possessed the burden of responsibility for defending the crossroads on his own at this point. As noted, General Gregg was not present.

Therefore, for a variety of reasons, Custer immediately made the smart decision to align his men in a lengthy line facing west and northwest toward the open fields that ascended northward toward the heavily timbered crest of Cress's Ridge and toward Gettysburg. He expected the main threat, if one emerged, to come down the Hanover Road from the west, or from Gettysburg, which was a logical conclusion based largely on his knowledge of the previous day's light combat by Gregg's men. After all, the Pennsylvania general had verbally informed the young brigade commander that the fighting was sure to resume on July 3. And of course this was the best road leading west from Gettysburg, and it was larger than the Low Dutch Road, which was nothing more than a country lane by comparison.

Without wasting time, because he was the sole guardian of the crossroads—now his responsibility and not General Gregg's, who remained at his headquarters—which he was determined to keep at all costs, Custer ordered his troopers of the 6th and 5th Michigan Cavalry, which had arrived first and second respectively, to dismount and prepare for action that might erupt at anytime for all he knew. He directed them to align in a defensive arrangement to protect the strategic crossroads, just in case the wily Rebels suddenly attacked down either road, but most likely down the Hanover Road from the west.

Most importantly, Custer now relied on one of the finest officers of the 6th Michigan, the dashing Captain Peter A. Weber, and his trust in this promising officer could not have been better placed. Weber was highly skilled in the soldierly arts of hard fighting, intelligence gathering, and reconnaissance, and just the kind of officer Custer needed when commanding a brigade on the verge of its first major battle.

Knowing that he could trust in the sound judgment of this handsome captain of exceptional ability, Custer smartly dispatched Weber and around fifty of his Company B boys about a mile and a half north up the Low Dutch Road to scout for Rebels and also to protect his right flank on the northeast. Custer felt more secure after having handed Captain Weber this key assignment, knowing that the versatile captain would quickly ascertain any existing threat.

From the view of Custer and located far closer—about half the distance to the crossroads—the patch of woods of farmer Lott loomed on the horizon to the northeast as the largest sheltered location close to the strategic intersection, and this position had to be occupied by boys in blue for safety's sake, because the Low Dutch Road ran through this heavily forested area on ground that was higher than at the crossroads. Spanning east–west just north of the Lott house, the Lott woods lay on both sides of the Low Dutch Road, and Custer was early concerned about what might lay in the shadowy woodlands, which seemed too quiet.

Therefore, in overall potential terms, the Lott woods, closer to the crossroads than the timbered crest of Cress's Ridge, posed the most immediate potential threat to Custer's toehold on the strategic intersection, especially if it was occupied by large numbers of Rebels, who might be hidden in the tall timber of this patch of hardwood forest that lay closer to the crossroads than the buildings, situated before Stuart's center, of the John Rummel farm to the northwest. Clearly and most importantly, Custer was not taking any chances after his recent promotion to brigade commander, for he still had to prove that he was worthy of the advancement.

Fortunately for Custer, the close call at Hunterstown had a sobering effect. Consequently, his initial actions and deployments were based on a careful reading of the terrain that lay before him. And in this regard, Custer acted with the thoughtful skill worthy of an experienced brigade commander. In addition, Custer remained extremely cautious and prudent because he was not familiar with this too quiet area in Meade's right-rear, and he could only depend upon what Gregg and the aide-de-camp had recently told him about the previous day's skirmishing.

Most importantly in General Gregg's absence, Custer now possessed the strategic crossroads with a firm and solid grip that would not be relinquished by him on July 3, but no one, especially General Gregg, who knew that he needed to keep Custer and his brigade at the crossroads at any cost, bothered to inform Kilpatrick, who was Custer's division commander, of this situation;

Custer was acting contrary to his division commander's orders, because Kilpatrick had planned an offensive effort on the southern end of the battle line and needed all of his troopers.

But the dark woodlands, especially to the north atop Cress's Ridge, were scattered around a central plain of open ground—the open fields and pastures of summer—located between the Low Dutch Road and the Hanover Road. Custer felt an eerie unease, and he was not taking any chances because this was his first key assignment in a major battle—protecting the vulnerable Army of the Potomac's rear, when Lee was about to unleash his greatest offensive effort of the war.

For all he knew, by this time, stealthy groups of Rebels—whole regiments or perhaps even a brigade or two—might well be hidden in the thickest woodlands, draped in heavy summer foliage that was impenetrable to the naked eye. In this sense, Custer was blind to what lay before him—a situation that forced him to rely on his scouts and especially Captain Weber, who was basically the head of scouts for the Wolverine Brigade. Therefore, Custer was wary about the high ground and dark patches of forests in the vicinity, ensuring that he remained careful because of the uncertainty of the overall situation. Most of all, the young man who had been born in Ohio knew that he could not afford to make a single mistake or miscalculation at this important position in the army's rear.

As mentioned, Custer knew that he had to first ascertain what lay before him in regard to both the terrain and any potential enemy positions, especially on the high ground or hidden in the woods, which might have been stealthily occupied. He saw Virginia skirmishers aligned before the forests of Cress's Ridge, and this sight was ominous, because they possessed the high ground. Most of all, he felt the responsibility of holding the strategic intersection because it was a key to the battlefield in this sector and was almost certainly the enemy's ultimate objective if they planned to strike Meade's rear.

In consequence, Custer was concerned about the dusty road—a mere thin artery—that led north to higher ground from the intersection, which was situated on lower ground. But as noted, the main threat was most likely to come not from the Low Dutch Road but the Hanover Road to the west. Putting up a bold front, as if more troops occupied the crossroads than was actually the case, to deter any potential attackers and to protect his front that guarded the intersection, Custer ordered the skirmishers of the 5th and 6th Michigan Cavalry to advance into the open fields to secure ground before the strategic crossroads. He reasoned that the more ground he secured, the better, just in case he faced more Rebels than anticipated.

Most of all, Custer was determined not to be caught by surprise if any large force of Rebels were lurking nearby, especially in the patches of woods, like the Lott woods north up the Low Dutch Road. On Custer's orders, the veteran skirmishers of the 6th Michigan Cavalry slowly advanced to extend the front to the west to provide greater protection to the crossroads by taking positions along the lengthy fences and along the small creek known as Little's Run that flowed north–south from the higher ground of the Rummel farm and ran perpendicular to the Hanover Road to protect his left flank on the southwest that faced north toward the York Turnpike and Cress's Ridge. By this time, some Virginia skirmishers on Stuart's right had advanced so far south down the slope that they were nearing a point just north of the head of Little's Run.

With prudent skill, Custer had ordered four companies of dismounted 6th Michigan Cavalry men to protect his left flank, which was anchored on both the Hanover Road and Little's Run north of the road, while four other companies protected the strategic crossroads. Most importantly, Custer had chosen his best top lieutenants of the 6th Michigan Cavalry in guardian roles under the ever-reliable Captain Peter A. Weber, who led Company B with consummate skill as demonstrated on past fields of strife, including recently in the cavalry clash at Hanover, and Lieutenant Charles E. Storrs, who led Company G. As Custer fully appreciated, the handsome young man named Weber, who was one of the most popular officers of not only his regiment but also of his hometown of Grand Rapids, was an expert in the art of intelligence gathering.

The highly skilled Captain Weber had just received word of his impending and well-deserved promotion to major. He now acted in that higher-rank capacity while in overall command of both flank protectors, although they were widely separated: Weber, who had advanced about a mile and a half north up the Low Dutch Road from the dusty crossroads and past the Jacob Lott house and the Lott woods, and Storrs, who had pushed forward around the same distance to the west—at least a mile and perhaps more—down the Hanover Road. Custer felt a sense of relief at the sight of the brave Captain Weber, a kindred spirit, and his men riding north up the ascending ground of the Low Dutch Road. If the Rebels attacked down the Low Dutch Road, then Custer would learn about that fact from Weber, who could be counted on to not only give early warning, but also to resist fiercely.

Any Confederate artillery, such as the fast-moving and highly mobile guns of Stuart's famed horse artillery—planted to the north on either side of the Low Dutch Road—could fire down the slope and sweep the crossroads with a devastating fire. Custer was not only concerned about the high ground north of the Lott woods, but also naturally the much larger forested area that covered the top of Cress's Ridge. For all of these reasons, Major Weber possessed a most crucial mission when he and his handful of troopers of Company B, 6th Michigan, pushed north with confidence but on full alert.

Custer watched the movement of Captain Weber and his boys with considerable satisfaction. If the men of Company B ran into any hidden Rebels, then Custer would receive early warning and not become a victim of a surprise attack streaming off the high ground and down the Low Dutch Road. As noted, Custer's sense of security increased immeasurably because he had taken wise precautions, especially after he had entrusted this key mission to Captain Weber, who always got the job done, no matter how difficult. After all, by this time and with his instincts paying dividends, Custer could almost sense the enemy's presence lurking nearby in the dark forests on the higher ground before the crossroads. For good reason and from the beginning, Custer had turned to the ever-reliable Weber, and he could now focus on other matters with no more concern about this right flank. In a strange way, Custer and Weber were very much alike, not only thinking alike but also fighting the same way—a no-holds-barred style—on the field of strife.

Therefore, to his credit, to compensate for the contours of geography that had placed him in a situation that was most disadvantageous, a prudent Custer was doing everything he possibly could to guard both main approaches to the crossroads by having sent out his dismounted troopers under his best commanders, Captains Weber and Charles E. Storrs, age twenty-nine and from the town of Blendon, Michigan, to anchor his flanks on the northeast to guard the Low Dutch Road (Weber) and southwest to protect the Hanover Road (Storrs). Like Weber, Storrs was every inch a fighter and a most reliable officer who could be depended on in an emergency situation.

With piercing eyes and an intelligent look that revealed a keenness of mind, Storrs was a man to be reckoned with by both friend and foe. During a deadly saber duel that he had initiated in a recent melee, Storrs had cut and drawn blood from the large-sized Brigadier General Wade Hampton, a true Achilles in gray and Stuart's top lieutenant, with a slashing blow from his saber during the fighting at Hunterstown that had raged north of Gettysburg on July 2.

With his main battle line facing toward Gettysburg, Custer wisely made these deployments just in case of a possible ambush or if any Confederates charged down either road, which was, in tactical terms, the most likely development, or so it seemed based on the limited information he possessed at that time. Presenting the appearance of a stronger force that was actually in possession of the crossroads before the arrival of the 1st and 7th Michigan Cavalry—now racing to the crossroads to join their two sister regiments—which would shortly be aligned by Custer along the Hanover Road just west of the crossroads to the right of Colonel Russell A. Alger's 5th Michigan, these seasoned men were especially formidable because they were armed with fast-firing Spencer rifles.[166]

A trooper of the 5th Michigan Cavalry, positioned on the Hanover Road west of the crossroads, described how, after dismounting in the rear of the 6th Michigan Cavalry, whose skirmishers began to advance north through the open fields from the Hanover Road and up the sloping ground along Little's Run, which pointed straight toward the huge Rummel barn, three stories tall with a spacious loft unlike anything seen in the South and that dominated the northern horizon, "we deployed in heavy line, then advanced toward a fence which ran along the edge of a wheat field."[167]

In part because the regiment was led by fine officers of outstanding ability, Custer had chosen Colonel Alger's 5th Michigan Cavalry to perform this early mission in the hope of ascertaining the enemy's dispositions and to provide any hint of the Rebels' tactical plan. While most of the Michigan men remained in a defensive stance near the intersection to protect the strategic crossroads and his newly arrived horse artillery under Captain Alexander Cummings McWhorter Pennington, Custer knew that he needed to utilize the 5th Michigan Cavalry to the fullest and in an aggressive manner, because the crossroads must be defended at all costs. This was only natural because this excellent regiment was armed with the most lethal weapon in the Army of the Potomac, the fast-firing Spencer, which was a killing machine.

Therefore, to allow him to complete all of his well-conceived dispositions in protecting the crossroads that Gregg wanted to be held at all costs and for ample good reason, Custer felt more secure after having ordered Alger and his troopers to gradually move north up the ascending terrain and through the open wheat, clover, and oat fields and grassy pastures that were nourished by the clear waters of Little's Run, which trickled south from the springhouse of farmer Rummel, and in the opposite direction of the largest woodlands in the area—the mysterious forest of heavy timber that covered the top of Cress's Ridge. With a mixture of confidence and prudent care, Colonel Alger led his men steadily north up through the open fields of this prosperous German farmer named Rummel and farther away from the Hanover Road to the south, while advancing parallel to Little's Run just to the west, or left.[168]

Contrary to the popular stereotypes and myths about Custer that have created the standard caricature of him as a military commander largely because of the tragic legacy of the fiasco at the Little Bighorn, he was the antithesis of the traditional negative portrait of a model of carelessness on the third day at Gettysburg. Instead of the popular image of the rash and reckless commander without common or tactical sense, Custer was extremely careful, smart, and prudent in having covered and protected his front and the crossroads on the north and west: the two main potential enemy approaches to the strategic intersection.

Upon the arrival of the troopers of the 1st Michigan Cavalry at the crossroads, which brought a sense of relief because of the regiment's superior quality, Custer assigned this closest regiment to guard the crossroads, while the troopers were aligned in a column of squadrons—a strategic reserve that was ready for action and any call to duty as ordered by Custer to meet any threat that might suddenly emerge from the high ground to the north, down both roads, or from the patches of timber, including the Lott woods. The 1st Michigan Cavalry was perhaps the finest regiment of the Wolverine Brigade.

Most of all, Custer's wise deployment of the six 3-inch guns (rifles) of Captain Alexander Cummings McWhorter Pennington's Battery M, 2nd United States Horse Artillery, in the southwest angle of the crossroads was also timely in protecting the skirmishers, mounted and on foot, who had extended the lengthy lines north and west with confidence engendered by the guns that would protect them if they were ambushed by hidden Rebels. Custer knew that he could count on his old West Point friend, Captain Pennington, who commanded his horse artillery.

Anticipating a possible Confederate strike in part because he could see Rebel skirmishers far away, just beyond, or south of, the tree line of Cress's Ridge, Custer ordered the guns of the highly capable Pennington to be positioned facing west to protect the approach down the Hanover Road, while the skirmishers in blue continued to fan out in that direction with eyes open for a clever Rebel ambush or any trouble brewing in the distance. Custer knew that he had to investigate every woodlot, low creek-bed position, and ravine for any hidden enemy troops, because any unexpected development might have the potential to cause him to lose the vital crossroads barely before he had taken possession of it. As mentioned, Custer was not taking any unnecessary risks or chances, because he felt the burden of responsibility and fully realized what was at stake.

An ambitious young man from Ionia, Michigan, who had studied Hardee's tactics in preparation for future challenges while serving as the captain of Company E, 6th Michigan Cavalry, Captain James Harvey Kidd, who possessed a high-quality education from the University of Michigan, concluded with insight that the "popular idea of Custer is a misconception. . . . He was not a reckless commander [and not] one who would plunge into battle with his eyes shut. He was cautious and wary, accustomed to reconnoiter carefully and measure the strength of an enemy as accurately as possible before attacking."[169]

The captain's description especially applied to the extremely prudent and careful actions of Custer on July 3, 1863, when the native Ohioan rose to the occasion. Kidd looked younger than his age, which was the same age as Custer. The son of a Grand Rapids businessman, Kidd had early formed a company of zealous students from the University of Michigan and christened the unit the Tappan Guards, which was named after the educational institution's president, Henry Tappan.[170]

For such reasons as explained with considerable insight by Captain Kidd, newly appointed Brigadier General Custer was allowed ultimate tactical flexibility and made decisions on his own and on the fly, because General Gregg was still absent from the vital crossroads sector and remained at his headquarters in the field. But Gregg actually had little reason for concern, because he trusted Custer and appreciated his abilities, despite the young man having commanded a full brigade of Wolverines for only a few days.

If anything, General Gregg felt less concern for the actions of a new brigadier general, because he knew that Custer would be eager to prove himself—ironically, much like Stuart at this time, but for entirely different reasons—and do everything by the book. Therefore, Custer's defense of the strategic crossroads was standard procedure without deviations or unorthodoxy. After all, too much was now at stake to take any unnecessary risks, and Custer went by the book in regard to orchestrating his defense of this vital intersection that had been suddenly made important by this showdown in Adams County. Despite his dismal performance during his years at the United States Military Academy, Custer had learned his lessons well, and he demonstrated as much in the crossroads' defense, which he conducted with great care.

At age thirty, or only seven years older than Custer, Gregg was not negligent in his duties in regard to his absence from the crossroads. He was ailing, which allowed Custer more flexibility and opportunity to orchestrate tactics on his own. In fact, Gregg's absence seemed to only invigorate Custer, who relished creating his defense of the road intersection on his own. This was a classic case of the ever-independent Custer enjoying doing things his own way and as he deemed proper in a situation of importance in the army's right-rear—not an example of youthful arrogance as it might seem at first glance, but actually more a case of an attitude stemming from a supreme confidence in one's ability. Gregg was fortunate because he could not have possessed a better top lieutenant in orchestrating a solid defense of the strategic crossroads than Custer.

General Gregg's nickname of "Old Steady"—an appropriate nickname because of his sensible and calm demeanor when in a crisis situation, like Custer—was ill placed at this time, but only because of his health. Gregg had come down with an intestinal illness acquired on the rapid and long march to Gettysburg. Consequently the ailing general was being treated by a physician. Therefore, he would not reach the crossroads sector until the early afternoon, and this development was actually to Custer's liking, because he thrived on the independence and the opportunity to do things as he saw fit. From the beginning, Custer consequently made the most of the opportunity not only in the absence of Gregg, but also because Kilpatrick, his division commander who led the Third Cavalry Division, was not aware of what Custer was doing, or even where he was located at this time, when he was preparing to attack the Confederate right, not knowing that Custer was making his own decisions and orchestrating his own defense of this key strategic position to protect the right-rear of the Army of the Potomac, while thriving because of the heightened responsibility and the extent of the challenge.[171]

Meanwhile, all remained relatively quiet in Custer's front, as if no Confederates were anywhere near this remote location in the right-rear of the Army of the Potomac. Custer summarized what he had already accomplished in making the strategic crossroads as safe and secure as possible, revealing the extent of his wise precautions: "Upon arriving at the point [the intersection of the Hanover and Low Dutch Roads] designated, I immediately placed my command in a position facing [west] toward Gettysburg. At the same time I caused reconnaissances to be made on my front, right and rear, but failed to discover any considerable force of the enemy [and] everything remained quiet" in this all-important sector.[172]

After having made his initial deployments with great care and having wisely protected his front in multiple directions, including his rear just in case, Custer felt that the strategic crossroads was now finally adequately protected if the Rebels were to launch an attack down either road. After having accomplished all he was able to do in regard to adequately protecting the key intersection of the Hanover and Low Dutch Roads, Custer almost certainly breathed a sigh of relief, because he had secured the ground surrounding the crossroads and for a good distance to the north and west without a fight or losing a single man. If in a battle situation, he knew that he would have lost a good many Michigan boys if he had been forced to gain this same ground that he now occupied and had secured so easily without a shot having been fired. In rapid fashion and with a marked degree of professionalism, the young man had not only quickly secured the crossroads, but he had also made it safe, after having effectively protected the approaches to the intersection that he had been ordered to hold at all costs.

After he had completed his dispositions to make the crossroads secure, and with his front quiet and not under any direct threat that he could see, Custer now needed to attend to another matter of equal importance, especially for a new commander of a full brigade in what was about to become his first major battle. Custer realized that he needed to brief and present a situation report to General Gregg to keep his commander informed of his actions and the overall situation, and to obtain his blessings for what he had achieved at this point.

First, such a timely and thorough report would relieve Gregg's mind if he had any concerns about the new brigadier general. Second, Custer was also covering himself just in case he met with a disaster, so that he would not be solely responsible for a possible setback if Gregg first gave his approval of

Custer's decisions and moves. Third, Custer knew the importance of gaining any new intelligence that might have arrived at Gregg's headquarters, and he needed an update of any recent developments. By this time, Custer knew enough about the world of the military to play the political game in regard to safeguarding his reputation as much as possible, like Gregg, Pleasonton, and other veteran leaders.

Fortunately, at this time, Pleasonton's messenger knew of the exact location of Gregg's headquarters, which was situated near White Run. Here, after riding at a rapid pace, Custer hastily briefed the brigade commander. General Gregg was fully satisfied with Custer's tactical decisions and dispositions, while realizing that the young man was indeed an excellent brigade commander by his well-conceived defense of the strategic crossroads. In fact, Gregg could not have done better himself, and he realized as much. After the hasty verbal presentation of his situation report, Custer drew himself up and stood at attention and then smartly saluted his division commander—a kindred spirit, especially in tactical terms on July 3.

Custer then quickly remounted his warhorse Roanoke. Without wasting any time, he galloped back to rejoin his command that was about to defend the strategic crossroads with the iron grip of a Wolverine, while the veteran Michigan skirmishers continued to advance over the open ground to the north toward Cress's Ridge to cover and protect the front as ordered by their young commander.[173]

Because the strength of Stuart's forces (four cavalry brigades and four batteries and a section of Louisiana artillery)—except for a thin line of Rebel skirmishers, who were not aggressive, just before the trees on the high ground—were hidden in the woods of Cress's Ridge, Custer's chances of achieving success were actually now relatively low. This situation was almost like when he had attempted to gain entry into West Point by way of a Democrat-hating Republican congressman, despite being from an outspoken Democratic family (Emmanuel Custer's legacy), or the task of courting pretty Libbie Bacon in the face of a disapproving father and the broad disparity that existed between their classes and social backgrounds. In all of these situations, the odds were almost insurmountable for Custer, but he was not deterred. In fact, despite the obstacles, he was even more determined to overcome each one of them. Indeed, as fate would have it, the odds were once again stacked against the young man on this afternoon. Once again, the strength of Custer's character and unique contrarianism, which defined his personality and fueled his actions, guaranteed that he was not cowed when he faced stiff odds whenever the challenge was greatest.[174]

In protecting the strategic intersection in the army's rear, Custer possessed another advantage that served him well on this day of destiny. He had learned a valuable lesson on the previous day, July 2, during the hot cavalry fight at Hunterstown. Here, amid the farmlands of Adams County situated around five miles just northeast of Gettysburg, he had led his first charge as a brigadier general with a misplaced zealousness. Overanxious with his first chance in commanding an entire brigade against Stuart's famed horsemen, Custer had acted impulsively and with a rashness that nearly cost him his life. He had taken the unnecessary risk of leading a foolish headlong attack with troopers of his 6th Michigan Cavalry, charging straight into an ambush. While his men fell around him in the torrent of bullets during the headlong charge against far too many Rebels, Custer had been nearly killed by troopers of Wade Hampton's Brigade, which served as the reliable rearguard of Stuart's cavalry.

In the end, Custer was lucky to have survived the wild charge against the odds, having his horse shot out from under him. He had learned from the harrowing experience and close brush with death, becoming aware of the danger engendered by his overenthusiasm in leading from the front and by example. By leading such a daredevil charge, he had almost established a record for having held the rank of brigadier general for the shortest period of time.

Therefore, Custer had learned his lesson by his first failure and mistake-ridden performance as a brigade commander at Hunterstown. He finally realized that he needed to be more careful and smarter when facing Stuart's veterans and talented officers, especially against the Virginian's finest top lieutenant, Wade Hampton. Fortunately for Custer, the close call at Hunterstown proved invaluable as a learning experience. Custer's first setback in having impulsively led the headlong charge of his Michigan troopers was inevitable because he had lacked proper knowledge of the enemy's numbers and position. Custer swore to himself that he would never again make the same tactical mistake, which set the stage for his wiser and more mature decision making on July 3. Ironically, and as fate would have it, these two key factors that nearly ended Custer's life at Hunterstown and his brief career as a brigadier general were destined to come full circle more than a dozen years after Gettysburg to spell his doom in his final charge at the Little Bighorn long after his glory days of the Civil War.[175]

Young Custer, extremely sensitive to the fact that he had recently failed to achieve any kind of a success at Hunterstown, which no doubt brought back memories of his lengthy list of failures at West Point, was certainly eager to make amends at the strategic crossroads. He was therefore determined to perform with greater wisdom and a higher degree of professionalism on July 3, because the previous day's fight had won him "no accolades," to say the least.[176]

Because of this hard-earned lesson from having led the headlong charge of the 6th Michigan troopers "so foolishly," Custer had early ordered out patrols in every direction to avoid any nasty surprises and to ascertain exactly what was around him to make doubly sure that the strategic crossroads was thoroughly protected and secure.[177] Unlike the wild charge in leading his Wolverines at Hunterstown where his overaggressiveness had very nearly caused him to lose his life, Custer was determined to ascertain the exact situation that he faced at the crossroads, and he made his tactical decisions with a newfound wisdom unseen on the previous day.

Meanwhile, with a quick eye but one that was deliberate and manifested greater care, Custer, when near the intersection of the Hanover and Low Dutch Roads, had closely studied the vast expanse of open terrain that lay before him and which gradually rose toward Cress's Ridge to the north, while his Michigan troopers were deploying and moving forward. He scanned the ground with his binoculars, attempting to detect any strange or unnatural anomalies in the lay of the land, searching for anything that looked out of place. As noted, he was especially concerned about the thick forests atop Cress's Ridge and the Lott woods just north up the Low Dutch Road and beyond, or north of the Lott house, which was located southeast of the Rummel buildings on high ground. Consequently, he had early dispatched patrols to investigate these darkened woodlands that seemed just too quiet, and Custer knew that he could not be complacent or make any assumptions, because too much was at stake.

Contrary to the stereotype of the careless young officer who was too rash, Custer continued to be extremely careful, like an experienced commander and not unlike the steady professionalism of General Meade, when it mattered the most on July 3. As would be demonstrated on this day in full in the army's rear, Custer possessed an uncanny ability to concisely sum up the overall situation with a quick eye, ascertaining opportunities and possibilities on a future battlefield in a mere glance. After having just won the coveted rank of brigadier general, he was not about to take any unnecessary risks that might prove the folly of such a rapid rise for someone of his age.

What Custer saw before him was a sweeping landscape that was a pristine pastoral scene, which was as quiet as it was serene. The entire landscape to the north, gently sloping ground that ascended to the southern spur of wooded Cress's Ridge, was open and picturesque, more so than his native hill country of east central Ohio. This isolated and remote place in the army's rear was less hilly and ideal wheat country, which was evident from the high standing wheat in the fields of farmers Rummel and Lott. A broad open plain existed between Little's Run and the Low Dutch Road—ideal terrain for unleashing a cavalry charge by both sides. In fact, this wide stretch of open ground north of the Hanover Road and south of the Rummel buildings fairly invited a Rebel cavalry attack south or a Union cavalry attack north by way of this plain of fields, pastures, and meadows, as early noticed by Custer.

The heavy timber of Cress's Ridge dominated the northern horizon just over a mile north of the strategic crossroads. Most of all, Custer noticed how the open ground and fields of a fertile limestone soil sloped gently up toward Cress's Ridge to the north. The entire crest of the high ground before him, especially the southern end of the strategic crest, was covered in heavy timber and the thick foliage of summer. Of course, he did not like the disadvantages of the low-ground position of the crossroads area that was dominated by the high ground of Cress's Ridge—not a good tactical situation when he possessed no knowledge of the enemy's strength and dispositions, except for the sight of the thin line of Rebel skirmishers just beyond, or south, of the tree line of Cress's Ridge. Nevertheless, the low-ground disadvantages of the intersection only made Custer more careful, which was necessary to achieve success on that day.

Custer had instantly seen that what lay before him presented an ideal landscape for cavalry operations—not only for dismounted cavalry to take advantage of the good cover provided by the stone and rail fences (of course, especially the fences of white limestone) that divided sections of the southern slope of Cress's Ridge, but also for a cavalry charge en masse across the wide open plain below the timbered ridge, as in the much-celebrated glory days of Napoleon, whose vastly superior mounted arm had become most effective on the open plains of central Europe because of its hard-hitting "shock tactics." As he had once read the thrilling narrative of Charles Lever's popular romance and historical fiction about the brave dragoon Charles O'Malley, no doubt Custer could now almost envision the finely uniformed men of the 14th Light Dragoons charging up the slope of the open ground with sabers flashing in the bright July sunlight, and perhaps all the way up to the dark green wood line of Cress's Ridge.

To Custer, however, the dense woodlands that covered the crest of Cress's Ridge appeared the most ominous because of the sight of distant Virginia skirmishers aligned before the tall timber, especially after he had learned around noon that Lee was planning to unleash a massive assault on Meade's defensive line about three miles to the east and southeast, and then, after the noon hour, Eleventh Corps pickets, who then relayed the crucial information to Union signal men atop Cemetery Hill, had spied Stuart's cavalrymen on the move toward the vital crossroads of the Hanover and Low Dutch Roads.

At first glance, the line of Rebel skirmishers—Jenkins's (Witcher's) Virginians—on the high ground consisted of too few men to cause serious concern to Custer, but they seemed to be protecting or screening something larger that might well now be positioned in the woods to their north and rear. Because of the reliable flow of intelligence that told him that the Rebel cavalry was on the move, General Gregg had realized since around noon that Stuart was headed toward the right flank of the Army of the Potomac. Suddenly, all of Stuart's careful efforts at concealment to mask his initial move toward Meade's rear by gaining Cress's Ridge had failed. Most importantly, this vital intelligence about thousands of Confederate horsemen having been seen riding forward on some unknown secret mission from Lee, because thousands of troopers were involved as revealed from the Yankees' sighting and the fact that large clouds of dust had been raised, had been passed to General Gregg in the nick of time.

Of course, by this time, Custer most of all wondered where Stuart and his cavalry had gone, and exactly where they were lurking and why, after having been informed of the latest intelligence from headquarters. If the Rebels were now hidden in the forest on the high ground, then why were they concealed, and for what sinister purpose in Meade's rear? If the thousands of Stuart's men held the strategic high ground of Cress's Ridge that dominated and controlled the lower ground to the south, and Custer and his men clung only to a mere toehold on the low ground around the crossroads, then disaster might well result if all of these Rebels were suddenly unleashed down the slope. Therefore, after gaining the disturbing intelligence of Southern cavalry on the move, Custer searched the northern horizon more intently with his binoculars, which he had used since serving as a zealous staff officer under his beloved General McClellan, when he had first earned an impressive reputation for boldness and daring. He then looked closer at the dark, thick forests that covered the top of Cress's Ridge, knowing that the wily Stuart might well have hidden his forces at this point, because this was the best cover and on the highest ground in the area.

The absence of any Confederate artillery positioned on the high ground before him made Custer even more suspicious. Only a thin line of Rebel skirmishers could be seen on the high ground at this time, but they were more than a mile away and remained close to the wood line north and northwest of the Rummel barn. As mentioned, these men had advanced only a relatively short distance before Jenkins's (Witcher's) Brigade that held Stuart's right on the southern spur of Cress's Ridge. As noted, Custer had recently learned a great deal—unlike Stuart in regard to Brandy Station—from his recent experiences and the close call on the previous day at Hunterstown.

Therefore, he would not commit the folly of hurling charges headlong at an enemy of unknown strength and in unknown positions, although screened by a weak line of skirmishers, on high ground that he was not familiar with— the potential recipe for not only a setback, but also perhaps disaster. But the sight of the line of Confederate skirmishers on the northern horizon was sufficiently significant to tell Custer that the main threat was most likely to the north and not from the west down the Hanover Road and not on lower ground. What was clear was the fact that this was a high-ground threat, and hence more ominous and potentially threatening to his low-ground position around the crossroads. Clearly, geography was not on Custer's side, and he would have to overcome a host of natural disadvantages to compensate as much as possible.

Fortunately for the Union, Custer's instincts and tactical insights were not only extremely good on July 3, but also right on target. In fact, he almost possessed a prophetic insight or a sixth sense about the enemy's whereabouts that he knew had to be in those mysterious woodlands to the north. Therefore, he was determined that he would not be surprised if large numbers of Confederates now filled the woods of Cress's Ridge, as he correctly suspected, and suddenly advanced down the slope with flags flying and Rebel yells.

In consequence, the reliable troopers of the 6th Michigan Cavalry, which consisted mostly of men from Grand Rapids and the surrounding area, held the left flank, which was anchored not only on the Hanover Road but also at Little's Run that flowed south from the Rummel springhouse to the north of the dusty road. Meanwhile, the 7th Michigan Cavalry held the center on the Hanover Road, and then the 1st Michigan Cavalry held the right on the road just west of the vital intersection. At this time, the troopers of both the 5th and 6th Michigan Cavalry were dismounted and ready for action, on the alert to make any additional tactical moves at a moment's notice on Custer's orders, depending on the next decision made by the young brigade commander.

As noted, Custer faced no ordinary threat. After all, Stuart's smart placement in the sheltering forest that covered the ridgetop to hide thousands of his troopers made good tactical sense because Cress's Ridge was ideal for serving as a high-ground launching pad to strike Meade's rear. This highest ground in the area stood in commanding fashion near—barely a mile from—the strategic crossroads just to the south, ensuring that this key position was under constant threat. But again, Custer sensed that the main force existed to the north, but of course it would have to be revealed before he was completely convinced with absolute certitude.

If Custer made one tactical mistake and allowed his vigilance to slip, then Stuart's veterans of four brigades, bolstered by four batteries and the section of Louisiana artillery, could suddenly swoop out of the woods and charge across the open fields to push aside any unwary Federal cavalry, even a full brigade, to gain the strategic crossroads that was most vulnerable on the low ground and held by too few Wolverines. From his ample experience as a staff officer in the Army of the Potomac and from what he had learned in his topographical engineering classes at West Point, Custer almost certainly knew that Lee and Stuart would have utilized a good topographical map, which was indeed the case, to have ascertained the significance of this high-ground position that was located so near the vital intersection that provided the way by which to eventually gain Meade's rear.[178] As noted, Custer's instincts and insights were right on target about the full nature of the threat on the high ground that he faced and looked at with an increasingly wary eye.

## NEW AND TIMELY ALIGNMENT OF CUSTER'S BATTLE LINE

Custer's mounting concerns were confirmed when General Stuart began to grow impatient. He began to contemplate the ordering of the guns of Captain Jackson's Charlottesville "Kanawha" Battery, Jenkins's (Witcher's) Virginia Brigade, to be pushed out of the thick woods and out into the open on the high ground. Evidently, Stuart was frustrated because he knew that the movements of his men had been spied, because Custer had made a host of wise dispositions of his Wolverine Brigade that told him that the strategic crossroads was now well protected.

Here, on a commanding perch that overlooked the large Rummel barn just to the southeast, Jackson's veteran artillerymen were attached to Jenkins's (Witcher's) Brigade that held the line of Stuart's right on the west. On Stuart's orders, they were about to take a commanding high-ground position in the open that overlooked the sprawling expanse of farmers' fields that spanned all the way to the strategic intersection.[179]

From his past experiences and instincts that were heightened by the increasing level of skirmishing to both the north and west of his advanced skirmish lines, Custer later pointed to Cress's Ridge and prophetically informed Colonel John Baillie McIntosh, upon his later (around 1:00 p.m.) arrival on the field and who commanded the First Cavalry Brigade, Gregg's Second Cavalry Division, which was destined initially to protect Custer's Brigade in a reserve position role, "I think you will find the woods out there [now] full of them"—the troopers of Stuart's cavalry.[180]

Custer might not have realized that Gregg's other brigade commander, Colonel J. Irvin Gregg, who would later occupy a reserve position behind the Wolverine Brigade, or perhaps even Colonel McIntosh, harbored jealousy and resentment toward him because of his youth (age twenty-three), recent rapid promotion, and favoritism garnered from Pleasonton and Gregg, and even Meade to a lesser degree. In a letter, an upset Colonel J. Irvin Gregg, who commanded the Third Brigade, Second Cavalry Division, wrote with a measure of disdain and disgust how the "Lieut Custer had never commanded even a squadron in the field" before he had been promoted and became a fellow brigade commander, but in Kilpatrick's Third Cavalry Division.[181]

But Custer was in the process of proving his ever-growing list of dissenters wrong on every score by his skillful orchestration of a well-conceived defense of the strategic crossroads. Custer learned that his prudence had been well placed because of the most recently gained intelligence that could not have been more timely or important to coincide with the intelligence from the vigilant men of the Eleventh Corps on Cemetery Hill. In his account of the battle written the next day from his own observation and personal knowledge, the special correspondent of the *Detroit Free Press* penned how at "about 12 o'clock we observed a column of cavalry [the late-arriving brigades of Hampton and Fitzhugh Lee] moving in the woods" of Cress's Ridge.[182]

For whatever reason, this Michigan journalist, who wrote his account on July 4, presented more detailed information than Custer in his own battle report.[183] Custer only wrote of the later development about how "the enemy appeared on my right flank."[184] This discrepancy cannot be readily explained, except that Custer had simply decided not to include this information and greater details in his report for some unknown reason.[185]

But what was no mystery was the fact that not only Stuart but also brigade commanders Hampton and Fitzhugh Lee had been incredibly careless in regard to their extension of the left of their battle line northeast of Jenkins's (Witcher's) right-flank position, especially because their movements were located on higher ground and were readily visible to the naked eye. Clearly, the latest-arriving Confederates should have demonstrated greater care because they were more exposed when riding across open ground to reach the timber of Cress's Ridge when on a higher-ground position. This almost casual deployment—a carelessness that nearly bordered on criminal neglect given the importance of the overall situation—seemed to indicate that neither Hampton nor Fitzhugh Lee were yet fully aware of the supreme importance of the day's crucial mission or of the crossroads. After all, they had never seen this area before, and neither commander had been present at the headquarters conference between Lee and Stuart on the night of July 2.

Custer's insights and deductions continued to prove to be right on target, which had been additionally verified by solid information and recent intelligence. Most importantly, he had earlier gained vital intelligence in real time that proved invaluable. In the beginning and as mentioned, he had prudently sent out not only skirmishers but also scouts to ascertain the location of possible enemy positions that might be hidden from his view from the disadvantageous low ground of the strategic crossroads, and the intelligence gained by doing this points out the wisdom of these moves.

Dispatched north up the Low Dutch Road to not only protect his right flank but also to gather much-needed information about what existed north of the crossroads, a patrol of Company B men of the 6th Michigan Cavalry had gained the day's most valuable intelligence for Custer. These trusty men,

Photograph of United States Military Academy Cadet Custer, fresh faced and not lacking in a sense of bravado, around 1858. He is holding a Colt Model 1855 Sidehammer Pocket Revolver, which was a weapon that was popular at the time.

George Armstrong Custer's high level of confidence and self-assurance can be readily seen in this photo. Unlike many Civil War officers of higher rank, he backed up his jaunty and flamboyant style with impressive accomplishments on the battlefield.

Profile of Custer, who led the Michigan Cavalry Brigade—the 1st, 5th, 6th, and 7th Michigan Cavalry regiments—with distinction, beginning on the East Cavalry Field, July 3, 1863. He early and skillfully orchestrated a masterful defense of the strategic crossroads—the key intersection of the Hanover Road and the Low Dutch Road—around three miles in the Union Army's right-rear on the final day at Gettysburg.

Formal portrait of Custer and his quite remarkable wife who was the love of his life and the most popular belle of Monroe, Michigan, Elizabeth "Libbie" Bacon-Custer. They wed on February 9, 1864.

Classic pose of a standing Custer, cocky and proud but for ample good reason. This young officer, only age twenty-three when recently promoted to brigadier general and the much-maligned "goat" of his West Point Class of 1861, played the leading role in saving the day on the East Cavalry Field by leading two audacious saber charges against an aggressive and more numerous opponent—first with the 7th Michigan Cavalry and then with the 1st Michigan Cavalry.

In his prime, Custer is shown with arms folded while wearing his favorite wide-brimmed hat at a jaunty angle. This photograph was taken by Mathew Brady at the end of the Civil War. As demonstrated on the East Cavalry Field, Custer had early emerged as one of the most aggressive and best cavalry commanders of the Army of the Potomac, ensuring his rise to the lofty rank of major general as revealed in this photo.

Formal portrait of Custer with arm resting on the barrel of a cannon in true Napoleonic style—a most symbolic pose because of his skillful use of horse artillery in defending the strategic crossroads throughout July 3, 1863.

Custer striking a more traditional pose of many Civil War soldiers, both officers and enlisted men, during the war years.

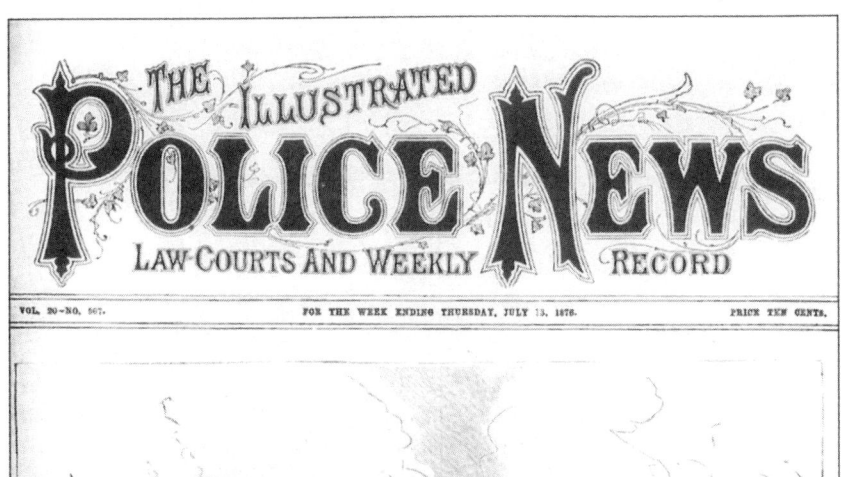

The American public across the United States viewed the artist's highly romanticized version of Custer's death at the Little Bighorn on June 25, 1876. The artist depicted Custer wearing the full dress uniform of a lieutenant colonel on one of the hottest days of the year, when he made the final charge of his illustrious career against the Sioux and Cheyenne in the remote Montana Territory.

Ink sketch of "Custer's Last Fight" by Alfred Waud. One of the best Civil War artists, Waud naturally emphasized Custer's heroism in the face of impossible odds on that fateful afternoon of June 25, 1876 atop Custer Hill above the clear waters of the Little Bighorn.

basically acting in the role of advanced scouts on the northeast, or right flank, of Custer's defensive line, were commanded by Captain Peter A. Weber.

Only twenty-three, Custer's own age, he was a tactically astute young officer who had long led Company B with distinction. Despite his age and known as "Bob," Weber was experienced as a former staff officer, highly capable, and certainly deserving of higher rank. Like Custer, Captain Weber reflected the rise of a new breed of Union cavalry officer, who had made the Michigan Cavalry Brigade more formidable: aggressive, dynamic, and intelligent, unlike less capable types—like Brigadier General Joseph T. Copeland, whom Custer had replaced in timely fashion—who had gained higher rank but proved unable to rise to the challenge in the early days.

In the past, Captain Weber had emerged as a talented officer who was especially skilled in the art of intelligence gathering and reconnaissance. He was tactically gifted, smart, and as handsome as Custer. Talented on multiple levels, Weber had also early played a key role in making the 6th Michigan Cavalry into a crack regiment. The resourceful Weber was a model officer, whom Custer now especially greatly appreciated and for ample good reason.

Most importantly, Weber had just brought crucial and valuable intelligence to Custer when he needed it most. He informed Custer around noon that two Rebel cavalry brigades (Hampton and Fitzhugh Lee) and accompanying horse artillery had been seen by him moving east into the western edge of the thick woods of Cress's Ridge. Clearly, this intelligence could not have been more vital or timely to Custer, who realized that Lee's most gifted cavalryman and thousands of seasoned Rebel troopers were hidden in the shadowy forests to the north for some sinister purpose—either Stuart was determined to attack the crossroads or he planned to ride southwest toward the Baltimore Turnpike to hit Meade's rear, or both. Of course, Custer could only guess what his enemy might do. Therefore, Custer's earlier prudence and care paid dividends for the possibility of meeting a variety of tactical scenarios.

For a variety of reasons, including that he would be killed in the days ahead, Captain Weber was one of the forgotten heroes of the Battle of Gettysburg. He played a key role in helping Custer rise to the challenge and save the day in the Army of the Potomac's rear. As an unfortunate fate would have it, this promising young officer, who was a self-made man who had risen up on his own merits and not based on civilian or army politics, was destined for death before the Gettysburg campaign's conclusion, dying heroically in leading a charge at Falling Waters, Maryland—a headlong cavalry charge that was so courageous as to have been suicidal.

Most importantly, thanks to Captain Weber's invaluable service in the key role of basically acting as a head scout, and a most resourceful one, Custer had just learned that thousands of Rebel troopers were now situated in hidden positions amid the dense woods of Cress's Ridge. Gaining the day's most crucial intelligence, Weber had seen a large number of members of the late-arriving brigades of Hampton and Fitzhugh Lee riding in formation, but carelessly, across the open ground in broad daylight, before they had gained the western edge of the timber that dominated Cress's Ridge. Clearly, to have moved stealthily into a secure, hidden position amid the tall timber on the high ground, thousands of Stuart's finest cavalrymen and artillerymen should have entered the woods from the north, which would have enabled them to move undetected south down the ridge to extend Stuart's left.[186]

In timely fashion and as soon as possible, an excited Captain Weber, knowing that he had gained the crucial intelligence that might literally save the day in regard to the crossroads' defense, had passed along the alarming word to Custer that "I have seen thousands of them over there [and] the country yonder is full of the enemy."[187] Unknown to Stuart and, of course, General Lee, the largest body of Southern cavalry at Gettysburg had been pinpointed at last and without any doubt, revealing the first indications of Gettysburg's most secret plan. In this regard, Custer could not have been more fortunate. But if he had not entrusted his northernmost position and right flank to such a capable man as Weber, this vital intelligence might not have been gained in such timely fashion. In this sense, therefore, Custer had made his own luck.

In addition, at some point, Custer had also gained equally important and timely information from General Gregg—dispatched by courier from Pleasonton's cavalry headquarters, which was located about three miles distant from Custer's position—about Major General Howard's message gained from sharp-eyed Federals who had seen Stuart's troopers moving northeast on the York Turnpike from the top of Cemetery Hill: "large columns of the enemy cavalry were moving toward the right," or east, of his position at the northern end of Cemetery Ridge.[188]

To confront this threat and to additionally feel out the enemy and their dispositions, Custer had ordered Colonel Alger and his dismounted troopers, who were armed with the fast-firing and deadly Spencers, to advance slowly north up the slope and through the open fields toward Cress's Ridge with greater caution. Most importantly, these 5th Michigan Cavalry troopers advanced northward in a defensive formation in the shape of a protective "shield" for his brigade and the overall defense of the crossroads.

This well-conceived tactical shield was a wise strategy in keeping with what Custer now knew lay before him, because the greatest danger lay to the north. Most importantly, every foot of ground gained by Alger's men in pushing north up through the open fields of gently ascending ground was important in securing a much-needed buffer between the crossroads and Stuart's position overflowing with Lee's best cavalrymen and horse artillery as revealed by Captain Weber's timely intelligence. Custer knew that he needed to keep Stuart as far away from the strategic crossroads as possible.

Clearly, serious trouble loomed up ahead to the north, and all hell could break loose at any moment. By this time, Custer had evidently informed Alger and his 5th Michigan Cavalry troopers in person—because he was literally riding over the field giving out orders and collecting the most recently acquired information from his most advanced troopers—of the fact that the dark haunts of the forest atop the commanding ridge were overflowing with Stuart's men: the finest troopers and horse artillerymen of the Army of Northern Virginia. Custer had benefited immensely from two timely intelligence sources: the report about Stuart's movement east that had been forthcoming from Cemetery Hill and Captain Weber's urgent warning about how the woods of Cress's Ridge were occupied by large numbers of Rebel cavalrymen of Stuart's command.[189]

Meanwhile, the foremost skirmishers of Jenkins's (Witcher's) Virginia Brigade, which held Stuart's right to the southwest of Hampton's and Fitzhugh Lee's Brigades, from right to left, while Chambliss's Virginia and North Carolina were positioned between Jenkins (Witcher) and Hampton, advanced south down the high ground farther beyond the dense forest of summer green that dominated the southern end of Cress's Ridge, after having been reinforced in timely fashion. Giving him some cause for concern and knowing that the boys in gray and butternut meant business, Custer saw that these Rebel skirmishers were now spread out in a "strong line."[190]

Even more at this time, these veteran dismounted cavalrymen possessed a distinct advantage over Colonel Alger and his 5th Michigan Cavalry, because they held the crucial high ground. They were not ordinary skirmishers from the Old Dominion cavalry brigade. The best sharpshooters of each regiment of Jenkins's (Witcher's) and Chambliss's Brigades had been sent forward with the purpose of killing as many Yankee boys as possible and inflicting havoc. Jenkins (Witcher) had been specifically assigned to Stuart to increase his offensive capabilities for this key mission in Meade's rear. These mostly Virginia skirmishers continued to advance down the open slope and toward the Rummel buildings, while benefiting from the fact that these seasoned men were armed with .577-caliber Enfield rifles. This was the favorite weapon of Lee's infantrymen because of its accuracy and long-range capabilities. These skirmishers were actually more formidable than they seemed, because Custer did not know they were armed with Enfield rifles during the long-range firefight across open ground, unless he or his men could identify the weapon by its sharp bark.

For good reason, Stuart began this fight by employing troopers who were more formidable than they appeared at first glance. Now at the beginning of the final chapter of the three days of the Battle of Gettysburg in Meade's right-rear, the gray-and-butternut skirmishers were more formidable than Custer's troopers because they possessed a weapon that was lethal at long range, unlike the less accurate weapons of the Michigan men. The deadly Enfield rifles, a reliable weapon imported from England, were more accurate and possessed a longer range than the carbines of Custer's men, who were exposed on the open ground while advancing north up the open slope toward the Rummel barn, making these Old Dominion skirmishers more formidable than the usual Southern cavalrymen by design, especially when advancing down higher terrain to possess a key advantage. However, the fast-firing troopers of the 5th Michigan Cavalry kept Jenkins's (Witcher's) Rebels—who steadily advanced down the slope, getting ever closer to the Rummel buildings, with a well-honed confidence that also revealed that they were supported by larger numbers of hidden men behind them in the woodlands—at bay by their fast-firing capabilities and accuracy.[191]

These Rummel buildings were about to become a major bone of contention because of their strategic location not far from Stuart's line that extended through the woodlands. One Union officer described the location of the Rummel farm buildings as being "situated in the plain about three-fourths of a mile north-west of the Lott house, and near the base of Cress's Ridge."[192]

Stuart certainly meant business, and more than usual, because this was Lee's last chance to win it all at Gettysburg. It was clear to Custer and other veterans in blue that it was no accident that Stuart's first skirmish line was actually stronger—more in terms of weaponry than in overall numbers—than was usually the case. Stuart was determined to reap a decisive success to redeem himself and his men. His close father-son relationship with Lee had been strained to the breaking point because of his recent far-flung raid devoid of significant results. And, most of all, he needed to restore that fractured bond, once so strong and impenetrable, in which he had long basked as Lee's best cavalry leader with a legendary reputation.

But more importantly at this time, Stuart was employing his own clever plan by relying on a strong line of skirmishers, who were armed with long-range Enfield rifles. In the words of historian Stephen Sears: "Stuart's plan had been to fix the Federals in place with aggressive [dismounted and veteran] skirmishers and then from the concealment of Cress Ridge swing around their left flank."[193]

Meanwhile, Custer continued to feel secure and satisfied in having orchestrated a well-conceived defense of the strategic crossroads and was not overly concerned about its safety, at least for the time being. After all, Stuart had launched no mounted attack down the slope. By this time, Custer had accomplished all that he could to achieve this goal of safeguarding the intersection. But that comforting sense of assurance was about to be suddenly shattered because Stuart was about to make his next move, as he had just targeted

Custer's right flank, which he now viewed as vulnerable, sensing a tactical opportunity.[194]

Significantly, Custer had already made a series of good tactical dispositions in complete confidence because of Weber's revealing intelligence report. But Custer was still vulnerable because he did not know Stuart's exact plan or when and where he would strike first. As mentioned, Captain Weber's contributions were invaluable in regard to enlightening Custer in a timely manner. As fully appreciated by Custer, Captain James Harvey Kidd said of Weber, he "was a born soldier, fitted by nature and acquirements for much higher rank than any he held."[195]

Yet Custer was surprised when after a short lull—clearly Stuart had not wanted to unleash an attack because his primary mission was to strike Meade's rear—which had fooled him for the first time that day, "the enemy appeared on my right flank and opened upon me with a battery of six guns. Leaving two guns [of Battery M, 2nd United States Artillery] and a regiment to hold my first position and cover the [Hanover] road leading to Gettysburg, I shifted the remaining portion of my command forming a new line of battle at right angles with my former position. The enemy had obtained correct range of my new position, and was pouring solid shot and shell into my command with great accuracy. Placing two sections of battery 'M,' Second regular artillery, in position, I ordered them to silence the enemy's battery" that was causing trouble on the right flank.[196] Custer was also proving that he knew how to manage horse artillery, especially in regard to eliminating a sudden threat that had surprised him.[197]

But he was demonstrating more skill with managing his brigade in a capable manner. In response to the first Rebel artillery fire that had raked his right flank and caught him by surprise because Stuart had hurriedly run the field pieces out of the woods and onto a commanding perch on the open ground, Custer swiftly made the correct tactical adjustments to meet the new threat, as he revealed in his own words: "My line [now] was shaped like the letter 'L.' The shorter branch, supported by one section of battery 'M' [while] supported by four squadrons of the Sixth Michigan Cavalry, faced toward Gettysburg, covering the [Hanover] pike; the long branch, composed of the two remaining sections of battery 'M,' supported by a portion of the Sixth Michigan cavalry on the left, and the First Michigan cavalry on the right—with the Seventh Michigan cavalry still further to the right and in advance—was held in ready to repel any attack on the" Low Dutch Road.[198]

Clearly, by hurriedly bringing forth six pieces of artillery on the open ground and opening fire, Stuart had upped the ante in the struggle for the crossroads by having moved forward artillery that targeted Custer's right flank to initiate the fight that had been only previously distinguished by nothing more than light and long-range skirmishing between Jenkins's (Witcher's) skirmishers and the men of the 5th Michigan Cavalry. At this time, Colonel McIntosh had been ordered by General Gregg to relieve Custer's command because these men were fresh and evidently because of the greater level of inexperience among the Michigan troopers, especially the 7th Michigan Cavalry, and their green brigadier general of age twenty-three. Even more, around noon, a courier (none other than an aide of Kilpatrick) arrived with orders from an upset Brigadier General Kilpatrick, who ordered the return of Custer's Wolverine Brigade to his Third Division where it rightfully belonged. Some of the foremost Michigan men began to retire as ordered.

This was now a key turning point of the battle. At this moment, General Gregg faced not only a crisis situation, but also a serious predicament of the first magnitude. Indeed, at this time, General Gregg, thanks to what Custer had first learned from Captain Weber about the enemy's large numbers in the woods of Cress's Ridge, "was already aware of Stuart's presence but was now concerned about the strength of his enemy. He had been charged with protecting the Union rear and could use all the troops he could muster."[199]

As noted, even the reporter of the *Detroit Free Press* (written on July 4 and published on July 15, 1863) evidently saw with his own eyes the carelessness of Hampton's and Fitzhugh Lee's almost casual approach to gain the excellent cover provided by Cress's Ridge, because "we observed a column of cavalry moving in the woods" on the high ground.[200]

Fortunately for the Union, Custer was the right commander on the right spot at the right time to fulfill Gregg's and Pleasonton's crucial mission to make sure that the Union never lost its now-firm grip on the strategic crossroads, while Stuart was the wrong commander at the wrong time to fulfill Lee's ambitious mission of striking Meade's rear, for a host of reasons that had become a lengthy list by this time. Although he did not realize this brutal fate, Stuart's heyday and glory days were already very much in the past because this war, especially the cavalry side of this increasingly brutal conflict, had changed so dramatically, and he had not adapted because he lacked flexibility. Meanwhile, a more open-minded and highly flexible Custer was a new man on the make with a good many new ideas, who brought a vibrant new energy about how to defeat the legendary "Invincibles."

Unlike Stuart, who had established his worth long ago when the war was still young and yet possessed a degree of innocence that revealed American novices on both sides at war, Custer still had to prove himself. He had to demonstrate to Generals Gregg, Pleasonton, and Meade, and to the wishy-washy Libbie, whose heart was torn by her good head and her disapproving judge of a father, that he was worthy of promotion to brigadier general. But while Stuart was fighting an old-fashioned war in which glory was out of date,

Custer had already perceived this new reality of the arrival of a new day. He knew that war was not only cruel, but also unfair to an inordinate degree. As recently penned in a letter, he was still disturbed by General McClellan's removal from command by President Lincoln for not having captured Richmond in the spring of 1862, when "he was left in a most precarious position [and] we should have been annihilated without McClellan to lead us."[201]

It is not known, but perhaps Custer now wondered if he had been left in a comparable "precarious position" at this strategic crossroads in Meade's right-rear that might result in his own removal if he failed to rise to the formidable challenge.[202]

## KEY TURNING POINT: CUSTER'S BOLD DECISION

As noted, Custer had received his recent orders to retire the troopers of his Wolverine Brigade because the arrival of the long-awaited verbal order had finally arrived from Pleasonton to confirm the wisdom of Gregg's decision to make a determined stand to protect the strategic crossroads of the Hanover and Low Dutch Roads to the bitter end if necessary. In this missive, Pleasonton ordered that Gregg should release Custer's Brigade for its return back to his division under Kilpatrick and his Third Cavalry Division on the left flank to the south because of a planned cavalry offensive by the ever-eager Kilpatrick, whose ambitions were as outsized as his ego, to attempt to turn Lee's right flank.

Knowing the extent of the brewing crisis situation, the growing threat of the strategic crossroads, and the pressing need to buy as much time as possible, General Gregg played a masterful hand. He successfully, if not brilliantly, played the red-tape game of delay to perfection by employing a clever pretext of requesting that the order to release Custer and his brigade be put into writing by Pleasonton, who was at his headquarters "not far from the cemetery" on Cemetery Hill.

For ample good reason, Gregg stalled for time because of the urgent need to keep Custer's Brigade of four regiments firmly in place to protect the crossroads, because he needed both Custer, the division's best fighting general, and his tough Wolverines in the upcoming offensive effort that was sure to come when Stuart unleashed his legions, which was only a matter of time. Doing everything possible to accomplish his goal, Gregg now made sure that Custer would stay at the crossroads until Pleasonton sent a written order, and that would take a good deal of time.[203]

At this key moment, and because of the timely intelligence that had been earlier gained by Captain Weber and based on his own instincts that told him that the crossroads must be defended at all costs with thousands of veteran

Rebels lying to the north in wait to strike a blow, Custer faced a quandary. First and foremost, he knew that his own division commander, Brigadier General Judson Kilpatrick, needed him and his brigade to rejoin his own Third Cavalry Division in the south. As mentioned, Kilpatrick was about to unleash his own offensive effort in a bid to turn Lee's weak right.

But this overall situation was not as conflicting as it seemed at first glance, because Custer knew that he faced large numbers of the opponent—thanks to Captain Weber's timely intelligence—and that the strategic crossroads needed to be protected at all costs. He concluded correctly that Gregg's sector (a defensive role) was far more important than Kilpatrick's sector (an offensive role) to the south, which was certainly the case on July 3. A general withdrawal in the face of the enemy and the entire abandonment of a strategic location—the vital crossroads—in Meade's rear, now under serious threat, was something that Custer simply could not do, regardless of the consequences for himself and his career. Indeed, as Custer fully realized by this time, abandoning the field at this point was not only folly but also something very close to cowardice, because it would be an act that might cost General Meade and the Army of the Potomac dearly.

Brigadier General Custer therefore decided to remain at the crossroads and disobey Kilpatrick's orders—with Gregg's blessing, since they (two kindred spirits in tactical terms and strategic thinking) thought the same—to stay and fight, because he knew that this crisis situation was far more crucial than whatever was occurring in Kilpatrick's sector, which remained quiet, and no cannon fire had been heard from the south on the far Union left at the Round Tops. To ease the young man's lingering concerns, Gregg was destined to eventually reach Custer at the crossroads and personally informed him that he would take full responsibility for keeping Custer and his Wolverines with him to defend the intersection in Meade's vulnerable right-rear. After all, Gregg now possessed the report of Stuart's movements from General Howard by way of observations of Union soldiers from the top of Cemetery Hill, and of course Custer had already gained the verbal reports from Captain Weber that verified the vital information about thousands of Rebels in the woods just ahead on the high ground to the north.

Indeed, Custer could not have been more delighted by these new developments because he and Gregg were in complete agreement about what needed to be accomplished and exactly how. On July 3, Custer battled the enemy with the same intensity as "Old Steady," who had fought like a man possessed at Brandy Station, to the amazement of his men. In contrast, Custer enjoyed no such warm relationship with Kilpatrick, who was another "boy general," but three years older than Custer. Kilpatrick was hot tempered and the antithesis of "Old Steady."

For such reasons, Custer's relationship with Kilpatrick was not good but professional, especially when compared with his personal and professional ties to Pleasonton and Gregg, which were strengthened by permanent bonds of mutual respect and admiration. Like many of his Michigan men, Custer lamented Kilpatrick's carelessness in regard to the lives of his men by relying too much on the tactical offensive—partly because he was ruthlessly ambitious and obsessively focused on self-promotion. Ironically, these are the same qualities that have forever branded Custer as an inferior commander, thanks to what happened at the Little Bighorn in June 1876. Custer knew that Kilpatrick would do anything to advance himself, even if it required a large number of dead and wounded troopers, who were nothing more than cannon fodder to him in regard to serving as expendable tools for his soaring ambitions. Significantly and to his great credit, Custer was the antithesis of Kilpatrick in many ways, and his Wolverines greatly appreciated that difference.

Even more, Custer possessed plenty of good reasons to have been critical of Kilpatrick's recent performances against Stuart, including in the recent cavalry clash at Hanover and his inability to determine the exact whereabouts of Stuart, who had slipped away and might well have then joined Lee's army after the battle. Even more, Custer might have detected some jealousy, which consumed a good many other cavalry officers because of his rapid rise. Custer, consequently, quite likely sensed that Kilpatrick felt that he was not ready to command a brigade in regard to his lack of overall command experience.

But the final decision had been made to hold firm and defend Meade's vulnerable right-rear, and Custer remained at center stage in the vital defense of the strategic crossroads. General Gregg later wrote with understatement about the extremely sound mutual agreement for Custer and his Wolverines to remain and defend the crossroads to protect the Army of the Potomac's rear by emphasizing how the young brigadier general was "fully satisfied of the intended attack [by Stuart's legions and was] well pleased to remain with his brigade" in defense of the key intersection.[204]

However and most importantly, despite the recent (early afternoon) reinforcements—Colonel J. Irvin Gregg's Third Brigade of Brigadier General Gregg's Division was destined to remain in reserve and not be engaged in the fight for possession of the crossroads on this day of destiny—and "Gregg's overall direction, it was left to the Boy General and his relatively untested Michiganders to meet the Invincibles out in the open, and it was they who would bear the brunt of the battle," when so much was at stake.[205]

Again, this was a key turning point in the battle, and Custer, although an extremely young and inexperienced officer, was about to engage in his first major battle, while holding the most strategic position in the army's rear with tenacity. In the words of historian Stephen Z. Starr in regard to Gregg's all-important decision to keep Custer in place against Generals Pleasonton's and Kilpatrick's orders, and Custer's own equally bold decision to remain, this was an all-important "decision that probably saved [Gregg]—and perhaps Meade—from a disastrous defeat."[206] A leading expert on the Union cavalry in his day, Starr was right on target in his analysis.[207]

On his own and with renewed vigor, therefore, Custer returned to the fight with a degree of enhanced confidence and his customary zeal, after having gained a new lease on life to hold the crossroads with a firm grip and never let go. In regard to location and situation, therefore, young Brigadier General Custer continued to be right where he wanted to be because this was exactly where the Battle of Gettysburg might be won and lost on what had now become the most important day of the war.

Beyond all doubt, Custer knew early on that this was the most vital sector of all in Meade's rear, and he had acted accordingly. Resuming their offensive to gain additional ground, the troopers of the 5th Michigan Cavalry continued their push far north of the crossroads across the open ground and past the Rummel barn and buildings. As mentioned, Custer had been most responsible for sending forth these reliable 5th Michigan Cavalry troopers, armed with Spencers, so far north to protect his grip on the crossroads, until their line extended as far north as the Rummel buildings, where the north–south skirmish line turned straight east. However, the 5th Michigan boys on the north, whose line extended east of the Rummel barn and toward the Low Dutch Road, were under the relentless punishment of long-range artillery fire and the fire of the deadly .577-caliber Enfield rifles of veteran Rebels who had long made sport of shooting down Yankees.[208]

## STUART RELIES ON THE 34TH VIRGINIA CAVALRY BATTALION

From the beginning, and because of its vital location so close to the left of Jenkins's (Witcher's) Brigade, which had been assigned to Stuart just for this special secret mission on Meade's rear, and to the right of Chambliss's Brigade, Stuart understood the tactical need to secure possession of the buildings, including the huge barn, of the Rummel farm and the surrounding stone fences—ideal defensive positions—which were situated about one thousand feet from the tree line of the southern spur of Cress's Ridge. Most of all, Stuart needed to secure this key position to keep it out of the Yankees' hands, because Custer's skirmishers had advanced so far north through the open fields of summer.

General Stuart had placed much faith in Lieutenant Colonel Vincent Addison Witcher. He was the former leader of the 34th Virginia Cavalry Battalion of Jenkins's Brigade. Witcher now commanded Jenkins's Brigade of hard-fighting Virginia boys. Born in Pittsylvania County, Virginia, in February 1837, Witcher was a young officer at age twenty-six, which was three years older than Custer. But he was capable and had excelled in commanding his tough cavalrymen from the forested mountains of Virginia in today's West Virginia.

Witcher commanded the 432 troopers of the 34th Cavalry Battalion, and only 96 of these men were destined to survive by not being wounded, killed, or captured on July 3. Because the Federals proved to be in force at the vital crossroads of the Hanover and Low Dutch Roads that he needed to possess, and because they had pushed so far north, Stuart had decided to first employ the trusty Witcher to push them back. Therefore, he ordered Witcher and his dismounted men to prepare to advance farther down the slope toward the Rummel buildings and across the lengthy expanse of open ground that spanned all the way south to the strategic crossroads.[209]

At this time, Stuart felt himself in a tactical dilemma because he had just "fired his signal shots to Lee, a signal that would have informed him that Stuart and his force had arrived safely on Cress Ridge and were ready to move into the Union rear with no apparent hindrance," but only if no Federals held the crossroads.[210] But now Custer and his Wolverine Brigade had disrupted that lofty ambition to a degree that frustrated Stuart, who had not envisioned that he would have to fight so many tough Michigan men, who did not know how to give up or surrender, like their feisty young commander. As noted, Stuart's plan to push southwest to gain the Baltimore Pike, located about halfway between the Low Dutch Road and Meade's Cemetery Ridge line, in order to strike Meade's rear was his top priority. Clearly, Stuart had his hands full, and far more than he realized at this time, in part because he knew little, if anything, about the blacksmith's son who opposed him.

Indeed, with so many Federals in his front, Stuart's plan of attacking into Meade's rear in conjunction with Pickett's Charge was interrupted and derailed more than he had initially imagined.[211] Therefore, Stuart planned to employ Lieutenant Colonel Witcher and his Virginia men on the right to advance down the slope and gain the Rummel house and barn and the nearby fences before the Yankees took over these key defensive points—close to where Stuart planned to position the field pieces of his batteries on the high ground—which the Federals could not be allowed to secure in large numbers, especially deploying additional horse artillery besides Captain Pennington's Battery.[212]

Meanwhile Custer faced his own tactical dilemma. What exactly was Stuart planning to do and when, if the woods of Cress's Ridge were overflowing with Rebels, as he not only suspected but now knew to be the case? Was Stuart about to attack the crossroads in full force, or was he only putting up a bold front to occupy the defenders of Meade's right-rear in order to ride southwest and assist in Lee's forthcoming offensive effort that was destined to become known as Pickett's Charge? Had Lee and Stuart concocted a daring plan to strike the thin defensive lines of the Army of the Potomac from two directions at the same time? If so, and if not stopped, then these two leading military men of the South might be on the verge of winning the greatest and most decisive victory of the war. Indeed, Stuart might well be planning to capture the crossroads and then ride southwest to strike Meade's rear along Cemetery Ridge. At this point in time, Custer could only guess, but he expected the worst, and he made his plans and dispositions accordingly.

## A PROPHETIC VISION

However, to his credit and before Witcher's attack with his hard-hitting Virginians, Custer had already put two and two together, because his instincts had early risen to the fore: An obviously large force of Rebels—Lee's most mobile fighting men—now occupying the highest ground near the strategic crossroads close to Meade's rear, at the time when Lee was about to unleash a massive offensive effort from the west, told him that Stuart and thousands of his veterans simply had to be hidden in the thick woods of Cress's Ridge. And, most of all, he realized that Stuart's men were there to cause all the mischief that they could inflict in the army's rear. In this regard, Custer was entirely correct. He was now thinking like a real West Pointer—and not the fun-loving clown of a cadet he had played at the academy for the amusement of others—because he had gotten into the minds of two fellow West Pointers, Lee and Stuart, in regard to their tactical thinking, like an experienced commander.

Custer's early decisions continued to pay dividends. Quickly, but carefully, after having ascertained the situation as much as possible and then making additional decisions in his usual rapid-fire manner that had been well honed by his scouting and reconnaissance missions as a staff officer since 1861, Custer had continued to size up the overall tactical situation, which had been made easier by having prudently ordered out patrols early on to ascertain if any opponents lurked nearby and could be flushed out. He had also ordered nearby wooden fences to be pushed down so as not to impede the advance of his skirmishers—and the possible unleashing of a mounted attack by his Wolverines—to confront the dismounted Rebels of Chambliss's and Jenkins's (Witcher's) Brigades, and to clear the way, including if he was forced by a disadvantageous situation to order a cavalry charge. He now saw the possibility of offensive thrusts by his Michigan men over the open ground: counterattacks that he now envisioned with clarity, which might be the best way to thwart a stronger opponent. Stuart was correct in anticipating an aggressive response to his own upping of the ante, because he now faced not only the youngest, but also the most aggressive cavalry brigade commander of the Army of the Potomac.

By this time, prospects had improved for Custer's chances of holding the strategic crossroads, and fortunately for him. Even more after the arrival of General Gregg, who had been absent from this vital section because of his illness, Custer's Michigan men benefited around 1:00 p.m. from having been bolstered by two other units of Gregg's Second Division, including Colonel John B. McIntosh's 3rd Pennsylvania Cavalry, which pushed toward Little's Run on the north, and the 1st New Jersey Cavalry just south of the Pennsylvanians, and a legion of cavalry known as the Purnell Maryland Legion Cavalry, First Brigade, which had bolstered the right flank west of the Low Dutch Road and roughly parallel to the Rummel buildings to the west after pushing north up the Low Dutch Road and past the Lott farm and into the Lott woods.

Initially under orders to replace Custer's men, McIntosh sent out his dismounted skirmishers over the open ground of the open fields beyond the Lott woods and west of the Lott farm. The dismounted troopers of the 1st New Jersey Cavalry, under a major, headed west across the open fields toward the Rummel buildings, which was countered by moving a long line of skirmishers farther south to gain a fence below the Rummel buildings—a first line of defense. Meanwhile, the 1st Maryland Cavalry, more than 250 troopers, was held near the Lott house in a reserve position to protect the crossroads and Union guns while serving as a fallback position just in case McIntosh's men ran into trouble and were forced to fall back to the east to regain the Low Dutch Road.

However, this reinforcement—rather than the initial plan to replace Custer's men—was not a sufficient number of troops to confront all of Stuart's cavalry that had been strengthened by additional units, both artillery and cavalry, for striking Meade's rear. These commands had been deployed on Custer's weak right flank to bolster this vulnerable position up the Low Dutch Road north of the intersection and to the Lott woods before pushing west and northwest out into the open fields and ever closer to the Rummel buildings and Little's Run to the northwest.

In this vital situation and on his own, Custer was still holding the strategic crossroads with too few men after he received Gregg's blessings to remain and ignore the orders from his superior. Custer was not going back to rejoin Kilpatrick's Third Division, because he now had a hot fight on his hands over a vital bone of contention—the strategic crossroads.

However, the disadvantages that Custer faced only stimulated him to greater exertions to protect the intersection. He possessed a new staff of young officers and naturally hoped that everything would work out smoothly during his first major action as a brigade commander. Unfortunately, it is not known what Custer's exact thoughts were at this time when facing his greatest challenge. However, he knew that he could trust his group of capable staff officers, his hard-fighting Wolverines, and his favorite sword with the "Toledo blade," with its inscribed motto, "Draw me not without provocation," by his side. On this day of destiny, General Stuart and his "Invincibles" were about to give Custer more provocation than he had ever faced or seen on any previous field of strife.

But at this time, what was the role of Brigadier General Gregg, the highest-ranking officer in this sector and now Custer's immediate superior, who commanded the Second Cavalry Division, when General Pleasonton had ordered him to serve as a blocking force by securing the crossroads with around 2,500 troopers—Custer's Cavalry Brigade—after Stuart's lengthy column of troopers had been spied on the move northeast along the York Turnpike by bluecoats atop Cemetery Hill? Under normal circumstances, Gregg should have been early on the spot in person to play the leading role in defense of the vital crossroads instead of allowing an extremely young and new brigadier general to literally sink or swim in this key situation on Meade's right-rear.

After all, Gregg had been sufficiently alarmed by the overall situation—attempting to defend the low ground of the vital crossroads that was dominated by Cress's Ridge and the woods on the high ground that was overflowing with Rebels and within easy striking distance of the dusty crossroads—to have requested Custer's Brigade to remain at the crossroads, despite the original desire of Generals Pleasonton and Kilpatrick for the Wolverines to be placed in position with the rest of the Third Division's cavalrymen at the southern end of the battle line, because he correctly sensed that he faced the full strength of Stuart's cavalry, which might have been augmented by Lee with additional manpower and guns—which was the case—after Stuart's exhaustive raid.

Nevertheless, Custer had been left to largely orchestrate tactical affairs on his own at the crossroads, while an ailing General Gregg, who still suffered from an intestinal infection, had only belatedly arrived in the early afternoon. He had then deployed most of his troopers elsewhere to locations safely out of harm's way, including Colonel Gregg's Brigade in a reserve position. But given Custer's distinctive, if not contrarian, temperament of being energized by embracing new challenges, especially formidable ones against the odds, this was actually something of an ideal situation for him under the circumstances, because he was largely responsible for holding the strategic crossroads on his own.

Some speculation has arisen that a conspiracy was at work to explain why Custer had been initially left on his own. In the words of one historian: "It seems clear that, by conveniently transferring nearly 80 percent of his troops off the field, Gregg was trying to avoid facing Stuart and his Invincibles, a cavalry force that had yet to be defeated by Union horsemen. His actions also show that he was willing to let Custer bear the ignominy that might come from his troops being trampled by Stuart."[213]

Of course this is a somewhat cynical conclusion by this historian, but the distinct possibility does exist that this situation was indeed the case. Even more, perhaps General Gregg, if a true Machiavellian type, which was only partly the case, might have envisioned creating a scenario that would have led to the elimination of a rising star and potential rival by realizing Custer's weakness for reckless bravery and leading cavalry charges in person—his penchant which had been fully demonstrated at Hunterstown on the previous day. Indeed, if Custer led an attack over such a wide stretch of open ground, between Little's Run to the west and the Low Dutch Road to the east, and against the overpowering might of Stuart's Corps, he might well never return from such a wild charge, which he was well known to favor.

Of course, these theories and possibilities in regard to the innermost depths of personal motivations cannot be proven conclusively. But General Gregg was a smart and savvy man. He was not about to risk his reputation and lofty standing by commanding too few troopers in the face of Stuart's entire cavalry division, which had probably been strengthened by Lee for this special mission in Meade's rear. Stuart's possible attack into the Army of the Potomac's rear might well change the course of the battle.

For whatever reason, Custer was early thrust into center stage in the brewing showdown for possession of the crossroads. As noted, the possibility does exist that General Gregg viewed Custer as a potential threat and worried that he might be eventually replaced by him. Unlike Custer, who was at a disadvantage because he had never seen this sector before, General Gregg knew all about the area around the crossroads because he had occupied this key position and skirmished here on the previous afternoon.

The many disadvantages of attempting to hold the strategic crossroads were obvious to one and all, and no one more than Gregg, who had needed no convincing of the extent of the inherent difficulties. As mentioned, making Custer's job most challenging was geography itself, because this key intersection in Meade's right-rear was located on low ground dominated by higher terrain, especially Cress's Ridge to the north, which loomed on the horizon like a threatening menace and was now the focus of Custer's attention. And a large-scale Rebel attack by cavalry and accompanying horse artillery (basically, highly mobile flying artillery) might come barreling down at any time from the two most likely directions—eastward down the Hanover Road and southward down the Low Dutch Road.

Of course, a greater threat might well come—which was eventually the case—from the wide plain located between the roads, if Stuart decided to launch an assault at this point, because Custer would be less likely to be prepared to resist such a threat. All in all, therefore, this was a vulnerable position in the army's vulnerable rear that young Custer had been ordered to hold to the last. As noted, a case could be made that Custer and his men were being used with less than noble purposes in mind (cannon fodder or sacrificial lambs to delay Stuart and buy time with their lives) by General Gregg, but this most likely was not the case. Nevertheless, the possibility does exist.

In this situation, either by accident or by design, if Custer met with a sharp reversal in his defense of the vulnerable crossroads, General Gregg would not be responsible for the defeat if he was not on the scene that morning and early afternoon, because Custer belonged to another division under Kilpatrick, who now possessed an aggressive plan to attack Lee's right flank on the south that was held by relatively few infantrymen, who had suffered heavily in attacking the high ground on July 2.

As mentioned, the odds improved dramatically for Custer to hold firm at the crossroads after General Gregg had belatedly arrived with the two brigades under Colonel John Baillie McIntosh and that of his cousin Colonel J. Irvin Gregg in the early afternoon after 1:00 p.m. But this last brigade, commanded by the colonel, was held in reserve, which did not enhance Custer's chances for a successful defense of the intersection because they were positioned to the rear. At this time and as noted, Gregg had decided to continue to keep Custer's Brigade in the key center position protecting the crossroads, while extending most of his troopers along a lengthier front, especially to the west beyond the crossroads, where Custer's left flank was held by companies of the 6th Michigan, and closer to Gettysburg.

As mentioned, McIntosh's men had originally moved north up the Low Dutch Road and then west toward the right of the 5th Michigan Cavalry. But again, Custer received no help from the other brigade under Colonel J. Irvin Gregg, who might have been more than happy to leave Custer on his own because of jealousy. All in all, and although it cannot be proven conclusively, there might well have been something entirely Machiavellian about this situation as well. Another historian, Tom Carhart, emphasized how General Gregg's deployments "effectively removed Colonel [J. Irvin] Gregg's [Third] brigade [around 1,000 troopers of the 4th and 16th Pennsylvania Cavalry, 1st Maine Cavalry, and 10th New York Cavalry of Gregg's Second Division] from the looming cavalry fight"—now held in reserve—which was all important in the Army of the Potomac's rear.[214]

For all of these reasons and perhaps others not yet proved conclusively, Custer and his men were left at center stage in the showdown at the crossroads because McIntosh's primary mission had been to guard Custer's right flank by taking a position north up the Low Dutch Road, while Colonel Gregg's Brigade held a reserve position well behind the Wolverine Brigade. Therefore, in the end, this tactical—if not political—situation meant that this fight was still going to be largely Custer's battle, just as Gregg and Pleasonton desired.[215] Initially and as noted, McIntosh's men were originally to have relieved all of Custer's troopers, who were low on ammunition and in need of rest, but such was not the case. After his arrival, Gregg had made sure that Custer and his troopers, especially Captain Pennington's guns, remained in place.[216]

Meanwhile, Custer was almost immediately back in action after the arrival of reinforcements. On Custer's advice, because of the growing threat to his right flank, which was vulnerable, as confirmed by the first fire of Rebel artillery that had caught him by surprise, McIntosh, who commanded around nine hundred men, had strengthened Custer's weak right on the Low Dutch Road north of the crossroads, where he naturally expected the main attack, or so it seemed in the beginning.[217]

In the end, and according to a recent estimation, therefore, "the total number of Union soldiers on East Cavalry Field that July 3 was probably about 2,700 [actually more than 3,000] facing 6,000 Confederates [as] Stuart had more than twice the number of Union soldiers standing in his patch, men he would have to get past to perform . . . his secret mission from Lee."[218]

However, in overall terms, the arrival of McIntosh's troopers proved less beneficial to Custer than expected. After McIntosh's men had initially advanced and begun to relieve the most advanced portions of Custer's foremost men of the 5th and 6th Michigan Cavalry, whose troopers were low on ammunition, they found themselves in a fix. The advanced dismounted skirmishers of Colonel McIntosh's Brigade just to the right, or east, of the Rummel buildings were under ever-increasing pressure from the sharpshooters of Jenkins's (Witcher's) Brigade and the fast-firing Confederate artillery. Clearly, a serious crisis was brewing, and Custer continued to be at the center of the storm. But he relished the thought of rising to the challenge to prove his worth.[219]

Most importantly, Custer realized "that the Battle of Gettysburg might be lost right here if Stuart got through to Meade's rear."[220] For such reasons, he prayed to God for mercy and success in the upcoming battle of such importance, as he did before every engagement. As he was destined to write at a future date, "I have so much to be thankful for [and] God grant that I may always prove as deserving as I am grateful to Him for what He has given me."[221]

## CUSTER'S DETERMINATION TO HOLD THE STRATEGIC CROSSROADS AT ALL COSTS

The strategic crossroads of the Hanover and Low Dutch Roads would certainly have fallen—thus opening the door for Stuart's attack into Meade's rear along Cemetery Ridge after riding southwest to gain the Baltimore Turnpike—if not for Custer's decisions and determination to continue to defend the crossroads because he understood—almost instinctively in the beginning—its crucial importance, despite his orders from General Kilpatrick, his superior and Third Division commander.

Custer was also concerned about what would happen if he met with defeat. After all, and as noted, in the early afternoon, and despite the initial plan for Custer and his men to have been officially relieved by Gregg's Brigade under McIntosh, Custer had decided otherwise by staying with the Second Division. Making the correct choice, Custer was proud of the fact that he had "decided not to abandon the road junction," even when he had been officially relieved by the fresh troopers of Gregg's Brigade, because he understood that this was the key point that had to be defended at all costs, since thousands of Stuart's troopers had targeted Meade's vulnerable rear with a nasty surprise.[222]

However, fate and his own smart decisions and strategic insights all combined to continue to place Custer at not only the right place, but also at center stage and largely on his own with an inferior force of Wolverines to literally do or die. He was in a key position to become a man of destiny if he could successfully defend the strategic crossroads, and seemingly destiny itself had placed him at this key location in the rear of the Army of the Potomac.[223]

Still largely on his own because General Gregg was sick and playing more of a passive role than usual in consequence, Custer realized that he had to hold this strategic crossroads at all costs to deny Stuart the open avenue into Meade's rear, when no other Union troops or natural obstacles stood between the new brigadier general and Cemetery Ridge. Therefore, Custer knew that the best defensive stance in defending the crossroads was an aggressive tactical offensive, especially when he was positioned in a vulnerable lower-ground position. Therefore, he ordered the 5th Michigan Cavalry troopers to advance north on foot and forward up the open slope and parallel to Little's Run all the way up to the Rummel buildings. Because he possessed prior knowledge from Captain Weber that Rebels were hidden in the dark forests, with the tall, hardwood trees in full foliage, which dominated the high ground of Cress's Ridge, and because McIntosh's most advanced men were under ever-increasing pressure, the men of the 5th Michigan Cavalry continued to play a key role while aligned in the open fields. After McIntosh's arrival, Custer then dispatched portions of the 6th Michigan Cavalry to extend his left to the west all the way to Little's Run.

The advancing troopers of the 5th Michigan Cavalry, which had been organized in Detroit, were protected by several companies playing guardian roles on their left, or west. And, as noted, McIntosh's foremost troopers, who had been skirmishing with Witcher's Virginians and were low on ammunition, also protected Custer's left, which was anchored on the Hanover Road west of the crossroads. Custer early envisioned launching cavalry attacks to counter any Rebels who might suddenly charge down the slope, in order to safeguard the crossroads. He therefore had ordered preparations for the launching of a mounted attack by the Wolverines, just in case an emergency situation developed, after the 5th Michigan Cavalry had advanced so far north to cover the front. Therefore, Samuel Harris, 5th Michigan Cavalry, described how "we came to Rummel's farm; here we threw down the fences and rode by his house [and large-sized German, or Dutch, barn] into the fields beyond."[224]

At this time, the 5th Michigan Cavalry troopers, especially those foremost troopers who had not been relieved by McIntosh's men, whose cartridge boxes were low, and then had been ordered to relieve McIntosh's most advanced troopers of the 1st New Jersey Cavalry and 3rd Pennsylvania Cavalry, who were low on ammunition, had continued to gain additional ground in steadily moving north, after having continued their push up the slope and ever closer to Cress's Ridge, after Custer ordered a battalion of the 5th Michigan Cavalry under Major Noah Henry Ferry—who had been born on April 30, 1831, on Mackinaw Island, Michigan—to reinforce McIntosh's hard-pressed dismounted men (initial replacements), who were caught in the open and exposed to hot fire. Custer had ascertained in timely fashion that dismounted Confederates were moving toward McIntosh's left, which was in the open west of the Low Dutch Road. He had therefore hurriedly dispatched Major Ferry to the rescue before it was too late.[225]

But Ferry and his boys ran into trouble. In consequence, casualties among the 5th Michigan men, exposed on open ground, steadily increased because they were hit by the fire of artillery and dismounted cavalrymen, who had targeted the left flank of Colonel Alger's men for turning because it was hanging in midair amid the golden wheat fields and green pastures. The sharpshooting skills of Lieutenant Colonel Witcher's men of the 34th Virginia Cavalry Battalion were well honed from years of experience in hunting for white-tailed deer and turkeys in western Virginia's mountains and in the art of killing Yankees, ensuring the spiraling of casualties among the Wolverines.

Consequently, the hard-hit Michigan troopers were forced to gradually give ground, after they had been allowed to advance too far north, which made them more vulnerable, and had fired away too much ammunition too quickly, and Major Ferry's men had literally walked into a clever ambush created by the savvy Witcher, whose superior level of experience had risen to the fore. Therefore, a blistering fire culled the ranks of the hard-hit 5th Michigan Cavalry in cruel fashion. Some of the regiment's finest officers were cut down, and the young bluecoats of the 5th Michigan Cavalry continued falling like autumn leaves under the hail of zipping bullets.

Bravely inspiring and encouraging his men, who were low on ammunition and were exposed in the open, Major Noah Henry Ferry, a fair-haired rising star of the Michigan Cavalry Brigade, rose to the challenge. While blasting away with a carbine, he was killed when a bullet whistled through his head, after having just screamed for his troopers to "Rally, boys! Rally at the fence!"[226] The talented Major Ferry, a hard-fighting officer with a full light-colored beard who hailed from the town of Grand Haven, Michigan, was one of the most dynamic and popular officers of the 5th Michigan Cavalry.[227] Lieutenant Colonel Witcher rejoiced in having achieved this sparkling success. He described the tactical sequence of events, including the clever ambush that he created with considerable tactical astuteness, that led to the deaths of a good many Wolverines of Ferry's ill-fated battalion of the 5th Michigan Cavalry: "The Battalion, which had alone rallied with me, opened upon the 5th Michigan Cavalry, sweeping down its ranks with a most deadly fire, killing its Major [Ferry], capturing its colors, and covering the ground with the killed and wounded men of the 5th Michigan. . . . I was within 30 yards and saw the Major fall, a gallant and heroic man he was."[228] Clearly, Witcher felt no hatred for an enemy who demonstrated great bravery.[229]

To exploit the opportunity in the hurling back of the boys of the 5th Virginia Cavalry and Major Ferry's death, in the words of one Union officer of the 2nd Pennsylvania Cavalry, "this opportunity, Fitz. Lee sent forward the 1st Virginia [Cavalry], which charged our right and left."[230]

Despite the punishment suffered by Major Ferry's hard-hit battalion of the 5th Michigan Cavalry, Custer continued to benefit immensely from the decisions made early on by both him and his superiors, especially General Gregg, whose judgments and insights certainly worked to his favor by this time. Indeed, the key decisions that had set the stage for Custer to perform beyond expectations had been most fortuitous.[231]

## TURNING POINTS:
## PLEASONTON'S AND GREGG'S SOUND DECISIONS

It was not only Custer and courageous officers, like Major Noah Henry Ferry, who had fought back with valor and in magnificent fashion, while meeting the most recent threat in an aggressive and timely manner. But of course it would be unfair to his superior to emphasize that Custer was the sole architect of a successful defense of the strategic crossroads, because of Gregg's timely insights and contributions as the grand orchestrator of events. Quite simply, and besides his command of elite troopers, Custer could not have succeeded on this day without the smart decisions of his two superiors, Pleasonton and Gregg. But in turn, Pleasonton and Gregg could not have been successful in safeguarding the strategic crossroads without Custer and his hard-hitting style and tactical skill on multiple levels. On this crucial day, Custer was destined to be the sharp sword that ultimately hacked Stuart's lofty ambitions to pieces until nothing remained of grandiose Confederate dreams of winning it all.

Like Custer, and after his belated arrival on the field just before Colonel McIntosh's Brigade had gained the crossroads, to the new brigadier general's relief, General Gregg's instincts had been right on target in a situation in which he could not afford to make any mistakes. To his great credit and as noted, Gregg had early realized that the threat could not have been greater at this point in Meade's right-rear, especially after having been warned that "large columns" of Stuart's brigades were in motion as seen from the vantage point of Cemetery Hill.

Gregg had played a more important role than Pleasonton. In defiance of the orders of Pleasonton, whose headquarters was located too far away—around three miles away on Cemetery Hill—which ensured that he was unable to issue orders based on the fast-paced flow of events at the crossroads, which now posed the greatest threat to Meade's rear, Gregg had wisely ordered Colonel McIntosh to march his brigade back to the crossroads where they had skirmished on the previous afternoon—a key decision that paid immense dividends to Custer, especially as this fight escalated.

Because Pleasonton—too far away from the strategic crossroads in Meade's rear—had little idea of the true tactical situation in the beginning, he had incorrectly believed that this strategic crossroads could be held by a single brigade. Of course, such was certainly not the case as ascertained by the ever-vigilant Captain Weber, who had immediately passed the intelligence on to Custer to enlighten him of the extent of the threat. As mentioned, an aide from General Pleasonton, who had dispatched Gregg to the crossroads after gaining the intelligence of Stuart's activity "moving toward the right," or east, that had been seen from the top of Cemetery Hill, arrived with a belated order to send Custer and his Michigan Brigade back to General Kilpatrick and his Third Cavalry Brigade now holding a position on the left-rear. But by this time, Custer had acted for hours contrary to Kilpatrick's orders, performing independently of his division and his commander's wishes. For ample good reason, an incensed Kilpatrick believed that a terrible mistake had been made, and he had issued orders around noon to Gregg to send Custer and his brigade back to him.

As noted, Generals Gregg and Custer were having none of it, because they fully realized the true extent of the threat to Meade's right-rear and fully realized what was at stake—perhaps even the life and death of the Army of the Potomac. At great risk to their future careers if they met with an ugly defeat or Kilpatrick met with disaster to the south in attacking Lee's right, the two generals had early seen eye-to-eye at this time about one thing, which was the most crucial point—that Stuart and thousands of his men were atop Cress's Ridge, and they were planning to strike Meade's rear in conjunction with Lee's upcoming offensive effort from the west to cut Meade's army in two. Therefore, and as mentioned, both officers had immediately decided that the Michigan Cavalry Brigade should remain firmly in place at the strategic crossroads and not ride south to rejoin Kilpatrick, because too much was at stake—an extremely wise decision.[232]

Custer consequently continued to fight well into the afternoon in defiance of the orders of his superior, Kilpatrick. As this situation is explained by historian Jay Monaghan: "Gregg kept Custer [because] Gregg believed, too [like Custer], that the Battle of Gettysburg might be lost right here, if Stuart got through to Meade's rear. He ordered Custer, for the second time that day, to serve in his command regardless of other orders. Jeb Stuart must be stopped!"[233]

But in fact it was more a case of Custer's decision to ignore the orders of his Third Division commander (Kilpatrick) and remain in defense of the crossroads, because he understood its strategic importance, and he now faced the day's greatest threat to Meade's vulnerable rear. From the beginning, and in spite of the fact that he was engaged in his first major battle, Custer's instincts not only continued to be right on target, but also his contrarian personality had risen to the fore.

Like at West Point, and fortunately for the Union on July 3, Custer was not only not a blind follower of the strict rules and regulations that bound other leaders and reduced their flexibility, but he had openly mocked them by ideas of his own, when he had firmly believed that his own ideas were more appropriate and better for a successful defense. And now, in much the same way, he had all but mocked the order from his superior, Brigadier General Kilpatrick, which he felt was unwise and outdated under the circumstances of what he had ascertained at the crossroads, by simply ignoring it.

One of Custer's strongest character traits, and one that served him well in Meade's right-rear, was that he often skirted the accepted standards and norms of convention to go his own way if he believed it was best for the army, as on July 3. Both on and off the battlefield, and as in the days of his youth, he had never been one to do things by the book, especially if they were wrong. Custer was always an officer who was just itching for an opportunity to go his own way and make his own decisions, and these contrarian qualities served him extremely well on July 3.[234]

Right on target, historian Stephen Z. Starr emphasized the importance of Gregg's decision to keep Custer and his crack brigade at the crossroads in this struggle in the rear of the Army of the Potomac and to ignore orders for the young brigadier general to return to Kilpatrick's Division: "a decision that probably saved him—and perhaps Meade—from a disastrous defeat."[235]

Clearly, Gregg had early understood the importance of this struggle for possession of the strategic crossroads, after he had belatedly reached the field to take charge—but more behind the scenes and accomplishing little more than formally approving Custer's decisions—from Custer, whose troopers continued to play the major role in defending the crossroads and advancing north. Indeed, as General Gregg, who maintained a field command position near the two horse artillery batteries after his arrival on the field, explained, because of the aggressiveness of Jenkins's (Witcher's) steadily advancing skirmishers, which indicated that a larger attack was about to be launched from the high ground, "the enemy had gained [his right] and were about to attack, with a view of gaining the rear" of the Army of the Potomac.[236]

Like Custer, General Gregg, who had demonstrated his aggressiveness at Brandy Station, knew that the best defense was to rely on the tactical offense. Therefore, after his arrival on the field in the early afternoon, he had ordered the 3rd Pennsylvania Volunteer Cavalry and 1st Maryland Volunteer Cavalry of Colonel J. Irvin Gregg's Brigade—both supported by companies of the 1st New Jersey—to advance up the Low Dutch Road to protect Custer's right flank on the native Ohioan's advice, since this was the vulnerable point where the first Confederate artillery had targeted their fire.

Gregg, like Brigadier General Custer, had early understood the supreme importance of this escalating battle and fully appreciated how much was at stake. He wrote about what was at stake on this hot afternoon in the Army of the Potomac's rear, because he was fully aware of the extreme "importance of resisting [Stuart's] attack . . . which, if succeeded . . . would have been productive of the most serious consequences."[237] Indeed, Generals Custer and Gregg, whose leg had been grazed by an iron fragment of an exploding Confederate shell in a recent skirmish, fully realized by this time that the Battle of Gettysburg—the largest engagement ever fought on the North American continent—might well be lost right there at that time and place "if Stuart got through to Meade's rear."[238]

And this battle in Meade's right-rear was steadily escalating and intensifying in accordance with its overall importance. Nevertheless, despite the extent of the challenge and added responsibility, Custer continued to remain calm and cool, in control of himself and the overall situation, as from the beginning, despite the fact that this was his first major battle, revealing that he was certainly not in over his head. For instance, he had made the key decision to send Major Noah Henry Ferry's battalion of the 5th Michigan Cavalry to reinforce McIntosh's hard-pressed units, whose left flank—on the west—had been threatened, to counter Confederate aggressiveness. But Custer and his men were about to face a more serious threat, because Stuart and his veterans had only fairly begun to fight on this afternoon of decision.[239]

Most of all, Custer possessed high motivations that were rooted in his strong moral faith and his belief that he was waging a holy war for the most righteous of causes on the third day at Gettysburg. This religious faith now fortified his resolve. In his own words that explained why he fought so well and hard against the odds on July 3, he was fueled "with the holy inspiration of a just and noble cause" of saving the Union and Meade's rear on the crucial third day at Gettysburg.[240]

## LIEUTENANT COLONEL WITCHER ATTACKS THE RUMMEL HOUSE AND BARN

With the battle escalating, Custer still felt anxious, because he knew that the woods of Cress's Ridge were full of mounted Rebels, due to the timely information early gained from vigilant Captain Weber. Custer must have wondered if he had made the right tactical decisions, and he hoped that no mistake had been made.

All of a sudden, the lengthy row of around 150 Confederate field pieces opened fire not long after 1:00 p.m. on that sweltering afternoon in Adams County, which Stuart knew was a prelude to the unleashing of Lee's greatest offensive effort of the war, Pickett's Charge. As could be expected, Stuart had been waiting for this moment, because he was fully aware—like Custer, who realized what the sound of so many roaring cannon meant—that the explosion of artillery fire was the long-awaited "signal to ready his men for an attack on the Union rear. But first he had to dispose of the blue cavalrymen that presently blocked his pathway" to the Army of the Potomac's rear.[241]

In addition, Stuart had been inching forward to advance farther down the slope of Cress's Ridge because Custer had become too aggressive, which seemed to indicate that he was determined to do something much more than just defend the crossroads, posing a threat not only to the Virginian's desire to capture the strategic intersection but also to his ultimate objective of striking Meade's vulnerable rear. In consequence, Stuart knew that something had to be done or there would be no chance of capturing the vital crossroads, which was the first step in turning to a final push from the Baltimore Road to strike into the Army of the Potomac's rear.

Not realizing that Custer and Gregg possessed the vital intelligence that had exposed his presence, and eager to redeem his sullied reputation, Stuart now envisioned unleashing a large-scale surprise attack from the woods atop Cress's Ridge. As noted, Stuart did not realize that Custer and Gregg knew that so many Rebel cavalrymen were hidden in the woods atop Cress's Ridge. All in all, this was partly a Virginia strategy gained from experience in having long battled in the woodlands of the Old Dominion, which possessed far fewer open fields than well-developed and heavily cultivated southeastern Pennsylvania.

Unrealized by Stuart, the acquisition of vital intelligence about the superior numbers of Southerners in the forests atop Cress's Ridge and Custer's wise deployments, having pushed his troopers so far north, and the wide stretch of open ground before the wood line of more than a mile, negated any possibility that a surprise attack could be achieved by attacking from the woodlands atop Cress's Ridge. Custer and his men could easily see any aggressive movements on the high ground because nothing impeded their view over such a wide area. Custer, relying on his binoculars, could quickly adjust his tactics and positions to compensate by strengthening the defensive effort or even launching the offensive if necessary to meet a larger threat. In this regard, consequently, attacking from the woodlands was not an effective offensive tactic like in Virginia as envisioned by Stuart, because too much open ground, including the plain, lay below Cress's Ridge, and any early Rebel movements could be quickly ascertained from the lower ground.

But Stuart still did not know what size of force was before him, because Custer also had many troopers, especially those in reserve, hidden in the woodlands near the strategic intersection, and McIntosh's men occupied the Lott woods to anchor the right of the battle line. Witcher's attackers, all of whom were dismounted, on Stuart's right would certainly flush out whatever Union force was in the area in defense of the crossroads—a couple of regiments, a brigade, or a full division, if the attack continued downhill. Stuart had to find out the Federals' numbers as soon as possible to develop his own tactics to fit the exact tactical situation that lay before him.

Meanwhile, Stuart had parried the threat of the arrival of McIntosh's reinforcements that had been dispatched to bolster the foremost Wolverines, after a lengthy line of dismounted cavalry skirmishers of the 5th Michigan, 1st New Jersey, and 3rd Pennsylvania—from west to east—had earlier surged forward to gain more ground on the north. Custer's men now held the large Rummel barn that dominated the northern horizon. Lieutenant Colonel Witcher commanded the troopers of the 34th Virginia Cavalry Battalion in person, and Stuart ordered them to advance down the slope to gain the Rummel house and barn and the surrounding fences.

By this time, Stuart worried that "now that he had been discovered [to have so many troopers hidden atop Cress's Ridge], this force might try to block his way [but he] was confident he could blow through what looked like no more than a single large brigade, perhaps two thousand men," that had been assigned to defend the crossroads."[242] In the words of Major Henry Brainerd McClellan: "Witcher's battalion [of seasoned veterans was] sent forward to hold the Rummel barn and a line of fence on its right," or west.[243]

Indeed, Custer understood the importance of his key mission and acted accordingly, because he fully realized that the woods of Cress's Ridge were full of Rebels, and that they were becoming more aggressive, with Stuart having finally stirred into taking more action; all indications that a much larger fight—it had always been only a matter of time—was developing to confirm his conviction that it was crucial to hold the strategic crossroads at all costs. The holding of the advanced skirmish line north of the head of Little's Run, which flowed south just below, or south, of the Rummel buildings, and at the massive Rummel barn and the surrounding stone fences, was a significant defensive stand in overall tactical terms.

Here, the dismounted skirmishers of the 5th Michigan, 3rd Pennsylvania, and 1st New Jersey (these last two regiments had reinforced the Wolverines) had "never attempted to go beyond that line [centered on the Rummel barn—located before the center of Stuart's line—because it was so close to the high ground and forests of Cress's Ridge]. Rather, they sought only to keep Stuart's troopers [Witcher's fast-firing skirmishers] at bay, especially from getting beyond them and into the Union rear."[244] After all and as mentioned, Custer fully realized, in regard to Stuart's troops, that the dense timber of Cress's Ridge was "full of them."[245]

Ironically, Custer's complete and thorough understanding of what lay before him with certitude and clarity—thanks mostly to the vital intelligence that had been gained in real time from Captain Weber—was the antithesis of the situation in which he was guilty of a refusal to accept the harsh realities that were destined to await him in the Little Bighorn valley on another summer afternoon in the future.[246] To his credit and revealing one secret of his success, Custer gave full credit to Captain Weber in his official report by emphasizing how Weber "kept me so well informed of the movements of the enemy, that I was enabled to make my dispositions with complete success."[247]

But this was a brewing crisis that only Custer could meet because he was the most aggressive and tactically gifted commander on the field. In truth, Stuart was now using Lieutenant Colonel Witcher and his Virginia aggressiveness to mask his main objective, which was to ascertain the best opportunity and means to avoid a major clash so as to fulfill his mission of delivering a devastating blow into Meade's rear. To his credit, Stuart was not swayed from his primary mission, which was to gain Meade's rear and not fight a battle on the scale of another Brandy Station. At this time, therefore, "after those signal shots, Stuart planned to wait with his men on Cress Ridge" and make final preparations for moving west and striking the rear of Meade's army, and he "began to busy himself with getting his unit ready to plunge into the Union rear" instead of getting involved in a full-scale battle.[248]

Meanwhile, because he could not see farther west from the highest point of Cress's Ridge since it was covered in heavy timber, Stuart realized that he needed to increase his visibility toward the southwest, where General Lee was orchestrating the greatest and most desperate offensive effort of his career, Pickett's Charge. The opening of the bombardment on Meade's Cemetery Ridge line naturally drew Stuart's attention to remind him of his orders to strike in conjunction with Pickett's Charge, and he needed to know more about what was occurring in the vicinity of the main army. Was the mass of Southern infantry now finally moving forward? Or was the artillery bombardment destined to take longer—if initially effective, which was the case—than planned before the infantry advanced, which would affect Stuart's timetable for hitting Meade's rear.

As noted, Stuart had been ordered to act in conjunction with this final offensive thrust as part of a three-part plan, which was envisioned by Lee to be the decisive formula for winning the day. To occupy the attention of the pesky Custer and his crossroads defenders while Stuart's main body, especially the elite brigades of Hampton and Fitzhugh Lee, prepared to slip around the Union cavalry and then dash for General Meade's rear, while Ewell struck on the north and Pickett's Charge targeted the right-center of Meade's forces—versus the center proper as originally planned—Stuart had first ordered Captain Jackson's Virginia guns (two 12-pounder howitzers and two 3-inch rifles) of the Charlottesville "Kanawha" Horse Artillery to not only rake Custer's right flank with hot fire, but also to support the advance of Lieutenant Colonel Witcher's Virginia mountaineers after the four pieces had fired from the open ground of Cress's Ridge that overlooked the shallow valley of the strategic crossroads.[249]

All the while, to the north, from behind the fence where they had retired on the major's orders before he was fatally cut down, Ferry's troopers watched Witcher's dismounted attackers advance to within 120 yards, when they unleashed an organized volley that inflicted damage on the Virginians. But surging south down the slope, the Rebel attackers possessed the momentum, and they exploited these advantages to the full. Despite their best efforts, the Michigan men could not stop the elated Virginians once they had been unleashed.[250]

Major Ferry's troopers of the 5th Michigan Cavalry were especially hard hit by the fire of the veterans of Witcher's 34th Virginia Cavalry Battalion, and good fighting men from the Wolverine command went down to rise no more.[251] Confederate artillery gained an early advantage. Samuel Harris, 5th Michigan Cavalry, described how the "rebels had run out six guns on a small rise in the ground, about three-fourths of a mile from where we were, and with these guns they began shelling our regiment" with intensity and accuracy that indicated that these were veteran gunners.[252]

This was all part of Stuart's two-part plan (dismounted cavalry in the open fields and an exposed Old Dominion battery that appeared alone and isolated on a high-ground perch relatively close to the Rummel barn to the south) to lure the Federals into a headlong attack to set the tactical stage for the ordering of Hampton's and Lee's hidden brigades, which were Stuart's crack commands, now basically serving as a strategic reserve, to spring their ambush and destroy the overconfident attackers.[253]

With enthusiasm because they enjoyed their high-ground advantage, therefore, the Virginia gunners hurled shells at Custer's right flank, and skirmishers aligned across the open fields of summer and continued to blast away at the dismounted Yankee skirmishers. This was a challenge that Custer could not ignore. He had the 5th Michigan Cavalry to not only reinforce McIntosh's hard-pressed troopers to the east, but perhaps with the ultimate design of making an attempt to capture the troublesome battery if the proper tactical opportunity arose, because these Michigan men were dismounted and basically acting as infantry.

But the concentrated artillery fire was too much for the men of the 5th Michigan Cavalry—now the most advanced position of any of Custer's men—and the casualty list steadily grew and the command became shaky under the pounding. Custer saw the punishment suffered by his men from the fast-firing Southern artillery and the blazing Enfield rifles of Jenkins's men, who possessed the advantage of firing downhill. He therefore ordered—either in person or by messenger—the 5th Michigan Cavalry troopers to retire down the slope and take good cover behind another sturdy fence from which they could fire back with greater accuracy and more overall security.

In the words of Samuel Harris, 5th Michigan, who explained Custer's countermove in what was the start of a tactical chess game over the possession of a strategic crossroads after the Virginia guns had opened fire: "Custer ordered us off to the right and to dismount and take position behind a rail fence, about a quarter of a mile in front of the rebel guns [and] we were ordered off to the right and front."[254]

## INVALUABLE ARTILLERY SUPPORT

But these smart and timely alignments were more defensive than offensive. As never before, Custer realized that he needed to rely on his best asset, because the Rebels, especially Lieutenant Colonel Witcher and his 34th Virginia Cavalry Battalion, had become more aggressive in pushing south down the slope to engage both Custer's and McIntosh's foremost skirmishers. Major Henry Brainerd McClellan never forgot how "the first sign of [artillery] activity on the Federal side came from a battery near the house of Joseph Spangler. This was fine horse battery M, 2nd United States Artillery, consisting of six three-inch rifles, and commanded by Lieutenant A[lexander]. C[ummings] M[cWhorter] Pennington."[255]

As mentioned, and as Custer earlier explained his initial surprise and in regard to his response to the first Confederate artillery fire from the looming heights, which had suddenly "appeared on my right and opened upon me with a battery" of half a dozen artillery pieces: "Placing two sections of battery 'M,' Second regular artillery, in position [in the southwestern corner of the crossroads], I ordered them to silence the enemy's battery" that was causing so much trouble, and this mission was accomplished by an accurate fire.[256]

Fortunately for him, and a forgotten secret to his success on July 3, Custer could not have possessed a better artillery officer than the gifted Pennington, one of the finest artillery leaders in the army, to command Battery M, 2nd United States Artillery. He was also his friend and an old West Point classmate—kindred spirits and aggressive young commanders who proved more than a match for Stuart's finest "Invincibles."[257]

Custer's most overlooked role at Gettysburg was in his skill demonstrated in deploying and coordinating the fire of his horse artillery. Upon ascertaining that the main threat was coming from the north and not the west toward Gettysburg by way of the Hanover Road, Custer had earlier ordered Captain Pennington to shift his guns, nestled in the southwest angle of the crossroads, more toward the north.[258]

As mentioned, the first fire of the Confederate guns from the high ground on his right flank had forced Custer to realign his defensive line by creating a new line at a right angle to his existing line, while maintaining his old position to create a new battle line shaped like the letter L. As could be expected, the Southern artillerymen had then turned their fire on the new line that Custer had created so quickly to counter the existing threat that was steadily growing.

At this time, and confident that he had made the right tactical decisions, especially in regard to the repositioning of Pennington's guns, Custer wrote how his defensive line had been well conceived in regard to both artillery and cavalry, because he had mixed and best utilized the two arms: "The shorter branch [of the letter "L"] formed one section [of two artillery pieces] of Battery M, supported by four squadrons of the 6th Michigan Cavalry, faced toward Gettysburg [while] the long branch [of the letter "L"], composed of the remaining two sections of Company M, 2d Artillery, [was ably] supported by a portion of the 6th Michigan Cavalry on the right," while holding the 7th Michigan further to the right in case any attack was forthcoming from the east.[259] Clearly Custer continued to take no unnecessary chances, and he continued to make well-conceived deployments based upon an accurate reading of the existing threats and overall tactical situation.[260]

From the beginning, after the first fire from the Confederate artillery from the commanding high ground to the north, Custer relied on the devastating firepower of his ace in the hole to quickly silence the troublesome battery, whose fire that hit his flank caused him to create his new L-shaped line: the half dozen ordnance rifles of the artillery unit, Battery M, 2nd United States Artillery, under the highly capable Lieutenant Alexander Cummings McWhorter Pennington. Still learning on the fly in his first major battle, Custer was not only impressed but also amazed by the masterful performance of Pennington and his lethal guns. As Custer wrote, "Notwithstanding the superiority of the enemy's [high-ground] position [his ordered silencing of the Rebel battery] was done in a very short space of time."[261] Actually, the artillery duel was longer, causing the commander of the 2nd North Carolina Cavalry, Chambliss's Brigade, to write with exaggeration, "I do not suppose it ever has been equaled by land forces in steadiness of discharge and roar of guns."[262]

Custer had learned that in a long-range artillery duel, and even when they held the high ground, the gunners—despite being seasoned veterans—of the Stuart Horse Artillery could not prevail in a showdown, especially a lengthy contest, against the superior Federal artillery. Stuart also knew as much from experience. But, as noted, he only desired to occupy the Federals at the crossroads in order to slip around the flank to strike Meade's rear to fulfill his primary mission.

In a one-sided artillery showdown, the inferior Confederate guns were no match for the superiority of the Union cannon, which possessed range and accuracy advantages. The inferiority of Southern artillery ammunition also bestowed a greater advantage to the Federal guns—especially Battery M, 2nd United States Artillery, which continued to prove that they were dominant on every level—the inevitable price of an agricultural nation without an adequate industrial and manufacturing base like the North during a lengthy war of attrition. Confederate audacity and courage could not compensate in an artillery showdown at long range.

But as part of his ambush and tactical trap, Stuart expected the relatively few guns to be quickly overpowered so that the Federals might become overconfident and unleash a reckless charge up the slope to provide an opportunity to strike a devastating blow by unleashing Hampton and Fitz Lee—his strategic reserve and ace in the hole. But Custer did not fall for the tactical trap, because he knew that Cress's Ridge was overflowing with Rebel cavalrymen just waiting for Stuart to order them downhill in an overwhelming charge.

Therefore, Custer wisely displayed good sense and prudence by not unleashing an attack uphill and over open ground—two distinct disadvantages—in a reckless manner as Stuart expected, sensing that elite troopers (Hampton's and Fitzhugh Lee's Brigades) were hidden in the woods. Instead, Custer maintained his composure and resisted the temptation to rely on his most aggressive instincts because he knew what was at stake, and because he correctly anticipated Stuart's tactical design as essentially a trap.

He consequently decided to rely on his superior artillery firepower rather than unleashing a wild charge up the slope to inflict damage at long range, while minimizing risks to his command. To his frustration, Stuart was learning that he could not easily fool his opponent as in the past and that Brandy Station might not have been a fluke after all. But Lee's top cavalier had no idea that he was destined to be outthought—and outfought as well—by one of the youngest generals in the annals of American history.

## INTENSIFYING ARTILLERY DUEL

Adding more superiority to considerably increase his firepower by relying on his artillery advantage, which he was determined to exploit to his maximum benefit, Custer had ordered up the four 3-inch ordnance rifles (the brigade's entire array of artillery) of McIntosh's horse artillery, Captain Alanson Merwin Randol's Battery. The long-arm command had accompanied McIntosh to the crossroads. The New York–born Captain Randol was a perfect complement to Captain Pennington, because he was a highly capable fellow West Pointer (class of 1860).

Custer possessed not only some of the best troopers in the Army of the Potomac, but also some of the finest artillery at his disposal. For such reasons, these advantages allowed his aggressive instincts to rise to the fore. Clearly Custer was not holding back and was upping the ante, but in regard to his artillery rather than his cavalry—a significant early command decision. After all, he instinctively knew of the importance of this showdown in the Union rear, because it was all about the safety of Meade's rear.

Most importantly on this day of destiny, Custer was performing extremely well and with consummate skill beyond one of his age and as a novice brigade commander. From the beginning, he had quickly developed tactics on the fly, while performing like a seasoned infantry brigade commander by skillfully integrating cavalry and artillery, both Pennington's and Randol's batteries, to create a masterful defense of the strategic crossroads situated amid the open fields. More important, he was successfully protecting the crossroads by not taking the risk of falling for Stuart's tactical trap or making himself vulnerable in overall tactical terms, because he had ascertained the tactical design of Lee's top cavalryman.

From what he had seen from June 9 through June 21, Custer knew that the morale of the Confederate gunners—like Stuart's cavalrymen in general—had been more deflated than usual because of successive recent artillery mismatches on Virginia and Pennsylvania soil over the past few weeks. Even more, the men and horses of Breathed's Virginia Battery (1st Stuart Horse Artillery, which was composed of four 3-inch guns) and a section of Captain McGregor's Battery (2nd Stuart Horse Artillery, which consisted of two 12-pounder Napoleons and two 3-inch guns) had been part of Stuart's exhausting raid nearly to the gates of Washington, DC, during which they had served no purpose. Significantly, they had been left behind near Gettysburg to refill their depleted ammunition chests and caissons when Stuart and his troopers had mounted up and galloped forth down the York Turnpike in mid-morning, another ill-fated development for the East Cavalry Field artillery showdown for which these worn Rebel artillerymen and their fagged horses were not prepared.

But worst of all, the guns and expert artillerymen of Breathed's and McGregor's batteries were still far behind Stuart's advanced position on Cress's Ridge. They were finally destined to reach Stuart's position on Cress's Ridge only belatedly in the afternoon, because they had to wait for ammunition wagons to refill their limbers and caissons, another Confederate logistical breakdown that came into play to Custer's advantage on the East Cavalry Field. At this time, Stuart's other batteries had already gained their resupply of ammunition and were ready for the stern challenges in facing the counterparts of Custer's and Gregg's horse artillery.

Then, after finally gaining their resupplies, these two absent batteries of the Stuart Horse Artillery were hurried toward Cress's Ridge: a lengthy and dusty race at full speed to reach the field of strife in Meade's right-rear, especially upon hearing the opening guns of opposing artillery firing around the strategic crossroads and the roaring cannon in preparation for Pickett's Charge.

In addition, Captain Breathed was also eager to reach the field because of the natural rivalry that existed between him and other battery commanders of Stuart's Horse Artillery.

Even more, the fresh Stuart Horse Artillery batteries, which had not been part of Stuart's overly long raid, which had been barren of results, with Brigadier General William Edmondson Jones's and Beverly Holcombe Robertson's Virginia cavalry brigades, had lingered too far in the rear of Lee's army, wasting time in guarding the mountain passes for too long until they could not be utilized by Stuart on the East Cavalry Field, where they were now most needed. Consequently, as fate would have it and fortunately for Custer, these guns of Stuart's Horse Artillery, now far to the west, never played a part in the crucial showdown in the Union army's rear on the afternoon of July 3.

## CUSTER THE ASTUTE ARTILLERYMAN

Relying on the greatest firepower—both artillery and repeating rifles—that was at his disposal, Custer wisely exploited his advantages on multiple levels, including the fact that Stuart's cavalrymen and artillery were not in top shape, after having endured the lengthy ordeal of Stuart's overly ambitious raid that had journeyed almost as far south as Washington, DC. Therefore, the better prepared and equipped, and more refreshed, gunners of Captain Alexander Cummings McWhorter Pennington's Battery were destined to dominate the day in Meade's rear. In response to the initial hail of shells from Confederate artillery fire, Custer had not only shifted and readjusted his lines into an L shape, but he also divided Pennington's guns of Company M, 2nd United States Artillery, with a section on each side of what was essentially a large right angle, with guns protecting both the Low Dutch Road and the Hanover Road.

Custer was most fortunate in possessing considerable firepower. Quite simply, Custer might not have emerged successful on this day without the advantage of his hard-hitting "long arm" assets of a decidedly superior quality. General McIntosh's horse artillery, Captain Alanson Merwin Randol's Batteries E and G (combined), 1st United States Artillery, which had arrived with General Gregg in the early afternoon, were aligned before the Low Dutch Road on the orders of General Gregg. Gregg and Custer had initially positioned Randol's 3-inch guns on the left center of his line, while one section of Pennington's guns, which were also 3-inch rifles, continued to blast away from his left flank just north of the Hanover Road, and the other fired from the other arm of Custer's defense line. One section of Randol's guns fired from among the fruit trees of an orchard located just behind the Lott house above the dusty crossroads and in the open fields situated just west of the Low Dutch Road.

These well-served guns roared in conjunction with Captain Pennington's artillerymen, whose "war hounds" and "bulldogs" continued to prove that they were decidedly superior in this intense artillery duel. Even before the first artillery shot was fired in anger, and as in the past, this was an unequal contest of artillery because of the existing realities beyond the control of Stuart and his hard-fighting artillerymen, who were once again badly outclassed by the boys in blue. General Gregg, like Custer, could not have been more impressed by the high-level performance of the horse artillery of both fast-firing batteries commanded by well-trained West Pointers. He therefore lavished praise on Captains Pennington and Randol for delivering the most accurate artillery fire he had ever seen.

Most importantly, Custer continued to demonstrate that he was not only a master of cavalry tactics, dismounted as well as mounted, but also of artillery tactics in regard to integrating them with cavalry tactics. Most of all, he understood the supreme importance of how artillery firepower needed to be used with cavalry in a carefully and closely integrated fashion to provide fire support, especially against an opponent whose full strength and exact battle plan was still undetermined.[263]

Indeed, the superior quality of Pennington's artillery had been fully demonstrated from the beginning. As noted, he had early gained the advantage over both opposing artillery when he had first outdueled the guns of Captain Jackson's "Kanawha" Charlottesville Virginia Battery of the Stuart Horse Artillery and dismounted troopers who were exposed in the open fields on the high ground of the Rummel farm. Even more, Pennington's deadly 3-inch rifles—generally more effective than Randol's 3-inch guns despite their own lethality, but not greatly so—had also punished Griffin's 2nd Baltimore Maryland Horse Artillery of four 10-pounder Parrotts. Confederate morale had been early deflated by the sight of the inferiority of their guns. In the words of Major James Brainerd McClellan, who described the one-sided duel that had early demonstrated the long-arm masters of the field: "The fire of these guns was most accurate and effective. The first shot [had] struck in Griffin's battery, and shot after shot came with such precision and rapidity that Griffin was soon disabled and forced to seek shelter."[264]

All in all and despite their high-ground perch, the Confederate artillery never had a chance of outmatching the superior Union guns from the beginning. Writing about the initial artillery fire from the Rebels—an unnecessary challenge against superior artillery—on the high ground, evidently on Stuart's orders, the reporter of the *Detroit Free Press* was early impressed by the superior firepower of Custer's horse artillery under Captain Pennington. He penned how a Confederate "battery was run out of the woods [atop Cress's Ridge] and opened on us with shell [but a] shell from battery M. [Pennington] destroyed one of their guns and the rest 'pulling out' on the double-quick."[265]

Most importantly, Custer's response to the Confederate artillery fire had been not only swift but also hard hitting in regard to not only artillery but also cavalry, because he utilized both to maximize his offensive capabilities and their full potential. He understood the importance of suppressive enemy firepower, especially when it had the advantage of a high-ground perch. In his journal, Corporal James Henry Avery, 5th Michigan Cavalry, on the left of Custer's line on the north and opposite McIntosh's most advanced skirmishers on the high ground just to the east, emphasized the fundamental basis of Custer's success that was in the process of being demonstrated in full on July 3: "The only way to succeed in cavalry is to work quickly, the more like lightning, the better, for this is the true mode of mounted fighting; this was the secret of many of Custer's victories."[266]

To slow any possible swift movements and to keep Custer's men at bay because they were becoming more aggressive and were acting like they not only wanted to staunchly defend the crossroads but also to push far north of this vital intersection, Stuart ordered more of Jenkins's (Witcher's) men to dismount and advance down the slope in larger numbers. Keeping the Rebels at a distance, meanwhile, Custer's foremost dismounted men of the 5th Michigan Cavalry continued to blaze away on the left like McIntosh's troopers to the right, while skirmishing reached new levels of intensity.[267]

Knowing that he faced a most formidable opponent who numbered in the thousands, Custer continued to wisely and fully utilize the combat prowess of the troopers of the 5th Michigan Cavalry because they were armed with the fast-firing Spencer rifles. Custer knew that he had to rely on superior weaponry, both in regard to his artillery and the fast-firing small arms, to keep the enemy at bay and as far from the strategic crossroads as possible.[268]

All the while, the fight for the strategic crossroads was picking up steam and momentum, with a will of its own, but Custer was managing it extremely well under the circumstances, despite performing under a host of disadvantages. At this time, Stuart needed to be present (he had been with Witcher but had departed by this time) on the front lines to either take control of the action or terminate it altogether, because he had a more important mission this afternoon: striking Meade's rear in conjunction with Pickett's Charge. With the Confederate artillery on the high ground having been punished by Pennington's and Randol's guns, these artillery pieces then turned their wrath on Witcher's Virginia men advancing on the open ground and those who held the Rummel barn and turned it into a fortress. Swept with an accurate fire of the guns of Captain Pennington's and Randol's Horse Artillery, the foremost

Rebels fell back and took shelter behind the nearest fence and buildings of farmer Rummel. Shells tore into the largest wooden structure (his pride and joy) of Rummel, raising a dark haze of dust and smoke that dominated the horizon. Then exploding shells ignited the barn, to the delight of the Union artillerymen who cheered their success, and the accurate fire caused a trail of black smoke to rise into the clear sky above the battered barn.[269]

Clearly, during this increasingly hot early afternoon, the struggle for the crossroads was escalating, and Stuart wanted not to engage in a large-scale battle, because his primary mission of striking Meade's rear remained paramount above all else. For such reasons, Stuart had "still not contemplated throwing Hampton's and Fitz Lee's commands against McIntosh [and Custer] on the skirmish line [because he] still saw the skirmish action as a diversion to mask a planned mounted attack around D. McD. Gregg's flank [to eventually strike Meade's rear. . . . In order for his surprise flank attack to work, however, Hampton's and Fitz Lee's presence had to remain undetected, and his skirmish line had to hold out" as long as possible.[270]

## STUART SEARCHING FOR THE BEST ROUTE TO MEADE'S REAR

This was a crucial moment in the struggle for the crossroads, because Stuart was looking for the right time and best chance to push southwest to unleash the attack into Meade's rear, and he had to gain this intelligence himself as best he could. He now faced two options: escalating the action for possession of the crossroads or slipping away in the attempt to launch his strike into Meade's rear whenever the opportunity presented itself, while ever mindful that he had been ordered to support the main offensive effort to the west. Of these two options, attacking the Army of the Potomac's rear was, of course, the most important.[271]

However, Stuart made a fundamental mistake—only one of many that day—at exactly the wrong time and place, assuming that he would be away from his command for only a short period of time, when a battle was escalating and his top officers and men were fueled by a powerful desire for revenge after the humiliation at Brandy Station. This situation guaranteed that he would remain out of touch with his top lieutenants, especially Hampton, for an extended period when they were not aware of the plan to attack Meade's rear.

With the upcoming mission to strike the Union rear in mind because it was all important, Stuart needed to ascertain developments to the southwest as much as possible. Therefore, Stuart wanted to peer to the west toward Gettysburg and southwest toward Cemetery Ridge to catch a glimpse of Union activity or the movements of Lee's army and positions to ascertain developments as best he could in order to make the proper decision. Was Pickett's Charge about to be unleashed or would it be delayed even longer? How long would the Confederate artillery bombardment continue before Longstreet ordered the attackers forward?

Therefore Stuart, who had departed from Witcher's sector, and some of his staff officers galloped out of the forests of Cress's Ridge to gain the top of an open ridge—Brinkerhoff Ridge—located on the other side, or west, of Cress Run and Little's Run, just to the east, which ran north–south before the crossroads and near the Hoffman Road (which he and the troopers had already crossed to reach Cress's Ridge) and then followed the ridge's western side that pointed south like Cress's Ridge—which roughly paralleled the Low Dutch Road at this point.

Significantly, this hasty reconnaissance to the top of a northern point of Brinkerhoff Ridge revealed Stuart's top priority, which continued to be first and foremost in regard to following Lee's orders: not a lengthy and costly fight at the crossroads—which he never wanted to evolve into a full-scale cavalry clash like at Brandy Station—but the planned Lee-Stuart strike into the Union rear in the opposite direction that was now most of all required by the commander in chief. Stuart, therefore, peered to the west and southwest while attempting to ascertain developments in the main army positions in preparation for striking Meade's rear.

Staff officer William Willis Blackford noted as much. He wrote how Stuart was trying to ascertain what exactly was happening to the west and southwest with the main army and the progress of the massive artillery bombardment in preparation for unleashing Pickett's Charge. Therefore, two staff officers wrote how Stuart was attempting to determine what was occurring to the west and southwest, peering toward the main army with his binoculars. Assistant Engineer Frank Smith Robertson, of Stuart's staff, described the situation at this time, writing, "Our cavalry was massed in woods [of Cress's Ridge] east of Gettysburg, a very big field [the open plain that led to the crossroads] in front of us. The General and staff rode out of the woods to a cleared hill [Brinkerhoff Ridge]. A Yankee battery [Pennington's Battery M, 2nd United States Artillery] at the far end of the big clearing opened on us and we rode back again. The General disappeared and the staff seemed scattered."[272]

This is one of the forgotten contributions of the accurate fire of Battery M, 2nd United States Artillery, and Captain Pennington, who had come close to eliminating the South's most famous cavalrymen and sabotaging one of the most aggressive battle plans—the Lee-Stuart plan for striking Meade's rear— that had been set in place on the night of July 2.

Fortunately for Custer and as repeatedly demonstrated, the West Pointer (a member of Custer's class of 1861, while Captain Randol was a member of the class of 1860) "Pennington was one of the best, if not the best in the Union horse artillery," which had come of age on the East Cavalry Field.[273] Clearly, Custer benefited immensely from the superior performance of his horse artillery on this day of destiny in the army's rear, when everything was at stake.[274]

This well-aimed shell fired from one of the half dozen 3-inch guns from Lieutenant Pennington's Battery near the crossroads was a close call for General Stuart, and it might have unnerved him to some degree. It is not known if this was indeed the case, but it might partly explain why Stuart virtually disappeared—to the consternation of his staff officers and top lieutenants, especially Hampton—for an extended period from playing a more active role in the combat that raged in the struggle for possession of the Hanover and Low Dutch Roads, and even from his own staff officers, who had also been scattered by the shell explosion.

For whatever reason on this crucial day when Lee launched his greatest offensive effort, General Stuart led no charges (the antithesis of Custer's stirring, if not audacious, performance) on the East Cavalry Field, because Lee's top cavalryman never wanted to fight a major cavalry clash at this point three miles from the Union army's rear—the ultimate tactical objective as planned by him and Lee at headquarters on the night of July 2.

By this time, seemingly everyone, especially his concerned staff officers, wanted to know what had happened to General Stuart, who was usually in the forefront and on the front lines, because he could not be found. Had Stuart been hit by a shell fragment? Was he lying alone and bleeding to death in the woods after having fallen from his horse? For instance, not long after the artillery fire from Pennington's Battery M, 2nd United States Artillery, had dispersed Stuart and his staff from their high-ground perch that presented a commanding view to the west and southwest, Stuart requested by a dispatched courier to hold a conference with both Hampton and Fitzhugh Lee to enlighten them on the exact details of the plan to strike into Meade's rear because they had not been previously told due to their late arrival at Cress's Ridge.

But Hampton, thinking more responsibly and sensibly than Stuart, balked at the idea of two brigade commanders leaving their commands at the same time in an attempt to find Stuart's field headquarters, whose location was unknown at this time, when the battle was escalating. After all, another shell from Pennington's sharp-eyed gunners could wipe out the top leadership—Stuart, Hampton, and Fitzhugh Lee—with a single shot. Hampton's precaution was wise.

Therefore, Hampton, the senior brigade commander and Stuart's top lieutenant, informed Fitzhugh Lee to stay with the brigade of five Virginia cavalry regiments and one Maryland cavalry battalion and that he would go first to find Stuart's field headquarters. But Hampton met only with frustration in the hunt for Lee's top cavalryman and wasted more valuable time in the process of searching in vain for Stuart. Quite simply, in the midst of a battle, the communications between Stuart and his top lieutenants was completely severed for an extended period of time. Assistant Engineer Frank Smith Robertson wrote, "A little later General Hampton asked me where General Stuart was. He said he had been trying in vain to find him. I also had been looking for him for some time, as were several members of his staff."[275]

Another member of Stuart's staff, Major Henry Brainerd McClellan, described the confusion and lack of communication among the top cavalry leadership of the Army of Northern Virginia in the right-rear of Meade's army in the middle of an escalating battle that resulted in the wasting of precious time: "Stuart's messenger was a longtime in finding Hampton; and before he, in turn, could find Stuart, the condition of the field required his presence with his own brigade."[276]

From ever-mounting frustration in failing to locate Stuart and with the battle raging, Hampton stopped searching for Stuart out of necessity, and Stuart evidently assumed that Hampton was coming to him, which was no longer the case. Whatever the exact situation, neither Hampton nor Fitzhugh Lee learned of the exact details of the plan to strike Meade's rear at this time. Of course, under the circumstances, this was an extremely important failure in communications—like Pickett not knowing that he had been assigned to spearhead the great infantry assault—at the highest levels, because, in McClellan's words, Stuart had "sent for Hampton and Fitz Lee, to arrange with them for an advance and an attack upon the enemy's rear."[277]

As expected by Stuart and as directed by him, Brigadier General Fitzhugh Lee, whose veteran brigade continued to hold Stuart's left flank on the high ground directly north of the crossroads and above the intervening open plain, also attempted to find Stuart. But Fitz failed to locate Stuart like Hampton, to reveal the full extent of the most embarrassing breakdown of high-level communications in the history of Stuart's cavalry in regard to such an important situation. Incredibly, in the greatest breakdown of Confederate communication on July 3, neither Hampton nor Fitzhugh Lee knew about Stuart's plan to attack Meade's rear!

Of course, at this time, it was absolutely vital for Hampton and Fitzhugh Lee to confer with Stuart for the formulation of the final plan of striking into the Union army's rear, because Stuart had not issued specific instructions about his secret mission—clearly one disadvantage of a secret plan that Stuart had closely guarded because of his mission's overall importance. And in a letter, Fitzhugh revealed exactly why this meeting between Stuart and Hampton and Fitzhugh Lee was so vital, because the commanders of his two elite brigades—the best units in Stuart's Division and basically his Imperial Guard in Napoleonic terms—were to have led the advance toward Meade's rear on Cemetery Ridge to the southwest: "Stuart sent for Hampton and I to come to his position to see about making the movement to the rear" of the Army of the Potomac.[278]

Quite simply at this time, Stuart had "disappeared" from his top lieutenants, who were focused on the battle raging in the open fields in front of them, primarily because he knew that finally playing a key role in the most important battle in American history as ordered by Lee now called for his full effort to be unleashed three miles away at the Union army's rear and not at the crossroads. However, not even his top lieutenant, Wade Hampton, knew of Stuart's location at this time in part because both men were focused on situations that existed in opposite directions: Hampton looking south toward the crossroads and Stuart focused on what was happening in the distance to the west and southwest.

Without having been apprised by Stuart of striking Meade's rear to the southwest along Cemetery Ridge, Hampton was naturally and most of all concerned about the tactical developments in the escalating struggle for possession of the strategic crossroads. Meanwhile, Stuart was not of a like mind. His more pressing tactical requirement of striking Meade's rear meant that he could not engage in a full-scale battle, because the real fight was far away, where General Lee needed him to attack in conjunction with the largest Confederate infantry assault in the history of the Army of Northern Virginia.[279]

Besides receiving new instructions from Stuart in regard to attacking the Army of the Potomac's rear, the other principal reason why General Hampton so desperately needed to see Stuart had nothing to do with the increasingly aggressive cavalry troopers, especially Custer but also McIntosh's men, who were aligned before them in the open fields of summer and at the strategic crossroads. This newly acquired intelligence was about something that was far more important and especially crucial, because it had a direct bearing on the future mission to strike the Army of the Potomac's rear.

Even more, this crucial information has provided a significant clue in regard to Stuart's future plans about striking the Union rear in conjunction with the greatest offensive effort in the history of the Army of Northern Virginia, according to the bold plan created by Generals Lee and Stuart on the previous night at the Widow Thompson house. By this time, Hampton so urgently needed to speak to Stuart to provide him with the startling new intelligence that also revealed that he had somehow gained information (evidently from one of Stuart's staff officers rather than from Stuart himself) about the overall plan of attacking Meade's rear, or perhaps from a courier or messenger from Stuart's field headquarters.

In Assistant Engineer Frank Smith Robertson's words about the more challenging tactical situation that now existed because of the arrival of this new intelligence that boded ill for the Lee-Stuart plan of striking Meade's rear, which was now obviously stronger than previously imagined when created at the Widow Thompson house: "General Hampton and his officers seemed excited. He told me, 'You must find him and tell him [Stuart] that we have just captured a man belonging to the Sixth Army Corps, who stated that his corps had just arrived and gone into Gettysburg's breastworks. It is most important that General Stuart know this."[280]

Indeed, this was crucial information as emphasized by this all-important primary account of one of Stuart's leading staff officers, Frank Smith Robertson, that has not been used by leading historians, who have been guilty of having missed and overlooked this vital information. If Stuart was assigned only to guard Lee's left flank as alleged today by what might be called the internet and blog-savvy anti-Stuart-in-the-rear advocates and non-PhD writers, who have built a cottage industry of outdated books on behalf of their self-serving agendas to make profits and fuel bloated egos, then why would General Hampton, who was Stuart's most capable top lieutenant, have become so excessively concerned that the mighty Sixth Corps—the Army of the Potomac's strongest corps—was now in position in Meade's defensive line to make it much stronger and less vulnerable to a surprise attack from the rear?

Indeed, the Sixth Corps was not only large, with more than ten thousand men and a good deal of artillery, but also a powerful strategic reserve that considerably strengthened Meade's overall defensive stance in the face of Lee's greatest offensive effort. However, if anything, this new situation placed more importance on Stuart's role in striking from the rear, which was the only tactic that might negate Meade's superiority in numbers and the strength of his high-ground defensive positions at this time.

All in all, this is clear evidence from the excessive concern, or the "excited" state, of Hampton and his staff officers that Stuart's mission was to strike into Meade's rear, because a considerable amount of well-placed excitement had reached a high point because the defensive stance of the Army of the Potomac was now obviously much stronger after the arrival of the Sixth Corps. For this reason alone in regard to his planned offensive strike into Meade's rear, this latest intelligence was "most important" and "General Stuart [needed to] know this."[281]

Assistant Engineer Frank Smith Robertson correctly concluded that the latest intelligence, not only about the arrival of the Sixth Corps, which had already joined the Army of the Potomac, but also its position in the overall strengthening of Meade's defensive stance, came as a stunning blow, because the primary mission was not to fight a major action at the crossroads, but to strike a blow into the vulnerable rear of the Army of the Potomac, which was thought to be weaker than was now actually the case: "This was a startling and unexpected reinforcement to Meade's army."[282] In this regard, Lee's plan to deliver an overpowering offensive blow was less likely to succeed because of the Sixth Corps' presence.[283]

But most importantly, this well-placed concern, if not outright fear, about the presence and availability to Meade of the mighty Sixth Corps was obviously not about a strong force that now threatened the Confederate cavalry now three miles from Meade's defensive line on Cemetery Ridge. Naturally, this heightened concern was all about what lay ahead in Meade's defensive lines to make them stronger or what might stop the projected cavalry attack into the Army of the Potomac's rear—more than 12,500 veterans of the Sixth Corps under the highly capable Major General John Sedgwick, a Mexican-American War veteran. Sharing Stuart's tragic fate of death on the battlefield in the same year, the Connecticut-born Sedgwick, age fifty, was fated to be killed on May 9, 1864, at Spotsylvania, Virginia, when a long-distance shot from a Confederate sharpshooter ended an impressive military career. Quite simply and obviously, Stuart and his top lieutenants and staff officers would have had absolutely no concern about the Sixth Corps strengthening Meade's defensive and having "gone into Gettysburg's breastworks" if Lee's legendary cavalry commander was not planning to strike Meade's rear.[284]

Clearly, such excessive alarm among the top leadership of the Confederate cavalry corps existed because they were indeed planning to strike Meade's rear, which suddenly now possessed thousands of additional defenders, and this fact had now become of great concern because Lee and Stuart had targeted Meade's rear for delivering their overpowering blow.[285]

After all, Generals Lee and Stuart had based their plans on the intelligence that had been available to leadership at the Widow Thompson house headquarters on the night of July 2, and it had not included anything about the last arriving corps of the Army of the Potomac, the Sixth Corps. Naturally, Lee's intelligence was outdated.

A member of the 2nd New York Cavalry, New York–born Lieutenant Willard W. Glazier, described the late arrival of this powerful corps, because the Army of the Potomac was aligned by the morning of July 2, all "except the Sixth Corps," which Meade badly needed to hold firm not only on July 2, but also for July 3.[286] Indeed, by around 4:00 p.m. on the afternoon of July 2, the foremost elements of the mighty Sixth Corps had finally reached Rock Creek, which was located about two miles from Meade's battered left flank.[287]

Nevertheless, Stuart still possessed the supreme advantage and opportunity to deliver a punishing blow into the Army of the Potomac's rear, even after the arrival of the Sixth Corps. Therefore, the Lee-Stuart plan remained in play because of the effectiveness of a surprise attack from the rear.[288]

## THE GOLDEN OPPORTUNITY

Significantly, a visit today to the East Cavalry Field, which is seldom visited by throngs of visitors like other sectors of the battlefield and exists today as little more than the forgotten stepchild of the main battlefield park, or even a brief look at a topographical map can convey the distinct possibilities of Stuart and Lee's bold plan of striking the Union rear when it was most vulnerable, at a time when Meade's defenders faced more than fifteen thousand attackers of Pickett's Charge. If this had been a planned infantry assault from the rear, the distance of three miles to Meade's rear ensured the impossibility of such a plan, because slow-marching infantrymen (dismounted cavalry in this case) would take too much time, especially after unleashing the massive Confederate bombardment in preparation for Pickett's Charge.

But with cavalry, the situation that bestowed an excellent tactical opportunity to yet fulfill General Lee's ambitions resulted in the exact opposite situation. If the Union cavalry under the upstart Custer and McIntosh could be defeated and pushed aside, then Stuart and his top lieutenants, especially Hampton, could then easily ride around the flank of this contingent of Union cavalry in a gallop at a rate of four hundred yards per minute—or fifteen miles per hour—over open and gently rolling terrain (open farmlands of mostly fields, pastures, and meadows that paved a smooth path all the way to the rear of Cemetery Ridge, which was Meade's main defensive position) that led to the Union army's vulnerable rear in less than fifteen minutes. No rivers, creeks, or swamps or Yankee troops now stood between Stuart and the vulnerable Federal rear on Cemetery Ridge, which was ripe for delivering an attack from the east. Or Stuart could turn his back on the fight at the crossroads and ride southwest to gain the Baltimore Road in Meade's rear along the Cemetery Ridge line.

Clearly, Stuart and his men could reach Meade's rear in less than a quarter of an hour at a gallop and deliver the key blow as envisioned by General Lee if everything went according to their very realistic but ambitious plan.[289] Historian Gregory J. W. Urwin described how from the combined offensive blow of Pickett's Charge "and Stuart whirling in from behind, the Army of the Potomac would be cut in half, thrown into a panic, and the South would gain the decisive victory she needed to win the war."[290]

For ample good reason, therefore, Custer and Gregg were firmly convinced and agreed "that the Battle of Gettysburg might be lost right here, if Stuart got through to Meade's rear."[291]

Also emphasizing as much, Brigadier General Fitzhugh Lee in a letter emphasized that Stuart's mission could not have been more crucial, because it was all about "effecting a surprise on the enemy's rear."[292] Almost the exact same wording appeared in Stuart's own official report in which he wrote that "he hoped to effect a surprise on the enemy's rear."[293]

## CUSTER DEFENDING THE CROSSROADS WITH SKILL

Meanwhile, Custer continued to enjoy a host of distinct advantages in his spirited defense of the sloping ground before the strategic intersection of the Hanover and Low Dutch Roads. For one, and especially in regard to the artillery duel, Custer continued to benefit from Captains Pennington's and Randol's superior fire and the ever-growing Confederate logistical failures that partly revealed the risks inherent in an invasion north of the Potomac River. McGregor's and Breathed's batteries—the two crack units of Stuart's Horse Artillery under Major Robert Franklin Breathed—were absent when the fight for the crossroads opened, because at this time the gunners were still filling their caissons and limbers with ammunition because of the late-arriving ammunition wagons.

Consequently, the two seasoned batteries were destined to finally reach Cress's Ridge at around 3:00 p.m., after a wild ride at a rapid pace to join the fight for possession of the vital intersection. Of course, this dusty race to gain Cress's Ridge additionally wore out the men and horses of two of the finest batteries of Stuart's Horse Artillery, to reduce their overall effectiveness on that afternoon. Here, on Cress's Ridge, Captain Breathed finally aligned his guns on the commanding high ground in the heat of mid-afternoon. In the words of one of his artilleryman: "We took position on the right slope [of the right] within sight" of the Union artillery deployed around the strategic crossroads.[294]

Meanwhile, the situation for Colonel McIntosh's most advanced men just east of the Rummel buildings worsened, and they were in trouble. Swept by artillery fire and the hot fire of Jenkins's (Witcher's) troopers whose bullets poured down the slope, McIntosh could not completely disengage without taking even heavier losses, because his men were in a tight spot on the open ground. As mentioned, after he called for help, Custer had to come to the rescue with the men of the 5th Michigan Cavalry, who had advanced a good distance north on the left and all the way to the west side of the Rummel buildings. Then, as noted, to protect the left flank of the 5th Michigan Cavalry, Custer also deployed several companies on the left because the flank was hanging in midair amid the open fields under the bright sunshine.

But this was an insufficient reinforcement for McIntosh's hard-pressed troopers, because the men of the 5th Michigan Cavalry were low on ammunition. The 5th Michigan Cavalry troopers were likewise exposed on open ground, because Custer had to ensure the safety of Pennington's guns situated on the low ground around the crossroads, and this meant having to send them far north of the intersection. This situation of the 5th Michigan troopers having advanced so far north meant that the 7th Michigan Cavalry was formed in position just north of the crossroads to guard against any Rebel attack that might suddenly come pouring down the Low Dutch Road, while the 1st Michigan Cavalry played a comparable role in protecting the intersection from a charge barreling down the Hanover Road. Basically, these two regiments, which had been trained in the saber charge, unlike the 5th and 6th Michigan Cavalry, were not only serving in the role of vital guardians to prevent a nasty surprise, but also in the role of Custer's strategic reserve, which could be hurled forward to parry any suddenly emerging threat. All in all, therefore, the most advanced troopers of the 5th Michigan Cavalry were increasingly exposed in the broad fields and pastures of farmer Rummel.

In playing a timely rescue role by having earlier reinforced McIntosh's most advanced skirmishers when they had been under increasing pressure from the steady advance of Jenkins's (Witcher's) dismounted cavalrymen down the slope and ever closer to the Rummel buildings, while running low on ammunition, Custer was basically playing the role of a vigilant fireman. His role now called for being on the alert and ever ready to make the necessary tactical moves and adjustments to put out the next fire, or threat in this case.[295] But hurling units into the fire piecemeal had its own risks in this escalating battle and fast-moving tactical situation, leaving relatively small numbers of men on their own and exposed on open ground, when ammunition ran low and without sufficient support.

Upon sighting a tactical opportunity, Custer then attempted a flanking movement, but it was quickly countered by the equally vigilant Fitz Lee, who was determined to utilize his hard-fighting dismounted men of the elite 1st Virginia Cavalry, under the capable Colonel William Augustine Morgan, to counter the advance of Custer's right center, where troopers fired from behind a post-and-rail fence.[296] Captain Leonard Williams, born on Sycamore Grove Plantation and a capable officer of the 2nd South Carolina Cavalry, described in a letter how "on the right on the 3rd, the enemy endeavored to flank us. Capt. Nesbit, of the 1st [Virginia Cavalry] Regt. and myself, each with about 50 men, were dismounted with rifles and opposed them and held them in check" by fast and accurate firing.[297] For ample good reason, he also wrote how Gettysburg was "the bloodiest fight of the war," including "on the right" where Stuart's men "succeeded in killing & capturing over two hundred of" the enemy.[298] During this time, "I took a position on the right on a hill when I could see the Yankees advancing which they did at a double quick, but were soon hurled in rapid Flight."[299]

But Custer's optimistic rescuers then found themselves in serious trouble, when Rebel gunners on the high ground turned their sights on the troopers of the 5th Michigan Cavalry, who were sitting ducks in the open fields on the left, a good distance northwest of the crossroads, after having advanced far north. Watching as his 5th Michigan boys were cut down in the sweeping artillery fire, Custer felt frustration and disgust while the casualty list continued to increase steadily. Therefore, Custer soon realized that he needed to do something to save his most advanced Wolverines, who were totally exposed in the open. With more of his troopers falling to rise no more in the open fields along ascending ground, Custer therefore contemplated sending an order for the men of the hard-hit 5th Michigan Cavalry south to the shelter of a fence from which they would be able to return fire with greater effect.[300] Even more, Custer explored his tactical options, hunting for an opportunity. Consequently, he also began to contemplate unleashing a cavalry charge to reverse the situation and rescue the hard-hit boys in blue in his front and to buy more time, because he possessed a strategic reserve in the 7th Michigan Cavalry.

Out of necessity, the withdrawal of the Michigan soldiers to the relative shelter of the fence, which left McIntosh's left unsupported, only emboldened Lieutenant Colonel Witcher and his Virginia boys, who had been reinforced by the elite 1st Virginia Cavalry, Fitzhugh Lee's best regiment of his brigade, by this time. Eager to strike a blow at an exposed flank (McIntosh) and with his fighting blood up, Witcher ordered his dismounted troopers to charge down the slope to exploit the opportunity of hitting the enemy during a withdrawal across open ground. In Lieutenant Colonel Witcher's words: "With a wild yell the whole line dashed forward, retook the fence and swept the Federal men back."[301] The sweeping attack of the tide of howling Confederates pushed the foremost Yankees farther down the body-strewn slope and captured the Rummel buildings, including the Rummel barn.

The howling attackers of the 1st Virginia Cavalry led the charge toward Custer's right-center and drove McIntosh's men, who were hit on the left, or western, flank from the open fields and all the way east into the shelter of the Jacob Lott woods for protection. This hard-hitting attack of the troopers of the elite 1st Virginia impressed Stuart and gave him more confidence for success. He wrote of how "the impetuosity of those gallant fellows, after two weeks of hard marching and hard fighting on short rations, was not only extraordinary, but irresistible. The enemy's masses vanished before them like grain before the scythe, and that regiment elicited the admiration of every beholder, and eclipsed the many laurels already won by its gallant veterans."[302]

## GENERAL STUART'S ABSENCE BECAUSE OF HIS FOCUS ON A MORE IMPORTANT TARGET

Bestowed with Lee's aggressive orders that gave him an opportunity to strike a blow that would ensure the endurance of his fame forever to the people of the South if victory was secured, Stuart seemed almost uninterested in the escalating fight for the crossroads in the fields below, because a large cavalry battle was not in his plans, as communicated by Lee at the Thompson house conference. Therefore, Stuart was wisely disinterested because he possessed more important orders that were the key to decisive victory.

For this reason, he failed to exploit the significant tactical gains achieved by the latest offensive effort, especially the charge of the crack 1st Virginia Cavalry, which continued to maintain its reputation for excellence on the field of strife. After all, Lee's objective for Stuart was to strike the Union rear and not to lose so many horses and men that it would reduce his combat capabilities and might eliminate the possibility of a successful attack to catch the Yankee defenders by surprise from the east. He therefore only wanted to inflict a light blow on the Union cavalry to occupy their attention and force them to commit a tactical error, a situation that would then allow him to slip away from the troublesome bluecoat cavalry to gain the Baltimore Turnpike and then ride away unopposed toward where the sun of July 3 would set and his true objective: the vulnerable Union rear to the southwest.

Therefore, while the rows of Confederate artillery continued to roar to the southwest in preparation for softening up the Union center before the unleashing of Pickett's Charge, Stuart continued to search the unfamiliar terrain to the southwest, which was mostly open ground over which his cavalrymen would ride to gain the Union rear and inflict the devastating blow that General Lee desired most of all. Stuart was forced to closely investigate the nature of the terrain to the southwest on his own to become familiar with the area over which he planned to lead his men to glory. However, more precious time slipped away for Southern fortunes. Like Fitzhugh Lee, not even his top lieutenant, General Hampton, had been able to locate Stuart.

After a lengthy search for the absent commander of Lee's cavalry, Assistant Engineer Frank Smith Robertson finally found the commander, who should have been orchestrating the battle before him in the open fields bathed in bright sunlight and stretching a long distance below Cress's Ridge at this time, if he was determined to first push the Federals aside to gain the strategic crossroads of the Hanover and Low Dutch Roads to ensure an unimpeded ride into Meade's rear by this route. Instead, Stuart was attempting to ascertain the best ground over which to push southwest and the best route to Meade's rear to deliver a masterstroke instead of the folly of engaging in a lengthy and costly fight for the crossroads around three miles northeast of the main battle, where Pickett's Division was about to spearhead Lee's greatest assault. Most of all, he continued to realize that he needed to avoid a large-scale fight at the crossroads since he possessed a more important mission.

In Frank Smith Robertson's words:

> I followed a lane near which I had seen General Stuart an hour earlier; I passed entirely out of sight of our men and headed straight [south] for the enemy, riding very cautiously and expecting every moment to strike a Yankee picket. After about a mile on this road [a farm lane known as the Hoffman Road that followed the western edge of Brinkerhoff's Ridge] parallel to the big field, I saw a man on a knoll behind a tree, his back to me, looking intently at something beyond. I recognized the General. I went up to the knoll [on Brinkerhoff's Ridge] to him and saw in the plain below [to the southeast] what looked like 20,000 cavalry,—the whole country was black with them. The General seemed worried by my message

about the arrival and deployment of the mighty Sixth Corps to strengthen Meade's defenses based on the high ground, especially Cemetery Ridge.[303]

Indeed, Stuart possessed ample good reason to be worried, because his all-important mission of striking Meade's rear was suddenly more daunting because Major General John Sedgwick's Sixth Corps was larger than all of Stuart's Cavalry Corps—more than twelve thousand men who had reached the field of Gettysburg on the afternoon of July 2. Meade had wisely plugged these troops into various defensive sectors along the line, including Cemetery Ridge, which Lee had targeted to split the Union army in two. Convinced that the numerical odds were in his favor and that the Army of the Potomac was on the ropes, Lee was eager to strike on July 3 in part because he believed that Meade's army had not yet been reinforced by fresh units, especially the powerful Sixth Corps. Quite simply, Lee did not know that thousands of troops of the Sixth Corps had arrived after a march of more than thirty miles when he formulated his tactical plan with Stuart at the Widow Thompson house.

Clearly and most importantly, this crucial evidence from an often-overlooked source of information reveals how Stuart, Hampton, and the officers of both staffs regarded this information as absolutely crucial for the future offensive operation, which was attacking the rear of Meade's army to "wreak havoc on a grand scale."[304] The entire Battle of Gettysburg might well have ended differently had Stuart fulfilled his crucial mission and "encircled Meade's right, as planned and cracked down on his rear" to deliver a devastating blow as planned.[305]

## CUSTER CONTINUES TO RISE TO THE CHALLENGE

To his delight, which bestowed greater confidence in regard to the stirring events to come, Custer continued to possess the key to the battlefield and the major bone of contention, the strategic crossroads of the Hanover and Low Dutch Roads that needed to be held at all costs, in case Stuart decided to make an all-out offensive effort to capture the intersection before riding to the southwest to gain the Baltimore Road and Meade's rear. And he was determined to hold his ground because he understood its importance as scores of Lee's artillery pieces roared in the distance from the direction of the bluish-hued Cumberland Mountains, while the strategic crossroads was now well defended by some of the best artillery units in the Army of the Potomac.[306]

Even more, Custer commanded perhaps the finest cavalrymen in the Army of the Potomac. Already, the Michigan Cavalry Brigade was a crack command of highly motivated and hard-fighting troopers, and their spirited performance in the tenacious defense of the crossroads had already revealed as much. The lofty motivations and fighting spirit of the Michigan men can be seen in the words of Corporal James Henry Avery, 5th Michigan Cavalry: "The Star Spangled Banner must and shall be saved, and again planted where it had been torn down by the hands of traitors."[307]

But even this lofty sentiment could not stop seemingly too many veteran Rebels to count, especially when they possessed the advantage of the high ground and had advanced aggressively down the slope with colorful battle flags flying. Behind the shelter of the fence on the far north, the men of the 5th Michigan Cavalry held firm under intensive fire as Custer's most advanced troopers on the field. But the increasing losses and declining ammunition left the 5th Michigan boys in an increasingly precarious position, while the Rebels mustered greater strength for a mightier push south down the slope.[308] Under these disadvantages, it was only a matter of time before the 5th Michigan troopers would have to give more ground or be cut to pieces.

Here, at the Rummel barn, which was located about three hundred yards from the foot of the ridge, and the house of this industrious farmer of German descent, the seasoned Virginians of Witcher's battalion held the buildings that stood in the open fields of plenty below the crest of Cress's Ridge, bolstered by reinforcements from Stuart to make sure they held this advanced position. In the words of Major Henry Brainerd McClellan: "Here the charge of the Confederate sharpshooters [dismounted] was a success. . . . The men sprang eagerly to their work, and the Federal line was driven back across the field for a long distance" down the sloping ground that led to the strategic crossroads.[309] But the greatest success had been achieved by the 1st Virginia Cavalry that had swept McIntosh's men, who had become vulnerable on the left flank by advancing too far north like the troopers of the 5th Michigan Cavalry, off the open plain and forced them to withdraw east and then to take shelter in the Lott woods to the east.[310]

Custer was not deterred by the sight of Witcher's Virginia mountaineers retaining possession of the Rummel house, barn, and nearby fences, which served as ideal defensive positions for excellent marksmen, who were now in a strong position—rather than completely exposed in the open fields—closer to the strategic crossroads, or the success of the 1st Virginia Cavalry's charge that had scattered McIntosh's troopers and hurled them back to the Low Dutch Road to the east.

But, as fully realized by Custer, this tactical advantage of a good defensive position among the buildings of farmer Rummel posed a threat to the overall safety of the strategic crossroads, and Custer was not going to back down because this was a true crisis situation. In fact, he was motivated now to up the ante, because he was determined to never relinquish his grip on the strategic intersection that he correctly knew was the key to the escalating battle. Most importantly, Custer refused to abandon the crossroads as Stuart hoped, regardless of the increasing level of pressure. Even more, he planned to unleash an offensive thrust to push the most advanced Rebels out of the buildings that needed to be regained because they posed a threat to the intersection.[311]

At this time and as noted, the most advanced Confederate defense and threat had increased to new heights after Witcher's 34th Virginia Cavalry Battalion had been "reinforced by [the 1st Virginia Cavalry—Fitzhugh Lee's Brigade and the] dismounted squadron from Chambliss' command, which took position on his left, and the line was still further extended in that direction by sharpshooters from Hampton's and Fitz Lee's Brigades. A stone fence extended from the Rummel Barn and to the right, or west, and behind this strong position were Jenkins' (Witcher) seasoned troopers, who were still dismounted and blasted away. The 2nd Virginia Cavalry [Fitzhugh Lee's Brigade] held the extreme left."[312]

Even more, Witcher's added reinforcements—a strengthening of a good defensive position on high ground to present a more formidable threat to the strategic crossroads situated on lower ground—caused him to become more aggressive, and "he not only maintained his ground, but even gained on the enemy," and against the odds.[313]

For such reasons, Custer planned a bold counterstroke to negate the extensive gains achieved by the increasingly aggressive Confederates. Watching from the high ground, Major Henry Brainerd McClellan viewed the escalating action, while the "enemy now advanced a strong line of dismounted men against Colonel Witcher's advanced position," which was protected by Rebel artillery poised on the high ground just to the north and northwest, and these men held the Rummel house, barn, and surrounding fences.[314] With his right flank about to be turned, reinforcements arrived in a timely manner. McClellan explained how the dismounted Federals had applied greater pressure, "overlapping [Witcher's] right [but now] Witcher was reinforced by a dismounted squadron from Chambliss' command, which took position on his left, and the line was still further extended in that direction by sharpshooters from Hampton's and Fitz Lee's Brigades."[315]

But as mentioned, this escalating battle was not something that Stuart wanted at this time in the hot afternoon of decision, because his primary mission was to strike the Army of the Potomac's rear to achieve a decisive result. If Stuart had desired to engage in a full-fledged battle, he would have exploited the gains achieved by the 1st Virginia Cavalry, which had pushed aside McIntosh's troopers and hurled them back toward the Low Dutch Road, but he let the tactical opportunity pass him by.[316]

Most of all, Stuart needed to stay focused and not allow his emotions to dominate his thinking or sway him from his all-important mission. He had to resist the temptation of getting sucked into an escalating battle for possession of the crossroads, because time was of the essence since the massive artillery bombardment in preparation for the unleashing of Pickett's Charge continued to roar in the distance.

By this time, General Stuart did not even need a good topographical map, especially since only open terrain—gently rolling hills covered mostly in fields of wheat and oats, which allowed for greater visibility, unlike land covered in a dense carpet of cornfields consisting of high standing stalks like on the rolling farmlands of western Maryland, because southeastern Pennsylvania was wheat country—led to Meade's rear along Cemetery Ridge to the southwest. In this regard, Stuart was most fortunate. He would face no natural obstacles, such as a river or creek or high hill, whenever he finally gave the order for his troopers to ride southwest to gain the Baltimore Road. But most of all, not a single Federal unit or artillery stood between thousands of Stuart's cavalrymen and artillery and the Army of the Potomac's rear, presenting a golden opportunity to strike a decisive blow from the east.

## THE SOUNDS OF THE ROARING GUNS

General Gregg emphasized the close connection (a symbiotic relationship in overall tactical terms) between Pickett's Charge and Stuart's mounted legions when he penned how, "during that terrific fire of artillery which preceded the gallant but unsuccessful assault of Pickett's Division on our line, it was discovered that Stuart's cavalry was moving to our right with the evident intention of passing to the rear to make a simultaneous attack there."[317]

In his official report of the Battle of Gettysburg, Gregg described the same life-or-death situation for the Army of the Potomac and what was at stake at the time: "the importance of *stubbornly resisting* an attack at this point [the crossroads], which, if successful, would have been productive of the most serious consequences."[318]

And in his own official report of the battle, Stuart penned how this position on Cress's Ridge "commanded a view of the routes leading to the enemy's rear [and] had the enemy's main body been dislodged, as was confidently hoped and expected, I was in precisely the right position to discover it, and improve the opportunity."[319]

Indeed, a great opportunity continued to exist for Stuart and his men at this time, and it lay ready and open for the taking. All Stuart had to do was merely follow the most basic and fundamental of military axioms that Napoleon and any other great captain had known since time immemorial—just march toward the sounds of the guns. And this was especially the case after General Lee had unleashed his massive artillery bombardment from more than 150 guns in preparation for unleashing Pickett's Charge. As mentioned, row upon row of Rebel field pieces had erupted in full fury just after 1:00 p.m. on this hot afternoon, especially where Lee and Longstreet had targeted Meade's right-center for piercing to the southwest of the East Cavalry Field.

Therefore, Stuart had only now to follow not only his instincts but also his orders from Lee for riding southwest to strike Meade's rear, which was now merely a case of following the sound of the guns. At this time, he had only to turn and lead his column toward the distant horizon where the sun would go down over the heavily timbered Cumberland Mountains that loomed on the western horizon. In regard to the time factor, and most importantly, Stuart was also in a race not only with the booming Confederate artillery pieces that foretold of the upcoming offensive effort spearheaded by Pickett's Division, but also with the sun before it went down, because this grand effort was already a much-belated attack as the result of a host of problems that had developed.

General James Longstreet, Lee's right-hand man and the orchestrator of the great assault, was about to unleash around fifteen thousand infantrymen when it was determined that the Confederate cannon had been effective in reducing the number of Federal artillery pieces on Meade's right-center at the clump of trees in the Angle sector of the bluecoat battle lines that ran along the strategic crest of Cemetery Ridge.

In much the same way and like Stuart, so Custer was also in a race of his own with the sun, but most of all in regard to the great artillery bombardment which he, or any seasoned veteran and West Pointer for that matter, knew was the preclude to a grand infantry attack that was Lee's most relied-upon offensive tactic for achieving success, as at Chancellorsville. Most of all, Custer realized that he needed to continue to fight in an aggressive manner as long as possible to buy precious time, which had become his top priority. And the very best way to guarantee that the contest continued for possession of the crossroads three miles in Meade's rear was to steadily up the ante to garner the attention, time, and focus of his opponent, when time was of the essence. Custer understood that he must continue to do whatever was necessary to ensure that Stuart and his men would fight the wrong battle in the wrong place and at the wrong time. Therefore, Custer needed to continue to ensure that what was wasted by the Rebels was even more precious time, while keeping them as far away from the Army of the Potomac's rear as possible, when Pickett's Charge was about to be unleashed.

So in this regard and in overall tactical terms, Custer knew that he had to outsmart his wily opponent who had become legendary for his combat prowess and tactical tricks. Most of all, Custer realized that he had to not only continue to distract his enemy in order to buy precious time but also commit himself to a new tactic to keep Stuart off balance, when the Lee-Stuart team was about to gamble everything on one throw of the dice. The more time that Stuart wasted in fighting at the wrong place and time instead of striking Meade's rear equated to a Union victory, if the bluecoat defenders of Cemetery Ridge held firm when Pickett's Charge was unleashed.

Brigadier General Custer's plan, consequently, was basically to keep Stuart and his top lieutenants engaged as long as possible and far from the Cemetery Ridge defensive line, which was relatively weak and vulnerable, especially in regard to a cavalry attack from the rear. And, under these circumstances, when time was of the essence, the very best way to accomplish this daunting task on a day of decision was by relying on a single tactic that was guaranteed to be most effective in a disadvantageous situation to buy time and keep the Confederates distracted far away from Meade's rear: a reliance on a hard-hitting tactical offensive, especially the headlong cavalry charge. Most of all, Custer had to keep Stuart occupied on this front and from gaining the strategic crossroads and the way southwest to Meade's rear along Cemetery Ridge.

As much as anyone else, Custer realized that these proud Southern cavaliers, especially Stuart and his "Invincibles," simply could not resist the ordering of a large-scale headlong attack of mounted cavalrymen to meet a comparable cavalry challenge—viewed as a professional and personal challenge to Southern cavaliers—because of their excessive pride and arrogance. Therefore, Custer realized that a preemptive strike was now necessary to garner the highest dividends under the circumstances: a guarantee that more time, focus, and attention would be directed by Stuart and his men at meeting a Federal cavalry charge instead of striking Meade's rear as ordered by Lee.

In fact, in overall psychological terms, Stuart and his men were more vulnerable in this regard than ever before, because of what had happened in their greatest recent embarrassments and because they now wanted to redeem themselves and their lofty reputations that had been tarnished, not only in regard to what occurred at Brandy Station, but also the recent raid that had taken them too far away for too long from Lee and the Army of Northern Virginia.

Therefore, the tactically savvy Custer, who knew the psychology of his opponent extremely well, which was one key to explain the success in helping to win the day in Meade's rear, was about to exploit the greatest weaknesses of Stuart and his men: an unprecedented amount of hubris, arrogance, and pride that fueled his opponent's desire to defeat the Federal cavalry in an open-field fight in which a much-touted Southern superiority—not only militarily but also culturally and morally in the thinking of the average Rebel—could be demonstrated in full in a man-to-man contest to demonstrate combat prowess. Custer understood that this long-existing Achilles' heel of Stuart and his men could be exploited to his full advantage precisely because they had been too successful in the past and now felt that they had to live up to their lofty reputations, which had been badly stained in the great cavalry clash at Brandy Station and then in the recent disastrous raid through such a large expanse of Maryland.

Indeed, nothing could now guarantee a more vigorous response—even an entirely misdirected one from Stuart and his top lieutenants—than a traditional saber charge, which would guarantee that these Southerners would automatically (almost without thinking) counter with their own charges instead of riding southwest to strike Meade's vulnerable rear. After all, the cavalry attack, especially the saber charge, was the most direct challenge of all for men of the South to prove manhood, character, and elite soldierly qualities. Of course, Custer knew as much from his days at West Point from what he had learned about cadets from the South.

Because of his small eastern Ohio hometown, lowly origins as the son of a talkative blacksmith, and isolated rural (almost frontier-like) background in the West, these factors had originally made him extremely curious about the well-bred and finely educated Southern cadets, from sophisticated cosmopolitan centers like Charleston, Mobile, and Richmond, of the aristocratic upper class. Custer, therefore, had gotten to know these peculiar Southerners and their unique way of life—many were the sons of wealthy planters who owned plenty of slaves—that supported their wealthy and elite status as the sons of the South's aristocratic order and rich families. Custer's close association with Southern cadets was quite unlike Judson Kilpatrick (Custer's division commander, who was known as "Kil" to other cadets, and who possessed the same last name as Custer's own Scotch-Irish mother), who argued and fought with them, including Custer's close friends from below the Mason-Dixon Line, because of his boldly stated anti-Southern sentiment, while Custer was decidedly pro-Southern in his prewar views.

Therefore, the popular Custer had befriended a good many Southern cadets, who were the South's young elite and future military, societal, and political leaders, unlike most northern-born cadets. Custer had learned a great deal after having departed the small farm community of New Rumley, and he was about to put some of these invaluable life lessons of his lowly upbringing and West Point—both in regard to academics and from what he had learned about Southerners—together to be utilized in full on the third day at Gettysburg. The homespun and provincial boy who had entered West Point had matured and evolved over time, after having gained life lessons in both war and peace to better face the stiff challenges of July 3. He was a long way from the picturesque hill country of eastern Ohio, and he had left that provincial world far behind in regard to distances and personal experiences.

Even when in the midst of battle, to fortify his resolve and courage, Custer now felt a degree of solace by his faith in God—after all, his mother had wanted him to become a preacher. He was a moral man who prayed before each battle, asking for God's blessings, forgiveness, and mercy. Custer knew that he needed spiritual protection, and he asked for it. As he penned in a letter, Custer commended himself "to God's keeping" at all times. But Custer definitely knew that he now possessed the moral high ground, unlike in geographic terms, because Stuart possessed the physical high ground of Cress's Ridge. But Custer, who had never himself owned a slave, nor had any of his family members, realized that slavery was the epitome of evil and that it needed to be destroyed once and for all.

Most importantly and as noted, Custer was determined to keep the minds of Stuart and his top lieutenants off their primary objective—striking a blow into Meade's vulnerable rear of an overextended battle line that spanned the length of Cemetery Ridge. And he knew exactly how best to accomplish this all-important objective in his own style and manner that best suited him. Leading a cavalry charge was Custer's tactic of choice and his ace in the hole when the chips were down. Most of all, Custer realized that the very best way to protect the Army of the Potomac's rear was by way of a bold tactical offensive: the old, time-honored axiom that the best defense was an aggressive offense—the unleashing of the cavalry charge. Quite simply, Custer understood that this exceptionally bold tactic was the key to not only protecting Meade's rear, but also in saving the hard-pressed Army of the Potomac in the end.

In this regard, Generals Meade, Pleasonton, and Gregg now had not only the right man but also the best man for achieving this all-important mission in the army's rear when everything was at stake—the most aggressive cavalry brigade commander in all of Pleasonton's Cavalry Corps. Significantly, these qualities alone negated Custer's relative inexperience and extreme youth.

But even more and as mentioned, Custer was as much a psychologist as an aggressive brigade commander, verifying the axiom that to wage war successfully, as emphasized by Sun Tzu, the brilliant ancient Chinese strategist, one must first get into the mind of one's opponent to understand his psychology to ascertain his weakness and to anticipate his impending moves. From his West Point experiences, Custer knew intimately about the mental strengths and weaknesses of the typical Southern mind, especially the haughty, proud cavalier from the wealthy families, which was so radically different from the northern mind based on widely divergent cultural experiences, which had partly guaranteed the bloodiest war in American history.

Here, during this dramatic showdown that was being played out on the East Cavalry Field, Custer was putting all his knowledge, past experiences, and instincts to the best use. And, most importantly, his instincts were now right on target in regard to the urgent need to unleash the tactical offensive that was almost certainly not expected by Stuart, who believed that the reputation of his cavalrymen and artillerymen would keep the Federals off balance and on the defensive at this time. Most of all, Custer realized that it was literally now or never, not only for the life of the Army of the Potomac, but also for the Union on this crucial third day at Gettysburg. At this time, General Meade and his hard-pressed men continued to hold firm under a fierce artillery bombardment of massive proportions, and they were facing their greatest threat of the war—Pickett's Charge—not only to the west, but also now to the east, because Stuart planned to fulfill Lee's ambitions of striking the Army of the Potomac's rear.

Ironically, at this crucial time, neither General Meade nor his weary men positioned along Cemetery Ridge—unlike Lee and Stuart, of course—knew of the extent of the threat to Meade's rear, because this had been the most secret plan on the third day. But by this time, Custer and Gregg knew intimately of the full extent of the danger, and that was all that really mattered at this point, because they were the trusty guardians of Meade's right-rear. Most of all, because of what Custer understood in his heart, he now was determined to perform even more aggressively out of urgent necessity and to the best of his ability, because of the existing tactical realities and escalating importance of the overall situation at the strategic crossroads that posed the most serious threat to the Army of the Potomac's rear at this key moment in the life of the North's principal eastern army.

It is, of course, not known, but perhaps Custer now thought back to his readings of Napoleonic history, which he had loved reading about since his youth. If so, then he perhaps recalled the hotheaded Marshal Michel Ney's repeated cavalry attacks that he led in desperate attempts to break through the redcoat center of the Allied Army, but entirely without the necessary coordinated infantry or artillery support, when he was going for broke in charging the neatly aligned British squares, whose disciplined members had unleashed volley upon volley to hold firm on June 18, 1815, at Waterloo, Belgium, in a desperate bid to gain the Brussels Road for a triumphant march of Napoleon's army into Brussels, when Europe's fate hung in the balance. In much the same way, so everything was now at stake for the Union on the afternoon of July 3, because both the Battles of Waterloo and Gettysburg were major turning points in world history and raged with unprecedented fury.

But even if Custer did not think about the historical analogies of the Napoleonic era, especially the epic clash at Waterloo, he nevertheless fully understood that what was happening in Meade's rear was not only all important, but also absolutely decisive and a key turning point of the Battle of Gettysburg. But quite unlike Marshal Ney's frantic cavalry attacks of determined men in fancy uniforms of bright colors and brass helmets and breastplates, who were the finest mounted force in all of Europe, in the futile bid to break through the thin British lines, which had deceptively appeared to the fearless marshal to be withdrawing (only maneuvering on orders) in panic, Custer was not now in the role of the Duke of Wellington, because he needed to break the threat of attacking cavalry by way of his own cavalry charge that would sap Stuart's initiative and momentum, while taking the Southerners' focus off their principal mission of striking the Army of the Potomac's rear. Under these circumstances, Brigadier General Custer now wanted to unleash an audacious cavalry charge that might well save the day in Meade's rear: the best, if not only, means of now providing protection against the greatest threat to Meade and his army from the east.

Therefore, it was not only Stuart who was going for broke—like Marshal Ney at Waterloo and on numerous other fields of strife in Napoleon's glory days—but now Custer, who realized that he needed to lead a cavalry charge across the wide open plain, which was nestled between Little's Run on the west and the Low Dutch Road on the east, because he knew that he had to go for broke himself to stop Stuart from fulfilling his lofty ambitions. And, most of all, this crucial requirement at this time called for the unleashing of a hard-hitting tactical offensive with Custer's typical aggressiveness, exactly when it was needed the most.

As a West Pointer who had studied Napoleonic history in detail, Stuart and his top lieutenants, like Hampton and Fitzhugh Lee, also knew all about what had happened on that fatal day at Waterloo, when Napoleon's great dream of revitalizing his empire came to an inglorious end on the grim killing fields of Belgium, which had reaped a glory harvest. However, because of overconfidence and hubris from having won too many past successes before the Union cavalry had become truly formidable by early 1863, Stuart and his top lieutenants almost certainly never imagined for a moment that they were in essence falling into a clever tactical trap as laid for the French cavalry at Waterloo: the overreliance on the launching of headlong saber charges in a determined bid to vanquish their hard-fighting opponent and win the day, which ensured the wasting of invaluable time exactly when time was of the essence in regard to striking Meade's rear. At this time on the East Cavalry Field, when everything was at stake, this was an especially dangerous tactical illusion—a legacy of 1861 and 1862 when glory was still in style and the war's innocence had not yet died an ugly death—and misplaced tactical concept, because time was running out for delivering a crushing blow to the Army of the Potomac's rear.

As Brigadier General Custer—like Gregg and Stuart—fully realized at this time because the thunderous Confederate cannonade to soften up the defenders of Cemetery Ridge on Meade's vulnerable right-center continued to roar in the distance, the stakes could not have been higher, because Stuart needed to turn and ride toward Meade's rear before it was too late. Quite simply, for Custer and the Army of the Potomac, this was a classic case of now or never, and the time factor was all important. A great deal—perhaps the battle itself—depended on what happened on the East Cavalry Field in the next hour or so.

Perhaps the young man well understood that he, his beloved Michigan Cavalry Brigade, and the reeling Army of the Potomac no longer had any real future in the days ahead if he now failed to rise to one of the day's greatest challenges and did not perform well beyond all expectations, because of the supreme importance of this key moment. Consequently, for all of these reasons, Custer knew what he had to do above all else at this crucial moment and at this place in Meade's right-rear: lead a daring saber attack north with his reserve regiment—Custer's ace in a hole—that had been specially trained in the art of the saber charge for just such a moment, the 7th Michigan Cavalry.[320]

At this time, after the success of the 1st Virginia Cavalry in having swept McIntosh's men off the field, including all the way east into the shelter of the Lott woods near the Low Dutch Road, Stuart was about to miss his best tactical opportunity to carry the field and win the day, while the cannon of Pickett's Charge continued to echo like thunder less than four miles to the southwest, because Custer, with General Gregg's blessing, was about to go on the offensive by leading a spectacular cavalry charge—a true turning-point moment of not only the escalating struggle for possession of the East Cavalry Field, but also the overall Battle of Gettysburg. Indeed, embracing a tactical opportunity because of this situation in which "the contest might have been decided," Custer rose to the challenge before Stuart "could bring more force to bear" by relying on the combat prowess of the highly motivated troopers of the 7th Michigan Cavalry.[321]

As if specifically made for this key moment in a crucial situation, Custer was now splendidly uniformed in a most conspicuous manner that well prepared him for what he knew he had to do against the odds. Because of this distinctive look so that his men would be able to follow him to hell and back if necessary on a smoke-covered battlefield and it would have an overall dazzling effect on the men in the ranks, Custer "captivated every one by his peculiar and picturesque appearance [while at the same time] keeping within the regulations . . . managed to produce one of the most brilliant and showy" uniforms.[322]

More importantly, he knew that he had to strike a blow to ensure that the Confederates failed to regain the initiative and momentum by launching another offensive effort to exploit the success and gains achieved by the hard-fighting Witcher and the 1st Virginia Cavalry. These elite troopers had advanced farther south after Witcher's Virginians had beaten the 5th Michigan Cavalry and exploited the tactical opportunity to achieve their greatest success. Hurled forth by Fitzhugh Lee, the 1st Virginia Cavalry continued to advance toward the strategic crossroads with flashing sabers and victory cheers. Indeed, at this time, which was absolutely critical, any "quick action by Stuart in support of the First Virginia might have given his forces the field, but he failed to follow up his advantage."[323]

Stuart only took action when it was too late because he had no choice, although he wanted no part of a large-scale battle for possession of the strategic crossroads, since of course his key mission continued to be to strike into Meade's rear as Lee fully expected when he was about to deliver his greatest offensive effort from the other direction. With events and fast-paced developments swirling beyond his control, and seeing that the worn-out men of the 1st Virginia Cavalry, the elite regiment of Fitzhugh Lee's Brigade, needed replacement after having advanced after Witcher's Virginians had severely punished Major Ferry's 5th Michigan Cavalry and killed the major, Wade Hampton ordered a fellow West Pointer, Colonel Laurence Simmons Baker, who commanded the 1st North Carolina Cavalry, Hampton's Brigade, to go to the assistance of the 1st Virginia Cavalry troopers. This withdrawal back up the slope came as a shock to Hampton, because the 1st Virginia Cavalry had been a model regiment since the war's beginning. As Brigadier General Hampton penned of the tactical situation when he was guilty of an escalation of the contest that was not wanted by Stuart: "I sent to Colonel Baker ordering him to send two regiments to protect Chambliss, who had made a charge . . . and who was falling back before a large force of the enemy."[324]

Therefore, time was of the essence for Custer to launch his own strike straight north toward Cress's Ridge before the Confederates dispatched significant numbers of reinforcements and unleashed a greater offensive effort from the high ground, because he possessed only a narrow window of opportunity to deliver a blow to catch an overconfident opponent by surprise. Custer retained the uncanny ability to rise to the challenge whenever the tactical situation looked darkest, and he was now determined to turn the tide by way of an aggressiveness that bordered on sheer audacity not expected by the most legendary cavalry leader in America.

At this crucial time, Custer faced the day's greatest crisis. However, whenever he found himself in a tight spot, Custer possessed the uncanny ability to somehow—some called it "Custer's Luck"—always get himself out of trouble of the most serious nature when there seemed to be no possible solution or chance to reverse the tide, a situation that continued to exist for Custer all the way up to that fatal June 25, 1876, when his fabled luck came to an abrupt end.[325]

# ⊂ 4 ⊃

# Custer Audaciously Leads the Way with the 7th Michigan Cavalry

*C*uster had become increasingly fearful about the overall tactical situation and his ever-declining chances for retaining possession of the crossroads because of his precarious toehold on the strategic intersection, while the Rebels, especially the 1st Virginia Cavalry and its sparkling recent success, became more aggressive after Major Ferry's 5th Michigan Cavalry had been hurled by Witcher's Virginians. In fact, the confident Rebels were threatening the major bone of contention of the crossroads as never before now that the fierce artillery barrage in preparation for the unleashing of Pickett's Charge continued to echo in the distance.

The Confederates were not only defending the buildings of the John Rummel farm of which the hardworking Teutonic farmer was rightly proud— a key launching pad for more aggressive action farther down the slope—but a strong line of dismounted skirmishers, supported by an even stronger reserve of cavalrymen, were also now advancing south through the open fields and ever closer to the strategic crossroads. As mentioned, the elite troopers of the 1st Virginia Cavalry had routed and pushed aside McIntosh's men, who had fled toward their main Low Dutch Road position to the east and into the shelter of the Lott woods, leaving the strategic crossroads, just to the south, more vulnerable. The attackers possessed the high ground that completely overlooked the crossroads, and the Rebels continued to exploit this advantage.

Most importantly, Custer began to see with greater tactical clarity and certitude that Stuart's plan was not to attack down either the Low Dutch Road or the Hanover Road as expected by him and other commanders, including General Gregg. Instead, it was now clear that Stuart's top lieutenants were planning to attack with mounted troopers between the two roads and across the open fields that led straight south to the strategic crossroads. Stuart, if he was the author of this offensive effort, had been clever in deciding not to apply pressure or launch attacks down either road, because he knew that these seasoned Federals would have prudently strengthened their flanks—ironically, basically Lee's tactical rationale for attacking Meade's right-center—to leave the crossroads more vulnerable.

Facing the growing threat and after ascertaining Stuart's plan of attacking over the open ground—the wide plain that was filled with crops, including wheat, and grassy pastures—between the two main roads by which Custer had originally expected no large-scale attack, Custer realized that as long as the Confederates retained possession of the barn, house, and other buildings of farmer Rummel (a high-ground launching pad for a major attack), the strategic crossroads continued to be under serious threat, because Stuart would almost certainly send in reinforcements to continue the attack southward down the slope.

Quite simply, at this time, the heavily pressured front all along the line was collapsing, with the 5th Michigan men, who had been forced to withdraw because they had fired too rapidly—a weakness and liability of using repeating rifles for an extended period—expending a great amount of ammunition in a relatively short time when combined with high losses. As noted, McIntosh's men had been pushed back toward where the sun had risen and the Low Dutch Road sector. Because of the extent of the heavy pressure at this time that continued to mount steadily, Captain Weber on the right flank and Lieutenant Storrs on the left flank had been forced to return to the crossroads because of the overwhelming advance of too many Rebels. Therefore, not only the strategic crossroads but also Pennington's guns of Battery M, 2nd United States Artillery (Custer's horse artillery of his brigade), and Randol's guns (McIntosh's horse artillery of his brigade) were now more vulnerable than ever before.

Clearly, in short order, something had to be done as soon as possible to regain the initiative and momentum gained by the success of Lieutenant Colonel Witcher and the 1st Virginia Cavalry, Fitzhugh Lee's Brigade, especially now that Lee was about to unleash thousands of infantrymen in Pickett's Charge. And this mounted counterattack had to be accomplished very quickly because the foremost lines of dismounted Confederates continued steadily to advance south down the open slope, heading straight toward the vital intersection, while maintaining a hot fire on the heavily pressured bluecoats, who continued to fight with the disadvantage of holding lower ground before the resurgent Rebels.

Even more, Custer saw through his field glasses that large numbers of Southerners were about to launch a larger offensive effort. At this time, he did not know that this strong force included one of the elite cavalry regiments of the South, the famed 1st Virginia Cavalry (the pride of Fitzhugh

Lee's Brigade), which had played a key role in scattering McIntosh's foremost troopers and had re-formed to resume the offensive. Custer feared that these crack Old Dominion troopers—Stuart's original regiment when only a colonel, when he had led them with distinction at First Manassas—would exploit their recent success by continuing the charge down the slope to slaughter his 5th Michigan boys, who were exposed in the open fields and in harm's way on lower ground.

Therefore, in this truly desperate situation, Gregg and Custer now looked to the 7th Michigan Cavalry, which had been supporting the booming guns of Pennington's Battery, consisting of around one hundred members, of six 3-inch rifles situated near the crossroads just in case Stuart launched a cavalry attack in force. This regiment was now serving as a strategic reserve for just such an emergency situation not long after these troopers had reached the vital intersection in a column of fours. Custer also knew that he possessed at least one tactical advantage besides the element of surprise, because the attacking Rebels, sensing victory as so often in the past, were overconfident and mostly dismounted men on open ground, and hence vulnerable to a sudden mounted charge if he struck before the 1st Virginia Cavalry launched its own attack downhill. And of course Custer also realized that he possessed the advantage of superior artillery support from two batteries commanded by capable West Pointers, who made the young brigadier general very proud on this day.

Although yet to engage in a major action and young rookies—the average age was only eighteen—of this green regiment, the 7th Michigan Cavalry was a very good command, and best of all, it was a fresh unit compared to a portion of the 6th Michigan Cavalry that had been bloodied in the recent clash at Hunterstown. Despite a small regiment of just over 450 men, the 7th Michigan troopers were highly motivated and ready for the challenge. They were now led by Colonel William D. Mann, whom they believed in and respected for his leadership ability. Mann had early gained solid experience as an officer of the 1st Michigan Cavalry before casting his fate with the 7th Michigan, where he had reached his full potential as a dynamic officer of considerable ability.[1]

Like the 6th Michigan Cavalry, the 7th Michigan Cavalry had been organized at Grand Rapids, whose sons were disproportionately represented in the ranks of the Wolverine Brigade. The 7th Michigan Cavalry troopers benefited not only because Colonel William Mann, of Detroit, was in command but also from superior horses, thanks to the tireless efforts of ingenious regimental officers, especially the capable quartermaster, who knew their business. As fate would have it, the 7th Michigan Cavalry was the most recently formed regiment of Custer's Wolverine Brigade, having been organized only in early 1863.

Then the new regiment of young, enthusiastic members had been dispatched to Washington, DC, embarking upon a distinguished career with the Army of the Potomac. All in all, therefore, these men of the 7th Michigan had much to prove, like Custer, because they were fully aware that they were considered rookies and novices by some of the seasoned troopers, especially the men of the 1st Michigan Cavalry, and they wanted to demonstrate their worth to one and all, including Custer.[2]

The chances for a successful charge were increased because Colonel Mann's regiment contained a high-quality and supremely motivated soldiery, especially among the officer corps. Adjutant George B. Briggs, who was raised in Battle Creek, Michigan, was one such high-quality officer, who was about to rise magnificently to the challenge of the upcoming charge over the open fields and straight north toward the largest number of Rebels in sight.[3]

Most of all, and despite their relatively small numbers compared to the brigade's largest regiment, the 5th Michigan Cavalry, which had taken a beating that afternoon, Custer knew he could rely on these highly motivated troopers—although mere youths of a green regiment who looked upon their brigade commander as an old man well past his prime—of the 7th Michigan Cavalry to turn the tide and ensure the safety of the strategic crossroads that the steadily advancing Confederates were descending upon with a mixture of arrogance and confidence. Most importantly, the 7th Michigan Cavalry troopers were good fighting men, although they had yet to prove it on the battlefield. Nevertheless, Custer trusted these exceptionally young men, mostly hardy farm boys of an unsophisticated nature. After all, they were from the western state of Michigan and possessed a feisty fighting spirit. Custer now needed these young men to reverse the tide of battle, which was going against the boys in blue to jeopardize their increasingly precarious toehold on the crossroads.

Although Colonel Mann's command was small and lacked experience, their morale and fighting spirit could not have been higher, which was exactly what was needed in this key battlefield situation. Nevertheless, like Gregg, who was of like mind, Custer now placed his faith in the immediate unleashing of an attack by the 7th Michigan Cavalry, positioned just south of the Hanover Road, north up the slope and through the open fields of the wide plain nestled between Little's Run on the west and the Low Dutch Road on the east. Custer knew that this desperate tactic was now absolutely necessary to drive the ever-aggressive Rebels back before it was too late. At this turning point, Custer correctly sensed that it was now or never, and the 7th Michigan Cavalry and the most aggressive tactic provided the best opportunity to strike a blow to reverse the tide of battle.

In the beginning, the far-sighted Colonel Mann, who was thinking along Napoleonic lines, had wisely created an elite guard of picked fighting men because of their size and combat prowess—two sturdy troopers from each company. Reminiscent of the days of Napoleon, who had long relied on his elite fighting men of the Imperial Guard, which included the Old Guard and the Young Guard, Mann had decided to call these chosen warriors the "Guard of Honor."[4]

Unknown to the young Wolverine troopers of the 7th Michigan Cavalry, including those who had yet to shave or make love to a pretty girl, General Gregg was thinking like a true Machiavellian, which boded well for a longtime military career in the U.S. military establishment. In cynical fashion but realizing that he had no choice under the circumstances, and perhaps not unlike Custer but to a lesser degree, Gregg had also realized that a high sacrifice was now required in the form of a hard-hitting counterattack. Again, he and Custer were of a like mind this afternoon in regard to their faith in the tactical offensive. Indeed, "considering a countercharge imperative but fearing it would take a dreadful toll, the division commander preferred to commit a rookie regiment . . . whose men would remain ignorant of the dangers until too late to turn back."[5]

To some degree, much the same case could have been made in regard to Custer, who was a daredevil type who led his men boldly by example, unlike the more cautious General Gregg, who was more concerned about his personal safety than his young brigadier general, who was absolutely fearless to the point of recklessness. Quite simply, Gregg would lead no attacks on July 3, like Stuart who had Hampton, because he knew that Custer would fill that vital role in an emergency situation like the one that held at this time.[6]

Therefore, more than 450 sabers of Colonel Mann's Wolverines were pulled from metal scabbards, while the sharp sound of metallic ringing echoed over the plain of the crossroads and the body-strewn lands of the Rummel farm now enveloped in clouds of slowly rising whitish smoke. All the while, a strong combined force of mounted and dismounted Rebels continued to advance down the slope, heading south with confidence and pushing nearly to the middle point of the wide plain. At this key moment, Custer knew it was now or never to turn the tide or be eventually hurled from the crossroads to bestow Stuart with an open avenue to charge into Meade's rear, because the threat to the strategic intersection was steadily mounting until it was the most serious one of the day. Realizing as much to galvanize him into action, the supreme moment had come for Custer, and he was determined to make the most of the crisis situation that he viewed as an opportunity to unleash the tactical offensive before it was too late.[7]

At this crucial time and place when the pressure was greatest and the advancing Rebels, moving forward in larger numbers than ever before, never seemed more confident for victory, Custer was completely in his element in this situation in which destiny and the battle's fate lay in his hands—the antithesis of what one might have expected from a young man commanding a brigade in his first major battle.

Ignoring the long list of disadvantages that diminished his overall chances for success, Custer realized that this was his time and that this high-stakes situation had seemingly been tailor-made for him. Indeed, more than just another cavalry brigade commander, Custer was not only a war lover but a lover of the awe-inspiring beauty and sheer majesty of the cavalry saber charge that he was about to unleash to shock Stuart's "Invincibles." Nothing appealed more to Custer than the intoxicating and exhilarating thought—which now applied to the 7th Michigan Cavalry troopers who were about to charge north—when "the command was given to draw sabre [and] as the bright blades flashed from their scabbards into the morning [afternoon in this case] sunlight [and] a most beautiful and wonderfully interesting sight was spread out before and around us."[8]

Perhaps Colonel Theodore Lyman, a Harvard graduate (class of 1855) and a Massachusetts-born member of Meade's staff, said it best in regard to the fighting spirit that now fueled Custer's motivations and ensured his rise to the challenge in splendid fashion: "Fighting for fun is rare. Only such men as . . . Custer and some others, attacked whenever they got a chance, and of their own accord."[9] For General Meade, the Army of the Potomac, and the Union, this young man with the long hair and unorthodox uniform was exactly the kind of commander now desperately needed in this key situation, when everything was at stake.

Custer only relied on audacity on the battlefield, and he was made fearless in leading the charge not from a mindless recklessness or a burning hatred of the enemy, but by the strength of his faith in God. In this sense, Custer was a true holy warrior. Therefore, even in this crisis situation on the East Cavalry Field, he felt calm and reassured because he had already "commend[ed] myself to God's keeping, asking him to forgive my past sins, and to watch over me while in danger" in leading the attack out in front of his men.[10]

The stage had been set for a dramatic charge. One trooper of the 6th Michigan Cavalry never forgot the breathtaking sight of the disciplined advance of the 7th Michigan Cavalry, which Custer was about to lead in its headlong charge into the open ground of the sprawling plain just above the Hanover Road and extending north nearly to the southern spur of Cress's Ridge: "Just then a column of mounted men were seen advancing from our right and rear squadron, until an entire regiment came into view with sabres gleaming and colors gaily fluttering in the breeze."[11]

As Custer had envisioned, the sight of the 7th Michigan Cavalry about to unleash the greatest Union cavalry charge of the day lifted the morale of the other Wolverines, especially those units, like the 5th Michigan Cavalry, that had taken the most severe beating. Incredibly, after "clearing" the guns of Pennington and receiving encouragement from the sweat-stained artillerymen who unleashed cheers, the 7th Michigan was about to unleash a saber charge with Custer at the head. Both the sight and situation was almost unbelievable to friend and foe for a number of reasons. First and foremost, the unleashing of a mounted saber charge over such a wide stretch of open ground was rare in this war and something out of the pages of the Napoleonic era, when Napoleon's cavalry had been invincible. But Custer was a modern warrior whose mind was not divorced from the romantic past, and this rather unusual quality now benefited Union fortunes.[12]

Hardly believing their eyes, the dismounted Rebels of Chambliss's Brigade and other boys in gray and butternut maintained their ground and advanced positions on the slope, while Custer and his 7th Michigan Cavalry troopers prepared to attack to regain the initiative that had been lost with the success of the 1st Virginia Cavalry. The sight of this splendid Wolverine regiment and knowing its vital mission of pushing aside the dismounted Confederates, not only Witcher's 34th Virginia Cavalry Battalion but also the 1st, 13th, and 19th Virginia Cavalry (the 1st Virginia was part of Fitzhugh Lee's Brigade, while the last two regiments were part of Chambliss's Brigade), was awe inspiring to the boys in blue.

The upcoming charge of the 7th Michigan Cavalry, led by Custer, would be straight north and parallel to the waters of Little's Run just to the west and parallel to the Low Dutch Road to the east. Unable to miss the tactical opportunity to strike a blow and knowing the attack's importance at such a critical moment, Custer decided that he now had to do whatever was possible to enhance the chances for success, and the headlong cavalry attack was not only the best, but also the only solution given the circumstances. He knew that the upcoming attack by the 7th Michigan Cavalry had to succeed in driving the increasingly aggressive and steadily advancing Rebels back from the crossroads and gain possession of farmer Rummel's buildings, which had become so important during this showdown. But, ironically, Custer did not realize that the designation of the regiment that he was about to lead in its first charge on this day of destiny was fated to be the same regimental number of bluecoat troopers whom he would lead in his final charge at the Little Bighorn on June 25, 1876.

Almost as if scripted by a skilled Hollywood writer, the man and the hour had met here on the East Cavalry Field at this key turning-point moment. Riding his muscular warhorse called Roanoke, after his favorite mount had been shot out from under him at Hunterstown, Custer dashed up to the head of the 7th Michigan Cavalry to personally lead the way in one of the most daring and audacious charges of the day.

Here he drew his saber, which glistened in the sun like the rows of swords of the Wolverines waiting patiently in a tight formation for Custer to say the word. The mostly teenagers of the 7th Michigan Cavalry had never unleashed a saber charge on the field of strife. In the past, the older men of Colonel Mann's regiment had wondered how such a boyish-looking officer, who appeared almost like he had just departed a classroom at West Point, could have been given command of the Wolverine Brigade. But because of what they had witnessed on this day, the last doubters of this young man's abilities now realized that Custer was the ideal commander, because he was about to risk his life in leading the 7th Michigan Cavalry in a rare saber charge and share the fate of the common soldiers when galloping into the midst of too many Rebels to count.

Clearly, as he demonstrated throughout this day, young Custer was the antithesis of the typical desk-and-headquarters commander who remained safely in the rear and far from danger. Despite yet to fully recover from his nasty fall and recent close brush with death in leading a foolish headlong attack at Hunterstown, when he had been flung over the head of his wounded horse to dash his head on the hard ground, Custer was ready for the challenge of leading the 7th Michigan Cavalry in its first charge. And as fate would have it, this was the first time that Custer led such a large body of Wolverines in an attack.

In preparation for the hard work that lay ahead, Custer had tucked his small, black felt hat into his pocket before pulling out his saber that sparkled in the sunshine and made him one with the command of mostly youngsters in blue wool uniforms that felt hot and almost suffocating under the early July sun. Instantly, when about to lead the way north in a steamrolling saber charge across a wide stretch of open ground, Custer became the idol of the 7th Michigan Cavalry for his upcoming role. By this time, the members of the 7th Michigan Cavalry were now willing to go to hell and back for the native Ohioan, and this was destined to be never more the case than on the afternoon of July 3.

Positioned before the regiment in the open fields just north of the Hanover Road and just northwest of the crossroads, the splendidly mounted Custer, now bareheaded despite the broiling sun, was in the exact critical and high-pressured situation in which he was known to excel where others most often failed, when the odds were stacked against him and large numbers of confident Rebels were advancing toward the crossroads with visions of victory. Incredibly, he was about to order a traditional saber charge that was something right out of the pages of the most exciting annals of Napoleonic history, and something that the Wolverines never forgot.

Here, before the eager young men of the 7th Michigan Cavalry, nothing looked or seemed more natural than Custer, without his beloved black slouch hat, about to lead the charge while wearing a resplendent uniform and with his "golden locks" flowing.[13] In Custer's own words: "I at once ordered the Seventh Michigan Cavalry to charge the advancing column of the enemy."[14] For whatever reason, Custer's exact final words to his men are not known to this day, before he ordered the charge straight north into the midst of the enemy. But the words shouted by Custer might have been comparable to those of Marshal Michel Ney on the fatal field of Waterloo, when he had ordered the leader of one cavalry charge to "crush them. Ride them down!"[15]

With drawn sabers, the 7th Michigan troopers, unleashing the "Michigan yell," sprang forth as one when Custer finally ordered the charge, moving at a trot, or walk, during this period before breaking into a gallop in the traditional Napoleonic way of cavalry rolling onward into a frontal charge. The Wolverines surged up the gradually ascending slope of open ground that ensured a perfect field of fire for the Southerners posted in good firing positions on higher terrain. Then Custer suddenly spurred his horse to accelerate, and the troopers of the 7th Michigan Cavalry broke out into a limited gallop, while the mounted Rebels, including the 1st Virginia Cavalry, continued to surge down the slope with regimental and company banners flying. In the surging line of Company A, 7th Michigan, alone, Privates Horace Brownlee, Edward J. Brickell, John Heinck, John Park, Nelson Walter, Charles Wilcox, and George A. Worthen were destined to be either killed or mortally wounded on this afternoon in hell.[16]

Other companies of the 7th Michigan Cavalry were fated to endure comparable losses. As fate would have it, the 7th Michigan Cavalry was destined to suffer not only the highest losses of Custer's Brigade, but also "exceeded those of any other cavalry regiment engaged in the battle of Gettysburg."[17] Custer might have believed that he would be killed in this steamrolling charge up gradually ascending terrain and over such a wide stretch of ground that was entirely open, but he was philosophical and fatalistic, which was understandable under the circumstances, believing that it would be only the case if "destiny wills me to die," as he penned in a letter.[18]

While the entire column gained more speed and momentum in surging up the slope of the open plain around one hundred yards north of the Hanover Road, and the pounding of hooves fairly thundered over the fertile fields of farmer Rummel, Custer's men still maintained discipline and alignment until they finally broke out into an extended gallop in pouring onward through the plain, as if nothing could stop them. Knowing the time was right for one last symbolic gesture to inspire the young troopers to even greater exertions at this key moment, Custer turned to his galloping troopers and shouted as loudly as possible, while waving his black hat over his head, "Come on, you Wolverines!"[19]

All the while, the dismounted Virginians, veterans of Chambliss's Brigade, maintained their nerve and ground in their advanced positions behind the fences, while the howling Michigan men surged through the open fields and ever higher up the slope with the steel blades of hundreds of sabers flashing in the sunlight. The escalating thunder of hundreds of pounding hooves grew louder to drown out the sharp crackle of gunfire, growing into a deafening roar. Then the Virginians, especially the seasoned troopers of the 9th and 13th Virginia Cavalry, after they had dismounted to take cover behind a sturdy fence, opened a hot fire as one. The hail of bullets dropped 7th Michigan men out of their saddles and hit horses that tumbled hard on the ground. But despite the losses and the torrent of Rebel bullets that tore through the regiment's ranks, the attack up the slope continued with a will of its own and to gained momentum, while Custer continued to lead the way.[20]

One 6th Michigan trooper never forgot the sight of how the "Seventh dashed into the open field and rode straight at the dismounted line, which, staggered by the appearance of this new foe, broke to the rear and ran for its [cavalry] reserves."[21] But Custer said it best: "The ground was very unfavorable for the maneuvering of cavalry, but, despite all obstacles, the regiment boldly advanced to the assault, which was executed in splendid style, the enemy being driven from field to field" during the sweeping charge.[22] The pounding hooves of hundreds of horses of Custer's attack fairly made the ground tremble to unnerve some of the most veteran Rebels in the ranks, while the battle cries of the 7th Michigan troopers reached a crescendo.

However, as usual in his official reports, Custer omitted the gory details of the horrors of this steamrolling cavalry charge for the hapless victims of Chambliss's Brigade that consisted of the 2nd North Carolina Cavalry and the 9th, 10th, and 13th Virginia Cavalry, when they were hit by the charge of the 7th Michigan Cavalry. Caught on the open ground without a prayer, these mostly Virginians of the foremost battle line were literally knocked down by pounding hooves and grotesquely cut up in nightmarish fashion by the slashing sabers of Colonel Mann's young attackers, who sensed the kill. Indeed, the charge of the 7th Michigan Cavalry "tore through the ranks of Chambliss's dismounted troopers, some of whom went down beneath the sabers of Mann's men and the flashing feet of their mounts," which pounded the fields of farmer

Rummel and unfortunate Confederates who were caught beneath the blue avalanche led by Custer.[23]

Of course the sight of the flight of the dismounted Rebel skirmishers of Chambliss's command higher up the gradually ascending terrain only fueled the determination of Custer to continue onward up the open slope with flashing sabers, while ignoring the high number of recently emptied saddles that he could see behind him and the mangled comrades littering the ground in ever-increasing numbers. In the words of one Wolverine, who revealed an obvious sense of pride in the sweeping attack that continued to gain momentum in pushing straight north toward Cress's Ridge: "There was no check to the charge. The squadrons [of the 7th Michigan Cavalry] kept on in good form. Every man yelled at the top of his voice until the regiment had gone probably one thousand yards straight toward the Confederate batteries" positioned on the high ground of the southern spur.[24]

The overall outstanding success and sheer excitement of Custer's charge resulted in a gradual breakdown of discipline, as could be expected under the circumstances, after having ridden through and down defenders. Henry C. Meyer, a New York cavalry commander, wrote, "Being a green regiment, many of the men rode wildly past McIntosh's command [to the east and well] beyond our guns."[25]

As the most dynamic brigade commander that the young men of the 7th Michigan Cavalry had ever seen, who faithfully led them to where few other cavalry brigade commanders, especially recently appointed ones, would have gone, Custer "led the charge half-way across the [open] plain, then turned to the left [or west]; but the gallant regiment swept on under its own leaders, riding down and capturing many prisoners," who were on foot and caught out in the open.[26]

This first-person account is somewhat misleading because Custer actually had a greater tactical objective than simply defeating the foremost defenders and chasing retreating Rebel cavalrymen attempting to escape up the slope while dismounted and caught in the open. Most importantly, after the first line of defenders had been swept aside, Custer and his followers—perhaps half of the regiment at most, according to some historians—veered away from the main attack column and toward the Rummel barn with the express purpose of "attacking a Confederate battery," which was booming away from the higher ground above the open plain.[27]

The other primary reason why the 7th Michigan veered to the west was because the head of the column had been swept with a hail of musketry from a concentrated volley unleashed by the men of the 13th Virginia Cavalry, Chambliss's Brigade, on the left of Jenkins's (Witcher's) Brigade, after the foremost Rebel line had been scattered. Therefore, Custer wisely attacked northwestward to bypass the right of Chambliss's Brigade and left of Jenkins's (Witcher's) Brigade to avoid its intense musketry as much as possible and to attack the guns that protected Jenkins's (Witcher's) Brigade, which was situated just south of Chambliss. With his fighting blood up, and after having spied the tactical opportunity, Custer aimed to strike the battery that stood on the high ground between these two brigades that held Stuart's right.

Fortunately, despite still being ahead of the regiment, Custer somehow escaped the devastating musketry that swept the Wolverines' surging formations and sapped the attack's momentum, emptying a good many additional saddles of the 7th Michigan boys. In consequence, however, this new direction, which promised a greater tactical opportunity, was now targeted to strike the battery between Jenkins's (Witcher's) Brigade, which was positioned on the right of Chambliss's Brigade, of mostly Virginians, except for the 2nd North Carolina Cavalry, under Colonel Chambliss.[28]

To stop the charge of the 7th Michigan Cavalry and punish Yankee audacity, Fitzhugh Lee had hurled forth his regiment, the 1st Virginia Cavalry. One of McIntosh's officers described the charge of the 1st Virginia Cavalry: "A more determined and vigorous charge than that made by the 1st Virginia it was never my fortune to witness."[29]

## THE FATAL FENCE

Symbolically, the section (the majority of regimental members) of the 7th Michigan Cavalry without Custer soon ran into serious trouble, after having been separated from the young brigadier general who continued to lead the way, when the head of the column (the leading squadron) continued to charge straight ahead, or north, only to run straight into a sturdy post-and-rail fence, which was heavily defended, that spanned obliquely before the huge Rummel barn.

This sturdy obstacle caused considerable confusion by completely disrupting the surging ranks, while thoroughly eroding the charge's momentum and then bringing it to a sudden halt. Meanwhile, from the field on the other side of the fence, Colonel Morgan's troopers of the 1st Virginia Cavalry loaded weapons and hurriedly mounted up to strike back. They then attacked south down the slope and gained the fence's other side to exploit the tactical opportunity posed by the serious tactical dilemma of this Custer-less section of the regiment, while confusion reigned supreme among the green Michigan men. Unlike a thin and anything but sturdy split-rail fence like those found all across rural Virginia, farmer Rummel's post-and-rail, which was made strong by deeply dug and solidly emplaced posts to hold the end of the lengthy rails, had stopped the attack like a high stone wall.

Undeterred by the formidable barrier—the fence having been constructed with longevity in mind—the men of the 7th Michigan hurriedly dismounted, because the charge was now effectively over. Then, without their officers barking orders above the noisy confusion, the Michigan men managed to draw weapons and then aligned along the length of the fence, while battle-hardened Virginia veterans, unlike the rookie bluecoats who took longer to get into an appropriate fighting form because of their greater inexperience, fired back from the other side of the fence, after having quickly dismounted. From this shelter provided by the fence that could not be knocked down because of its solid construction, the Michigan men then "pluckily began firing across it into the faces of the Confederates, who, when they saw the impetuous onset of the Seventh thus abruptly checked, rallied, and began to collect in swarms upon the opposite side."[30]

Dark-haired Lieutenant George G. Briggs, the capable regimental adjutant who had been raised in the town of Battle Creek, which lay directly west of Detroit and around 130 miles east of Lake Michigan, never forgot how the "bullets were flying mighty thick at this time, and the air was filled with the shouts of men—the bursting of shells—the cries of the wounded—and the commands of the officers on both sides."[31]

Leading the tough fighting men of the crack 1st Virginia Cavalry, Fitzhugh's Brigade, Colonel William Augustine Morgan, who had been born in Fairfax County, Virginia, in 1831, admitted that he had never faced a more stubborn opponent. He paid a compliment to these hard-fighting Wolverines: "Custer's men had now warmed up to the work [because] the fighting here was fierce, and terrible, they demanded our surrender, we telling them to go" to hell.[32]

Because they were young rookies, some 7th Michigan boys, unnerved by the prospect of hand-to-hand combat with Stuart's veterans blasting away with fast-firing revolvers and slashing with long sabers at close range, broke rearward to escape. Therefore, this place of death became known as the "deadly pocket," where Michigan troopers, because they were basically trapped by the sturdy fence, fell in greater numbers during what became a confused melee. One Michigan man wrote, "We [now] huddled together and the [Virginians were] pouring a destructive fire among us."[33]

Meanwhile, resourceful officers, especially Colonel William D. Mann, began to take charge in the confusing situation where the bullets flew thick in the exchanges of gunfire at point-blank range. They shouted for their men to create an opening in the immovable post-and-rail fence while under heavy fire and shooting back at the 1st Virginia Rebels. At this crucial time, the Old

Dominion men were still dismounted, while blasting away at point-blank range with abandon on the north side of the fence and putting up stubborn resistance.

Therefore, in the words of one of Custer's men: "The task was a difficult and hazardous one, the posts and rails being so firmly united that it could be accomplished only by lifting the posts, which were set deeply, and moving several lengths at once. This was finally done, however, though the regiment was exposed to not only a fire from the force in front, but to a flanking fire from a strong skirmish line along a fence to the right, and running at nearly right angles with the one through which it was trying to pass."[34]

All the while, the close-range combat continued to rage fiercely, with casualty lists lengthening on both sides. Heavily bearded and dark-haired Colonel Morgan, leading the 1st Virginia Cavalry with distinction and his usual skill, was appalled by the savagery of the contest that swirled along the fence line, which presented a scene of carnage in short order: "My men did not have time to reload their carbines, but were clubbing them to ward off and return the sabre cuts, and thrusts of the maddened enemy."[35]

Clearly, the 7th Michigan troopers were fighting like seasoned veterans instead of rookies, teaching the Virginia men some hard lessons about the toughness of Wolverines in a close-range contest. Perhaps the fact that the average age of Colonel Mann's troopers was only eighteen bestowed more agility and a confidence that they could defeat any number of Rebels (the typical overly confident Union soldier, a novice at war, the mind-set of 1861), because they were not intimidated by the so-called "Invincibles."[36]

However, this audacity and bravado of the plucky troopers of the 7th Michigan Cavalry came at a high price. Some of the finest men and officers of the 7th Michigan Cavalry were cut down because of the headlong attack due north and then the obstacle of the fence, which had left the regiment completely exposed in the open fields and at the mercy of multiple fires from seemingly all directions except the rear. In the ranks of Company D, Privates William H. Adams, Albert Fordham, Henry Haines, Orlando Jackson, Jehiel Karcher, John Milburn, and George E. Vaness were all either killed or mortally wounded. But, fortunately, excellent officers remained standing and leading their men, encouraging the hard-hit troopers of the enlisted ranks. Second Lieutenant James G. Birney was promoted for gallantry on this afternoon, and this recognition was well deserved for his inspiring performance.[37]

More importantly, the most resourceful officers, like Captain Heman N. Moore, of Grand Rapids, and an animated Lieutenant George G. Briggs, who had been the newly assigned adjutant and had a horse shot from under him, rose to the fore in a true crisis situation. Risking his life in the open and under a hail of lead from a good many Yankee-hating Rebels, the latter orchestrated the determined effort to create an opening in the sturdy fence, which stood in stubborn defiance to even the most vigorous efforts to reduce its strength, while Lieutenant John Clark, Company E, shouted for his Wolverines to "kill all you can" in the close-range contest. All the while, the furious hand-to-hand combat raged between the rookie men of the 7th Michigan Cavalry and the seasoned troopers of the elite 1st Virginia Cavalry, with slashing sabers and the firing of revolvers at close range, while the dust and casualty lists rose ever higher.[38]

With the gap finally laid bare in the post-and-rail fence by hard work under a hot fire, and after a handful of captured Old Dominion cavalrymen were hustled down the slope and destined for long stays in filthy prison camps across the North, the resurgent Michigan troopers poured through the gap in the fence. Then, displaying courage and discipline, they finally formed in a line on the north side of the fence—no small accomplishment while still under a heavy fire from Virginians only a short distance away. Not wasting any time and after having already suffered high losses in hurling back the 1st Virginia Cavalry veterans, the men of the 7th Michigan Cavalry—severely punished but not deterred in the least—still carried sabers and revolvers at the ready, after hurriedly reloading in the drifting smoke.

One Michigan man never forgot how "the regiment moved forward, the centre squadron leading, and resumed the charge [to the north and toward Cress's Ridge]. Before it the Confederates at once fell back [while] the charge was continued across a plowed field" swept by Rebel bullets.[39] Commanding Company G during the close-range combat that continued to swirl with unbridled savagery, Captain George Armstrong wrote how "the enemy recoiled and withdrew only as we cut or shot them down or rode over them."[40]

As if determined to wreak full revenge for having lost so many good men at the fence, the screaming troopers of the Custer-less section of the 7th Michigan Cavalry continued straight north up the slope with flashing sabers and a resolve to reap victory, while scattering the shocked troopers of the 1st Virginia Cavalry over a wide area by their onslaught. However, Colonel William D. Mann of Detroit and his reinvigorated section of the Wolverine regiment managed to sweep onward only a relatively short distance up the bullet-swept slope, because they were shortly forced to retire due to the intense artillery and small-arms fire that was concentrated on Mann's isolated section of the 7th Michigan Cavalry.

After not encountering the fence and continuing toward the main buildings of the Rummel farm and not losing time, meanwhile, Custer led his section of 7th Michigan men steadily northwestward and farther up the slope at a gallop, heading toward the gap between Jenkins's (Witcher's) Brigade and Chambliss's Brigade, because they had been spared the awful slaughter of the unfortunate Wolverines at the fence, as Custer had targeted the foremost battery on the commanding heights for capture. Not having encountered the fence ensured that Custer and his attackers lost no momentum during their own wild surge up the slope, like the majority of the 7th Michigan, under Colonel Mann, which had been recently stopped by the fence. Despite having lost more than half his force, which was no longer with him, Custer still adhered to his motto: "I allow nothing to swerve me from my purpose," this being especially the case three miles in the rear of the hard-pressed Army of the Potomac, when everything was at stake.

With Custer still leading the way on his contingent, the howling troopers of the 7th Michigan continued to gallop in a charge past the Rummel house and barn, which was situated to Chambliss's right and Jenkins's (Witcher's) left. After having already pushed aside Jenkins's (Witcher's) foremost dismounted men, the Wolverines then continued farther up the hill with Custer's steamrolling charge steadily gaining momentum. Just regaining possession of farmer Rummel's buildings was not enough, because Custer, with his fighting blood up, wanted to capture the foremost Confederate battery on the southern spur of Cress's Ridge. Consequently, this penetrating charge of Custer and his contingent of Wolverines up the slope continued "past Rummels, to a point within two or three hundred yards of the Confederate battery on the high ground of the southern spur of Cress's Ridge."

Meanwhile, Colonel Mann led his large portion of the 7th Michigan farther north of the slope to the right, or east, of Custer. Here, just east of the Rummel buildings, Mann's resurgent attack proceeded to gain more ground, when suddenly "another fence confronted it, the last one in the way of reaching the battery, the guns of which were pouring canister into the charging columns as fast as could be fired."[41]

Even more, Colonel Laurence Baker, acting on Hampton's orders, played a role in stopping this advanced portion of the 7th Michigan that had gained more ground. He was forming two regiments—his own 1st North Carolina Cavalry and the Jeff Davis Legion—to ride to the assistance of Chambliss's hard-hit units, whose members were retiring up the hill, when he spied the 7th Michigan Cavalry turning and dividing in two. Given this surprising situation that almost certainly shocked Custer, Hampton and Baker correctly sensed a golden tactical opportunity. Therefore, Hampton decided to strike back at the audacious Wolverines, and Baker hit the rear of Colonel Mann's contingent, forcing a hasty withdrawal down the slope by these Michigan men who continued to fight without Custer.[42]

Therefore, only a relative few of Colonel Mann's most determined Wolverines of his section had continued to charge over the wide, open ground beyond the second fence, where the regiment was again swept with a hail of lead from a merciless fire. The foremost troopers, only a handful of especially daring privates but no Michigan officers, actually gained a point farther north and higher up the slope and "certainly within two hundred yards of the enemy's cannon."[43]

Raked by hot fire from multiple directions and after having suffered heavy losses, what was left of the 7th Michigan Cavalry became shaky for ample good reason, especially because it had advanced a long distance and too far north, exhausting its horses and supplies of ammunition. Even more, not only the success in gaining ground but also the inexperience of this regiment almost ensured that it was only a matter of time before Mann's regiment was forced to ground because of its overaggressive pursuit of the withdrawing Rebels, especially when they continued toward another fence lined with fast-firing Southern boys, who seldom missed Yankee troopers out in the open. But most of all, fresh Confederate units were moving forward to confront the northward onslaught of the 7th Michigan Cavalry and hurl it back down the slope. To be fair, what this green regiment—the pride and joy of Colonel Mann—had already accomplished was far more than what could have been expected from any rookie command, infantry or cavalry.[44]

However, in the words of Henry C. Meyer, 2nd New York Cavalry, who watched the sweeping attack of an unleashed Custer and his Wolverines of the 7th Michigan Cavalry: "This charge was over a very considerable distance, with the result that the lines were somewhat extended" on the open ground.[45]

## CUSTER'S TROOPERS FINALLY STOPPED SHORT OF CAPTURING A BATTERY

Meanwhile, Custer was also beset by mounting losses in regard to his contingent and the lack of unity of the 7th Michigan Cavalry that had been split in two by the fence, with him commanding the smallest section of hard-riding troopers, and also by the counterattacking 1st North Carolina Cavalry and the Jeff Davis Legion, consisting of Mississippi, Alabama, and Georgia troopers, of Hampton's Brigade. Realizing that the Southern battery could not be taken by so few men and that it was supported by too many Confederates who held higher ground and fired down the slope, Custer found himself in a bad fix on higher ground near the northern end of the open plain between Little's Run and the Low Dutch Road.[46]

After having attached himself to Witcher's battalion, Assistant Engineer Frank Smith Robertson of Stuart's staff watched how Jenkins's (Witcher's) dismounted men had made a determined defensive stand behind the stone fence that led west from the Rummel barn, blasting away at the mounted Wolverine targets that were completely exposed out in the open. Here, these fast-firing

Rebels "were busily engaged in emptying saddles as the Yanks [under Custer] passed by a hundred yards off" in the open plain, including a plowed field, that had become a great killing field for Custer's most advanced attackers.[47]

Custer's determination to capture the troublesome Rebel battery on the high ground with only a minority of the 7th Michigan's available manpower was still another example that revealed his value as an aggressive commander, while attempting to capture the booming guns with too few men during a turning point of the battle. However, in the end, the might of the 1st North Carolina Cavalry and the Jeff Davis Legion—fresh troopers on fresh horses and with plenty of ammunition—proved overpowering to too few Wolverines and succeeded in the key mission that eventually "waylaid Custer's move toward the battery" on the high ground of the southern spur of Cress's Ridge.[48]

Watching from an elevated position situated just north of the Rummel barn, Chambliss ordered the 9th Virginia Cavalry to assist Witcher's hard-hit men and stop Custer's charge from pouring farther north. The solid leader of Company C (known as Lee's Light Horse), Lieutenant George W. Beale, who commanded a squadron of the 9th Virginia Cavalry, Chambliss's Brigade, described the belated reinforcements that went to the timely support of Lieutenant Colonel Witcher and his command, while summarizing the vicious combat: "Our dismounted men were giving way on Jenkins' line, and a body of mounted men [7th Michigan] were dashing forward to force a rout, when we moved [south down the slope] forward at a trot, passed Rummel's barn, and engaged the mounted men [of Colonel Mann's regiment] at close range across a fence. Some of our troops, dismounting, threw down the fence and we entered the field. A short hand to hand fight ensued, but the enemy speedily broke and fled" south down the sloping open ground that continued to decline all the way to the strategic crossroads.[49]

Much like on the morning of July 1 just northwest of Gettysburg when the battle began by accident and then gradually escalated with a will of its own, so the fight on the East Cavalry Field was also slowly but surely getting out of control by taking on a life of its own—something that Custer desired and Stuart did not. The turning point that began the process of transforming what was intended, in Stuart's mind because his secret mission remained paramount, to have been nothing more than skirmishing to occupy the Yankees' attention into a full-fledged battle was the 7th Michigan's attack (the portion led under Custer) that was calculated to capture the foremost battery on the southern spur, an especially bold offensive effort that had upped the ante to take the battle to a new level of intensity and seriousness. Now leadership on both sides realized that their respective artillery arms had to be protected at all costs, which called for additional offensive efforts, because the best defense was also the tactical offensive: the cavalryman's credo.[50]

From the highest ground of Stuart's position on the southern spur of Cress's Ridge on Stuart's left and northeast of the large Rummel barn, Fitz Lee sullenly watched the withdrawal of his fellow Virginians of Lieutenant Colonel Witcher's 34th Virginia Cavalry Battalion, which had been cut to pieces by this time, and other troopers, who had been routed from the shelter of the Rummel house and barn and the surrounding fence. To cover the withdrawal of Witcher's hard-pressed men, and evidently on Stuart's orders but perhaps not because of his aggressiveness, Fitz ordered a portion of his command to ride out of the woodlands and down the slope in still another offensive effort. However, the accurate fire of the Federal gunners, especially Captain Pennington's boys, shortly forced Fitz's cavalrymen back up the slope and into the shelter of the woods.[51]

But Witcher's own command had suffered far more than any of Fitzhugh Lee's boys. Of the 332 veteran troopers of the 34th Virginia Cavalry Battalion who entered the battle with confidence for an easy success as in the past, a mere 96 men were destined to survive the bitter contest.[52] These hardy mountaineers from today's West Virginia had performed magnificently, justifying Stuart's reliance on them and their experienced commander, Witcher, early in the battle.[53]

But Fitz's men, all Virginians except for one Maryland cavalry battalion, had accomplished a good deal, like Witcher's own battalion, despite having been thwarted and suffering losses. But advancing south far enough down the slope and nearly parallel to the exposed right flank of the 7th Michigan, the sight of Fitz's threat to his right, or east, had been sufficient to cause Colonel Mann to order his battered regiment, which had advanced too far north, to retire farther south through the open fields before it was too late. The sight of Confederate pioneer (like sappers of the Napoleonic era) details pulling down fences in preparation for a charge to outflank the 7th Michigan Cavalry was sufficient to discourage any thoughts about continuing to maintain this fight so far north and away from the remainder of Custer's Brigade located to the south. Therefore, Colonel Mann prudently ordered his men to return to the first fence and enter the field, covered with their dead and wounded comrades to the south, by way of the opening that had been earlier created in the sturdy post-and-rail fence.[54]

## COLONEL JOHN R. CHAMBLISS'S ATTACK

But Colonel Mann and General Custer possessed still another good reason to retire and as soon as possible, besides the threat posed by Fitz Lee's Brigade to the right, or east. Now filling in for General Lee's son "Rooney" Lee, Colonel

John R. Chambliss Jr. arose to the challenge, much like Custer on this day of destiny. Chambliss also spied a good tactical opportunity and was determined to exploit the advantage to the hilt.

Like Fitzhugh Lee had planned to strike the 7th Michigan's exposed right flank, Chambliss planned to deliver a blow to the exposed left flank of Colonel Mann's regiment. This tactical opportunity existed because the 7th Michigan Cavalry had attacked too far north and up the slope of the northern part of the open plain without support on either side, especially now that the regiment had been stopped at the second fence north of the Rummel place.[55] The 7th Michigan men under Custer had not only pushed north past the Rummel buildings, but as close as two hundred yards from the nearest Confederate battery perched on the high ground.[56]

By this time, Stuart had lost control of the battle and his own brigade commanders, with the battle escalating to new levels of intensity. Unlike Custer, Stuart had been unable to adequately adjust to the fast-paced tactical developments on the East Cavalry Field because he lacked a keen tactical focus, in part because he still planned to strike Meade's rear. One of these new levels of escalation was about to be caused by the unleashing of a large-scale charge that Stuart never authorized or ordered.[57]

Eager to prove himself in commanding the brigade of W. H. F. "Rooney" Lee, who had been wounded in the nightmarish combat at Brandy Station, Colonel Chambliss, who had only recently commanded the 13th Virginia Cavalry, which was not part of the counterattack, was determined to take advantage of the golden tactical opportunity that had to be exploited to the fullest if the 7th Michigan Cavalry remained in its advanced position too far north, with both flanks hanging dangerously in midair.

He, therefore, was not guilty of hesitation on the battlefield—which was a quality that had often cost victories in the past—knowing the importance of striking a blow when time was of the essence after the 7th Michigan had gotten itself into a bad fix by pushing too far north in pursing groups of fleeing Rebels and the overly ambitious dream of capturing the nearest Confederate battery—ever troublesome and steadily taking the lives of additional Michigan boys—that dominated the high ground of the southern spur of Cress's Ridge. But in overall terms, the mostly Virginia brigade was not quite the same after "Rooney" Lee had been wounded and Colonel Solomon Williams, the gifted commander of the crack 2nd North Carolina Cavalry, had been killed during the epic cavalry battle at Brandy Station, which had culled the ranks without mercy in close-range flurries of slashing sabers and fast-firing revolvers. Quite simply, both of these leaders were irreplaceable, and their presence was now much needed to increase the chances for success.

Colonel Chambliss now ordered the veterans of a portion of his brigade to draw sabers, after eyeing the ever-tempting target of the exposed right flank of the Wolverines that was hanging in midair amid the open fields of the Rummel farm. Chambliss had recently sent a dismounted squadron of his command to reinforce Witcher and his hard-hit battalion of Virginia mountaineers in the spirited defense of the main buildings of farmer Rummel, and had formed on his left. Chambliss then ordered an advance south down the slope covered in a broad expanse of open fields, green pastures, and meadows, heading toward Colonel Mann and what was left of his 7th Michigan.[58]

One of Chambliss's finest units was his lone non-Virginia regiment, the 2nd North Carolina, which served as a "pillar of strength" of the brigade because it was an elite command, and it was indeed destined to fight splendidly on this day.[59] The majority of the 2nd North Carolina troopers, including Rebels who now wore straw hats that had been recently confiscated from a store, hailed from the counties—former tobacco country—in the northern part of the state. Serving in the ranks of the "Cherokee Rangers" of Company A, the men from Cherokee County took pride in a Native American heritage and identity that were deeply interwoven with the history of their homeland.[60]

In the ranks of Colonel Chambliss's 9th Virginia Cavalry, Lieutenant George W. Beale described the action: "We moved forward at a trot, passed Rummel's barn, and engaged the mounted men at close range across a fence. Some of our troops, dismounting, threw down the fence and we entered the field."[61]

But before Brigadier General Fitz Lee, who held Stuart's left flank, and Colonel Chambliss, who held Stuart's right flank, could deliver a decisive blow with overpowering force on the Wolverines' flanks from opposite directions—Fitz from the east and Chambliss from the northwest—Colonel Mann and his survivors had already returned safely to the first fence and gained the field on the other side after pouring through the opening that had been created.[62] In his view of the success, Lieutenant Beale, who was every inch a fighter, described the "short" clash of arms at the first fence: "A short hand to hand fight ensued, but the enemy speedily broke and fled."[63]

Because of this rapid flight of the Wolverines of Mann's regiment that had been organized at Grand Rapids before the full horrors of war were realized, Chambliss failed to strike a blow at the targeted left flank of the 7th Michigan Cavalry, due to the swiftness of its withdrawal back to the first fence, which presented a good fallback position for the regiment to rally. But his 9th, 10th, and 13th Virginia Cavalry regiments and the 2nd North Carolina Cavalry had found an ideal target that remained too long in the open on the north side of the fence: Captain Heman N. Moore, from Grand Rapids, who had survived a recent wound in the nightmarish combat at Antietam, and his company of dismounted men were still performing exceptionally well in covering the regiment's withdrawal to the first fence in true heroic fashion, moving slowly down the slope and buying time, while exposed in the open.

These heroics came at a high price, however. Captain Moore and his men were practically ridden over by a wave of mostly Old Dominion attackers, including the seasoned troopers of the 13th Virginia Cavalry, Chambliss's Brigade, and the brave captain had a close call, while Moore fought beside his hard-pressed men, who blasted away at point-blank range. While "glancing over his shoulder, [Captain Moore suddenly] caught sight of the gleam of a sabre, thrust from the arm of a sturdy Confederate. He ducked to avoid the blow, but received the point upon the back of his head. At the same time a pistol ball crashed through his charger's brain, and the horse went down with Moore's leg under him. An instant later, Moore avenged his steed with the last shot in his revolver, and the Confederate fell dead at his side. Some dismounted men of the Thirteenth Virginia Cavalry took Moore prisoner" of war.[64]

But Moore had made a heroic last stand that bought precious time for the reeling survivors of the 7th Michigan Cavalry to escape and take a solid defensive at the next fence farther down, or south on, the slope, while, in Custer's words that described the precarious situation of his beloved Wolverines: "The Seventh was therefore compelled to retire, followed by twice the number of the enemy."[65] Lieutenant Beale, 9th Virginia Cavalry, described how the Virginia victors basked in the role of "pursuing them" to the next fence.[66]

Custer and Beale failed to mention how some members—in fairly large numbers—of the 7th Michigan had been systematically routed during the withdrawal to the next fence and the overall severity of the intense contest. While under heavy fire and tremendous pressure, a panic had swept many members of the 7th Michigan Cavalry after the rookie command had performed magnificently in its first charge. It was just a matter of time, as perhaps Custer realized, before the inexperience of the Michigan troopers was revealed in full when heavily pressured by seemingly too many attackers to count, when the fight escalated at the first fence and the bodies started piling up. Shocking him and shattering his youthful illusions about war, teenage Private William Glover Gage, Company C, 7th Michigan Cavalry, described the collapse of resistance in a letter, both astounding and shocking him to the core: "It was against my principle to be taken prisoner, at least without being hurt pretty badly, but when I saw a regiment [7th Cavalry] that I thought would fight [then] run all over like a flock of sheep, that is what they made me think when they were crowding to get back through the fence [the northernmost fence]. I thought I would not shoot on their account and so surrendered."[67]

But before he was captured by Virginians, Private Gage felt a sense of pride and admiration in regard to the heroic efforts of the courageous First

Lieutenant Bradley M. Thompson, a kindred spirit of Custer, to rally the regiment in this crisis situation. A thoughtful and intellectual University of Michigan man and a lawyer from East Saginaw in his late twenties, Thompson demonstrated a remarkable degree of bravery and resourcefulness in the face of all manner of adversity. In his words from a letter, Private Gage wrote glowingly about the courage and leadership ability of the die-hard Lieutenant Thompson, who "behaved the bravest of any officer in our reg. [on] 3rd of July. After the regiment broke he rallied about twenty men and charged the whole column of reb cavalry as the other officers were running helter skelter and did not know what to do."[68]

Relying upon his hands-on leadership style that had so often put him in the forefront of the action, Custer attempted to rally the hard-hit survivors, especially the shaken ones who had lost their nerve—little more than boys without the necessary combat experience—of the 7th Michigan Cavalry. Ignoring the hail of bullets, Custer proved successful in his efforts to stabilize the most panicked portion of Colonel Mann's regiment by his calm and cool leadership style—needed by the rattled rookies of the 7th Michigan Cavalry—to his credit in once again rising to the challenge in a crisis situation.[69] As was his habit on the battlefield but never off the field of strife, Custer swore "like a trooper" in attempting to rally as many 7th Michigan Cavalry boys as possible, while imploring them to stand firm before an enemy seemingly bent on revenge. In a later letter to Libbie, who naturally hung on every word from her warrior-knight, Custer admitted that he was "remarkably profane during the heat of battle," and this was especially the case because the love of her life was engaged in his first major battle, like his Wolverine Brigade, which had performed magnificently on that afternoon.[70]

Indeed, to be fair, the 7th Michigan Cavalry possessed ample good reason to lose some cohesion and give ground out of urgent necessity, and rapidly in the case of a good many of the inexperienced men of Colonel Mann's regiment. As mentioned, Chambliss had hurled the 9th Virginia Cavalry into the fray, and after hand-to-hand combat, these troopers continued south past the bodies of fallen Wolverines, "pursuing them" down the slope, in the words of one Virginia officer, Lieutenant George W. Beale of Company C, 9th Virginia Cavalry, who now led a squadron of veteran troopers of this excellent regiment.[71]

Evidently still atop Cress's Ridge and too far from the action, Major Henry Brainerd McClellan, of Stuart's staff, exaggerated the extent of Chambliss's tactical success and minimized the foremost penetration of the most aggressive troopers, under Custer, of the 7th Michigan Cavalry, writing, "This Federal charge was continued nearly to the original line held by the Confederates at the Rummel barn, where it was meet by Chambliss' brigade, aided by the 1st Virginia Cavalry" of Fitzhugh Lee's Brigade.[72]

Like members of other seasoned Rebel units, the victorious men of the 1st Virginia Cavalry who had taken possession of the Rummel barn meant to keep it out of Yankee hands to eliminate this advanced position as a potential threat to the center of Stuart's main line. In the words of William Augustine Morgan, born in Fairfax County, Virginia, and the former commander of Company F, Sheperdstown Troop of Stuart's original 1st Virginia Cavalry in 1861, who was a key player who explained why this was an elite regiment of veterans led by Colonel James H. Drake (former commander of Company A, Newtown Light Dragoons, of Stuart's original 1st Virginia Cavalry in 1861, who was fated to be killed in action on July 16, 1863, near the end of the Gettysburg campaign: "The barn, a large frame one, was [now] held by a portion of my regiment" and never relinquished their grip.[73]

Besides the 7th Michigan Cavalry, the foremost troopers of the 5th Michigan Cavalry were also pushed down the body-littered slope by the Rebel counterattack that had pushed everything before it. However, these men, whose fast-firing Spencers were unmatched by the limited firepower in the Confederate ranks except in regard to revolvers, shortly demonstrated their mettle in the heat of battle. After reorganizing and regaining supplies of ammunition, the troopers of the 5th Michigan Cavalry "for the third time this day [once again] advanced in support of embattled comrades," who were fighting for their lives in the fields of summer.[74]

Despite the sharp and bloody setback in the fierce Wolverine attack that had surged up the open plain for a considerable distance straight north, Custer could not have been more proud of the men of the 7th Michigan Cavalry. After all, he had bought precious time and had stolen the initiative from Stuart, while keeping his mind off striking Meade's rear. Custer was sensible and practical in his analysis, which was not marred by exaggeration in regard to summarizing the bitter contest, especially concerning what Colonel Mann and his fine regiment had accomplished against the odds, which had been driven back "until our advance reached a high and unbroken fence, behind which the enemy was strongly posted. Nothing daunted, Colonel Mann, followed by the main body of the regiment, bravely rode up to the fence, discharging revolvers into the very face of the foe. No troops could have maintained this [exposed] position."[75]

But the price that the young men of the 7th Michigan Cavalry paid had been frightfully high. In the ranks of Company F, which reflected comparable losses in other companies, Privates James T. Bedell, Robert Hoag, George W. Lundy, and Charles E. Minor were killed or wounded. Sergeant Asa B. Isham, of the 7th Michigan Cavalry, who had been born in Ohio like Custer, wrote of the high cost of reaping a measure of glory, although a gory one, on the East Cavalry Field:

Of the regiments composing [Custer's Michigan Brigade], none are entitled to more laurels for the part performed [at Gettysburg] than the Seventh Michigan Cavalry. Although the smallest regiment in the brigade, it suffered the greatest loss of any. With twenty-nine officers and four hundred and thirty-two men—four hundred and sixty-one in all—present for duty, thirteen men were killed, four officers and forty-four men wounded, and thirty-nine men were missing. This was nearly double the loss of the Fifth [Michigan Cavalry], with seven hundred and seventy present for duty, and over one-fourth greater than the loss of the First [Michigan Cavalry], with five hundred and two present for duty. The Sixth [Michigan Cavalry], with six hundred and eleven present for duty, suffered a loss of twenty-eight killed, wounded, and missing. It is a distinction we are not disposed to estimate lightly, that our casualties exceeded those of any other cavalry regiment engaged in the battle of Gettysburg."[76]

Meanwhile, Colonel Chambliss's success was short lived in a highly fluid battlefield situation that changed with great rapidity like the shifting currents of a flood after a torrential downpour. In the words of Major McClellan of Stuart's staff: "The Federal cavalry [7th Michigan Cavalry] was in turn forced back, but being reinforced, the tide was turned against Chambliss, and he was driven back to his starting point."[77] Lieutenant Beale, 9th Virginia Cavalry, described how the victory was significant, because farmer Rummel's buildings, including the barn, were now more firmly in Confederate hands, but these positions were still exposed and could yet be threatened by the resurgent Yankees if they unleashed another charge north in the manner of the recently hard-hitting attack by the 7th Michigan Cavalry.[78]

This development shocked Stuart because he retained great confidence in Chambliss, especially since he was a fellow Virginian, the son of an esteemed Confederate congressman, and a West Pointer. But again, Stuart had been guilty of being too political, and he had overestimated Colonel John Randolph Chambliss Jr. and his abilities. In truth, the men who served under Chambliss and fought hard to achieve victory on the East Cavalry Field on this bloody afternoon had good reason to lament that the capable Brigadier General "Rooney" Lee had been wounded at Brandy Station to open the door for Chambliss to take command. The extent of the growing chorus of complaints among the enlisted men revealed Chambliss's shortcomings never ascertained by Stuart.[79]

Therefore, Stuart made a rare admission in his battle report seldom revealed by any commander in regard to Chambliss's charge during an important part of the escalating battle: "I know not by whose orders" the offensive effort was ordered, admitting how the battle had been waged beyond his control.[80]

However, in overall terms, this situation of fast-paced tactical developments beyond his control forced Stuart to escalate the battle on a scale that he never wanted. Worst of all for Confederate fortunes, he was being gradually sucked into a battle that he could not control or win, which played a role in taking his mind off the more important mission of charging into Lee's rear.[81]

## FITZ LEE UNLEASHED

A crack command of Fitzhugh, consisting of the 1st, 2nd, 3rd, 4th, and 5th Virginia Cavalry and the 1st Maryland Cavalry Battalion, was one of Stuart's favorite brigades and possessed a well-deserved reputation. After having missed the combat at Brandy Station because of a serious outbreak of his case of inflammatory rheumatism, Fitzhugh Lee was overeager to engage the enemy, partly because he had missed the largest cavalry clash of the war in June.[82]

For such reasons, Stuart had wisely kept his two elite brigades, under his top lieutenant Hampton (his left-center) and Fitzhugh Lee (his left), as his strategic reserve. In the words of Captain James Harvey Kidd in regard to Stuart's ace in the hole: "The wily confederate had kept his two choicest brigades in reserve for the supreme moment."[83] And in this "supreme moment," Stuart, of course, still planned to strike the Army of the Potomac's rear, which continued to be his primary mission, because it was one that might well determine the fate of America. Indeed, as explained by one historian, who emphasized that Stuart continued to keep his main body (Hampton's and Fitzhugh Lee's Brigade) "concealed in the woods of Cress Ridge [because his primary mission and plan] was to execute a rapid flanking movement and then push onward to the true objective—the rear of the Army of the Potomac."[84]

Talented in leadership and tactics and good humored despite the war's increasing level of horrors and tragedies, Brigadier General Fitzhugh Lee, age thirty-two and the esteemed nephew of General Lee, was eager to fight the Yankees, as if wanting to redeem the sting and embarrassment of Brandy Station, where he had not been present because of illness. Now in command of Stuart's left after Stuart's top lieutenant, Hampton, had been absent for an extended period in attempting to locate Stuart, he now spied a tactical opportunity and planned to strike the exposed right flank (on the east) of the battered 7th Michigan, which had retired south from the second fence to the south. A dark-haired, handsome man with an irrepressible fighting spirit, Fitz had ranked just behind Wade Hampton in the chain of command, despite being more than a dozen years his junior in age, and Stuart trusted his good friend, fellow West Pointer, and Old Army comrade. Stuart was fortunate to have two very capable top lieutenants in Hampton and Fitzhugh Lee, and they had never failed him in the past.[85]

However, the more mature Brigadier General Hampton saw the popular Fitzhugh quite differently, as nothing more than a pampered and privileged member of the Virginia and West clique that he disliked intensely, and this rising tide of animosity included Stuart by this time. But Hampton detested Fitzhugh more than any other Virginian cavalry commander because of his cronyism and closeness to Generals Lee and Stuart, and because this often came at the expense of himself and his non-Virginia men.[86]

At this time, Hampton was the senior brigade commander, and while Stuart was still absent, Fitzhugh Lee was officially to take orders from the South Carolinian by rights of seniority. But in Hampton's absence, Fitz had command of both his brigade and Hampton's on the left and left-center, half of Stuart's battle line that spanned a considerable length along the high ground.[87]

Meanwhile, after the repulse of Custer's attack with the 7th Michigan, Hampton went in search of the absent Stuart, especially because he had been earlier requested to report to Stuart's field headquarters, although no one seemingly knew where it was situated. Hampton, therefore, failed to locate it or Stuart, who continued to be guilty of an extended absence from the front, leaving his top lieutenants guessing about what needed to be accomplished.[88]

But Fitzhugh Lee needed no directives from Stuart in regard to what needed to be done on the battlefield in tactical terms at this point, when he now possessed command of Stuart's left: his own brigade on the left flank and Hampton's Brigade on his right to the southwest. Most of all, Fitz Lee was a proud man and a fighter, who lusted to exploit any opportunity on the battlefield. Therefore, he was still frustrated and irritated because his command had been placed in the rear by Stuart and in what was basically a reserve position at the northernmost location of Stuart's battle line, despite holding the left flank, which was farther away from the action and the strategic crossroads than any other Confederate brigade. However, this was not Fitz's fault, which only irritated him more, because his brigade had been the last command to reach Cress's Ridge.

Indeed, as fate would have it, he had been saddled with Stuart's wagons and ambulances, which ensured that his seasoned command—one of Stuart's best—was the last brigade to arrive and had been relegated to the rearmost position, customarily an unflattering position that indicated less reliability and combat prowess, a situation that he almost certainly viewed as a personal insult to him and his veteran fighting men. He was also mad that some of his troopers had been pushed down the slope to protect the withdrawal of Witcher's Virginia troopers from the Rummel house, barn, and outbuildings and surrounding fences, and some very good soldiers had been lost by accurate

Union artillery fire, especially Pennington's fast-firing guns, when exposed on the open ground.[89]

For such reasons, Fitz was in an overly aggressive mood, wanting to compensate to redeem the reputation of himself and his men, who took great pride in their hard-won record. Taking advantage of the absence of Stuart's second in command and senior brigade commander, Hampton, who was still trying to locate Stuart, Brigadier General Fitzhugh Lee decided to act on his own and without proper authorization. Quite simply, this decision made in the heat of battle was actually an official case of abusing the power that he possessed in the absence of both Stuart and Hampton. He simply could not resist his aggressive impulses and instincts when he saw the troopers of the 7th Michigan Cavalry withdraw in some confusion—at least a portion of the regiment—across the open ground. The wide open fields before him offered an ideal stage for a sweeping cavalry charge, and he could not resist the temptation.[90]

Sergeant Robert S. Hudgins, of the 3rd Virginia Cavalry, Fitzhugh Lee's Brigade, described the situation: "We formed for a charge and rode to attack the skirmishers [aligned in the open fields]. About that same time, the enemy cavalry eventually approached just to the west of the infantry and prepared to meet us."[91]

After having advanced earlier down the slope until thwarted by a barrage of accurate shell fire about a half hour before, Fitzhugh now attacked with his full force of the 2nd, 3rd, 4th, and 5th Virginia Cavalry. Again, Fitzhugh's troopers were swept by the blistering fire of Pennington's and Randol's batteries that staggered the assault column, which the 3rd Virginia Cavalry suffered the most. In desperation, Fitzhugh then called up his elite 1st Virginia Cavalry to reinforce his hard-hit troopers, who were reeling from the shell fire. Undeterred and determined, Fitzhugh now targeted "the right center of Custer's and Gregg's adjoining positions."[92]

Meanwhile, Stuart wanted no part of the escalating combat that was raging for possession of the crossroads. He still had the main body of his troopers hidden in the dense forests of Cress's Ridge. All the while, he still continued to plan that the "main body of his force . . . was to execute a rapid flanking movement and then push onward to the true objective—the rear of the Army of the Potomac."[93] This was especially the case in regard to Stuart's keeping Hampton's and Fitzhugh Lee's Brigades as his strategic reserve on the high ground to fulfill his main mission of striking Meade's rear after riding to the southwest toward the Baltimore Turnpike, which he needed to gain.[94]

## WITH HIS FIGHTING BLOOD UP, FITZ LEE OUT OF CONTROL

But Fitz Lee, who commanded Stuart's left, which consisted of his and Hampton's Brigade, was only beginning to fight this afternoon. After searching for the long-absent Stuart, Brigadier General Hampton returned to his defensive line, where he needed to be just in case the Federals attacked once again. He returned just in time. To his great shock, Hampton now learned that Fitzhugh Lee had ordered Hampton's entire brigade of half a dozen units forward in a charge down to assist his own brigade: "a flagrant usurpation of a superior's authority"![95]

Revealing that his fighting blood was up, Fitz Lee's order was ill conceived and ill timed because he was escalating the fight, which neither Stuart nor Hampton, who had been apprised by Stuart of the larger plan to strike Meade's rear, unlike Fitz, wanted. As noted at this time, the hard-fighting Fitz wanted Hampton's men to advance downhill to support the hard-pressed troopers of Chambliss and Ferguson and ordered the attack. After riding onto the field, Hampton was shocked by the sight of his own brigade about to charge across the open fields sloping gently downhill toward the crossroads situated on the low ground. In desperation, he rode forward and reached the head of the column led by the capable Colonel Laurence Baker, who had served in Hampton's place in the past, just before the young buglers, including boys who had yet to shave, sounded the attack. He quickly countermanded Fitzhugh's order and directed his men to retire uphill.

This was the most ill fated of advances because Fitzhugh's orders resulted in his brigade and Hampton's Brigade departing the woods and aligning across the open ground to reveal them to the view of Custer and other leaders. Suddenly Stuart's plan of baiting the Federals to advance too far north with too much confidence and too few troopers and catch them by surprise, which was based on hiding his forces, or the alternate possibility of leading his two crack brigades to the southwest had been exposed. Even more, because it was launched with too few men by Fitz, they were bound to quickly run into trouble from Custer's and Gregg's reserves, as Hampton realized. For ample good reason, Hampton was incensed about the overall situation in which Fitzhugh Lee had been too aggressive, including with the lives of Hampton's own men. Therefore, Fitz was later charged with undue rashness and recklessness in prematurely launching an attack from an assigned defensive position that Stuart and Hampton wanted to be maintained: an unsupported attack without the authorization of either Generals Stuart or Hampton.[96]

Most of all, Hampton was worried about the devastating fire that would be unleashed by the two Union batteries, led by West Pointers Pennington and Randol, that now protected the vital crossroads, and that the attackers on the open ground would be cut to pieces by their accurate fire. Even when he managed to get Colonel Baker's men to withdraw back up the slope, they still took unnecessary punishment and losses from shell fire from the eager gunners in blue, thanks to the impatience and recklessness of Fitzhugh Lee. The unnecessary losses made Hampton sick, while fueling his anger toward Fitz and Virginians in general.[97]

Custer saw the tactical opportunity of Fitzhugh having prematurely ordered an advance without support and with too few troopers to make his opponent more vulnerable. To exploit the opportunity, he naturally went on the offensive with his typically aggressive style by leading a charge north and just to the left, or west, of where the 7th Michigan Cavalry had attacked. In his journal, James Henry Avery, 5th Michigan Cavalry, described their reaction: "We mounted our horses just in time to repel a charge of the enemy."[98]

As spied by Custer, a good opportunity now existed to outflank the victors who had gained possession of the Rummel barn on the west, or to the left of where the 7th Michigan had charged north into the expanse of the open plain situated between Little's Run to the west and the Low Dutch Road to the east. Battling along with Fitzhugh Lee's men in thwarting the attack of the 7th Michigan Cavalry, Lieutenant George W. Beale, 9th Virginia Cavalry, early spied approaching danger: "I observed another body of the enemy approaching rapidly from the right to strike us in the [right] flank [on the west] and rear [from the south and] I bore off in company with a portion of our men to meet and check this force," if possible.[99]

All the while, the Confederates were still reeling from Custer's first cavalry charge with the hard-hitting 7th Michigan Cavalry, which had inflicted considerable damage. In the words of Sergeant Robert S. Hudgins, Company B, 3rd Virginia Cavalry, Fitzhugh Lee's Brigade: "I will never forget the shock of that charge of unleashed Wolverines. We have always since referred to that charge as 'The Fight At Rummel's Barn' because of the presence of a huge red barn on that tract of land which was owned by a man of that name. We advanced at the charge with drawn sabres as the enemy did the same toward us. We met near the center of that field where sabre met sabre and pistol shots followed in quick succession. Because we tried to ride the enemy down, the individual encounters were often decided by the weight and strength of animals. The battle grew hotter and hotter, horses and men were overthrown or shot and many were killed and wounded."[100]

Lieutenant George W. Beale, who was leading some of Chambliss's best men (the 9th Virginia Cavalry and other Virginians), who were battling beside

Fitzhugh Lee's troopers at this point, admitted how "we soon found ourselves overpowered, and fell back closely pressed on two lines which converged at the barn" of farmer Rummel.[101]

Colonel Thomas H. Owen, 3rd Virginia Cavalry, had offered a bold new plan to Fitz, who eagerly accepted the tactical design because of existing opportunities, to strike Custer's dismounted men along the fence that ran behind the trickling waters of Little's Run, because they were aligned in a north–south direction to parallel the little creek, while Custer's main line was extending west–east along the Hanover Road west of the crossroads.[102]

But most of all, Owen and Fitzhugh wanted to capture the most destructive and lethal Federal guns that protected the crossroads, the booming field pieces of Pennington's Battery, which continued to cause extensive damage like Captain Randol's guns, but to a lesser extent. If Custer's dismounted men along Little's Run could be swept aside, then the charging Rebels could then gain the Hanover Road west of the intersection and the flank of Pennington's artillery pieces.[103]

Fitzhugh Lee's charge south down the open plain just on the east side of Little's Run was launched in a determined bid to outflank Custer's troopers, whose line extended north from the dusty Hanover Road and along the small watercourse to where it met the road, and it resulted in one of the greatest Confederate successes of the day, posing a threat to the left of Pennington's Battery on the west. In the words of Lieutenant James I. Lee, Company F, 2nd Virginia, Fitzhugh's Brigade: "We were in a lane [running north–south and paralleling Little's Run] between two stake-and-rider fences. We were ordered to charge the enemy, which we did, and drove them [south] for some distance. We had nearly reached their battery when we were charged by the enemy's cavalry, who were promptly met by our own, and a general fight began, which lasted only a short time, as the enemy withdrew and left us in possession of the field," now strewn with fallen troopers and dead horses.[104]

## INEFFECTIVE CONFEDERATE ARTILLERY

Unfortunately for Stuart's hard-fighting cavalrymen, they were receiving relatively little support from their guns, despite their advantageous position along the high ground: the antithesis of the situation enjoyed by Custer and his men, because Pennington's and Randol's Batteries were not only extremely accurate but also having their finest day, when it counted the most. By this time, in Major McClellan's words about the late arrival of two batteries of Stuart's Horse Artillery, which had already missed much of the battle, "Breathed and

McGregor had reached the field, and had taken position near where Griffin's battery was originally posted."[105]

Meanwhile, Captain Breathed finally barked out orders and had his battery ready for action, with his limbers and caissons full of ammunition, when he received the order to move his guns out of the woods of Cress's Ridge and onto the commanding open ground that overlooked the Rummel house and the strategic crossroads of the Hanover and Low Dutch Roads. But, continuing a trend of encountering one obstacle and problem after another since the beginning of that ill-fated July 3, a problem immediately developed for Breathed's gunners, who had been ordered to support the gray-and-butternut attackers on horseback.

In the words of Henry Matthews, Captain "Breathed brought the battery into position, but could not fire because of the continual mix up of the blue and grey in the [open] plains below. For many minutes the fight raged, pistol and sabre being used freely" among the mounted cavaliers in the tumult.[106]

Therefore, in some disbelief, Breathed's artillerymen—some of the finest gunners of Stuart's Horse Artillery—watched in amazement at the sight of the wide expanse of open fields below the high ground upon which the angry Rebel guns were perched and now roaring: "Neither force seemed willing to give way and held on tenaciously like two bull dogs."[107]

But unfortunately for General Stuart, even the newly arrived batteries of the famed Stuart Horse Artillery were destined to prove largely ineffective on this day, mirroring the overall performance of the Confederate batteries on the East Cavalry Field. Major McClellan, a respected member of Stuart's staff, lamented that the vast "inferiority of their ammunition was painfully evident. Many of their shells exploded before they had halfway crossed the plain."[108] For ample good reason, even the *Detroit Free Press* journalist gained a healthy disrespect for the inferiority of the Confederate artillery arm on this day, and even the best efforts of veteran Southern gunners was openly mocked.[109]

## GENERAL HAMPTON'S UNAUTHORIZED ATTACK

As a strange fate would have it, Fitzhugh Lee's ill-timed and ill-fated offensive effort was about to become part of a dismal trend for Southern fortunes. Meanwhile, the swirling combat of some of America's best cavalrymen on both sides continued to rage out of control across the open fields of farmer Rummel. During this period, elements of Chambliss's troopers had been fighting beside Fitzhugh's men, including the 9th Virginia Cavalry, to enhance their overall offensive capabilities to pack a hard-hitting punch. Lieutenant George W. Beale, who was leading a squadron of his 9th Virginia Cavalry boys under Chambliss, admitted how they had been forced back by Custer's attack with the 7th Michigan Cavalry.[110]

As mentioned, Stuart did not want to engage in a major cavalry battle over possession of the crossroads, because he continued to feel the burden of Lee's orders for the larger and more important mission of striking the Union rear. Therefore, as noted, he originally had only wanted to occupy the Federal cavalry in the fighting around the crossroads to allow him the opportunity to slip around them and ride unimpeded to the Army of the Potomac's rear in conjunction with Pickett's Charge.[111]

Nevertheless, either Hampton had other tactical ideas (he perhaps still did not know of Stuart's overall strategic goal of striking Meade's rear at this time because of the breakdown and lack of communication between Stuart and Hampton and his other top lieutenants, or he was being pulled into the escalating conflict like Fitzhugh Lee) and was determined to make the maximum effort—the "climactic drive" that was against Stuart's plans. All in all, this situation has remained a central mystery of the battle because the exact sequence of developments and events, including the tactical thinking at various times in regard to the actions of the top Southern leadership levels of Stuart's cavalry, are not known, and official records cannot be completely trusted in this regard.

Either way, and regardless of the exact sequence of developments, it almost seemed as if fate itself, especially the crucial lack of communication between Stuart and his brigade commanders when close communication was absolutely vital for success, especially a decisive one, on this afternoon, had decided that the final showdown was destined to be played out in full in the struggle for possession of the strategic crossroads. In consequence, what was now about to result was the final and main Confederate "effort against the Union rear [because now was] the hour of his advance to the Baltimore Pike [and therefore] no time remained in which to outflank the Union horsemen barring his path; he must slash through them as expeditiously as possible."[112]

Quite simply, the top Confederate cavalry of Lee's army was having one of its poorest days of the war, especially in the all-important area of close communications. While the enlisted men fought and died, Stuart and his top lieutenants were letting them down. Perhaps it was true what Major John Cheves Haskell lamented in regard to Lee's top cavalier: "His favorite companions were more or less buffoons, a part he, himself, greatly affected."[113]

But recent history—the great clash of cavalry at Brandy Station—and an older chapter of a most distinguished military history—Waterloo—still radiated a powerful pull on the minds of Confederate cavalry leaders, who knew that aggressiveness was the key to victory. Stuart's officers knew all about how a maniac, Marshal Michel Ney, Napoleon's top cavalry lieutenant, had led the French cavalry at the wrong time in an uncoordinated offensive effort without support of the all-important artillery or infantry, because he incorrectly believed that the Duke of Wellington's redcoats were retiring, when they were only redeploying into better defensive positions on more advantageous ground.

In the end, Ney's overaggressiveness, the hard-hitting style that had made him famous across Europe, cost the French and Napoleon dearly at a time when there was no margin for error during one of the most decisive battles in history. Ironically, in basic terms, Marshal Ney's overly aggressive actions were about to be repeated in the launching of an unauthorized and ill-fated cavalry attack by Stuart's finest cavaliers, who were about to go for broke in a final attempt to push aside the Yankees, especially Custer and his stubborn Wolverines. Indeed, as Marshal Ney had failed Napoleon miserably at Waterloo, so Stuart was destined to fail Lee and the Army of Northern Virginia miserably on the third day at Gettysburg.

Most of all and as mentioned, Stuart had wanted his elite brigade and top commander, General Hampton, who was to Stuart what Ney had been to Napoleon, to remain hidden in the dark forests of Cress's Ridge for the opportunity of launching a surprise attack on the crossroads or riding southwest to strike Meade's rear. As noted, the lack of communication between Stuart and his top lieutenants was not only extraordinary, but also entirely unprecedented on what was the most important day of the war, representing a gap that could not be bridged on that day. In the beginning and as noted, Stuart wanted to bait the enemy into advancing closer before striking by surprise with his finest top lieutenant and best brigade, which consisted of North Carolina, South Carolina, Georgia, and Mississippi veterans, who were known for their combat prowess.

Like General Lee, Stuart knew that he could not afford to lose too many men and horses in a major clash of arms on the scale of Brandy Station, because his main objective was to strike the Union rear. Therefore, he had originally envisioned slipping around the flank of the Union cavalry after they were sufficiently pushed aside to guarantee no pursuit, because Stuart did not want to be hit in the rear when he led his forces toward Meade's right-center, which Pickett's Division had targeted. As mentioned, therefore, neither Lee nor Stuart wanted a large cavalry fight on the war's most important day, especially when the Union rear was vulnerable and this golden tactical opportunity needed to be exploited when Pickett's Charge was about to be unleashed.[114]

Consequently, while observing the overall tactical situation and activities of Custer and his men from a commanding knoll, Stuart urgently informed Captain Frank Smith Robertson, his trusty staff officer, to reconfirm his earlier directives to General Hampton that were all important, because they were in preparation for eventually riding to and attacking Meade's rear. In Robertson's words: "He ordered me to ride back as quickly as possible and tell General

Hampton to keep his cavalry out of sight in the woods [of Cress's Ridge] and avoid an engagement. Riding full speed I was yet too late, ere I reached the place I had left General Hampton, I saw him on a full charge across the field with three brigades of cavalry."[115]

Indeed it was already too late. With so many troopers already drawn into the fight for the crossroads because of its steady escalation, Hampton now realized it was too late to hold anything back. Lieutenant Beale, 9th Virginia Cavalry, Chambliss's Brigade, wrote, "I was by General Stuart's side as we approached the [Rummel] barn. My horse fell at this point, placing me in danger of being made a prisoner. At this moment General Hampton dashed up at the head of his brigade. He was holding the colors in his hand" to inspire his troopers.[116]

But how and why had Hampton and his brigade—the finest of Stuart's command—attacked down the open slope at this time, when the primary mission was to attack the rear of the Army of the Potomac? Of course this has been one of the greatest mysteries of the dramatic showdown on the East Cavalry Field. Like other veteran commanders on July 3, and especially on the East Cavalry Field, Hampton had been swept up by events and tactical developments on the battlefield that were beyond his control.

First, Fitzhugh Lee's unauthorized charge had already upset Stuart's larger tactical plan and Hampton's wishes, which were based on Stuart's wishes, according to General Lee's plans as created on the night of July 2, because Hampton's Brigade had been exposed to the view of Custer and his men. Then even more trouble had developed of the same kind when a breathless staff officer from Chambliss, who had also charged in conjunction with Fitzhugh's orders, appeared. Hampton had then faced the same problem once again, but in fact the tactical situation was worse in having turned against the boys in gray and butternut. But this time the Confederates had charged too far south and were hit in the flank by a larger force of Yankees charging from the crossroads.

Consequently, a desperate Hampton had ordered Chambliss rearward and to get the ill-supported and too few troopers to withdraw back to the high ground to regain their former defensive stance on the heights, while ordering Colonel Baker and his men to hold back the Federals and buy precious time for Chambliss's withdrawal before it was too late. Baker proved successful in pushing the Federals back and allowing Chambliss time to withdraw, but he advanced too far and made himself vulnerable like Chambliss earlier. Therefore, Brigadier General Hampton was forced to take offensive action because Baker and Chambliss were in serious trouble, with Yankees hitting them from front and flank while threatening their rear.

Hoping to save his men and the day, Hampton rode instinctively and impulsively to the scene to take charge of a chaotic situation and assist Baker in getting his hard-hit troopers back up the hill. However, from the high ground, other Confederates saw Brigadier General Hampton, Stuart's top lieutenant by right of seniority and a towering figure in height and bulk, in the forefront, and they assumed that a general Southern advance was underway, which was incorrect.

Consequently, other and large numbers of Confederates charged forward to join the ever-escalating fray, with the battle swirling out of control and proving to have a life of its own—something that neither Stuart nor Hampton had ordered or desired.[117] In Hampton's words of a situation that was well beyond his control by this time: "To my surprise, I saw the rest of my brigade (excepting the Cobb Legion) and Fitz Lee's brigade charging," because Adjutant Theodore G. Barker believed that Hampton needed timely reinforcements, when he was only attempting to withdraw his troopers back up the hill.[118]

Complicating the situation, and a big part of the problem, was the fact that Hampton still evidently had no knowledge of Stuart's overall plan of striking Meade's rear, because Stuart had long kept it a secret and because Hampton had failed to confer with Stuart as requested by the overall commander. But Hampton, who rode his large and muscular bay, which was his favorite war charger, was now leading the charge down the slope and toward the strategic crossroads. After having been unhorsed by a shot, Lieutenant Beale saw Hampton hand over the colors "into the hands of a soldier at his side just as he swept by me." At this time, Hampton did not know that Stuart still wanted the troopers to remain hidden in the dark forests of Cress's Ridge for the overall purpose of obeying Lee's directives "to plunge into the Union rear," in one historian's words.[119]

Most of all, it was mostly left to Custer and his Wolverines to stop Stuart from achieving his great objective of inflicting a mortal blow on the Army of the Potomac, and this meant defending the crossroads to the last. As noted, this was Custer's primary mission, because he could not be pushed aside to allow the Rebels to ride southwest for Meade's rear, which was nothing less than the thwarting of the ambitions of not only Stuart but also Lee, if Custer continued to hold the strategic crossroads. Custer lived by the credo that now applied to the last-ditch bid to stop Stuart at all costs: "I allow nothing to swerve me from my purpose."[120] And in regard to this inexperienced twenty-three-year-old and new brigadier general, "my purpose" at this time was to stop Stuart from gaining the rear of the Army of the Potomac.[121]

Meanwhile, Custer watched the extent of the crisis that threatened to engulf the crossroads, which certainly would be lost to the resurgent Rebels if no significant action—especially of an aggressive nature—was taken, and he knew that something had to be done before it was too late, and this meant taking the tactical offensive. After all, the overall tactical situation was especially bleak on the East Cavalry Field after the repulse of the 7th Michigan Cavalry, which had suffered heavily. Not only the hard-riding Michiganders, but also some of McIntosh's men had been hurled back to find greater safety on lower ground and in decent cover. In desperation, General McIntosh rode among the fleeing bluecoats and screamed, "For God's sake, men, if you are going to stand, stand now, for you are on your free soil!"[122]

At this time, the survivors of the 7th Michigan Cavalry were in the overall worst shape, with many troopers fleeing in panic and heading toward the crossroads. Private William Glover Gage, Company C, 7th Cavalry, described how by this time the regiment had "broke" under the intense pressure, heavy losses, and lack of effective leadership among the officer corps.[123] One of McIntosh's officers described how the "1st North Carolina Cavalry and the Jeff Davis Legion coming up to [the] support [of the 1st Virginia Cavalry] crowded the 7th Michigan back, and it was obliged to fall back to their main body."[124]

James G. Birney, who hailed from Bay County, Michigan, summarized how "the Seventh Michigan Cavalry charged gallantly and drove them back, when Hampton's entire brigade charged us and we were obligated to fall back. My horse was shot twice and finally killed; a bullet went through the pommel of my saddle, two through my overcoat and one through my saber strap, and I was struck on the heel with a spent one. The regiment began to fall back and just then the color-sergeant [who also hailed from Bay County, Michigan] was killed by a pistol shot. I secured the colors and was charged by a large number of rebels, and I can assure you the bullets whistled merrily for a while but miraculously none touched me."[125]

Consequently, with Hampton unleashed and leading the way south down the slope, the overall tactical situation could not have been more critical for the Union, with the 7th Michigan Cavalry being steadily pushed south toward the crossroads, because Confederate strength had been steadily mustered during the escalating combat until Stuart's forces were fully prepared to deliver a knockout blow. And at this moment of supreme crisis, when the fate of the Federal defensive stand and the safety of the strategic crossroads was in doubt as never before, and with Stuart's finest top lieutenant leading the way in the greatest offensive effort of the day, there "was no organized Union resistance ready to receive the blow," which would be overwhelming.[126]

An officer of McIntosh's Brigade described how "there appeared moving us a large mass of cavalry . . . the remaining portions of Hampton's and Fitzhugh Lee's brigades. They were formed in close column of squadrons. . . . A grander spectacle than their advance has rarely been beheld. They marched with well-aligned front and steady reins. Their polished saber-blades dazzled in the sun. All eyes were turned upon them."[127]

## ᴄ 5 ᴐ

# The Day's Greatest Crisis

## *Custer Leads the Charge of the 1st Michigan Cavalry*

The offensive threat posed by Hampton's sweeping charge in overpowering numbers was the greatest of the day faced by Custer, his Wolverines, and the strategic intersection, but ironically, not only was it not orchestrated by Lee's top cavalryman, but it came without his knowledge. As noted, it was not General Stuart's deliberate decision to engage in a major battle in fighting to gain the crossroads, because he still planned to strike Meade's rear as ordered, and this meant avoiding a lengthy and costly showdown at the crossroads.

Quite simply, the fight for the crossroads had already swirled out of control and had taken on a life of its own until Hampton suddenly found himself leading the day's greatest cavalry charge almost by accident, because Confederate units had been earlier ordered to attack, but not by him, until he had a full-scale battle on his hands.[1]

At this time, and evidently because he was still gaining information from the direction of Meade's rear to the southwest toward the Baltimore Turnpike, Stuart was entirely absent in the last great clash on the East Cavalry Field. In the words of one of his perplexed staff officers: "I watched for the General [Stuart], who I suspected would follow . . . but I did not see him again until after the fighting was over."[2]

The reporter for the *Detroit Free Press* described the tactical setting for the climactic cavalry showdown of the day, writing how the long-range "artillery practice was all that was done [until] the enemy was seen forming in the edge of the woods for a charge."[3] And this was no ordinary Confederate cavalry charge that was pouring down the slope and through the broad fields of farmer Rummel, but one that was calculated to sweep the field clear of Federals and capture the vital crossroads for the all-important attack into the Army of the Potomac's rear, if the stubborn Wolverines and McIntosh's men could be hurled aside.

Knowing he must push the Federals, especially the hard-fighting Michigan troopers who were still the primary guardians of the strategic crossroads, aside now with precious time running out, a frustrated, if not furious, Hampton led eight regiments from Hampton's and Fitzhugh's Brigades in "one final desperate charge [because] if there was any conceivable hope of supporting Pickett by reaching the Union rear, Stuart must initiate his own version of Pickett's charge and force the Yankees from the pathway to his objective."[4]

Consequently, thousands of Rebel cavalry poured down the slope with Rebel yells and colorful flags flying, pushing aside the hard-hit survivors of the 7th Michigan Cavalry. Hardly believing his eyes, one Yankee wrote, "In close columns of squadrons, advancing as if in review, with sabers drawn and glistening like silver in the bright sunlight, the spectacle called forth a murmur of admiration."[5]

Indeed, "not long after 3:30 P.M.—while nearly 13,000 infantrymen were assaulting the midpoint in [Meade's line,] Hampton's intentions were obvious: to sweep his adversaries from the field."[6]

Knowing that everything was now at stake at this point in the afternoon, Custer realized that the decisive moment had come at last, especially now that the 7th Michigan Cavalry's survivors were under heavy pressure, after having been hurled farther down the slope and through the open fields torn by thousands of horses' hooves. Without any hesitation because he now knew that Hampton was launching "Stuart's last blow, Custer determined to parry and riposte."[7]

Captain William Miller, 3rd Pennsylvania Cavalry, described the massive might of Stuart's finest cavalry descending from the high ground with a grim determination to push every trooper in blue aside: "A grander spectacle than their advance has rarely been beheld! They marched with well-aligned fronts and steady reins. Their polished saber-blades dazzling in the piercing rays of a bright summer's sun [and] all eyes turned upon them" and their spectacular advance down the open slopes.[8]

Clearly, Custer faced the day's greatest threat, and it was now a case of do or die. Historian Thom Hatch was not guilty of exaggeration when he made the appropriate analogy that this great mass of cavalry was Stuart's own version of Pickett's Charge.[9]

For this reason and like so many other men on both sides, Captain Miller was overawed by the sight of thousands of the South's finest cavalrymen mounting their supreme offensive effort in a desperate bid to gain the Army of the Potomac's rear, if they could push aside the feisty Custer and his equally feisty Michigan men. He therefore simply concluded with an experienced soldier's fatalism that seemed right on target and unfortunate for the Union: "It seemed folly to resist them."[10]

But Custer was not deterred by the seemingly overpowering onslaught of gray-and-butternut troopers who were steadily descending in overwhelming numbers on the crossroads, nor by the extent of the day's greatest challenge. Once again, Custer demonstrated that the greater the challenge, the more he drew upon inner strength and resolve to rise to meet the day's greatest threat in the most aggressive and hard-hitting manner—the very essence of Custer's personality and most fundamental mind-set, which always brought out the best in him, not only on the battlefield, but also in life in general. Quite simply, Custer needed to overcome what seemed like an unstoppable attack and overwhelming odds, which set the stage to ensure a magnificent personal performance when it seemed like there was no hope or possibility for success.[11]

As mentioned, General Gregg, a kindred spirit, also realized, like Custer, that the best defensive was the tactical offensive in this key situation, when everything was at stake. During the afternoon after his superior's arrival on the field around 1:00 p.m., Gregg and Custer had acted together as a most effective team: a case of two dynamic cavalry officers rising to the challenge, with Gregg watching for tactical opportunities, while Custer was the man on the scene, who delivered that blow in his aggressive style, which was lacking in Gregg at this time. Quite simply, Custer was not only General Gregg's hardest-hitting lieutenant, but also his trusty right arm on July 3. And so now this symbiotic relationship was exactly what was needed by General Meade in facing the greatest cavalry threat of the day in the army's rear.

But General Gregg faced a serious quandary after the repulse of the 7th Michigan Cavalry, because that command had suffered heavy losses, and portions of the regiment had been thrown into panic by so many counterattacking Rebels. At this time, he lacked an adequate number of men, especially fresh troopers, because the fight for possession of the crossroads had escalated steadily. The severely punished 5th and 7th Michigan Cavalry were reeling, with the men needing rest and new supplies of ammunition, while the troopers of the 6th Michigan Cavalry were in formation to protect Pennington's fast-working guns, which had to be closely guarded at all costs now that Stuart's commanders and men had become more aggressive.

The 6th Michigan was now much needed for the attack because it was the largest regiment in the brigade, but such was not the case at this time, because the guns had to be protected. In fact, only the 1st Michigan Cavalry was left as a ready reserve for Gregg and Custer, but the relatively small size of this command made it less than an ideal strategic reserve. However, fortunately, the 1st Michigan was a veteran regiment, and this invaluable seasoned quality, especially in regard to a key combat situation when so much was at stake, was desperately needed in a truly desperate situation, because the Michigan command was badly outnumbered. Therefore, the possession of not only the strategic crossroads, but also the Federal artillery pieces of Pennington's and Randol's Batteries, were under direct threat and in jeopardy at this time. These exposed field pieces might well be lost by the onslaught of the massive concentration of Stuart's cavalry if aggressive action was not soon taken in the form of a desperate counterattack.

With the moment absolutely crucial, General Gregg officially ordered the attack, knowing what had to be done, because no other tactical options remained if the strategic crossroads was to be saved. But of course it was Custer who would lead the charge and do the fighting. No doubt, Gregg was greatly relieved that he possessed a hands-on subordinate, who was every inch a fighter in a crisis situation.

Colonel Charles H. Town of the 1st Michigan barked out orders for his troopers to draw sabers, and hundreds of men instantly obeyed. At this dramatic moment and without any hesitation, Custer naturally took over to lead the way, as in the recent attack of the 7th Michigan. He emphasized to the colonel how "the Seventh Cavalry has broke; I shall have to ask you to charge the Rebels," after he saluted Colonel Town smartly, as if he were on the West Point parade ground. Every inch a fighter, the highly capable Town led the 1st Michigan Cavalry with distinction. But the duty-minded colonel was ailing "in the last stages of consumption," in one trooper's words, and in overall bad shape. In fact, the irrepressible Colonel Mann was now tied to his leather saddle and had to have assistance in mounting his warhorse. But he would not miss the upcoming charge for anything in the world.

Significantly, the colonel's infirmities were not the reason Custer had decided to lead the way in still another charge north across the open plain between Little's Run and the Low Dutch Road. What was most important was that the upcoming cavalry charge had to be as hard hitting as possible to literally save the day by ensuring that Stuart would never capture the crossroads or ride southwest to strike Meade's vulnerable rear. Already, Stuart's largest offensive effort was descending rapidly down the slope, targeting the Union batteries for capture. Clearly, at this time, only a fierce counterattack by Custer and the Wolverines could save the batteries, the crossroads, and the day.

With a diplomatic flair that was all his own, Custer informed the colonel that he would lead the charge against the full might of the approaching gray-and-butternut avalanche of the best cavalry, in terms of experience and overall combat capabilities, in all of the Confederacy. Not discouraged, but fortified by the extent of the escalating crisis, which he faced head-on in true Custer style as on past fields of strife, the new brigadier general with long hair realized that he now confronted a seemingly no-win situation, which only caused him to rise higher to the challenge. As he penned, "The enemy had the advantage of position [high ground and in overall numbers] and were exultant over the repulse of the 7th Michigan Cavalry. All of these acts considered, would seem to render success on the part of the 1st [Michigan] impossible. Not so, however."[12]

Custer also understood that he only possessed the advantages of the high morale and confidence of his men, which were factors that helped to improve the odds to some degree when combined with his own hard-hitting leadership style and tactical skill, especially for the offensive. The journalist for the *Detroit Free Press* had noted the high spirits of the 1st Michigan troopers, who had been well trained in the art of fighting with the saber and unleashing the saber charge. He wrote with insight about how "our troops were panting for a chance to cross sabres with them" at this key moment, when everything was at stake.[13]

In addition and fortunately for the Union at this critical moment, Custer was not only the kind of strong-willed, if not outright contrarian, person who always performed better when the challenge was greatest, but he also relished the spotlight and the greatest place of danger in which he could take center stage. In the words of cavalry officer Captain George B. Sanford, who was right on target with his astute analysis of Custer's personality that made him such an ideal battlefield leader, especially for offensive operations: "He was perfectly reckless in his contempt of danger and seemed to take infinite pleasure in exposing himself" to the greatest risks.[14] Quite simply, Custer had been made for this crucial moment that might well decide the day on the East Cavalry Field, when so much was at stake.

Nevertheless, to all appearances, it seemed that this might well be Custer's "final charge," because he was about to be totally exposed in front of the 1st Michigan Cavalry, while leading the way during another daring attack straight north over the open plain that was nestled between Little's Run on the west and the Low Dutch Road on the east, the crossroads on the south, and the Rummel buildings to the north. After all, Custer was going to lead another daring saber charge like the 7th Michigan Cavalry in a classic case of literally going for broke. Custer had survived the recent saber charge of the 7th Michigan Cavalry, but he was now clearly pushing his luck to an extreme degree in his eagerness to lead the 1st Michigan Cavalry in the attack.[15]

All in all, Custer was about to do more than lead just another headlong cavalry charge across a wide stretch of open ground, because it would take much more than that to defeat Stuart's best men, such as the veterans of Colonel Morgan's crack 1st Virginia Cavalry. Most importantly, when the situation called for bold action, Custer would not only be aggressive, but he would also be on the lookout for exploiting any possible or existing tactical vulnerability among the lengthy lines of Rebel cavalry that continued to surge ever closer to the strategic crossroads.[16]

As noted, at this time, the stiff odds and the chances for any possible success seemed something now entirely out of reach for Custer and his men because of the massive array of Southern cavalry that was descending from higher ground and getting ever closer to the neat formations of the 1st Michigan Cavalry. One astonished Federal, feeling fatalistic and helpless before the Rebel offensive, wrote, "Great heavens! We will all be swallowed up!"[17] Indeed, in facing the concentrated might of Stuart's finest "Invincibles," which steadily advanced, this assignment of stopping the great onslaught seemed like nothing more than "a suicidal mission."[18]

But Custer was not discouraged by the situation or the high odds that had been stacked against him. In fact, he even relished this moment of decision precisely because it was such a critical one, sensing that he could turn the tide in such a key situation by relying on the tactical offensive and his tactical skill. Indeed, at this time, the situation could not have been more crucial. Despite being massed for a maximum offensive effort as designed by Lee, meanwhile, thousands of Confederate infantrymen of Pickett's Charge were about to fail miserably and tragically in the desperate bid to pierce Meade's right-center.

Therefore, it was now left to Stuart's cavalry to strike the key offensive blow. Lee's top lieutenant, General Longstreet, was about to fail the commander in chief like the leader of the Second Corps, General Ewell, who was described by one officer as "a queer character, very eccentric [and of] no very high talent," in their ill-fated offensive efforts on July 3. Therefore, it was still up to General Stuart to hit the Union army's rear to win the day. Quite simply, everything depended on Stuart and his "Invincibles" to win it all, now or never, and only Custer stood in their way.

In consequence, Custer realized that he could not win a decisive victory against such high odds because he would have to defeat the best and most experienced cavalry of the Confederacy, while possessing too few men. However, he realized that he needed to blunt the initiative and momentum of Stuart's maximum offensive effort as much as possible, wearing down the strength and resolve of Lee's famed cavaliers, thwarting and stopping Stuart's offensive effort to yet gain the Army of the Potomac's rear.

Most of all, Custer needed to buy precious time to keep thousands of Rebel cavalry as far away from Meade's vulnerable rear as possible, and for as long as possible. After all, the open and gently sloping ground east of Meade's right-center at the famed Angle and copse of trees—destined to be the apex or "high-water mark" of Pickett's Charge—was a strategic avenue that lay wide open for Stuart and his men: ideal terrain for striking the Army of the Potomac's rear.

Now representing Lee's largest mounted and most mobile strategic reserve in ample numbers and firepower (horse artillery and revolvers), Stuart still possessed the element of surprise, and more than sufficient strength in both cavalry and horse artillery, which would act in the role of "flying artillery" to batter a hole in Meade's rear. Clearly, the threat to the Army of the Potomac's rear could not have been greater. Even more, at this moment on the East Cavalry Field, Custer possessed the chance to prove that the concept of the invincibility of Stuart and his "Invincibles" was a myth, because times had changed for the fortunes of the Union cavalry.

## CUSTER AGAIN AT CENTER STAGE

At this time, Custer presented an especially dashing appearance. He wore a bright red tie around his neck so that his men could identify him on the field in the heat of combat, which made him a conspicuous target to the enemy, but he willingly took this considerable risk. Custer also wore a sailor's blue flannel shirt (acquired from the crew of a gunboat on the James River during the 1862 Peninsula Campaign and worn under his uniform coat) with a wide collar—lighter in color than the uniform coat, which was lined with a double row of gold gilt buttons—with brigadier general's stars. This ad hoc uniform stood out on the battlefield to both friend and foe, as Custer desired for purposes that were uniquely his own.

To complete his distinctive look, he also wore a black felt hat—in the style of a Southern planter's hat—captured from a Confederate soldier to complete his jaunty attire that set him apart from other Yankees. Custer's contrarian nature delighted in the wearing of this Southern hat, appealing to his sense of style and defiance of the traditional uniform of a brigadier general. Custer wore the Southern planter's hat at a jaunty angle that gave him a rakish air. He also wore high and stylish leather boots from a Philadelphia boot maker.

Of course, these distinctive personal touches of the young man represented Custer's core qualities and character, because he was basically flaunting the official uniform regulations of the United States Army to an extraordinary degree and with a deliberate relish that set him apart from the other Army of the Potomac generals, to the great delight of his ever-individualistic men from the ever-individualist West—still another secret of his popularity and magnetic effect that galvanized his Wolverine troopers to even greater exertions on the battlefield against the odds and helped to fuel their already lofty fighting spirit.

At this key moment, which was the turning point of the battle, Custer, "with his long, yellow curls flowing behind him," was positioned at the head of the 1st Michigan Cavalry, because "the Boy General, much to the surprise and admiration of his troops, had decided to lead the 1st Michigan on this dangerous charge [and he] rode in front, where every eye could see him, unsheathed his heavy blade, and trotted forward with his customary bravado."[19] One Michigan trooper, Private J. Allen Bigelow, explained the depth of Custer's popular appeal to the common soldiers, which made them even more determined to follow him to hell and back if necessary: "We followed Custer with his golden locks, and long straight sabre, putting the very devil into" the men.[20]

In a strange way, it was almost as if Custer somehow brought out the most primeval and killer instincts of his fighting men, especially in leading a saber charge that resembled the splendor of ancient combat from times immemorial. One staff officer, Captain George B. Sanford, of another "boy general" (Brigadier General Wesley Merritt, who now commanded the Reserve Cavalry Brigade of Pleasonton's Cavalry Corps), came close to understanding the strength of this analogy and unique symbiotic relationship between the commander and his hard-fighting Wolverines that paid such high dividends on the battlefield, because Custer's distinctive personal look—the blond hair and Nordic features inherited from his blacksmith father—"gave him the appearance of the Vikings of old."[21]

Corporal James Henry Avery never forgot the dramatic moment when "General Custer rode in front of our troops, and with his flag in one hand, and his sabre in the other, ordered us forward, and with a cheer [the Wolverines] rushed to meet the charging rebs," who poured onward in overwhelming numbers and banner flapping under the July sunshine.[22] The journalist of the *Detroit Free Press* described how Custer suddenly "rode to the head [of the 1st Michigan Cavalry] and ordered them forward, they obeyed with a shout [and] both parties advanced at once. It was a glorious sight to see those thousands of horseman, with drawn sabres, rushing at each other, yelling like demons."[23]

In part because the 1st Michigan Cavalry troopers were more experienced than the green boys of the 7th Michigan Cavalry, and since everyone knew that this was a true emergency situation on the East Cavalry Field that represented the battle's climax, this second saber attack of Wolverines led by Custer was destined to be more disciplined and organized, and accelerated at a greater rate as if to match the critical nature of the situation in the Army of the Potomac's rear when so much was at stake.[24]

As noted, this moment could not have been more crucial. In the words of one trooper of the 2nd New York Cavalry who was now with McIntosh's Brigade: "We discovered Stuart's final advance, by Hampton's and Fitz-Hugh Lee's brigades, which Hampton led past McIntosh's dismounted men, charging right up to within about fifty yards of our guns. Believing that, if the guns were taken, there was nothing to prevent the enemy from getting at the reserve artillery and ammunition trains in our rear, it seemed the crisis for us, as it was also about the time Pickett was advancing against the centre of our army's line of battle."[25]

As in only recently having led the 7th Michigan during the first saber charge north and up the same open plain, Brigadier General Custer encouraged the 1st Michigan troopers, who were mostly from the area around Detroit, with his inspirational commanding presence during the attack through the open fields. During another rare saber charge of this war, it clearly took great courage and nerve for the Michigan boys to rush headlong into the gray-and-butternut ranks of the cavalry formations pouring down the open plain between Little's Run on the west and the Low Dutch Road on the east, when now about halfway to the crossroads.

Fortunately for Custer and his 1st Michigan Cavalry troopers in the attack north up the open plain and straight toward the guns booming on Cress's Ridge, the fast-working bluecoat gunners, sweating and grimed in black powder, of the half dozen 3-inch rifles of Captain Pennington's Horse Artillery and four 3-inch rifles of Captain Randol's Horse Artillery, McIntosh's Brigade, picked up the pace at exactly the right time. Consequently, these gunners now performed "like madmen," pouring an avalanche of projectiles into "the cream of Stuart's corps" of veterans. Working at a rapid rate in the intense heat and swirls of whitish smoke, these seasoned Union artillerymen even fired blasts of canister (the cavalryman's nightmare) that ripped through the assault waves of Stuart's so-called "Invincibles."[26]

The journalist of the *Detroit Free Press* described the effectiveness of the Union artillery, which was having its finest day, like Custer and his Wolverines of the Michigan Cavalry Brigade, writing about the key equation that existed from the beginning to the end during the decisive showdown for possession of the strategic crossroads: "The rebels' fire was tremendous as soon as our troops came within range, but our artillery more than compensated for that."[27]

All the while, the finest cavalrymen of both sides continued to surge toward each other at a rapid rate in the open fields and meadows bathed in the early summer sunshine, but Custer's men were heavily outnumbered by at least three or four to one, when they were about to engage in the largest cavalry clash during the three days at Gettysburg—not an optimistic tactical situation and a scenario that seemed to bode ill for Custer and his Wolverines, who would be battling for their lives as much as anything else. But Custer and his 1st Michigan men were not deterred by the extent of the daunting challenge that lay before them.

As could be expected, and like his 1st Michigan Cavalry attackers surging north at a gallop across the open plain situated between the crossroads on the south and the Rummel buildings on the north, Custer felt encouragement at the sight of the initial decimation of Stuart's vanguard attackers when they were swept with canister from Pennington's and Randol's guns, which cut down men and horses in gory piles stained in red. Custer saw the destruction and then the natural hesitation among the hard-hit attackers for the first time, which gave him reason to be more hopeful for success: an inviting tactical opportunity that needed to be exploited in full and as soon as possible. Therefore, issuing a shout that was actually as much a dare and challenge to his men as a war cry when the seemingly endless ranks and dense formations of Stuart's "Invincibles" were only about one hundred yards distant from the onrushing horse soldiers in blue, Custer turned back to the galloping troopers of the 1st Michigan Cavalry and screamed, "Come on, you Wolverines!"[28]

Clearly, Custer was now leading no ordinary cavalry charge over the open plain at this point in time, and hundreds of his determined troopers of the 1st Michigan Cavalry seemed to know as much given the crisis situation. Quite simply, Custer's most daring offensive effort of the day with too few men was the last tactical opportunity to stop Stuart's bid to push aside the defenders, capture the crossroads, and then gain the Army of the Potomac's rear, when everything was at stake on that hot afternoon. Veteran fighting men considered Custer's headlong attack—still another old-fashioned saber charge over the same open plain and straight north as in having led the 7th Michigan Cavalry's saber charge earlier—to have been "the most gallant charge of the war," in the words of dark-haired Colonel Russell A. Alger, who commanded the 5th Michigan Cavalry with great skill on this afternoon of decision.[29]

At this time, one observer never forgot the remarkable sight of Custer, who seemed like a man possessed, leading the way over a wide stretch of open ground with an unprecedented degree of audacity that imbued a sense of awe among onlookers on both sides: "The First Michigan rushed on, Custer four lengths ahead."[30] One of Colonel McIntosh's officers described the importance of Custer's audacious attack at this key moment, because it was delivered at the most crucial possible time, as "the finest thing I witnessed during nearly three years" of fighting for the Union.[31]

A sweat-stained Captain Pennington, Custer's former West Point classmate who performed magnificently on this afternoon, admired the sight while standing beside his guns that continued to roar and inflict damage: "I saw the charge and in all I never saw a more picturesque sight."[32] Lieutenant William Brooke Rawle, 3rd Pennsylvania Cavalry, McIntosh's Brigade, never forgot the sight to the west: "The charge of the 1st Mich. led by Custer himself . . . was the finest thing I witnessed during nearly three years of war."[33]

What now occurred was the mightiest crash of two masses of cavalrymen in the war when the two massive columns of opposing cavalrymen finally ran into each other head-on and clashed in a melee on the open plain situated north of the Hanover Road and south of the Rummel buildings. In the words of Captain Miller, 3rd Pennsylvania Cavalry: "As the two columns approached each other, the pace of each increased, when suddenly a crash, like the falling of timber. . . . So sudden and violent was the collision that many of the horses were turned end over end and crushed their riders beneath them. The clashing of sabers, the demands for surrender, the firing of pistols and cries of the combatants now filled the air" of the Rummel farm.[34]

Because the 1st Michigan Cavalry was a seasoned command, unlike the 7th Michigan Cavalry, which had been trained in the art of delivering a saber assault, it had hit the less disciplined Confederates a harder blow fueled by greater momentum, despite attacking up ascending ground that led to the top of Cress's Ridge. Therefore, the charging horsemen of the 1st Michigan Cavalry cut a wedge through the middle of the dense gray-and-butternut formations, and then charged all the way through their opponents to reach the Rummel farm lane before turning back to reengage the hard-hit Rebels, who were still stunned after having just received the powerful blow from the fiercely fighting Wolverines.[35]

As usual, Custer was in the forefront and in the thick of the hand-to-hand combat that raged beyond all control in the wide open plain. Custer's favorite mount, Roanoke, was shot from under him, and he went flying through the air like a rag doll. But the agile Custer seemed indestructible and extremely lucky in not having been fatally shot or cut down during the combat, while leading two saber charges—first the 7th Michigan Cavalry and then the 1st Michigan Cavalry—nothing less than a minor miracle. Custer quickly jumped to his feet and ran down a mount. Proving that he was a true Wolverine, he then leaped atop the riderless horse to continue fighting beside his troopers to inspire greater exertions against the odds.[36]

One cavalryman in blue admitted, "Such fighting I never saw before" or since.[37] In a letter to his wife in which he revealed a fundamental basis of Custer's popularity and his personal appeal to the common Wolverine soldiers in the ranks, Private Victor E. Comte, a Frenchman in his early thirties, emphasized how during the intense hand-to-hand combat Custer was every inch a fighter, and he "commanded in person [from the front despite the rank of brigadier general] and I saw him plunge his saber into the belly of a rebel who was trying to kill him. You can guess how bravely soldiers fight for such a general."[38]

Meanwhile, the savage combat raged out of control and continued with a will of its own across the open plain that was situated below the Rummel barn. One Michigan trooper swore how this vicious fighting in the open fields, like a famous fight on a Napoleonic battlefield on Europe's central plains, was "the most furious dragoon fight I ever saw or engaged in."[39]

Thanks to the blistering artillery fire that had played a key role in culling the Southerners' ranks before he struck, Custer's charge had ripped a hole into the heart of the sprawling length of Stuart's formations to create a wedge that was driven home by a smaller command into the depths of an overpowering foe like the ancient Spartans, who had battled heroically against the insurmountable odds of the Persian Empire at Thermopylae in 480 BC.[40]

Even more, the 1st Michigan Cavalry's attack also gave new life and confidence to other bluecoats on the field, especially the hard-hit men of the 7th Michigan and McIntosh's troopers, who protected the Low Dutch Road sector. In the words of Private William Glover Gage, Company C, 7th Michigan Cavalry, from a letter that revealed the importance of Custer leading the way in the second Wolverine saber charge of the day: "They [the men of his 7th Michigan Cavalry] did not hold the field until the First [Michigan Cavalry] came to their support [and] I saw about one-half of them rally once but they ran again almost before the [counterattacking] rebel Cavalry got to them."[41]

Clearly, the savage combat had initially been too much for these brave Wolverines, who were learning of the harshness and nightmarish qualities of engaging Stuart's veterans at close range. However, it was quite remarkable that the green troopers of the 7th Michigan Cavalry fought as well as they did, especially having earlier launched their first saber charge, against battle-hardened veterans.

Custer described the charge of the 1st Michigan Cavalry, which covered a good deal of ground in surging north: "I challenge the annals of warfare to produce a more brilliant charge of cavalry."[42]

Custer was not guilty of exaggeration, but the hard-fighting men of the 1st Michigan Cavalry had needed some assistance to prevail because they were so few in number against an experienced and highly motivated opponent, who outnumbered them by three or four to one. While Custer had smashed into the center of Stuart's column and the 1st Michigan boys battled hand-to-hand against Stuart's "Invincibles," he gained timely assistance from resurgent elements of the 5th and 7th Michigan Cavalry—the mostly teenagers of the Wolverine Brigade's youngest regiment—and McIntosh's troopers of a squadron of the 1st New Jersey Cavalry and two squadrons of the 3rd Pennsylvania Cavalry struck the right and left flank of Stuart's assault column.[43] Therefore, Corporal James Henry Avery, with some exaggeration, wrote how the entire "brigade rushed to meet the charging rebs, driving them back in confusion; but they rallied and came again" with a determination to wipe out Custer and his hard-fighting Wolverines.[44]

And as mentioned, the fast-firing two batteries under the dynamic team of Captains Pennington and Randol had played a key role in punishing Stuart's assault formations, exposed in the open fields, during their final descent off the high ground to meet Custer and the 1st Michigan Cavalry in an epic duel of slashing sabers and blazing revolvers.[45] For such reasons, Custer lavishly praised the invaluable role of these fast-firing guns that inflicted so much damage and provided so much timely assistance.[46]

## THE IRREPRESSIBLE HAMPTON WOUNDED

The confusion and dysfunction among Stuart's top lieutenants and their fellow officers created an opportunity that Custer exploited to the fullest. After gaining the upper hand, the Federals, including elements of McIntosh's Brigade that struck the exposed left flank of the attackers from the east, applied heavier pressure on Lee's, Hampton's, and Chambliss's men, while Union artillery sent shells screaming into the Rebel troopers, who were having anything but their finest day.

In fact, it seemed that everything that could go wrong for Southern fortunes was now going wrong. In a desperate situation, Hampton seemed to instinctively realize that this was the last chance to win a decisive victory over the obstinate Wolverines and their young commander, whose experience level—in not only battle but also life—could not come close to matching his older opponent.[47]

Not realizing that Custer and the Wolverines could not be beaten on this afternoon in Meade's right-rear, Hampton was last heard shouting, "Charge them, my brave boys, charge them!"[48]

Corporal James Henry Avery described how during this "desperate fight" to the death, "Major [Luther S.] Trowbridge of the Fifth, had his horse shot under him, and being likely to be taken prisoner, Billy Dunn of Company I, gave him his horse, and was himself taken prisoner."[49]

During the melee with Custer's and McIntosh's troopers, Hampton was slashed on the head by a Federal saber. Fortunately, the blow was cushioned by the brigadier general's slouch hat and thick hair, or skull, as his critics said. Rebel horsemen then rode up to the bleeding general and used reason and exaggeration to finally break off the bitter combat: "General, General, they are too many; for God's sake leap your horse over the fence."[50] In his journal, Corporal James Henry Avery, 5th Michigan Cavalry, described how the resurgent Rebels, howling like demons, were "repulsed a second and third time," when Hampton was a guiding spirit of Rebel resistance and resolve to capture the crossroads.[51]

But Hampton's fight was finally over for the day. In one bound in clearing the fence, he escaped, but not before a bullet struck him in the side. Clearly, it was not a good day for Hampton, who had taken a beating in more than one way, and his hard-hit brigade lost more good men in this ill-fated campaign north of the Potomac than any other cavalry brigade in Lee's army.[52]

Fortunately for Custer and his 1st Michigan Cavalry boys, as noted, they had received timely assistance when elements of McIntosh's fresh brigade struck Hampton's flanks, especially on the east. Colonel Alger, who led the 5th Michigan Cavalry in his fourth offensive effort, also assisted in timely fashion by hitting Hampton's right flank in conjunction with not only McIntosh's men, but also portions of the 6th and 7th Michigan Cavalry.[53]

And, of course, Pennington's and Randol's guns, especially when blasting away with canister with the Rebels so close, had also played a key role in decimating the attackers of the final charge. Again, Custer could not have possessed more effective artillery support on this day of destiny, and he benefited immensely.[54]

But all the while, Stuart's artillerymen blazed away at the Yankees from their high-ground perch. Corporal James Henry Avery described a close call from the fire of Rebel artillerymen, who possessed an excellent and wide field of fire: "I noticed a cannon smoke in front, and a little to the left [on the southern spur of Cress's Ridge]; the ball came past my horse's head, brushed my knee, and struck the man beside me, tearing his leg and passing through his horse, rolling them together on the ground."[55]

The reporter for the *Detroit Free Press* described the fierce combat and then the moment of a sparkling success—more due to Custer's stirring performance than any other Union officer on the field—when the Confederates "were broken [and then] followed by our troops to the very edge of the woods. Here they reformed and our men fell back only to form and charge. This was repeated some four times, when the enemy [finally] broke and fled in the wildest confusion, while our victorious boys followed, sabring them down without mercy to the very muzzles of their guns" on the high ground.[56]

Caught in the swirl of the savage combat, Sergeant B. J. Haden, 1st Virginia Cavalry, described the unique nature of this contest, which was quite unlike any other cavalry fight of the war: "The fight . . . raged with fury [but] mounted fights never lasted long, but there were more men killed and wounded in this fight than I ever saw on any field where the fighting was done mounted. I shall not attempt to say who got the better of this engagement, as they seemed to mutually agreed to quit. One party [Stuart] afraid to advance, and the other [Custer] glad of it."[57]

Custer also emphasized how Stuart's men only briefly resisted the onslaught until overpowered and forced to flee the fiercely fighting Federals, who simply could not be beaten by the finest cavalrymen of the Confederacy: "For a moment, but only a moment, that long, heavy column stood its ground; then, unable to withstand the impetuosity of our attack, it gave way in a disorderly rout, leaving vast numbers of dead and wounded in our possession, while the First, being masters of the field, had the proud satisfaction of seeing the much-vaunted chivalry, led by their favorite commander, seek safety in headlong flight."[58]

Commanding Company K, 3rd Virginia, Captain Richard H. Watkins described in a letter to his wife about the final clash of cavalry in the Army of the Potomac's rear and why it had so suddenly concluded: "On the 3rd we (the Cavalry) engaged the cavalry of the enemy on our left wing & had a very severe engagement, finally repulsing them but finding that they are supported by infantry could gain no advantage" over the Union cavalry and highly effective guns of the horse artillery, especially Captain Pennington's Battery of six 3-inch guns.[59]

Henry Matthews, a member of the Stuart Horse Artillery, summarized how at long last "the fierce attack of the Federals [1st Michigan Cavalry] was broken at last [and] both forces withdrew to the lines held at the opening of the fight" for the strategic crossroads.[60]

But Custer was determined to only withdraw to better defensive ground after he ascertained that Stuart's threat was over for good. Custer rallied the troopers of the 1st Michigan and re-formed them in line, just in case another Confederate attack was suddenly forthcoming by Rebels troopers charging off the high ground and out of the darkened forests atop Cress's Ridge. Once he had determined that Stuart's threat to the strategic crossroads no longer existed, Custer then led what was left of the bloodied troopers of the 1st Michigan Cavalry, "with defiant deliberation, to the rear," with the satisfaction of having completed his vital mission.[61]

"At the close of the battle General Gregg had a reserve of one strong brigade which had hardly been engaged at all, and which was drawn up ready for action in full view of the Confederate position [while General] Stuart had no fresh troops with which to renew the fight," wrote Major Henry Brainerd McClellan of the general's staff.[62]

After Custer withdrew his men off the body-strewn plain like a protective mother who looked closely after the welfare of her children, General Stuart and his trusty staff officer, Major McClellan, had surveyed the field. They were shocked by the carnage and the large number of dead and wounded cavalrymen. In the major's words: "After the fighting had ceased, I accompanied Stuart as he rode over part of the field in the vicinity of the [Rummel] barn, and often in close rifle range of it. We were the only horsemen visible on the plain. The fire from the opposing batteries passed over our heads; and we were so much endangered by the premature explosion of shells from our own guns, that I at length ventured to expostulate with him for what I considered an unnecessary exposure of his person."[63]

Because of the high losses in manpower and the wasting of so much precious time in battling Custer and his tough Wolverines, Stuart had belatedly called off the fight at the East Cavalry Field with the grim knowledge that he had failed miserably in his most crucial mission of striking Meade's rear in conjunction with Pickett's Charge. That awful realization for the most famed and proudest cavalry leader in the Army of Northern Virginia resulted from absolute exhaustion, high losses, and utter frustration after the last and best Confederate offensive effort sputtered to an inglorious conclusion in a massive clash of cavalry that Lee and Stuart had never wanted. Stuart had been defeated in an open-field fight and thwarted in every possible way. He rode away with no laurels or victories because the best efforts of Stuart and his top lieutenants had been wasted and were in vain. However, in the end, this monumental failure can best be explained by who Stuart had primarily faced on this day of destiny.

Indeed and most of all, a young brigadier general named George Armstrong Custer had stood in his way and refused to relinquish the initiative and the strategic crossroads to Stuart. With so much at stake on July 3, a full-scale cavalry engagement on the Rummel farm—like at Brandy Station—had proved to be entirely counterproductive for the men of the South and the last outcome that Stuart and his men had expected or even imagined for that matter. Ironically, General Stuart, the South's greatest cavalier and one of its most iconic heroes, had failed General Lee and the army when a sparkling success was needed the most. Stuart had once proclaimed with his usual bravado: "All I ask of fate is that I may be killed leading a cavalry charge."[64]

But in regard to General Stuart, there were far too many forthcoming dances, pretty girls, and acclaim to be sacrificed on the altar of leading a heroic charge and dying at its head, especially if it was doomed like at Gettysburg; a sentiment not shared by Custer, who had gone for broke as never before on July 3, and this meant having repeatedly risked his life. Despite his brave words that had garnered so much admiration, Stuart never led a cavalry charge either on the East Cavalry Field or into Meade's rear as envisioned on the night of July 2 at Lee's headquarters. In fact, his top lieutenants and staff officers believed that he had "disappeared" and had failed to locate Stuart for an extended period of time. When his presence was needed for such a key role in leading from the front because so much was at stake on July 3, Stuart was not there to lead the way to any kind of victory like Custer on the all-important third day at Gettysburg.[65]

Instead, Stuart simply came off the field when he realized that Custer and his hard-fighting Wolverines could not be beaten. This no doubt was an easy response because the East Cavalry Field was the site of his greatest defeat and humiliation (even more than Brandy Station) in overall strategic terms, because of the supreme importance of his vital role to "wreak havoc on a grand scale" in Meade's rear when facing Pickett's Charge. After all, by this time, "Stuart was also well aware that Lee's effort to break through Meade's center had ended badly."[66]

Brigadier General Hampton, whose bitter resentment toward the highly respected nephew of General Lee only increased at Gettysburg, blamed the defeat on Fitzhugh Lee, who had prematurely initiated the Confederate offensive effort by his unordered and unauthorized charge. This offensive effort had set the stage for an escalation of the fighting that resulted in a full-scale battle, which was something that Stuart and Hampton had never wanted in the first place, because a larger and more important mission had been assigned to them by General Lee at the Widow Thompson house: the striking of the vulnerable rear of the Army of the Potomac in conjunction with Pickett's Charge.[67]

But far more than Brigadier General Fitzhugh Lee, Major General Stuart was actually the true architect of the failure on that day, born of overconfidence and hubris that had been created in 1861 and 1862, before the arrival of a new day with the enhanced superiority of the Union cavalry now led by younger and more aggressive commanders. Custer was only the most shining example of this key development that heralded the dawn of a new dispensation for the much-maligned Union cavalry of the Army of the Potomac.

But this central weakness of the famed Southern cavalry arm of the most successful army in the annals of American military history would not have been so fully exploited by any ordinary Union cavalry commander on the third day at Gettysburg in Meade's right-rear. Indeed, in the end, Stuart simply was unable "to foresee a young general who might lead a suicidal attack on him and stop him with a far smaller force. He failed to anticipate Custer, and that was to be his undoing."[68]

All in all, Custer was the true architect of the final victory that was won on the East Cavalry Field, because he had thwarted and stopped Stuart, who possessed a superior force, when time was of the essence. In the end, because of the combination of Custer's aggressiveness and tactical skill, Stuart "had missed the narrow window of opportunity" to strike the Army of the Potomac's rear, when it had been the most vulnerable during the unleashing of Pickett's Charge.[69]

But Stuart had missed this golden opportunity because of the superior performance of Custer and his tough Michigan men, who proved to be elite fighting men on July 3. As Custer penned without exaggeration in regard to the aggressive role of himself and the 1st Michigan Cavalry: "I challenge the annals of warfare to produce a more brilliant or successful charge of cavalry" in this war.[70] By his own heroics and leading of two daring saber charges of highly motivated Wolverines who surged forth with sabers in hand, Custer had saved not only Captain Pennington's Battery of a half dozen guns, but also Captain

Randol's Battery in a true crisis situation, an appropriate development because these fast-firing and accurate guns had saved the lives of so many Michigan boys throughout the afternoon.[71] Like his surviving comrades, a member of the 6th Michigan Cavalry described how this great cavalry clash in the Army of the Potomac's rear at Gettysburg—a suitable mounted counterpart to Pickett's Charge—was nothing less than "the hardest Battle of the war."[72]

For ample good reason, Major General George Gordon Meade fully understood and, therefore, greatly appreciated the splendid performance of Custer and his Wolverines and what had happened in the rear of his defensive line that spanned such a long distance north–south down Cemetery Ridge's length: "Meanwhile, during the time of Lee's assault [known as Pickett's Charge], General Gregg had won an extremely important cavalry engagement with General Stuart on the right of the Union line of battle. While Stuart was proceeding toward the Baltimore Pike [and toward Gettysburg], where he hoped to create a Diversion in aid of the Confederate infantry [of Pickett's Charge], and, in case of Pickett's success, to fall upon the retreating Federal troops, he encountered Gregg, who was guarding the right flank of the Federal army, and was well out of the path of Stuart's movement. The contest was fast and furious, with the result that Stuart was compelled to fall back."[73]

In his diary, one enlisted man of the 6th Michigan Cavalry echoed Meade's words about the climactic nature of the great clash on the East Cavalry Field. He wrote, "This was the most furious dragoon fight I ever saw or engaged in."[74] Custer's report was full of lavish praise and heartfelt thanks for the remarkable performance of the 1st Michigan Cavalry: "I cannot find language to express my high appreciation of the gallantry and daring displayed by the officers and men of the First Michigan cavalry. They advanced to the charge of a vastly superior force with as much order and precision as if going upon parade" back in Michigan.[75]

A New York trooper of Gregg's Second Cavalry Division concluded in regard to the last shot fired in anger on the East Cavalry Field, where everything had been at stake: "This ended General Gregg's cavalry fight at Gettysburg, the fortunate outcome of which undoubtedly contributed greatly to the victory" at Gettysburg.[76]

Ironically, in contrast to General Meade's words, the importance of the intensity of the cavalry combat that swirled in the Union rear cannot always be found in the ranks of the common soldiers of Stuart's cavalry, because striking the Army of the Potomac's rear was a secret plan that had been recently developed between Lee and Stuart at the Widow Thompson house on the night of July 2, and its secrecy was well guarded. These men knew nothing of Stuart's conference with Lee at the Widow Thompson house on the night of July 2, nor the specific orders given by the army's commander. Captain

Watkins, Company K, 3rd Virginia Cavalry, said in a July 18 letter to his wife that was not far from the truth: "I reckon you know more of the particulars of the Gettysburg fight than I do."[77]

In a strange way, it was almost as if Stuart and his men wanted to most of all forget about the Gettysburg campaign and its long list of failures, especially their dismal defeat on July 3, and as soon as possible. After all, Stuart and his men had failed Lee, who had delegated too much authority to his subordinates, especially his top lieutenant, Longstreet. As usual, he had embraced the vain hope for the best in what was essentially an audacious leadership gamble. These men, who possessed sterling reputations, failed Lee and let the army down—and badly—in a disastrous and miserable performance, despite their best efforts, or reluctant efforts as in Longstreet's case. Likewise, and despite Stuart's recent disastrous raid that had garnered no positive results, Lee had gambled on his top cavalry commander "to clinch the victory" and lost his high-stakes bet that was calculated to win it all.[78] In the end, perhaps a Union soldier said it best in a letter that explained why Stuart's final offensive effort failed in Meade's rear: An overconfident Lee "supposed he could walk right over the Army of the Potomac" and young brigade commanders like Custer.[79]

This kind of overly optimistic thinking was basically Lee's own view about what thousands of his infantrymen, especially the fresh troops of Pickett's Division of three Virginia brigades, could achieve before Meade's right-center on Cemetery Ridge, which equaled what he thought his cavalry under Stuart, despite his recent failures at Brandy Station and his overly long and pointless raid, could accomplish on the ridge's other side. One modern historian, despite the cost of Stuart's failure on the third day, wrote how "both parties [of cavalry forces] withdrew to their original lines. Scattered over the fields adjacent to the Rummel barn 181 of Stuart's cavalrymen lay dead. Stuart, Fitz Lee, Hampton . . . had done all they could, but it wasn't enough to overtake Gregg's force and gain access to the Federal rear as Lee had hoped."[80] A saddened Lieutenant Colonel Witcher described the frightful cost of Stuart's failures: "I shall never, no never forget [when I] saw with tears in my eyes, my brave fellows from away over the mountains in West Virginia, laid out in windrows, torn and bleeding" from some of the most fierce cavalry fighting of the Civil War.[81]

A member of the 5th Michigan Cavalry also realized the decisiveness of the struggle on the East Cavalry Field, writing how Custer and his men had successfully thwarted "the much larger force of Stuart's Cavalry in their determined effort to break through our lines and get to our trains."[82] Like other members of the Union cavalry corps, Lieutenant Willard W. Glazier was worried about the fate of the ammunition and supply wagons of the Army of the

Potomac, writing about "Stuart, who had hoped to break in upon our flank and rear, and to pounce upon our trains" behind the Round Tops.[83]

Indeed, General Meade and his men along Cemetery Ridge had been concerned for the overall safety of "our ammunition and other trains [that] had been parked in rear of Round Top, which gave them splendid shelter" from the attacks of Lieutenant General "Old Bull" Longstreet's First Corps on the afternoon of July 2.[84] A New York trooper of Gregg's Division who witnessed Custer in action on the East Cavalry Field emphasized that "General Gregg's division was, at this suggestion, moved to a position farther to the right and rear, to guard against the enemy's breaking through to where our reserve artillery and ammunition were parked."[85]

But in truth, these ammunition and supply trains were only a secondary target, because they could be captured after the Army of the Potomac was destroyed at will and with impunity during Lee's greatest offensive effort from two directions, if in fact they had succeeded at this. Indeed, most of all, Stuart's mission was to strike Meade's rear in conjunction with Pickett's Charge to inflict a decisive blow, not to capture wagons.[86] After all, Stuart had already learned about the folly of not capturing wagons during his recent raid that had removed him from his vexed commander and the Army of Northern Virginia for an extended period of time, an absence that had helped to set the stage for the Battle of Gettysburg. Confederate leaders, especially Lee, were not at all impressed on the night of July 2 when General Stuart "brought with him 200 wagons and 1,200 horses and mules [all of which slowed Stuart's movements to a crawl when time was of the essence], captured in the vicinity of Washington city," penned one Rebel cavalryman in his diary.[87]

## BITTER AFTERMATH

In the end, the total number of casualties from the East Cavalry Field contest had been "moderately heavy on both sides," and for Stuart, "who had failed to reach the rear of Meade's army, there was no gain whatsoever."[88] Perhaps historian Ken Allers Jr. said it best, writing how in regard to the bitter end of the dramatic showdown of thousands of cavalrymen that was played out on the East Cavalry Field: "For Stuart, it was an ignominious end of a dreadful campaign."[89]

For ample good reason, Stuart felt not only humiliation in having suffered his greatest reversal but also considerable anger because he had failed when handed his most important assignment of the war by General Lee. After all, he had failed miserably to vanquish the Union cavalry and strike the Army of the Potomac's rear in conjunction with Pickett's Charge. Therefore,

Stuart's mood was extremely foul and even vengeful. The Widow Mary Thompson recalled to a Philadelphia newspaperman in September 1863 her thoughts of General Stuart, after he had rejoined Lee at this headquarters—her stone house atop Seminary Ridge just west of town—after his greatest failure of the war: "The impression which she had of him was not favorable. Stuart wanted to enter Gettysburg, and burn and make an indiscriminate plunder of all property, but to this Gen. Lee would not consent. She thought Stuart was a bad man" in consequence.[90]

Captain Charles Minor Blackford, 2nd Virginia Cavalry, concluded in a July 18, 1863, letter to his wife about the much-celebrated Virginia-born commander, who had played a large role in the Confederate defeat throughout the course of the all-important Gettysburg campaign, when Lee and the army simply could not afford to have committed so many glaring mistakes and misjudgments when no margin of error had existed: "General Stuart is much criticized for his part in our late campaign. . . . During his many reviews at Culpeper he was said to have twelve thousand cavalry ready for duty. He crossed the [Potomac] river with six thousand, but they played a small part in the great drama either as the 'eyes of the army' or any other capacity. In his anxiety to 'do some great thing' General Stuart carried his men beyond the range of usefulness and Lee was not thereafter kept fully informed as to the enemy's movements as he should have been, or as he would have been had Stuart been nearer at hand."[91]

Captain Blackford, of course, meant an offensive role when he lamented that Stuart failed to play a significant role at Gettysburg, when Lee had needed every available man to rise to the occasion on July 3.[92] Major Henry Brainerd McClellan, of Stuart's staff, concluded with some bitterness: "The result of this battle shows that there is no probability that Stuart could successfully have carried out his intention of attacking the rear" of the Union army, because of the aggressive and high quality of Union leadership, especially Custer, but also General Gregg.[93]

Significantly, the nightmarish combat that had raged across the East Cavalry Field, and Custer's magnificent performance, demonstrated that the most popular concept about Stuart's cavalry was a myth. In the words of British observer Arthur Fremantle, who mocked Stuart and his cavalrymen and their overall ineffective way of waging war that certainly was not appropriate for the final day at Gettysburg as demonstrated by Custer leading the way in two saber charges: "These cavalry fights are miserable affairs. Neither party has any idea of serious fighting with the sabre. They approach one another with considerable boldness, until they get to within about forty yards, and then, at the very moment when a dash is necessary, and the sword alone should be used, they hesitate, halt, and commence a desultory fire with carbines and revolvers."[94]

Indeed, the intense combat that had taken place between opposing cavalry in Meade's right-rear on the afternoon of July 3 was the most important battle of the Civil War, in which the cavalrymen on both sides had principally relied upon the saber, as in the days of Napoleon during a bygone and more romantic age, to demonstrate the falseness of Fremantle's words.[95]

## AMERICA'S GREATEST KILLING FIELD

Reflecting the leading role played by Custer and his Wolverine Brigade on the crucial third day, the Michigan Cavalry Brigade suffered the lion's share of the losses at nearly 90 percent of Gregg's casualties: an astounding 219 men out of 254 total losses.[96] In writing back to the people of Michigan on July 4, the special correspondent to the *Detroit Free Press* presented the grim news to the home folk about the high cost of Custer's last attack that had turned the tide: "The First Michigan had four Captains and two Lieutenants wounded, and four of them taken prisoner, one of whom afterwards escaped."[97]

This correspondent, who had seen what happened on July 3, gave credit where it was due like Custer, who lavishly spread the praise where it was deserved: "In all this desperate fighting the noble old First was first to advance and the last to fall back."[98] But perhaps General Stuart said it best in regard to the high sacrifice that was necessary for victory: "The 34th [Virginia Cavalry Battalion led by Witcher] had made the worse massacre of [Colonel Russell A.] Alger's command [6th Michigan Cavalry, but actually this was the 7th Michigan Cavalry, under Colonel William D. Mann, that had lost the most men in the Wolverine Brigade] and had piled more dead and wounded men and horses on as little space as . . . ever seen on any field."

Clearly, Custer's "Michigan Brigade paid a steep price for besting America's best cavalryman [because] the First and Fifth lost about fifty men; the Sixth lost fewer than a dozen; and the Seventh about one hundred—25 percent of the regiment's strength" on July 3.[99] In the analysis of Edward G. Longacre: "Official casualty figures for the Michigan Cavalry Brigade in the fighting on July 3 are largely incorrect [because] Custer enumerated the command's losses" for the entire Gettysburg campaign.[100]

However, Custer's losses of 219 were not only correct, but also significant, because they represented "more than six times as many casualties as General Gregg's Second Cavalry Division suffered on the third . . . the Wolverines' losses testify to the severity of the contest and the scope of the brigade's commitment to a critical phase of a pivotal battle."[101] Captain Daniel H. Darling, who commanded Company C, 7th Cavalry, emphasized in a letter with sadness how the regiment lost "many killed and wounded" in this "fierce engagement."[102] Lieutenant Colonel Witcher was proud of the fact that his Virginia mountaineer boys had fired with such great accuracy that they succeeded in "covering the ground with the killed and wounded" Wolverines.[103]

Custer's two audacious saber charges—first the 7th Michigan and then the 1st Michigan—in which he had bravely led the way north up the open plain, saved the day by stopping Stuart and his lofty ambitions of striking the Army of the Potomac's rear, while saving not only the strategic crossroads but also the artillery commanded by Captains Pennington and Randol. Because of his aggressiveness in key turning-point situations during the dramatic showdown on the East Cavalry Field, Custer had lost not a gun or a regimental battle flag in an amazing accomplishment, which represented a future trend that was destined to continue throughout the war.[104] More importantly, Custer had demonstrated in full and in convincing fashion that the lofty reputation and name of Stuart's "Invincibles" was something of the past and no more.[105]

As noted, the cost to the hard-fighting Wolverines was frightfully high, creating widows and orphans across Michigan. Writing his column that appeared under the heading "From the Michigan Cavalry," the special correspondent of the *Detroit Free Press* lamented to the people of Michigan, "Our loss was heavy."[106] After narrowly surviving the holocaust at Gettysburg, one Michigan soldier penned in a letter how "the battlefield of Gettysburg was one vast slaughter pen. Dead & wounded lay in all directions. A man that went through the carnage unhurt may call himself a lucky man."[107]

Some of the finest men and officers of this incredibly tough and resilient Wolverine Brigade were no more. Handsome and dashing Colonel Russell A. Alger, who led the 6th Michigan Cavalry with great courage and distinction, and the survivors of the Michigan Cavalry Brigade especially lamented the loss of Major Noah Henry Ferry, 5th Michigan Cavalry. He was buried on the field after having been killed with a bullet through the head. In Alger's heartfelt words: "Every moment brings a sad gloom over all our hearts for the noble Ferry."[108] Even the Confederates rejoiced in the killing of the inspirational Ferry, who fought like a demon and inspired his Wolverines to heroics. Lieutenant Colonel Witcher's Virginia men killed Ferry, and their commander noted that his men triumphed over the boys of the 5th Michigan Cavalry in no small part because they succeeded in "killing its Major."[109] To his credit, Witcher praised Major Ferry as a most worthy opponent, who was "a gallant and heroic" who gave his life for his country.[110]

And no one had been luckier than Custer on July 3. He had at least one horse shot from under him while leading the charge of the 1st Michigan Cavalry. And one trooper "heard him remark after the fight that he would have been captured except for the fact that one of his buglers [either Joseph Fought or Peter Boehn] caught a horse for him and held off the man who wanted him to surrender."[111]

Indeed, Custer survived a number of close calls in leading two saber charges and then in the hand-to-hand combat that raged through the open fields. In the years ahead, the legendary phenomenon known as "Custer's Luck" was destined to continue to thrive unabated, until he and his five ill-fated companies of the 7th Cavalry rode with unbridled confidence—like Stuart's men when they rode into the East Cavalry Field—into the timbered valley of the Little Bighorn. A good number of impressive victories and glory lay in the future for Custer, especially in 1865. He had demonstrated his winning ways and outstanding promise on July 3, which was only the beginning of one of the most remarkable careers of any officer of not only the Army of the Potomac, but also the North.

Meanwhile, General Stuart was fated for future defeats and an unnecessary 1864 death on a Virginia battlefield just north of Richmond in a fight of relatively little importance, especially when compared to Gettysburg. Ironically, Stuart's reputation would have been largely preserved if he had been killed on July 3. That dark future for Lee's most famous cavalryman had been forecast by what happened during the Gettysburg campaign, when Stuart performed at his worst.

Nevertheless, General Stuart continued to bask in the romance and unimportant absurdities of the pageantry of war as if it was still 1861, and as if he was an ancient crusader on the long march to the Middle East to win victories for God and country during the struggle in the Holy Land to gain possession of the sacred city of Jerusalem. In an insightful and extremely diplomatic letter to his wife, Susan Leigh Blackford, that revealed Stuart's ever-growing central character flaws, which had reached a high point in the 1863 campaign and partly explained why Lee's famed cavalry leader had performed so poorly in repeated fashion, Captain Charles Minor Blackford, an older and more mature man than the flamboyant Stuart, wrote, "I was much amused to see Stuart pass through Martinsburg [Virginia] with a large cavalcade of staff and couriers and two buglers blowing most furiously. Lee, Hill, Ewell and Longstreet [the last three were all corps commanders] respectively passed the point at which I was standing, each with one or two persons with them and not even a battleflag to make their rank [and Stuart] rode up to The Bower, (Mr. Dandridge's), with the same pomp and show. I scarcely like to write this of so gallant an officer, but all of us have some weaknesses and should be very liberal to each other."[112]

And of course General Lee's own personal weaknesses, an overconfidence that bordered on hubris and an excessive delegation of authority to his top lieutenants during the war's most important campaign, had also played their part in paving the way for Stuart's defeat behind the Army of the Potomac on July 3. Lee's fatal delegation of far too much authority and discretion to General Stuart, which resulted in his ill-fated raid and denied him the benefit of his most dependable "eyes and ears" during the first two days at Gettysburg, was simply inexcusable on every level.

Handed the opportunity by the army's commander, Stuart, like a kid in a candy store, eagerly took full advantage of the broad latitude that Lee had bestowed upon him. Therefore, he had raided to his heart's content as if the Southern army deep in enemy territory would never become engaged in the most decisive battle of the war, while riding nearly to the outskirts of the heavily fortified Washington, DC, for little gain—a disastrous scenario that also helped to lay the groundwork for Stuart's failure on July 3.

When General Lee had needed to keep Stuart close at hand, he had let him go in what can only be described as an irresponsible manner that was not only shortsighted, but also entirely too risky under the circumstances. Because of the wearing down of men and horses for nearly a week and a half because Lee had given his blessing and permission to conduct this wide-ranging raid, Stuart and his cavalry were in extremely poor shape to perform their assigned mission on the third day at Gettysburg.[113]

## THE GREAT SILENCING

First and foremost, there was absolutely no reason for Lee and Stuart to put anything at all in their official reports about one of the greatest Confederate failures by the South's primary leaders and heroes (themselves) that had a decisive impact on the most important battle of the war. Of course, the primary reason was obvious, because nearly two more years were left in the war, and the already severely damaged resolve of the Southern people needed to be kept high in the wake of the two reversals at Vicksburg and Gettysburg. This great silencing was necessary to preserve the long-existing myths about the superiority of the Southern cavalry and Stuart, because the Union cavalry had now become dominant on the battlefield for the first time in the war in what was nothing less than a remarkable transformation. Two central Southern myths—the superiority of Confederate cavalry and the inevitability of winning the war—had to be kept alive by the top leadership, especially Lee, and this fact has obscured the ambitious plan for Stuart's cavalry to strike into the rear of the Army of the Potomac.

The 1966 movie *The Blue Max* presented an insightful view of the detailed interworking and personal dynamics of the upper-class elite of the German officer corps, especially when it came to reinforcing a people's morale during the dark days of World War I. But what was most intriguing was this fascinating story about not only the rise but also the fall of a young, fiercely ambitious pilot named Lieutenant Bruno Stachel, the main character, who was played by actor George Peppard.

A former German infantryman who had survived the slaughter of trench warfare on the western front, he was a commoner who aspired to escape a tragic lower-class fate—wounding, maiming, or death in the nightmarish trenches. Therefore, after his transfer to one of Germany's elite flying squadrons that ruled the skies over war-torn France, he had to endlessly prove himself to aristocratic superiors and haughty comrades of the old nobility, including wealthy counts of the upper crush, to prove his worth and equality—a situation that fueled his ambitious and relentless pursuit of his nation's highest military decoration for valor, the Blue Max medal.

With Germany's defeat in 1918, which had been inevitable after the fresh manpower and military might of industrialized America entered the war, this well-directed movie ended in an especially spectacular and memorable manner. Stachel, a member of the lower class and a former infantry private, was set up by his aristocratic and elitist superior to die in a test flight of a dangerous new monoplane that the count ordered the young airman to fly before a large crowd, because he knew it would be a fatal and final flight that would end his controversial career, which was about to become scandalous due to an upcoming exposure. As the count realized, the beleaguered German nation, on the brink of defeat, needed heroes, not scandals, to inspire the people, who had been at war since August 1914. Therefore, Stachel's death was cleverly orchestrated by top German leadership for the overall good of the nation and the unblemished reputation of the German officer corps, whose image must remain stainless.

In much the same way, so the beleaguered Confederacy and its war-weary people needed heroes and not scandals to tarnish the reputation of the army and the Confederate officer corps, especially in regard to who was responsible for the decisive defeat at Gettysburg and the last northern invasion by the Army of Northern Virginia, which needed victory north of the Potomac to survive. After all, Lee's failure in his second invasion on northern soil eliminated the future possibility of achieving decisive success over the Army of the Potomac in this war of attrition. And the new superiority of the Union cavalry and dynamic commanders like Custer were other factors that pointed the way to the bitter end for this fabled army at Appomattox Court House.

Indeed, Lee's decisive defeat at Gettysburg was a monumental setback, representing a wasted opportunity and one that would never come again for the steadily declining combat capabilities of the Army of Northern Virginia in 1864–1865. Only one day after Lee's and Stuart's failures on the third day at Gettysburg, the strategic bastion of Vicksburg on the "Father of Waters" surrendered to General Ulysses S. Grant, who proved that he was the ultimate hard-nosed fighter and brilliant strategist in the western theater. Not only the loss of the key city on the east bank of the Mississippi River to divide the Confederacy in two, but also an entire army was lost for the South on that fateful July 4, 1863, only one day after Stuart's failure to strike Meade's rear the day before.

These twin defeats in the western and eastern theaters were devastating blows from which the Confederacy never recovered, ordaining the South's ultimate fate. Therefore, the two strategic setbacks in Pennsylvania and Mississippi were so great that the very last thing the reeling South needed was the morale-damaging exercise of finger-pointing and accusations, especially formal charges, against those top Confederate officers who were most responsible for the failure at Gettysburg. Above all else, morale-sapping scandals needed to be avoided at this time.

At this low point in Confederate fortunes during the darkest summer in the nation's young lifetime, Southern leadership, especially Lee, could not afford to lay blame for defeat at Gettysburg, regardless of how grievous the mistakes made by leadership. And, of course, under such circumstances, this situation especially applied to laying blame on one of the most cherished national heroes of the Confederacy, who had become an icon across the nation. First and foremost during this tragic summer for Confederate fortunes, Lee had to seriously think about doing whatever was best for his beleaguered country—now on the road to decisive defeat—and what was most of all necessary to bolster the will of the people, which called for doing whatever was possible to eliminate dissension and divisions that would inevitably sap the strength of the war effort.

In this situation in which the domestic and political consensus was all important for the nation's survival, General Lee naturally took all blame for the decisive defeat at Gettysburg in the proper Virginia gentleman tradition, and, of course, with these key considerations in mind. Stuart garnered no blame for what happened on July 3, because the East Cavalry Field fight and why it was so important were simply covered up and quickly forgotten.

But of course and in truth, this rightful allocation of blame was simply not the case, because Lee's top lieutenants, from Longstreet to Stuart, had let him down on both sides of Cemetery Ridge. Lee was not the primary person to blame, although he certainly made his fair share of mistakes that paved the way to defeat. So who was the most responsible for the Confederate defeat at Gettysburg? During the postwar period, James Longstreet garnered most of the blame, but largely for political reasons since he became a Republican. Stuart drew far less blame than Longstreet, and it was mostly for his ill-fated raid. Most revealing, however, Stuart never gained the rank of lieutenant general from Lee, and for ample good reason, which has provided a hint of the extent of his dismal performance at Gettysburg. But because of political and domestic reasons, Lee simply could not point his finger at Stuart. Instead and as noted, he took all the blame for defeat, and Stuart's monumental failure on the critical third day has been overlooked and ignored for generations.

Therefore, the case can be made—as in regard to a central thesis of this book—that Lee's top lieutenant was most responsible for the Confederate defeat, and the main culprit for missing a golden opportunity of striking Meade's rear with a surprise attack was the South's greatest cavalry leader, General Stuart. Ironically, Stuart had been mostly blamed because of his far-flung raid by critics and historians since the Civil War and even to this day, but it was his more significant and decisive failure on the afternoon of July 3 that ensured Confederate defeat because of what he failed to accomplish, when Lee and the army depended on him.[114]

Pulitzer Prize–winning historian Walter A. McDougall was correct when he wrote how Lee deliberately "kept the fact of [the July 3] failure secret out of concern for his army's morale."[115] The official reports of Stuart's commanders make relatively little mention of the strategic importance of what happened on the East Cavalry Field on July 3, and it is almost certain that Lee deliberately suppressed the little existing information and knowledge of the extent of the monumental lapse of Stuart for his failure to charge into the Army of the Potomac's rear in conjunction with Pickett's Charge.[116]

But to be fair and as noted, Lee possessed ample good reason to suppress the ugly truths and the failures of his top lieutenants, because he could not afford "to see grievances and recriminations finish off his wounded army."[117] Even Pickett had failed the general. Major John Cheves Haskell, who had lost an arm in battle and a brother on the killing field of Gettysburg, wrote with bitterness how "neither Pickett nor any of his staff . . . was touched" during Pickett's Charge, "when near all of his officers outside of him and his staff were killed and wounded [because] he was not leading the charge of his division as his admirers assert" and celebrate.[118]

Certainly no accident on any level, this general silencing of Stuart's failure on the East Cavalry Field was evident in regard to Lee's official report of the battle. He spared his reluctant and hesitant top lieutenant, Longstreet, from censure, although the Georgian was guilty of a lengthy list of failures, including improperly orchestrating Pickett's Charge and because of his desire to outflank the Union left on July 3, contrary to Lee's orders, and had even prepared to move around Little Round Top and Big Round Top. Even more, Lee did not blame Major General Longstreet for his failures to hurry forward Pickett's Division to be in a proper position to attack at dawn on July 3. In conclusion, because of such reasons, historian Edwin B. Coddington wrote with considerable understatement how Lee's official report "was a model of restraint," because some historians have accused Longstreet of deliberately sabotaging Lee's offensive plans.[119]

Even more, the plan to strike Meade's rear had been a secret mission, and not even Stuart's top lieutenant, Brigadier General Wade Hampton, was early informed about the commander's plan on July 3, if at all. In fact, Stuart "never revealed his intention" to General Hampton, or his other top lieutenants, to ensure the lack of information about Gettysburg's most secret mission, which exists to this day.[120]

In the end and even more than Longstreet, therefore, Stuart escaped widespread condemnation for his failure to attack Meade's rear in part because it was not revealed to the Southern people in order to preserve morale and keep spirits as high as possible during the crisis summer of 1863; hence, the great silencing of the importance of what happened on the East Cavalry Field and exactly why. With the twin defeats at Gettysburg and Vicksburg, the Confederacy was reeling as never before and needed to keep faith in heroes like Stuart, who was the people's idol. Therefore, the laying of blame to transform Stuart into a culprit would send Southern morale into free fall, as he was one of the South's most idolized and revered figures, who symbolized the South and its war effort.

For all of these reasons, and certainly not in his two official reports (July 31, 1863, and then in early 1864) that were meant for publication in Southern newspapers, Lee never blamed any of his top lieutenants, including Longstreet—who directed Pickett's Charge with less skill than was necessary for success—for having played key roles in the defeat at Gettysburg, when in truth they had let their commander down and failed to perform to his lofty expectations. And this was especially the case in regard to Stuart's failures on that third day, especially his long absence from the front during the struggle for the East Cavalry Field and his lack of proper communication with his top lieutenants, which was inexcusable on many levels.

Of course, no one realized the painful reality of the many failures of his top lieutenants at Gettysburg more than General Lee. But he still blamed no one but himself in his two reports of the battle, which were actually written by his staff officer Colonel Charles Marshall, a former attorney who wrote most judiciously and with skill like he was still working on an important legal case, especially in safeguarding Lee's every move and decision, particularly with regard to possible criticism. For all his famous battles, Lee left behind "the sketchiest and least satisfactory" report in regard to Gettysburg, especially July 3, when Stuart was guilty of his greatest and most important failure of the war.[121]

And as mentioned, this silencing was much needed for the overall welfare of the Southern nation on multiple levels. Indeed, under the circumstances, after Lee "learned that Stuart had been stopped on East Cavalry Field . . . destroying the entire effort save only for the massacre of Pickett's men, such information was only poison for the Confederate cause. Nothing good for the South could come out of Lee admitting to anyone that he [and Stuart had failed]. And the worst part of all was that it had failed because Jeb Stuart and his Invincibles, the flower of southern horsemen, had been stopped by a Yankee cavalry unit less than half its size. . . . And if it were ever made public, it would only boost the morale of Union forces while at the same time administrating a blow to that of Confederate forces. So Lee just swallowed it and never mentioned it to anyone."[122]

In addition, the continued obscurity and silencing of what actually happened on July 3 and exactly why was additionally guaranteed when Stuart was mortally wounded on May 11, 1864, at Yellow Tavern, Henrico County, Virginia, just west of the Telegraph Road and less than six miles from Richmond. General Grant unleashed a cavalry raid toward Richmond, and Stuart had met the threat to the nation's capital, where President Jefferson Davis clearly heard the musketry crackling to the north from his office. Davis visited the dying Stuart the next day, and he and his wife, Varina, prayed for his speedy recovery in vain, because he was still the South's premier cavalryman.

But nothing could save Stuart. He died on the following evening in Richmond, and the knowledge and exact details of his secret mission of striking Meade's rear on July 3, 1863, was buried with him. But most of all, the man who possessed all the secrets, General Lee, died in October 1870 before he wrote his memoirs. So neither Lee nor Stuart wrote their memoirs, guaranteeing additional obscurity in the historical record. And Lee left behind no collection of personal papers to shine a proper light on Stuart's role on July 3. What has survived, including Lee's official reports, not written by him (most after-action battle reports were written by Colonel Charles Marshall) but merely signed by him, are not only incomplete, brief, and sketchy, but also extremely misleading.[123]

However, in a hasty and totally incomplete analysis of the battle written on July 4, Lee only informed President Davis in writing that "a more extensive attack was made" on July 3 in contrast to July 2, because of "the third division of General Longstreet having come up"—General Pickett's Division of three seasoned Virginia brigades.[124]

General Lee failed to mention some of the most significant tactical decisions of July 3, especially in regard to how he had to modify his offensive plans—attacking the right-center instead of the center on the third day—because of Longstreet's disregard for Lee's previous orders to attack at dawn. The persistent Longstreet, who proved more stubborn and headstrong than usual on July 3 for a variety of reasons, still wanted to ease around the Union army's left flank beyond the Round Tops. Ironically, more attention has been given by historians to Longstreet's contrarianism and reluctance in regard to following Lee's orders than Stuart's more significant failures, which were more important in leading the way of decisive defeat.

In his careful analysis presented in an excellent study, historian William Garrett Piston correctly concluded with some degree of amazement how in regard to Lee's July 4 report to the president in Richmond, "This is so cursory that it scarcely sounds like the battle of Gettysburg at all."[125]

In his official report of the battle that was finally submitted to President Davis in January 1864, Lee strongly hinted at Stuart's failure in his incomplete report, that the key to success on July 3 was due to the lack of a "proper concert of action" that he believed he possessed on July 3 and not only the previous day. The greatest difference on July 3 was that Lee utilized all three branches—infantry, artillery, and cavalry in the Napoleonic tradition—together for the first time at Gettysburg for a maximum offensive effort, because he now possessed Stuart's cavalry, unlike on the previous two days at Gettysburg.[126]

Longstreet's deep-seated reluctance to abide by Lee's orders, which resulted in an outrageous degree of foot-dragging, if not open defiance—including not having Pickett's Division up and ready to attack at dawn on July 3 as Lee had planned and ordered—had forced Lee to modify his plan to assault farther north in the early afternoon instead of at dawn. But, most importantly, this final offensive effort when Lee went for broke was actually closer (farther north by targeting Meade's right-center instead of center) to actual developments on the third day, which allowed Stuart an even better opportunity to play an offensive role in conjunction with the main offensive effort—Pickett's Charge.[127] Because Lee knew that the key to decisive victory on the third day was the utilization of all branches of his army in "proper concert of action," he was relying on the old Napoleonic formula (his secret for success), and "this is why Lee sent Stuart and his cavalry on a sweeping end run around Ewell's left flank with orders to threaten the Federal rear."[128]

Or, although it is not known, Stuart might well have been informed by courier or a staff officer from headquarters of Lee's change of plans in launching the main offensive effort past dawn on July 3. If not, then Stuart would have known as much from the lack of firing, which indicated that the planned grand offensive effort had not been unleashed early that morning. Again, Stuart was not censured in Lee's written documentation—battle reports—about the battle, not only because of their briefness and incompleteness in regard to exact details of the battle, but also because the Confederacy and the Southern people needed to not know about the greatest failure of their most revered hero after Lee. Piston concluded in frustration how "given the vast attention accorded the battle of Gettysburg, it is sobering to realize that information on key issues such as Confederate direction of the battle on the night of July 2 and the morning of July 3 is limited to a few pages of sketchy and conflicting evidence."[129]

However, despite documentation and all the facts, Piston summarized how "the fact remains that Lee's First Plan [an attack that targeted the Cemetery Ridge defensive line farther south of the clump of trees and with all of Longstreet's Corps, or General John B. Hood's and Lafayette McLaws's Divisions that occupied the southern end of Lee's battle line since July 2] was a monumentally bad one, almost as certainly doomed to failure as Pickett's Charge [farther north], which replaced it."[130]

But, like most American historians without detailed knowledge and expertise on Napoleon's campaigns and how these long-overlooked factors were key to understanding the extent and depth of Lee's tactical thinking, Piston failed to take into account the generally forgotten role of Stuart in conjunction with the overall offensive effort that might have changed the tactical equation in regard to making more sense of the complexity of Lee's plans, which was far more than the stereotypical mindless frontal assault of Pickett's Charge as long emphasized and alleged by generations of historians.[131]

For his own reputation and high standing in the eyes of the Southern people on both sides of the Mississippi, Stuart was extremely fortunate because of the simple fact, in the words of one historian, that "there are no written orders for the cavalry, and the messages are not preserved, and we cannot tell exactly what orders [because they were oral and given late on the night of July 2] Stuart had from this Commanding General, or what arrangements were made for liaison, between the cavalry and the Confederate infantry."[132]

For such reasons and as in Stuart's case, even the capable commander of the veteran Stuart Horse Artillery Battalion and his key role has not been documented, obscuring the importance of the climactic contest that was played out on the East Cavalry Field. Bewildered by the glaring lack of documentation about the contributions of Major Robert Franklin Beckham: "Of the three individuals who held the command of the Stuart Horse Artillery Battalion Beckham is the least known, yet he led the battalion during the most famous campaign of the war in which the horse artillery played a major role. . . . Of Beckham there is nothing after Brandy Station [and including the Battle of Gettysburg]. It is as if he disappeared amidst the rising columns of dust as the army trudged north."[133]

This general silence over Beckham's role in leading the Stuart Horse Artillery Battalion at Gettysburg was deserved for another reason that mirrored the overall situation in regard to the obscurity of Stuart's own role on July 3: Major Beckham, like General Stuart, failed in his all-important mission on the final day. Both Stuart and Beckham, who demonstrated that his true skills lay in organization and management rather than fighting, proved to be miserable failures as leaders on the afternoon of July 3. Not surprising after his failures at Gettysburg, Beckham was shuffled off to the western theater, where inferior and mediocre officers who failed to live up to expectations had long been banished from the Army of Northern Virginia by Lee, who was an excellent judge of leadership ability.

In regard to the historical record, consequently, Beckham's general obscurity, like Stuart's, especially at Gettysburg, is complete, because his specific orders, mission, and directives on July 3 are nonexistent to this day. But, as with Stuart, this situation does not mean that Beckham was not there and played no important role on the East Cavalry Field. Indeed, the role of the guns of the Stuart Horse Artillery Battalion was all important in the final showdown on July 3. Naysayers have long argued that the lack of evidence means that nothing happened and that Stuart possessed no important mission (still another popular myth of Gettysburg historiography aggressively fueled by self-serving deniers), because official orders to do so do not exist at this time, while forgetting that Stuart received oral orders from Lee on the night of July 2.

Despite knowing that Confederate records and documentation are terribly incomplete, because much was lost or destroyed either in wartime or after the conflict, which has made the Confederate record at Gettysburg, especially on the critical last day, also incomplete, revisionist historians have attempted to argue that this lack of physical writing evidence in the form of official records, especially reports, means that an event could never have possibly happened—a self-serving and one-sided generalization that has overlooked even the most fundamental facts, situations, and realities about the Pennsylvania invasion and the chaotic final day, and an extremely limited interpretation of history by the most narrow and often most inaccurate means. Today's armchair types, especially those who have been emboldened by becoming cyber-propagandists (with cyber-courage) on the internet and self-serving Civil War blogs to spread propaganda and lies, have ignored the fact that this was a risky invasion, the army had been decimated, and a dangerous retreat back to Virginia was required to save what was left of the Army of Northern Virginia—a situation also explained by the lack of records.

Quite simply, there was no time or inclination to write detailed reports of every movement, including what happened on the East Cavalry Field. But this does not mean that events did not happen when supported by ample evidence, just because something was not explained in great detail in an official report, which are noted (on both sides) for their inaccuracy and incompleteness under such circumstances. Even more, official reports, which were written by officers who desired promotion and fame in most cases, are incredibly self-serving and often more fiction than fact and should be taken with a grain of salt by modern historians, unfortunately a situation that too often is not the case. In the end, the truth of the plan to strike Meade's rear would have been almost certainly forthcoming in greater detail from their own words, but these words were buried with the deaths of Lee and Stuart to guarantee no memoirs, and all within five years after the war's end.

One historian has correctly lamented the lack of written orders from Lee's headquarters, especially for the three-day battle, when he summarized the importance of the cavalry fight in the Army of the Potomac's rear: "Pleasanton's troopers have done what they should have done: kept Stuart off of Meade's rear."[134]

Ironically, even the Union side, but of course much less than the Southern side, has also been guilty of ignoring the importance of what happened on the East Cavalry Field for a variety of reasons, including because Pickett's Charge cast such a giant shadow. In his memoir and emphasizing a long-overlooked historical truth, James H. Kidd lamented this silencing of what really happened, and exactly why, on the East Cavalry Field, which has continued to this day:

> For more than twenty years after the close of the civil war, the part played by Gregg, Custer, and McIntosh and their brave fellows in the battle of Gettysburg received but scant recognition. Even the maps prepared by the corps of engineers stopped short of Cress's Ridge and Rummel's fields. 'History' has been practically silent upon the subject, and had not the survivors of those commands taken up the matter, there might have been no record of the invaluable services which the Second cavalry division and Custer's Michigan brigade rendered at the very moment when a slight thing would have turned the tide of victory the other way. In other words, the decisive charge [led by Custer at the head of the 1st Michigan Cavalry] coincided in point of time with the failure of Pickett's assault upon the center, and was a contributing cause in bringing about the latter result.[135]

Ironically, survivors of the bloody holocaust at Gettysburg laid blame on Confederate leadership to an excessive degree, which also played a role in overlooking Custer's key contributions to victory in Meade's right-rear. John N. Opie, who enlisted at age seventeen and served as a hard-riding cavalryman of the Army of Northern Virginia, concluded that "the plain truth and incontestable solution [was that] Lee blundered, Stuart blundered [and] some of them blundered forward and others blundered backwards."[136] But no one blundered more than Stuart on the crucial last day at Gettysburg, when the fate of two republics hung in the balance.

Not only has the importance of the achievements of Custer and his men been long ignored in regard to their true significance, but even credit for their splendid performance against the odds and in defeating Lee's best cavalry commander has been obscured. The fact that Custer was killed in the remoteness of the Montana Territory on the hot afternoon of June 25, 1876, presented a greater opportunity to do even more disservice to the achievements of Custer and his Wolverines, who literally saved the day for General Meade, the Army of the Potomac, and the Union to a degree seldom achieved by so few troopers in the course of a war.

After all, Custer could hardly refute any of the growing body of critics and challengers of what he had accomplished on the afternoon of July 3, 1863, after he met a cruel fate at the Little Bighorn. Captain Kidd, a young Wolverine cavalry officer, compared how one writer and orator, a former member of a Pennsylvania cavalry regiment, gave more recognition to others than to the native Ohioan and adopted Michigander, while "he did not estimate Custer's part at its full value, an omission" that has also played a part in obscuring the exact details of the historical record to disguise the importance of what happened on the East Cavalry Field.[137] By comparison, Stuart's role on July 3 went almost entirely unnoticed by the giant shadow cast by Pickett's Charge, especially because he was not entirely forthcoming in his official report in order to minimize his long list of failures.[138]

## FORGOTTEN TRUISMS OF AMERICA'S MOST IMPORTANT BATTLE

A widely accepted scholar who won the Pulitzer Prize in 1986 emphasized how Lee's "plan for the third day was the most brilliant of all; he just kept the fact of its failure secret out of concern for his army's morale. That plausible plan concerns something everyone knows—J. E. B. Stuart's belated return on July 2—and something many people may not know: the action Stuart's men fought on July 3 well beyond Culp's Hill. It is always assumed that Stuart just meant to disrupt the federal troops' supplies and reinforcements or harry their expected retreat."[139]

In truth, Stuart was part of the planned three-part offensive effort to win the day, because his primary mission was to ride into Meade's rear to strike his center from the east, and to "wreak havoc on a grand scale" in conjunction with Pickett's Charge—essentially a pincer movement from the west (Pickett's Charge) and the east (Stuart's Charge).[140] In the end, therefore, Stuart was even more guilty of the cover-up of this secret plan than Lee to ensure a thorough silencing in the historical record. In the on-target analysis of historian Stephen Z. Starr, he correctly maintains how "Stuart's claim that he was only protecting the left flank of the Confederate army is not worth a moment's credence."[141] A member of McIntosh's Brigade, Captain William

E. Miller, who survived the bitter combat that had raged on the East Cavalry Field, basked in the sparkling July 3 success, because Stuart's "avowed object was to strike the rear of the Federal army in co-operation with Pickett's grand attack upon its center."[142]

Historian Roger L. Rosentreter, an expert on the Michigan Cavalry Brigade and its campaigns, concluded that "if Lee's plan of pressing the Union center from both the front ("Pickett's Charge") and rear [by Stuart] succeeded, the enemy line would be broken and the Yankees routed."[143]

Even in the cavalry volume of *The Photographic History of the Civil War*, Francis Trevelyan Miller, who edited this classic ten-volume set that was first published in 1911, wrote with on-target analysis of the fighting behind the Army of the Potomac on July 3: "Finally the Confederate brigades withdrew behind their artillery, and the danger that Stuart would strike the rear of the Union army simultaneously with Pickett's charge was passed."[144]

In his book *Custer's Road to Disaster*, historian Kevin M. Sullivan summarized how "Stuart was determined to strike at the Federals' rear on that decisive day by smashing General Meade's forces, thereby assisting Pickett in his advance. Very adept at striking the Army of the Potomac at will, Stuart, commanding the Invincibles, had every reason to believe his plan of attack would come off beautifully. But here again, fate, chance, and the unexpected tide of battle would be dealing the cards, and the star of George Armstrong Custer would ascend even higher in history."[145]

Another historian, Ron Field, emphasized how "Stuart attempted to get into the Federal rear" on the afternoon of July 3.[146] Historian Roger H. Harrell wrote how Union cavalry leadership, including Custer, had accomplished its most vital mission on the third day, because they eliminated "the threat to Meade's rear and flank."[147]

On target with his analysis, Fairfax Downey, a respected writer of an earlier generation, wrote how at Gettysburg, "on the third, Stuart and his cavalry attempted to circle the Federal right and strike the enemy's rear."[148] Although the writer of more traditional history of the 1950s and 1960s like the prolific Downey, Glenn Tucker still emphasized how Stuart's "assignment for July 3 was to reach the rear of the Federal center," which had been targeted by Pickett's Charge.[149]

But Emory M. Thomas, a respected academic and college professor, later provided some of the most thoughtful and on-target analysis, while emphasizing the irony of Stuart's forgotten July 3 role and its longtime absence from the annals of Civil War historiography:

> In all the emphasis and attention heaped on Stuart's role in the Gettysburg campaign [his lengthy and time-consuming raid to the outskirts of Washington, DC] before he reached the scene of the great battle, his contem-

poraries and historians alike all ignore Stuart's significant cavalry battle on July 3. To be sure, reasons exist to overlook the mounted action on the battle's third day. George Pickett's charge on the center of the Federal line was the climactic moment in the conflict and maybe of the entire war [but nevertheless] Stuart's participation in the events of July 3 usually rates no more than an afterthought, a meager mention, in the accounts of Gettysburg. The cavalry battle that took place beyond the Confederate left flank about three miles east of Gettysburg does not even appear on most maps of the battle. Yet that battle was ferocious and for those who witnessed or participated, it must have seemed every bit as dramatic as Pickett's charge. Further, Stuart's cavalry fight generated one of the most fascinating might have been/what-ifs in all of American military history.[150]

This insightful view of Thomas's agrees with the words of Major McClellan, of Stuart's staff, who emphasized how Stuart's objective was to unleash "an attack upon the enemy's rear."[151] Therefore, generations of historians have been in agreement with those individuals, both Union and Confederate, who fought on the East Cavalry Field, a fact not understood or appreciated by today's aggressive community of self-serving deniers—not unlike the thoroughly contemptible Holocaust deniers—on the internet and blogs.

As noted, Custer's key role on July 3 has long been either ignored or minimized by historians, largely because of the legacy of the Little Bighorn disaster, for which he was to become the most convenient scapegoat for one of America's most famous military disasters. Historian B. H. Liddell Hart, an experienced military man who knew intimately of the inner workings and core dynamics of the military establishment, understood a truism about the unreliability of official records that has been seldom realized by Civil War historians, especially those who have explored the dramatic showdown on the East Cavalry Field: "Official documents often fail to reveal their real views and aims, while sometimes even drafted to conceal them."[152]

Unfortunately and sadly, the ever-aggressive revisionists, especially today's Civil War blogging community, have relied upon the simple fact of the lack of orders not found in the *Official Records of the War of the Rebellion* as having provided definite evidence that Stuart never planned to act in conjunction with Pickett's Charge—the creation and perpetuation of a cyber-myth, thanks to the powerful advantages of the internet where coordinated denials are artificially manufactured by puppet masters for their own personal gain in regard to book sales and egos. Even Custer's official report of the fight at the East Cavalry Field was omitted from the 128 volumes for the *Official Records* for reasons that are not known to this day—an enduring mystery. But the absence of Custer's report in the *Official Records* certainly does not mean that he played no leading role on July 3, 1863, a simple fact ignored by the cyber-propagandists.

But the ultimate truth not found in the *Official Records* can be seen in the words of Stuart's adjutant, Major Henry Brainerd McClellan, who emphasized that Stuart's primary objective was to unleash "an attack upon the enemy's rear."[153] This is in agreement with Stuart's own words: "I [had] hoped to effect a surprise upon the enemy's rear."[154]

## UNION GENERALS AND LEADING HISTORIANS AGREE

But in truth, the highest levels of the Union leadership understood what was at stake and appreciated the supreme importance of the showdown on the East Cavalry Field. As noted, the Army of the Potomac's commander, George Gordon Meade, emphasized how "during the time of Lee's assault [known as Pickett's Charge], General Gregg had won an extremely important cavalry engagement [when] Stuart was proceeding toward the Baltimore Pike, where he hoped to create a diversion in aid of the Confederate infantry" of Pickett's Charge.[155]

Historians from Michigan—significantly more than Gettysburg historians in general—have more fully understood the importance of the dramatic story of the East Cavalry Field correctly because they have looked more closely at the Michigan Cavalry Brigade and Custer's experiences on July 3 and have a greater appreciation for the heroics and sacrifice of Custer's Wolverines. For example, Roger L. Rosentreter, a college professor and the editor of the *Michigan History Magazine*, emphasized how "Stuart's mission was to strike the rear of the Union center as Pickett's men converged on the Copse of Trees. If everything worked as planned, the Army of the Potomac would be cut in half and Lee would win a decisive victory."[156] Likewise, historian James S. Robbins concluded, "The outnumbered and disorganized Union troops had mounted a fierce enough resistance to halt Stuart [from ever reaching] the Baltimore Pike and [Meade's rear was] saved."[157]

Michigan historian Richard Bak emphasized how "Stuart attempted to crash into the rear of the Union line," and this "was a critical moment [because] had Stuart succeeded in converging his forces with Pickett's, the outcome of the battle—and the war—may very well have been different."[158]

But it was not to be. Perhaps Virginia cavalryman John N. Opie, who had enlisted at age seventeen, pinpointed one of the primary reasons for Stuart's failure on the East Cavalry Field: "This great disaster [at Gettysburg] was brought upon us by our overweening confidence, which induced us to imagine that we could conquer the 'Army of the Potomac,' in any position it might occupy, however, impregnable [and] the plain truth and incontestable [fact was that] Lee blundered, Stuart blundered," to ensure defeat on July 3.[159]

But as mentioned, General Stuart escaped blame for his failures to assist Lee and his army in a decisive manner on the third day, especially in conjunction with Pickett's Charge. As noted, another general became the scapegoat for Confederate defeat at Gettysburg to take off the possible spotlight on Stuart: James Longstreet. In part because he became a Republican after the war and personally profited from his loyalty to the party that had been dedicated to slavery's destruction and the South's defeat, an extremely effective anti-Longstreet faction, including former Confederate leaders, of the "Lost Cause" period transformed Longstreet into the main culprit of defeat at Gettysburg. He was systematically made into the dark villain of the South and even a Judas, who ultimately betrayed not only Lee but also the South to doom in its desperate bid for independence, a development which heavily influenced generations of historians who dutifully painted Longstreet as the primary villain and foil to the canonized Lee for the creation of enduring myths, both negative and positive. This thorough distortion of the historical record was made easier by the fact that Longstreet was a native Georgian—hence an outsider from the Virginia establishment—and Stuart was a Virginian like Lee, and it was the pro-Virginia school of writers who were the most dominant in writing the romanticized version of "Lost Cause" history of the South.

Therefore, in the end, it was Longstreet, not Stuart, who became the architect of decisive defeat at Gettysburg and the perfect scapegoat during the postwar period, when the vanquished South struggled in emotional and psychological terms with its defeated self during a bleak time. Clearly, Stuart was most fortunate in regard to his legacy in the historical memory because of the glorification of Confederate heroes from the "Lost Cause" school and the excessive focus of generations of historians on Longstreet's failures in regard to Pickett's Charge west of Cemetery Ridge, while forgetting about Lee's other top lieutenant on the ridge's other side and Stuart's all-important role and complete lack of success when it mattered most. Instead of becoming a scapegoat as he deserved for his failures on the third day, which played a large role in the decisive Confederate defeat, Stuart joined Lee as a revered romantic idol in the mythic and idealized past that was believed in by generations of not only Southerners but also Americans in general in the postwar period.

Clearly, the vilification of Longstreet—especially in regard to Pickett's Charge, which he orchestrated—because of his hesitation and reluctance, which helped to ensure defeat, to the point that it should be more properly known today as "Longstreet's Charge," has played a large role in casting a giant shadow over the supreme importance of the East Cavalry Field showdown.[160]

Meanwhile, Stuart's fame continued to grow in the postwar years like that of Lee, thanks to the Virginia school of historians, who painted the most romanticized and glowing portrait of Stuart. Stuart's blemishes and warts were covered by a dense romantic shroud, which included a silencing of what happened on the East Cavalry Field and why.

But a feisty Virginia lady's letter to President Jefferson Davis placed Stuart in a more realistic and accurate perspective that helped to explain why Stuart was defeated by Custer and his hard-fighting Wolverines at Gettysburg on July 3: "General Stuart's conduct since in Culpeper is perfectly ridiculous, having repeated reviews for the benefit of his lady friends, he riding up and down the line thronged with those ladies, he decorated with flowers, apparently a monkey show on hand and he the monkey. In fact General Stuart is nothing more or less than one of those fops devoting his whole time to his lady friends' company."[161]

The roots of Stuart's failure on July 3 were already early evident, but no one, including Lee, seemed to notice or much care. From the beginning Stuart had been promoted well beyond his abilities, and this came back to haunt the army and the South on the East Cavalry Field, where he failed in his crucial mission. In late December 1861, Stuart had exercised independent command when he embarked on an expedition to Dranesville, Virginia, to gather forage. But Stuart had received a nasty surprise when suddenly confronted by a sizeable force of Federals. As revealed in a journal, one Confederate general correctly described this "fight as a blunder on the part of Gen. Stuart who was surprised by finding the enemy where he did not expect him." Ironically, this was not unlike the situation on July 3, where Stuart failed in much the same way, when the stakes were truly high, unlike at Dranesville, in Fairfax County, Virginia, on a cold December 20, 1861.[162] Clearly Stuart had failed to learn from his mistakes by the time of the dramatic showdown on the East Cavalry Field. Even more, Stuart then presented a report of the affair that, in diplomatic terms, was "highly colored."[163]

In striking contrast, Custer proved to be quite the opposite of Stuart in almost every way on the afternoon of July 3—not only more moral, but also a tough and hard-nosed fighter, who took the business of soldiering much more seriously than the South's most revered cavalryman. Ironically, Custer seemed to have learned more about what was necessary for victory on July 3 not from his dry lessons in the classrooms at West Point, but from having read stirring words from his beloved Charles O'Malley in *Irish Dragoon*, from a war during an earlier era and long before the native Ohioan entered the United States Military Academy: "I have felt all the glorious enthusiasm of a fox-hunt, when the loud cry of the hound, answered by the cheer of the joyous huntsman, stirred the very heart within, but never till now did I know how far higher the excitement reaches when, man to man, saber to saber, arm to arm, we ride forward to the battle-field. On we went, the loud shout of 'forward' still ringing in our ears. One broken, irregular discharge from the French guns shook the head of our advancing column, but stayed us not as we galloped madly on" to victory.[164]

Fortunately for General Meade, the Army of the Potomac, and the Union, Custer had possessed a cavalry brigade—hardy and highly motivated Wolverines—that was far more formidable than anything seen or imagined by military men, including Napoleon, of the Napoleonic era. Not only were the Michigan men masters in the art of the headlong cavalry charge and the use of the cavalry saber, but also in the unleashing of the heavy firepower from the Spencer rifle and carbine, which provided the most hard-hitting power of any small-arms weapon in the Army of the Potomac. Clearly, Custer had been extremely well served by these distinct advantages on July 3, 1863.[165] But Custer's moralistic sense and faith also played a key role in his rising to the challenge of the crucial third day because of "the holy inspiration of a just and noble cause": saving the Union.[166]

## FORGOTTEN TACTICAL LESSONS OF THE CLASH OF CAVALRY ON JULY 3

Ironically, the most forgotten architect of Custer's victory on the East Cavalry Field was one of the most ridiculed of all Army of the Potomac commanders, General "Fighting Joe" Hooker. What has been most forgotten was the fact that Hooker had wisely initiated the key cavalry reforms that had well prepared the Union cavalry, especially in setting the stage for the rise of a new generation of young and dynamic fighting generals like Custer, for achieving success in the climactic cavalry showdown on July 3. As revealed in a letter, the insightful Lieutenant Edward G. Granger, Custer's aide-de-camp, realized as much, penning how "the credit belongs to the defeat of Lee at Gettysburg I think is due Hooker, who was not relieved [of command] till the army was ready for the battle."[167]

Perhaps one of Stuart's staff officers, William Willis Blackford, said it best in summarizing the fight of July 3 that doomed Stuart's crucial mission, because possession of ground—the traditional criterion for measuring victory—no longer mattered, when everything was at stake and this day was the last chance for the Confederate to win it all: "Stuart held his ground . . . and the enemy withdrew after about as bloody and hot an affair as any we had ever experienced. The cavalry of the enemy were steadily improving and it was all we could do sometimes to manage them."[168] Of course, Blackford's words were not only an understatement, but also a distortion of the facts. Quite simply, Stuart had been defeated, and badly, primarily by Custer and his Wolverines, who had fought better and harder than the opposition on the third day. Stuart had failed General Lee and the Army of Northern Virginia on the ultimate day of destiny, and the primary source of that failure was Custer.

Stuart's ill-advised decision to fight for possession of the strategic crossroads in a conventional and predictable manner revealed his lack of tactical flexibility and his overall failure to rise to the stiff tactical challenge of July 3. One of Stuart's staff members, aide-de-camp Theodore S. Garnett Jr., emphasized the truth about the cavalry fight on July 3: "It is common error to suppose that the sabre was during our war a useless lesson. It is true that it played no such formidable part here as in European wars, but" this much-maligned tactic rose to the fore when least expected on the East Cavalry Field, when Custer led the audacious saber attacks of the 7th Michigan Cavalry and then the 1st Michigan Cavalry north toward the buildings of farmer Rummel.[169]

Quite simply, as learned the hard way on the East Cavalry Field by Stuart and his troopers, the reliance on such Napoleonic tactics in the face of fast-firing Spencer repeaters of Custer's men was absolute folly, especially when the boys in blue were defending home soil, which fortified their resolve and determination to hold firm regardless of the cost. In the commonsense and on-target reasoning of one of Stuart's horse artillerymen, who lamented with a sense of grim humor an undeniable reality that rose to the fore on July 3: "I believe that the confounded Yankees can shoot better in the United States [northern soil] than they can when they come to Dixieland."[170]

On July 3, the superior and rapid firepower of the state-of-the-art Spencer rifles of the hard-fighting Wolverines was a key factor that had not only defeated but also unnerved Stuart and his men, because they had never before faced such massive firepower in a major battle.[171] For ample good reason, stunned Confederates, victims of the immense and rapid firepower of the Spencer, described these weapons as "*Hell-fire* guns."[172]

Conversely, Custer excelled in relying on Napoleonic tactics, especially the classic saber charge, in part because he faced no superior firepower from his opponents. Even the fire of Confederate artillery proved inferior on this day of decision in Meade's right-rear. The East Cavalry Field was ideally suited for the sudden rebirth of Napoleonic tactics—which had been made largely obsolete by the rugged and heavily wooded terrain of Virginia and elsewhere across the South—because of the open fields, pastures, and meadows of the East Cavalry Field.

In a strange paradox that distinguished the cavalry showdown on the afternoon of July 3, the Union army's cavalry proved its superiority and a dominance that revealed how a new day had come by a reliance on the old Napoleonic tactics, and especially Custer's headlong cavalry charges with the 7th Michigan Cavalry and then the 1st Michigan Cavalry. In this regard and in a tactical sense, the Napoleonic era–minded Custer proved that he was an anachronism—but a good one—when it came to the tactics of the saber charge, when he led the Wolverines not once but twice in attacks straight north up the open plain, because of a true emergency situation when such desperate and aggressive tactics were entirely called for. Therefore, what had been demonstrated by Custer at the East Cavalry Field was a timely and symbiotic meeting of the old with the new, when the shock power of old-fashioned Napoleonic charges were resurrected far from the plains of central Europe in a European-like battlefield in Adams County, Pennsylvania.

By leading the saber charges of the 7th Michigan Cavalry and then the 1st Michigan Cavalry, Custer demonstrated that what was thought to have been obsolete (Napoleonic tactics, especially the saber charge) in America's first modern war was actually the very key to success in regard to stopping Stuart and saving the day. In convincing fashion, he proved that the popular concept that Napoleonic cavalry tactics, especially the sheer power of the shock tactics of the frontal cavalry charge in the Murat tradition, were obsolete was nothing more than a myth by employing exactly those Napoleonic tactics, which were needed to protect Meade's vulnerable rear and win the day: two sweeping saber charges of a kind that was seen on one Napoleonic battlefield after another, when Napoleon's cavalry arm was the toast of all of France and the finest in Europe and perhaps the world. Appropriately and even more ironic in a classic inverse equation, Custer thwarted the best-laid Napoleonic strategic plans of Lee and Stuart by way of his own set of extremely bold Napoleonic tactical plans, not once, but twice, in leading the saber charges of the 7th Michigan Cavalry and then the 1st Michigan Cavalry—the long-forgotten tactical recipe for a most impressive success on the afternoon of July 3 on the East Cavalry Field, which revealed Custer's talents and skills as a battlefield commander.

In addition, Custer's timely Napoleonic tactics succeeded in part because of the overall poor performance of the Confederate artillery, which failed to rise to the occasion for reasons that had more to do with logistics and the poor quality of ammunition, including faulty fuses, than the experience levels of the gunners. Perhaps the commander of the 1st Stuart Horse Artillery, Major James Williams Breathed, said it best in his September 1863 resignation letter in regard to Stuart, his cavalry, and the artillery on the afternoon of July 3, because all should have been able to "do better service" at Gettysburg, when the stakes were especially high.[173]

Indeed, in the words of gifted historian Bradley M. Gottfried, PhD, the superior performance and "the heroics of the Federal cavalry and artillery blunted the Confederate drive toward the Federal rear, and Stuart again failed Lee."[174] But of course what Gottfried did not explain in greater detail in this isolated statement was the fact that this was Stuart's greatest failure of the war in overall strategic terms. In truth, however, both Lee and Stuart had failed the

Army of Northern Virginia and the Confederacy at Gettysburg, ensuring that the South never recovered. But in fact, and as mentioned (a primary thesis of this book), no one was more responsible for the outstanding success that saved the day in the Army of the Potomac's rear than Custer.

In his classic work, Edward G. Longacre, PhD, emphasized Custer's significant contributions to victory by leading two dramatic charges of his highly motivated Wolverines that swept north up the open plain and thwarted Stuart and his so-called Invincibles: "They had been decisively repulsed largely as the result of two of the most dramatic saber charges of this or any other war. Stuart would not reach the Union rear in time to salvage the doomed attack against Meade's center that would become known as Pickett's Charge."[175] But in regard to the supreme importance of Union artillery, Captains Pennington's and Randol's guns played a key role in making Custer's last charge with the 1st Michigan an outstanding success, and these were important and timely contributions to victory.[176]

Custer was thankful for the highly effective artillery support when he and his men were going for broke in attempting to save the day, and they succeeded in no small part because of the horse artillery. In his report, therefore, Custer stated, "Nor must I forget to acknowledge the invaluable assistance by Battery M, Second Regiment of Artillery, in this charge [of the 1st Michigan Cavalry]. Our success in driving the enemy from the field, is due, in a great measure, to the highly efficient manner in which the battery was handled by Lieutenant A. C. Pennington, assisted by" his top lieutenants.[177]

All in all, Custer played the leading role in relying on aggressive tactics, especially the saber charge, but also in successfully utilizing the superior firepower of his horse artillery under Pennington, thwarting what was the most nightmarish of all tactical scenarios for General Meade and the Army of the Potomac. As explained by respected historian Emory M. Thomas, Regents' Professor of History at the University of Georgia: "Had Stuart been able to overwhelm his enemies, the direction of his advance would have carried his troopers into the rear of those Federal foot-soldiers on Cemetery Ridge. And had Pickett's charge succeeded in breaking the Union battle line, Stuart would have been in the right place at the right time to provoke a rout. Stuart might have been the hero of a climactic battle that destroyed Meade's army and quite possibly won the war. Even had Pickett failed as he did, Stuart still had the chance to thunder down on the Federal infantry posted on Cemetery Ridge and rescue the day for the Confederacy [when] Pickett and Stuart would have shaken hands on Cemetery Ridge" on that afternoon of decision.[178]

For those deniers who might think Thomas's words an exaggeration, these astute insights and evaluations are in fact in general agreement with the views of many of the boys in blue who fought on the East Cavalry Field. In no uncertain terms, Corporal James Henry Avery, one of Custer's reliable Wolverine troopers, emphasized as much in his journal in regard to the final showdown on July 3: "We were beating back the columns of Lee, who was trying to push around the flank of our army. If he had succeeded, he would probably have beat us, but [Custer and] the Michigan brigade was there, and no rebel troops could move it out of the way."[179]

As noted, what Custer thwarted by his aggressive tactics was the tactical offensive formula that had been created by Lee and Stuart at the Widow Thompson house for the winning of a decisive success by striking Meade's rear in a surprise attack, as he emphasized in July 1863: "An attack of cavalry should be sudden, bold, and vigorous [when] the cavalry arrives noiselessly but steadily near the enemy, and then, with one loud yell leaps upon him without a note of warning, and giving no time to form or consider anything but the immediate means of flight."[180]

Therefore, during what "was the last great saber battle of the Civil War in which cavalry alone participated . . . Stuart's threat to Meade's rear had been thwarted."[181]

Major John Cheves Haskell, young Major General John Bell Hood's Division, was exactly right when he laid blame for Confederate defeat at Gettysburg on West Point and its highly esteemed graduates, which included Lee, Longstreet, Stuart, and other top Virginians who dominated the army at all levels, especially the highest echelon, to the never-ending disgust of non-Virginians. Haskell emphasized, "We were handicapped by West Point [which] certainly gave us some great soldiers, but it also gave us some dummies, who were grievous stumbling-blocks in our way."[182]

Haskell was not guilty of exaggeration in this regard. A former brigadier general and dynamic leader of a hard-fighting Georgia Brigade, Army of Northern Virginia, a disillusioned Robert "Bob" Toombs famously emphasized that the final epitaph of the Confederate Army should be "Died of West Point."[183]

Ironically, one of the best examples of these West Point "dummies" who cost the lives of quite a few good men was Marcus A. Reno. Graduating in the class of 1855, Reno accumulated more demerits than Custer—more than a thousand. Not surprisingly, as one of Custer's top lieutenants of the 7th Cavalry on its most fateful and tragic day, Reno was a key player in ensuring that Custer and his five companies were destroyed at the Little Bighorn, in part because of his lack of tactical and leadership ability, which ensured that Custer was left on his own on June 25, 1876.[184]

Even Brigadier General Wade Hampton, the model citizen-soldier from South Carolina who gained widespread recognition as a gifted leader without having attended a military school, realized that the root of the army's problems was that it was dominated by so many West Pointers. In a revealing wartime letter, he emphasized with considerable insight and wisdom that "if we mean to play at war, as we play a game of chess, West Point tactics prevailing, we are sure to lose the game."[185]

However, Major Haskell and Brigadier General Hampton did not know before the dramatic showdown at Gettysburg that Custer was one of the "great soldiers" produced by West Point until it was entirely too late. Indeed, despite his poor academic record, and although one of its youngest graduates, West Point had produced one of its best and most capable fighting men who rose splendidly to the fore on July 3 and in the years afterward. In the end and because of an abundance of tactical skill, flexibility, and "raw personal courage," Custer played the leading role in ensuring that the projected tactical scenario of Stuart's attacking into Meade's rear—the key to decisive success that would have been absolutely catastrophic for Union fortunes—never happened on the crucial afternoon of July 3.[186]

And of course it had also taken a great deal of courage from the Michigan men in the ranks, like Edward Corselius, 5th Michigan Cavalry, to save the day. He described what seemingly everyone on both sides who survived the bitter contest in the rear of the Army of the Potomac had experienced: "Such fighting I never saw before."[187] Major Henry Brainerd McClellan paid tribute to the Union cavalry leadership in regard to winning the day on the East Cavalry Field: "As soon as General Gregg was aware of Stuart's presence he wisely assumed the aggressive, and forced upon Stuart a battle in which he had nothing to gain."[188] Indeed, in the end, Stuart's effort was a wasted one far from any kind of glory.

But this was mostly Custer's own personal battle and that of the Michigan Cavalry Brigade, which suffered nearly 90 percent of the Union cavalry losses on July 3 and had played the decisive role in stopping Stuart in his tracks and thwarting his grandiose ambitions. Historian Edward G. Longacre, who wrote in summary how Stuart's best efforts "had been decisively repulsed largely as a result of two of the most dramatic saber charges of this or any other war. Stuart would not reach the Union rear in time to salvage the doomed attack against Meade's center that would become known as Pickett's Charge. And for that outcome, Custer's Wolverines could claim a heroic share of the credit."[189]

This keen and insightful analysis by America's dean of Civil War cavalry studies is right on target. The journalist of the *Detroit Free Press* emphasized as much when he wrote of how "the enemy, galled by our terrible cannonade, and decimated by our [two] charges [led by Custer leading the way before the 7th Michigan Cavalry and then the 1st Michigan Cavalry] broke and fled," to decide the day in the rear of the Army of the Potomac.[190] The reporter's words are in agreement with those of Edward G. Longacre, who emphasized how Stuart's units were "decisively repulsed, largely as a result of two [charges led by Custer to ensure that] Stuart would not reach the Union rear in time" to meet the infantrymen of Pickett's Charge.[191]

Even more, historian Paul Andrew Hutton summarized how "Custer justified Pleasonton's trust with a spectacular debut at Gettysburg [on the crucial third day] that thrashed Jeb Stuart's vaunted cavalry and saved General George Meade's line" from being struck from behind.[192]

For such reasons, it is especially ironic today that the East Cavalry Field is the least visited part of the Gettysburg National Military Park. Most of this hallowed ground is covered in farmlands—looking much the same today as on July 3, 1863—that have been only slightly marred by the encroachment of modernity. In fact, the East Cavalry Field is the most forgotten and overlooked part of America' most visited battlefield.

The crowds of tourists and buffs that converge in throngs on popular sites like Little Round Top, Cemetery Hill, and the Peach Orchard are not seen on the East Cavalry Field, which lies in relative obscurity in its pristine isolation. Ironically, few people today who have visited the battlefield are even aware that Custer played a crucial role at this isolated place on that hot afternoon when the life of the Army of the Potomac and the Union were at stake. It was here that General Meade and his heavily pressured forces were saved by Custer's aggressive actions, which were unprecedented in their boldness and timeliness.

But as mentioned, the price had been high, which became evident when burial parties scoured the field on the morning of July 4—a sad beginning of the Fourth of July. A trooper of a New York regiment, Henry C. Meyer, of German descent, described how

> the following morning our burial parties were at work, when a man from a Michigan regiment came and asked me if I would help him look for some of his comrades in a wheat field; the wheat being about three feet high it was not easy to notice a body in it unless one stumbled right on it. In a few minutes he called out that he had found one and then he said he had another. As the burial party was digging a trench on a ridge just beyond, I suggested that he stay where he was to mark the location and I would ride over and get some of the citizens, whom we noticed plundering the battlefield of horse equipments, to help carry the bodies over so they might be buried. I rode up to two or three men who had harness, saddles, and horse equipments in their possession and told them to drop them and come over to help me carry the bodies that we might bury them, as we had to move on shortly. They were the type of Pennsylvania Dutchmen that lived in that country, who seemed utterly indifferent to the war and anything pertaining to it, beyond securing such spoils as they got on the battle-field. They at once demurred and said they had no time, whereupon I flew into

a rage at their heartless conduct, drew my sabre, and threatened to sabre them if they did not come at once. They then sulkily complied. When we got back to where the bodies were I told them to take some fence rails and carry them as though they were a stretcher. We put the bodies across the rails, the men holding the ends of them. When we had two bodies on this improvised stretcher I discovered a Confederate soldier, a sergeant, with a bushy head of red hair and a red beard. A sabre had split open the top of his head so you could put your hand in the gash. I suggested that he be cared for too, and when we attempted to put him on the stretcher they complained that they could not carry the load. Then I rode after some more citizens whom I also compelled to come over and help us. With their assistance we succeeded in getting a number of bodies up to where the burial party was at work. When I told my Michigan comrade of my experience with these men he became so angry that I thought he would shoot them then and there."[193]

The large number of missing men was tabulated by officers, who were shocked by the high losses. Private William Glover Gage, Company C, 7th Michigan Cavalry, never returned from the first audacious charge led by Custer to help turn the tide of battle. Captain Daniel H. Darling, who was born in June 1836, commanded Company C, and was destined for the rank of lieutenant colonel in 1865, wrote a letter on July 6, 1863, to young William's father: "My Dear Sir: I take this opportunity to write you in reference to Glover. He rode in to the engagement with us on Friday [July 3] and did not return. It was reported [by his comrades] that he was killed. . . . As soon as I could ride I went over the field but did not find him. The reg. in charge of the burial party had his name and [a sergeant] told me where he was buried. I immediately made arrangements with him taken up and buried by himself in the churchyard but on uncovering the bodies his was not among them. . . . He is still missing, but I can give you the hope that . . . he is not dead but a prisoner. We had a fierce engagement with many killed and wounded."[194]

Indeed, teenage Private William Glover Gage, Company C, 7th Michigan, was extremely fortunate on July 3. He survived the "fierce engagement," but he was now in Confederate hands and bound for the hell of Libby Prison, Richmond. In a September 9, 1863, letter, he paid a glowing compliment to his fearless brigade commander, whom he greatly admired because of the dynamic performance that he witnessed on the East Cavalry Field: "The General sat on his horse as cool as could be in front of the men, calling on them to rally. I would ask [for] no braver General than Custer."[195] During the savage combat of July 3, the Michigan men had learned, to their great delight, "By God Custer is a brick!" which was one of the day's highest compliments for a highly capable commander, who exceeded all expectations.[196]

This was the kind of high quality leadership ability that helped to inspire Custer's Michigan men and caused them to play the key role in saving the day in the army's rear on July 3 at Gettysburg. But Custer's all-important contributions on the East Cavalry Field were doomed to become even more forgotten when he was killed at the Little Bighorn at one of the most isolated and remote places on the North American continent, which Americans of 1876 had not previously heard about or seen. Here, Custer's death at age thirty-six ended a most distinguished record and legacy that began on the East Cavalry Field at Gettysburg, when he was more personally and directly responsible for success in Meade's rear on July 3 than any other Union commander.[197]

In the year following Custer's death at the hands of Sioux and Cheyenne warriors, Captain William E. Miller, 3rd Pennsylvania Cavalry, McIntosh's Brigade, returned to Gettysburg. Here, on the East Cavalry Field—which looked the same as in early July 1863—he recalled how Custer had played such a stirring role. During the intense combat on the bloody afternoon of July 3, Miller had the blade of his sword broken near the hilt by a strike from a Confederate saber blow. At that time, he had tossed the useless hilt on the ground.

Then, upon his visit, he made a stunning discovery that surprised him. In looking through the rusted pieces of old junk and relics that had been picked up by farmer John Rummel, who had long plowed up the iron, bronze, brass, and metal fragments of a bygone day from his fields where some of America's finest cavalry had clashed with flashing sabers and a great deal of bravery on the third day, Miller found his old rusted saber with the broken steel blade and the tarnished brass hilt that had been broken during the hand-to-hand combat with Confederate troopers nearly a decade and a half earlier. This occurrence happened at a reunion of veterans, while Custer's bones lay on the remote hilltop in the faraway Montana Territory, far from his beloved Michigan and Ohio home.[198]

Miller's sword was only one of many blades that had been cut off near the hilt from saber blows during the hand-to-hand combat on that day. Lieutenant Beale wrote how two troopers—a private and a corporal—of his Company C, 9th Virginia Cavalry, Chambliss's Virginia and North Carolina Brigade, "after the hand to hand fight in the field, showed me their sabres cut off close to the hilt."[199]

# Epilogue

What happened on the East Cavalry Field in regard to the successful defense of the strategic crossroads in Meade's right-rear was nothing short of miraculous, and Custer was the primary architect of that amazing success against the odds, especially in regard to his leading of the two saber charges. Historians Scott Bowden and Bill Ward summarized the true cause of Confederate failure on July 3: "Most students of the battle seem to accept the proposition that Pickett's attack on the third day at Gettysburg was a hopeless proposition from the start, generally overlooking the fact that significant errors were made by several Southern commanders that contributed to its bloody failure. There is no doubt that assault that finally materialized on July 3 bore little resemblance to the one General Lee had envisioned."[1]

These two distinguished authors correctly emphasized that one of the key failures that led to Southern disaster on July 3 was the most forgotten one because it has been the most overlooked part of Lee's overall battle plan that was developed to secure decisive victory on the final day: "Stuart's successful movement to threaten the Federal rear."[2]

Author Thom Hatch wrote how "Stuart and his 6,000 troopers were poised to support Pickett by attacking the Union rear, which would in all probability turn the tide in their favor [but] blocking Stuart's access to the battlefield in support of Pickett was only one brigade of Union cavalry" led by Custer, who saved the day in the rear of the Army of the Potomac.[3]

But instead of the views of modern historians, perhaps Lieutenant William Brooke Rawle, 3rd Pennsylvania Cavalry, Colonel McIntosh's Brigade, said it best: "Had Stuart succeeded in his well-laid plan and, with his large force of cavalry, struck the Army of the Potomac in the rear of its line of battle, directly towards which he was moving, simultaneously with Longstreet's magnificent and furious assault at its front, when our infantry had all it could do to hold on to the line of Cemetery Ridge, and but little more was needed to make the assault a success," then decisive victory would have been achieved by the dual attacks from the west (Pickett's Charge) and the east (Stuart's cavalry).[4]

In agreement with other historians, Tom Carhart, a distinguished Vietnam War veteran and scholar, also concluded that General Lee "expected Pickett's men to be met at the Clump of Trees by the thousands of grey cavaliers" under Stuart.[5] Historian Thom Hatch agreed: "Stuart's part in this offensive would be to wade into the Union rear in coordination with Pickett's charge [and] this one-two punch [might well] result in an overwhelming Confederate victory."[6]

But perhaps Gregory J. W. Urwin said it best by emphasizing how the Army of the Potomac, by the combined offensive thrusts of Pickett's Charge from the front and Stuart's attack from the rear, "would be cut in half, thrown into panic, and the South would gain the decisive victory she needed to win the war."[7] One officer of the cavalry correctly stated an undeniable truth: "Just as Gettysburg was the turning point of the great war, so, to my thinking, was the grapple with and overthrow of Stuart on the fields of the Rummel farm the turning point of Gettysburg. Had he triumphed there; had he cut his way through or over that glorious brigade of Wolverines and come sweeping all before him down among the reserve batteries and ammunition trains, charging furiously at the rear of our worn and exhausted infantry [defending Cemetery Ridge] even as Pickett's devoted Virginians assailed their front, no man can say what scenes of rout and disaster might not have occurred."[8] And, as noted, no single cavalry commander was more responsible for this amazing success in stopping Stuart than Custer in the view of America's top cavalry expert of the cavalry at Gettysburg.[9]

What has been forgotten by historians about what happened on the East Cavalry Field was that it was actually a turning point in history because Stuart never closed in to attack into the rear of Meade's defenders on Cemetery Ridge while they faced Pickett's Charge. A cavalry attack in the rear had already played a decisive role in Western history. Not only western Europe but also Christendom had been saved just outside the gates of a besieged Vienna, Austria, in 1683 when Polish cavalry under John Sobieski, the dynamic king of Poland, struck into the rear of the besieging Islamic Ottoman Turk invaders. This famous cavalry attack into an opponents' rear inflicted a decisive defeat, saved the day, and won one of the greatest of all Western victories to end the greatest threat to Western civilization at the time: the spread of Islam and almost certainly the wiping out of Christianity in Europe.[10]

In many ways, this was the kind of decisive cavalry strike from the rear that had been envisioned by Lee and Stuart at the Widow Thompson house conference on the night of July 2, which might well have resulted in nothing less than a turning point not only in the Battle of Gettysburg, but also in American history. After all, in the words of Captain William E. Miller, 2nd Pennsylvania Cavalry, McIntosh's Brigade, to reveal the full extent of one of the day's greatest threats to Union fortunes on July 3: "Stuart had with him the main strength and flower of the Confederate cavalry, led by their most distinguished commanders. His force comprised 4 brigades with 20 regiments and battalions and 4 batteries. His avowed object was to strike the rear of the Federal army in cooperation with Pickett's grand attack upon its center."[11]

Nevertheless, to this day and after more than a century and a half after the Battle of Gettysburg raged for three days through the fields, forests, and hills of Adams County, Pennsylvania, Brigadier General George Armstrong Custer's contributions to that decisive victory have been long minimized or ignored to an inordinate degree. But even more and most importantly, what has also been overlooked was the all-important role that Custer played in bestowing the newly formed cavalry corps with a new confidence and spirit for defeating an enemy that had been long considered invincible—hence their name of the "Invincibles"—at the time, beginning with his stirring performance on the afternoon of July 3, 1863.

For the next two years, Custer's achievements and fame continued to rise at an unprecedented rate to reach seemingly impossible heights for someone so young and with such an undistinguished West Point record. In the process and in a true Horatio Alger story, this lowly son of a blacksmith and farmer from a small Ohio town in the middle of nowhere and his Wolverines helped to instill the army's cavalry corps and the Army of the Potomac with a new confidence, hard-hitting style, and swagger that helped to pave the way to Lee's surrender at Appomattox Court House on Palm Sunday 1865—an impossibility without first winning an all-important success in the Union army's rear by the Union cavalry on the third day at Gettysburg.

## THANK GOD FOR CUSTER

In the war's beginning, when Michigan troops had arrived early in May 1861 to protect the capital when under direct Rebel threat with Virginia just across the Potomac River, President Abraham made the comment, "Thank God for Michigan." But in fact, the president's statement would have been more appropriate and fitting in regard to the die-hard troopers of the Michigan Cavalry Brigade, because they had not only thwarted but also defeated the finest cavalry of the Army of Northern Virginia, and primarily by aggressive tactics that were always Custer's high card in emergency situations. But in regard to the decisive afternoon of July 3, 1863, at Gettysburg, President Lincoln might well have said, "Thank God for Custer."[12]

Indeed, General Lee had handed Stuart his most crucial mission of the war because his most highly valued cavalry leader was placed in a position and situation "to clinch the victory" that would save the nation from death in a lengthy war of attrition.[13] Therefore, because of this critical situation, what resulted, in the words of a letter from a fortunate survivor of the 7th Michigan Cavalry, was a universal sentiment: "Cavalry never did such fighting before in America."[14]

The faithful correspondent of the *Detroit Free Press* who witnessed the bitter fighting on the East Cavalry Field at close range wrote his very first sentence to the people of Detroit and Michigan with obvious pride in what Custer and his Michigan men had achieved against the odds: "The battle is fought, the victory is won, and Michigan troops are still ahead."[15] Ironically, however, he hardly knew the correct name—in regard to the spelling—of the young man who had only recently been promoted to command the Michigan Cavalry Brigade. This newspaperman, therefore, wrote in his article from the field how the hard-fighting Wolverines were led by "General Coster."[16]

After the afternoon of July 3, 1863, Custer's name was not again to be misspelled in the bloody course of the war. Ironically, after having been swept off the field by Custer leading the charge of the 7th Michigan Cavalry, Steven, or Stephen, Gaines, a member of the 14th Virginia Cavalry, Jenkins's Brigade, which consisted mostly of hardy mountain boys from today's West Virginia, was impressed by the daredevil style and heroics of the young brigadier general on his finest day. During the struggle for possession of one hard-fought position at a fence, he asked a Michigan prisoner, an officer, who was the dynamic officer who was leading his regiment with such bravery and audacity. In Gaines's words, which explained a strange situation in which Stuart's men learned of Custer's name even before the people of Michigan were bestowed with an iconic hero, after he posed his question: "He told me it was Gen. Custer [and] that was the first time I had ever heard his name."[17]

In the words of historian Emory M. Thomas in his summary of the supreme importance of the cavalry clash on the East Cavalry Field on July 3: "Stuart had the greater opportunity [because] had Stuart been able to overwhelm his enemies, the direction of his advance would have carried his troopers into the rear of those Federal foot-soldiers on Cemetery Ridge. And had Pickett's charge succeeded in breaking the Union battle line, Stuart would have been in the right place at the right time to provoke a rout. Stuart might have become the hero of a climactic battle that destroyed Meade's army and quite possibly won the war. Even had Pickett failed as he did, Stuart still had the chance to thunder down on the Federal infantry posted on Cemetery Ridge and rescue the day for the Confederacy."[18]

As noted, the possibility of Stuart having fulfilled his lofty goals of a truly decisive nature—as emphasized by the astute Thomas, a university professor of distinction—was certainly the case because he was within easy striking distance of the Union rear with thousands of the Army of Northern Virginia's best cavalrymen and ample horse artillery (four batteries and a section of artillery), a most potent strike force that could have caused extensive damage in Meade's rear, including piercing the center of the Cemetery Ridge defensive line from the rear if the cavalry attack from the rear was unleashed in time. At a gallop from the East Cavalry Field, Stuart and his men could have reached Meade's rear in less than fifteen minutes to deliver what would have been nothing less than a masterstroke.[19]

For such reasons, historian Jay Monaghan concluded in regard to Stuart and his cavalrymen and the Army of the Potomac's fate that "a sudden attack on the rear might lose the Battle of Gettysburg."[20] And of course this was the one battle that the Union could not afford to lose, because so much was at stake. For this reason, General Lee and Stuart had planned to deliver their "coup de grace," in the words of Professor James M. McPherson, by unleashing Stuart's cavalry into the Union rear in conjunction with Pickett's Charge to deliver a one-two knockout punch to the Army of the Potomac.[21]

Clearly the story of the dramatic events that played out on the East Cavalry Field was one of the forgotten turning points of not only the Battle of Gettysburg but also of the Civil War in general. Here, as emphasized by Edwin B. Coddington, Stuart "and Lee [had] worked out a scheme to put Stuart's entire cavalry force in a position from which he could separate the Union cavalry from the main body of the army and at the proper moment swoop down onto its rear."[22]

After the war, one Confederate cavalry veteran, who knew that the highest levels of Southern leadership had badly let the common soldiers down and failed them miserably on the final bloody day of Gettysburg, asked, "We, of to-day, veterans of the gray and the blue, who fought at Gettysburg, and the few survivors of Pickett's fatal charge, can we [now] truthfully and positively determine . . . who lost that great and decisive battle of the war, the Waterloo of the Confederacy?"[23] In truth and not realized by this Southern veteran because he was obviously not aware of the details of the secret Lee-Stuart plan to strike the Army of the Potomac's vulnerable rear, no one deserved greater blame for losing the Battle of Gettysburg than Stuart, as revealed in no uncertain terms in this current book.

In the end and for plenty of good reason, General Lee correctly emphasized how if Pickett's division of three Virginia brigades "had been supported as they were to have been," then a decisive victory might have been won. Of course, Lee was not laying blame or looking for scapegoats, but Stuart had failed him miserably on July 3, and the South paid dearly for this failure.[24] Lee knew that if Pickett's attacking troops had been properly supported in a timely manner as ordered, then "we would have held the [advanced] position [the breakthrough penetration at the copse of trees and the Angle on Meade's right center] and the day would have been ours."[25] Again, in the words of one veteran, General Lee "was the only man of them [all his top lieutenants, including Stuart] magnanimous enough to bear the burden [of full responsibility for defeat], and he drew the sting of censure" that was avoided by Stuart.[26]

A fortunate survivor of a wound suffered during the nightmarish Pickett's Charge, which was doomed in part from Stuart's failure in the rear, and captivity in the North, Lieutenant John E. Dooley, an educated young man from Richmond, lamented, "But a little well timed support and Gettysburg was ours."[27] Ironically Dooley was not even including Stuart's secret mission of attacking from the rear in the tactical equation, which would have guaranteed decisive victory. Therefore, almost any support in the form of an offensive role by Stuart's cavalry to hit Meade's rear along the Cemetery Ridge line in conjunction with Pickett's Charge would have changed the course of the Battle of Gettysburg in the most dramatic way.

Even more ironic and for ample good reason, a prophetic General Lee, who had been correctly alarmed by the increased aggressiveness and combat capabilities of the Union cavalry after General Hooker's timely reorganization earlier in the year, had for the first time expressed to President Jefferson Davis on May 9, 1863, in regard to General George Stoneman's raid, how this newly enhanced Union cavalry must be stopped and defeated "or we shall be ruined."[28]

Lee's well-founded growing concern for the more formidable Union cavalry arm finally became an awful reality on July 3, 1863, when the Confederacy's chances for a long life were "ruined," largely because Custer rose magnificently to the fore to verify the Southern commander in chief's worst fears. By relying on tactical mobility, flexibility, and superior firepower and cavalry charges, Custer thwarted the grandest ambitions of Lee's and the Army of Northern Virginia's greatest cavalry commander, while demonstrating that a new day had dawned: the superiority of the Union cavalry arm had become a permanent equation, and the golden age of Southern cavalry had passed by forever. While the myth of the superiority of Stuart's cavalry had been first shattered at Brandy Station, it was buried for all time and in a decisive manner in the most vital of battlefield situations—unlike at Brandy Station—on July 3: one of Custer's most important forgotten contributions of his career.

Indeed, more than any other Union cavalry commander on July 3, Custer shattered the myth that the importance and effectiveness of cavalry had already passed by because of the advances of modern weaponry and superior firepower, especially from artillery but also small arms, which he exploited in full on the East Cavalry Field. Historian Jay Monaghan summarized how Custer "could hardly forget that he had successfully evaded a superior's order and, by doing so, became a gallant—perhaps a key—figure in winning the greater battle" of the Civil War.[29]

But perhaps General Pleasonton said it best in regard to why the Union cavalry won the crucial victory on the East Cavalry Field: "Custer is the best cavalry general in the world, and I have given him the best [cavalry] brigade to command."[30]

Therefore, Custer was the key player who had been able to not only thwart but also defeat Stuart, the highly touted Virginians, and his well-laid plans that had been formed with Lee at the army's headquarters on the night of July 2. Especially in leading two daring cavalry charges—saber attacks—north across the wide open plain, the young man from Ohio and West Point (class of 1861) also vanquished one of the oldest and most enduring myths of the war: the alleged superiority of Stuart and his "Invincibles." Custer had demonstrated that these veteran cavalrymen who were the pride of the South were anything but invincible when he was leading his Wolverines with distinction on the all-important third day at Gettysburg.[31]

Clearly, on the East Cavalry Field, the American nation's destiny hung in the balance only a relatively short distance northeast of the famous clump of trees on Cemetery Ridge, where Pickett's Charge struck Meade's right-center in the all-out and desperate bid to cut the Army of the Potomac in two. But the key tactical equation for decisive victory—Stuart's attack into Meade's rear—had been missing on the afternoon of July 3, to doom the Confederacy to the ash heap of history. Had Stuart been able to strike Meade's rear—less than a fifteen-minute gallop away just to the southwest from the East Cavalry Field—with thousands of cavalrymen in conjunction with thousands of infantry attackers of Pickett's Charge at this crucial turning point of American history, the outcome of the Battle of Gettysburg would have been entirely different. For this reason, the misnamed Pickett's Charge should perhaps be known more correctly as not only Longstreet's Charge, but even more correctly as the Longstreet-Pickett-Stuart Charge, because generations of historians have failed to fully understand and appreciate the supreme importance of Stuart's vital role on the final crucial day of Gettysburg.

More than any other cavalryman on July 3, Custer proved that no one was a more aggressive, tactically flexible in his skillful employment of cavalry and artillery, resourceful, or daring cavalry leader on this hot afternoon of decision in General Meade's right-rear, reversing the roles that had once made his opponent the best cavalryman in America. In a decisive manner, the tide had turned in this war on July 3, not only in regard to the Battle of Gettysburg, but also in regard to the Union cavalry, which had proved not only dominant, but also unbeatable on the third day when it had mattered most.

Custer was at the center stage of these important and timely developments in the army's rear that helped to pave the way to Appomattox Court House because he outfought and outthought the South's greatest cavalryman (Stuart) on the afternoon of July 3. Fortunately, Custer was sufficiently young, confident, and cocky that he never succumbed on the third day to the myth of the superiority of Stuart and his men, who had been partly successful in the past because of this aura of invincibility that had bewitched older and more traditional Union cavalry leaders, who became victims because they were guilty of falling under the romantic spell and committing the cardinal sin of overevaluating their opponent.

Most importantly, the bitter fight at the East Cavalry Field was the place where one of the South's greatest myths and any chances for success died ugly deaths that boded ill for the Confederacy's future, which ceased to shine brightly after the third day—including the superiority of its cavalry and its revered leader—while heralding the day when Lee finally surrendered his Army of Northern Virginia at Appomattox Court House.[32]

The finest cavalry leader and the best cavalry of the Army of Northern Virginia had been primarily thwarted by the son of a lowly blacksmith, whose tactical skills far exceeded and shown brighter on July 3 than the aristocratic sons of the South. In the end, not only the Union cavalry but also the young general named Custer came of age on the third day at Gettysburg, when the blacksmith's son outsmarted, outmaneuvered, outfought, and defeated the very best that the South had to offer. Perhaps historian Tom Carhart said it best: "It was [Custer's] raw personal courage alone that prevented a Confederate victory at Gettysburg and thus truly saved the Union."[33]

In another book by the same author titled *Sacred Ties*, he also emphasized "the spectacular personal courage shown by George Armstrong Custer on East Cavalry Field [where he] stopped Stuart's column and in so doing probably saved the Union."[34] Most importantly, this conclusion was no exaggeration but a right-on-target analysis. Edward G. Longacre also concluded, "Stuart's troopers had been decisively repulsed—they would be in no position to support Robert E. Lee's offensive at Gettysburg."[35]

The accurate and concise analyses by these historians all agree with those of General Gregg, who emphasized how in regard to Stuart's most important mission of the war, his goal "was to do, ours to prevent. Could he have reached the rear of our army . . . disastrous consequences might have resulted."[36] For such reasons, historian Jay Monaghan correctly wrote how on

July 3, "General Custer had made an auspicious start [and] became a gallant—perhaps a key—figure in winning the greatest battle of the war."[37]

Another fine historian, Roger H. Harrell, professor emeritus at California State University in Northridge, concluded that "Gregg was content that the threat to Meade's rear and flank was over [because] Stuart [simply] could not break through Gregg's cavalry and do damage to Meade's infantry" at the key moment.[38] And in the words of historian Stephen Z. Starr, who summarized with his usual insight and broad breadth of knowledge, while exploding the popular myth—increasingly fashionable today because of zealous deniers who have abused the internet and Civil War blogs in true propagandistic fashion—that Stuart was only guarding the army's left: "What was the result of the fight? Stuart's claim that he was only protecting the left flank of the Confederate army is not worth a moment's credence. The course of the battle from its beginning makes it evident that his objective was to brush Gregg [and Custer] out of the way and attack the rear of Meade's infantry on Cemetery Ridge, at the same time that it was attacked frontally by Pickett."[39]

Indeed, in a letter, Fitzhugh Lee emphasized the most fundamental truth of the struggle for possession of the East Cavalry Field and exactly why it was so crucially important, because Stuart's mission was for the overall "purpose of effecting a surprise on the enemy's rear" on the afternoon of July 3.[40] Even more, in this same letter, Fitzhugh Lee described how "Stuart sent for Hampton and I to come to his position [field headquarters] to see about making the movement to the rear" of the Army of the Potomac.[41] Lee's words coincided with those of Edward G. Longacre, who emphasized that Stuart's "main effort [was] against the Union rear."[42] The same author, a former Department of Defense historian, also concluded, "Stuart's attempt to reach the rear of Meade's army in time to influence the outcome of Robert E. Lee's grand offensive had failed."[43]

For such reasons, historian Tom Carhart, PhD, and a West Point graduate, concluded, "Lee ordered Stuart to try to travel those roads at the bottom of Cress Ridge and 'effect a surprise on the enemy's rear.' But despite the fact that he had a much larger force, Stuart was simply unable to get past Custer; [the] cavalry charge by Stuart's force that was blunted by Custer and his Wolverine Brigade was the more important high-water mark of the Confederacy [because in the end] finally this battle really comes down to Custer and his seemingly suicidal attack [and] it seems very reasonable to say that, at Gettysburg, Custer truly saved the Union."[44]

Corporal James Henry Avery, 5th Michigan Cavalry, revealed as much in his journal when he summarized the furious battle that raged with intensity on the East Cavalry Field: "We were beating back the columns of Lee, who was trying to push around the flank of our army. If he had succeeded, he would probably have beat us" to achieve Confederate victory at Gettysburg.[45]

Without exaggeration, Lieutenant George G. Briggs, 7th Michigan Cavalry, concluded that "the world has never seen such Cavalry fighting as we have done, which is the testimony of the best Cavalry officers in the service."[46]

These words were no exaggeration, because Stuart had been thoroughly beaten, and like never before, after some of the most bitter cavalry combat of the war. In the end after Custer's two saber charges that kept him off balance, Stuart had lost all confidence and desire for unleashing any offensive attempt, as ordered by Lee, to strike Meade's rear, because he had been outfought and outthought by the goat of his West Point class of 1861 who was still far from seeing his mid-twenties. Custer had ensured that Stuart was just another one of Lee's top lieutenants who had failed him miserably on July 3 by failing to fulfill his orders. Generations of historians have long focused on the romance, heroism, and grandeur of Pickett's Charge, and the most famous attack in American history has cast a giant shadow to obscure the overall importance of the decisive showdown on the East Cavalry Field: the forgotten other half of Pickett's Charge.

But instead of their longtime focus, if not obsession, with the sheer majesty of Lee's greatest assault that was doomed because of Stuart's failures, they should have been focused on the equally important and dramatic story of the East Cavalry Field, because Stuart's attackers possessed the potential to inflict a more damaging blow than Pickett's Charge by striking Meade's Cemetery Ridge defenders from the rear, the surprise attack from the east that actually possessed a better chance of achieving decisive victory than the doomed infantry attack, which never had a chance without Stuart's assistance, in the open fields before Meade's right-center. Stuart had expected an easy victory over the opposing cavalry at the Hanover and Low Dutch Roads, but he had never counted on the boldness and aggressiveness of Custer in leading two daring charges that stunned the so-called "Invincibles," and decisively turned the tide in favor of Union fortunes.

Clearly, for determining the fate of the Army of the Potomac on the afternoon of July 3, young Custer was exactly the right man, at the right place, at exactly the right time—a classic case of a man having met his hour. What had been most important was that General Meade and his hard-hit army, which was only hoping to survive Lee's last great offensive effort on the afternoon of July 3 after the Army of the Potomac had been severely bloodied on the first two days, had a dynamic and aggressive young officer who was tactically flexible and opportunistic and had much to prove, in the army's rear. Much like the Army of the Potomac itself on Gettysburg's day of decision, Custer had much to prove to himself and his men.

Consequently, given these powerful motivations when combined with the moment when everything was at stake for the life of the Union and despite being only twenty-three, Custer was ideally suited for his all-important role in the army's rear in orchestrating a brilliant performance that made a significant contribution to not only saving the Army of the Potomac, but also the Union during the most decisive battle of the Civil War.

Contrary to the orders of his superior (Third Cavalry Division commander Kilpatrick), Custer decided with single-minded assurance that the key to the safety of Meade's rear was in staying with the Second Cavalry Division and defending the strategic crossroads of the Hanover and Low Dutch Roads. Custer understood that this position was vital to hold at all costs. Custer was correct in his early strategic insights and tactical evaluations that he made on the fly, because this strategic intersection was the immediate objective of an overconfident Stuart before he struck Meade's rear in the most important surprise attack of the war, if the Wolverines and their feisty commander could be pushed aside.

Therefore, even when recalled by his superior (the division commander), Custer still refused to depart the crossroads that he was determined to defend to the last, because he understood that this was the key to the Battle of Gettysburg. In this regard, Custer's instincts and distinctive contrarianism (especially in regard to doing what no one expected and regardless of odds or situation) served him and the Union extremely well, which partly explained how the last—graduating thirty-fourth, which even included a poor grade in his study of cavalry tactics—in his West Point class could rise so splendidly to the greatest challenge on July 3.

In the end, Custer's determination not to relinquish the initiative and then his sheer aggressiveness in leading two of the war's most daring cavalry charges—first the 7th Michigan Cavalry and then the 1st Michigan Cavalry—saved the day in the army's rear more than the superior firepower of either the fast-firing Spencers or his horse artillery, by thwarting Stuart's best offensive efforts and taking him away from his primary mission, disarranging the entire Lee-Stuart battle plan to strike the Army of the Potomac's vulnerable rear. No one more than Stuart's men realized that Custer's two saber attacks straight north across the open plain had turned the tide and saved the day in the army's rear, thwarting their best efforts. Clearly, this was Custer's finest day and that of his Michigan Brigade, cementing an unbeatable team bond between the young brigadier general and his hard-fighting Wolverines. He excelled like no other cavalry commander at Gettysburg, surpassing the achievements of the much-celebrated John Buford on July 1 in overall importance, because the situation on the final day was far more crucial as much more was at stake for the army and the nation.

On the decisive afternoon of July 3, Stuart possessed a relatively simple mission that was all important: He simply had to either bypass or gain the strategic crossroads of the Hanover and Low Dutch Roads and then the Baltimore Pike before riding southwest and striking the Army of the Potomac's rear in conjunction with Pickett's Charge to deliver an attack from the east that possessed unlimited possibilities for decisive success. But Stuart was stopped from ever achieving his great goal upon which Lee and his top cavalry commander had staked everything to achieve decisive victory. Custer not only thoroughly disrupted and thwarted the best-laid tactical plans of Lee and Stuart, but also ended their lofty ambitions by some of the hardest cavalry fighting of the war, including leading two saber charges in person, in a dramatic showdown that was far more important than the Battle of Brandy Station. In the end and as mentioned, no man was more responsible for frustrating of ambitions of both Lee and Stuart than the "goat" of his West Point class.

Therefore, like few, if any, other brigadier generals on either side, Custer saved the day in Meade's rear during a true crisis situation when everything was at stake for the army and the Union. The true turning point of the East Cavalry Field fight was when Custer boldly led two Napoleonic-era charges in the same manner as Marshal Murat during Napoleon's glory days, when the armies of France had dominated Europe, the antithesis of Custer's disastrous last fight along the Little Bighorn in the middle of nowhere, which has cast a giant shadow to obscure the supreme importance of his vital contributions to decisive victory at Gettysburg. While the fight along the Little Bighorn in the remote Montana Territory was a minor and insignificant clash of arms, the dramatic showdown on the East Cavalry Field was America's most decisive cavalry battle of the Civil War.

Prophetically, during the war years, Major General George Gordon Meade, who was a Pennsylvanian who enjoyed his own greatest day at Gettysburg like Custer, remarked in regard to Custer's ultimate fate far from Gettysburg and the eastern theater: "That man will die at the head of his command."[47] Ironically, the aide-de-camp who had brought General Pleasonton's order to depart from the strategic crossroads and return south to rejoin his Third Cavalry Division under Kilpatrick was Captain George Yates, who had gained his position by way of Custer's recommendation for his old Monroe, Michigan, friend. As a cruel fate would have it, Captain Yates was destined to die with him on a barren hill above the Little Bighorn.[48]

But by Custer not following the directive delivered by Yates, he was more responsible than any other cavalry brigade commander for saving the day, because, in the analysis of Dr. Lawrence A. Frost, "had Stuart's seemingly invincible cavalrymen not been [defeated then] they would have been free to attack the rear of the Union forces on Cemetery Ridge [and] the Union chance of stopping them at that point would have been zero and Pickett's Charge could have been successful."[49]

Even the vanquished Confederates of Stuart's mauled command were "full of admiration for the Federal troops who so gallantly charge our lines," especially the two most dramatic and important attacks led by Custer himself.[50] In the end, Custer looked fondly upon what he had accomplished against the odds and all expectations, including having "successfully evaded a superior's order and, by doing so, became a gallant—perhaps a key—figure in winning the greatest battle of the war."[51]

Clearly, this early July 1863 was a heady time when achieving military glory, and thoughts about the great saber charges of finely uniformed cavalry during Napoleon's European wars filled Custer's imagination as he led his tough Wolverines on the East Cavalry Field, where he saved the strategic crossroads, the horse artillery, and the reputations of his men, before his disillusionment with fighting Native Americans battling for their freedom, because, in his own words, "if he survives the campaign he can feel assured of this fact, that one-half of his fellow-citizens at home will revile him for his zeal and pronounce him success, if he achieves any, a massacre of poor, defenseless, harmless Indians; while the other half, if his efforts to chastise the common enemy are not crowned with satisfactory results, will cry 'Down with him.'"[52]

Custer was invigorated by the remarkable success he achieved on July 3, penning with ample good reason on July 19, 1863, "I believe more than ever in Destiny."[53] Most of all, he thanked God for his outstanding success and for having survived the awful bloodletting at Gettysburg and other fights. But even in achieving such a sparkling success in the Army of the Potomac's rear, the young man remained humble and well grounded, despite his heady achievements and young age. Reflecting on his many close calls in the heat of battle, especially at Gettysburg, Custer emphasized in a letter to Libbie how his brush with death only "strengthens my grateful dependence on the Merciful Being Who has so often shielded me. . . . May I live to glorify Him and keep His commandments!"[54]

On the hot afternoon of June 25, 1876, no one knows Custer's last thoughts just before he met his final doom and Maker at the Little Bighorn. It is not known, but perhaps while facing the hordes of enraged Sioux and Cheyenne warriors of the Northern Great Plains, he might have briefly wondered what kind of a strange fate and odd destiny had brought him nearly two thousand miles from the East Cavalry Field, where he had enjoyed the finest day of his career, to the sage-covered hilltop that overlooked the blue waters of the Little Bighorn River, where he launched his final charge against odds that could not be overcome, unlike his day of glory on the East Cavalry Field. In the end, Custer could never have possibly imagined that his greatest day in the most important battle of the Civil War, when everything was at stake, would become completely overshadowed by a short, insignificant fight in the faraway Montana Territory, when nothing was at stake.

In part because no one knows—no survivors of Custer's five companies—about the exact details of Custer's last moments on earth, the story of the famous "Custer's Last Stand" evolved into one of America's great myths. The battle has long been shrouded in romance and legend to an excessive degree because so many writers have allowed their imaginations to soar. Ironically, such has not been the case of Custer's greatest day on July 3, 1863.

A symbolic sacrifice in the "winning of the West," Custer's death at the Little Bighorn catapulted him into the realm of national myth that has endured to this day.[55] When his old commander, General Phil Sheridan, who was his commander during the campaigns of 1864 and 1865, first heard of Custer's death, he retorted with confidence, "Nonsense! Don't believe it!"[56] After all, larger-than-life commanders "like Custer didn't die."[57]

Indeed, as revealed in his memoir, one Confederate officer never forgot a truly impressive sight when General Lee was about to surrender at Appomattox Court House in a glorious early April for the Army of the Potomac on the verge of decisive victory: "Just then a Union officer came dashing up [and] he was a most striking picture: a rather young man, dressed in a blue sack with the largest shoulder-straps of a major general I ever saw; with long, red hair hanging in oily curls down near to his shoulders, a gorgeous red scarf in which there was a gold pin, nearly two inches in length and breadth, with big letters, 'George A. Custer, Major General.'"[58]

In a final tribute to Custer after he made his last charge of June 25, 1876, the reporter of the *Detroit Free Press* summarized after the victor of the East Cavalry Field met a dismal end at the Little Bighorn, which cast the giant shadow that has obscured Custer's finest day on July 3, 1863: "It is said that those who live by the sword shall perish by the sword, but the manner of his death is a sad shock. He who led a hundred charges against brave men, riding through storms of shot and shell [especially in leading the 7th Michigan Cavalry and then the 1st Michigan Cavalry on the final day at Gettysburg], should have been spared to die at home among his loved ones, or should have been struck down at the head of his troopers when leading some fierce and glorious charge [as opposed to the alleged "massacre" by the Sioux and Cheyenne]. No man had a better heart—no braver hand ever held a sabre," including in the climactic showdown at Gettysburg, which was a day of destiny for the American nation.[59]

Indeed, Custer's hard-hitting role in leading the 7th Michigan and then the 1st Michigan in headlong cavalry charges against the odds saved the day in Meade's rear by buying precious time and sapping the strength and determination of Stuart and his "Invincibles," while keeping their attention focused on the wrong objective—beating Custer—and not on fulfilling the primary mission of striking Meade's rear, by keeping them as far away from the Union army's main defensive line and thwarting what was basically Lee's pincer movement— from the west and east—in conjunction with Pickett's Charge. Therefore and not surprisingly, in a letter Custer revealed the extent of his feisty fighting spirit and the key to his success on July 3: "Oh, could you but have seen some of the charges that we made! While thinking of them I cannot but exclaim, 'Glorious War!'"[60] For such reasons, a highly respected general, Nelson Miles, who investigated the fiasco at the Little Bighorn, where Custer launched his last charge against even greater odds than on the East Cavalry Field, concluded with pride that "Custer's flag went down in disaster, but with honor."[61]

Again, Custer's audacity, courage, and daring can hardly be overstated in regard to reaping success on the crucial third day. Only a few days after his promotion to brigadier general and becoming the Wolverine Brigade's commander on June 29, 1863, Custer had achieved a stunning success in the Army of the Potomac's rear because Stuart's best offensive efforts "had been decisively repulsed, largely as a result of two of the most dramatic saber charges of this or any other war [to ensure that] Stuart would not reach the Union rear in time to salvage the doomed attack against Meade's center that would become known as Pickett's Charge."[62]

It was here on the hallowed ground of the most important battle of the war that the inexperienced West Pointer, age twenty-three, played the leading role in protecting the vulnerable rear of the battered Army of the Potomac, saving the day when everything was at stake. Although still known primarily for the tragic outcome of an entirely insignificant clash of arms along the Little Bighorn on the afternoon of June 25, 1876, Custer's impressive tactical performance and demonstrated leadership ability in his first major battle was nothing short of remarkable and has been long deserving of greater attention —the genesis for the writing of the current book.[63]

What has been most forgotten was the fact that July 3, 1863, was Custer's finest day when he stopped the most legendary cavalry commander from striking a blow in the Army of the Potomac's rear in conjunction with Pickett's Charge, because Lee was making his final and most determined bid to win it all, before it was too late for the Army of Northern Virginia. In the end, perhaps Corporal James Henry Avery, 5th Michigan Cavalry, best summarized in his journal the supreme importance of Custer's vital role and the true meaning of the bloody struggle that raged for hours on the East Cavalry Field in terms of overall decisiveness: "The rebels had again, and again, pushed forward a heavy force to break our line, so as to strike Meade's rear. And were as often repulsed by our brigade, and Meade was saved."[64] What cannot be denied was the fact that America would have been a very different nation if Custer and his Wolverines had not emerged victorious in the right-rear of the hard-pressed Army of the Potomac on the war's most decisive day on July 3, 1863: although long overlooked and forgotten, this great clash of cavalry was a true turning point of not only the Battle of Gettysburg and the Civil War, but also of American history.

# Notes

## CHAPTER 1

1. Stephen Z. Starr, *The Union Cavalry in the Civil War: From Fort Sumter to Gettysburg, 1861–1863*, 2 vols. (Baton Rouge: Louisiana State University Press, 2007), 1:437–38.
2. Karla Jean Husby, comp., and Eric J. Wittenburg, ed., *Under Custer's Command: The Civil War Journal of James Henry Avery* (Dulles, VA: Potomac Books, 2002), 35.
3. Ibid.
4. Henry B. McClellan, *I Rode with Jeb Stuart: The Life and Campaigns of General J. E. B. Stuart* (New York: Da Capo, 1994), 339.
5. Edward G. Longacre, *Fitz Lee: A Military Biography of Major General Fitzhugh Lee* (New York: Da Capo, 2005), 125.
6. Jay Monaghan, *Custer: The Life of General George Armstrong Custer* (Lincoln: University of Nebraska Press, 1971), 3–10.
7. Ibid., 10.
8. John M. Carroll, comp. and ed., *Custer in the Civil War: His Unfinished Memoirs* (Mattituck, NY: J. M. Carroll, 1977), 78; Monaghan, *Custer*, 10–11.
9. Carroll, *Custer in the Civil War*, 86.
10. Ibid., 86; Louise Barnett, *Touched by Fire: The Life, Death, and Mythic Afterlife of George Armstrong Custer* (New York: Henry Holt, 1996), 28.
11. Carroll, *Custer in the Civil War*, 87.
12. Ibid., 88.
13. Ibid., 88–89.
14. Ibid., 89.
15. Barnett, *Touched by Fire*, 28.
16. James S. Robbins, *Last in Their Class: Custer, Pickett and Goats of West Point* (New York: Encounter Books, 2017), xiii.
17. Ibid.
18. Carroll, *Custer in the Civil War*, 90–91.

19. Ibid., 90.
20. Ibid., 91–92.
21. Ibid., 93, 100.
22. Robert J. Trout, *They Followed the Plume: The Story of J.E.B. Stuart and His Staff* (Mechanicsburg, PA: Stackpole Books, 1993), 3; Carroll, *Custer in the Civil War*, 101.
23. Willard W. Glazier, *Three Years in the Federal Cavalry* (Middletown, NY: Pantianos Classics, 2018), 9–10.
24. William C. Davis, *Jefferson Davis: The Man and His Hour, a Biography* (New York: HarperCollins, 1992), 501–6.
25. Ibid.
26. Marguerite Merington, *The Custer Story, The Life and Intimate Letters of General Custer and His Wife* (Elizabeth, NY: Devin-Adair, 1950), 10.
27. Glazier, *Three Years in the Federal Cavalry*, 63.
28. Edward G. Longacre, *Custer: The Making of a Young General* (New York: Skyhorse Publishing, 2018), 119–20. Ron Field, *Confederate Cavalryman versus Union Cavalryman, Eastern Theater, 1861-65* (South Yorkshire: Osprey, 2015), 4–5; Glazier, *Three Years in the Federal Cavalry*, 9, 17; Starr, *The Union Cavalry in the Civil War*, 1:57, 316–23, 336–40; Stephen W. Sears, *Chancellorsville* (New York: Houghton Mifflin, 1996), 41–373; Philip Katcher, *The Army of Robert E. Lee* (London: Arms and Armour, 1994), 137; Philip Katcher, *Confederate Cavalryman, 1861-65* (Oxford: Osprey, 2002), 4, 6; Dan Beattie, *Brandy Station 1863: First Steps towards Gettysburg* (Oxford: Osprey, 2008), 8–9.
29. Jay Luvaas and Herold W. Nelson, eds., *Guide to the Battle of Gettysburg* (Lawrence: University Press of Kansas, 1994), 210–11.
30. Glazier, *Three Years in the Federal Cavalry*, 63.
31. Ibid., 63–64, 83.
32. Heros von Borcke, *The Confederate War for Independence: A Prussian Officer with J.E.B. Stuart in Virginia* (Nashville, TN: J. S. Sanders, 1999), 364; Editors of Time-Life Books, *Echoes of Glory: Arms and Equipment of the Confederacy* (Alexandria: Time-Life Books, 1991), 74–75.
33. Glazier, *Three Years in the Federal Cavalry*, 63–64.
34. Wilbur Sturtevant Nye, *Here Come the Rebels!* (Dayton: Morningside Bookshop, 1988), 15.
35. Edwin B. Coddington, *The Gettysburg Campaign: A Study in Command* (New York: Scribner, 1979 ), 220–21; Starr, *The Union Cavalry in the Civil War*, 1:416; Jeffry D. Wert, *Custer: The Controversial Life of George Armstrong Custer* (New York: Simon and Schuster, 1996), 81.
36. Coddington, *The Gettysburg Campaign*, 220–21; Beattie, *Brandy Station 1863*, 8; Starr, *The Union Cavalry in the Civil War*, 1:337–39; Wert, *Custer*, 82; Husby and Wittenburg, *Under Custer's Command*, 1.
37. Wert, *Custer*, 82.
38. Ibid., 81; David F. Riggs, *East of Gettysburg: Custer vs. Stuart* (Fort Collins, CO: Old Army Press, 1970), 25–26; Husby and Wittenburg, *Under Custer's Command*, 1–2.
39. Miscellaneous Newspaper Collection, Author's Collection.
40. Wert, *Custer*, 81–82.

41. James S. Robbins, *The Real Custer: From Boy General to Tragic Hero* (Washington, DC: Regnery, 2014), 74.
42. Gregory J. W. Urwin, *Custer Victorious: The Civil War Battles of General George Armstrong Custer* (Lincoln: University of Nebraska Press, 1990), 51.
43. Frederick Whittaker, *A Complete Life of General George A. Custer: Though the Civil War*, 2 vols. (Lincoln: University of Nebraska Press, 1993), 1:171.
44. Carroll, *Custer in the Civil War*, 74–75.
45. Tom Carhart, *Sacred Ties: From West Point Brothers to Battlefield Rivals; A True Story of the Civil War* (New York: Berkley, 2011), 193.
46. Robbins, *The Real Custer*, 3.
47. Merington, *The Custer Story*, 57.
48. Robbins, *The Real Custer*, 74.
49. Robbins, *Last in Their Class*, 261–62.
50. Urwin, *Custer Victorious*, 53–54.
51. Robbins, *The Real Custer*, 11.
52. Monaghan, *Custer*, 42.
53. Robbins, *Last in Their Class*, 260, 262.
54. Starr, *The Union Cavalry in the Civil War*, 1:416; Paul Johnson, *Napoleon: A Life* (New York: Penguin, 2002), 15–57.
55. Roy Bird, *The Better Brother: Tom and George Custer and the Battle for the American West* (New York: Turner, 2011), 2–9, 30–34, 239–40; Longacre, *Custer*, 2–5; Merington, *The Custer Story*, 3–5; Monaghan, *Custer*, 3–8; Robbins, *The Real Custer*, 1–3.
56. Monaghan, *Custer*, 3, 9.
57. Merington, *The Custer Story*, 13.
58. Ibid., 6.
59. Longacre, *Custer*, 2; Paul Andrew Hutton, "Libbie Custer: 'A Wounded Thing Must Hide,'" *Wild West*, June 2012, 30; Merington, *The Custer Story*, 14–16, 24, 39, 41–43, 48–51; Barnett, *Touched by Fire*, 19–24; Thom Hatch, *Clashes of Cavalry: The Civil War Careers of George Armstrong Custer and Jeb Stuart* (Mechanicsburg, PA: Stackpole Books, 2001), 61.
60. Barnett, *Touched by Fire*, 21–24; Hatch, *Clashes of Cavalry*, 61; Merington, *The Custer Story*, 46–51.
61. Merington, *The Custer Story*, 50–51; Barnett, *Touched by Fire*, 24.
62. Barnett, *Touched by Fire*, 24.
63. Merington, *The Custer Story*, 48–51.
64. Barnett, *Touched by Fire*, 24–25.
65. Richard Bak, *A Distant Thunder: Michigan in the Civil War* (Ann Arbor, MI: Hudson River Press, 2004), 3, 8–19, 31; Seamus Metress and Eileen K. Metress, *Irish in Michigan* (East Lansing: Michigan State University Press, 2006), 5–10; Bruce Catton, *Michigan: A History* (New York: Norton, 1976), 149; Edward G. Longacre, *Custer and His Wolverines: The Michigan Cavalry Brigade, 1861–1865* (New York: Da Capo, 1997), 9–10, 17–18; Starr, *The Union Cavalry in the Civil War*, 1:433, 437–38; McClellan, *I Rode with Jeb Stuart*, 339; Coddington, *The Gettysburg Campaign*, 520–21; Husby and Wittenburg, *Under Custer's Command*, 1, 10.

66. Bruce A. Rubenstein and Lawrence E. Ziewacz, *Michigan: A History of the Great Lakes State* (Wheeling, IL: Harlan Davidson, 1981), 102.

67. Donald L. Smith, *The Twenty-Fourth Michigan* (Harrisburg, PA: Stackpole Books, 1962), 9–10; Bak, *A Distant Thunder*, 115–26; Rubenstein and Ziewacz, *Michigan*, 106.

68. Rubenstein and Ziewacz, *Michigan*, 106–7.

69. Husby and Wittenburg, *Under Custer's Command*, 2; Longacre, *Custer and His Wolverines*, 9–10.

70. Longacre, *Custer and His Wolverines*, 9.

71. Hatch, *Clashes of Cavalry*, 97.

72. Robbins, *Last in Their Class*, 260.

73. Merington, *The Custer Story*, 35.

74. Catton, *Michigan*, 3–101.

75. *Grand Rapids Enquirer*, Grand Rapids, Michigan, April 20, 1861.

76. Roger L. Rosentreter, *Grand Rapids and the Civil War* (Charleston, SC: History Press, 2018), 16–18.

77. Ibid., 29–30.

78. Ibid., 33–38.

79. Samuel Harris, *Personal Reminiscences of Samuel Harris* (Chicago: Rogerson Press, 1897), 1, 10.

80. Richard L Hamilton, *"Oh! Hast Thou Forgotten," Michigan Cavalrymen in the Civil War, The Gettysburg Campaign, A Civil War Memoir of Sgt. Thomas Patten, 1862–1863* (Charleston, SC: BookSurge Publishing, 2008), xvi–xxii, 1–2, 6, 11, 14, 16–17, 30, 34; Rubenstein and Ziewacz, *Michigan*, 101.

81. Hamilton, *"Oh! Hast Thou Forgotten,"* 33–34.

82. Husby and Wittenburg, *Under Custer's Command*, 4.

83. Asa B. Isham, *Seventh Michigan Cavalry of Custer's Wolverine Brigade* (New York: Town Topics, 2000), 7–10.

84. Longacre, *Custer and His Wolverines*, 9–10.

85. Isham, *Seventh Michigan Cavalry*, 148.

86. Ibid., 154.

87. Ibid.

88. William Glover Gage Letters, Gettysburg Letter Lot, November 2016, Nate D. Sanders Auctions, Fine Autographs and Memorabilia, Los Angeles, California. Hereafter cited as Gage Letters, SA.

89. James Harvey Kidd, *Personal Recollections of a Cavalryman, One of Custer's Wolverines, The Civil War Letters of Brevet General James H. Kidd*, introduction by Paul Andrew Hutton (New York: Skyhorse Publishing, 2018), 67, 74.

90. Ibid., 4.

91. Mark S. Stowe, *Company B, 6th Michigan Cavalry* (North Charleston, SC: CreateSpace, 2012), 3–4, 39.

92. Urwin, *Custer Victorious*, 90–91.

93. Michael Stephenson, *The Last Full Measure: How Soldiers Die in Battle* (New York: Broadway Paperbacks, 2012), 132; Ernest L. Reedstrom, *Bugles, Banners and War Bonnets* (New York: Bonanza Books, 1977), 246–48; Husby and Wittenburg, *Under Custer's*

*Command*, 3; David Harsanyi, *First Freedom: A Ride through America's Enduring History with the Gun* (New York: Threshold Editions, 2018), 123–27.
  94. Husby and Wittenburg, *Under Custer's Command*, 18.
  95. Harsanyi, *First Freedom*, 127.
  96. Husby and Wittenburg, *Under Custer's Command*, 7.
  97. Longacre, *Custer and His Wolverines*, 9.
  98. Stowe, *Company B*, 7.
  99. Bak, *A Distant Thunder*, 104–5, 108.
  100. Husby and Wittenburg. *Under Custer's Command*, 2.
  101. Whittaker, *A Complete Life of General George A. Custer*, 1:179.
  102. John E. Norvell, "General Custer Comes to Dinner," An American Family, July 22, 2013, internet.
  103. Sandy Barnard, ed., and Thomas E. Singelyn, comp., *An Aide to Custer: The Civil War Letters of Lt. Edward G. Granger* (Norman: University of Oklahoma Press, 2018), xiv–xvi, 8–11, 19.
  104. Ibid., 115.
  105. Neil McKinstry, Grantsville, Utah, emails to author, May 9 and 12, 2018.
  106. Barnard and Singelyn, *An Aide to Custer*, 116.
  107. Ibid., 117–18.
  108. Ibid., 118–19.
  109. Harris, *Personal Reminiscences of Samuel Harris*, 23–24.
  110. Henry C. Meyer, *Civil War Experiences with the New York Cavalry, Under Bayard, Gregg, Kilpatrick, Custer, Raulston and Newberry, 1862–1864* (London: Leonaur, 2010), 33.
  111. Rosentreter, *Grand Rapids and the Civil War*, 40.
  112. Whittaker, *A Complete Life of General George A. Custer*, 1:169–70.
  113. Johnson, *Napoleon*, 57.
  114. Hatch, *Clashes of Cavalry*, 113–17.
  115. Garland C. Hudgins and Richard B. Kleese, *Recollections of an Old Dominion Dragoon: The Civil War Experiences of Sgt. Robert S. Hudgins II Co. B, 3rd Virginia Infantry* (Orange, VA: Publisher's Press, 1993), 39; Edward G. Longacre, *The Cavalry at Gettysburg: A Tactical Study of Mounted Operations during the Civil War's Pivotal Campaign, 9 June–14 July 1863* (Lincoln, NE: Bison Books, 1993), 27.
  116. John W. Thomason Jr., *JEB Stuart* (New York: Mallard Press, 1992), 2–3, 5–6, 12–13; Hatch, *Clashes of Cavalry*, 169.
  117. John Camden West, *A Texan in Search of a Fight, Being the Diary and Letters of a Private Soldier in Hood's Texas Brigade* (Memphis, TN: General Books, 2012), 1, 11.
  118. Hatch, *Clashes of Cavalry*, 169.
  119. Ibid., 171.
  120. Thomason, *JEB Stuart*, 9–10, 16.
  121. Ibid., 398; Fairfax Downey, *Clash of Cavalry: The Battle of Brandy Station* (New York: David McKay, 1959), 3–5, 76–147; Glazier, *Three Years in the Federal Cavalry*, 109; Carhart, *Sacred Ties*, 188–89; Beattie, *Brandy Station 1863*, 5–17; Nye, *Here Come the Rebels!*, 16; David Bridges, *Fighting with Jeb Stuart: Major James Breathed and the Confederate Horse Artillery* (Arlington, VA: private printing, 2006), 149.

122. Bcattic, *Brandy Station 1863*, 5-81; David Douglas, *A Boot Full of Memories: Captain Leonard Williams, 2nd South Carolina Cavalry* (Camden, SC: Gray Fox Publishing, 2003), 225; George Michael Neese, *Three Years in the Confederate Horse Artillery* (New York: Neale, 1911), 166-69; Bridges, *Fighting with Jeb Stuart*, 149.

123. Neese, *Three Years in the Confederate Horse Artillery*, 170.

124. Douglas, *A Boot Full of Memories*, 225; Susan Leigh Blackford, comp., *Letters from Lee's Army* (New York: A. S. Barnes, 1962), 175.

125. Starr, *The Union Cavalry in the Civil War*, 1:393.

126. Robert N. Rosen, *The Jewish Confederates* (Columbia: University of South Carolina Press, 2000), 126-28.

127. Edward B. Williams, *Rebel Brothers: The Civil War Letters of the Truehearts* (College Station: Texas A&M University Press, 1995), 77-78.

128. W. W. Blackford, *War Years with Jeb Stuart* (London: Endeavor Press, 2016), 106.

129. Carhart, *Sacred Ties*, 188.

130. Blackford, *Letters from Lee's Army*, 42.

131. Neese, *Three Years in the Confederate Horse Artillery*, 178.

132. *Charleston Mercury*, Charleston, South Carolina, June 17, 1863.

133. Neese, *Three Years in the Confederate Horse Artillery*, 168.

134. Bridges, *Fighting with Jeb Stuart*, 157.

135. Von Borcke, *The Confederate War for Independence*, 353, 449; Web Garrison, *Civil War Stories, Strange Tales, Oddities, Events, and Coincidences* (New York: Promontory Press, 1997), 67; Sheridan R. Barringer, *Fighting for General Lee: Confederate General Rufus Barringer and the North Carolina Cavalry Brigade* (El Dorado Hills, CA: Savas-Beatie Publishing, 2016), 119-20; Field, *Confederate Cavalryman versus Union Cavalryman*, 6-7; Glazier, *Three Years in the Federal Cavalry*, 63-64; Longacre, *The Cavalry at Gettysburg*, 33.

136. Von Borcke, *The Confederate War for Independence*, 364; Glazier, *Three Years in the Federal Cavalry*, 72.

137. Robert J. Trout, ed., *Memoirs of the Stuart Horse Artillery Battalion, Moorman's and Hart's Batteries* (Knoxville: University of Tennessee Press, 2008), 192.

138. Ibid., 203.

139. Ibid., 195.

140. Douglas, *A Boot Full of Memories*, 215-16; Downey, *Clash of Cavalry*, 82-83; Nye, *Here Come the Rebels!*, 15.

141. Glazier, *Three Years in the Federal Cavalry*, 83.

142. Thomason, *JEB Stuart*, 364; Nye, *Here Come the Rebels!*, 15; Downey, *Clash of Cavalry*, 25; Garrison, *Civil War Stories*, 67.

143. Garrison, *Civil War Stories*, 67; Nye, *Here Come the Rebels!*, 15.

144. Starr, *The Union Cavalry in the Civil War*, 1:393.

145. *Dispatch*, Richmond, Virginia, April 5, 1896.

146. Meyer, *Civil War Experiences with the New York Cavalry*, 39.

147. Jeff Toalson, ed., *Send Me a Pair of Old Boots & Kiss My Little Girls: The Civil War Letters of Richard and Mary Watkins, 1861-1865* (Bloomington, IN: iUniverse, 2009), ix-x, xv, 1-3, 11.

148. Ibid., 134.
149. Ibid., 187–88.
150. Sears, *Chancellorsville*, 430.
151. Bak, *A Distant Thunder*, 71.
152. Merington, *The Custer Story*, 56.
153. Ibid., 42.
154. Carroll, *Custer in the Civil War*, 156.
155. Ibid., 155.
156. Merington, *The Custer Story*, 29.
157. Ibid., 34.
158. Ibid., 35.
159. Ibid., 65–66.
160. Field, *Confederate Cavalryman versus Union Cavalryman*, 4.
161. Husby and Wittenburg, *Under Custer's Command*, 2.
162. Field, *Confederate Cavalryman versus Union Cavalryman*, 4, 22–23; Starr, *The Union Cavalry in the Civil War*, 1:50–53; Barnett, *Touched by Fire*, 28; Katcher, *The Army of Robert E. Lee*, 137; Johnson, *Napoleon*, 49–57; Merington, *The Custer Story*, 3–65; R. F. Delderfield, *March of the Twenty-Six* (South Yorkshire: Pen and Sword, 2004), 12, 43, 57; Longacre, *Custer and His Wolverines*, 153.
163. Merington, *The Custer Story*, 7; Monaghan, *Custer*, 6–8.
164. Kevin M. Sullivan, *Custer's Road to Disaster: The Path to Little Bighorn* (Guilford, CT: Globe Pequot Press, 2013), 11.
165. Ibid.; Longacre, *Custer and His Wolverines*, 153.
166. Merington, *The Custer Story*, 13.
167. Burke Davis, *They Called Him Stonewall: A Life of Lt. General T. J. Jackson, C.S.A.* (New York: Fairfax Press, 1974), 148–49.

## CHAPTER 2

1. Douglas, *A Boot Full of Memories*, 226, 229; William Garrett Piston, *Lee's Tarnished Lieutenant: James Longstreet and His Place in Southern History* (Athens: University of Georgia Press, 1987), 46; Davis, *Jefferson Davis*, 504–5.
2. Thomason, *JEB Stuart*, 12, 412; Blackford, *Letters from Lee's Army*, 175.
3. Douglas, *A Boot Full of Memories*, vii, 216.
4. Katcher, *Confederate Cavalryman 1861–65*, 7.
5. Glazier, *Three Years in the Federal Cavalry*, 79.
6. Barringer, *Fighting for General Lee*, 117.
7. Meyer, *Civil War Experiences with the New York Cavalry*, 31.
8. Barringer, *Fighting for General Lee*, 119–20; Glazier, *Three Years in the Federal Cavalry*, 112–14.
9. Glazier, *Three Years in the Federal Cavalry*, 114.
10. Meyer, *Civil War Experiences with the New York Cavalry*, 32.
11. Ibid.

12. Glazier, *Three Years in the Federal Cavalry*, 63–64, 72.
13. Bridges, *Fighting with Jeb Stuart*, 165.
14. Robert K. Ackerman, *Wade Hampton III* (Columbia: University of South Carolina Press, 2007), 45.
15. Jeb Stuart to M. R. H. Garnett, Confederate Congress, April 16, 1863, Seth Keller Inc., White Plains, New York.
16. Guy R. Everson and Edward W. Simpson Jr., eds., *Far, Far from Home: The Wartime Letters of Dick and Tally Simpson, 3rd South Carolina Volunteers* (Oxford: Oxford University Press, 1994), 213.
17. Meyer, *Civil War Experiences with the New York Cavalry*, 33–34.
18. Jeffry D. Wert, *A Glorious Army: Robert E. Lee's Triumph, 1862–1863* (New York: Simon and Schuster, 2011), 225–26; Piston, *Lee's Tarnished Lieutenant*, 46–47; Joseph B. Mitchell, *Military Leaders of the Civil War* (McLean, VA: EPM Publications, 1972), 140–41; Emory M. Thomas, *Robert E. Lee: A Biography* (New York: Norton, 1995), 291–93, 302–3; McClellan, *I Rode with Jeb Stuart*, 339; Glazier, *Three Years in the Federal Cavalry*, 63–64, 72; Carhart, *Scared Ties*, 196; Edward G. Longacre, *Gentleman and Soldier: The Extraordinary Life of General Wade Hampton* (Nashville, TN: Rutledge House Press, 2003), 142–43.
19. Thomas, *Robert E. Lee*, 292–93; *Philadelphia Weekly Times*, Philadelphia, Pennsylvania, February 8, 1879; Carhart, *Scared Ties*, 196.
20. Toalson, *Send Me a Pair of Old Boots*, 200–201.
21. Thomas, *Robert E. Lee*, 293; Joseph T. Durkin, *John Dooley: Confederate Soldier His War Journal* (Tuscaloosa: University of Alabama Press, 2005), ix, xi, 97.
22. Toalson, *Send Me a Pair of Old Boots*, 201; Longacre, *Gentleman and Soldier*, 144.
23. Neese, *Three Years in the Confederate Horse Artillery*, 102.
24. James M. Pugh, July 12, 1863, letter to his wife, Southern Historical Collection, James M. Pugh Papers, Louis Round Wilson Library, University of North Carolina, Chapel Hill, North Carolina.
25. Stephen W. Sears, *Gettysburg* (Boston: Houghton Mifflin, 2003), 459.
26. Glazier, *Three Years in the Federal Cavalry*, 63–64, 72; Barringer, *Fighting for Lee*, 107.
27. John Singleton Mosby, *Stuart's Cavalry in the Gettysburg Campaign* (New York: Moffat, Yard, 1908), 77–222.
28. Gilbert E. Govan and James W. Livingood, eds., *The Haskell Memoirs: The Personal Narrative of a Confederate Officer* (New York: Putnam, 1960), 19.
29. *Charleston Mercury*, Charleston, South Carolina, June 17, 1863.
30. Ibid.
31. Merington, *The Custer Story*, 63.
32. Robbins, *Last in Their Class*, xiv.
33. Longacre, *The Cavalry at Gettysburg*, 27–28; Ackerman, *Wade Hampton III*, 1–13, 36, 42–44.
34. Longacre, *The Cavalry at Gettysburg*, 28; Ackerman, *Wade Hampton III*, 2–3, 13–27.
35. Ackerman, *Wade Hampton III*, 1–41.
36. McClellan, *I Rode with Jeb Stuart*, 336–37.

37. Merington, *The Custer Story*, 98.
38. Blackford, *Letters from Lee's Army*, 187.
39. Longacre, *Fitz Lee*, ix, 1–38; Monaghan, *Custer*, 28–41.
40. Longacre, *Gentleman and Soldier*, 122.
41. Ackerman, *Wade Hampton III*, 33.
42. Ibid., 40–41.
43. Merington, *The Custer Story*, 9.
44. *Dispatch*, Richmond, Virginia, April 5, 1896.
45. Durkin, *John Dooley*, 96–97.
46. Neese, *Three Years in the Confederate Horse Artillery*, 186.
47. Glazier, *Three Years in the Federal Cavalry*, 128.
48. Ken Allers Jr., *The Fog of Gettysburg: The Myths and Mysteries of the Battle* (Naperville: Cumberland House, 2008), 45.
49. Husby and Wittenburg, *Under Custer's Command*, 32.
50. Hudgins and Kleese, *Recollections of an Old Dominion Dragoon*, 82; Longacre, *Gentleman and Soldier*, 146; Hatch, *Clashes of Cavalry*, 104–5; Bridges, *Fighting with Jeb Stuart*, 172–73.
51. Hudgins and Kleese, *Recollections of an Old Dominion Dragoon*, 82.
52. Bridges, *Fighting with Jeb Stuart*, 173.
53. Hatch, *Clashes of Cavalry*, 104.
54. Roger H. Harrell, *The 2nd North Carolina Cavalry* (Jefferson, NC: McFarland, 2004), 164.
55. Carroll, *Custer in the Civil War*, 110.
56. Thomason, *JEB Stuart*, 9.
57. Merington, *The Custer Story*, 75.
58. Husby and Wittenburg, *Under Custer's Command*, v.
59. Hatch, *Clashes of Cavalry*, 106.
60. Husby and Wittenburg, *Under Custer's Command*, 34.
61. Barnard and Singelyn, *An Aide to Custer*, 104; Hatch, *Clashes of Cavalry*, 106.
62. Hatch, *Clashes of Cavalry*, 97, 105–6.
63. Merington, *The Custer Story*, 95.
64. Ibid.
65. Scott Bowden and Bill Ward, *Last Chance for Victory: Robert E. Lee and the Gettysburg Campaign* (New York: Da Capo, 2001), 385–93, 422–23; Blackford, *Letters from Lee's Army*, 187; Longacre, *Custer*, 161; Timothy H. Smith, *The Story of Lee's Headquarters* (Gettysburg, PA: Thomas Publications, 1995), 1, 5, 40–41; Robert J. Trout, *Galloping Thunder: The Stuart Horse Artillery Battalion* (Mechanicsburg, PA: Stackpole Books, 2002), 289–90; Nye, *Here Come the Rebels!*; 16, Thomas, *Robert E. Lee*, 298; Longacre, *Fitz Lee*, 121; Mosby, *Stuart's Cavalry in the Gettysburg Campaign*, 77–222; Longacre, *Custer*, 161; Trout, *Memoirs of the Stuart Horse Artillery Battalion*, 55.
66. Faye Acton Axford, *The Journals of Thomas Hubbard Hobbs* (Tuscaloosa: University of Alabama Press, 1976), 225.
67. Rosen, *The Jewish Confederates*, 116.
68. Bowden and Ward, *Last Chance for Victory*, 423; McClellan, *I Rode with Jeb Stuart*, 339.

69. Bowden and Ward, *Last Chance for Victory*, 423; Samuel Carter III, *The Last Cavaliers: Confederate and Union Cavalry in the Civil War* (New York: St. Martin's, 1979), 169; McClellan, *I Rode with Jeb Stuart*, 339; Coddington, *The Gettysburg Campaign*, 520-21.
70. McClellan, *I Rode with Jeb Stuart*, 339.
71. Starr, *The Union Cavalry in the Civil War*, 1:433, 437-38; Coddington, *The Gettysburg Campaign*, 520-21; Thomas, *Robert E. Lee*, 53; Bowden and Ward, *Last Chance for Victory*, 422-31, 437-39, 472; Johnson, *Napoleon*, 49, 56-58; Longacre, *The Cavalry at Gettysburg*, 29-35, 220; Phillip Thomas Tucker, *Pickett's Charge: A New Look at Gettysburg's Final Charge* (New York: Skyhorse, 2016), 1-40; Field, *Confederate Cavalryman versus Union Cavalryman*, 4; Katcher, *Confederate Cavalryman 1861-65*, 31; Albert F. Harris, *Fated Stars: Virginia Brigadier Generals Killed in the Civil War, 1861-1865* (Gettysburg, PA: Thomas Publications, 2000), 78-82; Bridges, *Fighting with Jeb Stuart*, 1-2, 28-29, 43; Bradley M. Gottfried, *The Artillery of Gettysburg* (Nashville, TN: Cumberland House, 2008), 235; Hatch, *Clashes of Cavalry*, 110; Starr, *The Union Cavalry in the Civil War*, 1:392-95; Tom Carhart, *Lost Triumph: Lee's Real Plan at Gettysburg—And Why It Failed* (New York: Putnam, 2005), xi-269; Harris, *Fated Stars*, 80; Urwin, *Custer Victorious*, 73; Carhart, *Sacred Ties*, 205-7; Trout, *Galloping Thunder*, 289-90; McClellan, *I Rode with Jeb Stuart*, 339; Noah Andre Trudeau, *Gettysburg: A Testing of Courage* (New York: HarperCollins, 2002), 307; Trout, *They Followed the Plume*, 6, 17; Bridges, *Fighting with Jeb Stuart*, 174; Sears, *Gettysburg*, 460.
72. Urwin, *Custer Victorious*, 73.
73. Coddington, *The Gettysburg Campaign*, 520-21.
74. McClellan, *I Rode with Jeb Stuart*, 339.
75. Coddington, *The Gettysburg Campaign*, 520-21; Hatch, *Clashes of Cavalry*, 110; McClellan, *I Rode with Jeb Stuart*, 339.
76. Thomas, *Robert E. Lee*, 292; Bowden and Ward, *Last Chance for Victory*, 429-31, 472.
77. Starr, *The Union Cavalry in the Civil War*, 1:433, 437-38; McClellan, *I Rode with Jeb Stuart*, 339; Coddington, *The Gettysburg Campaign*, 520-21; Bowden and Ward, *Last Chance for Victory*, 422-31, 438, 472; Thomas, *Robert E. Lee*, 30-31, 292; Carhart, *Sacred Times*, 205-7; Field, *Confederate Cavalryman versus Union Cavalryman*, 26; Carhart, *Lost Triumph*, xi-269; Urwin, *Custer Victorious*, 73; Carter, *The Last Cavaliers*, 169; Bridges, *Fighting with Jeb Stuart*, 174; Trout, *Galloping Thunder*, 289-90.
78. Edward G. Longacre, *Lincoln's Cavalrymen: A History of the Mounted Forces of the Army of the Potomac* (Mechanicsburg, PA: Stackpole Books, 2000), 7.
79. Ibid., 5-9; Coddington, *The Gettysburg Campaign*, 520-21; McClellan, *I Rode with Jeb Stuart*, 339.
80. Longacre, *Custer*, 161.
81. Carter, *The Last Cavaliers*, 169-70.
82. McClellan, *I Rode with Jeb Stuart*, 337.
83. Husby and Wittenburg, *Under Custer's Command*, v; Bowden and Ward, *Last Chance for Victory*, 429-31, 472; Carhart, *Sacred Ties*, 205-7.
84. Starr, *The Union Cavalry in the Civil War*, 1:433, 437-38; Coddington, *The Gettysburg Campaign*, 520-21; McClellan, *I Rode with Jeb Stuart*, 339; Urwin, *Custer Victorious*,

73; Carhart, *Lost Triumph*, xi-269; Bowden and Ward, *Last Chance for Victory*, 429-31, 472; Bridges, *Fighting with Jeb Stuart*, 174.

85. Merington, *The Custer Story*, 10.

86. Jeffry D. Wert, *Cavalryman of a Lost Cause: A Biography of J. E. B. Stuart* (New York: Simon and Schuster, 2008), 284.

87. Starr, *The Union Cavalry in the Civil War*, 1:433, 437-38; Coddington, *The Gettysburg Campaign*, 520-21; McClellan, *I Rode with Jeb Stuart*, 339; Urwin, *Custer Victorious*, 73; Carhart, *Lost Triumph*, xi-269; Thomason, *JEB Stuart*, 9, 441, 444; Carhart, *Sacred Times*, 205-7; Bowden and Ward, *Last Chance for Victory*, 429-31, 472.

88. Bowden and Ward, *Last Chance for Victory*, 423, 429-31, 472; McClellan, *I Rode with Jeb Stuart*, 339; Coddington, *The Gettysburg Campaign*, 520-21; Starr, *The Union Cavalry in the Civil War*, 1:433, 437-38.

89. McClellan, *I Rode with Jeb Stuart*, 339.

90. Bowden and Ward, *Last Chance for Victory*, 439; Starr, *The Union Cavalry in the Civil War*, 1:433, 437-38; Coddington, *The Gettysburg Campaign*, 520-21; McClellan, *I Rode with Jeb Stuart*, 339.

91. Sears, *Gettysburg*, 459; McClellan, *I Rode with Jeb Stuart*, 339; Carhart, *Lost Triumph*, xi-269; Bridges, *Fighting with Jeb Stuart*, 174.

92. Gottfried, *The Artillery of Gettysburg*, 235.

93. Riggs, *East of Gettysburg*, vi.

94. Hatch, *Clashes of Cavalry*, 110.

95. McClellan, *I Rode with Jeb Stuart*, 339.

96. Longacre, *The Cavalry at Gettysburg*, 221.

97. McClellan, *I Rode with Jeb Stuart*, 339; Carhart, *Lost Triumph*, xi-269.

98. Starr, *The Union Cavalry in the Civil War*, 1:433, 437-38; McClellan, *I Rode with Jeb Stuart*, 339; Coddington, *The Gettysburg Campaign*, 520-21.

99. Riggs, *East of Gettysburg*, 45.

100. Harris, *Personal Reminiscences of Samuel Harris*, 28.

101. Sears, *Gettysburg*, 459.

102. Katcher, *The Army of Robert E. Lee*, 137.

103. Carhart, *Lost Triumph*, xi-269.

104. McClellan, *I Rode with Jeb Stuart*, 337.

105. Gottfried, *The Artillery of Gettysburg*, 245; Starr, *The Union Cavalry in the Civil War*, 1:392-95, 433, 437-38; McClellan, *I Rode with Jeb Stuart*, 339; Urwin, *Custer Victorious*, 73; Carhart, *Lost Triumph*, xi-269; Bowden and Ward, *Last Chance for Victory*, 429-31, 472; Bridges, *Fighting with Jeb Stuart*, 174.

106. Richard F. Selcer, *Lee vs. Pickett: Two Divided by War* (Gettysburg, PA: Thomas Publications, 1998 ), 49; Starr, *The Union Cavalry in the Civil War*, 1:433, 437-38; McClellan, *I Rode with Jeb Stuart*, 339; Urwin, *Custer Victorious*, 73; Carhart, *Lost Triumph*, xi-269; Bridges, *Fighting with Jeb Stuart*, 174; Bowden and Ward, *Last Chance for Victory*, 429-31, 472.

107. Carhart, *Lost Triumph*, xi-269.

## CHAPTER 3

1. Wert, *Custer*, 83.
2. Husby and Wittenberg, *Under Custer's Command*, 22.
3. Wert, *Custer*, 84.
4. Husby and Wittenburg, *Under Custer's Command*, 32.
5. Kidd, *Personal Recollections of a Cavalryman*, 67.
6. Wert, *Custer*, 85.
7. Longacre, *Custer and His Wolverines*, 143.
8. Ibid.; Longacre, *Custer*, 154.
9. Longacre, *Custer*, 154.
10. *Detroit Free Press*, Detroit, Michigan, July 15, 1863.
11. Ibid.; Robbins, *The Real Custer*, 80; Longacre, *Custer and His Wolverines*, 144; Hatch, *Clashes of Cavalry*, 110; Longacre, *The Cavalry at Gettysburg*, 223; Longacre, *Custer*, 157–60; Robbins, *Last in Their Class*, 263.
12. Longacre, *Custer and His Wolverines*, 144.
13. *Detroit Free Press*, July 15, 1863.
14. Ibid.
15. Robbins, *Last in Their Class*, 263.
16. *Detroit Free Press*, July 15, 1863; Longacre, *Custer and His Wolverines*, 144; Starr, *The Union Cavalry in the Civil War*, 1:432; Longacre, *Custer*, 154.
17. Husby and Wittenburg, *Under Custer's Command*, 34.
18. Longacre, *Custer*, 159.
19. Merington, *The Custer Story*, 65.
20. Robbins, *The Real Custer*, 64.
21. Ibid.
22. Wert, *Custer*, 83; Longacre, *Custer and His Wolverines*, 9–10, 19; Kidd, *Personal Recollections of a Cavalryman*, 73–82; Isham, *Seventh Michigan Cavalry*, 22–28.
23. Monaghan, *Custer*, 9.
24. Merington, *The Custer Story*, 35; Monaghan, *Custer*, 8.
25. Luvaas and Nelson, *Guide to the Battle of Gettysburg*, 210.
26. Ibid.; Longacre, *The Cavalry at Gettysburg*, 33–34; Ackerman, *Wade Hampton III*, 40–41; Johnson, *Napoleon*, 56–57.
27. George Gordon Meade, *The Life and Letters of General George Gordon Meade*, 2 vols. (New York: Scribner, 1913), 2:95.
28. Husby and Wittenburg, *Under Custer's Command*, 22.
29. Luvaas and Nelson, *Guide to the Battle of Gettysburg*, 211.
30. Grady McWhiney and Perry D. Jamieson, *Attack and Die: Civil War Military Tactics and the Southern Heritage* (Tuscaloosa: University of Alabama Press, 1990), 126.
31. Longacre, *Gentleman and Soldier*, 151; Starr, *The Union Cavalry in the Civil War*, 1:433, 437–38; Coddington, *The Gettysburg Campaign*, 520–21; McClellan, *I Rode with Jeb Stuart*, 339; Carhart, *Lost Triumph*, xi–269; Urwin, *Custer Victorious*, 73; Bridges, *Fighting with Jeb Stuart*, 174.

32. McWhiney and Jamieson, *Attack and Die*, 126; Starr, *The Union Cavalry in the Civil War*, 1:433, 437–38; McClellan, *I Rode with Jeb Stuart*, 339; Urwin, *Custer Victorious*, 73; Carhart, *Lost Triumph*, xi–269; Bridges, *Fighting with Jeb Stuart*, 174.

33. Gottfried, *The Artillery of Gettysburg*, 235.

34. McWhiney and Jamieson, *Attack and Die*, 127–28; Starr, *The Union Cavalry in the Civil War*, 1:433, 437–38; Coddington, *The Gettysburg Campaign*, 520–21; Urwin, *Custer Victorious*, 73; McClellan, *I Rode with Jeb Stuart*, 339; Carhart, *Lost Triumph*, xi–269; Bridges, *Fighting with Jeb Stuart*, 174.

35. Gabor S. Boritt, ed., *The Gettysburg Nobody Knows* (New York: Oxford University Press, 1997), 114; Starr, *The Union Cavalry in the Civil War*, 1:433, 437–38; McClellan, *I Rode with Jeb Stuart*, 339; Coddington, *The Gettysburg Campaign*, 520–21.

36. Robert J. Trout, *"The Hoss": Officer Biographies and Rosters of the Stuart Horse Artillery Battalion* (N.p.: JebFlo Press, 2003), 29–30.

37. Ibid., 26.

38. Ibid., 84.

39. Blackford, *War Years with Jeb Stuart*, 9, 29.

40. McClellan, *I Rode with Jeb Stuart*, 339; Coddington, *The Gettysburg Campaign*, 520–21; Trout, *Memoirs of the Stuart Horse Artillery*, xiii; Trout, *Galloping Thunder*, 4–6; Bridges, *Fighting with Jeb Stuart*, 28–29; Carhart, *Lost Triumph*, xi–269; Urwin, *Custer Victorious*, 73; Johnson, *Napoleon*, 49–57.

41. Starr, *The Union Cavalry in the Civil War*, 1:433, 437–38; McClellan, *I Rode with Jeb Stuart*, 339; Coddington, *The Gettysburg Campaign*, 520–21; Trout, *"The Hoss,"* 4–7; Bridges, *Fighting with Jeb Stuart*, 66; Trout, *Galloping Thunder*, 289–90.

42. Trout, *"The Hoss,"* 8; Longacre, *The Cavalry at Gettysburg*, 32.

43. Trout, *"The Hoss,"* 13–15, 27–28.

44. Ibid., 21–22.

45. Ibid., 226–27; Starr, *The Union Cavalry in the Civil War*, 1:433, 437–38; McClellan, *I Rode with Jeb Stuart*, 339; Coddington, *The Gettysburg Campaign*, 520–21.

46. Starr, *The Union Cavalry in the Civil War*, 1:433, 437–38; McClellan, *I Rode with Jeb Stuart*, 339; Coddington, *The Gettysburg Campaign*, 520–21; Trout, *Galloping Thunder*, 6.

47. Starr, *The Union Cavalry in the Civil War*, 1:433, 437–38; Coddington, *The Gettysburg Campaign*, 520–21; Carhart, *Lost Triumph*, xi–269; Urwin, *Custer Victorious*, 73; McClellan, *I Rode with Jeb Stuart*, 339.

48. Starr, *The Union Cavalry in the Civil War*, 1:393, 433, 437–38; Coddington, *The Gettysburg Campaign*, 520–21; McClellan, *I Rode with Jeb Stuart*, 339.

49. *Charleston Mercury*, Charleston, South Carolina, June 17, 1863.

50. Thomason, *JEB Stuart*, 398.

51. Starr, *The Union Cavalry in the Civil War*, 1:393; McClellan, *I Rode with Jeb Stuart*, 339; Carhart, *Lost Triumph*, xi–269; Urwin, *Custer Victorious*, 73; Bridges, *Fighting with Jeb Stuart*, 174.

52. Thomason, *JEB Stuart*, 439–40; Downey, *Clash of Cavalry*, 25.

53. Trout, *Memoirs of Stuart Horse Artillery Battalion*, 195; Katcher, *Confederate Cavalryman 1861–65*, 5.

54. Bowden and Ward, *Last Chance for Victory*, 423; McClellan, *I Rode with Jeb Stuart*, 339; Carhart, *Lost Triumph*, xi–269; Urwin, *Custer Victorious*, 73; Starr, *The Union Cavalry in the Civil War*, 1:432.
55. Blackford, *War Years with Jeb Stuart*, 115–16.
56. Cadwallader J. Iredell, June 13, 1863, letter, Cadwallader J. Iredell Papers, Southern Historical Collection, Louis Round Wilson Library, University of North Carolina, Chapel Hill, North Carolina.
57. Ackerman, *Wade Hampton III*, 40–41.
58. Longacre, *Custer and His Wolverines*, 153.
59. Ibid., 9–10.
60. Kidd, *Personal Recollections of a Cavalryman*, 77–78.
61. Govan and Livingood, *The Haskell Memoirs*, 57.
62. Trudeau, *Gettysburg*, 69.
63. Ibid.; Blackford, *Letters from Lee's Army*, 195; Starr, *The Union Cavalry in the Civil War*, 1:393; Thomason, *JEB Stuart*, 409.
64. Monte Akers, *Year of Glory: The Life and Battles of Jeb Stuart and His Cavalry, June 1862–June 1863* (Philadelphia, PA: Casemate, 2017), 326–27.
65. Hatch, *Clashes of Cavalry*, 106.
66. Blackford, *Letters From Lee's Army*, 195.
67. Ibid., 175, 195; Bowden and Ward, *Last Chance for Victory*, 422–23.
68. Thomason, *JEB Stuart*, 4.
69. Mitchell, *Military Leaders of the Civil War*, 140–41; Bridges, *Fighting with Jeb Stuart*, 174; Carhart, *Lost Triumph*, xi–269; Urwin, *Custer Victorious*, 73; Starr, *The Union Cavalry of the Civil War*, 1:433, 437–38; McClellan, *I Rode with Jeb Stuart*, 339; Coddington, *The Gettysburg Campaign*, 520–21; Trudeau, *Gettysburg*, 69; Downey, *Clash of Cavalry*, 149; Bowden and Ward, *Last Chance for Victory*, 429; Longacre, *The Cavalry at Gettysburg*, 221.
70. Starr, *The Union Cavalry in the Civil War*, 1:433, 437–38; McClellan, *I Rode with Jeb Stuart*, 339; Coddington, *The Gettysburg Campaign*, 520–21.
71. Glazier, *Three Years in the Federal Cavalry*, 132.
72. Bridges, *Fighting with Jeb Stuart*, 174.
73. Starr, *The Union Cavalry in the Civil War*, 1:433, 437–38; McClellan, *I Rode with Jeb Stuart*, 339; Coddington, *The Gettysburg Campaign*, 520–21.
74. McClellan, *I Rode with Jeb Stuart*, 339; Carhart, *Lost Triumph*, xi–269; Urwin, *Custer Victorious*, 73.
75. Starr, *The Union Cavalry in the Civil War*, 1:433, 437–38; McClellan, *I Rode with Jeb Stuart*, 339; Coddington, *The Gettysburg Campaign*, 520–21.
76. Starr, *The Union Cavalry in the Civil War*, 1:43, 437–38; McClellan, *I Rode with Jeb Stuart*, 339; Coddington, *The Gettysburg Campaign*, 520–21; Ackerman, *Wade Hampton III*, 47.
77. Ackerman, *Wade Hampton III*, 47; Trudeau, *Gettysburg*, 69.
78. Akers, *Year of Glory*, 310; Jeffry D. Wert, *Cavalryman of the Lost Cause: Biography of J.E.B. Stuart* (New York: Simon and Schuster, 2008), 251–52.
79. Wert, *Cavalryman of the Lost Cause*, 251–52.
80. Ibid.

81. Monaghan, *Custer*, 9.
82. Ibid., 12.
83. Ibid., 3, 9–10; Hatch, *Clashes of Cavalry*, 60–61, 168.
84. Riggs, *East of Gettysburg*, iv.
85. Sears, *Gettysburg*, 92–93.
86. Starr, *The Union Cavalry in the Civil War*, 1:391–95.
87. Nye, *Here Come the Rebels!*, 16–17; Bridges, *Fighting with Jeb Stuart*, 174; McClellan, *I Rode with Jeb Stuart*, 339; Urwin, *Custer Victorious*, 73; Carhart, *Lost Triumph*, xi–269; Longacre, *The Cavalry at Gettysburg*, 220; Starr, *The Union Cavalry in the Civil War*, 1:433, 437–38; Coddington, *The Gettysburg Campaign*, 520–21.
88. McClellan, *I Rode with Jeb Stuart*, 337.
89. Wert, *A Glorious Army*, 197–202; Nye, *Here Come the Rebels!*, 16–17; Beattie, *Brandy Station 1863*, 8–9.
90. Wert, *A Glorious Army*, 194–95, 209; Blackford, *War Years with Jeb Stuart*, 115.
91. Akers, *Year of Glory*, 317.
92. Johnson, *Napoleon*, 67–68; Rosentreter, *Grand Rapids and the Civil War*, 44.
93. Merington, *The Custer Story*, 65.
94. Hatch, *Clashes of Cavalry*, 110.
95. McClellan, *I Rode with Jeb Stuart*, 337.
96. Ibid.
97. Longacre, *The Cavalry at Gettysburg*, 221.
98. Ibid., 220; Coddington, *The Gettysburg Campaign*, 520–21; Longacre, *Fitz Lee*, 121; Hatch, *Clashes of Cavalry*, 110; McClellan, *I Rode with Jeb Stuart*, 337–38.
99. Starr, *The Union Cavalry in the Civil War*, 1:433, 437–38; Coddington, *The Gettysburg Campaign*, 520–21; Carter, *The Last Cavaliers*, 170; Hatch, *Clashes of Cavalry*, 110; Longacre, *Lincoln's Cavalrymen*, 193–94; Hatch, *Clashes of Cavalry*, 110; Carhart, *Lost Triumph*, 196; Longacre, *The Cavalry at Gettysburg*, 220–22; McClellan, *I Rode with Jeb Stuart*, 339; Bowden and Ward, *Last Chance for Victory*, 385–93; Wert, *Custer*, 91.
100. Carhart, *Lost Triumph*, 197.
101. Hatch, *Clashes of Cavalry*, 110.
102. Starr, *The Union Cavalry in the Civil War*, 1:433, 437–38; McClellan, *I Rode with Jeb Stuart*, 339; Coddington, *The Gettysburg Campaign*, 520–21.
103. Longacre, *The Cavalry at Gettysburg*, 221.
104. McClellan, *I Rode with Jeb Stuart*, 337; Longacre, *The Cavalry at Gettysburg*, 221.
105. McClellan, *I Rode with Stuart*, 337–38.
106. Starr, *The Union Cavalry in the Civil War*, 1:433, 437–38; McClellan, *I Rode with Jeb Stuart*, 339; Coddington, *The Gettysburg Campaign*, 520–21.
107. Riggs, *East of Gettysburg*, 45.
108. Wert, *Cavalryman of the Lost Cause*, 285; Trudeau, *Gettysburg*, 455; Harrell, *The 2nd North Carolina Cavalry*, 166.
109. Blackford, *War Years with Jeb Stuart*, 261.
110. Bowden and Ward, *Last Chance for Victory*, 429.
111. Riggs, *East of Gettysburg*, 43.
112. Blackford, *War Years with Jeb Stuart*, 260.
113. McClellan, *I Rode with Jeb Stuart*, 338.

114. Ibid., 339; Starr, *The Union Cavalry in the Civil War*, 1:433, 437–38; Coddington, *The Gettysburg Campaign*, 520–21; Wert, *Cavalryman of the Lost Cause*, 285–86.
115. Wert, *Cavalry of the Lost Cause*, 290.
116. Hatch, *Clashes of Cavalry*, 111.
117. Robert U. Johnson and Clarence C. Buel, eds., *Battles and Leaders of the Civil War*, 4 vols. (Edison, NJ: Castle Books, 1965), 3:401–2.
118. Katcher, *Confederate Cavalryman 1861–65*, 17, 21; Starr, *The Union Cavalry in the Civil War*, 1:433, 437–38; McClellan, *I Rode with Jeb Stuart*, 339; Urwin, *Custer Victorious*, 73; Carhart, *Lost Triumph*, xi–269; Bridges, *Fighting with Jeb Stuart*, 174.
119. Starr, *The Union Cavalry in the Civil War*, 1:433, 437–38; Coddington, *The Gettysburg Campaign*, 520–21; Riggs, *East of Gettysburg*, 43; McClellan, *I Rode with Jeb Stuart*, 339; Hudgins and Kleese, *Recollections of an Old Dominion Dragoon*, 82.
120. Longacre, *Gentleman and Soldier*, 150.
121. Blackford, *War Years with Jeb Stuart*, 261; Longacre, *Gentleman and Soldier*, 150; Coddington, *The Gettysburg Campaign*, 520–21; McClellan, *I Rode with Jeb Stuart*, 339; Starr, *The Union Cavalry in the Civil War*, 1:433, 437–38.
122. Bridges, *Fighting with Jeb Stuart*, 174.
123. John B. Bachelder Papers, vol. 3, New Hampshire Historical Society, Concord New Hampshire, 1377.
124. Starr, *The Union Cavalry in the Civil War*, 1:433, 437–38; Coddington, *The Gettysburg Campaign*, 520–21; McClellan, *I Rode with Jeb Stuart*, 339.
125. Starr, *The Union Cavalry in the Civil War*, 1:433, 437–38; McClellan, *I Rode with Jeb Stuart*, 339; Coddington, *The Gettysburg Campaign*, 520–21; Harrell, *The 2nd North Carolina Cavalry*, 166; *Dispatch*, Richmond, Virginia, April 5, 1896.
126. James M. Paradis, *African Americans and the Gettysburg Campaign* (Lanham, MD: Scarecrow Press, 2013), 31; Starr, *The Union Cavalry in the Civil War*, 1:433, 437–38; Coddington, *The Gettysburg Campaign*, 520–21; McClellan, *I Rode with Jeb Stuart*, 339; Urwin, *Custer Victorious*, 73; Carhart, *Lost Triumph*, xi–269; Bridges, *Fighting with Jeb Stuart*, 174.
127. *Dispatch*, Richmond, Virginia, April 5, 1896.
128. Starr, *The Union Cavalry in the Civil War*, 1:433, 437–38; McClellan, *I Rode with Jeb Stuart*, 338–39; Coddington, *The Gettysburg Campaign*, 520–21.
129. Bowden and Ward, *Last Chance for Victory*, 427–31; Starr, *The Union Cavalry in the Civil War*, 1:433, 437–38; McClellan, *I Rode with Jeb Stuart*, 339; Coddington, *The Gettysburg Campaign*, 520–21; Carhart, *Sacred Ties*, 205–7.
130. Bowden and Ward, *Last Chance for Victory*, 430–42; Starr, *The Union Cavalry in the Civil War*, 1:433, 437–38; Coddington, *The Gettysburg Campaign*, 520–21; McClellan, *I Rode with Jeb Stuart*, 339; Carhart, *Sacred Ties*, 205–7.
131. Blackford, *War Years with Jeb Stuart*, 261; Carhart, *Sacred Ties*, 205–7; Bowden and Ward, *Last Chance for Victory*, 429, 431.
132. Starr, *The Union Cavalry in the Civil War*, 1:433, 437–38; McClellan, *I Rode with Jeb Stuart*, 339; Coddington, *The Gettysburg Campaign*, 520–21.
133. Blackford, *War Years with Jeb Stuart*, 261–62; Carhart, *Sacred Ties*, 205–7.
134. Harrell, *The 2nd North Carolina Cavalry*, 166; Longacre, *Fitz Lee*, 122–23; McClellan, *I Rode with Jeb Stuart*, 338.

135. McClellan, *I Rode with Jeb Stuart*, 339.

136. Ibid., 338–39; Harrell, *The 2nd North Carolina Cavalry*, 166.

137. McClellan, *I Rode with Jeb Stuart*, 338–39; *Charleston Mercury*, Charleston, South Carolina, June 17, 1863.

138. Sears, *Gettysburg*, 459; Riggs, *East of Gettysburg*, 45; Starr, *The Union Cavalry in the Civil War*, 1:433, 437–38; McClellan, *I Rode with Jeb Stuart*, 338–39; Coddington, *The Gettysburg Campaign*, 520–21.

139. Carhart, *Lost Triumph*, 206; McClellan, *I Rode with Jeb Stuart*, 338–39.

140. McClellan, *I Rode with Jeb Stuart*, 338.

141. Ibid., 338–39.

142. Starr, *The Union Cavalry in the Civil War*, 1:433, 437–38; Coddington, *The Gettysburg Campaign*, 520–21; Carhart, *Lost Triumph*, xi–269; McClellan, *I Rode with Jeb Stuart*, 338–39.

143. Carhart, *Sacred Ties*, 207; Hudgins and Kleese, *Recollections of an Old Dominion Dragoon*, 84.

144. Gottfried, *The Artillery of Gettysburg*, 235; McClellan, *I Rode with Jeb Stuart*, 338–39.

145. Trout, *They Followed the Plume*, 197–202; Longacre, *The Cavalry at Gettysburg*, 32.

146. Longacre, *The Cavalry at Gettysburg*, 32.

147. McClellan, *I Rode with Jeb Stuart*, 339.

148. Hatch, *Clashes of Cavalry*, 111.

149. McClellan, *I Rode with Jeb Stuart*, 338–39; Carhart, *Sacred Ties*, 207.

150. Riggs, *East of Gettysburg*, 45.

151. Stowe, *Company B*, 37; McClellan, *I Rode with Jeb Stuart*, 338–40.

152. Harris, *Personal Reminiscences of Samuel Harris*, 28; Bridges, *Fighting with Jeb Stuart*, 174.

153. Bridges, *Fighting with Jeb Stuart*, 174; Harrell, *The 2nd North Carolina Cavalry*, 166.

154. Hudgins and Kleese, *Recollections of an Old Dominion Dragoon*, 82; Coddington, *The Gettysburg Campaign*, 520–21; McClellan, *I Rode with Jeb Stuart*, 339; Starr, *The Union Cavalry in the Civil War*, 1:433, 437–38.

155. Trout, *"The Hoss,"* 226; Bridges, *Fighting with Jeb Stuart*, 174; Starr, *The Union Cavalry in the Civil War*, 1:433, 437–38; Coddington, *The Gettysburg Campaign*, 520–21; Gottfried, *The Artillery of Gettysburg*, 235.

156. Gottfried, *The Artillery of Gettysburg*, 235; Hudgins and Kleese, *Recollections of an Old Dominion Dragoon*, 82; Starr, *The Union Cavalry in the Civil War*, 1:433, 437–38; Coddington, *The Gettysburg Campaign*, 520–21; McClellan, *I Rode with Jeb Stuart*, 338–39; Urwin, *Custer Victorious*, 73; Carhart, *Lost Triumph*, xi–269; Riggs, *East of Gettysburg*, 45; Hatch, *Clashes of Cavalry*, 110; Bridges, *Fighting with Jeb Stuart*, 174.

157. Bridges, *Fighting with Jeb Stuart*, 174; Carter, *The Last Cavaliers*, 169; Starr, *The Union Cavalry in the Civil War*, 1:433, 437–38; Coddington, *The Gettysburg Campaign*, 520–21; McClellan, *I Rode with Jeb Stuart*, 339.

158. McClellan, *I Rode with Jeb Stuart*, 339.

159. Starr, *The Union Cavalry in the Civil War*, 1:432.

160. Ibid., 433, 437–38; Coddington, *The Gettysburg Campaign*, 520–21; McClellan, *I Rode with Jeb Stuart*, 339; Carter, *The Last Cavaliers*, 169.
161. Riggs, *East of Gettysburg*, 45.
162. Stowe, *Company B*, 19; Riggs, *East of Gettysburg*, 45; Robbins, *The Real Custer*, xv.
163. Longacre, *Custer*, 157; Monaghan, *Custer*, 140–41.
164. Robbins, *Last in Their Class*, xvi–xvii, 188–89.
165. Harrell, *The 2nd North Carolina Cavalry*, 166; Longacre, *Custer and His Wolverines*, 144–45; Longacre, *Custer*, 160.
166. Monaghan, *Custer*, 143; Rosentreter, *Grand Rapids and the Civil War*, 36–37, 43–44; Longacre, *Lincoln's Cavalrymen*, 193–95; Hatch, *Clashes of Cavalry*, 110–12; Longacre, *The Cavalry at Gettysburg*, 223; Longacre, *Custer*, 160, 164; Urwin, *Custer Victorious*, 81; Stowe, *Company B*, 32–36, 39; Longacre, *Custer and His Wolverines*, 144–45; Robbins, *The Real Custer*, 80–81.
167. Husby and Wittenberg, *Under Custer's Command*, 35.
168. Johnson and Buel, *Battles and Leaders of the Civil War*, 3:402; Longacre, *Custer*, 163; Kidd, *Personal Recollections of a Cavalryman*, 77.
169. Kidd, *Personal Recollections of a Cavalryman*, vii–viii, 69; Rosentreter, *Grand Rapids and the Civil War*, 33–35; Longacre, *Custer*, 160–63.
170. Rosentreter, *Grand Rapids and the Civil War*, 33–35.
171. Longacre, *Lincoln's Cavalrymen*, 197; Starr, *The Union Cavalry in the Civil War*, 1:432; Longacre, *The Cavalry at Gettysburg*, 223; Longacre, *Custer*, 161; Robbins, *The Real Custer*, 71.
172. Kidd, *Personal Recollections of a Cavalryman*, 73.
173. Longacre, *Custer*, 161.
174. Longacre, *Lincoln's Cavalrymen*, 196; Monaghan, *Custer*, 10, 108–12; Riggs, *East of Gettysburg*, 39, 42; Hatch, *Clashes of Cavalry*, 61.
175. Hatch, *Clashes of Cavalry*, 106–9; Wert, *Custer*, 91; Phillip Thomas Tucker, *Death at the Little Bighorn* (New York: Skyhorse, 2007), 183–300.
176. Longacre, *Lincoln's Cavalryman*, 195.
177. Hatch, *Clashes of Cavalry*, 109, 111; Longacre, *Lincoln's Cavalrymen*, 194–95; Longacre, *Gentleman and Soldier*, 151.
178. Monaghan, *Custer*, 8, 25–43, 143–44; Longacre, *Lincoln's Cavalrymen*, 196; Wert, *Custer*, 91; Carhart, *Sacred Ties*, 207–9; McClellan, *I Rode with Jeb Stuart*, 339; Coddington, *The Gettysburg Campaign*, 520–21; Starr, *The Union Cavalry in the Civil War*, 1:51–52, 432–33, 437–38; Robbins, *The Real Custer*, xv; Longacre, *Custer*, 163; Riggs, *East of Gettysburg*, 27, 37; Trudeau, *Gettysburg*, 456; Stowe, *Company B*, 2; Hatch, *Clashes of Cavalry*, 110–12.
179. Riggs, *East of Gettysburg*, 51; *Detroit Free Press*, July 15, 1863; Johnson and Buel, *Battles and Leaders of the Civil War*, 3:402.
180. Longacre, *Lincoln's Cavalrymen*, 196.
181. Longacre, *Custer*, 151, 164.
182. *Detroit Free Press*, July 15, 1863.
183. Whittaker, *A Complete Life of General George A. Custer*, 1:175.
184. Ibid.

185. Ibid.
186. Stowe, *Company B*, 4–5, 32–36, 39; Hatch, *Clashes of Cavalry*, 110–11; Robbins, *The Real Custer*, xv; Kidd, *Personal Recollections of a Cavalryman*, 78.
187. Urwin, *Custer Victorious*, 73.
188. Starr, *The Union Cavalry in the Civil War*, 1:432; Longacre, *Custer*, 164.
189. Longacre, *Custer*, 164–65; Stowe, *Company B*, 39.
190. Starr, *The Union Cavalry in the Civil War*, 1:433; Longacre, *Custer*, 164.
191. Starr, *The Union Cavalry in the Civil War*, 1:433; Harrell, *The 2nd North Carolina Cavalry*, 166.
192. Johnson and Buel, *Battles and Leaders of the Civil War*, 3:402.
193. Sears, *Gettysburg*, 460–61.
194. Kidd, *Personal Recollections of a Cavalryman*, 73.
195. Ibid., 73–74, 77.
196. Ibid., 73.
197. Ibid., 73.
198. Ibid., 73–74.
199. Ibid., 73; Stowe, *Company B*, 39; Hatch, *Clashes of Cavalry*, 113; Urwin, *Custer Victorious*, 73.
200. *Detroit Free Press*, July 15, 1863.
201. Merington, *The Custer Story*, 52.
202. Ibid.
203. Robbins, *The Real Custer*, 82; Robbins, *Last in Their Class*, 264; Meyer, *Civil War Experiences with the New York Cavalry*, 43.
204. Urwin, *Custer Victorious*, 55–56, 73–74; Robbins, *The Real Custer*, 82; Longacre, *Custer*, 153–54, 158; Meyer, *Civil War Experiences with the New York Cavalry*, 30.
205. Urwin, *Custer Victorious*, 74–75.
206. Starr, *The Union Cavalry in the Civil War*, 1:434.
207. Ibid.
208. Hatch, *Clashes of Cavalry*, 114; Robbins, *Last in Their Class*, 264; Stowe, *Company B*, 39.
209. Colonel Vincent Addison Witcher (1837–1912), Find A Grave, internet; Harrell, *The 2nd North Carolina Cavalry*, 168.
210. Carhart, *Lost Triumph*, 214.
211. McClellan, *I Rode with Jeb Stuart*, 339.
212. Ibid.
213. Monaghan, *Custer*, 10, 143–44; Carhart, *Sacred Ties*, 207–9; McClellan, *I Rode with Jeb Stuart*, 339; Coddington, *The Gettysburg Campaign*, 520–21; Starr, *The Union Cavalry in the Civil War*, 1:433, 437–38; Wert, *Custer*, 91; Kidd, *Personal Recollections of a Cavalryman*, 73–75; Longacre, *Lincoln's Cavalrymen*, 196; Trudeau, *Gettysburg*, 456; Harrell, *The 2nd North Carolina Cavalry*, 168; Carhart, *Lost Triumph*, 207–8; Robbins, *Last in Their Class*, 263–64; Whittaker, *A Complete Life of General George A. Custer*, 1:179.
214. Johnson and Buel, *Battles and Leaders of the Civil War*, 3:402; Carhart, *Lost Triumph*, 203; Harrell, *The Second North Carolina Cavalry*, 168.
215. Urwin, *Custer Victorious*, 73–81.
216. Johnson and Buel, *Battles and Leaders of the Civil War*, 3:402–3.

217. Kidd, *Personal Recollections of a Cavalryman*, 73; Harrell, *The 2nd North Carolina Cavalry*, 168.

218. Harrell, *The 2nd North Carolina Cavalry*, 168; Johnson and Buel, *Battles and Leaders of the Civil War*, 3:402; Carhart, *Lost Triumph*, 212.

219. Robbins, *Last in Their Class*, 264; Hatch, *Clashes of Cavalry*, 114; Robbins, *The Real Custer*, 82.

220. Riggs, *East of Gettysburg*, 50.

221. Robbins, *The Real Custer*, xi, xiv.

222. Longacre, *Fitz Lee*, 122.

223. Carhart, *Sacred Ties*, 208-9, 213; Longacre, *Fitz Lee*, 122.

224. Bridges, *Fighting with Jeb Stuart*, 174; Johnson and Buel, *Battles and Leaders of the Civil War*, 3:402-3; Longacre, *Lincoln's Cavalrymen*, 196; Coddington, *The Gettysburg Campaign*, 520-21; Hatch, *Clashes of Cavalry*, 114; Starr, *The Union Cavalry in the Civil War*, 1:433, 437-38; Stowe, *Company B*, 4; Harris, *Personal Reminiscences of Samuel Harris*, 28.

225. Hatch, *Clashes of Cavalry*, 114; Johnson and Buel, *Battles and Leaders of the Civil War*, 3:403; Robbins, *The Real Custer*, 83; Kidd, *Personal Recollections of a Cavalryman*, 78; Robbins, *Last in Their Class*, 264.

226. Kidd, *Personal Recollections of a Cavalryman*, 78; Robbins, *The Real Custer*, 83; Johnson and Buel, *Battles and Leaders of the Civil War*, 3:403; Robbins, *Last in Their Class*, 264.

227. Rosentreter, *Grand Rapids and the Civil War*, 44; Johnson and Buel, *Battles and Leaders of the Civil War*, 403.

228. "34th Virginia Cavalry—Wayne County, West Virginia," RootsWeb, internet.

229. Ibid.

230. Johnson and Buel, *Battles and Leaders of the Civil War*, 3:403.

231. Wert, *Custer*, 92.

232. Longacre, *Lincoln's Cavalrymen*, 196; Monaghan, *Custer*, 143-45; Trudeau, *Gettysburg*, 456; Coddington, *The Gettysburg Campaign*, 520-21; Longacre, *The Cavalry at Gettysburg*, 223; Starr, *The Union Cavalry in the Civil War*, 1:433, 437-38; Longacre, *Custer*, 164-65; Meyer, *Civil War Experiences with the New York Cavalry*, 43.

233. Monaghan, *Custer*, 144.

234. Sullivan, *Custer's Road to Disaster*, 4-5; Monaghan, *Custer*, 6-13.

235. Starr, *The Union Cavalry in the Civil War*, 1:434.

236. Ibid., 1:433; Meyer, *Civil War Experiences with the New York Cavalry*, 44.

237. McClellan, *I Rode with Jeb Stuart*, 338-39; Longacre, *Fitz Lee*, 122; Starr, *The Union Cavalry in the Civil War*, 1:433; Kidd, *Personal Recollections of a Cavalryman*, 73; Meyer, *Civil War Experiences with the New York Cavalry*, 30-31.

238. Riggs, *East of Gettysburg*, 50; Meyer, *Civil War Experiences with the New York Cavalry*, 38-39.

239. Robbins, *Last in Their Class*, 264.

240. Merington, *The Custer Story*, 103.

241. Robbins, *Last in Their Class*, 264; Hatch, *Clashes of Cavalry*, 113-14; Stowe, *Company B*, 39.

242. McClellan, *I Rode with Jeb Stuart*, 340; Carhart, *Lost Triumph*, 214-15; Kidd, *Personal Recollections of a Cavalryman*, 73-74.
243. McClellan, *I Rode with Jeb Stuart*, 339.
244. Longacre, *Lincoln's Cavalrymen*, 196; Carhart, *Lost Triumph*, 214-15, 224.
245. Longacre, *Lincoln's Cavalrymen*, 196.
246. Ibid.; Sullivan, *Custer's Road to Disaster*, ix; Kidd, *Personal Recollections of a Cavalryman*, 74.
247. Kidd, *Personal Recollections of a Cavalryman*, 74.
248. Carhart, *Lost Triumph*, 208; Starr, *The Union Cavalry in the Civil War*, 1:434; McClellan, *I Rode with Jeb Stuart*, 338-39; Coddington, *The Gettysburg Campaign*, 520-21.
249. Gottfried, *The Artillery of Gettysburg*, 235; McClellan, *I Rode with Jeb Stuart*, 339; Carhart, *Lost Triumph*, 208, 214-15; Bridges, *Fighting with Jeb Stuart*, 174; Starr, *The Union Cavalry in the Civil War*, 1:433, 437-38; Carhart, *Sacred Ties*, 205-7; Riggs, *East of Gettysburg*, 46; Coddington, *The Gettysburg Campaign*, 520-21.
250. Hatch, *Clashes of Cavalry*, 114.
251. Robbins, *The Real Custer*, 83.
252. Harris, *Personal Reminiscences of Samuel Harris*, 28.
253. Bridges, *Fighting with Jeb Stuart*, 174.
254. Hatch, *Clashes of Cavalry*, 114; Riggs, *East of Gettysburg*, 46; Harris, *Personal Reminiscences of Samuel Harris*, 28-29.
255. McClellan, *I Rode with Jeb Stuart*, 339; Harrell, *The 2nd North Carolina Cavalry*, 168.
256. Kidd, *Personal Recollections of a Cavalryman*, 73.
257. Robbins, *Last in Their Class*, 260, 262.
258. Kidd, *Personal Recollections of a Cavalryman*, 73-74; Longacre, *Custer*, 161-63.
259. Riggs, *East of Gettysburg*, 46; Longacre, *Custer*, 163; Kidd, *Personal Recollections of a Cavalryman*, 73-74.
260. Longacre, *Custer*, 163; Riggs, *East of Gettysburg*, 48.
261. Kidd, *Personal Recollections of a Cavalryman*, 73.
262. Harrell, *The 2nd North Carolina Cavalry*, 168.
263. Gottfried, *The Artillery of Gettysburg*, 235-36; Trout, *Galloping Thunder*, 7-9, 268, 274, 279-80, 283-84, 287-88; Starr, *The Union Cavalry in the Civil War*, 1:434; Longacre, *Custer and His Wolverines*, 149; McClellan, *I Rode with Jeb Stuart*, 337-39; Harrell, *The 2nd North Carolina Cavalry*, 169; Riggs, *East of Gettysburg*, 50; Bridges, *Fighting with Jeb Stuart*, 174-75; Longacre, *The Cavalry at Gettysburg*, 223; Kidd, *Personal Recollections of a Cavalryman*, 73-78.
264. McClellan, *I Rode with Jeb Stuart*, 339; Longacre, *Custer and His Wolverines*, 149; Riggs, *East of Gettysburg*, 50; Kidd, *Personal Recollections of a Cavalryman*, 73-74.
265. *Detroit Free Press*, July 15, 1863.
266. Husby and Wittenburg, *Under Custer's Command*, 26; Blackford, *War Years with Jeb Stuart*, 261; Kidd, *Personal Recollections of a Cavalryman*, 73-74.
267. Carhart, *Sacred Ties*, 209-10.
268. Stowe, *Company B*, 39; Kidd, *Personal Recollections of a Cavalryman*, 73-74.

269. Robbins, *Last in Their Class*, 264; Riggs, *East of Gettysburg*, 53; Kidd, *Personal Recollections of a Cavalryman*, 73-74; Harrell, *The 2nd North Carolina Cavalry*, 168.
270. Harrell, *The 2nd North Carolina Cavalry*, 169.
271. Ibid.; McClellan, *I Rode with Jeb Stuart*, 339.
272. Robert J. Trout, *In the Saddle with Stuart: The Story of Frank Smith Robertson of Jeb Stuart's Staff* (Gettysburg, PA: Thomas Publications, 1998), 80; Thomas, *Robert E. Lee*, 302-3; Gottfried, *The Artillery of Gettysburg*, 235; Bridges, *Fighting with Jeb Stuart*, 174-75; McClellan, *I Rode with Jeb Stuart*, 338-39; Carhart, *Lost Triumph*, xi-269; Urwin, *Custer Victorious*, 73; Harrell, *The 2nd North Carolina Cavalry*, 168-69; Starr, *The Union Cavalry in the Civil War*, 1:433, 437-38.
273. Bridges, *Fighting with Jeb Stuart*, 104.
274. McClellan, *I Rode with Jeb Stuart*, 339; Kidd, *Personal Recollections of a Cavalryman*, 73.
275. Trout, *In the Saddle with Stuart*, 80, 83; Gottfried, *The Artillery of Gettysburg*, 235; McClellan, *I Rode with Jeb Stuart*, 339; Urwin, *Custer Victorious*, 73; Harrell, *The 2nd North Carolina Cavalry*, 169; Carhart, *Lost Triumph*, xi-269; Starr, *The Union Cavalry in the Civil War*, 1:433, 437-38; Bridges, *Fighting with Jeb Stuart*, 174; Longacre, *Gentleman and Soldier*, 151-52.
276. McClellan, *I Rode with Jeb Stuart*, 339.
277. Ibid.; Harrell, *The 2nd North Carolina Cavalry*, 169.
278. Bachelder Papers, vol. 3, 1377.
279. Bridges, *Fighting with Jeb Stuart*, 174; Trout, *In the Saddle with Stuart*, 80; Starr, *The Union Cavalry in the Civil War*, 1:433, 437-38; McClellan, *I Rode with Jeb Stuart*, 339; Urwin, *Custer Victorious*, 73; Carhart, *Lost Triumph*, xi-269; Harrell, *The 2nd North Carolina Cavalry*, 169; Longacre, *Gentleman and Soldier*, 151-52; Gottfried, *The Artillery of Gettysburg*, 235.
280. Trout, *In the Saddle with Stuart*, 80; Bridges, *Fighting with Jeb Stuart*, 174; McClellan, *I Rode with Jeb Stuart*, 339; Urwin, *Custer Victorious*, 73; Carhart, *Lost Triumph*, xi-269; Starr, *The Union Cavalry in the Civil War*, 1:433, 437-38; Gottfried, *The Artillery of Gettysburg*, 235; Bridges, *Fighting with Jeb Stuart*, 174.
281. Trout, *In the Saddle with Stuart*, 80; Bowden and Ward, *Last Chance for Victory*, 570.
282. Trout, *In the Saddle with Stuart*, 80.
283. Ibid.
284. Ibid., 80-81; Bowden and Ward, *Last Chance for Victory*, 570.
285. Trout, *In the Saddle with Stuart*, 80-81.
286. Glazier, *Three Years in the Federal Cavalry*, 130.
287. Trudeau, *Gettysburg*, 332.
288. Carhart, *Lost Triumph*, xi-269.
289. Garrison, *Civil War Stories*, 67; McClellan, *I Rode with Jeb Stuart*, 339; Gottfried, *The Artillery of Gettysburg*, 235; Urwin, *Custer Victorious*, 73; Carhart, *Lost Triumph*, xi-269; Bridges, *Fighting with Jeb Stuart*, 174; Coddington, *The Gettysburg Campaign*, 520-21.
290. Urwin, *Custer Victorious*, 73.
291. Monaghan, *Custer*, 144.

292. Bachelder Papers, vol. 3, 1377.
293. Ibid., 247.
294. Bridges, *Fighting with Jeb Stuart*, 175.
295. Hatch, *Clashes of Cavalry*, 114; Riggs, *East of Gettysburg*, 48; Carhart, *Sacred Ties*, 209–10.
296. Longacre, *Fitz Lee*, 124.
297. Douglas, *A Boot Full of Memories*, xiii, 250.
298. Captain Leonard Williams, 2nd South Carolina Cavalry, July 29, 1863, letter to wife Anna Laval Williams, Raynor's Historical Collectibles Auction, Burlington, North Carolina.
299. Ibid.
300. Hatch, *Clashes of Cavalry*, 114.
301. Hatch, *Clashes of Cavalry*, 114; Robbins, *The Real Custer*, 83.
302. Robbins, *Last in Their Class*, 264–65.
303. Trout, *In the Saddle with Stuart*, 80–81; Bachelder Papers, vol. 3, 1377; McClellan, *I Rode with Jeb Stuart*, 339; Urwin, *Custer Victorious*, 73; Robbins, *Last in Their Class*, 265; Carhart, *Lost Triumph*, xi–269; Bridges, *Fighting with Jeb Stuart*, 174; Starr, *The Union Cavalry in the Civil War*, 1:433, 437–38; Coddington, *The Gettysburg Campaign*, 520–21; Carter, *The Last Cavaliers*, 169; Gottfried, *The Artillery of Gettysburg*, 235.
304. Trout, *In the Saddle with Stuart*, 80–81; Starr, *The Union Cavalry in the Civil War*, 1:433, 437–38; McClellan, *I Rode with Jeb Stuart*, 339; Urwin, *Custer Victorious*, 73; Carhart, *Lost Triumph*, xi–269; Bridges, *Fighting with Jeb Stuart*, 174; Bowden and Ward, *Last Chance for Victory*, 427, 431, 570; Meyer, *Civil War Experiences with the New York Cavalry*, 43.
305. Monaghan, *Custer*, 149.
306. Gottfried, *The Artillery of Gettysburg*, 235–36.
307. Husby and Wittenburg, *Under Custer's Command*, 8.
308. Hatch, *Clashes of Cavalry*, 114; Robbins, *Personal Recollections of a Cavalryman*, 78.
309. McClellan, *I Rode with Jeb Stuart*, 340.
310. Robbins, *Last in Their Class*, 264–65.
311. Ibid.; McClellan, *I Rode with Jeb Stuart*, 339.
312. McClellan, *I Rode with Jeb Stuart*, 339; Robbins, *Last in Their Class*, 264; Trout, *In the Saddle with Stuart*, 82.
313. McClellan, *I Rode with Jeb Stuart*, 339–40.
314. Ibid., 338–39.
315. Ibid., 339.
316. Robbins, *Last in Their Class*, 265.
317. J. Edward Carpenter, "Gregg's Cavalry at Gettysburg," in *Annals of the War: Written by Participants North and South* (Edison, New Jersey: Blue and Grey Press, 1966), 527.
318. Ibid., 529.
319. Ibid., 531.
320. Coddington, *The Gettysburg Campaign*, 520; Monaghan, *Custer*, 4–41; Hatch, *Clashes of Cavalry*, 18, 110–15; Robbins, *The Real Custer*, xi, xiv, 83; Alan Schom, *Napoleon Bonaparte* (New York: HarperCollins, 1997), 755–58; Tucker, *Pickett's Charge*,

1-375; Raymond Horricks, *Marshal Ney: The Romance and the Real* (New York: Hippocrene Books, 1982), 238-40; Merington, *The Custer Story*, 34-35, 95.
  321. Robbins, *The Real Custer*, 83; Robbins, *Last in Their Class*, 265.
  322. Whittaker, *A Complete Life of General George A. Custer*, 1:168.
  323. Robbins, *Last in Their Class*, 265; Johnson and Buel, *Battles and Leaders of the Civil War*, 3:403.
  324. Johnson and Buel, *Battles and Leaders of the Civil War*, 3:403; Robbins, *Last in Their Class*, 264-65.
  325. Monaghan, *Custer*, 10, 146-49, 386-91.

## CHAPTER 4

  1. Isham, *Seventh Michigan Cavalry*, 7-22, 26; Longacre, *Custer and His Wolverines*, 149; Stowe, *Company B*, 37-39; Robbins, *The Real Custer*, 79; Johnson and Buel, *Battles and Leaders of the Civil War*, 3:403; Longacre, *Custer*, 174; Hatch, *Clashes of Cavalry*, 115; Robbins, *Last in Their Class*, 265.
  2. Rosentreter, *Grand Rapids and the Civil War*, 38-40.
  3. Ibid., 44-45.
  4. Isham, *Seventh Michigan Cavalry*, 14, 22-23, 26; Longacre, *Custer and His Wolverines*, 149; Robbins, *The Real Custer*, 83; Johnson, *Napoleon*, 58; Robbins, *Last in Their Class*, 265; Hatch, *Clashes of Cavalry*, 115.
  5. Longacre, *Custer and His Wolverines*, 149.
  6. *Detroit Free Press*, July 15, 1863.
  7. Longacre, *Custer and His Wolverines*, 149-50.
  8. Sullivan, *Custer's Road to Disaster*, 70-71.
  9. Stephen A. Ambrose, *Crazy Horse and Custer: The Parallel Lives of Two American Warriors* (New York: Anchor, 1996), 195.
  10. Merington, *The Custer Story*, 95.
  11. Isham, *Seventh Michigan Cavalry*, 23.
  12. Johnson, *Napoleon*, 56-57.
  13. Isham, *Seventh Michigan Cavalry*, 23; Longacre, *Custer*, 157; Robbins, *The Real Custer*, 83-84; Hatch, *Clashes of Cavalry*, 115; Robbins, *Last in Their Class*, 265; Monaghan, *Custer*, 10.
  14. Isham, *Seventh Michigan Cavalry*, 26; Horricks, *Marshal Ney*, 221, 233-39.
  15. Horricks, *Marshal Ney*, 221.
  16. Isham, *Seventh Michigan Cavalry*, 99-101; Horricks, *Marshal Ney*, 221; Longacre, *Custer and His Wolverines*, 150; Hatch, *Clashes of Cavalry*, 115; Merington, *The Custer Story*, 98.
  17. Isham, *Seventh Michigan Cavalry*, 28.
  18. Merington, *The Custer Story*, 103.
  19. Longacre, *Custer and His Wolverines*, 150.
  20. Kidd, *Personal Recollections of a Cavalryman*, 80; Robbins, *Last in Their Class*, 265; Robbins, *The Real Custer*, 84.

21. Isham, *Seventh Michigan Cavalry*, 23.
22. Ibid., 26.
23. Longacre, *Custer and His Wolverines*, 150.
24. Isham, *Seventh Michigan Cavalry*, 23.
25. Meyer, *Civil War Experiences with the New York Cavalry*, 47.
26. Isham, *Seventh Michigan Cavalry*, 23.
27. Hatch, *Clashes of Cavalry*, 115; Kidd, *Personal Recollections of a Cavalryman*, 79; Isham, *Seventh Michigan Cavalry*, 25; Robbins, *Last in Their Class*, 265.
28. Robbins, *Last in Their Class*, 265; Longacre, *Custer and His Wolverines*, 150.
29. Johnson and Buel, *Battles and Leaders of the Civil War*, 3:404.
30. Isham, *Seventh Michigan Cavalry*, 23–24; Robbins, *The Real Custer*, 84; Hatch, *Clashes of Cavalry*, 115.
31. Rosentreter, *Grand Rapids and the Civil War*, 44–45; Robbins, *The Real Custer*, 84.
32. Robbins, *The Real Custer*, 84.
33. Longacre, *Custer and His Wolverines*, 150.
34. Isham, *Seventh Michigan Cavalry*, 24–25.
35. Robbins, *The Real Custer*, 84; Kidd, *Personal Recollections of a Cavalryman*, 79.
36. Robbins, *The Real Custer*, 84; Hatch, *Clashes of Cavalry*, 115.
37. Isham, *Seventh Michigan Cavalry*, 104–6, 130.
38. Rosentreter, *Grand Rapids and the Civil War*, 44–45; Longacre, *Custer and His Wolverines*, 150.
39. Isham, *Seventh Michigan Cavalry*, 25.
40. Longacre, *Custer and His Wolverines*, 150–51.
41. Isham, *Seventh Michigan Cavalry*, 25, 95; Robbins, *Last in Their Class*, 265; Longacre, *Custer*, 155; Kidd, *Personal Recollections of a Cavalryman*, 79; Robbins, *The Real Custer*, 84.
42. Robbins, *Last in Their Class*, 265–66.
43. Isham, *Seventh Michigan Cavalry*, 25; Hatch, *Clashes of Cavalry*, 115.
44. Gage Letters, SA.
45. Meyer, *Civil War Experiences with the New York Cavalry*, 47.
46. Robbins, *The Real Custer*, 84; Isham, *Seventh Michigan Cavalry*, 25; Hatch, *Clashes of Cavalry*, 115.
47. Trout, *In the Saddle with Stuart*, 82; Kidd, *Personal Recollections of a Cavalryman*, 79.
48. Hatch, *Clashes of Cavalry*, 115; Isham, *Seventh Michigan Cavalry*, 25; Robbins, *The Real Custer*, 84.
49. McClellan, *I Rode with Jeb Stuart*, 343–44.
50. Isham, *Seventh Michigan Cavalry*, 25.
51. McClellan, *I Rode with Jeb Stuart*, 339, 344; "34th Virginia Cavalry—Wayne County, West Virginia," RootsWeb, internet; Longacre, *Fitz Lee*, 123.
52. "34th Virginia Cavalry—Wayne County, West Virginia," RootsWeb, internet.
53. Ibid.
54. Isham, *Seventh Michigan Cavalry*, 25–26; Kidd, *Personal Recollections of a Cavalryman*, 79.

55. Isham, *Seventh Michigan Cavalry*, 25–26.
56. Kidd, *Personal Recollections of a Cavalryman*, 79.
57. Robbins, *Last in Their Class*, 265.
58. Bridges, *Fighting with Jeb Stuart*, 175; Isham, *Seventh Michigan Cavalry*, 25–26; Kidd, *Personal Recollections of a Cavalryman*, 80; Harrell, *The 2nd North Carolina Cavalry*, 125–26; Meyer, *Civil War Experiences with the New York Cavalry*, 47.
59. Harrell, *The 2nd North Carolina Cavalry*, 1, 10.
60. Ibid., 6–7, 149.
61. Rod Gragg, *The Illustrated Gettysburg Reader: An Eyewitness History of the Civil War's Greatest Battle* (Washington, DC: Regnery, 2013), 295.
62. Isham, *Seventh Michigan Cavalry*, 26.
63. Gragg, *The Illustrated Gettysburg Reader*, 295.
64. Ibid.; Kidd, *Personal Recollections of a Cavalryman*, 80; Isham, *Seventh Michigan Cavalry*, 26, 96.
65. Isham, *Seventh Michigan Cavalry*, 27.
66. Gragg, *The Illustrated Gettysburg Reader*, 295.
67. Ibid.; Private William Glover Gage to Family, August 8, 1863, Gage Letters, SA.
68. Private William Glover Gage to Family, September 10, 1863, Gage Letters, SA.
69. Ibid.
70. Merington, *The Custer Story*, 114.
71. McClellan, *I Rode with Jeb Stuart*, 343–44.
72. Ibid., 340.
73. Ibid., 343.
74. Longacre, *Custer and His Wolverines*, 151.
75. Isham, *Seventh Michigan Cavalry*, 27.
76. Ibid., 28, 191–92.
77. McClellan, *I Rode with Jeb Stuart*, 340.
78. Gragg, *The Illustrated Gettysburg Reader*, 295.
79. Harrell, *The 2nd North Carolina Cavalry*, 126–27, 146.
80. Robbins, *Last in Their Class*, 265.
81. Ibid., 265.
82. Harrell, *The 2nd North Carolina Cavalry*, 146.
83. Kidd, *Personal Recollections of a Cavalryman*, 80–81.
84. Ibid.; Riggs, *East of Gettysburg*, 53.
85. Harrell, *The 2nd North Carolina Cavalry*, 146, 169; Longacre, *The Cavalry at Gettysburg*, 27–29.
86. Ackerman, *Wade Hampton III*, 36, 42–44, 47.
87. Ackerman, *Wade Hampton III*, 50; Harrell, *The 2nd North Carolina Cavalry*, 169.
88. Harrell, *The 2nd North Carolina Cavalry*, 169; Longacre, *Gentleman and Soldier*, 151–52.
89. Longacre, *Fitz Lee*, 122–23; McClellan, *I Rode with Jeb Stuart*, 339.
90. Ackerman, *Wade Hampton III*, 50; Harrell, *The 2nd North Carolina Cavalry*, 169.
91. Hudgins and Kleese, *Recollections of an Old Dominion Dragoon*, 82.
92. Longacre, *Fitz Lee*, 124.
93. Riggs, *East of Gettysburg*, 53.

94. Kidd, *Personal Recollections of a Cavalryman*, 80–81; Riggs, *East of Gettysburg*, 53–54.
95. Harrell, *The 2nd North Carolina Cavalry*, 169; Longacre, *Gentleman and Soldier*, 153.
96. Ackerman, *Wade Hampton III*, 50, 53; Longacre, *Gentleman and Soldier*, 153; Harrell, *The 2nd North Carolina Cavalry*, 169.
97. Harrell, *The 2nd North Carolina Cavalry*, 169; Longacre, *Gentleman and Soldier*, 153.
98. Husby and Wittenberg, *Under Custer's Command*, 35, 37.
99. McClellan, *I Rode with Jeb Stuart*, 344.
100. Hudgins and Kleese, *Recollections of an Old Dominion Dragoon*, 82, 84.
101. McClellan, *I Rode with Jeb Stuart*, 344.
102. Longacre, *Fitz Lee*, 124.
103. McClellan, *I Rode with Jeb Stuart*, 345; Longacre, *Fitz Lee*, 124.
104. McClellan, *I Rode with Jeb Stuart*, 345; Longacre, *Fitz Lee*, 124.
105. McClellan, *I Rode with Jeb Stuart*, 341.
106. Bridges, *Fighting with Jeb Stuart*, 178.
107. Ibid.
108. McClellan, *I Rode with Jeb Stuart*, 341.
109. *Detroit Free Press*, July 15, 1863.
110. McClellan, *I Rode with Jeb Stuart*, 343–44.
111. Starr, *The Union Cavalry in the Civil War*, 1:433, 437–38; Coddington, *The Gettysburg Campaign*, 520–21; McClellan, *I Rode with Jeb Stuart*, 339; Carhart, *Lost Triumph*, 208.
112. Longacre, *The Cavalry at Gettysburg*, 237; Trout, *In The Saddle with Stuart*, 79–83.
113. Trout, *In the Saddle with Stuart*, 79–83; Govan and Livingood, *The Haskell Memoirs*, 20.
114. McClellan, *I Rode with Jeb Stuart*, 339; Carhart, *Lost Triumph*, 208; Coddington, *The Gettysburg Campaign*, 520–21; Ackerman, *Wade Hampton III*, 38–50; Trout, *In the Saddle with Stuart*, 79–83; Schom, *Napoleon Bonaparte*, 755–58.
115. Trout, *In the Saddle with Stuart*, 80–81; Gottfried, *The Artillery of Gettysburg*, 235.
116. Gragg, *The Illustrated Gettysburg Reader*, 295–96.
117. Ackerman, *Wade Hampton III*, 50.
118. Longacre, *Gentleman and Soldier*, 40, 153.
119. Longacre, *Gentleman and Soldier*, 151, 154; McClellan, *I Rode with Jeb Stuart*, 339; Carhart, *Lost Triumph*, 208; Coddington, *The Gettysburg Campaign*, 520–21; Starr, *The Union Cavalry in the Civil War*, 1:433, 437–38; Gragg, *The Illustrated Gettysburg Reader*, 296.
120. Longacre, *Custer*, 155.
121. Ibid.
122. Robbins, *Last in Their Class*, 266.
123. William Glover Gage to Family, September 10, 1863, Gage Letters, SA.
124. Johnson and Buel, *Battles and Leaders of the Civil War*, 3:404.

125. James G. Birney, *The Gateway*, vol. 3, August 1904.
126. Ibid.; Robbins, *Last in Their Class*, 266; Gragg, *The Illustrated Gettysburg Reader*, 296.
127. Johnson and Buel, *Battles and Leaders of the Civil War*, 3:404.

## CHAPTER 5

1. Trout, *In the Saddle with Stuart*, 82.
2. Ibid., 83.
3. *Detroit Free Press*, July 15, 1863.
4. Hatch, *Clashes of Cavalry*, 116; Birney, *The Gateway*, vol. 3, August 1904.
5. Hatch, *Clashes of Cavalry*, 116; Urwin, *Custer Victorious*, 79.
6. Birney, *The Gateway*, Vol. 3, August 1904; Longacre, *Custer and His Wolverines*, 151.
7. Longacre, *Custer and His Wolverines*, 151.
8. Robbins, *The Real Custer*, 85.
9. Hatch, *Clashes of Cavalry*, 116.
10. Robbins, *The Real Custer*, 85.
11. Monaghan, *Custer*, 10.
12. Ibid.; Meyer, *Civil War Experiences with the New York Cavalry*, 47–48; Robbins, *The Real Custer*, 85; Hatch, *Clashes of Cavalry*, 116–17; Longacre, *Custer*, 150, 174.
13. *Detroit Free Press*, July 15, 1863.
14. Urwin, *Custer Victorious*, 58.
15. Ibid., 79.
16. Robbins, *The Real Custer*, 85.
17. Hatch, *Clashes of Cavalry*, 116–17.
18. Ibid., 117.
19. Urwin, *Custer Victorious*, 57–59; Longacre, *Custer and His Wolverines*, 151–53; McClellan, *I Rode with Jeb Stuart*, 337–41; Hatch, *Clashes of Cavalry*, 117; Monaghan, *Custer*, 10; Govan and Livingood, *The Haskell Memoirs*, 18.
20. Urwin, *Custer Victorious*, 59.
21. Ibid., 58; Longacre, *Custer*, 5.
22. Husby and Wittenburg, *Under Custer's Command*, 35, 37.
23. *Detroit Free Press*, July 15, 1863.
24. Longacre, *Custer and His Wolverines*, 152.
25. Meyer, *Civil War Experiences with the New York Cavalry*, 47.
26. Urwin, *Custer Victorious*, 79–80.
27. *Detroit Free Press*, July 15, 1863.
28. Urwin, *Custer Victorious*, 67; Hatch, *Clashes of Cavalry*, 117.
29. Hatch, *Clashes of Cavalry*, 117; Urwin, *Custer Victorious*, 80.
30. Urwin, *Custer Victorious*, 80.
31. Longacre, *Custer and His Wolverines*, 152.
32. Longacre, *Custer*, 173.
33. Ibid.

34. Hatch, *Clashes of Cavalry*, 118.
35. Longacre, *Custer and His Wolverines*, 152.
36. Hatch, *Clashes of Cavalry*, 118; Longacre, *Custer and His Wolverines*, 152.
37. Longacre, *Custer and His Wolverines*, 152.
38. Urwin, *Custer Victorious*, 93.
39. Longacre, *Custer and His Wolverines*, 152.
40. Urwin, *Custer Victorious*, 79–81; Ernie Bradford, *Thermopylae: The Battle for the West* (New York: Da Capo, 1993), 125–42; Stephenson, *The Last Full Measure*, 18, 29–30.
41. Private William Glover Gage to Family, September 4, 1863, Gage Letters, SA.
42. Hatch, *Clashes of Cavalry*, 118.
43. Hatch, *Clashes of Cavalry*, 115, 117–19; Urwin, *Custer Victorious*, 81.
44. Husby and Wittenburg, *Under Custer's Command*, 37.
45. Urwin, *Custer Victorious*, 79–80; Whittaker, *A Complete Life of General George A. Custer*, 1:178–79.
46. Whittaker, *A Complete Life of General George A. Custer*, 1:178–79.
47. Longacre, *Gentleman and Soldier*, 153; Meyer, *Civil War Experiences with the New York Cavalry*, 47.
48. Longacre, *Gentleman and Soldier*, 154; Meyer, *Civil War Experiences with the New York Cavalry*, 47.
49. Husby and Wittenburg, *Under Custer's Command*, 37.
50. Ackerman, *Wade Hampton III*, 50.
51. Ibid.; Husby and Wittenburg, *Under Custer's Command*, 37.
52. Ackerman, *Wade Hampton III*, 50–51.
53. Meyer, *Civil War Experiences with the New York Cavalry*, 47; Longacre, *Custer and His Wolverines*, 153.
54. Meyer, *Civil War Experiences with the New York Cavalry*, 47; Whittaker, *A Complete Life of General George A. Custer*, 1:179.
55. Husby and Wittenburg, *Under Custer's Command*, 37.
56. *Detroit Free Press*, July 15, 1863.
57. B. J. Haden, *Reminiscences of J. E. B. Stuart's Cavalry* (Charlottesville, VA, n.d.), 24–25.
58. Whittaker, *A Complete Life of General George A. Custer*, 1:178.
59. Toalson, *Send Me a Pair of Old Boots*, 201.
60. Bridges, *Fighting with Jeb Stuart*, 178.
61. Longacre, *Custer*, 173.
62. McClellan, *I Rode with Jeb Stuart*, 341.
63. Ibid., 343.
64. Ibid., 341; Mark E. Neely Jr., Harold Holzer, and Gabor S. Boritt, *The Confederate Image: Prints of the Lost Cause* (Chapel Hill: University of South Carolina Press, 1987), 204; McClellan, *I Rode with Jeb Stuart*, 339; Carhart, *Lost Triumph*, xi–269; Bridges, *Fighting with Jeb Stuart*, 174–78; Starr, *The Union Cavalry in the Civil War*, 1:433, 437–38; Gottfried, *The Artillery of Gettysburg*, 235.
65. Neely et al., *The Confederate Image*, 204; Trout, *In the Saddle with Stuart*, 80–81, 83; Carhart, *Lost Triumph*, xi–269; Urwin, *Custer Victorious*, 73; Starr, *The Union Cavalry in the Civil War*, 1:433, 437–38; Bridges, *Fighting with Jeb Stuart*, 174, 178.

66. Bridges, *Fighting with Jeb Stuart*, 174, 178; Starr, *The Union Cavalry in the Civil War*, 1:433, 437–38; Carhart, *Lost Triumph*, xi–269; Urwin, *Custer Victorious*, 73; McClellan, *I Rode with Jeb Stuart*, 339.

67. Ackerman, *Wade Hampton III*, 50; McClellan, *I Rode with Jeb Stuart*, 339; Starr, *The Union Cavalry in the Civil War*, 1:433, 437–38; Coddington, *The Gettysburg Campaign*, 520–21.

68. Carhart, *Sacred Ties*, 213.
69. Ibid., 214.
70. Wert, *Custer*, 95.
71. Longacre, *Custer*, 174.
72. Wert, *Custer*, 95.
73. Meade, *The Life and Letters of General George Gordon Meade*, 2:109.
74. Wert, *Custer*, 95.
75. Whittaker, *A Complete Life of General George A. Custer*, 1:178.
76. Meyer, *Civil War Experiences with the New York Cavalry*, 48.
77. Toalson, *Send Me a Pair of Old Boots*, 205.
78. Thomas, *Robert E. Lee*, 302–3; Coddington, *The Gettysburg Campaign*, 520–21; Carter, *The Last Cavaliers*, 169.
79. William A. Allison to Stock, July 18, 1863, Allison Letters, New York Historical Society, Gilder Lehrman Collection, New York.
80. Douglas, *A Boot Full of Memories*, 238–39.
81. "34th Virginia Cavalry—Wayne County, West Virginia," RootsWeb, internet.
82. Harris, *Personal Reminiscences of Samuel Harris*, 28.
83. Bridges, *Fighting with Jeb Stuart*, 132.
84. Ibid., 135.
85. Meyer, *Civil War Experiences with the New York Cavalry*, 43.
86. Bridges, *Fighting with Jeb Stuart*, 174; Starr, *The Union Cavalry in the Civil War*, 1:433, 437–38; Carhart, *Lost Triumph*, xi–269; Urwin, *Custer Victorious*, 73; McClellan, *I Rode with Jeb Stuart*, 339.
87. *Dispatch*, Richmond, Virginia, April 5, 1896.
88. Bridges, *Fighting with Jeb Stuart*, 178.
89. Allers, *The Fog of Gettysburg*, 159.
90. *Lutheran and Missionary*, Philadelphia, Pennsylvania, September 24, 1863.
91. Blackford, *Letters From Lee's Army*, 195.
92. Ibid.
93. McClellan, *I Rode with Jeb Stuart*, 341.
94. Katcher, *The Army of Robert E. Lee*, 138.
95. Ackerman, *Wade Hampton III*, 40–41; Whittaker, *A Complete Life of General George A. Custer*, 1:176–78.
96. Longacre, *Custer and His Wolverines*, 154; Robbins, *The Real Custer*, 87.
97. *Detroit Free Press*, July 4, 1863.
98. Ibid.
99. Rosentreter, *Grand Rapids and the Civil War*, 46.
100. Longacre, *Custer*, 175.
101. Ibid., 175.

102. Captain Daniel H. Darling to father of Private William Glover Gage, July 6, 1863, Gage Letters, SA.
103. "34th Virginia Cavalry—Wayne County, West Virginia"—RootsWeb, internet.
104. Longacre, *Custer*, 174; *Detroit Free Press*, July 7, 1876; Longacre, *Custer and His Wolverines*, 153.
105. Urwin, *Custer Victorious*, 82.
106. *Detroit Free Press*, July 15, 1863.
107. Bak, *A Distant Thunder*, 119.
108. Rosentreter, *Grand Rapids and the Civil War*, 46.
109. "34th Virginia Cavalry—Wayne County, West Virginia," RootsWeb, internet.
110. Ibid.
111. Meyer, *Civil War Experiences with the New York Cavalry*, 47; Whittaker, *A Complete Life of General George A. Custer*, 1:179.
112. Blackford, *Letters from Lee's Army*, 195–96.
113. Thomas, *Robert E. Lee*, 302–3; Toalson, *Send Me a Pair of Old Boots*, 200–201; Piston, *Lee's Tarnished Lieutenant*, 46–47; *Dispatch*, Richmond, Virginia, April 5, 1896.
114. Mosby, *Stuart's Cavalry in the Gettysburg Campaign*, 77–222; Kim Newman, "The Blue Max Review," April 28, 2006, internet; *Dispatch*, Richmond, Virginia, April 5, 1896.
115. Carhart, *Sacred Ties*, 206.
116. Carhart, *Lost Triumph*, 241–42.
117. Edward G. Longacre, *Pickett: Leader of the Charge; Biography of General George E. Pickett, C.S.A.* (Shippensburg, PA: White Mane, 1995), 128–29.
118. Govan and Livingood, *The Haskell Memoirs*, 51–52.
119. Coddington, *The Gettysburg Campaign*, 458.
120. Longacre, *Gentleman and Soldier*, 151.
121. Gary W. Gallagher, editor, *The Third Day at Gettysburg and Beyond* (Chapel Hill: University of North Carolina Press, 1998), 33; Mosby, *Stuart's Cavalry in the Gettysburg Campaign*, 207–9; Coddington, *The Gettysburg Campaign*, 458; Piston, *Lee's Tarnished Lieutenant*, 168; Trout, *In the Saddle with Stuart*, 79–83.
122. Carhart, *Lost Triumph*, 245.
123. William C. Davis, *Jefferson Davis: The Man and His Hour; A Biography* (New York: HarperPerennial, 1992), 556; Gallagher, *The Third Day at Gettysburg and Beyond*, 33–34; Mosby, *Stuart's Cavalry in the Gettysburg Campaign*, 203, 207–9; Thomas, *Robert E. Lee*, 329.
124. Gallagher, *The Third Day at Gettysburg and Beyond*, 33.
125. Ibid., 33–35.
126. Ibid., 34; Bowden and Ward, *Last Chance for Victory*, 429–30, 439.
127. Gallagher, *The Third Day at Gettysburg and Beyond*, 33–37, 45; Bowden and Ward, *Last Chance for Victory*, 431–39; McClellan, *I Rode with Jeb Stuart*, 339; Urwin, *Custer Victorious*, 73; Carhart, *Lost Triumph*, xi–269; Starr, *The Union Cavalry in the Civil War*, 1:433, 437–38.
128. Gallagher, *The Third Day at Gettysburg and Beyond*, 34; Bowden and Ward, *Last Chance for Victory*, 437–39.
129. Gallagher, *The Third Day at Gettysburg and Beyond*, 46.

130. Ibid.

131. Bowden and Ward, *Last Chance for Victory*, 437-39; McClellan, *I Rode with Jeb Stuart*, 339; Carhart, *Lost Triumph*, xi-269; Urwin, *Custer Victorious*, 73; Starr, *The Union Cavalry in the Civil War*, 1:433, 437-38.

132. Thomason, *JEB Stuart*, 441.

133. Trout, "The Hoss," 4.

134. Ibid., 8-9; Thomason, *JEB Stuart*, 444.

135. Kidd, *Personal Recollections of a Cavalryman*, 82.

136. John N. Opie, *A Rebel Cavalryman* (Dayton, OH: Morningside Bookshop, 1997), 167.

137. Kidd, *Personal Recollections of a Cavalryman*, 83.

138. Trudeau, *Gettysburg*, 473.

139. Carhart, *Sacred Ties*, 205-7.

140. Bridges, *Fighting with Jeb Stuart*, 174; McClellan, *I Rode with Jeb Stuart*, 339; Carhart, *Lost Triumph*, xi-269; Urwin, *Custer Victorious*, 73; Starr, *The Union Cavalry in the Civil War*, 1:433, 437-38.

141. Starr, *The Union Cavalry in the Civil War*, 1:437.

142. Riggs, *East of Gettysburg*, 67.

143. Rosentreter, *Grand Rapids and the Civil War*, 44.

144. Francis Trevelyan Miller, ed., *The Cavalry: The Photographic History of the Civil War*, 10 vols. (New York: Castle Books, 1957), 29 (Vol. 4).

145. Sullivan, *Custer's Road to Disaster*, 32.

146. Field, *Confederate Cavalryman versus Union Cavalryman*, 43.

147. Harrell, *The 2nd North Carolina Cavalry*, 172.

148. Downey, *Clash of Cavalry*, 149.

149. Glenn Tucker, *Lee and Longstreet at Gettysburg* (Dayton, OH: Morningside Bookshop, 1982), 205.

150. Emory M. Thomas, "Eggs, Aldie, Shepherdstown, and J.E.B. Stuart," in *The Gettysburg Nobody Knows*, ed. Gabor S. Boritt (New York: Oxford University Press, 1997), 111-12.

151. McClellan, *I Rode with Jeb Stuart*, 339.

152. B. H. Liddell Hart, *History of the Second World War* (Old Saybrook, CT: Konecky and Konecky, 1970), v.

153. McClellan, *I Rode with Jeb Stuart*, 339.

154. Riggs, *East of Gettysburg*, 67.

155. Meade, *The Life and Letters of General George Gordon Meade*, 2:109.

156. Roger L. Rosentreter, "Thank God for Michigan!," *Michigan History Magazine* 82, no. 4 (July-August 1998): 119.

157. Robbins, *Last in Their Class*, 267.

158. Bak, *A Distant Thunder*, 131, 133.

159. John N. Opie, *A Rebel Cavalryman* (Chicago: W. B. Conkey, 1899), 163, 167.

160. Piston, *Lee's Tarnished Lieutenant*, ix-xi, 1, 163-85.

161. Downey, *Clash of Cavalry*, 83.

162. Thomas Hubbard Axford, editor, *The Journals of Thomas Hubbard Hobbs* (Tuscaloosa: University of Alabama Press, 1976), 249-50.

163. Ibid., 251.
164. Monaghan, *Custer*, 6–8; Downey, *Clash of Cavalry*, 159; Merington, *The Custer Story*, 7, 26, 30, 67, 95; Sullivan, *Custer's Road to Disaster*, 7, 11.
165. Longacre, *Custer and His Wolverines*, 9–10.
166. Merington, *The Custer Story*, 103.
167. Barnard and Singelyn, *An Aide to Custer*, 114.
168. Blackford, *War Years with Jeb Stuart*, 262.
169. *Philadelphia Weekly Times*, February 8, 1879.
170. Neese, *Three Years in the Confederate Horse Artillery*, 114.
171. Longacre, *Custer and His Wolverines*, 151–74; *Detroit News*, July 15, 1863.
172. Harsanyi, *First Freedom*, 127.
173. Longacre, *Custer and His Wolverines*, 153; Monaghan, *Custer*, 8; Starr, *The Union Cavalry in the Civil War*, 1:51–52; Trout, "The Hoss," 15; Johnson, *Napoleon*, 57–58.
174. Gottfried, *The Artillery of Gettysburg*, 238.
175. Longacre, *Custer and His Wolverines*, 153.
176. Urwin, *Custer Victorious*, 79–80.
177. Whittaker, *A Complete Life of General George A. Custer*, 1:178.
178. Ibid., 174–79; Longacre, *Custer and His Wolverines*, 153; Boritt, *The Gettysburg Nobody Knows*, 114.
179. Husby and Wittenburg, *Under Custer's Command*, 35.
180. Ibid., v.
181. Carter, *The Last Cavaliers*, 172.
182. Govan and Livingood, *The Haskell Memoirs*, 19, 55–56.
183. Axford, *The Journals of Thomas Hubbard Hobbs*, 250, note.
184. Robbins, *Last in Their Class*, 189.
185. Ackerman, *Wade Hampton III*, 36.
186. Carhart, *Lost Triumph*, 6.
187. Wert, *Custer*, 95.
188. McClellan, *I Rode with Jeb Stuart*, 341.
189. Longacre, *Custer and His Wolverines*, 153.
190. *Detroit Free Press*, July 15, 1863.
191. Longacre, *Custer and His Wolverines*, 153.
192. Kidd, *Personal Recollections of a Cavalryman*, ix.
193. Meyer, *Civil War Experiences with the New York Cavalry*, 49–50.
194. Longacre, *Custer and His Wolverines*, 153; Captain Daniel H. Darling to Father of Private William Glover Gage, July 6, 1863, Gage Letters, SA.
195. Private William Glover Gage to Family, September 10, 1863, Gage Letters, SA.
196. Merington, *The Custer Story*, 115.
197. Longacre, *Custer and His Wolverines*, 153.
198. Gregory A. Coco, *On the Bloodstained Field, I and II: 262 Human Interest Stories of the Campaign and Battle of Gettysburg* (Orrtanna, PA: Colecraft Industries, 2013), 49.
199. Gragg, *The Illustrated Gettysburg Reader*, 296.

## EPILOGUE

1. Bowden and Ward, *Last Chance for Victory*, 471-72; Longacre, *Custer and His Wolverines*, 153.
2. Bowden and Ward, *Last Chance for Victory*, 472.
3. Hatch, *Clashes of Cavalry*, xi-xii.
4. Commander-in-Chief Biographies, Major General David McMurtrie Gregg, Mollus Website, internet.
5. Carhart, *Lost Triumph*, 244.
6. Hatch, *Clashes of Cavalry*, 110.
7. Urwin, *Custer Victorious*, 73.
8. Kidd, *Personal Recollections of a Cavalryman*, 83-84.
9. Longacre, *Custer and His Wolverines*, 153.
10. Louis L. Snyder, *Great Turning Points in History* (New York: Barnes and Noble, 1971), 75-77.
11. Johnson and Buel, *Battles and Leaders of the Civil War*, 3:406.
12. Longacre, *Custer and His Wolverines*, 153; Bak, *A Distant Thunder*, 31.
13. Carter, *The Last Cavaliers*, 169; Starr, *The Union Cavalry in the Civil War*, 1:433, 437-38; Coddington, *The Gettysburg Campaign*, 520-21; McClellan, *I Rode with Jeb Stuart*, 339.
14. Wert, *Custer*, 95.
15. *Detroit Free Press*, Detroit, Michigan, July 15, 1863.
16. Ibid.
17. Urwin, *Custer Victorious*, 78.
18. Boritt, *The Gettysburg Nobody Knows*, 114.
19. Garrison, *Civil War Stories*, 67.
20. Monaghan, *Custer*, 144.
21. Starr, *The Union Cavalry in the Civil War*, 1:433, 437-38; McClellan, *I Rode with Jeb Stuart*, 339; Carhart, *Lost Triumph*, xi-269; Urwin, *Custer Victorious*, 73.
22. Starr, *The Union Cavalry in the Civil War*, 1:433, 437-38; McClellan, *I Rode with Jeb Stuart*, 339; Coddington, *The Gettysburg Campaign*, 520-21.
23. John N. Opie, *A Rebel Cavalryman* (Dayton, OH: Morningside Bookshop, 1997), 10.
24. Thomas, *Robert E. Lee*, 301; Gottfried, *The Artillery of Gettysburg*, 236.
25. Thomas, *Robert E. Lee*, 301.
26. Opie, *A Rebel Cavalryman*, 167.
27. Durkin, *John Dooley*, 107.
28. Nye, *Here Come the Rebels!*, 15.
29. Monaghan, *Custer*, 149.
30. Husby and Wittenburg, *Under Custer's Command*, 2; Longacre, *Custer and His Wolverines*, 153.
31. Longacre, *Custer and His Wolverines*, 153.
32. Monaghan, *Custer*, 149; McClellan, *I Rode with Jeb Stuart*, 339; Longacre, *Custer and His Wolverines*, 153; Urwin, *Custer Victorious*, 73; Carhart, *Lost Triumph*, xi-269; Longacre, *The Cavalry at Gettysburg*, 27.

33. Carhart, *Lost Triumph*, 6; Longacre, *Custer and His Wolverines*, 153.
34. Carhart, *Sacred Ties*, 215.
35. Longacre, *Gentleman and Soldier*, 155.
36. Sears, *Gettysburg*, 462.
37. Monaghan, *Custer*, 149.
38. Harrell, *The 2nd North Carolina Cavalry*, 172.
39. Starr, *The Union Cavalry in the Civil War*, 1:437–38.
40. Bachelder Papers, vol. 3, 1377.
41. Ibid.
42. Longacre, *The Cavalry at Gettysburg*, 237.
43. Longacre, *Fitz Lee*, 125.
44. Carhart, *Lost Triumph*, 267–69.
45. Husby and Wittenberg, *Under Custer's Command*, 35.
46. Rosentreter, *Grand Rapids and the Civil War*, 47.
47. *Detroit Free Press*, July 7, 1876; Riggs, *East of Gettysburg*, 68; Sullivan, *Custer's Road to Disaster*, 4–5, 10–11; Longacre, *Custer and His Wolverines*, 153.
48. Monaghan, *Custer*, 123; Riggs, *East of Gettysburg*, 50.
49. Riggs, *East of Gettysburg*, 68–69.
50. Longacre, *Custer*, 173.
51. Monaghan, *Custer*, 149.
52. Milo Milton Quaife, ed., *General George A. Custer* (New York: Promontory Press, 1995), 17; Longacre, *Custer and His Wolverines*, 153.
53. Merington, *The Custer Story*, 62.
54. Ibid., 141.
55. Brian W. Dippie, *Custer's Last Stand: The Anatomy of an American Myth* (Lincoln: University of Nebraska Press, 1994), 1–3.
56. Carter, *The Last Cavaliers*, 320.
57. Ibid.
58. Govan and Livingood, *The Haskell Memoirs*, 94.
59. *Detroit Free Press*, July 7, 1876; Longacre, *Custer and His Wolverines*, 153.
60. *Detroit Free Press*, July 7, 1876; Merington, *The Custer Story*, 66; Longacre, *Custer and His Wolverines*, 153.
61. Carter, *The Last Cavaliers*, 319.
62. Longacre, *Custer and His Wolverines*, 153.
63. Ibid.
64. Husby and Wittenburg, *Under Custer's Command*, 38.

# Index

Page numbers in italics indicate photos or illustrations. Numbers starting with "*p*" indicate photos section after page 225.

Achilles, 33
Adams, William H., 312
Alger, Horatio, 7
Alger, Russell, A., 83, 226, 227; Cress's Ridge and, 240–41; on Ferry's death, 359; on 1st Michigan Cavalry saber charge, 346; 6th Michigan Cavalry of, 166; Witcher and, 358
Anderson, Jubal, 146
Antietam, 86, 120; Army of the Potomac at, 55; cavalry at, 58–59; Custer, G., at, 110–11; Lee, R., at, 55; Moore at, 319
Appomattox Court House, 26; Custer, G., and, 394; Lee, R., at, 400
Armistead, Lewis, 133
Army of Northern Virginia: artillery of, 24; cavalry of, 56; Copperhead Party and, 187; Harrisburg and, 116; horse purchase for, 107; of Lee, R., 7, 53, 138; Vicksburg and, 54; Weber and, 88. *See also specific individuals, units, and topics*

Army of the Potomac: at Antietam, 55; artillery of, 269–70; cavalry of, 56, 60; at Cemetery Hill, 170; Cemetery Ridge and, 9, 41, 170; at Chancellorsville, 109; at Culp's Hill, 170; Custer, G., in, 12, 41–42; at East Cavalry Field, 169; of Lee, R., 8–9, 53; McPherson and, 31; Meade in, 64; Pickett's Charge and, 37, 38–39; Stuart and, 184; at Williamsburg, 109. *See also specific individuals, units, and topics*
artillery: of Army of Northern Virginia, 24; of Army of the Potomac, 269–70; at Brandy Station, 100–101; cavalry and, 392–93; comparison of Union and Confederate, 268–69; at Cress's Ridge, 237, 239, 243–44, 249, 255, 266, 267–74; Custer, G., and, 20, 25, 271–74; 1st Michigan Cavalry saber charge and, 348–49, 350, 380; at Fredericksburg, 59; at Gettysburg, 145–53; at Gettysburg day 3, 207; at Hanover Road, 228; from higher ground, 268; infantry and, 291; at Low Dutch Road, 225, 248, 261; of Napoleon, 147–48, 174; Pickett's Charge and, 38, 285, 289, 290–98;

439

of Sixth Corp, 279–80; of Stuart, 15, 24. See also Charlottesville "Kanawha" Horse Artillery; 2nd United States Artillery; Stuart Horse Artillery

Avery, James Henry, 85, 133–34, 136, 170–71, 287; on Custer, G., 401; on 1st Michigan Cavalry saber charge, 344, 348, 349, 350; on Gettysburg day 3, 381, 395–96; on Lee, R., 45–46; on 7th Michigan Cavalry saber charge, 328; on Spencer repeating rifles, 90; on Stuart, 45–46

Bacon, Daniel Stanton, 73–77
Bacon-Custer, Elizabeth. See Custer, Elizabeth Bacon "Libbie"
Bak, Richard, 374
Baker, Laurence Simmons, 297–98, 314, 328
Baltimore Road (Turnpike): Cemetery Ridge and, 217; Cress's Ridge and, 201, 214; Stuart and, 8–9, 156, 165, 197, 239, 249, 256, 285, 287, 289, 354, 374, 398
Barker, Theodore G., 334
Barnes, James, 2
Barringer, Rufus, 117
Baylis, R., 91
Beale, George W., 135, 319, 320, 333, 385; Chambliss and, 328–31; of 9th Virginia Cavalry, 330–31; 7th Michigan Cavalry saber charge and, 316
Beckham, Robert Franklin, 100, 144, 149; of Stuart Horse Artillery, 174–77, 368–69
Bedell, James T., 322
Beverly Ford, 100
Big Black River, 54
Bigelow, J. Allen, 344
Bingham, John A: on Custer, G., beauty of, 72; on Custer, G., bravery of, 114; on Napoleon, 114; West Point sponsorship by, 47–48

Birney, James G., 312, 335
Blackford, Charles Minor, 101, 357; on Stuart, 182, 360
Blackford, Launcelot, 173
Blackford, Susan Leigh, 360
Blackford, William Willis, 102, 157, 174, 275; at Brandy Station, 180; Cress's Ridge and, 199, 202; on Gettysburg day 3, 377
"Black Hat" Brigade (Iron Brigade), 78–79
Black Horse Cavalry. See 1st Virginia Cavalry
The Blue Max (movie), 361–62
Boehm, Peter, 359
Bonaparte, Napoleon. See Napoleon Bonaparte
"Boots and Saddles," 165
von Borcke, Johann Heinrich Heros: at Middleburg, 105; Stuart and, 62
Boritt, Gabor S., 26
Boteler, Alexander Robinson, Jr., 173
Botts, John Minor, 99
Bowden, Scott, 387
Brady, Mathew, p6
Brandy Station: artillery at, 100–101; Blackford, W., at, 180; Chambliss at, 145; Custer, G., at, 67, 261; Gettysburg day 3 and, 178–81; Gregg, D., at, 261; Hampton, F., at, 130; Hooker at, 96–97, 99–200; Lee, R., at, 11; no-quarter warfare at, 117; Pleasonton at, 99–200; Stuart at, 94–104, 107, 116, 117–18, 122, 123, 178–81, 183–84, 274, 292, 398; Williams, S., at, 318
Breathed, James Williams, 173, 175; at Cress's Ridge, 270–71, 282; of Stuart Horse Artillery, 176–77, 379
Brickell, Edward J., 307
Bridges, David P., 184
Briggs, George B., 302, 311, 396
Brinkerhoff Ridge, 275
Brownlee, Horace, 307
Bruno Stachel (fictional character), 362

Buchanan, James, 48
Buford, John, 133, 160, 397; Custer, G., and, 36–37; First Cavalry Division of, 34; as heroic figure, 4–5, 37; in political and social elite, 7; Spencer repeating rifles of, 89–90
Bull Run, 52
Burnside, Ambrose E., 57, 59

Carhart, Tom, 212, 254, 388, 394, 395
cavalry: at Antietam, 58–59; of Army of Northern Virginia, 56; of Army of the Potomac, 56, 60; artillery and, 392–93; "Custer Luck" with, 69; at East Cavalry Field, 45; at Fredericksburg, 59; at Gettysburg, 157; Glazier on, 63; of Hampton, Wade, 127–30; of Hooker, 57, 58, 59–62, 65; horse purchase for, 107; horse shortage for, 105–7, 119; importance of, 59; infantry and, 59, 60, 61, 172; of Lee, R., 56, 60, 104, 151–52; of McClellan, H., 60; of Meade, 63; in Mexican-American War, 56; morale of, 62; of Napoleon, 94, 112–13, 169, 180, 378–79; of Pleasonton, 61–64; power of charge from, 152–53; reorganization of, 59–61; shortage of horses for, 105; of Stuart, 56–57, 59–60, 94–104; West Point and, 113–14. *See also specific units*
*Cavalry Tactics* (Poinsett), 113
Cemetery Hill: Army of the Potomac at, 170; Cress's Ridge and, 246; Eleventh Corps at, 221, 238; Pleasonton at, 163; York Turnpike and, 240
Cemetery Ridge: Army of the Potomac at, 9, 41, 170; Baltimore Road and, 217; Cress's Ridge and, 196, 200; East Cavalry Field and, 14; Meade at, 13, 45, 138, 153, 161, 196, 249, 250, 256, 280, 281, 291, 356, 388,
396; Sixth Corps at, 286; Stuart and, 274–75. *See also* Pickett's Charge
Chamberlain, Joshua Lawrence: as heroic figure, 2–5, 16, 37; at Little Round Top, 34; in political and social elite, 7; report rewriting by, 6
Chambliss, John Randolph, Jr., 121, 145; attack by, 317–24; Beale and, 328–31; Cress's Ridge and, 193, 199, 213, 215, 241; Hampton, Wade, and, 298, 333; McClellan, H., and, 321, 323; at Rummel buildings, 321; 2nd North Carolina Cavalry of, 268, 319; 7th Michigan Cavalry and, 305, 314; 7th Michigan Cavalry saber charge and, 308–10, 313, 316, 317–24; Stuart and, 323; 13th Virginia Cavalry of, 318; Witcher and, 289
Champion's Hill, 54
Chancellorsville, 54–55, 86; Hooker at, 58; horse shortage from, 106; Jackson, J., at, 108, 115, 158, 191; Lee, R., at, 291; Watkins, R., at, 108–9
Charlottesville "Kanawha" Horse Artillery, 214; Custer, G., and, 265; Jackson, T., of, 178, 237, 265; Pennington and, 272
"Christmas Raid," on Dumfries, Virginia, 126
Clark, John, 313
Coddington, Edwin B., 150, 156, 184, 195–96, 197, 364–65, 391
Colerick, William, 91
Colt revolver, 201
Comte, Victor E., 347
Copeland, Joseph T., 65; Custer, G., and, 239
Copperhead Party, 186; Army of Northern Virginia and, 187
Corselius, Edward, 382
Cortez, Hernando, 169
court-martial, at West Point, 49–50, 51
Cress Run, 275

Cress's Ridge, 150, 156; Alger, R., and, 240–41; artillery at, 237, 239, 243–44, 249, 255, 266, 267–74; Baltimore Road and, 201, 214; Blackford, W., and, 199, 202; Breathed at, 270–71, 282; Cemetery Hill and, 246; Cemetery Ridge and, 196, 200; Chambliss and, 193, 199, 213, 215, 241; Custer, G., and, 193–298; Enfield rifles at, 241–42, 266; Ewell and, 197, 202; fences of, 234, 264, 284, 310–15; 5th Michigan Cavalry and, 240–42, 255, 273, 284; 1st Maryland Cavalry at, 251; 1st Virginia Cavalry at, 283–85; forests on, 223–25, 227, 235–36, 239, 240, 256, 265; Gregg, D., and, 252–53; Hampton, Wade, at, 193, 194, 198, 199, 215, 238, 239, 240, 244, 269, 276, 332–33; Hanover Road and, 194, 198, 199, 214; Jackson, T., at, 237; Jenkins and, 193, 196, 197, 199, 210, 215, 235, 237; Lee, F., at, 193, 194, 198, 199, 202, 214, 238, 239, 240, 244, 269, 276; Lee, R., and, 217; Lee, W., and, 193; Low Dutch Road and, 194, 198, 199, 214, 275; McClellan, H., and, 196–97, 217; McGregor at, 270, 282; McIntosh at, 282–83; Meade and, 201; Michigan Cavalry Brigade and, 193–298; Old Dominion Brigade and, 201, 214; Pennington at, 249, 267–69; Pleasonton and, 215; Second Cavalry Division and, 215; 7th Michigan Cavalry and, 268; 6th Michigan Cavalry and, 255, 268; skirmishes at, 237, 241; Spencer repeating rifles and, 240; Stuart and, 193–298, 317; Stuart Horse Artillery at, 270–71, 282; 3rd Virginia Cavalry and, 201; Third Cavalry Division and, 245–46; 34th Virginia Cavalry at, 193, 248–50, 257; Weber and, 88, 238–43, 246, 256; Witcher and, 235, 237,

265. *See also* 1st Michigan Cavalry saber charge; Rummel buildings; 7th Michigan Cavalry saber charge

Culp's Hill, 371; Army of the Potomac at, 170; Ewell at, 143, 149, 151, 154; Meade at, 154

Custer, Elizabeth Bacon "Libbie" (wife), 8; courtship of, 73–77; with Custer, G., *p4*; on Stuart's death, 130

Custer, Emmanuel Henry (father), 47, 70–72, 186

Custer, George Armstrong: advancement of, 51; Appomattox Court House and, 394; in Army of the Potomac, 12, 41–42; artillery and, 25, 271–74; as boy general, 8, 12; at Brandy Station, 67, 261; bravery of, 114; Buford, John and, 36–37; Charlottesville "Kanawha" Horse Artillery and, 265; childhood of, 72; confidence of, *p3*; Copeland and, 239; Cress's Ridge and, 193–298; Custer, Elizabeth, with, *p4*; Custer, T., and, 71–72; death of, 18–19, 39, 385, 400; as Democrat, 68, 185–87; disobedience of orders by, 38, 165–66, 245–48, 260; "disposition" of, 127; at East Cavalry Field, 8–10, 11, 12, 16, 21, 25, 28, 30, 33, 35, 36, *p5*; embarrassment of, 119–20; faith of, 137–38, 293, 399; Farnsworth and, 166; as fighter, 68, 169, 347; 1st Michigan Cavalry saber charge of, 337–85; 1st Virginia Cavalry and, 283; as forgotten hero, 5–6, 12–13, 19, 27, 373; formal portrait of, *p7*; 14th Virginia Cavalry and, 390; at Gettysburg day 1, 133–38; on Gettysburg day 3, 167–385; as glory hunter, 20, 42; good looks of, 72, 168–69; Grant and, 28–29; Gregg, D., and, 164, 213, 229, 230–31, 240, 245, 246, 247–48, 252–54, 255, 256, 258–62, 338; Hanover Road and, 10, 25, 34, 37, 166, 197, 219–37,

256–59, *p2*; with hat, *p5*; Hollywood misrepresentation of, 16; horrors of war and, 109–11; humble beginnings of, 7, 28–29, 46, 70–71, 73, 292–93; at Hunterstown, 232–33; importance of in battle, 6–7, 11–12; Kilpatrick and, 165–66, 244, 247, 254, 260, 397; leadership of, 9, 17, 28, 92–94, 167, 341, 384–85; Lee, F., and, 283; Lee, R., and, 392; Lincoln and, 40, 186–87, 389–90; at Little Bighorn, 18–21, 28, 39, 264, 371, 385, 399–400, *p7*, *p8*; at Little Round Top, 16; Low Dutch Road and, 10, 25, 34, 37, 166, 197, 219–37, 256–59, *p2*; Manifest Destiny and, 6, 32; McClellan, H., and, 235; Meade and, 9–10, 24–25, 38, 40, 41–42, 165, 170, 293–94, 354, 398; in Michigan Cavalry Brigade, 65, 81–88, 111, 159–67; modesty of, 67, 68, 167; monument to, 12; Napoleon and, 35, 40, 69, 111–14, 295, 378, 398, 399; official report of, 6; Pennington and, 353–54; Pickett's Charge and, 291; Pleasonton and, 64, 67, 68, 119, 255, 258–62, 294, 383, 393; popularity of, 293, 347; on potential blood spilling in Civil War, 55–56; promotion of, 64–67, 87, 187; Randol and, 354; relationships of, 67–68; Republicans and, 186–87; reputation of, 74; Rummel buildings and, 263, 282–83; as scapegoat, 6, 19–20; in 2nd United States Cavalry, 51–52, 109–11; 7th Michigan Cavalry saber charge and, 299–335, 379; slavery and, 293; stereotypes of, 20, 227, 233; Stuart and, 12, 16–17, 30, 32, 38, 42–43, 45, 180, 235, 244–45, 352, 353; unconventional thinking of, 260–61; uniform of, 8, 94, 343; unorthodox nature of, 51; as war lover, 80; at West Point, 8, 10, 28, 42, 43, 137, 219, 236, 382, 396; in Wolverine Brigade, 55; writings of, 18–19. *See also* Michigan Cavalry Brigade

Custer, Maria Ward Kilpatrick (stepmother), 71; kindness of, 72–73

Custer, Matilda Viers (mother), 71

Custer, Paul (grandfather), 70

Custer, Thomas Ward "Tom" (brother), Custer, G., and, 71–72

"Custer Luck," 298; with cavalry, 69; with court-martial, 49, 50; at Gettysburg saber charges, 359–60; with promotion, 67

"Custer's Last Fight" (Waud), *p8*

"Custer's Last Stand," 10, 19, 34, 35, 400

*Custer's Road to Disaster* (Sullivan), 113, 372

*Custer Victorious* (Urwin), 41, 150

Darling, Daniel H., 384

Davis, Jefferson: Grant and, 54; Lee, R., and, 187, 366, 392; Lincoln and, 55; as scapegoat, 55; as Secretary of War, 48, 185; Stuart and, 366, 367, 376; Vicksburg and, 115

Democrats: Custer, G., as, 68, 185–87; Custer family as, 47; McClellan, H., as, 68

Denton-Patten, Lydia Ann, 84–85, 113

*Detroit Free Press*, 39, 161, 164, 238, 244, 330, 382; on Custer, G., 390; on 1st Michigan cavalry saber charge, 341, 345, 350, 358; on Little Bighorn, 400; on Michigan Cavalry Brigade, 390; on Pennington's artillery, 272–73

Divisional Artillery Battalion. *See* Stuart Horse Artillery

Dooley, John E., 124–25, 392

Downey, Fairfax, 372

Drake, James H., 322

Drew, G. A., 91

Dumfries, Virginia, 126

Dunn, Billy, 349

East Cavalry Field: Army of the Potomac at, 169; battle maps of, *vii–ix*; cavalry at, 45; Cemetery Ridge and, 14; Custer, Elizabeth, and, 76–77; Custer, G., at, 8–10, 11, 12, 16, 21, 25, 28, 30, 33, 35, 36, *p5*; as forgotten, 281; Lee, F., and, 395; Lee, R., and, 217; Meade and, 10–11; Pickett's Charge and, 13, 39; saber charge at, 295–96, 299–317; 7th Michigan Cavalry at, 86; Stuart and, 276; Weber at, 88. *See also specific locations and events*
Eleventh Corps, 221, 238
Elliott, Sam, 4
Enfield rifles: at Cress's Ridge, 241–42, 266; at Low Dutch Road, 248
Ewell, Richard S., 342, 367; Cress's Ridge and, 197, 202; at Culp's Hill, 143, 149, 151, 154; at Gettysburg day 1, 134; Meade and, 142, 154, 265; at Picket's Charge, 10; Second Corps of, 115, 121, 122, 123, 133, 134, 142, 171, 175, 202; Stuart and, 175, 199, 202

Falling Waters, 84; Weber at, 88, 239
Farnsworth, Elon John: Custer, G., and, 166; in First Brigade, 65, 162; promotion of, 64–65
Ferguson, Milton Jameson, 145, 207
Ferry, Noah Henry, 257–58, 262; death of, 359; Witcher and, 266, 359
Field, Ron, 372
15th Alabama Infantry Regiment, 16
5th Michigan Cavalry, 81; Avery in, 45, 85, 170–71, 287; Baylis of, 91; casualties of, 86; Copeland in, 65; Cress's Ridge and, 240–42, 255, 273, 284; from Detroit, 257; Ferry of, 257–58, 262, 266; fighting greatness of, 78; 1st Michigan Cavalry saber charge and, 349; 1st Virginia Cavalry and, 297; at Gettysburg day 1, 135, 136; at Hanover Road, 226–27; Harris of, 83–84, 93, 157, 257, 266; at Little's Run, 256–57; at Lott woods, 288; at Low Dutch Road, 248, 254; McIntosh and, 266; McKinstry, H., of, 92; at Rummel buildings, 264, 282–83, 287–88; saber charges by, 89; 7th Michigan Cavalry saber charge and, 322; Spencer repeating rifles of, 89, 167, 226, 248, 300; 34th Virginia Cavalry and, 266; Wheeler of, 91
Fifth Corps, at Little Round Top, 175
1st Maine Cavalry, 254
1st Maryland Cavalry, 193; at Cress's Ridge, 251; at Low Dutch Road, 261
1st Michigan Cavalry, 16, 81, 111; Colerick of, 91; elite reputation of, 86; fighting greatness of, 78; at Gettysburg day 1, 135; at Hanover Road, 227–28, 236; at Low Dutch Road, 283; 6th Michigan Cavalry and, 83
1st Michigan Cavalry saber charge, 25, 38, 40, 167, 181, 283; aftermath of, 356–57; Alger, R., on, 346; artillery and, 348–49, 350, 380; Avery on, 344, 348, 349, 350; casualties from, 358–61; at Cress's Ridge, 345, 347; of Custer, G., 337–85; 5th Michigan Cavalry and, 349; 1st New Jersey Cavalry and, 348; 1st Virginia Cavalry and, 350; Gage, William Glover on, 348; of Gettysburg day 3, 337–85; Gregg, D., and, 338, 340, 351; Hampton, Wade, and, 344–45; Hanover Road and, 347; Lee, F., and, 344–45; Little Round Top and, 356; Little's Run and, 340; Longstreet and, 356; Low Dutch Road and, 340, 348; McClellan, H., and, 351; Meade and, 340; Pennington and, 345, 346, 348–49,

350, 380; Pickett's Charge and, 342; Randol and, 345, 346, 348–49, 350, 380; Rummel buildings and, 347; 7th Michigan Cavalry and, 337–85; Stuart and, 337–85; 3rd Pennsylvania Cavalry and, 348; 3rd Virginia Cavalry and, 351

1st New Jersey Cavalry, 251, 257; 1st Michigan Cavalry saber charge and, 348; at Rummel buildings, 264

1st North Carolina Cavalry, 117; Pugh of, 125; 7th Michigan Cavalry saber charge and, 316, 335

1st United States Artillery, 271, 273–74. *See also* Randol, Alanson Merwin

1st Virginia Cavalry: at Cress's Ridge, 283–85; Custer, G., and, 283; 5th Michigan Cavalry and, 297; 1st Michigan Cavalry saber charge and, 350; Hampton, Wade, and, 297–98; of Lee, F., 258; at Low Dutch Road, 289; McIntosh and, 284–85, 288, 296; at Rummel buildings, 321–22; 7th Michigan Cavalry and, 299–317; Stuart in, 52, 53; 34th Virginia Cavalry and, 288; Witcher and, 284

First Cavalry Brigade (Division), 4; of Buford, 34; Farnsworth in, 65, 162; McIntosh of, 237; Spencer repeating rifles of, 89–90

First Corps, of Longstreet, 102, 154, 175, 195, 356

First Division, Army of the Potomac, 2

First Manassas: Custer, G., at, 109, 110; Hampton, Wade, at, 129; McDowell at, 52; Old Dominion Brigade at, 301; Stuart at, 301

Fleetwood Hill, 100, 101

Ford, Henry, 32

Fordham, Albert, 312

Fought, Joseph, 359

14th Virginia Cavalry, 108; Custer, G., and, 390; on Gettysburg day 3, 193

Fredericksburg, 86; Burnside at, 57, 59; Hooker at, 58; Lee, R., in, 96, 97, 115

Fremantle, Arthur, 357–58

Frost, Lawrence A., 398–99

Gage, William Glover, 87, 320, 321, 335; on 1st Michigan Cavalry saber charge, 348; as prisoner, 384

Gaines, Stephen, 390

*Galaxy Magazine*, 18–19

Garnett, Richard B., 173

Garnett, Theodore S., Jr., 123, 378

Germans, 108, 141; in World War I, 362

Gettysburg: artillery at, 145–53; cavalry at, 157; forgotten truisms of, 371–74; secret plan for, 142–45, 154–59, 240, 354–55; shoes and, 133; Waterloo and, 295. *See also specific individuals, units, events, and topics*

*Gettysburg* (movie), 3, 4, 16, 34–35, 36

*Gettysburg* (Sears), 155

*The Gettysburg Campaign* (Coddington), 150

Gettysburg day 1: Custer, G., on, 133–38; Ewell on, 134; 5th Michigan Cavalry on, 135, 136; 1st Michigan Cavalry on, 135; Kilpatrick on, 136; Lee, W., on, 135; Michigan Cavalry Brigade on, 135–38; Pleasonton on, 136; 7th Michigan Cavalry on, 135; 6th Michigan Cavalry on, 135; Stuart Horse Artillery on, 135; Stuart on, 134–38; 3rd Virginia Cavalry on, 134–35; Third Cavalry Brigade on, 136

Gettysburg day 2: Hunterstown on, 232–33; Little Round Top on, 160

Gettysburg day 3: artillery at, 207; battle maps of, *vi–ix*; Brandy Station and, 178–81; burial parties after, 383–84; Custer, G., on, 167–385; delayed

offensive of, 203–6; forgotten tactical lessons of, 377–85; 14th Virginia Cavalry on, 193; Jenkins on, 193; Lee, R., on, 167–385; Michigan Cavalry Brigade on, 167–385; 17th Virginia Cavalry on, 193; Stuart Horse Artillery on, 174–78; Stuart on, 167–385; 34th Virginia Cavalry on, 193, 248–50; 36th Virginia Cavalry on, 193; Virginians on, 173. *See also specific locations and events*
Gettysburg National Military Park, 383
*The Gettysburg That Nobody Knows* (Boritt), 26
Glazier, Willard Worcester, 53, 56, 125–26, 133, 355–56; at Brandy Station, 118; on cavalry, 63; on Hooker, 62; of 2nd New York Cavalry, 280–81; on Stuart, 183–84
Gottfried, Bradley M., 155, 216, 379
Grand Rapids, Michigan, 82–83, 88, 225; Heman from, 312–13; Kidd from, 228–29; 7th Michigan Cavalry from, 301, 319; 6th Michigan Cavalry from, 236, 301
Granger, Edward G., 91–92; on Custer, G.'s leadership, 92–93; Lee, R., and, 377
Grant, Ulysses S., 21; Custer, G., and, 28–29; Davis and, 54; Lee's surrender to, 362–63; Lincoln and, 53; Mississippi River and, 53–54; at Vicksburg, 54, 116
Green, Charles A., 146, 175
Gregg, David McMurtrie "Old Steady," 27, 217; at Brandy Station, 261; Cress's Ridge and, 252–53; Custer, G., and, 164, 213, 229, 230–31, 240, 245, 246, 247–48, 252–54, 255, 256, 258–62, 338; 1st Michigan Cavalry saber charge and, 338, 340, 351; Gregg, J., and, 254; Hanover Road and, 41, 245; Kilpatrick and, 161, 246; Lee, F., and, 326; Low Dutch Road and, 41, 195, 245, 271; McIntosh and, 244, 259; Meade and, 162–63, 170, 195, 374, 395; Pennington and, 272; Pleasonton and, 163, 231, 252; Randol and, 272; Second Cavalry Division of, 237, 251, 252; 7th Michigan Cavalry and, 303; sound decisions of, 258–62; Stuart and, 45, 165, 190, 234–35, 382, 394; Witcher and, 261
Gregg, J. Irvin, 247; Gregg, D., and, 254; at Low Dutch Road, 261; of Third Brigade, 237
Griffin, William H., 209, 212, 272

Haden, B. J., 350
Haines, Henry, 312
Halleck, Henry W. "Old Brains," 64
Hampton, Frank, 117–18; at Brandy Station, 130
Hampton, Preston, 130
Hampton, Wade, 100–101, 121; cavalry of, 127–30; Chambliss and, 298, 333; at Cress's Ridge, 193, 194, 198, 199, 215, 238, 239, 240, 244, 269, 276, 332–33; 1st Michigan Cavalry saber charge and, 344–45, 349–56; 1st Virginia Cavalry and, 297–98; Hanover Road and, 276; Lee, F., and, 131–32, 327–28, 333–34, 353; Lee, R. and, 181; Low Dutch Road and, 276; McIntosh and, 274; Meade and, 265, 277; 7th Michigan Cavalry and, 314; 7th Michigan Cavalry saber charge and, 330–35; Stuart and, 127–30, 232, 274, 276–78, 332, 365; Stuart Horse Artillery and, 105; on West Point problems, 381–82; wounding of, 349–56
Hampton, William Preston, 130
Hanover Road, 161; artillery at, 228; Cress's Ridge and, 194, 198, 199, 214; Custer, G., and, 10, 25, 34, 37, 166, 197, 219–37, 256–59, *p3*; 1st Michigan Cavalry saber charge and, 347; Gregg, D., and, 41, 195,

245; Hampton, Wade, and, 276; Kilpatrick at, 247; Low Dutch Road and, 162–64; Pennington at, 271; 2nd United States Artillery at, 271; 7th Michigan Cavalry at, 236, 283, 306; 6th Michigan Cavalry at, 236, 243; Stuart and, 8–9, 165, 212–13, 299–300, 398; 34th Virginia Cavalry and, 249; Weber at, 88
Harrell, Roger H., 372, 395
Harris, Samuel, 83–84, 157, 257, 266; on Custer, G.'s leadership, 93
Harrisburg: Army of Northern Virginia and, 116; Ewell at, 123
Hart, B. H. Liddell, 373
Hart, James Franklin, 175
Haskell, John Cheves, 126, 181, 331, 381; on Pickett, 364
Hatch, Thom, 156, 211, 338, 387, 388
Heinck, John, 307
Hill, Ambrose Powell, 133
Hoag, Robert, 322
Hoffman Road, 275
Hood, John Bell, 195, 368, 381
Hooker, Joseph K. "Fighting Joe," 57–58, 377; at Brandy Station, 96–97, 99–200; cavalry of, 58, 59–62, 65; Lee, R., and, 58, 63, 392; Lincoln and, 79; Stuart and, 121, 122
Houck's Ridge, 195
Howard, Oliver Otis, 221, 240, 246
Hudgins, Robert Scott, 134–35, 201–2, 210, 214, 328
Humphrey, Annette, 111
Hunterstown, 218; Custer, G., at, 232–33; at Gettysburg day 2, 232–33; 6th Michigan Cavalry at, 301
Hutton, Paul Andrew, 383

infantry: artillery and, 291; cavalry and, 59, 60, 61, 172. *See also specific units*
"Invincibles," of Stuart, 11, 14–15, 33, 35, 103, 247, 252, 291–92, 304, 312, 345, 359, 380, 393

Irish Brigade, 59
*Irish Dragoon* (O'Malley), 376
Iron Brigade ("Black Hat" Brigade), 78–79
Isham, Asa B., 322–23

Jackson, Jonathan Thomas "Stonewall": at Chancellorsville, 108, 115, 158, 191; Stuart and, 191
Jackson, Orlando, 312
Jackson, Thomas Edwin, 144, 146, 175, 214; of Charlottesville Battery, 178, 237, 265; at Cress's Ridge, 237; Pennington and, 272
Jenkins, Albert G., 108, 132–33, 145, 175; Cress's Ridge and, 193, 196, 197, 199, 210, 215, 235, 237; Enfield rifles of, 266; on Gettysburg day 3, 193; Gettysburg secret plan and, 144; McIntosh and, 282–83; Meade and, 151; 7th Michigan Cavalry and, 314; 7th Michigan Cavalry saber charge and, 310, 313; Stuart and, 153; Virginia Brigade of, 241
Jews, 101, 141

Karcher, Jehiel, 312
Kearney, Philip, 66
Kelly's Ford, 100; Pelham at, 144
Kidd, James Harvey, 39, 87–88, 228–29, 370, 371; on Weber, 243
*The Killer Angels* (Shaara), 3, 4, 16
Kilpatrick, Judson, 33, 160; Custer, G., and, 165–66, 244, 247, 254, 260, 397; at Gettysburg day 1, 136; Gregg, D., and, 161, 246; at Hanover Road, 247; at Little Round Top, 194–95, 246; Pleasonton and, 162; Spencer repeating rifles and, 90; Third Cavalry Brigade of, 64, 161, 229–30, 237, 244–46, 259–60
Kirkpatrick-Reed, Lydia-Ann, 55–56
"Knight of the Golden Spurs," Stuart as, 182

Lea, John W. "Gimlet," 80
Lee, Fitzhugh, 33, 101, 102, 116, 121, 141; at Cress's Ridge, 193, 194, 198, 199, 202, 214, 238, 239, 240, 244, 269, 276; Custer, G., and, 283; East Cavalry Field and, 395; 1st Michigan Cavalry saber charge and, 344–45; 1st Virginia Cavalry of, 258, 297; Gregg, D., and, 326; Hampton, Wade, and, 131–32, 327–28, 333–34, 353; Little's Run and, 329; McIntosh and, 274; Meade and, 265, 277; Pennington and, 326; Randol and, 326; 2nd Virginia Cavalry of, 288; 7th Michigan Cavalry saber charge and, 317, 324–29; Stuart and, 276–78, 282, 379–80
Lee, Henry "Light Horse Harry," 131, 152
Lee, James I., 329
Lee, Robert E., 1; at Appomattox Court House, 400; Army of Northern Virginia of, 7, 53, 138; Army of the Potomac of, 8–9; Avery on, 45–46; at Brandy Station, 11; cavalry of, 56, 60, 104, 151–52; Cemetery Ridge and, 138; at Chancellorsville, 109, 291; Cress's Ridge and, 217; Custer, G., and, 392; Davis and, 187, 366, 392; death of, 366; East Cavalry Field and, 217; in Fredericksburg, 96, 97, 115; Gettysburg artillery and, 145–53; Gettysburg blame to, 363–64; on Gettysburg day 3, 167–385; Gettysburg secret plan of, 142–45, 154–59, 240, 354–55; Granger and, 377; Hampton, Wade, and, 181; as heroic figure, 27; Hooker and, 58, 63, 392; Longstreet and, 23, 290–91, 364–65; McClellan, H., and, 67; Meade and, 150; in Mexican-American War, 141; Napoleon and, 147–48, 155, 368; offensive of, 45–46; Pickett and, 388; Pickett's Charge and, 14–15, 33, 34, 39, 250, 262, 265, 290, 372, 391–92; Providence and, 151; Stoneman and, 392; Stuart and, 17–18, 29, 31, 39, 41, 96, 98–99, 102, 120–27, 138–41, 172–73, 178–79, 190, 195–96, 209–12, 216, 242, 279, 357, 360–61, 391, 395; surrender by, 362–63, 400; Vicksburg and, 54–55
Lee, William Henry Fitzhugh "Rooney," 105, 121, 141; at Brandy Station, 118; Chambliss and, 317, 318, 323; Cress's Ridge and, 193; at Gettysburg day 1, 135; Stuart Horse Artillery and, 105
Lever, Charles, 113
*Life and Letters of George Gordon Meade* (Meade), 11
Lincoln, Abraham: Custer, G., and, 40, 186–87, 389–90; Davis and, 55; Grant, Ulysses S. and, 53; Hooker and, 79; McClellan, G., and, 57, 67–68, 186, 245; Meade and, 15; Michigan Cavalry Brigade and, 78; Mississippi River and, 53; 6th Michigan Cavalry and, 218; Twenty-First Cavalry and, 62
Little Bighorn: Custer, G., at, 18–21, 28, 39, 264, 371, 385, 399–400, p8, p9; Custer, T., at, 71; massacre at, 35; Reno at, 381; 7th Cavalry at, 19–20, 28, 30, 35, 79; Yates at, 398
*Little Big Man* (movie), 16
Little Round Top, 2; ammunition stored at, 356; Chamberlain at, 3, 4, 6, 34; Custer, G., at, 16; Fifth Corps at, 175; 1st Michigan Cavalry saber charge and, 356; on Gettysburg day 2, 160; Kilpatrick at, 246; Lee, R., and, 23; Longstreet at, 195; Meade at, 142, 162, 194–95; O'Rorke at, 68–69; 20th Maine Volunteer Regiment at, 16
Little's Run, 225, 227; Brinkerhoff Ridge and, 275; 5th Michigan Cavalry at, 256–57; 1st Michigan

Cavalry saber charge along, 340;
Lee, F., and, 329; McIntosh at, 251,
256–57; 7th Michigan Cavalry saber
charge along, 305, 315; 6th Michigan
Cavalry at, 236; 3rd Pennsylvania
Cavalry at, 251
Longacre, Edward G., 152–53, 156,
192–93, 196, 358, 380, 382–83, 394;
on Stuart, 395
Longstreet, James "Old Bull," 342;
at Devil's Den, 195; 1st Michigan
Cavalry saber charge and, 356;
First Corps of, 154, 175, 195, 356;
Gettysburg blame to, 363, 375; Hart,
J., and, 175; at Houck's Ridge, 195;
Lee, R., and, 23, 290–91, 364–65; at
Little Round Top, 195; "Lost Cause"
and, 375; Moses and, 102; Pickett's
Charge and, 165, 217, 367, 375, 393;
Stuart and, 181, 184
"Lost Cause," 13, 14, 35; Longstreet
and, 375; Stuart and, 15, 18
Lott, Jacob, 199, 225, 233
Lott woods: 5th Michigan Cavalry at,
288; Low Dutch Road and, 223,
225; McIntosh at, 263
Louisiana Guard Battery, 146, 175
Low Dutch Road: artillery at, 225,
248, 261; Cress's Ridge and, 194,
198, 199, 214, 275; Custer, G., and,
10, 25, 34, 37, 166, 197, 219–37,
256–59, *p3*; Enfield rifles at, 248;
5th Michigan Cavalry at, 248,
254; 1st Maryland Cavalry at, 261;
1st Michigan Cavalry at, 283; 1st
Michigan Cavalry saber charge along,
340, 348; 1st Virginia Cavalry at,
289; Gregg, D., and, 41, 195, 245,
271; Gregg, J., and, 261; Hampton,
Wade, and, 276; Hanover Road and,
162–64; Kilpatrick and, 162; Lott
woods and, 223, 225; McIntosh at,
254, 255, 300; Purnell Maryland
Legion Cavalry at, 251; 2nd United
States Artillery at, 271; 7th Michigan
Cavalry at, 243; 7th Michigan
Cavalry saber charge along, 315; 6th
Michigan Cavalry at, 238–39; Stuart
and, 8–9, 212–13, 299–300, 398; 3rd
Pennsylvania Cavalry at, 261; 34th
Virginia Cavalry and, 249; Weber
at, 88
Lundy, George W., 322
Lyman, Theodore, 304
Lyman, William Remsen, 173

Manifest Destiny, 6, 32
Mann, William D., 301, 302–3, 308–9,
311–15, 317, 340, 358
Marshall, Charles, 365
Matthews, Henry, 118–19, 135, 351
McClellan, George B., 66; Lincoln and,
57, 67–68, 186, 245
McClellan, Henry Brainerd "Harry,
Little Mac": cavalry of, 60; Chambliss
and, 321, 323; confidence of, 153;
Cress's Ridge and, 196–97, 217;
Custer, G., and, 235; as Democrats,
68; 1st Michigan Cavalry saber
charge and, 351; Gettysburg secret
plan and, 142; Lee, R., and, 67;
Meade and, 277; Stuart and, 46, 130,
156, 207, 211, 357, 373; Witcher
and, 264, 289
McClellan, James Brainerd, 272
McDougall, Walter A., 364
McDowell, Irvin, 52
McFarland, Sara, 72, 168
McGregor, William Morrell, 144, 146;
at Cress's Ridge, 270, 282; of Stuart
Horse Artillery, 177–78
McIntosh, John Baillie, 217, 335; at
Cress's Ridge, 282–83; 5th Michigan
Cavalry and, 266; 1st Virginia
Cavalry and, 284–85, 288, 296; of
First Cavalry Brigade, 237; Gregg,
D., and, 244, 259; Hampton, Wade,
and, 274; Jenkins and, 282–83; Lee,
F., and, 274; at Little's Run, 251,
256–57; at Lott woods, 263; at Low

Dutch Road, 254, 255, 300; Randol and, 269; at Rummel buildings, 282–83; Witcher and, 257
McKinstry, Henry, 92
McKinstry, Neil, 92
McLaws, Lafayette, 368
McPherson, James M., 146, 153, 156, 184, 391; Army of the Potomac and, 31; at Pickett's Charge, 10
Meade, George Gordon, 2; in Army of the Potomac, 64; cavalry of, 63; at Cemetery Ridge, 13, 45, 138, 153, 161, 196, 249, 250, 256, 280, 281, 291, 356, 388, 396; Cress's Ridge and, 201; at Culp's Hill, 154; Custer, G., and, 9–10, 24–25, 38, 40, 41–42, 165, 170, 293–94, 354, 398; East Cavalry Field and, 10–11; Ewell and, 142, 154, 265; 1st Michigan Cavalry saber charge and, 340; Gregg, D., and, 162–63, 170, 195, 374, 395; Hampton, Wade, and, 265, 277; Jenkins and, 151; Lee, F., and, 265, 277; Lee, R. and, 150; Lincoln and, 15; at Little Round Top, 142, 162, 194–95; McClellan, H., and, 277; Pennington and, 271; Pickett's Charge and, 152, 265, 281; Pleasonton and, 63–64, 160; Second Cavalry Division and, 195; Sixth Corps and, 286; Stuart and, 23, 39, 43, 146, 171–72, 184, 192–203, 235, 243, 249, 255–56, 260, 265, 274–82, 285–87, 371, 392; Stuart Horse Artillery and, 178
Merritt, Wesley, 64–65
Mexican-American War, 46; cavalry in, 56; Grant in, 53; Lee, R., in, 141; Scott in, 169; Sedgwick, John in, 280; Stuart in, 174
Meyer, Henry C., 93, 117, 118, 309, 314; on Gettysburg burial parties, 383–84
Michigan Cavalry Brigade, 6, 7, 8, 11, 16–17, 36, 40, 41; Avery in, 45; casualties of, 382; Copeland in, 65; Cress's Ridge and, 193–298; as elite group, 35, 77–80, 287; fighting greatness of, 78; on Gettysburg day 1, 135–38; on Gettysburg day 3, 167–385; horses of, 90; monument to, 12; officers of, 91–92, 93; Spencer repeating rifles for, 89–90; Stuart and, 91; Third Cavalry Brigade and, 244–46; troopers of, 81–88; uniforms of, 78–79; weaponry of, 89–92. *See also* 5th Michigan Cavalry; 1st Michigan Cavalry; 7th Michigan Cavalry; 6th Michigan Cavalry
*Michigan History Magazine*, 374
Middleburg, Virginia, 105
Milburn, John, 312
Miller, Francis Trevelyan, 372
Miller, William E., 338, 371–72; on Custer, G., 385; on Stuart, 389
Minor, Charles E., 322
Mississippi River, 115; Grant and, 53–54; Lincoln and, 53. *See also* Vicksburg, Mississippi
Monaghan, Jay, 391, 393; on Custer G., 394–95
Moore, Heman N., 312–13, 319–20
Morgan, William Augustine, 283, 310, 311, 322, 341
Moses, Raphael J., 101–2
Munford, Thomas T., 134
Murat, Joachim, 94, 112, 169

Napoleon Bonaparte, 9; artillery of, 147–48, 174; cavalry of, 94, 112–13, 169, 180, 378–79; Custer, G., and, 25, 35, 40, 69, 111–14, 295, 378, 398, 399; Lee, R., and, 147–48, 155, 368; Mann and, 303; McClellan, H., and, 57; "Old Guard" of, 303; Pickett and, 143; Pickett's Charge and, 367; saber charge and, 378–79; Scott and, 52; 7th Michigan Cavalry saber charge and, 379; Spencer repeating rifles and, 378; Stuart and,

97, 191–92, 296; Waterloo and, 295, 296, 307, 331–32; "Young Guard" of, 303
National Battlefield Park, 3
Neese, George Michael, 103, 125, 133
Nesbit, Captain, 283–84
"New Rumley Invincibles," 67
Ney, Michel, 295, 307, 331–32
19th Virginia Cavalry, 305
9th Virginia Cavalry, 135; Beale of, 330–31; 7th Michigan Cavalry saber charge and, 308, 316, 319, 328
no-quarter warfare, at Brandy Station, 117
Norvell, Dallas, 91
Norvell, Edwin Forrest, 91

Oden, James Skinner, 173
*Official Records of the War of the Rebellion*, 373–74
Old Dominion Brigade, 17, 108, 131, 144, 172–73; Cress's Ridge and, 201, 214; at First Manassas, 301; at Rummel buildings, 266; 7th Michigan Cavalry saber charge and, 320
"Old Guard," of Napoleon, 143, 303
O'Malley, Charles, 113, 376
*O'Malley, the Irish Dragoon* (Lever), 113
Opie, John N., 370, 374–75
O'Rorke, Patrick Henry "Paddy," 4, 68–69
Owen, Thomas H., 329

Park, John, 307
Patten, George Thomas, 84–85, 108
Peace Party, 55, 186
Peach Orchard, 175, 383
Pelham, John, 144, 176
Pelican State, 146
Peninsula Campaign, 19; Custer, G., at, 109–10; Hampton, Wade, at, 130; Lea at, 80; McClellan, H., at, 57; Stuart in, 171

Pennington, Alexander Cummings McWhorter, 69, 168, 228; Charlottesville "Kanawha" Horse Artillery and, 272; at Cress's Ridge, 249, 267–69; Custer, G., and, 353–54; 1st Michigan Cavalry saber charge and, 345, 346, 348–49, 350, 380; Gregg, D., and, 272; at Hanover Road, 271; Jackson, T., and, 272; Lee, F., and, 326; Meade and, 271; 2nd United States Artillery of, 267–69, 271–72, 275–76; 7th Michigan Cavalry saber charge and, 317
Peppard, George, 362
*The Photographic History of the Civil War* (Miller, F.), 372
Pickett, George Edward, 133; Gettysburg secret plan and, 143; Haskell on, 364; Lee, R., and, 388; Stuart and, 173, 380, 387; at West Point, 42
Pickett's Charge, 1, 36, 143–44, 147, 150, 156, 158, 184, 217; Army of the Potomac and, 38–39; artillery and, 38, 285, 289, 290–98; Custer, G., and, 291; East Cavalry Field and, 13, 39; failure possibility of, 46; 1st Michigan Cavalry saber charge and, 342; heroism at, 396; high-water mark of, 342; horse exhaustion at, 23, 24; Lee, R., and, 14–15, 33, 34, 39, 250, 262, 265, 290, 372, 391–92; Longstreet and, 165, 367, 375, 393; Meade and, 152, 265, 281; Napoleon and, 367; Stuart and, 11, 14–15, 23–24, 37–39, 182, 212, 249, 275, 352, 364, 371, 375, 380, 388, 392; Stuart Horse Artillery and, 270; Trimble at, 151; Virginians at, 13–14, 35; Witcher and, 273
Piston, William Garrett, 367
Pleasonton, Alfred, 66; at Brandy Station, 99–200; cavalry of, 61–64; at Cemetery Hill, 163; Cress's Ridge

and, 215; Custer, G., and, 64, 67, 68, 119, 255, 258–62, 294, 383, 393; at Gettysburg day 1, 136; Gregg, D., and, 163, 231, 252; Kilpatrick and, 162; Meade and, 63–64, 160; sound decisions of, 258–62
Plum Run, 162
Poinsett, Joel R., 113
Pollard, Edward Alfred, 101, 183
Port Gibson, Mississippi, 54
Port Hudson, Louisiana, 107, 115
Providence, Lee, R., and, 151
Pugh, James M., 125
Purnell Maryland Legion Cavalry, 251

Randol, Alanson Merwin: Custer, G., and, 354; 1st Michigan Cavalry saber charge and, 345, 346, 348–49, 350, 380; 1st United States Artillery of, 271, 273–74; Gregg, D., and, 272; Lee, F., and, 326; at Lott House, 271–72; McIntosh and, 269; at West Point, 276
Rawle, William Brooke, 346, 387
Rebel yell, 98, 109–10; at Cress's Ridge, 236
Reed, David, 113
Reno, Marcus A., 381
repeating rifles. *See* Spencer repeating rifles
Republicans: Bingham as, 47; Custer, G., and, 186–87; of Ohio, 68
Riggs, David F., 156
Rinehart, Levi, 196
Roanoke (Custer, G.'s horse), 231, 306; at 1st Michigan Cavalry saber charge, 347
Robbins, James S., 165, 374
Robertson, Frank Smith, 275, 279–80, 285–86, 315, 332–32
Rock Creek, 280
Rosen, Robert N., 141
Rosentreter, Roger L., 372, 374
Rummel, John, 194, 199, 213, 233, 378

Rummel buildings: Chambliss at, 321; Custer, G., and, 263, 282–83; 5th Michigan Cavalry at, 282–83, 287–88; 1st Michigan Cavalry saber charge and, 347; 1st Virginia Cavalry at, 321–22; McIntosh at, 282–83; Old Dominion Brigade at, 266; 7th Michigan Cavalry and, 314; 7th Michigan Cavalry saber charge to, 305, 313, 321, 323; Stuart at, 317; 34th Virginia Cavalry at, 262–66; Witcher at, 262–66, 287, 319

saber charge, 16, 25, 38, 40, 180, 299–317; Napoleon and, 378–79. *See also* 1st Michigan Cavalry saber charge; 7th Michigan Cavalry saber charge
*Sacred Ties* (Carhart), 394
Sanford, George B., 341
Schuricht, Hermann, 108, 133
Scott, Winfield: Grant and, 54; meeting with, 51–52; in Mexican-American War, 169
Sears, Stephen W., 155, 242
2nd Baltimore Maryland Horse Artillery, 272
2nd Brandenburg Dragoons, 105
2nd Michigan Cavalry, 83
2nd New York Cavalry, 53, 56, 118; Glazier of, 133, 183–84, 280–81
2nd North Carolina Cavalry, 118; artillery and, 268; of Chambliss, 268, 319; 7th Michigan Cavalry saber charge and, 308, 310, 319; Solomon, W., of, 318
2nd Pennsylvania Cavalry, 258
2nd South Carolina Cavalry, 100–101, 116, 130; Hampton, F., of, 118; Williams, L., of, 283
2nd United States Artillery, 243, 267–69, 271–72; Brinkerhoff Ridge and, 275–76; at Hanover Road, 271; at Low Dutch Road, 271. *See also* Pennington, Alexander Cummings McWhorter

## Custer at Gettysburg 453

2nd United States Cavalry, 51–52, 109–11
2nd Virginia Cavalry, 101, 288; Blackford, C., of, 357; horse shortage of, 116–17
Second Cavalry Division: Cress's Ridge and, 215; of Gregg, D., 237, 251, 252; Meade and, 195
Second Corps, of Ewell, 115, 121, 122, 123, 133, 134, 142, 171, 175, 202
Sedgwick, John, 280, 286
Seminary Ridge, 140, 141, 150, 172
17th Virginia Cavalry, 193
7th Cavalry: East Cavalry Field and, 30; at Little Bighorn, 19–20, 28, 30, 35, 79; Reno of, 381
7th Michigan Cavalry, 16, 81, 111; Chambliss and, 305; Cress's Ridge and, 268; on drill field, 86; at East Cavalry Field, 86; fighting greatness of, 78; 1st Michigan Cavalry saber charge and, 337–85; 1st Virginia Cavalry and, 299–317; Gage of, 87; at Gettysburg day 1, 135; from Grand Rapids, 301, 319; Gregg, D., and, 303; at Hanover Road, 236, 283, 306; at Low Dutch Road, 243
7th Michigan Cavalry saber charge, 25, 38, 40, 89, 167, 283, 296–97; Avery on, 328; Beale and, 316; Chambliss and, 308–10, 313, 316, 317–24; Custer, G., and, 299–335, 379; 5th Michigan Cavalry and, 322; 1st North Carolina Cavalry and, 316, 335; Hampton, Wade, and, 330–35; Jenkins and, 310, 313; Lee, F., and, 317, 324–29; Little's Run and, 305, 315; Low Dutch Road and, 315; Napoleon and, 379; 9th Virginia Cavalry and, 308, 316, 319, 328; Old Dominion Brigade and, 320; Pennington and, 317; to Rummel buildings, 305, 313, 321, 323; 2nd North Carolina Cavalry and, 308, 310, 319; Stuart and, 317;

10th Virginia Cavalry and, 308; 13th Virginia Cavalry and, 308, 319, 320; 34th Virginia Cavalry and, 317; Witcher and, 310, 313, 316
Shaara, Michael, 3, 4, 16, 36
Shakespeare, William, 90–91
Sharpsburg, 110; Lee, R., at, 55
Sheridan, Phil, 400
6th Michigan Cavalry, 81, 167; of Alger, R., 166; Cress's Ridge and, 255, 268; Drew of, 91; fighting greatness of, 78; 1st Michigan Cavalry and, 83; at Gettysburg day 1, 135; from Grand Rapids, 236, 301; at Hanover Road, 225, 236, 243; at Huntersrown, 232–32, 301; Kidd of, 87–88; Lincoln and, 218; at Little's Run, 236; at Low Dutch Road, 238–39; Patten of, 84, 85, 108; Weber of, 87–88, 238–39
6th New York Cavalry, 93–94
Sixth Corps: artillery of, 279–80; at Cemetery Ridge, 286; Meade and, 286; at Rock Creek, 280
slave patrols, 59
slavery, Custer, G., and, 293
Smith, Kirby, 116
Smith, William F. "Baldy," 66
Sobieski, John, 388
Spangler, Joseph, 267
Spanish Conquistadors, 169
Spencer, Christopher, 89
Spencer repeating rifles, 9, 25, 26–27; Cress's Ridge and, 240; early firing of, 300; of 5th Michigan Cavalry, 89, 167, 226, 248, 300; of Michigan Cavalry Brigade, 89–90; Napoleon and, 378
Stallsmith, Daniel, 194, 200
Starr, Stephen Z., 39, 45, 247–48, 261, 395; on Stuart, 371
Stevens, Thaddeus, 141
Stoneman, George D., 62, 64; Lee, R., and, 392
Storrs, Charles E., 225, 226

Strong, George Templeton, 187
Strong, Vincent, 2, 4
Stuart, James Ewell Brown (J. E. B.): ambitious raid by, 120–27; Army of the Potomac and, 184; artillery of, 15, 24; Avery on, 45–46; Baltimore Road and, 8–9, 156, 239, 249, 256, 285, 287, 289, 354, 374, 398; von Borcke and, 62; at Brandy Station, 94–104, 107, 116, 117–18, 122, 123, 178–81, 183–84, 274, 292, 398; at Brinkerhoff Ridge, 275; cavalry of, 56–57, 59–60, 94–104; Cemetery Ridge and, 274–75; Chambliss and, 323; at Chancellorsville, 108; character flaw of, 178–79, 182–85; confidence of, 60–61; Cress's Ridge and, 193–298, 317; criticisms of, 101–3, 122, 126–27, 182–85, 208; Custer, G., and, 12, 16–17, 30, 32, 38, 42–43, 45, 180, 235, 244–45, 352, 353; Davis and, 366, 367, 376; death of, 17, 360, 366; East Cavalry Field and, 276; Ewell and, 175, 199, 202; failures of, 27, 30, 31–32, 35; 1st Michigan Cavalry saber charge and, 337–85; in 1st Virginia Cavalry, 52–53; at First Manassas, 301; Gettysburg artillery and, 145–53; Gettysburg blame to, 363; on Gettysburg day 1, 134–38; on Gettysburg day 3, 167–385; Gettysburg secret plan of, 142–45, 154–59, 240, 354–55; Gregg, D., and, 165, 190, 234–35, 382, 394; Hampton, Wade, and, 127–30, 232, 274, 276–78, 332, 365; Hanover Road and, 8–9, 212–13, 299–300, 398; as heroic figure, 17–18, 27, 29–30, 31, 32, 95, 102–3, 375–76; Hooker and, 121, 122; horse purchase for, 107; horse shortage for, 105–7; "Invincibles" of, 11, 14–15, 33, 35, 103, 247, 252, 291–92, 304, 312, 345, 359, 380, 393; Jackson, J., and, 191; Jenkins and, 153; as "Knight of the Golden Spurs," 182; Lee, F., and, 276–78, 282, 379–80; Lee, R., and, 17–18, 29, 31, 39, 41, 96, 98–99, 102, 120–27, 138–41, 172–73, 178–79, 190, 195–96, 209–12, 216, 242, 279, 357, 360–61, 391, 395; Longstreet and, 181, 184; "Lost Cause" and, 15, 18; Low Dutch Road and, 8–9, 212–13, 299–300, 398; McClellan, H., and, 46, 130, 156, 207, 211, 357, 373; Meade and, 23, 39, 43, 146, 171–72, 184, 192–203, 235, 243, 249, 255–56, 260, 265, 274–82, 285–87, 371, 392; in Mexican-American War, 174; Michigan Cavalry Brigade and, 91; Napoleon and, 97, 191–92, 296; objective of, 45; in Peninsula Campaign, 171; Pickett and, 173, 380, 387; Pickett's Charge and, 11, 14–15, 37–39, 182, 212, 249, 275, 352, 364, 371, 375, 380, 388, 392; reputation restoration obsession of, 182–85; reviews by, 97–99, 106–7; at Rummel buildings, 317; 7th Michigan Cavalry saber charge and, 317; social life of, 95–96; 34th Virginia Cavalry and, 248–50; trooper casualties of, 117; troopers of, 108–9; uniform and appearance of, 94–95; on veterinary surgeons, 119; at West Point, 52; Witcher and, 355; women and, 95, 96, 102; at Yellow Tavern, 130, 366; on York Road, 192, 193, 240, 252, 270
Stuart Horse Artillery, 15, 100–101, 105, 133, 149; Beckham of, 174–77, 368–69; Breathed of, 176–77, 379; at Cress's Ridge, 270–71, 282; on Gettysburg day 1, 135; on Gettysburg day 3, 174–78; horses stolen for, 106; Mathews of, 118–19; McGregor of, 177–78; Meade and, 178; Oden of, 173; Pelham of, 144; Pickett's Charge and, 270

Sullivan, Kevin M., 113, 372
Sumner, Edwin V., 66
Sumter, Thomas "Fighting Gamecock," 129
Sun Tzu, 294
*A System of Military Tactics*, 112–13

Tappan, Henry, 228
Tappan Guards, at University of Michigan, 228
Taylor, James B., Jr., 118
10th New York Cavalry, 254
10th Virginia Cavalry, 118; 7th Michigan Cavalry saber charge and, 308
Texas Brigade, 195
3rd Pennsylvania Cavalry, 217, 338; 1st Michigan Cavalry saber charge and, 348; at Little's Run, 251; at Low Dutch Road, 261; at Rummel buildings, 264
3rd Virginia Cavalry, 108, 124, 210; Cress's Ridge and, 201; 1st Michigan Cavalry saber charge and, 351; at Gettysburg day 1, 134–35
Third Cavalry Brigade (Division), 2; Cress's Ridge and, 245–46; at Gettysburg day 1, 136; Gregg, J., of, 237; of Kilpatrick, 64, 65, 161, 229–30, 237, 244–46, 259–60; at Little Round Top, 194–95; Michigan Cavalry Division and, 244–46
Third Corps, 133
13th Virginia Cavalry: of Chambliss, 318; 7th Michigan Cavalry and, 305; 7th Michigan Cavalry saber charge and, 308, 319, 320
34th Virginia Cavalry: at Cress's Ridge, 193, 248–50, 257; 5th Michigan Cavalry and, 266; 1st Virginia Cavalry and, 288; on Gettysburg day 3, 193, 248–50; at Rummel house barn, 262–66; 7th Michigan Cavalry and, 305; 7th Michigan Cavalry saber charge and, 317

36th Virginia Cavalry, 193
Thomas, Emory M., 26, 173, 372–73, 380; on Stuart, 390–91
Thompson, Bradley M., 321
Thompson, Henry E., 83
Thompson, Mary, 14, 141, 150, 157, 172, 191, 210, 357
Toombs, Robert "Bob," 381
Town, Charles H., 340
Trimble, Isaac R., 151
Trojan War, 33
Trowbridge, Luther S., 349
Trudeau, Noah Andre, 181
Trueheart, Charles William, 102
Tucker, Glenn, 372
20th Maine Volunteer Regiment, 2; at Little Round Top, 16
Twenty-First Cavalry, 62
24th Michigan Volunteer Infantry, 78
24th Virginia Infantry, 173
Two Taverns, 161, 163, 195

*The Union Cavalry in the Civil War* (Starr), 45
United States Military Academy. *See* West Point
University of Michigan, Tappan Guards at, 228
Urwin, Gregory J. W., 41, 150, 388

Vallandigham, Clement L., 186
Vaness, George E., 312
veterinary surgeons, 119
Vicksburg, Mississippi, 53; Army of Northern Virginia and, 54; Davis and, 115; Grant at, 54, 116; Lee, R., and, 54–55
Virginia Brigade, 101; of Jenkins, 241
Virginians: on Gettysburg day 3, 173; of Jenkins, 145; at Pickett's Charge, 13–14, 35; of Witcher, 257. *See also specific individuals and units*

Walker, Emma, 92
Walter, Nelson, 307

Ward, Bill, 387
*The War of the Rebellion: A Compilation of the Official Records of the Union and Confederate Armies*, 6
Warren, Gouverneur K., 2, 3
Washington, George, 131; Lee, R., and, 144
Waterloo: Gettysburg and, 295; Napoleon and, 295, 296, 307, 331–32; 7th Michigan Calvary saber charge and, 307
Watkins, Mary, 108
Watkins, Richard Henry, 108–9, 124, 351, 354–55
Waud, Alfred, *p8*
Weber, Peter A. "Bob," 83, 87–88, 181, 225, 226; Cress's Ridge and, 88, 238–43, 246, 256; at Falling Waters, 88, 239
Wert, Jeffry D., 154
West, John Camden, 95
West Point: Baker at, 297; Beckham at, 174; Bingham sponsorship for, 47–48; Carhart at, 395; cavalry and, 113–14; Chambliss at, 145, 323; court-martial at, 49–50, 51; Custer, G., at, 8, 10, 28, 42, 43, 137, 219, 236, 382, 396; demerits at, 48–49, 219; entry into, 47–48; example to be avoided at, 68; Gettysburg defeat from, 381; "goat" at, 8, 10, 42, 51, 137, 218–19, *p5*, 396, 398; Hampton, Wade, at, 127; Lea at, 80; McDowell at, 52; McGregor at, 177; O'Rorke at, 68–69; Pennington at, 69, 168, 228, 276; Pickett at, 42; Pleasonton at, 68; Randol at, 276; Reno at, 381; Stuart at, 52

Wheeler, William H., 91
White Run, 231
Wilcox, Charles, 307
Williams, Anna Olivia Laval, 116
Williams, Leonard, 100–101, 116, 283
Williams, Solomon, 118, 318
Williamsburg: Custer, G., at, 109; Lea at, 80
Williamsport. *See* Falling Waters
Witcher, Vincent Addison, 197–98, 202–3, 207, 210; Alger, R., and, 358; Chambliss and, 289; Cress's Ridge and, 235, 237, 265; Ferry and, 258, 266, 359; 1st Virginia Cavalry and, 284; Gregg, D., and, 261; McClellan, H., and, 264, 289; McIntosh and, 257; Pickett's Charge and, 273; at Rummel buildings, 262–66, 287, 319; 7th Michigan Cavalry and, 305, 314; 7th Michigan Cavalry saber charge and, 310, 313, 316; Stuart and, 248–50, 355; 34th Virginia Cavalry of, 248–50
Wolverine Brigade. *See* Michigan Cavalry Brigade
women: Hampton, Wade, and, 128; Stuart and, 95, 96, 102
World War I, 361–62
Worthen, George A., 307

Yates, George, 398
Yellow Tavern, Virginia, 17; Stuart at, 130, 366
York Road (Turnpike), 161, 188, 192–94; Stuart on, 192, 193, 240, 252, 270
"Young Guard," of Napoleon, 143, 303
"Young Turks," 64